CANADIAN SOCIETY *in the* TWENTY-FIRST CENTURY

CANADIAN SOCIETY *in the* TWENTY-FIRST CENTURY

AN HISTORICAL SOCIOLOGICAL APPROACH

Fourth Edition

TREVOR W. HARRISON
JOHN W. FRIESEN

CANADIAN SCHOLARS
Toronto | Vancouver

Canadian Society in the Twenty-First Century: An Historical Sociological Approach, Fourth Edition
Trevor W. Harrison and John W. Friesen

First published in 2021 by
Canadian Scholars, an imprint of CSP Books Inc.
425 Adelaide Street West, Suite 200
Toronto, Ontario
M5V 3C1

www.canadianscholars.ca

Library and Archives Canada Cataloguing in Publication

Title: Canadian society in the twenty-first century : an historical sociological approach / Trevor W. Harrison, John W. Friesen.
Names: Harrison, Trevor W., 1952- author. | Friesen, John W., author.
Description: Fourth edition. | Includes bibliographical references and index.
Identifiers: Canadiana (print) 20200339052 | Canadiana (ebook) 20200339087 | ISBN 9781773382203 (softcover) | ISBN 9781773382210 (PDF) | ISBN 9781773382227 (EPUB)
Subjects: LCSH: Canada—Civilization—Textbooks. | LCSH: Canada—Civilization—21st century—Forecasting—Textbooks. | LCSH: Canada—English-French relations—Textbooks. | LCSH: Indigenous peoples—Canada—Textbooks. | LCSH: Indigenous peoples—Canada—Government relations—Textbooks. | LCGFT: Textbooks.
Classification: LCC FC95.5 .H37 2021 | DDC 971—dc23

Cover design by Em Dash
Page layout by S4Carlisle Publishing Services

21 22 23 24 25   5 4 3 2 1

Printed and bound in Ontario, Canada

Dedicated to our wives:

Terri Mae Saunders and Virginia Lyons Friesen

Contents

Acknowledgements

As with the first three editions, I want to thank the many students whom I have instructed in courses on Canadian society, first at the University of Alberta and, since 2002, at the University of Lethbridge. Their keen interest and probing questions have led me to think hard about the nature of societies and Canadian society in particular.

Thanks go to Canadian Scholars' Press Inc., particularly the many editors and designers with whom John and I have worked over the years. Thanks to Lizzie Di Giacomo for shepherding this text through the various stages. An especially grateful thanks to Jenn Harris for her outstanding work on this edition's final preparation. Jenn's attention to detail, probing questions, and knowledgeable insights represent the finest text editing I have ever witnessed.

Thanks go also to a host of friends and colleagues for their many contributions to my thinking over many years about Canadian society and to my departmental colleagues for their general support.

I would also like to acknowledge Dr. P. B. Waite for the use of his words quoted in Chapter 5 and John Robert Colombo for the use of various quotations from *Colombo & Company*.

Finally, I must also acknowledge the support of my wife, Terri, and my children, Jayna and Keenan. They are a constant source of inspiration and the cause of my dedication to a better Canada.

I apologize to any whose contributions I have unintentionally overlooked. I take sole responsibility for any errors or omissions contained in the text.

T. W. H.

To begin, I want to acknowledge the consistent support of my wife, Dr. Virginia Lyons Friesen, who shares my research interests and with whom I have co-authored more than a dozen books. Virginia shines in the areas of computer technology, Internet research, editing, and putting up with my whims. I owe her a debt that cannot be repaid in this life.

Second, I want to say thanks to the Indigenous peoples who graciously hosted us while we were conducting research through the years on reservations (reserves) from Alberta and Saskatchewan to Texas and Mexico. Locally, our gratitude must be extended to the Four Band Plains Cree, Siksika, Stoney (Nakoda Sioux), and Tsuu T'ina First Nations, from whom we have learned a great deal. My own formal attachment to the Stoney First Nation, as minister of the Morley United Church from 1986 to 2016, gave me the opportunity to be mentored by some of the most accepting individuals I have ever met. This includes a lengthy list, some of whom have since passed away. They are: Chief John and

Alva Snow, Lazarus and Lily Wesley, Frank and Glenda Crawler, Ivan and Trudy Wesley, Rod and Reatha Mark, Lucy Daniels, Clara Rollinmud, Fred and Beatrice Powder, and Reba Powderface. There are many more people to list, but space will not allow, and I apologize for that. Still, I want to express my thanks for their influence on my life.

Finally, I want to thank my colleague, Trevor W. Harrison, for the hard work he put into this project. He never seemed to weary of deadlines, but worked prodigiously and perseveringly to bring this production to its birth as a book. I only hope that our readers will appreciate the effort involved in producing this work.

J. W. F.

Note to the Fourth Edition

Short decades ago, Canadian textbooks customarily referred to the original inhabitants of North America as Indians or sometimes natives. In more recent years, the term most often used has been *Aboriginal*. This was the term regularly used in the first three editions of this text. The chosen term employed throughout this edition is *Indigenous*, except where citations and quotations or administrative offices and documents (e.g., Department of Indian and Northern Affairs; Royal Commission on Aboriginal Peoples) use the previous terms, or where otherwise using the term *Indigenous* would be anachronistic.

INTRODUCTION

What Is Society?

Going Up. Photo by Alex Powell from Pexels.

Ours is not the only nation which has out-travelled its own soul and now is forced to search frantically for a new identity. No wonder, for so many, the past Canadian experience has become not so much a forgotten thing as an unknown thing.
　　—novelist Hugh MacLennan, 1974

How could we have believed that there is such a thing as time, the self, or the nation?
　　—author John Gray, 1994

As a country or a society, Canada might always be a work in progress.
　　—political scientist Peter Russell, 2017

INTRODUCTION

Since Canada's founding in 1867, its imminent demise has been regularly predicted or encouraged. Throughout much of the 19th and early 20th centuries, two threats were particularly prominent: the internecine battles between Canada's French and English communities as well as the equally looming presence of the United States. English-born journalist Goldwin Smith (1891/1971) enunciated the first of these threats in 1891 with the publication of *Canada and the Canadian Question*, a text that somewhat too gleefully pronounced the conflict between English Canada and French Canada as intractable. The second threat, that of American absorption, found its voice in a duet sung across the borders, from the Canadian side by Sarah Jane Duncan (1904/1971) in *The Imperialist* (1904) and from the American side by Samuel Moffett (1908/1972) in *The Americanization of Canada* (1908). Later, as the western provinces were opened up for development, a third peril reared its head—that of western alienation.

In one form or another, these same threats found an echo in later years. Quebec's escalating demands for recognition, if not outright sovereignty, after the 1960s resulted in a plethora of books predicting, as before, an end to Canada's national experiment. One of them, Peter Brimelow's (1986) *The Patriot Game*, faithfully replicated Smith's arguments of nearly a century previous. Similarly, changes in Canada's political economy after the Second World War led George Grant (2005/1965), in *Lament for a Nation*, to decry the loss of British influence as a buffer against the American embrace. The adoption of free trade after 1988 heightened these warnings: Witness, for example, Lawrence Martin's *Pledge of Allegiance: The Americanization of Canada during the Mulroney Years* (1993). These twin pillars of discontent were joined in the late 1980s by rising western discontent in the guise of the Reform Party (Harrison 1995). These more traditional fears were joined in some quarters by warnings centred on Indigenous demands for the redress of historic wrongs (Smith 1995). And though a new confidence—even cockiness—has in recent years emerged, there are voices still heralding Canada's demise, to wit columnist Diane Francis's (2013) lauding the benefits of a merger with the United States and the resurgence of separatist murmurings in Alberta spurred on by troubles in that province's oil-based economy.

Canada faces challenges and always will. As with individuals, the scars that define nations are always ripe to be opened again. To the historic and more recent internal challenges and threats must also be added the growing and interrelated challenges of globalization, terrorism, resource scarcity, and climate change (especially global warming). These issues—some old, some new—and the processes by which Canadians have attempted to resolve them frame this text. In particular, this text deals with the thorny problem of Canadian society.

Given Canada's geographical vastness, its historical and cultural diversity, and its political and social complexity, one might ask how it is possible to grasp Canadian society. On the one hand, and only scant years ago, even speaking of "Canadian society" seemed increasingly impossible, as we were repeatedly told that cultural, economic, and political borders were breaking down (see Ohmae 1990). Yet on the other, the vastness of the object contemplated led one sociologist to comment that "the task of 'constituting society,' of creating knowledge about, and articulating a wholist account of, the total society, is no longer central to current concerns of sociologists in Canada" (Whyte 1992, 313). To borrow from Frisby and Sayer (1986, 121), Canadian society seemed "too grand an abstraction by far for modern sociological tastes."

The reader is thus forewarned: In opening this text, you begin the daunting task of journeying into a territory that many scholars avoid, where existing maps may be unclear, where the terrain is constantly shifting, where fact and myth coexist, and where abstractions run wild. To assist in this journey through Canadian society, this introductory chapter provides a set of rudimentary tools: terms, concepts, theories, and an explanation of historical sociology as a method of study. Learn to use these tools well. The chapter begins with an attempt at defining the object of study.

THE "PROBLEM" OF SOCIETY

What is society? At first, the question may seem strange. After all, we use the term *society* frequently. But try to touch it or point a finger to it. It cannot be done, of course, because—unlike a rock, for example—society is not a concrete thing; it is an abstract concept.

This comparison touches on the first problem with the concept of society. Abstract concepts are very powerful and necessary tools for assisting us to think about complex social phenomena. Abstract concepts become problematic, however, when we engage in **reification**, the process of coming to believe that our mental constructs actually exist materially. Many of the terms we will deal with in this chapter, such as *state* and *nation*, share with *society* the frequent problem of being reified.

A second problem with the term *society* is its diverse meanings. Take, for example, the following definition of the term appearing in *Merriam-Webster's Collegiate Dictionary* (Merriam-Webster, Incorporated 2003, 1115):

> **1** : companionship or association with one's fellows : friendly or intimate intercourse : COMPANY **2** : a voluntary association of individuals for common ends; *esp* : an organized group working together or periodically meeting because of common interests, beliefs, or profession **3 a** : an enduring and cooperating social group whose members have developed organized patterns of relationships through interaction with one another **b** : a community, nation, or broad grouping of people having common traditions, institutions, and collective activities and interests **4 a** : a part of a community that is a unit distinguishable by particular aims or standards of living or conduct : a social circle or a group of social circles having a clearly marked identity <literary society> **b** : a part of the community

that sets itself apart as a leisure class and that regards itself as the arbiter of fashion and manners **5 a** : a natural group of plants usu. of a single species or habit within an association **b** : the progeny of a pair of insects when constituting a social unit (as a hive of bees); *broadly* : an interdependent system of organisms or biological units.

Such a definition is very broad. Clearly, Canada is not a society like that of a group of plants or the progeny of insects, or even members of the Flat Earth Society (www.tfes. org). Moreover, the problem of definition is only partially remedied by adding a descriptive modifier, such as *Canadian*.

When sociologists refer to society, they often mean something more narrowly defined yet conceptually larger. A popular introductory text in sociology (Brym 2020, 34), for example, states, "A society involves people interacting socially and sharing culture, usually in a defined geographical area." Another introductory text (Murray, Linden, and Kendall 2017, 4) defines society as follows: "A society is a large social grouping that shares the same geographical territory and is subject to the same political authority and dominant cultural expectations, such as Canada, the United States, and Mexico." This definition suggests that a society's social boundaries are coexistent with its political boundaries. But which political boundaries are to be used: federal, provincial, or municipal?

This question points to a third problem with the concept of society: Where does one society end and another begin? While Canadian society courses are common throughout Anglo-Canadian universities, Quebec's francophone universities focus on Quebec society courses, while a popular anglophone text (Fournier, Rosenberg, and White 1997) also deals with Quebec society. Add to this the fact that the University of Calgary some years offered an Alberta society course, or that Memorial University in St. John's, Newfoundland, still mounts a course titled "Newfoundland Society and Culture," and we may understand Denis's (1993, 255) frustration:

> Where does it stop? If "English Canada" and Quebec can both be distinct societies within Canada, which is itself a distinct society relative to (or within?) the US, does this also mean that American society is within . . . etc.? In this socio-geographic chain, shouldn't a number of statements be mutually exclusive?

A fourth problem with the concept of society is its conflation with several other concepts, notably those of country, state, and nation (see Denis 1993). Note, for example, the inclusion in *Merriam-Webster's* of *nation* in its definition of society, and Murray et al.'s (2017) equation of the concepts of country and society. How can we distinguish among concepts such as country, state, and nation? And how are they related to the concept of Canadian society?

COUNTRY, STATE, NATION

Turning once again to our *Merriam-Webster's* dictionary, one of its definitions of *country* is as follows: "a political state or nation or its territory" (Merriam-Webster, Incorporated 2003, 266). In other words, country *equals* nation *equals* state. There are problems with this formulation, as we will see. For now, however, we will define a **country** as a territorial area, politically recognized as a country both by people within the territory and by governments outside it, on the basis of historical, material, and geographical factors (see Lane and Ersson 1994; Deutsch 1980).

In these terms, Canada is a country consisting of 10 provinces and three territories, spanning a total land area of 9,093,507 square kilometres (*Time* 2020, 730). This makes Canada the fourth-largest country in the world according to land area, next to Russia (16,377,742 square kilometres), the People's Republic of China (9,326,410 square kilometres), and the United States (9,148,655 square kilometres)—though when areas of water are included, Canada is the world's second-largest country, next to Russia. Compared with Russia, China, and the United States, however, Canada is quite sparsely populated, with roughly 35 million people (see table 0.1).[1] By comparison, Russia's population is 142 million, China's population is 1.4 billion, and the United States is 332 million (*Time* 2020, 730).

Defining Canada, Russia, or China as countries is unproblematic because each has diplomatic recognition of its sovereignty from the rest of the world. Contrast this reality with that of the Kurdish people—whose would-be homeland is divided among the countries of Iran, Turkey, Syria, and Iraq—or, for that matter, the small but militant Aryan Nations movement in the northwest United States. While the former has established a quasi-state within northern Iraq, there is no likelihood of the latter gaining a similar homeland in the foreseeable future.

A term frequently employed offhandedly as synonymous with *country* is that of *state*. However, *state* is also often used when referring to issues of governance and the use of political power. In the former sense, an individual might argue that Canada *is* a state. In the latter sense, however, the same individual might ask what kind of state Canada *has* and what its characteristics are.

The latter meaning of *state* is rendered even more diverse in scholarly accounts. For example, pluralist theorists tend to ignore the state altogether, choosing instead to narrowly analyze the formal institutions of government (such as parties, legislatures, bureaucracies), which they view as open to the influence of competing political interests (see Orum and Dale 2009). By contrast, neo-Marxist scholars, such as Miliband (1969) and Poulantzas (1973), have tended to view the state more broadly, the former seeing the state as an instrument of capital accumulation, the latter, as a relatively autonomous ensemble of social and political institutions. For others, like Skocpol (1979), the state is a wholly autonomous actor with its own powers, goals, and interests.

Table 0.1: Canadian Population, by Province and Region, 1851–2016 (in thousands)

Year	CANADA	NL[1]	PEI	NS	NB	QC	ON	MB[2]	SK	AB[3]	BC	YT	NT	NU[4]
1851	2,436	n.a.	63	277	194	890	952	n.a.	n.a.	n.a.	55	n.a.	6	n.a.
1861	3,230	n.a.	81	331	252	1,112	1,396	n.a.	n.a.	n.a.	52	n.a.	7	n.a.
1871	3,689	n.a.	94	388	286	1,192	1,621	25	n.a.	n.a.	36	n.a.	48	n.a.
1881	4,325	n.a.	109	441	321	1,360	1,927	62	n.a.	n.a.	49	n.a.	56	n.a.
1891	4,833	n.a.	109	450	321	1,489	2,114	153	n.a.	n.a.	98	n.a.	99	n.a.
1901	5,371	n.a.	103	460	331	1,649	2,183	255	91	73	179	27	20	n.a.
1911	7,207	n.a.	94	492	352	2,006	2,527	461	492	374	393	9	7	n.a.
1921	8,788	n.a.	89	524	388	2,361	2,934	610	758	588	525	4	8	n.a.
1931	10,377	n.a.	88	513	408	2,875	3,432	700	922	732	694	4	9	n.a.
1941	11,507	n.a.	95	578	457	3,332	3,788	730	896	796	818	5	12	n.a.
1951	14,009	361	98	643	516	4,056	4,598	777	832	940	1,165	9	16	n.a.
1961	18,238	458	105	737	598	5,259	6,236	922	925	1,332	1,629	15	23	n.a.
1971	21,962	531	113	797	643	6,137	7,849	999	932	1,666	2,241	19	36	n.a.
1981	24,820	575	124	855	706	6,548	8,811	1,036	976	2,294	2,824	24	48	n.a.

1991	28,031	580	130	915	746	7,065	10,428	1,110	1,003	2,593	3,373	29	61	n.a.
1996	29,672	561	136	931	753	7,274	11,101	1,134	1,020	2,781	3,882	32	68	25
2001	31,021	522	137	932	750	7,397	11,898	1,151	1,000	3,057	4,078	30	41	28
2006	32,571	511	138	938	746	7,632	12,662	11,484	992	3,421	4,242	32	43	31
2011	33,477	515	140	922	751	7,903	12,852	1,208	1,033	3,645	4,400	34	41	32
2016	35,152	520	143	924	747	8,164	13,448	1,278	1,098	4,067	4,648	36	42	36
2016%	100	1.5	0.4	2.6	2.1	23.2	38.3	3.6	3.1	11.6	13.2	0.1	0.1	0.1

Notes: 1. Newfoundland figures before its confederation in 1949 are not included. 2. Population figures for Manitoba before 1871 are included in figures for the Northwest Territories. 3. Population figures for Saskatchewan and Alberta before 1901 are included in figures for the Northwest Territories. 4. Population figures for Nunavut before 1996 are included in figures for the Northwest Territories.

Sources: Adapted from Statistics Canada. 1983. Data Table 11-516: *Historical Statistics of Canada.* Ottawa: Statistics Canada. 2001. Canada Year Book, Cat. no. 11-402. Ottawa: Statistics Canada; Statistics Canada. 2011a. "Focus on Geography Series." 2011 Census. Ottawa: Statistics Canada; and Statistics Canada. 2017a. Data Table 98-316-X2016001: "Canada [Country] and Canada [Country] (table). Census Profile." 2016 Census. Totals rounded up by authors.

In each of these interpretations, the state is described more or less as a thing. Recent definitions of the state, however, have taken a more radical turn. Beginning with Abrams (1988), the state has increasingly been described as an abstract concept, the reification of which is a weapon for enacting, legitimating, and ultimately condoning "violence" (Sayer 1987; Denis 1989).

Despite important differences, the definitions reviewed here agree that the concept of state has something to do with the exercise of political power. In this text, therefore, a **state** is defined as a set of institutions successfully claiming a monopoly over political rule-making and the legitimate use of violence and coercion within a given territory—that is, a country (see Weber 1958; Lane and Ersson 1994). The important question of globalization's impact upon states is taken up later in the chapter.

The third term requiring definition is *nation*. Note, at the onset, how the terms *nation* and *state* are often linked together—that is, as *nation-state*. (Note also how *Merriam-Webster's* definition equates the concepts of country and nation.) We have looked at the meanings of *country* and *state*. What exactly is a nation?

A **nation** is defined as a mass of individuals who define themselves collectively as a people. But on what bases might individuals define themselves as a nation?

Scholars differentiate between two types of nations: civic nations and ethnic nations (Webber 1994). Civic nationalism is determined by citizenship. Membership in the civic nation, at least in theory, is open to anyone. By contrast, ethnic—sometimes also termed *tribal*—nations are based on supposedly fixed biological (e.g., racial) and cultural (e.g., linguistic or religious) markers. Note, however, how malleable even these markers are. Biological descriptors are particularly uncertain measures of difference, and people can readily acquire a new language, convert to a different religion, or adopt new cultural practices.

Both civic and ethnic nations are tied to a specific territorial homeland. In the case of civic nations, however, the territorial referent is quite concrete: no territory, no citizenship. By contrast, ethnic nations may continue to exist, even thrive, after the territorial homeland has disappeared from political maps. Both civic and ethnic nations, however, constitute what Anderson (1983) terms "imagined communities." A person can never know all the other members of his or her nation. Rather, the other members are idealized figments, our relationship with them the product of collective stories that we tell each other.

As stated previously, the term *nation* is often conflated with *state* to produce *nation-state*. This conjoining of these terms is both unfortunate and imprecise. The term *nation-state* suggests that every nation must be a state, and that every state must consist of only one nation. The actions of the Nazi regime in Germany (1933–1945) and the Balkan and African wars of the 1990s suggest the dangerous consequences that may result from such a belief. Beyond these extremes, however, the term *nation-state* is simply misleading in describing reality. As Hobsbawm (1992) notes, no more than a dozen of today's 180-plus nation-states house only a single ethnic or linguistic group. Indeed, van den Berghe

(1992) argues that only Japan, Swaziland, and Somalia are genuine nation-states—and even these are, today, finding their "purity" challenged.

As Laxer (2000, 56) points out, most countries are heterogeneous and "cannot, even mythically, pretend all citizens are kith and kin." A lot of countries, in fact, are "state-nations," that is, nations organized—indeed, "created"—under the guidance of the state, while other nations are "stateless." In short, the assumption that country *equals* state *equals* nation is historically, politically, and socially constructed. Determining the exact fit between these terms in any particular case is a matter of empirical reflection. This point brings us to Canada.

A central thesis of this text is that while Canada is indisputably a country, it is one founded on not one but three historic nations—English, French, and Indigenous—and consequently requires a complex federal state structure. Efforts to make Canada conform to the European model—for example, repeated attempts by the English majority to coerce and otherwise assimilate either the French or Indigenous peoples—have usually foundered, threatening Canada's continuance. The text's second thesis, however, is that these internal differences over nation and state, combined with external threats of absorption by the United States, have rendered Canada unique among 21st-century countries. The result, in turn, is a country in which civil and state relations are also unique—in short, something that we may consider a society.

BACK TO SOCIETY

The concept of society emerged in the 19th century. **Sociology** arose at the same time. For early sociologists, the concept of society was meant to locate the site of the many changes wrought, both directly and indirectly, by the Industrial Revolution and the rise of capitalism. For Karl Marx (1818–1883), feudal relationships, based on tradition and fealty, were being replaced by capitalist relationships based on private property and the cash nexus (Marx 1977a). For Ferdinand Tönnies (1855–1936), rural and small-town life was being replaced by urban life, and kinship and tradition were being replaced by anonymity and self-interest (Tönnies 1887/1957). For Émile Durkheim (1858–1917), the changes were marked by a transformation in the basis of social solidarity from similarity-in-kind ("mechanical solidarity") to differentiation and, hence, greater interdependence ("organic solidarity") (Durkheim 1893/1964). For Max Weber (1864–1920), traditional authority was giving way to legal-rational forms of authority, reaching its apex in bureaucratic institutions (Weber 1958).

Early on, however, the concept of society also came to define "one half of an antithetic tandem in which the other is the state" (Wallerstein 1997, 315). Wallerstein adds,

> In this formulation, the state could be observed and analysed directly. It operated through formal institutions by way of known (constitutional) rules. The "society" was taken to mean that tissue of manners and customs that held a

group of people together without, despite or against formal rules. In some sense, "society" represented something more enduring and "deeper" than the state, less manipulable and certainly more elusive.

This perspective is very much alive today. Consider, for example, how often you have heard someone—perhaps on talk radio—complain about the state or, just simply, "the government." For many people, including some academics, society is an abstract concept defined by its opposition to another abstract concept, the state.

It was not always the case, however, that society and state were viewed as separate (and perhaps opposed). Knuttila and Kubik (2000) suggest, for example, that both Auguste Comte (1798–1857), who first coined the term *sociology*, and Durkheim, who held the first chair in sociology, viewed the state as an integral part—*but only a part*—of a functional modern society. From this perspective, society and state are not merely "coterminous" (Giddens 1984); they are indivisible.

Denis (1989) has argued forcefully for a restoration of the links between the two concepts. For him, "'states' are a historically specific type of society, whose institutions take the legal-constitutional discursive form which has enabled capitalism to rise—*a state is not in (or above) society, a state is a society*" (Denis 1989, 347–348, italics added). Similarly, Teeple (2000, 15) argues that the form of state that has emerged since the Second World War in most Western countries, the welfare state (see Chapter 7), "can also be seen as a capitalist *society*" (italics in original).

This formulation may seem at first extreme, positing that the capitalist state is everything and everything is the capitalist state. Yet it is hard to think of any activity today that is not codified, regulated, and occasionally prohibited in some way by the state, often for the purposes of enabling markets and ensuring profits. This is true whether speaking of a state-capitalist country such as the "communist" People's Republic of China, the social democratic country of Sweden, or the laissez-faire capitalist country of the United States.

It is also true of Canada. The creation of Canada—of Canadian *society*—cannot be understood separately from the role of the state. A prime example of this is the National Policy of 1878 (see Chapter 6), which dramatically altered Canadian economic development and immigration policy. The real challenge in conceptualizing state and society as one thing involves determining which social actors have gained either influence or outright control of the state's machinery at given times and what this has meant, in turn, for defining and shaping socio-cultural, economic, and political relations within Canada.

What, then, is society? A **society** is defined as the product of relatively continuous and enduring interactions within a political territory, between people more or less identifying themselves as members of the society, these interactions being maintained by an ensemble of political, economic, cultural, and other institutions, the sum of such interactions being in excess of interactions occurring with similarly defined societies external to the given territory.

This definition raises several points requiring elaboration. First, note that societies, like states and nations, are processes, not things. Whether any of these labels has substantive meaning for a group of people is dependent upon the maintenance of "relatively continuous and enduring interactions." We may presume further that, on balance, positive interactions are more fruitful than negative interactions.

Second, note also that individuals may have either greater or lesser attachment to a society, just as they may have greater or lesser attachment to other social groups (such as the family) or may have different reasons for feeling they are part of a group. Third, note the important role of various institutions in acting as intermediaries between individuals, small groups, and society as a whole. Fourth, note that no society today is hermetically sealed off from external influences. This last point is brought home by globalization.

GLOBALIZATION, THE STATE, AND SOCIETY

The term *globalization* became popular in the late part of the 20th century as a shorthand means of describing global integration. But what does globalization actually mean? Current **globalization**—often prefaced with the word "neo-liberal" (see Chapter 8)—is defined as a series of integrative economic, political, and cultural changes, sometimes contradictory and even opposed, occurring throughout the world (see Harrison 1999). Economically, globalization involves a complex series of worldwide exchanges in labour, trade, technology, and capital (Stubbs and Underhill 1994; Laxer 1995) and the reorganization over space of production itself (Mittelman 1996; Lairson and Skidmore 1997). Politically, globalization similarly manifests itself in increased interconnectedness and interdependence among countries, though not necessarily unification (Boyer and Drache 1996). Culturally, globalization involves the spread of primarily Western liberal practices and notions of individualism and civil and political rights, as well as consumerism (Mittelman 1996; Boyer and Drache 1996; Sklair 2002; Robbins and Dowty 2019).

A central debate surrounding globalization has been its impact upon the state. One school of thought holds that globalization has severely curtailed the power and capacity of states, if not actually signalled their outright demise. Economic historian Eric Heilbroner (1992, 60), for example, states:

> The global market system stretches beyond the political authority of any single government. Faced with a network of connections that escape their powers of surveillance and regulation, national governments become increasingly unable to cope with the problems that arise from the intrusion of the global economy into their territories.

Or, in Daniel Bell's words, "the national state has become too small for the big problems of life, and too big for the small problems" (D. Bell 1993, 362). In partial consequence, the state is being "decomposed" by globalization from above (by transnationals, the World

Bank, the International Monetary Fund, etc.) and the re-emergence of smaller communities from below (McDonald 1994, 241). In effect, nation and state are viewed as decoupling (Paquet 1997), perhaps devolving into smaller, regional states (Ohmae 1995). While hardly a case of peaceful devolution, the breakup of the former Yugoslavia in the 1990s provides an example.

Note that not everyone views the state's supposed decline equally. In the early days of globalization, some applauded the decomposition of the state as allowing for greater economic efficiency and consumer choice (Ohmae 1995) and the end of state-orchestrated violence (Rummel 1994; van den Berghe 1992). Others, however, fear the state's eclipse will result in the sweeping away of 200 years of hard-won civil, political, and social rights (Teeple 2000). Likewise, some believe that the fragmentation of states signals the decline of civic nationalism, replaced instead by anarchism, terrorism, or the rebirth of tribalism in the form of xenophobic, far-right nationalism (Ehmsen and Scharenberg 2018).

If traditional states are in decline, does this mean their powers of regulation and coercion have been dispersed? A second school of thought disputes this, arguing instead that the powers previously held by territorial states remain concentrated but have been transferred to undemocratic quasi-states—transnational corporations—and other unaccountable international organizations (see Robbins and Dowty 2019; Strange 1996; Korten 2001). From this perspective, the state itself is being globalized (Albrow 1997). In the words of David Korten (2001, 54), "Corporations have emerged as the dominant governance institutions on the planet." An even more radical perspective, grounded in Marxist political economy (see later in this section), argues that states are not the creators of the international system; rather, the international system of capitalist class relations has been the primary instrument of specific state formations (see Holloway 1994; Van der Pijl 1998).

Clearly, either the outright demise of the state or its resurrection at the global level would have important implications for societies such as Canada's. What might be the fate of Canadian society in such a world? Malcolm Waters (1994, 233) provides a succinct answer: "If the nation-state is dissolving, or at least attenuating, then so too must national societies." One logical extension of this dissolution is that national societies will be replaced by a global society, also known as "the global village." Is such a thing possible, or is this merely Utopian theorizing?

A third school of thought argues that the death of the state has been greatly exaggerated (Laxer 1995). From this perspective, the world economy has not been globalized but rather "internationalized," with states themselves the architects reorganizing capitalist production. While many of the world's wealthiest economies are not countries but corporations (Robbins and Dowty 2019), the latter are not stateless, let alone "virtual." Most multinationals retain headquarters in the economically dominant states, especially the United States. Put another way, states peripheral to the world capitalist economy were weak before globalization and remain so now, while states that were central to that economy remain powerful actors, not merely despite but as a *consequence of* globalization

(Burbach et al. 1997). Note, however, that the rise of China as a major economic actor challenges this deterministic view of the world system being unalterable.

Finally, from an historical perspective, it should be noted that globalization is not a new phenomenon (Laxer 1995). Of an earlier episode of capitalist globalization in the mid-19th century, Marx (1977a, 224) wrote, "The need of a constantly expanding market for its products chases the bourgeoisie over the whole surface of the globe. It must nestle everywhere, settle everywhere, establish connections everywhere." At the same time, however, capitalist expansion has not always proceeded in a straightforward manner; there have been periods of contraction, such as during the Depression of the 1930s. Faced with increasing challenges brought about by war, resource scarcity, and climate change, some argue the world may experience deglobalization and a return to localism (Bello 2002). The credit crisis that spread like a virus through the world economy in the fall of 2008, leading to the widespread nationalization of banks and the overnight depreciation of stock values, bears witness to the negative side of global interrelatedness and dependency, as does the spread of an actual virus—a coronavirus—that shut down the world's economy in early 2020. In the context of the latter, some have begun arguing that a "global decoupling" will occur as governments seek to lessen future dependencies upon global supply chains, instead ensuring that their populations are protected against critical shortages of food or energy (Ivison 2020).

Whatever its final disposition, the recent period of globalization has not left states unscathed. Technological and organizational changes as well as the freer flow of capital associated with the growth of multinationals have had an impact on state roles, functions, and policies (see Jessop 1993; Teeple 2000). At the same time, states remain central actors, organizing economic life, providing political legitimacy, employing means of coercion, and generally exercising control over their populations (Boyer and Drache 1996). Moreover, states have become the main site of a cultural, political, and economic backlash to globalization (Crouch 2018)—witness, for example, the United Kingdom's Brexit referendum vote in June 2016 to leave the European Union, a decision finalized in early 2020.

This fact remains true for Canada. Globalization has not left Canada and Canadian society untouched. As a wealthy but semi-peripheral country, Canada faces the challenge of residing next to the United States, both the chief architect of globalization and more recently, under the administration of Donald Trump (1946–), an advocate for greater isolationism. Yet Canada also remains a sovereign country, its cultural symbols and political state intact. And within these geographic and political boundaries, Canadian society also continues to exist as an object worthy of study. Sociology is particularly suited for the task of carrying out this examination.

THEORIZING SOCIAL RELATIONSHIPS

Students approaching sociology for the first time are frequently confounded by an array of theories. This reaction is both unfortunate and unnecessary. Theories are like tools.

A wrench is a poor instrument for pounding nails. Likewise, a hammer is useless for saw-ing wood. But, used properly, a wrench or a hammer can be very helpful.

The same goes for theories. Theories are neither good nor bad. They are either useful or not in assisting us to sort out and understand particular phenomena.

The sociological "tool box" contains several theories for understanding how individ-uals and groups (large and small) interact. For students at a beginning level of instruc-tion, four theories, with their own perspectives on human behaviour, are particularly useful: structural functional, conflict, symbolic interaction, and post-structural theories. **Structural functional theory** has roots in the work of early anthropologists, including Herbert Spencer (1820–1895), an English sociologist who adopted evolutionary theory for the study of human societies (the idea of social Darwinism, or the "survival of the fittest"). It was the American sociologist Talcott Parsons (1902–1979) who primarily codified the theory's tenets, however. Drawing upon earlier work by Weber and Durkheim (among others) and emerging ideas of systems theory and cybernetics, Parsons arrived at a grand theory of social action that emphasized the relationships among various institutions—the church, family, schools, the state—each of which, he argued, fulfill specific functions necessary for the continuation and survival of a given society (Parsons 1951). An institu-tion's function may be *manifest* or *latent* (Merton 1968). For example, schools are mani-festly intended to educate students, but they also control young people and socialize them for later participation in the labour market.

Structural functionalism draws our attention to how various social elements are inter-connected. A change in one part of society—for instance, a downturn in the economy—may thus have unforeseen consequences for other parts (Merton 1968), such as family structure. Where change in one sphere occurs and other spheres are not able to adapt, or do so slowly, disequilibrium or *dysfunctions* may occur. In general, however, the theory suggests that the interconnectedness of functions slows the rate of social change.

The second perspective, **conflict theory**, has its roots in the work of Karl Marx and Max Weber. Marx, whose writings champion social revolution, argued that world history was the result of class struggle and, more widely, of structural contradictions. Weber's contribution to conflict theory was to suggest that conflict is not necessarily based on class alone but also upon differences in status and power. Conflict theorists today recognize the many non-class bases of inequality and conflict, such as ethnicity, language, region, age, and gender, and that conflict frequently cuts across several lines (Curtis, Grabb, and Guppy 1999). For example, labour conflict at a bank may involve workers and owners/shareholders (class conflict). At the same time, it is likely that the majority of low-level employees are female while upper-level managers are male (gender conflict).

Within the Marxist stream of conflict theory, particular emphasis is given to the notion of **praxis**, defined as purposeful action in contrast to abstract theorizing. As Marx (1977b, 158) himself said, "The philosophers have only interpreted the world, in various ways; the point is to change it." This tradition of activism continues today in feminist and anti-oppressive approaches to research (see box 0.1).

Box 0.1: Feminism and Anti-oppressive Research

There are several types of feminism: liberal, socialist, radical, cultural, and postmodern feminism. Despite some differences, however, each of these types of feminism encourages activist research, especially meant to oppose **patriarchy** (the system of male domination in society) and **sexism** (the belief that one sex is inherently superior to another).

The tenets of anti-oppressive research, as described by Potts and Brown (2016, 91–93), similarly invokes the notion of praxis:

1. Anti-oppressive research is social justice and resistance in processes and outcomes.
2. Anti-oppressive research contends that all knowledge is socially constructed, political, and, currently, shaped by the neo-liberal context.
3. Anti-oppressive research foregrounds relationships.

Source: Potts, Karen, and Leslie Brown. 2016. "Becoming an Anti-Oppressive Researcher." In *Rethinking Sociology in the 21st Century: Critical Readings in Sociology*, 4th ed., edited by M. Webber and K. Bezanson, 90–106. Toronto: Canadian Scholars' Press.

Structural functionalism and conflict theory are generally viewed as the yin and yang of sociological perspectives. Nonetheless, the theories also share similarities. Both are macro theories, examining society as a whole using broad social categories, such as class, occupation, or gender. Both emphasize the interrelatedness of society's parts. Both also emphasize the social reality of the objects of study (e.g., class, family). By contrast, the other two theories examined here—symbolic interaction theory and post-structuralism—argue that social reality is largely constructed.

Symbolic interaction theory generally deals with the role of symbols in facilitating interactions between individuals and small groups. Symbolic interaction is a sociological offshoot of social psychology. While social psychological concepts are embedded in the work of Marx, Weber, and Durkheim, symbolic interaction theory is chiefly a product of American pragmatism, particularly the work of George Herbert Mead (1863–1931) (see Morrow 1994; Collins 1982). Whereas both conflict and structural functional theories emphasize the structures within which action occurs or is constrained, symbolic interaction theory emphasizes that all human behaviour is meaningful but that these meanings are collectively constructed and defined in the course of interaction. To give an example drawn from Durkheim (1912/1978), the flag for which a soldier dies represents symbolically more than a piece of cloth. In this sense, the methodological approach of Weber (1958), known as *verstehen*—that is, an understanding of the meaning that others attach to events, symbols, and experiences—is entirely congruent with this theory.

Like symbolic interaction theory, **post-structural theory** deals with the social construction of meanings. Unlike the former, however, its origins lie in the structural linguistics of Ferdinand de Saussure (1857–1913), hence the theory's primacy of language as the medium by which reality is understood. Specifically, post-structural theorists argue that language operates through a system of signs that point not to a definite referent but gain their meaning through difference from other signs. In turn, any text (written or spoken) involves a combination, or string, of signs, each pointing to another sign, such that any "meaning" is both arbitrary and unstable. Put another way, post-structuralists argue there is an endless slippage between the words we use and the meanings (we think) we are conveying and the meanings that others derive. From this perspective, while humans may engage in meaningful behaviour, the exact meanings are not precisely discernable.

At the extreme, post-structuralism would suggest "the impossibility of sociology" (Scott and Marshall 2005, 512; see also Giddens 1987). Especially as practised by theorists such as Jacques Derrida (1930–2004), post-structuralism questions the possibility of establishing taken-for-granted meanings (as suggested by symbolic interaction theory) or apprehending objective reality (as sought by structural functionalists and conflict theorists).

The work of theorists such as Michel Foucault (1926–1984) restores post-structuralism's radical potential, however. In a series of books, Foucault (1973, 1977, 1980) examined the discursive practices that define and categorize individual behaviour. Take criminal behaviour, for example. Rather than existing per se, Foucault argues it is a category produced by a social discourse produced within a set of social institutions (prisons, the criminal justice system) using a set of historical statements (theories, statistics, etc.). More important, however, post-structural theorists such as Foucault connect language with a rethinking of ideology and power (Fairclough 1989). Post-structuralism thus provides a link to structural functionalism and conflict theory as well as to the work of theorists such as Antonio Gramsci and Noam Chomsky. To give an example, a post-structural analysis might question the role of data gathered by Statistics Canada (a source we will use throughout this text) in formulating our notion of Canadian society (see box 0.2).

How might a sociologist use structural functional, conflict, symbolic interaction, and post-structural theories? A typically Canadian example makes the case.

THINKING THEORETICALLY: CANADA'S GAME

The theory you choose as your lens for examining a topic will provide you with particular questions and insights. Take hockey as an example. From a structural functional point of view, a sociologist might examine the functions that hockey plays in our society. She or he might emphasize that hockey provides a source of national pride and cohesion, such as occurred in 1972 when Paul Henderson scored the goal that clinched Canada's victory over the Soviet Union. Our sociologist might also remark on the role of hockey (and sports in general) in providing a safe outlet for male aggression, both at the interpersonal level and as a substitute for war between countries. (The 1972 series was widely viewed in the context of the Cold War as pitting the respective communist and capitalist systems

Box 0.2: Government Statistics: Information for the People or Power for the State?

The practice of states' gathering statistical data about populations within their borders goes back thousands of years and continues today in every country, by various means. Many European countries use mandatory population registers to obtain constantly updated data on births, deaths, marriages, divorces, address changes, and migration, but this data is often combined with survey data. Additionally, each member state of the European Union collects statistics that are comparable, reliable, relevant and usable, data that is then compiled in the European Statistical System (Poulain and Herm 2013).

The first census on Canada's present territory dates to New France in 1666; the first census after Confederation was conducted in 1871 and has been done regularly since that time (Statistics Canada 2013). Over the years, the census has grown in importance and scope not only to enumerate Canadians but to provide a statistical profile of Canadian life.

Rather than using registers, Canada relies on a census conducted by Statistics Canada. A major census is conducted in every year ending in "1," with a less fulsome census conducted in the interim years ending in "5." In each year, Statistics Canada conducts both a mandatory long-form census (MLFC) and a mandatory short-form census (MSFC). In 2016, the MLFC was given to 25 percent of Canadians to "collect information on the demographic, social and economic situation of people across Canada, and the dwellings they live in." The MSFC was given to the other 75 percent of Canadians and requires information on the number of people living in a given household, their ages, and genders. The more extensive information gathered through the MLFC is used in a wide variety of ways, including social planning, marketing, school construction, and social transfers—not to mention genealogical research.

In June 2010, however, the federal Conservative government ordered Statistics Canada to cease using the MLFC. The decision was made without consultation with any experts or affected community leaders, and the change was quickly denounced by virtually every segment of Canadian society, including several of the provinces, union and business leaders, nursing and religious organizations, non-profit groups, and university administrators and academics. The head of Statistics Canada resigned his position on a matter of principle.

The government defended its decision, citing privacy concerns and complaints it had received about the MLFC being coercive—a state intrusion into personal liberty. Critics noted, however, that the confidentiality of census data is protected by the Statistics Act and that there had only been two complaints about the census in recent memory. Many critics argued that the decision appeared to be based on the government's desire to control the information available to Canadians, particularly disadvantaged groups who might use it to promote their claims for greater social justice. Others suggested the government's decision reflected an extreme libertarian streak borne of neo-liberalism.

The MLFC was replaced in 2011 with the (voluntary) National Household Survey (NHS). When the federal Liberal party returned to power in 2015, it immediately restored the MLFC and it was used in 2016. The differences between a census and a survey is important. A census is a record of an entire population, while a survey is only a sample, which may or may not accurately reflect the population. This means that data collected in 2011 is not methodologically comparable with that collected before or after 2011—an important point to consider in some of the statistical tables used in this text.

At the same time, it is worth noting that Statistics Canada is considering, primarily for financial reasons, replacing the MSFC with the kind of information registry found in Europe.

Sources: Central Statistics Office (Ireland). n.d. "European statistical system"; Statistics Canada. 2013. "History of the Census of Canada." Ottawa: Statistics Canada; Statistics Canada. 2017b. "2016 Census of Population Long-Form Guide"; McDaniel, Susan, and Heidi MacDonald. 2012. "To Know Ourselves—Not." *Canadian Journal of Sociology* 37(3): 253–272; Ramp, William, and Trevor W. Harrison. 2012. "Libertarian Populism, Neoliberal Rationality, and the Mandatory Long-Form Census: Implications for Sociology." *Canadian Journal of Sociology* 37(3): 273–294; *Maclean's.* 2016. "Statistics Canada eyes the end of the short-form census," September 25.

against one another.) She or he might finally note that hockey has traditionally provided a means of social mobility for working-class youth.

A conflict perspective forces us to examine professional hockey quite differently. The 2012–2013 dispute that saw half the National Hockey League (NHL) season wiped out highlighted a conflict between capitalist owners and workers (albeit very well-paid ones). Analyzing the events that led the Winnipeg Jets to move to Arizona in 1996 (see Silver 1996)—then return in 2011–2012, the result of the relocation of a team from Atlanta—provides a similarly provocative view of corporate capitalism in an age of globalization. Alternatively, a conflict theorist might note that professional hockey seems stratified along ethnic lines. For example, most players in the NHL are white, whether Canadian, American, or European. The first Black player in the National Hockey League was Willie O'Ree, with Boston in 1958. Since then, other Black players (such as Evander Kane and P. K. Subban), as well as some Indigenous players (such as T. J. Oshie), have entered the league, but ethnic minorities remain few and, as in arenas beyond sports, have often faced racist taunts from other players and fans.

Likewise, a conflict theorist employing a feminist critique might note how women's professional hockey players remain unrecognized, underpaid, and under-resourced, resulting in their forming a players union in 2019 to fight for improvements. The feminist approach might also draw our attention to how women in hockey, and sports in general, receive publicity only when they are sexually attractive; that mainstream sports appear often to enforce and reward a kind of male machismo whose aggressiveness is sometimes carried into the personal lives of players, with dire consequences for girlfriends, spouses, and children; or that women's professional hockey players remain woefully underpaid—a situation that caused the players to threaten to strike in 2019.

A symbolic interaction theorist might concentrate on the meanings that fans bring to hockey. What, for example, is the process by which an individual becomes a fan? How is it that people come to see their own success as reflected in a team? How do people at a hockey game learn to act like fans (and not like uninformed wannabes)? From the players' point of view, what is the process by which one becomes accepted as a team member? What is team bonding, and how is it achieved?

Finally, a post-structural theorist might begin by examining a set of binary elements surrounding hockey's place in fans' psyche (the individual versus the team; playing for fun versus playing for money; gentlemanly play—for which the NHL awards the Lady Byng Trophy—versus often violent aggression) and how these are connected to other shifting signs. A post-structural theorist might also note the role played by sportswriters, cultural institutions (e.g., the Hockey Hall of Fame), and record keepers in lodging hockey within a series of classical tropes dealing with athletics, sport, and society. Finally, post-structural theorists, as well as those versed in feminist approaches (see Allain 2012), employing discourse analysis, would undoubtedly note the remark of Mike Modano, a former NHL player who, leading up to the women's 2014 gold-medal-deciding game between Canada and the United States, said that there was "nothing like a good cat fight."

Note that none of these theories is exclusive. For example, a sociologist might argue that fan disenchantment during the 2004 NHL lockout resulted from a specific set of cultural meanings (a symbolic interaction perspective) manufactured through a set of discursive statements within the institution of professional sports (a post-structural argument) that was upset by the increased corporatization of professional hockey (a conflict argument) and the subsequent breaking of the irrational—but very real—emotional bonds of solidarity (a structural functionalist's concern) that male fans in particular (again, a feminist insight) have traditionally felt for their teams.

METHODOLOGY: SOCIOLOGY AND WHY HISTORY MATTERS

The methodological approach used in this text is termed **historical sociology**. Historical sociology combines historical detail with sociological generalization. Harrison (1995, 261) notes the following specific characteristics of the method:

- deliberate use of time as a variable
- the explicit use of narrative structure
- the tendency to deal simultaneously with events and processes at different levels
- the use of comparisons of distinct cases or between elements of a single case

Many students are familiar with sociology as the study of society, but often this understanding is focused on society as it exists *at the moment*. This focus is comparable to that of a digital camera taking a single shot. By contrast, the focus of historical sociology is comparable to that of a video camera. An underlying assumption of historical sociology is that *our material institutions, actions, and beliefs are shaped, though not determined, by past events and our understanding (or misunderstanding) of those events.* Some of the sources of historical material a researcher might examine include official government and organizational records, including statistics; newspapers and magazines; public speeches and sermons; private letters and diaries; photographs, drawings, and audio recordings; cemetery tombstones; and interviews with participants.

For a time, the study of history fell out of fashion. At the end of the Cold War, the title of a bestselling book proclaimed "the end of history" (Fukuyama 1992), meaning that the victory of capitalism over communism had resolved the major questions of how to organize society. About the same time, a line from a popular song by the British band Jesus Jones spoke of "watching the world wake up from history." Some people appeared to view history as a kind of personal affront to their claims of individualism and self-achievement. Many agreed with Henry Ford Sr. that "history is more or less bunk." Others, reflecting the legitimate concerns of post-structural theorists, questioned the "taken-for-granted" categories—men/women, black/white—that historians have traditionally employed in constructing their accounts (Mills 2005).

History has made a recent comeback, however. Eminent historian Margaret MacMillan (2008, 3) notes that history is "widely popular these days, even in North America where we have tended to look toward the future rather than the past."

To understand the value of historical sociology as a methodological approach, think for a moment about the role of history—and memory—in your own life. Consider your own personal relations with others. Do you begin each meeting with your friends anew? Of course not. Your friendship is based on experiences, ideas, and feelings you have shared. In short, you have a history together. If you were to suddenly lose that history—if you contracted total amnesia, for example, like the protagonist in the film *Memento*—the friendship would also be lost.

Looking around us, we can see where history continues to play a role in shaping current events: long-simmering disputes in Ireland, the Middle East, and Kashmir provide ample evidence. Likewise, the echoes of history can be heard in the breakup of Yugoslavia in the 1990s. Not even the United States—surely the world's most proudly modern country—can escape history. Witness, for example, the plethora of Hollywood movies that continue efforts at coming to terms with *the* meaning of the Vietnam War or that attached to more recent conflicts in Afghanistan and Iraq, or the continuing civil unrest in the American South over whether to remove statues erected to the memory of those who fought for the Confederacy—or, indeed, the protests in Canada over statues erected to several historical figures. As the controversy over statues especially shows, the meaning of events is not carved in stone.

What of Canada? In an oft-quoted remark, Prime Minister William Lyon Mackenzie King (1874–1950) once stated, regarding Canada, "If some countries have too much history, we have too much geography." As John Gray (1994, 124) notes, such arguments really mean that Canada "lacks *European* history," conveniently ignoring 50,000 years of Indigenous existence in North America. But even by Eurocentric standards, the argument is false, as one glance at Quebec's licence plates will attest: *Je me souviens* (I remember). Remember what? History . . . although which particular historical events and how they are remembered often differ between groups of people.

We need not refer, however, merely to centuries-old history. Ask Indigenous Canadians about the continuing impact of residential schools, some of which remained open until the mid-1990s. Or ask Albertans about the National Energy Program of 1980–1986 and how it still colours a widespread understanding of political relations between that province and Ottawa (or at least the federal Liberal Party).

Note, however, that the facts of history often vary with people's understanding, valuation, and interpretation of history. People may agree on the former but not on the latter. Alternatively, they may disagree about *both* the facts *and* the meaning of events—a problem increasing manifested through the spread of social media.

The late Palestinian scholar Edward Said (1993, xiii) remarked that "nations are narrations." But the history that makes up our narratives is often contested terrain (Francis 1997). History, in this sense, is not "dead" but, rather, a source of constant rediscovery, re-creation, reinterpretation, and *power*. As George Orwell (2008, 37) wrote in his novel *1984*, "Who controls the past controls the future: who controls the present controls the past."

Every society possesses a dominant narrative. Always, however, there are also counter-narratives seeking expression—the voice, in too many cases, of the **subaltern**—that is, the oppressed subject. Among the questions an historical sociologist asks are the following: Who determines the "official" historical narrative? How does this narrative square with the facts? Are unofficial, alternative, anti-oppressive, and even multiple histories heard and respected within the society? What are the lessons—myths, really—that a people construct around their collective histories? In what forms (institutions, laws) is history enunciated and enshrined in the present?

Of course, our historical narratives can sometimes trap us. It *is* possible for some countries to have "too much history," to be (as it were) stuck in the past; but not remembering—living in a state of amnesia—is also a trap.

History *determines* nothing (Carr 1990). But our understanding—our *imagination*—of it locates us, both individually and collectively, in time in the same way that geography locates us in space. Put another way, our understanding of history organizes material in a manner that shapes our interpretation of current events. Meaning and meaningful action are impossible without a temporal context (see Rickman 1961; Dilthey 1961).

Moreover, the consequences of historical events (as set down in institutions, treaties, laws, etc.), as well as our understanding and interpretation of these events, often set off chains of meaning and action long after the specific events themselves have ceased. Thus, in Canada, two lines can be drawn—one leading directly, the other indirectly—from the Royal Proclamation of 1763. The first of these lines leads to the Oka Crisis of 1990 and recent efforts at resolving long-standing treaty and other jurisdictional disputes (Chapter 11). The second of these lines leads to the Meech Lake Accord and the Quebec referendum of 1995 (chapters 3 and 4).

One way to comprehend the role of history in shaping Canadian society is to employ a methodological technique termed **counterfactual history**, defined as a simulation based on calculations about the relative probability of plausible outcomes (Ferguson 2003; see also Showalter and Deutsch 2010).

What is counterfactual history? While once condemned as a pointless parlour game, counterfactual history properly employed is not just history "made up." Rather, it is based on factual information and interpretive and extrapolative logic, held together by an historical sociologist's imagination.

The use of counterfactual history is not new (Honan 1998). Recalling, for example, the events that led to the dissolution of the Austro-Hungarian Empire in 1918, Oszkar Jaszi (1929/1961, 380) wrote,

> Opposed to the materialistic point of view, I accept the . . . reversibility of the historical process, and regard the chief utility of all historical and sociological investigations to be to admonish us of the alternative possibilities of history.

Counterfactual history provides a means of separating what is important in history from that which is merely incidental. It alerts us to the importance of history by asking the question, "What if people involved in an event had made different decisions, or events had otherwise transpired in different ways?" The reader is invited throughout this text to ask similar questions about Canada. What if New France had not been surrendered to the British in 1763 (Chapter 1)? What if the Meech Lake Accord had been passed in 1990 (Chapter 3)? What if the United States had decided to invade Canada following its own civil war (Chapter 5)? What if the Liberals had won the 1988 election and not signed the Free Trade Agreement (Chapter 7)? What if Indigenous Nations had been treated as equals in the founding of Canada after 1867 and not as colonized subjects (Chapter 9)?

Finally, counterfactual history also alerts us to the fact that individuals and the decisions they make matter—again, that history does not determine the present. For Canadians, repeatedly advised that globalization is inevitable and that the invisible hand of the marketplace cannot be resisted, or that Canada is too small to forever resist absorption into the American Empire, reminders of personal efficacy are to be valued.

OUTLINE OF THE TEXT

The book is divided into three sections. These sections deal with what both Canadian philosopher John Ralston Saul (1997) and political scientist Peter Russell (2017) argue are

Canada's three foundational pillars, or experiences—the Indigenous, francophone, and anglophone—and whose relationship to each has shaped the specificity that is Canadian society. Each of these pillars is a kind of "master narrative" that is used to structure the overall text while, at the same time, dealing with other important relationships, based (for example) on differences of gender, ethnicity, race, and class.

Part 1 (chapters 1–4) examines francophone Quebec's relationship with the rest of Canada, while Part 2 (chapters 5–8) examines English Canada's relationship with the United States. In a manner calculated to disrupt the usual historicized narrative of Europeans' arrival and Indigenous peoples' gradual disappearance from the scene, the Indigenous/non-Indigenous relationship is dealt with in Part 3 (chapters 9–12).

At another level, each of these sections deals with larger issues impacting all societies in the early 21st century: nationalism, neo-liberalism, and cultural values of social solidarity that persist, despite modernity, because—some would argue—they define what it means to be human. These larger themes are returned to in a final chapter that again examines the complex relationship between the state, globalization, and society while comparing Canada with other countries on issues of inequality, social development, and democracy.

CONCLUSION

Sociology is the study of society. But what is society? This chapter has established a framework and a set of theoretical and methodological tools for answering this question. The remainder of this text applies these tools to the study of a specific phenomenon—Canadian society.

In keeping with the narrative structure employed by historical sociologists, the story of Canadian society that follows enlists all the usual literary devices: myths (the Conquest); metaphors (are Quebec and Canada "two solitudes," in the phrase made famous by novelist Hugh MacLennan [1998], or "Siamese twins," as described by Saul [1997]?); symbols (Canadian hockey, the maple leaf, the fleur-de-lis); heroes, villains, and tragic figures (Louis Riel was all three, depending upon whom you ask); and recurrent subtexts (regional alienation, Americanization, ethnic divisions).

For hundreds of years—longer, in the case of Indigenous peoples—people in this part of North America have been creating, together and alone, a story as broad as the prairie landscape, as deep as the Hudson Bay basin, and as rich as ore from the Canadian Shield. It is a story worthy of many books. This is one of them.

NOTE

1. Statistics Canada (2019a) has devised three projections of Canada's population by 2068. The low-end projection is that Canada's population at that time will be 44.4 million; the high-end projection is 70.2 million.

CRITICAL THINKING QUESTIONS

1. Is higher-level thinking possible without employing abstractions?
2. In what concrete ways is the world both globalizing and becoming more localized?
3. Should sociologists strive to change the world?
4. How might you apply the four main theoretical perspectives discussed in this chapter to current issues in your community?
5. How does an historical sociological methodology help in studying a society such as Canada's?

RECOMMENDED READINGS

Anderson, Benedict. 1983. *Imagined Communities*. London, UK: Verso.
  Imagined Communities remains a central book in nation studies, its title capturing a central idea of nationhood as a social-psychological construct.

Ferguson, Niall. 2003. *Virtual History: Alternatives and Counterfactuals*. London, UK: Pan Books.
  This book provides a fun and interesting introduction to the idea of counterfactual history.

Knuttila, Murray, and Wendee Kubik. 2000. *State Theories: Classical, Global, and Feminist Perspectives*. Halifax: Fernwood.
  This book is an excellent review of theoretical perspectives on the state.

MacMillan, Margaret. 2008. *The Uses and Abuses of History*. Toronto: Viking.
  MacMillan's short and very readable book is an excellent introduction to the importance of the historical perspective in social research and a warning regarding the improper uses of history.

Robbins, Richard H., and Rachel A. Dowty. 2019. *Global Problems and the Culture of Capitalism*. 7th ed. Toronto: Pearson.
  This text, now in its seventh edition, provides a comprehensive sociological examination of globalization, including numerous case studies.

RELATED WEBSITES

Canadian Historical Association
www.cha-shc.ca
  Founded in 1922, this is Canada's leading bilingual organization for the scholarly study of history.

Canadian Sociological Association

www.csa-scs.ca

> Founded in 1965 as the Canadian Sociology and Anthropology Association (CSAA) but renamed the Canadian Sociological Association in 2007, the CSA is Canada's pre-eminent organization for sociologists. It holds professional meetings every year in a Canadian city and works closely with other international organizations in the field.

Statistics Canada

www.statcan.gc.ca

> The Dominion Bureau of Statistics was created in 1918. In 1971, it was renamed Statistics Canada. It is the primary source of statistical information for the Canadian public about their country.

CANADIAN SOCIETY ON VIDEO

> *Postcards from Canada.* 2001. National Film Board of Canada, 41 minutes, 20 seconds. A breathtaking photographic sweep of Canada, narrated by the late Peter Gzowski, from the frozen vistas of the Arctic to the frenzy of rush-hour traffic, from deep within the Canadian Shield to the orbiting Radarsat satellite.

PART 1

CANADA AND QUEBEC

For a brief moment, on the evening of October 30, 1995, it seemed that Quebec had decided, via a referendum on sovereignty, to separate from Canada; the endless debates between English- and French-speaking Canada had reached a fatal climax. Like deer caught in winter headlights, stunned Canadians watched Quebec's vote results unfold on their television screens.

In the end, the *No* side narrowly defeated the *Yes* side by just over a percentage point (50.6 percent to 49.4 percent), a mere few thousand votes. For supporters of sovereignty, the sadness of defeat was lessened by the true believers' faith that next time their side would win. For federalists, nervous relief dampened the ecstasy one would expect of victory. By the skin of its teeth, Canada had narrowly escaped a venture into an unknown, uncertain, and, some argued, dangerous territory.

The time since the 1995 referendum has seen a different Quebec and a different Canada emerge. Much of what French-speaking Quebecers demanded for decades has come to pass, including recognition by the Canadian House of Commons in the fall of 2006 of Quebec as a "nation." As such, the issues that historically aroused the separatist spirits seem rendered dormant, replaced by a new confidence and a détente with the rest of Canada. Nonetheless, to understand Canada it is necessary to examine the history of English-French relations in Canada, how those relations have structured both Quebec and Canadian society as a whole, and why a country reputed by many outsiders to be "the best in the world" has seemed at times to teeter perilously close to dissolution. Part 1 examines this history in the context of sociological insights into the origins of societal relations and conflicts, the symbolism surrounding these, and their transformation over time.

CHAPTER 1

Living with the Consequences of 1760

Notre-Dame-des-Victoires Roman Catholic Church, Old Quebec City. Photo by DEZALB from Pixabay.

Valour gave them a common death / history a common fame / posterity a common monument.
—words engraved on the Wolfe and Montcalm Monument, Quebec City

I expected to find a contest between a government and a people: I found two nations warring in the bosom of a single state.
—Lord Durham's *Report*, 1839

The human tragedy, or the human irony, consists in the necessity of living with the consequences of actions performed under the pressure of compulsions so obscure we do not and cannot understand them.
   —Hugh MacLennan, 1959; words later adapted by The Tragically Hip for their 1992 song "Courage"

INTRODUCTION

The 1980 and 1995 Quebec referendums on sovereignty and the threat of others in the future bring into sharp relief two very different views of Canada. Is Canada a partnership of two founding peoples, the French and English, or even a third, the First Nations, as discussed in Part 3 of this text? Or is Canada a federation of 10 equal provinces: Quebec, and what has been termed "the rest of Canada" or ROC? Most francophone Quebecers believe the former, sometimes referred to as the "two nations theory." They further believe that as a minority nation within Canada, they have an historically distinctive patrimony that must be protected; that they constitute a "distinct society" within Canada.

Thanks to decades of political wrangling, many people in English-speaking Canada know something of the history of Quebec-Canada and French-English relations. But this knowledge is often partial or inexact. In any case, facts do not automatically produce meaning; even less do they constitute truths.

This chapter goes beyond the historic facts to explore the emotional and symbolic meaning of English and French relationships in Canada, and the early evolution of this unique relationship. Embedded in the discussion are important sociological questions regarding dominant-subordinate relationships and the responsibilities and consequences imposed by history upon conquerors and conquered alike.

THE AGE OF MERCANTILISM

Between 1689 and 1763, the French and the English fought a series of wars. The last of these wars (1756–1763) was known in Europe as the Seven Years War, but in British North America as the French and Indian War (Hofstadter et al. 1957). North America was merely one outpost, albeit an important one, in these wars. To understand these wars, it is necessary to reflect briefly on the political economy of European expansion beginning in the 15th century.

Before that time, the basic structures of European society had remained fundamentally unchanged since (roughly) the collapse of the Roman Empire (see Manchester 1992). In Thomas Hobbes's (1651/2014) memorable phrase, life was "poor, nasty, brutish, and short." People lived predictable lives in small rural communities. Families were large, class structures and age and gender roles were fixed, trade was local, and barter was the chief means of exchange.

Slowly, however, European feudal society began to change. Central to the changes was the growth of states in which power was centralized and monarchs became all-powerful, a corresponding decline in the temporal power of churches (though religion itself remained important), and the emergence of a new merchant class. In earlier times, churches had frowned upon trade, especially such practices as the granting of monopolies, usury, and profiteering (Hofstadter et al. 1957). Between the 16th and 18th centuries, however, there arose a new economic arrangement. Now the new merchant class and the state encouraged commercial trade. Merchants paid the state levies and taxes, and even lent money at favourable rates to support the state's armies. In return, merchants induced states to enact policies, including war, designed to protect their business interests (La Haye 1993).

The new economic arrangement was called **mercantilism** (Hofstadter et al. 1957; La Haye 1993; Norrie and Owram 1996). The chief aim of mercantilist policies was to preserve the mother country's supply of precious metals and to make it less vulnerable during times of war. Colonies were fundamental to mercantilist policy. In practice, because mercantilism and colonialism also meant the enrichment of one state and its merchant allies at the expense of other states and their business friends, conflict was a frequent result. In North America, the conflict primarily involved the English on the eastern seaboard and around Hudson Bay and the French in Nova Scotia and along the St. Lawrence, the colony of New France. The Indigenous peoples of the region soon found themselves caught up in the conflict.

THE RISE AND FALL OF NEW FRANCE

The history of New France begins in 1534. That year, French explorer Jacques Cartier (1491–1557) first made landfall on the shores of the Gaspé Peninsula (see Miller 2000). Like the Spanish far to the south, Cartier came in search of gold. He was discredited, however, when the "gold" he brought back from his third voyage in 1541–1542 turned out to be iron pyrite. Diverted by a series of European conflicts, France temporarily forgot about North America (Morton 1997, 24).

Early in the next century, however, France returned in the person of Samuel de Champlain (1570–1635). A "navigator, soldier, visionary," "a Protestant turned Catholic by conviction," and "a man of Renaissance curiosity and eternal fortitude" (Morton 1997, 25), Champlain in 1608 founded a trading post at what is now Quebec City. Thus began New France.

From the beginning, the post's survival was perilous. Life was harsh. Champlain's efforts to forge alliances with the Huron Confederacy brought the colonists into conflict with the Huron's chief enemies, the tribes of the Iroquois Confederacy. Despite Champlain's efforts to build a colony, Quebec City in 1627 still had fewer than 100 people. In that year, France's chief minister, Cardinal Richelieu, formed a private company made up of 100 merchants and aristocrats. The Compagnie des Cent-Associés was given a monopoly over the fur trade in exchange for promises to colonize the territory (Moore 2012).

Still, the settlement did not thrive. Military threats continued. In 1629, an English trading company seized Quebec City; the city was returned to France in 1632 only after diplomatic negotiations (Moore 2012). The fact is, Quebec City and the surrounding area were far less politically and economically valuable to France than its posts in Cape Breton, Nova Scotia, and Newfoundland, which protected the valuable cod fishery. Dickinson and Young (2008, 16) note that, until 1760, "France imported far more cod than fur and the fishery employed many more seamen and ships than all other French colonial trade combined" (see also Eccles 1993a). By contrast, New France's fur trade economy was unstable. European demand fluctuated according to fashion. Supply was equally unpredictable. Weather conditions, the needs and good fortune of Indigenous suppliers, the actions of middlemen (Norrie and Owram 1996), and conflict between Indigenous tribes, exacerbated by competition between the French and Dutch trading companies in Port Albany, all affected supply. In the 1630s, disease ravaged the Huron population, delivering a severe blow to the trade (Dickinson and Young 2008; Innis 1962; Morton 1997).

In 1650, about 1,200 French European colonists lived in New France (Dickinson and Young 2008, 65). In theory, the Huron Confederacy's destruction opened up new opportunities to attract French immigrants into the fur trade and agriculture. However, war and the Cent-Associés's near bankruptcy prevented the colony from taking advantage of the changed circumstances (Moore 2012). In 1663, the colony's population was still only around 3,000 people. That year, Louis XIV dissolved the company and made New France a royal colony. An active immigration policy was pursued. Encouragement and financial inducements were given to disbanded military officers and their men, civilian workers, and—in an effort to redress a long-standing gender imbalance in the colonies—women. By 1681, the population of New France was 10,000. Most of Canada's francophone population today traces its roots to these original 10,000 inhabitants (Moore 2012, 119; see also Dickinson and Young 2008). New France's population thereafter increased primarily from births rather than immigration.

Growth and development create their own problems and natural contradictions. After 1663, the internal contradictions and conflicts facing New France mounted: the Catholic Church versus the state; rural versus urban; fur trading versus agriculture and industry. As historian Desmond Morton (1997, 27) asks, "Were the people of New France to be habitants, cultivating their small colony in the valley of the St. Lawrence, or were they to be voyageurs, carrying the fur trade, Catholicism, and French influence throughout the continent?" Yet the colony also began to develop. Visitors to New France in the mid-18th century regularly commented on its growing prosperity and cultural sophistication (Eccles 1993b).

In 1756, however, New France faced a growing threat from England and its southern colonies. The 13 British colonies that eventually became the United States had a more developed and diverse economy than New France. Agriculture and commerce were thriving. The English colonists—roughly 1.5 million compared with New France's 75,000 (Eccles 1993a, 171)—were eager to expand into the Ohio Valley. There, however, they faced a belt of French forts constructed along the Ohio and Mississippi rivers, established both to support the fur trade and to hem off British expansion (Innis 1962; Morton 1997; Eccles 1993a). In 1754, a series of armed clashes occurred between British and French forces. These events partially set off the Seven Years War in Europe, which began two years later (Dickinson and Young 2008; Eccles 1993a).

As the war began, the English in North America possessed several advantages over the French. Besides a larger population in the colonies, the English also had a larger and more powerful navy, with which they could blockade the French colonies, and a larger standing army. In 1756, there were roughly 22,000 English regulars and militia in the colonies, to which were later added another 20,000 regular troops. By contrast, New France had no more than 7,000 regular troops, along with several thousand militiamen and Indigenous allies (Dickinson and Young 2008, 47; Moore 2012, 177; but see also Eccles 1993a, 171).

Despite these overwhelming odds, the French in the early stages successfully defended their colony, in part because the British had difficulty in marshalling their superior resources. Gradually, however, the British gained the upper hand. In 1758, the British seized the fort of Louisbourg in Nova Scotia. The following summer, a British fleet sailed up the St. Lawrence, while troops on the ground scorched the countryside, burning barns and houses, killing villagers and livestock as they went (Henderson n.d.), in what today we would recognize as an act of **terrorism**: the deliberate use of acts of violence or the threat of violence by individuals, groups, or the state for the purpose of furthering political ends—in this instance, orchestrated by the state.

Gradually, Quebec City was isolated from the surrounding territory, and the siege began. Throughout the following months, the British, led by General James Wolfe (1727–1759), conducted a constant bombardment of the city in hopes of forcing the French under the Marquis Louis-Joseph de Montcalm (1712–1759) out of their defensive position. Much of lower Quebec City was laid to rubble. The British also torched the surrounding countryside (Dickinson and Young 2008; Dufour 1990; Moore 2012), yet the French did not surrender.

Frustrated, Wolfe tried a final tactic. On the night of September 12, the British forces seized a path up the cliffs to west Quebec City, setting the stage for the historic battle of the next day, as related by Moore (2012, 178):

> On the Plains of Abraham, Wolfe's red-coated army formed one line, facing east towards the city. After some fierce skirmishing, Montcalm's troops in their white coats moved west towards them, drums beating, regimental banners flying. The two armies were roughly equal in numbers. These were precisely the conditions Wolfe had sought all summer, and in a battle that lasted barely fifteen minutes, the close-range volleys of his skilled regulars tore the French army apart.

Wolfe died that day in battle, Montcalm succumbed the next day to his wounds, and part of a national mythology was born (see Francis 1997). In effect, the war was over, although fighting continued for another year. In August 1760, Montreal capitulated, the French humiliation completed by a public surrender of arms (Dufour 1990). The Treaty of Paris in 1763 formally ended the war. France ceded its former colony along the St. Lawrence to Britain.

THE ROYAL PROCLAMATION AND QUEBEC ACT

In 1760, New France, now known as Quebec, was in a state of ruin. Roughly a tenth of the colony's population had been killed (Moore 2012, 180). Quebec City and the area around it were in ruins, the colony's economic infrastructure destroyed. Famine and disease were rampant. All in all, the war and its immediate aftermath were terrifying for the residents of the colony.

Adding to their abject circumstances was the French's fear of their conquerors. The French had good reason to fear the British—the torching of homes and villages along the St. Lawrence gave ample proof of the enemy's barbarity. The forced expulsion of roughly 7,000 Acadian people in 1754 from what is now Nova Scotia, followed by 6,000 more in 1758, many of them from what is now Prince Edward Island, was also fresh on French minds (Dickinson and Young 2008, 47; Conway 2004, 22; Russell 2017, 26). (Many of the Acadians resettled in Louisiana; hence that region's "Cajun" culture.)

The French were surprised, therefore, by the generally courteous and respectful behaviour of the British. In the years between 1760 and 1764, Quebec was under martial law. Yet the British did little to interfere with French traditions, and indeed they helped in the province's reconstruction. In the words of Dufour (1990, 27), the conqueror's behaviour was "correct. Even exemplary."

The Royal Proclamation of 1763, however, gave the French a taste of the iron fist. Designed to assimilate the French, the proclamation declared that British institutions would henceforth govern Quebec, with an elected assembly and British laws. British immigration would be encouraged. Finally, in an effort to head off further wars with Indigenous peoples, the interior hinterland of the Ohio Valley was made a vast reserve (Innis 1962; Dickinson and Young 2008).

In an act of surprising civility, however, British governor James Murray (1721–1794) refused to enact many of the proclamation's provisions. In part, Murray's actions were based on his recognition that the provisions were not enforceable (Russell 2017). Eighty-five percent of the colony's inhabitants lived in rural areas beyond administrative control (Dickinson and Young 2008). There was little likelihood soon of a wave of English immigration that might change the colony's predominantly French and Catholic character. Under existing British law, no Catholic could hold office, making impossible the notion of a representative legislative assembly. Montreal fur traders were already demanding that the Ohio Valley be reopened for business. Moreover, given growing unrest in England's southern colonies on the continent, the last thing the British needed was agitation in the north. But it is also true that Murray himself *actually liked and admired the French* and, setting a tradition followed for a time by his successors, acted, albeit paternalistically, as a protector of French interests (see Conway 2004). Conqueror and conquered were mutually seduced (Dufour 1990).

Thus, in 1774, the British passed the Quebec Act, which reversed much of the Royal Proclamation. The law was changed to allow Catholics to hold elected office, and seigneurial land tenure was confirmed. The colony's territorial boundaries were increased to include some of the First Nations territories. Catholics were given the right to practise their religion. The Catholic Church was once more allowed to collect tithes. And while English criminal law was retained, French law was allowed in civil cases (Dickinson and Young 2008).

In a curious sense, the Conquest seemed to have changed little. Nonetheless, its effects were real. In the most profound sense, the Conquest forged a people, a sociological—but not a political—nation.

BEING *CANADIEN*

A people somewhat distinct from the European French were arising in the colony even before the Conquest. In contrast to the town-dwelling French administrators, the peasant farmers—*habitants*, as they described themselves—were mostly rural. In their everyday lives, they experienced greater independence and social equality, including gender equality, than people living in France (Rioux 1978). This basic equality, combined with isolation, the harshness of their existence, and the constant fear of attack by Indigenous tribes, developed a strong sense of solidarity among the *habitants* over time (Dickinson and Young 2008; Rioux 1978). By the 1750s, visitors to New France "claimed that a new kind of French people was emerging along the banks of the St. Lawrence" (Morton 1997, 28), a people distinguished by different beliefs, customs, behaviours, and even dialect (Rioux 1978; see also Eccles 1993b; Thompson 1995). They called themselves *Canadiens* and their country Canada. There was no need to copyright the *Canadien* identity. By definition, *Canadiens* were French-speaking Catholics settled permanently along the St. Lawrence. Moreover, in their own minds at least, the territorial boundaries of their nation extended well beyond their colony's borders into areas traversed and imagined by French voyageurs and missionaries.

But distinctiveness, though necessary, is not a sufficient basis of nationalism. The Conquest transformed—though not all at once—New France's distinctiveness into nationalism (Cook 1995).

Try to put yourself for the moment in the shoes of a *habitant* after 1763. You have been conquered, not merely defeated, by the English (Dufour 1990). Equally, you have not been merely orphaned by the mother country, but, as the Treaty of Paris cruelly attests, abandoned. The past cannot be reversed. Finally, to add to your confusion, your enemy is actually magnanimous in victory. As a conquered subject, you welcome the difference; the fact that you are not tortured, raped, and killed is clearly important. Still, as Dufour (1990) remarks, the conqueror's magnanimity changes nothing; indeed, it actually makes your subordinate status more humiliating because now you must also be grateful.

New France in 1760, like the British colonies to the south, was growing apart from France and no doubt one day would have sought independence, but the Conquest truncated this normal development. Quebec's sense of self-identity was not positive in the sense of one chosen by the people; rather, it was an identity thrust upon them, forged in war, trauma, and the torturous severing of the colony's umbilical cord from France. Time and circumstances conspired to make Quebec's French population a distinct people—*les Canadiens*—before their time. By contrast, the few hundred British who occupied Quebec after 1763 remained, even to themselves, "the British."

Political circumstances were unstable, however. As the British feared, the American colonists in 1775 revolted. In consequence, 40,000 United Empire Loyalists fled to the northern British colonies, about 10,000 of them settling in Quebec (Dickinson and Young 2008). The contest for political, territorial, and economic power and national identity began again.

THE LOYALISTS AND THE CONSTITUTION ACT OF 1791

Imagine now that you are a United Empire Loyalist recently arrived in Canada. The American revolutionaries have stolen your property and distributed it among themselves, their friends, and small farmers to garner political support for the new republic (Zinn 1995). Your financial circumstances and physical health, and that of your family, are poor. By contrast with the 30,000 Loyalists who arrived in Nova Scotia by ship, you came to Canada by horse cart overland and on foot, bearing little. You are bitter and angry; a historian will later remark that "quarrelsomeness" marked your character and that of your compatriots (Brown 1993, 246). You were loyal to Britain (you say to yourself and anyone who will listen) and now have lost everything (Morton 1997; but see also Francis 1997). The free land, clothing, and farming utensils supplied by the British administration (Dickinson and Young 2008) do not assuage your bitterness.

Such, in part, was the view of the Loyalists as they arrived in the northern British colonies. Like the French, the Loyalists were a conquered people. In Canada, however, the roughly 10,000 who arrived found their humiliation increased by the fact that they were a minority surrounded by more than 70,000 French Catholics. For their part, the French were no more thrilled with their new neighbours, viewing them as an advance guard of future anglophone settlement. In an age when ethnic and religious bigotry were rife, the arrival of the Loyalists was like gasoline thrown on a fire.

Elsewhere, the arrival of Loyalists created similar tensions. In Nova Scotia, the arriving Loyalists quickly swamped the existing population of 4,000 New Englanders and Acadians. The 1,000 Loyalists who arrived on the Island of St. John (renamed Prince

Edward Island in 1799) equalled those already living there, while the 400 Loyalists who arrived on Cape Breton doubled that island's existing population (Brown 1993, 241–242).

Anxious to prevent conflict, the British thus segregated the respective populations. Nova Scotia was divided and a new province, New Brunswick, created, while Cape Breton (temporarily) became a separate colony. The colony of Quebec, formally New France, likewise was divided.

The instrument of this latter division was the Constitution Act of 1791. The Constitution Act amended the Quebec Act but left intact many of the latter's provisions protecting the French language, the Catholic Church, French civil law, and the seigneurial system. The Constitution Act, however, divided the colony into Upper Canada (where many of the Loyalists had settled) and Lower Canada (French Canada), the term *Canada* having historically been a loose synonym for New France. The act further maintained strong executive power in the office of the governor, an executive council (made up of the governor's advisers), and a non-elected legislative council (a colonial House of Lords). But it also allowed, for the first time, popularly elected assemblies in both Canadas and extended the franchise. Finally, the act envisaged the creation of a colonial aristocracy, a state church, and public education. The first idea was soon abandoned, but substantial land holdings were set aside for the Anglican Church and education (Careless 1970; Dickinson and Young 2008).

Even at the time, the Constitution Act pleased few people. The merchants of Montreal had not wanted Canada divided. The English in Lower Canada did not like being separated from the English in Upper Canada. The agrarians and rising bourgeoisie in both provinces did not like the act's openly mercantilist bent. Democrats, believing that the elected assemblies did not go far enough, railed against oligarchic rule. But perhaps the major flaw in the Constitution Act was that it institutionalized ethnic conflict (Cook 1995). Thereafter, as Quebec premier Pierre-Joseph-Olivier Chauveau would later remark, the English and French met each other only "on the landing of politics," frequently in conflict.

THE CONQUEST'S IMPACTS

Social stratification is the system by which a society ranks categories of people (e.g., by occupation, race, ethnicity, or gender) in a hierarchy involving inequalities of various sorts. At the top of New France's stratification system before the Conquest were royal officials: the governor, the *intendant* (the business manager), and the senior military officers. The clergy were somewhat parallel to the royal officials, but after 1663 clearly subordinate in the final instance to the state. The *seigneurs*, some of whom came from the French nobility, came next in the social order, followed by a sizable middle class (composed of merchants and small vendors), the urban working class, then the *habitants* (Eccles 1993a). (Note that this stratification system does not include women or Indigenous peoples.) The Conquest changed Canada's economic and political order. The degree and type of changes, however, are somewhat disputed.

One dispute involves the actual number of people who left New France. The articles of capitulation in 1760 gave inhabitants the right to return to France. Perhaps only a few hundred took advantage of the opportunity (Dickinson and Young 2008, 49), perhaps 4,000 (Eccles 1993a, 173). Most of those who left were French bureaucrats and soldiers (though some decommissioned soldiers remained), quickly replaced by British bureaucrats and soldiers.

A second, more important dispute arose during the 1950s and 1960s over the Conquest's impacts upon New France's economic classes and the colony's future. Early on, scholars of "the Montreal School" (Saul 1997, 19)—Maurice Seguin, Guy Fregault, and Michel Brunet—developed the **decapitation thesis** (Cook 1995, 92; Dickinson and Young 2008). This thesis holds that the Conquest had destroyed New France's "embryonic bourgeoisie" (Brunet 1993; see also Rioux 1978, 39; Conway 2004, 24–25). The English and Scotch merchants subsequently stepped into the void left by the French bourgeoisie, while the French who remained retreated to a rural existence. There, dominated by the Catholic Church, they espoused conservative values inimical to capitalist development (Norrie and Owram 1996; Dickinson and Young 2008). Lower Canada's economic development was thus truncated.

In direct refutation of the decapitation thesis, a second argument holds that New France in 1763 had no "viable business community" (Dickinson and Young 2008, 51), no middle class (Hamelin 1993) to be destroyed. More recently, a synthesis of both arguments has emerged. This third argument suggests that the Conquest resulted in the departure of agents and merchants directly connected to France's trading companies, but that local merchants, storekeepers, and traders stayed. That is, the transatlantic French bourgeoisie was eliminated, but the local French bourgeoisie, albeit small, remained (Norrie and Owram 1996; see also Dickinson and Young 2008).

More broadly, these debates point to how historical interpretations can have current sociological and political significance. For example, while the decapitation thesis lends itself to support for the Quiet Revolution (Chapter 2) and sovereignty (Cook 1995; Saul 1997), the second and third arguments provide much less support for the belief that the conquest held back Quebec's early development.

There is no dispute, however, that Canada's economy immediately after 1760 was in crisis. The war's devastation, the permanent disruption of its mercantile (metropolitan-hinterland) arrangements with France, and the outbreak of wars with Indigenous tribes on the frontier were all contributing factors. Within a short time, however, Lower Canada's economy began to rebound. The colony was rebuilt; the Indigenous wars ended in 1763 (see Chapter 9), restoring the Ohio Valley fur trade; and trade links were re-established, this time with Britain. Capital also began to enter Lower Canada from Britain and merchants in England's southern colonies.

The direct economic impacts of the Conquest should not be minimized. In the long term, however, the Conquest's social and political consequences were more important. After 1763, the English held the balance of **power**: the ability to impose his or her will upon others even against their resistance (see box 1.1). The imposition of English upon

---

Box 1.1: Means of Exercising Power

Power can be exercised by three means, each of which may be effective depending on a particular situation, but each also has limits and none is effective in all situations. Often one means of power is used in combination with another. The three means of power are as follows:

Force or the threat of force: The English expulsion of the Acadians in 1754, the Canadian government's use of the RCMP against protesters at Regina in 1935 (Chapter 6), the use of the Canadian military to deal with the Front de libération du Québec (FLQ) Crisis in 1970 (Chapter 2), and the use of military troops to deal with the Oka Crisis in 1990 (Chapter 11) provide examples of the use of force.

Reward: Whereas force involves use of the stick, reward involves the use of the carrot. Rewards may be material (e.g., money), but not always; status, for example, is also a form of reward. Because systems of social stratification differentially reward individuals and groups on the basis of class, race, ethnicity, gender, and so on, such systems are themselves means of power. (Note that withholding instrumental rewards results in economic coercion—the use once more of force.)

Authority: Authority gains its power by being recognized as legitimate. Authority frequently coincides with the means of force and reward but often includes elements of tradition, law, status, or prestige that tend to legitimize current power relations (see chapters 2 and 7) of any period.

Lower Canada was a fact of life, despite the newcomers' frequent conciliations and sensitivity to the French majority. With the arrival of the Loyalists after 1775 (see Chapter 5), ethnicity came to play an even greater role in Canada's social structure. The effects of ethnicity, however, were mitigated somewhat by the granting of elected assemblies under the Constitution Act of 1791, which opened up opportunities for a nascent *Canadien* political class.

By the early 19th century, ethnicity had become a defining feature of Lower Canada's system of social stratification. The English controlled the executive and judicial branches in the political realm, but the French dominated the legislative branch. The English controlled the upper reaches of the economy: international trade, banking, and finance. The French business class was restricted to local trade. At the lower levels, British labourers, contractors, and producers—often favoured by British administrators—competed with their French counterparts (Dickinson and Young 2008; Innis 1962; Norrie and Owram 1996). Finally, the *habitant* majority occupied the bottom level of Lower Canada's social structure (Rioux 1978).

The ethnic division of Lower Canada was not merely social, but also demographic. Gradually, the English "captured" the urban portion of the colony, while the French retreated to the colony's villages and rural farms (Rioux 1978). Early in the 19th century, 40 percent of Quebec City and 33 percent of Montreal were anglophone (Norrie and Owram 1996, 98). In this context, the Catholic Church, especially its parish priests, grew in importance.

By the 1830s, these social, political, and economic divisions, built on a foundation of Conquest, had nurtured among Lower Canada's French population a growing sense of grievance and a rising spirit of nationalism. Finally, the grievances boiled over.

THE REBELLIONS OF 1837–1838

In 1837, after years of political discord and in the midst of a prolonged recession, rebellions broke out in both Upper and Lower Canada. The causes of the rebellions in the two Canadas were similar. Popular anger focused on the corrupt oligarchies that governed the provinces—the Château Clique in Lower Canada, the Family Compact in Upper Canada—and their political masters in London.

In Upper Canada, the rebels demanded "responsible government." They wanted real power to rest with an elected legislative assembly. The Upper Canadian rebels also wanted economic reform, believing—correctly—that current policies were designed to protect mercantilist interests. The rebels wanted instead increased immigration, greater access to capital, and more land opened up for agriculture (Careless 1970; Norrie and Owram 1996).

Though the movements in both Upper and Lower Canada were informed by liberal democratic ideals, inspired by the French and American revolutions (Rioux 1978; Cook 1995; Conway 2004; Romney 1999), a fundamental difference existed between the two rebellions. In contrast with Upper Canada, the rebellion in Lower Canada was inspired not only by demands for representative democracy, but also by nationalism (Conway 2004). In consequence, the conflict in Lower Canada could only be more serious—and bloody.

In Lower Canada, the rebellion's leader was Louis-Joseph Papineau (1786–1871), a member of the new middle class and speaker of the Assembly. The rebellion occurred in several stages. In October 1837, Patriote leaders issued a "Declaration of the Rights of Man," based on the American declaration of 1776 (Ouellet 1993, 360). At Saint-Denis on November 23, 800 Patriotes defeated 200 British regulars. This was followed by a British victory two days later at St. Charles, then a massive British attack on the rebels at Saint-Eustache, north of Montreal, on December 14. Many of the rebels hid in the village church. The British, however, set the church alight and shot the rebels as they fled through the windows. Estimates of the number of Patriotes killed range from 58 to 100. The village of Saint-Eustache was razed. The fight continued into the countryside, where British troops left behind them a trail of scorched *habitant* homes, farms, and villages (Morton 1997, 37; Dickinson and Young 2008, 165; Conway 2004, 37).

In the wake of the Lower Canada rebellion, martial law was declared, the Canadian constitution suspended, and a new governor of British North America, Lord Durham (1792–1840), was named (Dickinson and Young 2008). By now, Papineau had fled to the United States. The rebellion, however, soon flared anew.

A second uprising occurred in late November 1838, with its leader, a follower of Papineau, declaring Lower Canada a republic and issuing a "Proclamation of Independence." The uprising was soon put down, however. While a degree of leniency followed the first wave of rebellions in Lower Canada, no leniency was shown after the second rebellion. Twelve Patriotes were hanged and 58 deported to Australia's penal colonies, while two more were banished (Dickinson and Young 2008, 167; Conway 2004, 37; Wynn 2012, 204).

By contrast, the rebellion in Upper Canada was, in the words of historian Jack Granatstein (1996, 29), a "small-bore affair." There, William Lyon Mackenzie (1795–1861)—publisher, editorialist, social critic, *and* grandfather to a later prime minister—led the rebellion. Since the 1820s, he had argued against the Family Compact and for democratic reform, to no avail. Finally, emboldened by events in Lower Canada— Mackenzie was in frequent contact with Papineau—the rebels took up arms in December 1837. On December 7, after a night of heated discussion at Montgomery's Tavern, 800 of Mackenzie's followers (mostly farmers, small-town tradesmen, and some professionals) marched up Yonge Street in Toronto. There, untrained militia recruited by Upper Canada's elite met them. Shots rang out. The rebellion soon ended. Mackenzie fled disguised as a woman to the United States—he would return 12 years later and be elected to the legislature—but two of his lieutenants died on the gallows. Ninety-two more of Mackenzie's followers were sent to the penal colonies, while hundreds more, disenchanted with the rebellion's outcome, eventually left for the United States. As in Lower Canada, a few cross-border skirmishes occurred in 1838, led by groups trying to liberate Canada from "the British yoke." In 1840, Mackenzie supporters also burned a British steamship at the Thousand Islands and blew up General Brock's monument at Queenston Heights. These events were mere sideshows, however. Upper Canada's rebellion was over (Morton 1997; Dickinson and Young 2008; Conway 2004; Wynn 2012).

Neither rebellion had widespread popular support. The movements were primarily middle class in origin (Morton 1997; Ouellet 1993; Trofimenkoff 1993), no match for the power of the state and its allies. In Upper Canada, the rebels were easily tainted with the labels "American" and "republican" (Granatstein 1996). In Lower Canada, the movement's avowed anticlericalism evinced even stronger condemnations from the Catholic Church (Trofimenkoff 1993).

The rebels' final defeat in 1838 was decisive. French nationalism would not rise again with force until the 1960s (Cook 1995). For Canada as a whole, defeat meant the throttling of liberal democracy (see Laxer 1989; Trofimenkoff 1993; Conway 2004). Thereafter, conservatism, exercised both in the political-economic and religious realms, gained an increased hold on Canadian society.

LORD DURHAM AND THE ACT OF UNION

The new governor, Lord Durham, spent only five months in Canada before resigning in anger. On his return to England, he produced his analysis of the rebellions, based on his short time in Canada, which included a 10-day steamboat trip and conversations with a few close acquaintances (G. Martin 1993a). Durham's *Report on the Affairs of British North America* condemned the ruling oligarchy, the abuses of land granting, and Anglican privileges in the colonies, while also dealing with a host of other issues, from immigration to canal building (see Careless 1970). It further made some of the most derogatory statements ever directed at the *Canadiens*, including this one, quoted in Colombo (1994, 38):

> There can hardly be conceived a nationality more destitute of all that can invigorate and elevate a people, than that which is exhibited by the descendants of the French in Lower Canada, owing to their peculiar language and manners. They are a people with no history and no literature.

Finally, Durham's report included a particularly memorable paragraph (Colombo 1994, 38):

> I expected to find a contest between a government and a people: I found two nations warring in the bosom of a single state: I found a struggle, not of principles, but of races; and I perceived that it would be idle to attempt any amelioration of laws or institutions until we could first succeed in terminating the deadly animosity that now separates the inhabitants of Lower Canada into the hostile divisions of French and English.

Durham's analysis reflected European views of the time about the "necessary" relationship between state and nation (see the Introduction); as such, it is a textbook example of material reality being shaped to fit theory and of the problems of biases in conducting research (see box 1.2). Theories have consequences, and in this case two significant consequences resulted from Durham's report.

Durham's report contained two major recommendations: first, that the British North American colonies be granted responsible government and, second, that Upper and Lower Canada be united (Careless 1970). In effect, the sundering of the two colonies by the Constitution Act of 1791 would be reversed. There was now, however, an important difference. In 1791, the French had been in the majority; it was to protect the English minority that the colonies had been split. By 1840, however, the demographics had changed. Lower Canada still had the larger population, between 600,000 and 650,000, compared with Upper Canada's population of 450,000 (Dickinson and Young 2008, 183; see also Conway 2004). But virtually all of Upper Canada's population was anglophone, while approximately 150,000 people in Lower Canada were also of British heritage. Thus, the English could dominate in a united Canada. Moreover, Durham argued that English

Box 1.2: Observer Bias: A Tale of Two Journeys

Lord Durham travelled through Upper and Lower Canada in 1838. Only a few years earlier (in 1830), Alexis de Tocqueville (1805–1859) journeyed to the United States. Both Lord Durham and Tocqueville were European aristocrats; both travelled in the respective countries for only a few months, yet the latter produced *Democracy in America*, still considered an accurate depiction of the United States' developing political culture, while the former's *Report* is viewed as biased and inaccurate. The result raises the question of why observer bias occurs and how it might be prevented.

Durham arrived with fixed notions of the situation in Lower Canada, and his informants were a relatively small number of the existing elite who supported his beliefs. By contrast, Tocqueville arrived in the United States to study that country's penal system, not US society as a whole. As a result, he was relatively open to experiencing the new environment and supplemented his observations by reading widely and interviewing a large number of Americans.

The tale of Durham and Tocqueville also raises the question of the proper distance researchers should have from the object of study. On the one hand, group members have an advantage over outsiders in understanding what is observed. On the other hand, insiders are sometimes too close to see what outsiders can observe.

immigration should be strengthened to ensure over time the complete assimilation of the French, thereby blunting the nationalism that had fuelled the recent rebellions.

In 1840, the British government implemented much of Durham's report through the Act of Union, but what they did not implement was crucial. First, they denied outright responsible government, with the result that reformers in Upper Canada remained angry. Second, the union was not total. The Quebec Act's major provisions protecting French civil law, the rights of the Catholic Church, and local control of education remained extant. Even more importantly, the Act of Union meant that elected legislative assemblies in Canada East (Lower Canada) and Canada West (Upper Canada), each with 42 seats, would govern Canada (see Conway 2004).

The seeds for further crisis, leading ultimately to Confederation in 1867, were thus sown. The French population would not—could not—be assimilated; indeed, the legislative structure actually gave the French minority power disproportionate to its numbers, power that they sensibly used, voting *en bloc*, to protect their interests. The English in Upper Canada, meanwhile, complained bitterly that they had cast off the oligarchic power of the Family Compact only to find themselves now dominated by Lower Canada and a French-speaking minority that was Catholic to boot (see Romney 1999).

The rebellions of 1837–1838 had seen French Canada conquered a second time. Both Papineau's dream of an independent French republic and Durham's hope of French assimilation were equally chimerical. Nonetheless, the conflicts remained. It would take the forces of modernity, a major depression, two world wars, and the rise of a new intellectual class before Quebec nationalism would again rise, but rise it would, in unexpected ways, with consequences for conquered and conqueror alike.

CONCLUSION

New France gave Canada its name, its history, its founding myths (see Chapter 6), and one of its languages—according to Dufour (1990), its "heart." After 1840, however, the English increasingly put their stamp on the rest of Canada. A series of events symbolized the ongoing rejection of the French language and its near confinement to the province of Quebec: the hanging of Riel in 1885; the school acts adopted in several provinces, beginning with Manitoba in 1890; and, of course, the conscription crises of the two world wars.

Why does this matter? From the perspective of historical sociology, five later aspects of Canadian society derive, directly or indirectly, from these events. First, these events (beginning with the Conquest) help explain Canada's system of stratification until recent times, with those of English ethnic origin disproportionately occupying elite positions and people of French (and other) ethnic origins disproportionately occupying lower rungs (see Porter 1965; Clement 1975; Nakhaie 1997).

Second, these events suggest why francophone Quebecers might feel a sense of grievance toward the rest of Canada (see Conway 2004). Third, attention to historical and political contexts also sheds light on Quebec's continuing claims to linguistic, cultural, and religious distinctiveness.

A fourth, less obvious, consequence of this early history is that no "strong national myth" could cement Canadian federalism, as in the United States (Balthazar 1997, 45; see Part 2 of this text). In the words of political scientist Reg Whitaker (1987, 23), "Nationalism as legitimation is a weak, derisory ploy in Canada." Any attempt by political demagogues to "fly the flag" has quickly run aground on ethnic divisions and the Canadian tendency, perhaps inborn, toward skepticism.

Finally, a fifth related consequence (which we shall explore further) involves the complex nature of Canadian federalism. Some of the Fathers of Confederation no doubt wanted to create a strong, centralized government, leaving the provinces with only meagre powers. Quebec's presence, however, as well as that of the smaller Maritime provinces, made this impossible. Canada's flexible and significantly decentralized system of powers and responsibilities—sometimes a benefit, sometimes not—is a product of efforts to solve real problems and conflicts among Canada's constituent communities.

Sociologically, an examination of Quebec's relationship with Canada draws attention to how social inequality exists as an historically structured relationship with deep material and ideological underpinnings, in turn creating the basis of group identity and conflict.

To a degree, political institutions and cultural traditions before the 1950s restrained the conflict between Canada's English and French communities. Where these might have proved insufficient to reduce conflict, social isolation provided additional restraint. But the world would not let the two communities go on this way. War and the relentless forces of modernity—capitalism, industrialism, and secularism—were about to throw the separate worlds together, altering the trajectory of Canadian society.

CRITICAL THINKING QUESTIONS

1. What are the similarities and differences between mercantilism and global capitalism today?
2. What are the processes by which social conflict between different groups emerges and is transformed over time?
3. Under what conditions are some means of power more effective than others?
4. Is it possible to overcome observer bias?
5. In what sense is nationalism always based on a myth?

RECOMMENDED READINGS

Dickinson, John, and Brian Young. 2008. *A Short History of Quebec*. 4th ed. Montreal and Kingston: McGill-Queen's University Press.
This book provides an excellent social history of Quebec, from pre-European times to the present.

Dufour, Christian. 1990. *A Canadian Challenge/Le défi québécois*. Halifax: Oolichan Books and the Institute for Research on Public Policy.
In a Weberian manner, this book allows anglophones to understand the world from the point of view of francophone Quebecers, while also showing the unrecognized influence that each community has had upon the other.

Manchester, William. 1992. *A World Lit Only by Fire: The Medieval Mind and the Renaissance*. Boston: Little, Brown.
This book brings to life, in a very readable way, Medieval Europe and shows how very different it was from the present day.

Moore, Christopher. 1997. *1867: How the Fathers Made a Deal*. Toronto: McClelland & Stewart.
This book tells the engaging story of how the Fathers of Confederation created Canada's first constitution.

Porter, John. 1965. *The Vertical Mosaic.* Toronto: University of Toronto Press.
Porter's book is a classic in sociology, detailing Canada's complex stratification system in the 1960s and paving the way for subsequent studies of the changing dynamics of power and inequality in Canada.

RELATED WEBSITES

Acadian-Cajun Genealogy, Culture, History, and Music Group
www.acadian.org/acadfounding.html
This group preserves and promotes the Acadian cultural heritage.

CanGenealogy
www.cangenealogy.com/quebec.html
Quebec's demographic history is among the best recorded anywhere. Cangenealogy has a list of sites for those interested in genealogical history.

Library and Archives Canada
www.collectionscanada.gc.ca
Extensive birth, marriage, death, and other records for Canada as a whole.

CANADIAN SOCIETY ON VIDEO

Canada: A People's History. 2000–2001. CBC, 17 episodes, 32 hours. history.cbc.ca.
This 17-episode documentary television series, which first aired on the CBC, portrays the history of Canada.

Canadian History Series. 1959–1961. National Film Board of Canada, six videos of roughly 28 minutes each.
The historically accurate videos deal with six individuals important to Confederation in 1867: Robert Baldwin, Lord Durham, Lord Elgin, Joseph Howe, William Lyon Mackenzie, and Louis-Joseph Papineau.

A License to Remember—Special Edition/Un certain souvenir—Édition spéciale. 2007. National Film Board of Canada, 121 minutes, 2 seconds.
Examines the meaning of the words on Quebec licence plates, *Je me souviens*, at the heart of Quebec history and society.

CHAPTER 2

100 Years of Solitudes

Chateau Frontenac. Photo by Jean-François Gagnon from Pixabay.

English and French, we climb by a double flight of stairs toward the destinies reserved for us on this continent, without knowing each other, without meeting each other, and without even seeing each other, except on the landing of politics.
   —Pierre-Joseph-Olivier Chauveau, first Quebec premier after
   Confederation, 1876

He shall hang though every dog in Quebec howl in his favour.
   —Prime Minister John A. Macdonald, refusing to pardon Riel, 1885

Society must take every means to prevent the emergence of a parallel power which defies the elected power.
   —Prime Minister Pierre Trudeau, at the peak of the FLQ Crisis, 1970

INTRODUCTION

In the spring of 1955, Canadians were transfixed by television pictures of hundreds of hockey fans rioting in the streets of Montreal to protest the suspension, for the rest of the regular season and playoffs, of Maurice "Rocket" Richard (1921–2000). Store windows were smashed, cars overturned, and property looted, leading to the arrest of 37 adults and four juveniles. The Richard riot ended only when Richard went on radio and television the next day to ask the rioters to stop.

We noted in the Introduction the importance of symbols to societies. In 1955, Quebec was on the verge of *La Revolution Tranquil*, the Quiet Revolution. In this context, the Richard riot had little to do with hockey. Richard, the first player in NHL history to score 50 goals in a regular season, was hero to a French-speaking population dominated by an anglophone minority. For francophones, Richard's suspension was symbolic of this unequal and discriminatory relationship. In turn, the riot was a symbolic protest against what many Quebecers viewed as 200 years of subjugation and humiliation. As we will see in this and subsequent chapters, however, symbols not only unite, they also divide. Indeed, much of French-English conflict in Canada can be viewed as a clash of symbols.

This chapter provides a necessarily short account of Quebec during the period between Confederation and the Second World War. It then provides a more detailed account of the events, individuals, and ideas that transformed Quebec, leading to the historic Quebec election of 1960 and the turbulent years of the Quiet Revolution, which ended with the October Crisis of 1970, a moment when, once more, English-speaking Canada watched transfixed by events on their television screens. Competing concepts of nationalism are discussed in what follows, too.

ENGLISH EXPANSION AND THE ISOLATION OF QUEBEC

Confederation in 1867 recognized Quebec as distinct, with its own majority French-Canadian population, Catholic religion, and civil law tradition, combined with autonomous political powers. For many French-Canadians, the historic province on the shores of the St. Lawrence was their homeland. At the same time, significant French-Canadian communities existed outside Quebec, especially in New Brunswick, but also in Nova Scotia, Prince Edward Island, Ontario, and the western territories (Silver 1997). Confederation partially disentangled issues of Quebec's governance from those of the other, majority-English, provinces. Confederation did not, however, separate French and Catholic sensibilities from the issue of how their compatriots were treated in the other provinces—indeed, from the issue of respect.

Some French Quebecers in 1867 no doubt viewed diaspora French as "dead ducks," to use Parti Québécois leader René Lévesque's expression from the 1970s. In their minds, only Quebec could provide security for French language and culture. Nonetheless, French-Canadians in general also viewed Canada as a bargain between French and English.

Yes, Quebec for all practical purposes would always be the citadel of French culture in Canada, but the rights of French Catholics outside Quebec were also to be respected. By 1900, a broader understanding that "the two races" were not to be compartmentalized but rather were to forge a new nation had emerged within French Canada (Silver 1997). Henri Bourassa (1868–1952), grandson of Louis-Joseph Papineau, was a chief spokesperson for this "pan-Canadian" view (Rioux 1993).

Not all French-Canadians held this view; even fewer English-Canadians did so. Alexander Muir's poem "The Maple Leaf Forever," written in the year of Confederation, says volumes about English Canada's view of the country just created:

> In days of yore, from Britain's shore,
> Wolfe the dauntless hero came,
> And planted firm Britannia's flag,
> On Canada's fair domain.

A hundred years of history had taught the English that the French could be neither defeated nor assimilated. However, the French could, it was believed, be contained. The French could have their separate language, religion, and civil laws, but only in Quebec. The rest of Canada would carry a distinctly British stamp.

These conflicting views of Confederation, and of the rights of minorities, inevitably met on the political landing. The rendezvous did not take long to occur. At Red River in the western territories in 1869, Canadian and American expansionism ran headlong into an established community of Métis (see chapters 6 and 9). Led by a young intellectual and visionary, Louis Riel (1844–1885), the Métis firmly rejected American efforts at annexation but also demanded from the Canadian government full provincial status and protections for their French language and Catholic religion. The Conservative government of Prime Minister John A. Macdonald (1815–1891) acceded to the demands. Thus, the Manitoba Act was passed in 1870, guaranteeing French-language rights in the legislature and schools, and the right to a Catholic education in the new province of Manitoba.

The battle for French and Catholic rights outside Quebec was not over, however. The social conflicts and political intrigues of 1869 were repeated again in 1885, this time against the wider canvas of the entire western territories. This time, the demands of Riel and the Métis, and other Indigenous and non-Indigenous peoples, were rejected. The "rebels" were hunted down and tried, and Riel hung amid outcries from French-Canadian politicians and the Quebec press, convinced that he would not have been executed had he not been French and Catholic.

Riel's hanging was a blow to both French-Canadian and Métis hopes on the Prairies. For French Quebecers, Riel's hanging symbolized their exclusion from the rest of Canada. Incensed by Prime Minister Macdonald's refusal to pardon Riel (see chapter epigraph quotation), French Quebec thereafter generally refused to vote Conservative, the major exceptions being two landslide victories in 1958 and 1984, under John Diefenbaker

(1895–1979) and Brian Mulroney (1939–), respectively (appendices 1 and 2). More than ever, French Quebecers retreated behind their provincial walls, where the Catholic Church and conservative political leaders urged them to remain (see Dufour 1990; Rioux 1993; Conway 2004).

In the aftermath of 1885, immigrants quickly filled the West (see Chapter 6). In the early stages, many of these were from Ontario: English, Protestant, and often decidedly anti-Catholic. Soon they were a majority. In 1890, the English-speaking and Protestant legislature of Manitoba abolished Catholic separate schools and declared that French was no longer an official language (Careless 1970; Conway 2004). Declared unconstitutional by the Supreme Court in 1979, this legislative act nonetheless served its purpose: In the interim, French was reduced to a minority language in Manitoba. The legislature of the Northwest Territories in 1892 passed similar language legislation that remains contested today (see box 2.1). In 1912, Ontario eliminated French from its public education system. In 1916, Manitoba broke an agreement made with Sir Wilfrid Laurier (1841–1919) when he was prime minister and abolished French and any other language except English from its schools (Conway 2004; Silver 1997).

Throughout the 20th century, the minority status of French-Canadians and the political impotence of Quebec within Confederation were thus reinforced again and again. Symbolically, French-Canadians were "put in their place"—that is, the place of a vanquished people. Canada was British.

The maintenance of British constitutional symbols, such as the monarchy and the Union Jack, was particularly grating to French-Canadians. For nationalists, such symbols were constant reminders of defeat. For pan-Canadianists, such symbols revealed English-Canadians as slavish colonials unable or unwilling to get on with the task of creating a new nation. Tensions heightened in 1903 with the Boer War, leading to Bourassa's break with the Laurier government. French-English conflict escalated into a full-blown political crisis during the First World War (see also Chapter 6).

Many French-Canadians viewed the First World War as not being Canada's fight, and they were offended that English-Canadians had allowed themselves and the country to be dragged into the conflict. By contrast, many English-Canadians were still emotionally tied to the British Empire and could not understand the lack of a similar French-Canadian need to defend France. That the umbilical cord between French-Canadians and France had been severed in 1763 entirely escaped most people in English Canada, who viewed French-Canadians *en masse* as disloyal, if not cowardly.

As the war dragged on, the need for fresh troops (and British demands that Canada "pull its weight") caused the Unionist government of Prime Minister Robert Borden (1854–1937) to intensify its efforts at recruitment. These efforts were botched, leading in 1916 to anti-recruitment riots in several Quebec towns. Amid continued Quebec opposition, the next year Borden introduced the Military Conscription Bill and called an election on the issue. Though many Canadians, farmers and labourers among them, opposed conscription, the election results revealed a particularly massive fissure between Quebec

Box 2.1: The Case for Alberta as a Bilingual Province

In 2003, a 54-year-old truck driver, Gilles Caron, was ticketed for making an unsafe left turn and fined $54. He fought the ticket, wanting it and his hearing on the matter in French, but was denied under Alberta's 1988 Languages Act. That act states that "all Acts and regulations [in Alberta] may be enacted, printed and published in English only."

In 2008, a provincial court judge—after 89 days of hearings involving legal arguments and the testimony of several historical experts—threw out Caron's ticket. The judge ruled that bilingualism was an established part of Rupert's Land legislature and the Northwest Territories as early as 1845 and that bilingualism remained in force. In consequence, Alberta's Languages Act was unconstitutional and the ticket given to Caron invalid.

The Alberta government appealed this ruling. In 2009, a judge of the Court of Queen's Bench in Alberta sided with the government, ruling that historical documents and orders did not enshrine language rights in what became Alberta. In early 2014, the Alberta Court of Appeal upheld this ruling but Caron rejected this finding. His lawyer argued that French language rights were entrenched in the Royal Proclamation of 1869, which annexed western land and the Northwest Territories into Canada. In 1870, the Manitoba Act created that province and was specific about the legal right to legislative bilingualism for Manitobans. He argued further that the Manitoba Act still reached beyond Manitoba's borders because that province's authority stretched into the Northwest Territories.

Justice Frans Slatter, of the Alberta Court of Appeal, rejected these historical arguments, however. In his ruling, Justice Slatter wrote, "Parliament knew full well how to entrench language rights, yet neither elected to do so in any constitutional document relating to what is now Alberta." Slatter wrote further that the 1905 Alberta Act, which founded the province, purposefully did not include French language rights.

Further complicating the issue is a Supreme Court of Canada decision made in 1988—the same year that Alberta's Languages Act was passed—that provinces have the power to determine their own language rights legislation. The matter was finally settled in November 2015. In a 6–3 split, the Supreme Court ruled that Alberta is not constitutionally required to enact, print, or publish laws in both English and French.

What do you think? The Supreme Court's decision was based on existing constitutional law. But should the legislatures and the laws of Alberta—and the rest of Canada—be recognized as formally bilingual? What would be the pros and cons of such a change?

Source: Cormier, Ryan. 2014. "Alberta Court of Appeal Rules Provincial Laws Don't Have to Be Bilingual," *Edmonton Journal*, February 21; *National Post*. 2015. "Supreme Court Says Alberta Doesn't Have to Make Its Laws in Both English and French," November 20.

and the rest of Canada (see appendices 1 and 2). Borden's government won, but there were no French-Canadians from Quebec or Acadia among his MPs (Silver 1997). The will of the English majority ruled over the French minority, and the Conscription Bill was passed. The riots resumed throughout Quebec (Careless 1970; Conway 2004).

In the end, only 60,000 men were actually drafted. A large number of French recruits—as many as 40 percent—did not report (Dickinson and Young 2008, 254). Few of the conscripts reached the front before the war ended. Bitterness lingered, however, between the French and English communities.

The Conscription Crisis of 1917 was reprised during the Second World War. In 1940, the Liberals, under Prime Minister William Lyon Mackenzie King, won re-election, partly on a promise made to Quebec that they would not bring in conscription. Two years later, however, as casualties again mounted, King sought political absolution from his promise through a national referendum. Since the promise had been made to them alone, French Quebecers viewed the matter as one that should have been resolved only with them, not all of Canada (Silver 1997). Nonetheless, the referendum was held. The outcome was quite predictable: Once again, Quebec was isolated. Quebec voted 73 percent against releasing King from his promise, while the rest of Canada voted 80 percent in favour of the release and, thereby, conscription (Conway 2004, 54).

In the end, King's adroitness—some would say dithering—forestalled the sort of flare-up that had occurred in 1917. Though anti-conscription riots did occur in parts of Quebec, they were less intense than during the previous war (see Fraser 1967). Most Quebecers understood that King had gone the extra mile in attempting to meet their objections to conscription.

For many French Quebecers, the hanging of Riel, Canada's ongoing British connection, the conscription crises, and the school controversies symbolized their minority status within Confederation. Too often, when conflicts arose, Quebec's views and interests were ignored. By the late 1940s, the idea of a pan-Canadian French and English Canada had all but retreated from Canada's political map. More than ever, Canada consisted of "two solitudes."

By then, however, the consequences of three historical world events were rapidly pushing the French and English communities together. The first two events were the world wars of 1914–1918 and 1939–1945. The third event was the intervening economic depression (see Chapter 6). All of these events had the consequence of enlarging and centralizing state power, the first two in making Canada a giant war factory, the third in creating the liberal welfare state (Rice and Prince 2013). A further consequence was the emergence from the Second World War (in particular) of a new spirit of nationalism in English-speaking Canada. The stage was thus set for a clash over the nature of Canada and Quebec's place within it. These changes in English-speaking Canada cannot be understood, however, without reference to the profound social, economic, and, ultimately, political changes also occurring inside Quebec.

SOCIAL AND ECONOMIC CHANGE IN QUEBEC, 1867–1960

Quebec's population grew from 1.36 million in 1881 to 2.36 million in 1921, then to 5.25 million in 1961. Its proportion of the Canadian population declined from 31.4 percent in 1881 to 26.8 percent in 1921, but rebounded to 28.8 percent by 1961 (see table 0.1). In part, this decline during the middle period resulted from decreased birth rates. Quebec's birth rate fell from a pre-industrial high of 50 per 1,000 to 41.1 in 1884 and 1885 to 29.2 during the period from 1931 to 1935, when Quebec was rapidly industrializing (Dickinson and Young 2008, 202). Birth rates in rural areas remained higher than in urban areas, but high death rates, especially infant deaths, reduced overall population growth. During and after the Second World War, however, the birth rate once more rebounded—part of the broader Canadian phenomenon known as the baby boom (Chapter 7)—while life expectancy gradually increased.

The larger reason, however, for Quebec's relative decline in population during this period, compared with the rest of Canada, lay in immigration and emigration. The early 20th century witnessed massive European immigration into Canada, especially the West (see Chapter 6). At the same time, despite the exhortations of church leaders and politicians, many francophone people left the boundaries of Old Quebec. Fearful of their treatment elsewhere in Canada but finding themselves unable to survive farm life economically, some were convinced to move into the Shield country north of the St. Lawrence. Thus began Quebec's period of northern expansion. Work in New England's lumber mills, however, proved a far greater attraction. Between 1840 and 1930, perhaps 900,000 Quebecers, along with many francophone people from Nova Scotia, moved (in particular) to the New England states (Cook 1995, 91; see also Dufour 1990).

Of course, immigrants also came to Quebec. This was not a new occurrence. The potato famine of the 1840s, for example, saw the arrival in Quebec of large numbers of Irish, many of whom, as orphaned children, were welcomed into francophone families (Dufour 1990). Immigration intensified during the period from 1911 to 1915, however, resulting in large and thriving Italian and Jewish communities arising in Montreal (Dickinson and Young 2008). As in the rest of Canada, immigration declined during the two world wars and the intervening depression years. After 1945, however, as immigrants streamed into Canada, many again located in Quebec. Indeed, the proportion of immigrants to Canada settling in Quebec increased steadily, from 13.6 percent in 1946 to 23.7 percent in 1951 and remained at 23.6 percent in 1961 (GRES 1997, 97). Nonetheless, Quebec remained about 80 percent francophone, while the actual number of anglophones declined and became more confined to the Montreal region.

These demographic changes were accompanied by other social and economic changes. For example, agriculture was still an important element of Quebec's economy in 1891, employing 45.5 percent of Quebec's labour force. Even then, however, Quebec was rapidly industrializing. Quebec's transition from a rural and pre-industrial society to an urban, industrial society intensified in the early 20th century, fuelled by the flow of foreign (mainly American) capital into Canada (see Chapter 6). By 1941, agriculture in Quebec employed only 19.3 percent of the workforce (Dickinson and Young 2008, 213). As noted, some of the "surplus" workers left Quebec. Many more, however, found employment in manufacturing (based on Quebec's abundant hydro power) and resource extraction (especially timber and mining).

The decline in rural Quebec was matched in both relative and absolute terms by growth in urban Quebec. In 1901, 36.1 percent of Quebec's population lived in urban areas; by 1931, the figure was 63.1 percent (Dickinson and Young 2008, 203). Montreal was the hub of much of this urban growth, spurred by the presence of the head offices for the Bank of Montreal, Sun Life, the Canadian National Railway, and the Canadian Pacific Railway. Other urban centres, many of them resource towns, sprang up across the province.

Again, however, the interrelated social and economic changes that Quebec experienced after Confederation and up until the end of the Second World War were not particularly unusual. Industrialization, urbanization, and assorted social changes occurred throughout Canada (see Chapter 6). What made Quebec's situation different was that the changes it experienced brought into sharp relief the social, political, and ideological structures that had arisen around the Conquest.

As we have seen, Quebec after 1760 was stratified along (among other things) ethnic lines. Whether an individual was French or English influenced his or her occupational status, class position, chances for social mobility, and even the town and neighbourhood in which he or she lived. Curiously, the arrangement "worked"—if that term can be used—after the years 1837 and 1838 precisely because French and English did live in separate worlds.

Industrialization and urbanization disrupted this arrangement, forcing French and English into renewed contact and conflict. For example, industrialization created a (largely) **francophone proletariat**. At work sites, francophone workers found themselves in regular conflict with their anglophone bosses. Class conflict merged with ethnic conflict, creating a dangerous mix that finally exploded at the company town of Asbestos in 1949 (Finkel 2012). The Asbestos strike became a symbolic rallying point for opponents of the conservative government of Maurice Duplessis (1890–1959) and an economic structure that favoured anglophone-dominated corporations.

Likewise, industrialization, mass communication, and rising levels of literacy also gave rise to new occupations and professional groups. Quebec's new francophone middle class felt thwarted in its aspirations for social and economic advancement (Taylor 1993; Rioux 1993). Inevitably, these changes resulted in challenges to the old political order. These challenges came from trade unionists, progressive intellectuals (including some within the Catholic Church), and members of the new middle class and were directed first at replacing Duplessis's Union Nationale government, but the challengers also had the broader goal of changing Quebec's role within Confederation. These challengers were not homogeneous, however. In particular, each possessed a different ideological notion of Quebec's identity and its relation to the rest of Canada.

IDEOLOGY AND IDENTITY

What is ideology? **Ideology** is the set of assumptions, beliefs, explanations, values, and unexamined knowledge through which we come to understand reality (Marchak 1988). As we have seen (Chapter 1), the dominant ideology tends to legitimize existing power relations; as Marx (1977a, 236) stated, "The ruling ideas of each age have ever been the ideas of its ruling class."

Throughout the late 20th century, federalists and sovereigntists in Quebec argued vehemently about Quebec nationalism and its future. They agreed, however, on one thing: Quebec's past (Couture 1998), in particular that Quebec had been governed, in the words of Rioux (1993), by an "ideology of conservation"—alternatively, "conservative nationalism" or (reflecting the influence of the Catholic Church during this period) "**clerico-nationalism**" (Cook 1995, 91). After the rebellions of 1837–1838, they argued, Quebec had been in a 100-year "time warp," dominated by the Catholic Church, a bourgeois and anglophone business establishment, and an anti-democratic and authoritarian state, resulting in a reactionary and backward society (Trudeau 1996).

Conservative nationalism stressed French Quebec's unique cultural heritage, glorifying the past and rural life. Engaging in business or seeking material rewards, by contrast, was denounced. So also were Quebecers warned against leaving their homeland, either for the United States (though many did so) or for Canada's opening West: There, the dragons of certain assimilation waited. Furthermore, French Quebecers were charged with a historic and sacred mission to defend and preserve their culture against the English, the last bastion of "true" Catholic France. (It was viewed as providential that Quebec had been saved from the radicalism and anticlericalism that had befallen the mother country after the French Revolution of 1789.) Large families were applauded. Catholic, French-speaking, agricultural, and traditional: these were the idealized traits, federalists and sovereigntists both agreed in the 1950s, that marked Quebec society in the second half of the 19th century and continued largely unchallenged until the end of the Second World War (Rioux 1993).

There frequently is a kernel of truth in generalizations. The Catholic Church *did* grow more powerful after the failed rebellions, as was reflected in the Ultramontane movement, and continued to exercise considerable influence over Quebec society until the 1950s (Dickinson and Young 2008). Anglophones *did* dominate Quebec's increasingly capitalist economy after 1880, especially its financial and manufacturing sectors. Quebec's political culture *was* strongly conservative, as represented by the Catholic priest, teacher, and historian Lionel-Adolphe Groulx (1878–1967), whose fierce nationalism also mixed with anti-secularism and, some argue, anti-Semitism. Its political system likewise *did* have anti-democratic and authoritarian aspects. Women, for example, did not get the vote until 1940, civil rights were sometimes abridged, and the state's coercive powers were frequently abused, particularly under the reign of Duplessis from 1936 to 1939 and again from 1944 to 1959 (see Black 1977), against labour and in defence of private property (Dickinson and Young 2008).

Nonetheless, dominant ideologies rarely go unchallenged. Recently, Couture (1998) has argued that pre-1960s Quebec was never entirely homogeneous. Equally important, he points out that Quebec was not much different from other Canadian provinces of the period. The Ultramontane movement had its counterpart in the Orange movement, which swept Ontario and much of the West (see also Saul 1997). Into the 1960s, Canada as a whole was socially conservative and highly religious. With the exception of Saskatchewan after 1944 (see Chapter 6), Canadian governments at all levels were business-oriented and, on occasion, authoritarian. Likewise, the economic and social changes (such as urbanization and industrialization) occurring in Quebec during the 20th century were similar in broad terms to those in the other provinces. In short, while displaying some distinct features, Quebec historically was neither entirely monolithic nor dissimilar from much of the rest of Canada.

In the early 1950s, however, the dominance of conservative ideology in Quebec declined in the face of two other ideological views of Quebec's future. The first of these ideologies was liberal, federalist, and anti-nationalist. Its leaders were Pierre Trudeau (1919–2000), a lawyer and political economist who rose to political prominence during the Asbestos strike, and Gérard Pelletier (1919–1997), a journalist, social activist, and long-time friend of Trudeau's. They founded a radical magazine, *Cité libre*, in 1950 to articulate their vision of Quebec's future in Canada. The magazine denounced the insularity and conservatism of Quebec. Though Catholic, the editors also denounced the power of the Catholic Church. Finally, taking a stance that marked his later adult life, Trudeau also denounced Quebec nationalism—indeed, all forms of nationalism, new and old—as retrograde, a reversion to tribalism. Trudeau's vision of Quebec and Canada was essentially liberal, ostensibly valuing the individual over the collective (but see Couture 1998). He and Pelletier argued that Quebec had all the powers it needed under the British North America Act. What was needed to address Quebec's rising demands was increased democracy within the province and greater power in Ottawa (McCall-Newman 1982; Clarkson and McCall 1990; Balthazar 1993).

The second ideological strain challenging conservative Quebec was sovereigntist and nationalist. Quebec's intellectual class, especially historians, provided early impetus for the nationalist cause by reinterpreting the history of Quebec in light of neo-Marxist notions of class and colonial oppression. But other members of the new middle class, such as journalists, broadcasters, and teachers, were also prominent (Rioux 1993; Cook 1995). The old Quebec nationalism was cultural rather than political, largely unconcerned with economic development, based on a set of mainly Catholic values, inward looking and defensive, and rejected newcomers. By contrast, while the new nationalism shared with the old a belief in the French language and was perhaps even more dedicated to preserving the French fact in North America, it was otherwise opposed, even scornful, of Quebec's traditional culture.

Like the liberal anti-nationalists, the new nationalists favoured modernization and political reform. Unlike the liberals, however, the new nationalists were often stridently anticlerical and highly secular, and their reforms extended into the economy. Most importantly, the new nationalists argued that French culture could survive only if Quebec had the powers of an autonomous state (Balthazar 1993; Taylor 1993; Conway 2004). These powers could be exercised within a loose federal arrangement, if not, however, within an independent country.

Embedded in this idea was an important transformation in identity. Prior to the Second World War, Canada's two identities, French-Canadian and English-Canadian, had existed (distantly) side by side. The war, however, fuelled a new sense of nationalism in English-speaking Canada and, by the close of the 1950s, fuelled increasing demands for an end to "hyphenated" Canadianism (see Chapter 6). In Quebec, however, these demands and the federal government's increasing encroachment into areas of provincial jurisdiction were viewed as threats. Quebec's long isolation and rejection by the rest of Canada produced, finally, an identity coincident with the new nationalism. The old nationalism identified with the French language and the Catholic faith; its people were *French-Canadian*. By contrast, the people of the new nationalism were *Québécois* (Webber 1994).

Revolutions require not only symbols but ideological justifications and blueprints. Quebec's *Tremblay Report* of 1956 provided both of these, and the report became a bible for the Quiet Revolution. In four volumes, it "gave ideological and statistical support to provincial autonomy and to the idea that the Quebec government was the primary defender of a threatened culture" (Dickinson and Young 2008, 296). In some ways profoundly traditional and nostalgic, the report nonetheless contained two ideas that have since been important to debates about Canada and Quebec. First, the report gave voice to a belief already existing in Quebec that Confederation involved a pact between two equal peoples, French and English. Quebec was not "just one" of several provinces. Second, the *Tremblay Report* argued that Quebec was distinct from the other provinces and required continued jurisdictional autonomy in some areas into which the federal government was moving (Cook 1995).

When Maurice Duplessis died in 1959, the last vestiges of conservative nationalism died with him. The Liberals, led by Jean Lesage (1912–1980), defeated Duplessis's Union Nationale government the next year. Quebec's Quiet Revolution had begun.

CLASHING NATIONALISMS AND QUIET REVOLUTIONS

Lesage's Liberal Party contained elements of both the new liberal and new nationalist factions. In time, that marriage would break down. At first, however, the goals of replacing the Union Nationale and modernizing Quebec provided sufficient cement to hold the coalition together.

The Liberals, in their first mandate, moved to bring Quebec's public services (health, education, labour laws, social welfare) up to the level of the other provinces (Conway 2004). They also made political changes: The voting age was lowered from 21 to 18, new laws governing election expenses were passed, and patronage and gerrymandering were attacked. Much of English Canada applauded these steps. Two years later, however, Lesage won re-election using the slogan *"Maîtres chez nous"* ("Masters in our own house"). English Canada grew more wary.

In 1962 the Liberals called an election seeking a mandate to nationalize Quebec's private electric companies. The idea was that of René Lévesque (1922–1987), a former journalist and prominent television commentator, now Lesage's minister of natural resources. Like many Québécois, Lévesque believed Quebec's distinctiveness could be protected only if francophone Quebecers had control over the economy, a belief that in time caused him to leave the Liberal Party and to lead the Parti Québécois.

In the meantime, however, the Liberals created Hydro-Québec, which quickly became a symbol of Quebec nationalism. Other measures followed, such as the creation in 1965 of the Caisse de dépôt et placement du Québec, made responsible for Quebec's own pension plan. These actions were popular among Quebec francophones who saw in economic nationalism a means of addressing entrenched inequalities between themselves and the English minority. Quebec's English-dominated business community viewed these actions with alarm, however.

The fears of English-speaking Canadians within Quebec were matched by those of their counterparts outside the province, concerned that Quebec nationalism threatened their ideal of "One Canada." Few Canadians were yet travelling across their country; the Trans-Canada Highway was not formally opened until the summer of 1962. Television and radio provided a kind of link, but also reinforced regional and cultural divisions. Indeed, French television in Quebec after 1950 became a chief breeding ground for cultural nationalism (Balthazar 1993). In consequence, Canadian nationalism exhibited what Rotstein (1978) described as **mapism**, the tendency of English-speaking Canadians to identify with the shape of Canada as learned in school by looking at the map, but to know nothing about the history or culture of their fellow citizens, especially those in Quebec. They knew only that Quebec was geographically at Canada's heart, and that Quebec nationalism now seemed to be a dagger pointed at that heart.

For most Quebecers, Canada outside Quebec also remained a mystery; more than a century of parochial education had ensured that. The new nationalists did not harbour any hatred toward English Canada. In the main, French Quebecers were simply indifferent to the rest of Canada.

For a few Quebec nationalists, however, the pace of social and political change was too slow. In the early 1960s, the Front de libération du Québec (FLQ) was formed for the sole purpose of taking Quebec out of Canada, by force if necessary. The FLQ and many of its sympathizers drew their revolutionary ideals from broader social currents of the time, in Canada and abroad. While in English Canada, anti-establishment politics focused upon opposition to the United States, in Quebec the spirit of revolution focused on anglophone symbols and institutions and their supporters. In the revolutionaries' view, Quebec was still a colony. In the blunt—and intentionally offensive—words of the nationalist writer Pierre Vallières (1971), francophone Quebecers were "White N_____s," and they needed to be liberated.

In 1963, the FLQ began a terrorist campaign directed at symbols of English privilege and power, including robbing banks, stealing weapons, and bombings. The campaign began with the bombing of the Wolfe monument in Quebec City—what more symbolic target could there be? Over the next seven years, the FLQ proceeded to other targets: McGill and Loyola universities; the Westmount district of Montreal; the Eaton's department store and the Montreal Stock Exchange; the RCMP and the Black Watch Regiment; a monument to Queen Victoria and the Queen's Printer. Six lives were lost. Some of the terrorists were caught, tried, convicted, and sentenced (Conway 2004, 64).

The FLQ's tactics never had strong support in Quebec; indeed, they were denounced. The bombings served a purpose, however, in garnering English-speaking Canada's attention. Thus began English-speaking Canada's education on Quebec and the history of French-English relations.

COMMISSIONS AND THE "THREE WISE MEN"

In the context of growing civil strife in Quebec and rising angst elsewhere, Liberal Prime Minister Lester Pearson (1897–1972) created the Royal Commission on Bilingualism and Biculturalism (Government of Canada 1963) in 1963. In its preliminary report of 1965 and a final report, encompassing six books, the commission detailed the second-class status of francophones within Quebec and Canada's federal structures. In 1961, for example, unilingual anglophones had the highest average income in Quebec ($6,049), followed by bilingual anglophones ($5,929), bilingual francophones ($4,523), and finally unilingual francophones ($3,107) (Webber 1994, 45; see also Conway 2004). Most of Quebec's private-sector economy was owned by anglophone Canadians or non-Canadians. Francophones were similarly disadvantaged in the federal civil service, significantly underrepresented and concentrated in the lower tiers of administration. Both inside and outside Quebec, English was the language of work in the federal service. Francophone hospitals, schools, and universities were inferior to those of anglophones (see also Porter 1965). In short, the pattern of social stratification in Quebec, set in motion by the Conquest, seemed largely unbroken 200 years later.

Even before the commission's final report, acting on its preliminary recommendations and spirit, the Pearson Liberals took several steps. There was never any intent that all of Canada could or should become a completely bilingual country. At the level of federal institutions, however, an intensive French- and English-language training program was instituted for civil servants. In keeping with its demands for greater control over internal economic affairs, Quebec was allowed to opt out of the Canada Pension Plan

(Webber 1994). A new Canadian flag also was created (see Chapter 6), one that broke with Canada's long-standing fealty to Britain (Conway 2004).

These measures had their critics, both among Quebec nationalists, who viewed the commission as obscuring their demands, and some in English-speaking Canada who were unsympathetic to francophone demands for equality. Yet many English-speaking Canadians also accepted, even embraced, the administrative and linguistic changes.

More problematic was the commission's vision of Canada—specifically, the idea that Confederation involved a partnership of the French and English "nations." Very quickly, some academics, including eminent historian Donald Creighton, denounced this **two nations theory** (a.k.a. **compact theory**) as revisionist (Creighton 1970). For them, Canada was not a partnership between the French and the English, but rather a partnership of equal provinces (see Romney 1999). In Weberian terms, French- and English-speaking Canadians had very different understandings of the basis of their relationship with the country. The resultant disagreement continues to frame Canada-Quebec relations and constitutional debates into the present (see Chapter 4).

The federal Liberal party recruited three prominent Quebecers in an effort to win over the hearts and minds of francophone Quebecers: the aforementioned Pierre Trudeau and Gérard Pelletier, and a labour leader, Jean Marchand (1918–1988). Soon referred to as Quebec's "three wise men," Trudeau, Pelletier, and Marchand believed Quebec's demands for cultural protection could best be met by securing representation within Ottawa. For the Liberal Party, they also represented the resurrection of an old idea that Canada was the home of both English and French. In English Canada, however, another message was frequently understood: that Quebec's new ministers would stop the nationalist agitation and put Quebec back in its place.

The year 1967 was Canada's centennial. English-speaking Canada was optimistic, its cheery enthusiasm captured by Bobby Gimby's song, "Canada." All of Canada and much of the world seemed to congregate that summer in Montreal, home of the Man and His World exposition, to celebrate. But France's president, Charles de Gaulle (1890–1970), came to Canada in July on a state visit. Steaming up the St. Lawrence on a French cruiser, he disembarked at Quebec City and proceeded by cavalcade to Montreal. There, overcome by the occasion, speaking from the balcony of city hall, de Gaulle shouted "*Vive le Québec libre!*" The Canadian government was not amused with this break in diplomatic protocol—Quebec and Quebecers did not, in its view, require liberation—and quickly insisted on de Gaulle's exit (see Clarkson and McCall 1990, 103–104). Nonetheless, for English-speaking Canadians, the Quebec "problem" had reared its head once more.

In 1968, Pierre Trudeau succeeded Lester Pearson as leader of the Liberal Party and prime minister. As justice minister in the previous Cabinet, Trudeau had reformed Canada's divorce laws and made liberal amendments to Criminal Code laws on abortion and homosexuality (Clarkson and McCall 1990). Now, in 1968, Canadians experienced "Trudeaumania" and became familiar for the first time with the word **charisma**, a term coined by Max Weber (1958, 295), meaning an extraordinary quality of a person, regardless of whether this quality is actual, alleged, or presumed.

As prime minister, one of Trudeau's first acts was to bring in the policy of official bilingualism. Following in the footsteps of Henri Bourassa, Trudeau held a pan-Canadian vision of the country, one in which French and English were equal from sea to sea. Quebec nationalism, he believed, would wither as francophones came to feel at home in the rest of Canada. Two years later, however, the Canadian state and society faced a serious challenge from those in Quebec who believed Trudeau did not understand their demands and was selling the rest of Canada a false vision.

THE OCTOBER CRISIS AND ITS AFTERMATH

On October 5, 1970, members of the FLQ kidnapped James Cross (1921–), a British trade commissioner. The terrorist cell quickly made seven demands in exchange for Cross's release. The Quebec and Canadian governments rejected all demands at first. They soon relented, however, granting one request: the broadcast and publication of the FLQ's manifesto.

Few Quebecers supported the FLQ's actions. Nonetheless, the manifesto, a broadly Marxist polemic laced with invective and dark humour, drew much applause. In its way, the FLQ touched on real frustrations and anger felt by francophones in the province.

Faced with unexpected public support within Quebec for the FLQ's position, the Quebec government declared on October 10 that no further concessions would be made to the kidnappers. A few hours later, the crisis escalated. Pierre Laporte (1921–1970), Quebec's labour minister, who had only months before nearly been elected provincial Liberal leader, was kidnapped by another FLQ cell acting independently.

René Lévesque, union leaders, and some others demanded negotiations with the FLQ for Cross's and Laporte's lives. Rejecting, however, the notion of a "parallel government," and thereby also invoking a classical definition of the state (see the Introduction), Pierre Trudeau ordered Canadian troops be positioned in Ottawa and the province of Quebec. On October 16, the federal government declared the War Measures Act (WMA). Under this act, since replaced, all civil rights and liberties in Canada were technically suspended. Those suspected of criminal offences were arrested without charge and held without bail and without trial. The focus was upon Quebec and those suspected of being FLQ supporters, but the act's application was wider. Under the WMA, 465 FLQ "supporters" were arrested, 403 of whom were released without charge. Of the remainder, 32 were charged but not prosecuted, while 18 were convicted of minor offences (Conway 2004, 82–83).

The day after the WMA was declared, Laporte's kidnappers murdered him. The killing intensified feelings of fear and panic, both inside and outside Quebec. Support for the Trudeau government rose, especially in English-speaking Canada. Feelings were more mixed in Quebec, but many accepted the presence of tanks and the suspension of civil liberties without question.

Laporte's killers were eventually caught, tried, and convicted using regular police methods. Shortly thereafter, in early December, Cross was located and freed in return for his kidnappers' safe passage to Cuba. Over time, all of Cross's kidnappers voluntarily returned to Canada, where they too were tried, convicted, and sentenced (*Maclean's* 2000).

Thus, the October Crisis—and the Quiet Revolution—came to an end. Today, the crisis and the imposition of the War Measures Act, though replaced in 1988 by the Emergencies Act, remain controversial (see Gagnon 2000). Was invoking the WMA necessary? Or was it an overreaction? What is the best way to protect civil society from threat? (Indeed, which was threatened—civil society or the state?) When is state coercion justified? (Is it ever justified?)

In the short term, Trudeau's government was praised for its handling of the situation, while the use of violence to achieve sovereignty, never widely supported in Quebec, was thoroughly repudiated. Yet, if invoking the WMA was meant to render Quebecers fearful of pursuing nationalism, it utterly failed. Within a few years, support for Quebec nationalism among francophones was stronger than ever.

CONCLUSION

The story of Quebec in the 20th century is one of sociological change. These changes occurred early in the century but became more obvious (especially to English-speaking Canada) after 1945. Still largely Catholic and conservative at war's end, Quebec only 25 years later was essentially secular and liberal. Birth rates fell remarkably and divorce rates rose. Likewise, sexual mores and social views changed, with Quebecers becoming more generally liberal in these matters than people elsewhere in North America.

Industrialization, long a fact in Quebec, also continued apace and expanded into the province's north, bringing Quebec society into increasing contact and conflict with Indigenous communities, but economic development also remained uneven. After 1960, social stratification along French-English lines began lessening, and a new francophone bourgeoisie emerged. Rural-urban and gender differences remained, however.

Sociologically, these changes were not dissimilar to those occurring elsewhere in Canadian society. Growing urbanization and industrialism, the rise of the welfare state, and the changing role of women in society: these were also occurring in English-speaking Canada. What gave Quebec's changes particular cogency, however, was their occurrence against the historic backdrop of French-English relations going back to the Conquest. Additionally, Quebec's demands during this period coincided, clashed with, and reinforced changes occurring in English-speaking Canada's structure, beliefs, and identity. Sometimes, English-speaking Canada even changed in response to demands it *imagined* French Quebec had made (e.g., bilingualism). Throughout the 1960s, Canada and Quebec danced together, each reacting to the other, tailoring their steps, measuring the other's performance. As the fall of 1970 ended, however, the two seemed more separate than ever. Ironically, conflict increased between the French and English groups as the two communities became more functionally integrated and more sociologically similar as, to continue the metaphor, their steps became more synchronized. In 1970, no one could be certain how or when the dance would end.

CRITICAL THINKING QUESTIONS

1. In what ways did English expansion during the 19th and 20th centuries lead to both Quebec isolation and a strengthened nationalism in that province?
2. How might structural functionalists and conflict theorists view the political, economic, cultural, and social changes that occurred in Quebec during the 20th century?
3. Why is symbolism so important in shaping human relations?
4. In what ways do maps help or hinder our ideas about what is real?
5. Do individuals possess charisma, or is it something that their followers "read into" them?

RECOMMENDED READINGS

Conway, John. 2004. *Debts to Pay: The Future of Federalism in Quebec*. 3rd ed. Toronto: James Lorimer & Company.
Written with passion, this book calls upon English-speaking Canada to discover its real history and thereby to understand the legitimate grievances of French-speaking Canada.

Gavreau, Michael. 2005. *The Catholic Origins of Quebec's Quiet Revolution, 1931–1970*. Montreal and Kingston: McGill-Queen's University Press.
This book argues that debates and reforms within the Roman Catholic Church played a part in paving the way for the Quiet Revolution.

Romney, Paul. 1999. *Getting It Wrong: How Canadians Forgot Their Past and Imperilled Confederation*. Toronto: University of Toronto Press.
This book tells the story of how Confederation came about and holds lessons for Canadians today who seek constitutional reform.

Saul, John Ralston. 1997. *Reflections of a Siamese Twin: Canada at the End of the Twentieth Century*. Toronto: Penguin Books.
Almost a classic, Saul's book outlines the complicated relationship that has arisen between Canada's "two solitudes," creating the kind of society Canada has today.

Zubrzycki, Geneviève. 2016. *Beheading the Saint: Nationalism, Religion, and Secularism in Quebec*. Chicago: University of Chicago Press.
Examining Quebec's national holiday—the Feast of St. John the Baptist, held every June 24—the author shows how that celebration became a venue for publicly contesting the heretofore dominant ethno-Catholic conception of French Canadian identity and, via a violent rejection of Catholic symbols, provided for the articulation of a new, secular Québécois identity during the Quiet Revolution.

RELATED WEBSITES

CBC Digital Archives (October Crisis)

www.cbc.ca/archives/categories/politics/civil-unrest/the-october-crisis-civil-liberties-
suspended/topic---the-october-crisis-civil-liberties-suspended.html

This archive contains numerous video clips of important events in Canadian
history, including "October Crisis: Civil Liberties Suspended."

CBC Digital Archives (Richard Riot)

www.cbc.ca/archives/categories/sports/hockey/the-legendary-9-maurice-rocket-
richard/the-1955-richard-riot.html

The archive also contains useful footage of the Richard riot.

Manitoba Métis Federation

www.mmf.mb.ca

This non-profit organization was founded in 1967 to give an independent voice
to Métis people.

CANADIAN SOCIETY ON VIDEO

The Champions Series, Part One: Unlikely Warriors. 1978. National Film Board of
Canada, 57 minutes, 27 seconds.

Examines the lives of Pierre Trudeau and René Lévesque from the early 1950s
through to 1967, the year Lévesque left the Liberal Party and Trudeau became
the federal minister of justice.

The Champions Series, Part Two: Trappings of Power. 1978. National Film Board of
Canada, 55 minutes, 44 seconds.

Examines the period from 1967 to 1977, during which Pierre Trudeau won
three federal elections, the October Crisis occurred, and the Parti Québécois
came to power under Rene Lévesque.

The Great Resistance. 2008. National Film Board of Canada, 77 minutes, 22 seconds.

In the 1930s, in the throes of the Great Depression, the government relocated
more than 80,000 citizens to found a new settlement in the virgin forests of
Quebec's Abitibi region. After enduring back-breaking work to clear the land,
however, many left, seeking a better life in the city or as labourers for the large
corporations that came to exploit the North's valuable resources.

CHAPTER 3

The Constitutional Years and Their Aftermath

Signing of the Proclamation of the Constitution Act, 1982, Ottawa, April 17, 1982. © Government of Canada. Reproduced with the permission of Library and Archives Canada (2020). Source: Library and Archives Canada/National Archives of Canada fonds/e002852801.

The Magnificent Obsession
  —subtitle to Clarkson and McCall's 1990 examination of the Trudeau years and efforts at constitutional reform

Quebec constitutes, within Canada, a distinct society.
  —the Meech Lake Accord, 1987

The process of constitutional reform in Canada has been discredited.
  —Quebec premier Robert Bourassa after the failure of the Meech Lake Accord, 1990

INTRODUCTION

This chapter examines events in Quebec and the relationship between Canada and Quebec during the 20 years that followed the FLQ Crisis of 1970. As noted in the previous chapter, the FLQ Crisis ended the Quiet Revolution in Quebec. Thereafter, nationalist and separatist impulses within the province took a less violent but, in the long term, potentially more lethal turn. Between 1980 and 1995, two referenda on Quebec independence were held, the latter only narrowly defeated. In between these major events, Canada rewrote its Constitution—of which Quebec, however, was not a signatory—while two other efforts at constitutional renewal failed. The chapter begins with a discussion of the sociological importance of political constitutions.

SOCIOLOGY AND THE CANADIAN CONSTITUTION

The events of the 1960s, culminating in the FLQ Crisis in 1970, set off a profound re-thinking of Canada's Constitution. Sociology and sociologists played a major role in this rethinking. This should not surprise us. After all, one of sociology's main interests involves **social norms**.

While many social norms are simply understood, some are formally inscribed by the state. These latter are called laws, the most profound of which is a constitution. The term **constitution** refers "both to the institutions, practices, and principles that define and structure a system of government and to the written document that establishes or articulates such a system" (taken from Hemberger 1993, 189). A constitution defines a state's sphere of authority, the means of its governance, and the claims that may be made in the political realm, broadly defined and contested. More broadly, constitutions represent symbolically a statement of spirit or intent, for example, that "all people are created equal." Beginning with the American and French revolutions, constitutions arose as a means of formally specifying the relationship between individuals and groups and their relationship to the state, a chief interest of early sociologists such as Tönnies, Weber, and Durkheim (see the Introduction). Finally, while some constitutions are more easily changed than others, none are written in such a way that they can be changed at whim. Constitutions are meant to represent a more or less firm statement of a country's legal foundation. By comparison, the American Constitution is relatively "fixed" while the Canadian Constitution is sometimes referred to as a "rolling compromise." Beginning in the 1960s, the compromise picked up speed.

Until 1982, Canada's key constitutional document, of course, was the British North America (BNA) Act (later renamed the Constitution Act, 1867), creating the Dominion of Canada (Dunn 1995) (see Chapter 5). Long before 1867, however, Canada's existence was structured by a series of constitutional acts: for example, the charter of the Hudson's Bay Company in 1670, the Royal Proclamation of 1763, the Quebec Act of 1774, the Constitution Act of 1791, and the Act of Union of 1841 (see Chapter 1). The BNA Act repealed some elements contained in these previous legal documents. Other commitments, however, remain in effect; for example, current Indigenous land claims date from the Royal Proclamation Act (see Chapter 12).

The BNA Act was repeatedly altered after 1867 to meet changing conditions and demands. A partial list of these changes includes the various acts that incorporated the lands of the Hudson's Bay Company and the Northwest Territories into Canada, made Manitoba, British Columbia, Alberta, and Saskatchewan provinces, established the Yukon Territory, and brought Newfoundland into Confederation.

Constitutional reform stalled, however, after the 1920s, even as the need for it became greater. The Statute of Westminster in 1931 declared Canada (along with Australia, New Zealand, and South Africa) sovereign and equal to Britain. Canada, however, declined at that time to take control over the Constitution because the federal and provincial governments could not agree on how the Constitution would be amended in the future.

Why was the issue of an amending formula problematic? It was problematic because it dealt with issues of power between levels of government and between government and individual citizens. For example, would the federal government be constitutionally able to make changes unilaterally? Or would provincial consent for constitutional changes be required? If so, how many provinces, and would all provinces, large and small, be equal? If not provinces, would Canadian citizens have the ultimate say over constitutional changes through, for example, a Canada-wide referendum? How would the rights of smaller provinces and, in the case of Quebec, minorities be protected against the majority provinces or population? Would some elements of the Constitution be more easily changed than other elements? These were only some of the constitutional questions facing Canadian politicians after 1931. With no clear answers in sight, the Constitution remained "housed" in Britain, even as Canada symbolically distanced itself from Britain in other ways. (In 1950, for example, the British Privy Council ceased to be Canada's Supreme Court.)

Constitutional questions would not go away, however. Two issues with constitutional implications dominated federal-provincial relations in Canada during the 1950s. The first was the ongoing search for an amending formula. The second was the fiscal relations between the two levels of government (Webber 1994), a by-product of the federal government's control of revenues and the expansion of welfare state programs after 1945 (see Chapter 6). With the Quiet Revolution of the 1960s, a third issue was added to the mix: Quebec's historical relation to the rest of Canada. Was Canada a confederation of 10 equal provinces, or was it a bargain between two nations, French and English (Chapter 2)?

The events of the Quiet Revolution, culminating in the October Crisis of 1970, made obvious the necessity of resolving these issues. Quebec, however, was not the sole impetus for demands for constitutional change. In particular, the western provinces in the 1970s also demanded constitutional changes in two areas: first, "control over the taxing and marketing of natural resources" and, second, "reform of federal institutions, especially the Senate" (Webber 1994, 103) (see chapters 7 and 8). Quebec and many of Canada's "hinterland" provinces demanded *both* a greater devolution of federal powers and, concomitantly, more inclusion at the centre of federal decision-making.

The Trudeau government's interpretation of Canada's "problem" was quite different. Among developed countries, Canada was significantly decentralized already. The problem was not an excess of power at the centre but too much power in the regions. Giving into Quebec's nationalist demands would only encourage more demands. Already other provinces were piggybacking on Quebec's demands, threatening further weakening of the Canadian state. The solution to Canada's problems, in Trudeau's eyes, lay in constitutional reforms that would bring Quebecers and Quebec into the "Canadian nation" (see Balthazar 1997).

By 1971, the federal and provincial governments were seeking constitutional reform. At a federal-provincial meeting held in Victoria, the two levels of government appeared at last to have reached an accord on some principles for renewing Confederation. Quebec's premier, Robert Bourassa (1933–1996), faced strong opposition from nationalists, unionists, business groups, and the media, however, upon his return to Quebec. These opponents feared the agreement would enhance federal authority while reducing Quebec to the status of just another province. Constitutional reform thus was put on hold. In the absence of a constitutional solution to Quebec's demands, new coalitions of social and political forces soon arose in Quebec, proffering different solutions to the Quebec-Canada "problem."

THE ELECTION OF THE PARTI QUÉBÉCOIS

On November 15, 1976, René Lévesque's Parti Québécois (PQ) was elected to govern Quebec. The election result panicked much of English Canada and the province's elite, who feared both the PQ's avowed separatism—Lévesque promised to hold a referendum on sovereignty sometime during his party's electoral mandate—and social democratic platform. What led to the PQ victory?

The PQ's election reflected an evolution in Quebec society and in the idea of Quebec nationalism. By the 1970s, the economic changes undertaken during the Quiet Revolution were bearing fruit. New middle and entrepreneurial classes were emerging, dominated by francophone Quebecers. Labour unions, long suppressed in Quebec, were also growing in power, and labour militancy was on the rise, exemplified in an extreme manner by workers' intentional destruction of the James Bay hydroelectric site in 1974. Quebec culture and arts, no longer insular or defensive, were also thriving. The PQ's positive message of creating a more autonomous, social democratic, and progressive society appealed to a wide cross-section of francophones within the blue- and white-collar, intellectual, and cultural communities.

Like all Quebec political parties, going back to the previous century, the PQ was nationalist, but the PQ's nationalism was fundamentally different from that of previous Quebec governments. First, reflecting changes among Quebecers themselves, the PQ's nationalism was more positive and future-oriented than in the past (Dufour 1990; Thompson 1995). Second, where Quebec governments in the past had defended the French "nation"—albeit with its obvious homeland in Quebec, still within Canada—the PQ rejected both the notion of allegiance to Canada and to a broader pan-Canadian French nation (Webber 1994). For the PQ and many of its followers, there was only a Québécois nation, its interests represented by Quebec's quasi-state, on the verge of becoming a sovereign country. All that was needed to make Quebec sovereign was a decision by its people to assert their rights of self-determination.

Third, where the Union Nationale had been authoritarian and conservative, and the Liberals classically liberal, the PQ was unabashedly democratic socialist as reflected in several progressive policies enacted during its first term in office. Labour laws were amended, outlawing strike-breaking and adopting the Rand formula (see Chapter 7) for deducting union dues. Reflecting the strength of emergent feminism within the party, the rights of women also were extended (see Dickinson and Young 2008). Finally, Quebec's minimum wage became the highest in Canada, and the sales tax was removed on such necessary items as shoes, clothing, and furniture (Conway 2004). The PQ's most important moves, however, were in defence of the French language.

THE LANGUAGE OF QUEBEC NATIONALISM

Language is a central element of national identity, as it represents continuity with the past and future (see Chapter 4). It is also central to much sociological thought. From a symbolic interaction perspective, for example, language is the chief vehicle for understanding and expressing a group's history, beliefs, and values, but from a post-structural perspective, language and its putative efforts at defining a precise "meaning" are tied up with issues of power. Likewise, while structural functionalists view language as a means of facilitating mutual exchanges, conflict theorists view it as a contested terrain between the dominant culture and minority groups.

Until the Constitution Act of 1982, only the BNA Act of 1867 (later renamed the Constitution Act of 1867) dealt constitutionally with language, and then only in Section 133 and in a limited context. Section 133 states that either French or English can be used in the legislatures of Canada and Quebec and courts under their authority, and that records and journals of both Parliament and the Quebec legislature must be bilingual. Section 23 of the Manitoba Act of 1870 replicated the Quebec provisions of the BNA Act (Dunn 1995), as did arrangements in the Northwest Territories in 1874 (Cook 1995).

The cultural wars of the 1890s and early 20th century, recounted in Chapter 2, saw English majorities abuse French-language protections, however. Meanwhile, the majority French in Quebec found their social and cultural status gradually declining against the minority and unilingual anglophone population. In effect, where constitutional bilingualism existed, it provided greater protection for English speakers, minority or otherwise, than it did French speakers.

By the 1960s, survival of the French language and culture in Quebec was further threatened by a combination of declining birth rates and rapidly increasing immigration into the province (Dickinson and Young 2008; Fournier et al. 1997). Many of the new arrivals spoke neither French nor English. However, surrounded by a North American sea of English, increasingly available through television and radio, and experiencing the economic and social benefits of English within the province, most immigrants were choosing to speak English. Moreover, schools were pressed into the debate as immigrants demanded that their children receive education in English. For many francophones, their ancestral homeland and culture were once more under siege. Official bilingualism, enacted in 1969, did not address these fears. Indeed, official bilingualism was the answer to a question most francophone Quebecers had not asked, satisfying only Canadian nationalists outside the province. In 1968, violence broke out in Montreal between francophone nationalists and immigrant Italians over language instruction in schools (Dickinson and Young 2008; Thompson 1995; Fournier et al. 1997).

The Quebec government in 1974 attempted to deal with the issue through the Official Languages Act (Bill 22). The act made French Quebec's official language in certain key areas, such as business, labour, education, some professions, and public administration (Conway 2004). It did not demand the exclusive use of French, however. Education matters, for example, were left largely untouched, with immigrant parents still able to enrol their children in English-language schools.

After its election in 1976, the Parti Québécois moved quickly to remove any ambiguity concerning the status of French in Quebec. The Charter of the French Language of 1977 (Bill 101) made French the province's official language and the "normal language of work, education, communications, and business." Bill 101 also restricted English instruction to those whose parents were educated in English in Quebec. (An exception was granted to Indigenous peoples and Indigenous languages.) Bill 101 further placed limits on bilingual signs and restricted the use of English in business and government (see Fournier et al. 1997; Dickinson and Young 2008; Webber 1994).

Anglophones within Quebec, many of whom had deep ancestral roots, felt themselves under attack. Their anger found support outside Quebec among English-speaking Canadians who could not understand the Quebec government's moves to make the province predominantly French at a time when they were (grudgingly) accepting bilingualism. Anger outside Quebec was aided and abetted by some English-Canadian politicians pandering to anti-French, anti-Quebec sentiment in search of cheap votes.

Supporters of Bill 101 pointed out, however, that its provisions dealt solely with Quebec's public and symbolic realms, not with cultural institutions (e.g., McGill University) or private interactions (Webber 1994). They noted the failure of governments elsewhere to protect and promote the French language (see Conway 2004). However, few in English-speaking Canada listened to such arguments. Following the passage of Bill 101, Sun Life announced it was moving its headquarters from Montreal to Toronto. Other businesses soon followed. Many young anglophone Quebecers also left the province during this period (Morton 1997).

By 1979, the Parti Québécois was entering the bottom half of its electoral mandate. It had been elected on a promise to hold a referendum on sovereignty that would make the Quebec state the political embodiment of that expression. Now time was running out to fulfill the promise. The stage was set for the 1980 referendum and one of the most compelling political rivalries of the late 20th century.

A STUDY IN PERSONAL AGENCY: THE 1980 REFERENDUM

One of sociology's ongoing central debates involves the relationship between individual behaviour and the constraints and imperatives of social structure. Do individuals really make a difference, or are we merely creations of our time and place? In a famous passage, Marx (1977c, 300) once wrote that people "make their own history, but they do not make it just as they please, they do not make it under circumstances chosen by themselves, but under circumstances directly encountered, given, and transmitted from the past." American sociologist C. Wright Mills (1961, 6) viewed agency and structure as a meeting place for what he termed the **sociological imagination**, the ability "to grasp history and biography and the relations of the two within society." From this perspective, Pierre Trudeau and René Lévesque can be seen as products of pre-war 1939 Quebec society and the political and ideological struggles of their time.[1] Yet each also influenced the shape and manner of those struggles (Cook 1995).

Trudeau and Lévesque are often viewed as opposites: Trudeau the reasoned intellectual and committed federalist, Lévesque the passionate "man of action" and Quebec nationalist. Certainly, their public styles were at odds (Clarkson and McCall 1990), yet they were both children of the post–First World War French-Canadian bourgeoisie, had fought to end the Duplessis regime, and were social liberals dedicated to modernizing Quebec. Both believed in a "large role for the state in public affairs" (Chodos and Hamovitch 1991, 195). Moreover, each in his way represented a form of Quebec nationalism (see Dufour 1990), Trudeau as passionately as Lévesque, Lévesque in as calculated a manner as Trudeau. In their time, each received mixed responses from Canadians. Loved by francophone Quebecers, loathed by their anglophone counterparts, Lévesque was at the same time both respected and feared in English-speaking Canada. For his part, Trudeau likewise was loathed and hated, admired and respected, often by the same people. Yet Lévesque's death in 1987 resulted in a profound outpouring of grief in Quebec (Conway 2004), while Trudeau's death in September 2000 was mourned by much of Canada, his funeral perhaps the largest attended and watched in Canadian history (*Maclean's* 2000).

In 1979, Trudeau's and Lévesque's different visions of Quebec's relationship to Canada were on a collision course. Trudeau believed in a strong Quebec, but as a province among other provinces, within a bilingual Canada. As already noted, Trudeau held a pan-Canadian vision of a bilingual Canada, a vision with deep roots in Quebec (Chapter 2), but his idea of a strong central state was European while the notion of constitutionally equal provinces was American (see Dufour 1990; Balthazar 1997).

For many Quebecers, this vision of Canada was at odds with the historic reality of Quebec's relationship with the rest of Canada, going back at least to the Quebec Act of 1774. Perhaps worse, Trudeau's vision created a kind of straitjacket for constitutional change (Dufour 1990). Many francophones supported Lévesque's vision of a strong Quebec with unique powers within a decentralized Canadian federation. By 1979, a sizable number of Quebecers believed the only option, if their nation could not be protected within Canada, was Quebec independence.

Lévesque's vision of the Canadian federation was neither radical nor recent. Debates about how centralized or decentralized Canada should be, or about jurisdictional responsibilities, had gone on since before Confederation and were a key aspect of discussion at Charlottetown and Quebec leading up to 1867 (Moore 1997; Romney 1999) (Chapter 5). Beginning with the Depression and the Second World War, however, Ottawa's role had increased in Quebec and Canada at large (Balthazar 1997; Thompson 1995). In the wake of Quebec's separatist threat, and faced with a stagnating economy in the 1970s, the Trudeau Liberal government attempted to reassert federal authority both politically and economically. These actions elicited hostility from Quebec, as well as other provinces, especially in the West (see Chapter 7). The stage was set for the constitutional conflict.

The Ottawa-Quebec, Trudeau-Lévesque showdown was briefly postponed when the Liberals were defeated in the 1979 federal election. But Trudeau's government was returned to office only months later (see appendices 1 and 2). In the meantime, Lévesque's government had called for a sovereignty referendum to be held on May 20, 1980.

The debates and speeches leading up to the referendum vote were impassioned, occasionally nasty. Families were divided, friendships dissipated (Chodos and Hamovitch 1991). In the end, 60 percent of Quebecers voted *No* in the referendum. Why did the first Quebec referendum turn out as it did?

In part, for older francophone Quebecers, the question represented a kind of "Sophie's choice" between two heritages, Canada and Quebec, and, for that matter, between two respected "sons," Trudeau and Lévesque. Many Quebecers in general also feared the economic consequences of sovereignty, a fear magnified by the *No* side throughout the campaign. But the reasons for the referendum's outcome were also reflected in the demographics of the voters. Quebec's anglophones and allophones, making up roughly 20 percent of the population, voted nearly en masse for the *No* side, meaning that francophone voters were split 50/50. In short, half of Quebec's large francophone population had publicly voiced their displeasure with their place in Canada's constitutional arrangements. Moreover, *Yes* supporters could take hope from the fact that the young and the educated among francophones had voted overwhelmingly in favour of sovereignty (Conway 2004, 110). The future seemed theirs to grasp.

The referendum outcome left *Yes* supporters with a sense of bitterness and gloom, feelings of "collective trauma," and a mood of "political exhaustion" (Chodos and Hamovitch 1991, 107). By contrast, for *No* supporters, the predominant feeling was one of relief (Conway 2004). They understood too well that, in the words of Balthazar (1993), Quebecers had said *no* to sovereignty but had not said *yes* to Canada.

In the closing days of the referendum campaign, Trudeau repeated promises that if the *No* side won, he would work to revitalize Confederation (Clarkson and McCall 1990; Conway 2004). Trudeau's pledge, repeated the day after the referendum, set the stage for the most substantial revision of Canada's Constitution since 1867.

THE 1982 CANADIAN CONSTITUTION

Trudeau's statements before and immediately after the referendum were not always clear, occasionally suggesting changes to federal institutions and a redistribution of powers. His only certain statement was that the patriated Constitution must contain a Charter of Rights and Freedoms. He viewed such a charter as a means of ensuring the individual equality of all Canadians, especially against the "collective assaults of Quebec nationalism" (Conway 2004, 111).

By long-standing tradition, Quebec held a veto over constitutional changes. Quebec did not oppose per se the constitutional entrenchment of individual rights; after all, Quebec had passed its own Charter of Human Rights and Freedoms in 1975 (see Fournier et al. 1997). Quebec nationalists, however, feared Trudeau's Charter could be used against Quebec's national interests—for example, in attacking Quebec's language laws.

Quebec's possible veto was not the Trudeau government's only problem. Many Conservative premiers also feared the Charter's application, believing that judicial activism would replace legislative supremacy. Several provinces also wanted changes in other areas. The western provinces wanted institutional reforms, notably dealing with the Senate. They also wanted clarification over provincial control over resources.

Finally, new political actors also appeared on the scene. Indigenous Canadians, women's groups, and other social organizations, heretofore largely excluded from elite consultations, also demanded input into constitutional changes.

The constitutional negotiations began in earnest in the fall of 1980 and continued throughout the next year. They were frank and often acrimonious (*Maclean's* 2000; Clarkson and McCall 1990). As talks began, only the provinces of Ontario and New Brunswick supported the federal plans. The other premiers, known as the "gang of eight," posed a seemingly solid front, but the Trudeau government held a winning card. The public at large liked the idea of the Charter and also wanted Canada's Constitution "brought home." In the negotiations that followed, the alliance of provincial premiers slowly began to unravel. Equally important, Lévesque had agreed in the course of negotiations to give up Quebec's traditional constitutional veto. When the final agreement was reached on the Constitution, Lévesque stood alone, Quebec—in the eyes of nationalists—defenceless (Clarkson and McCall 1990; Conway 2004).

The new Canadian Constitution, proclaimed on April 17, 1982, has six parts (Government of Canada 1982; Webber 1994; Dunn 1995). Part I deals with the Canadian Charter of Rights and Freedoms. These rights and freedoms include the fundamental freedoms of conscience, religion, thought, belief, opinion, expression, peaceful assembly, and association, as well as democratic, mobility, legal, equality, and language rights. Part I makes French and English the official languages of Canada. It further designates New Brunswick as Canada's only officially bilingual province. The Charter of Rights and Freedoms, however, also includes a "notwithstanding" clause that allows provinces to opt out of a provision if they choose.

Part II of the Constitution Act, 1982, recognizes Aboriginal rights, including those existing by way of land claims, and formalizes the holding of conferences between first ministers and Indigenous peoples (Chapter 11). Part III commits governments to promoting equal opportunities for all Canadians, reducing regional disparities, and providing essential public services. Part IV commits the government to holding two future constitutional conferences on Aboriginal peoples and the representatives of Yukon and the Northwest Territories, since held. Part V sets out a procedure for future amendments to the Constitution. Amendments may henceforth be made with the agreement of Parliament and seven provinces totalling 50 percent of the population. Part VI amends the British North America Act of 1867, renaming it the Constitution Act of 1867.

THE CONSTITUTION'S AFTERMATH

By and large, English-speaking Canadians were happy with the new Constitution. Gallup polls in May 1982 found strong support throughout Canada, and substantial, though not majority, support even in Quebec. Likewise, the political elite outside Quebec was also generally pleased with the new Constitution. Finally, the provinces outside Quebec also welcomed the act's clarification of provincial powers over natural resources—a key sticking point for provinces such as Alberta—and the insertion within the Charter of a "notwithstanding clause" that limited the Charter's application.

The PQ government and francophone nationalists in Quebec were embittered, however. For them, the promises of constitutional renewal had been hollow. Ottawa and the rest of the provinces had gotten what they wanted. What had Quebec gotten? In the eyes of nationalists, Quebec had been "humiliated," "betrayed," "stabbed in the back." Quebec had lost its traditional veto and now was constitutionally defenceless against Canada's anglophone majority. The Charter of Rights and Freedoms, it was feared, could and would be used to advance anglophone rights and attack French language laws. Thus, the Constitution Act of 1982, meant to heal the rifts of past years, became yet another source of Quebec grievance. Lévesque's government refused to put Quebec's signature on the Constitution and did not participate in the ceremonies marking the occasion.

Whether the PQ would ever have signed a constitutional agreement is a moot point. Trudeau, the provincial leaders, and most Canadians outside Quebec doubted that a government dedicated to separatism would ever have signed. Yet the referendum defeat had left the PQ with few options, and Lévesque himself was viewed as a "soft" separatist.

In 1984, however, Lévesque's old nemesis, Pierre Trudeau, retired, and was soon replaced as Liberal leader by a former finance minister, John Turner (1929–2020). The Tories, meanwhile, also had a new leader, Brian Mulroney, a bilingual Quebecer and lawyer with strong ties to American business. When Mulroney promised Quebecers a deal that would allow them to sign the Constitution "with dignity," Lévesque and Quebec nationalists as a whole threw their support behind the Tories.

The 1984 election saw Mulroney's Tories take the largest number of seats ever won by a federal party. The victory reflected the broad sweep of Mulroney's electoral coalition, which featured at its core western Canadian conservatives, pro-business advocates of free trade, and Quebec nationalists.

No sooner was the election over than Mulroney moved to make good his promise to Quebecers on constitutional reform. By the spring of 1987, informal discussions had proved sufficiently positive that a federal-provincial meeting was held at Meech Lake, a resort a few miles outside Ottawa. Much to everyone's surprise, that meeting ended in a formal agreement signed by the federal government and all the premiers.

Signing the Meech Lake Accord did not immediately change the Constitution, however. Both Mulroney and the premiers were required to take the accord back to the people, in the form of passage through their respective legislatures. The time frame for doing so was three years from the date that the first legislature passed the accord, and failure by any legislature (federal or provincial) thereafter to do so would result in the accord's rejection. Quebec passed the accord quickly. The clock hence began ticking on its acceptance by the various levels of government.

Opposition to the Meech Lake Accord was slow in mobilizing, in part because the impact of constitutional changes is not always apparent and such documents are far from easy (or enjoyable) reading. Slowly over the next few years, however, opposition mounted based on a mixture of ancient grievances and grudges, misconceptions, lofty but unmet expectations, and legitimate concerns. Three years after its signing, the accord collapsed, dividing Canada more than at any time since the FLQ Crisis and fuelling support for a second sovereignty referendum in 1995.

Of all the issues, what most brought down the Meech Lake Accord was a provision that would have recognized Quebec as a **distinct society**. Why was the notion of Quebec as a distinct society so controversial in 1990? Would it still be controversial today?

IS QUEBEC A "DISTINCT SOCIETY"?

At least on the surface, few could seriously argue that culturally, Quebec is a province *comme les autres*, a difference reflected also in the distinctive focus of Quebec sociologists (see box 3.1). Two measures of culture—language and religion—support this point.

Across Canada, the number of bilingual individuals has steadily grown since the early 1960s, reaching 17.9 percent in 2016, with the highest rate observed in Quebec, followed by New Brunswick (Statistics Canada 2017c). But French remains the dominant language in

Box 3.1: Quebec Sociology and Quebec Society

Marcel Fournier argues that Quebec sociology developed over three particular periods: (1) a pioneering stage before 1939, when Quebec scholars focused on the province's ethnic particularity, often as a handicap or historicized artifact; (2) an institutional period between 1940 and 1969 when academic scholars, including many from the United States, examined the province's transition (according to modernization theory) from a traditional to a modern society; and (3) the nationalization period of Quebec sociology, beginning in 1970 and continuing today, during which descriptions of Quebec as a "distinct society" or even "sociological nation" became *de rigueur*. His central argument is that sociological studies over the decades have made "significant contributions to the formation of national identity" within Quebec, contributing to such characteristics as race, ethnicity, group, society, and nation.

What contributions might sociology make to your community?

Source: Fournier, Marcel. 2001. "Quebec Sociology and Quebec Society: The Construction of a Collective Identity," *Canadian Journal of Sociology* 26(3): 333–347.

Quebec; indeed, that province is the only domain in Canada and in North America in which the French language dominates, although New Brunswick is Canada's only officially bilingual province. Table 3.1 shows that, in 2016, French was the mother tongue of 77 percent of Quebecers, a small decline from 10 years earlier, but also less than 4 percent of people outside Quebec. On the other side, English was the mother tongue of only 7.5 percent of Quebecers in 2016, slightly less than in 2006, but was the mother tongue for nearly 71 percent of Canadians outside of Quebec. In this sense, terming Canada a "bilingual country" is misleading. Canada is marked at the federal level by **institutional bilingualism**. At the level of everyday usage, however, **territorial bilingualism** predominates, much as it does in Belgium or Switzerland (Dunn 1995, 368–369). For francophones inside and outside of Quebec, the general pattern of decline plays into fears of assimilation.

If language remains a significant marker of cultural difference, religion historically has also played such a role. As indicated in table 3.2, nearly 39 percent of Canadians in 2011 identified themselves as Roman Catholic, while 28.5 percent identified themselves as belonging to another Christian religion. As with the French language, however, this figure is misleading. The largest majority of Roman Catholic identifiers are located within Quebec, with nearly 75 percent of people in that province describing themselves, at least nominally, as Roman Catholic. By contrast, only 28 percent of people outside Quebec identify themselves as Roman Catholic, while 34.7 percent of people adhere to another variant of Christian religion. Finally, one should note the joint processes of secularization and decline in identification with organized religion, with more than 27 percent of Canadians today stating an adherence to no religious faith. Indeed, the category "none" now makes up the third-largest category among Canadians' religious preferences.

Table 3.1: Population with English, French, or English and French Mother Tongue, Canada, Provinces, and Territories, and Canada less Quebec, 2006 and 2016 (in thousands and percentage)

	2006						2016					
	English	**%**	**French**	**%**	**Both**	**%**	**English**	**%**	**French**	**%**	**Both**	**%**
Canada	**17,882.9**	**57.2**	**6,817.7**	**21.8**	**98.5**	**0.3**	**19,460.9**	**56.0**	**7,166.7**	**20.6**	**165.3**	**0.5**
Newfoundland and Labrador	488.4	97.6	1.9	0.4	0.3	0.1	499.7	96.9	2.4	0.5	0.6	0.1
Prince Edward Island	125.3	93.3	5.3	4.0	0.5	0.4	128.0	90.8	4.9	3.5	0.5	0.4
Nova Scotia	832.1	92.1	32.5	3.6	2.1	0.2	830.2	91.0	29.5	3.2	3.4	0.4
New Brunswick	463.2	64.4	233.0	32.4	4.5	0.6	472.7	64.2	231.1	31.4	7.3	1.0
Quebec	575.6	7.7	5,877.7	79.0	43.3	0.6	601.2	7.5	6,219.7	77.1	72.4	0.9
Ontario	8,230.7	68.4	488.8	4.1	32.7	0.3	8,902.3	66.9	490.7	3.7	54.0	0.4
Manitoba	838.4	74.0	44.0	3.9	2.6	0.2	900.6	71.4	40.5	3.2	4.4	0.3
Saskatchewan	811.7	85.1	16.1	1.7	1.1	0.1	892.6	82.4	15.1	1.4	2.0	0.2
Alberta	2,576.7	79.1	61.2	1.9	5.4	0.2	2,991.5	74.3	72.2	1.8	10.2	0.3
British Columbia	2,875.8	70.6	54.7	1.3	5.9	0.1	3,170.1	68.9	57.4	1.2	10.1	0.2
Yukon	25.7	84.9	1.1	3.7	0.1	0.4	29.1	81.7	1.6	4.5	0.2	0.6
Northwest Territories	31.5	76.8	1.0	2.4	–	–	31.8	76.8	1.2	2.9	0.1	0.2
Nunavut	7.8	26.5	0.4	1.3	–	–	11.0	30.8	0.6	1.7	–	–
Canada less Quebec	17,307.3	72.7	940.0	3.9	55.2	0.2	18,859.7	70.6	947.0	3.5	92.9	0.3

Sources: Adapted from Statistics Canada. 2006. "Population by Mother Tongue, by Province and Territory, 2006 Census." Ottawa: Statistics Canada; and Statistics Canada. 2019b. "Language Highlight Tables, 2016 Census: Mother Tongue by Age (Total), 2016 Counts for the Population Excluding Institutional Residents of Canada, Provinces and Territories, 2016 Census—100% Data." Figures rounded and percentages calculated by authors.

Table 3.2: Population by Selected Religions, Canada, Provinces, and Territories, and Canada less Quebec, 2011 (in percentage)[1]

	Roman Catholic[2]	Other Christian[3]	Buddhist	Hindu	Jewish	Muslim	None[4]	Other	Total
Canada	**38.7**	**28.5**	**1.1**	**1.5**	**1.0**	**3.2**	**23.9**	**2.0**	**99.9**
Newfoundland and Labrador	35.9	57.4	–	–	–	–	6.1	0.2	99.6
Prince Edward Island	43.1	41.6	–	–	–	–	14.6	–	99.3
Nova Scotia	32.9	43.4	0.2	0.2	0.2	1.0	21.9	0.2	100.0
New Brunswick	49.7	34.1	0.1	0.1	0.1	0.4	15.1	0.4	100.0
Quebec	74.6	7.6	0.7	0.4	1.1	3.1	12.1	0.3	99.9
Ontario	31.2	33.3	1.3	2.9	1.5	4.6	23.1	2.0	99.9
Manitoba	25.0	43.4	0.6	0.7	0.9	1.0	26.5	1.9	100.0
Saskatchewan	28.4	43.6	0.4	0.4	0.1	1.0	24.4	1.7	100.0
Alberta	23.8	36.5	1.2	1.0	0.3	3.2	31.6	2.4	100.0
British Columbia	15.0	29.7	2.1	1.1	0.5	1.8	44.1	5.7	100.0
Yukon	18.2	27.3	0.9	0.6	0.1	0.1	51.5	1.5	100.2
Northwest Territories	39.0	26.8	0.5	0.2	–	0.7	29.3	2.4	98.9
Nunavut	25.0	59.4	–	–	–	0.3	12.5	1.6	98.8
Canada less Quebec	28.0	34.7	1.3	1.8	1.0	3.2	27.1	2.5	99.6

Notes: 1. Some percentages may not add up to 100 due to rounding. 2. There are several varieties of Catholic, including Ukrainian Catholic, but those defining themselves as Roman Catholic make up 99.4 percent of this total. 3. Includes all "other" Christians. The other Christian category comprises primarily United Church (21.4 percent), Anglican (17.4 percent), Baptist (6.8 percent), Pentecostal (5.1 percent), Lutheran (5.1 percent), and Presbyterian (5.0 percent) adherents. 4. "None" includes agnostic, atheist, humanist, no religion, and no religious affiliation.

Source: Adapted from Statistics Canada. 2011b. Data Table 99-010-X2011032: "Religion (108), Immigrant Status and Period of Immigration (11), Age Groups (10) and Sex (3) for the Population in Private Households of Canada, Provinces, Territories, Census Metropolitan Areas and Census Agglomerations." 2011 National Household Survey.

Clearly, Quebec is distinct from the rest of Canada in terms of both language and religion. Moreover, this distinctness is historically and constitutionally grounded. (Remember, for example, that the Quebec Act of 1774 granted Quebec control over language and religion, as well as a distinct legal system.) Most English-speaking Canadians, inside and outside of Quebec, acknowledge that the province of Quebec is distinct. Some even embrace Quebec's difference as a corner of their identity. So why did the notion of a "distinct society" lead to the failure of the Meech Lake Accord in 1990 and threaten Canada's survival?

Much of the furor revolved around the vagueness of society as a concept (Cook 1995), previously discussed in the Introduction. For example, does the term mean that Quebec is distinct? Or does it refer to the francophone community within Quebec?

Opponents, like Pierre Trudeau and the newly created Reform Party, led by Preston Manning (1942–), successfully argued that the Meech Lake Accord's distinct society clause went against the notion of equality of the provinces, granting Quebec powers or claims to a status not held by others (Denis 1993; Harrison 1995). They further argued that distinct society status implied something greater than mere difference: that it could be used later on by Quebec governments to leverage further demands for nationhood and perhaps separate statehood.

Interestingly, hard-line separatist factions in Quebec argued just the opposite. For them, Quebec was not merely a distinct society, but a sociological nation. The vapidity of distinct society was underlined by arguments that Canada was made up of "ten distinct societies" (see Bourgault 1991, 35). In this context, Denis (1993) argued the term "distinct society" seemed merely a clever way of avoiding the "two nations" concept fundamental to many Quebecers' understanding of Canada.

At the more general level, the passions unleashed in English-speaking Canada by the notion of a distinct society can be traced to the fragility of Canadian identity itself. Author Joseph Conrad once wrote that underlying every great emotion is a great fear. What is English-speaking Canada's great fear? Just as Quebec's overarching fear has been assimilation into English Canada, Canada's fear has been a fatal embrace by the United States. For many Canadians, Quebec's assertions of difference and its refusal to unreservedly become Canadian nationalists threaten Canada's integrity. In the spring of 1990, English Canada's demands for uniformity, swelling in the aftermath of the recently signed Free Trade Agreement with the United States, ran up against Quebec's long-standing demands for respect and recognition of its differences.

THE FAILURE OF THE MEECH LAKE AND CHARLOTTETOWN ACCORDS

The Meech Lake Accord unravelled in the spring of 1990. The unravelling occurred simultaneously from both the top and the bottom, attacked at one end by prominent politicians—such as Trudeau, Manning, and the premiers of New Brunswick, Newfoundland, and Manitoba—and at the other end by popular grassroots elements (Conway 2004). In the end, despite last-minute efforts to save it, the accord died on the order paper, the three-year time frame for its ratification (June 23) having passed. An Indigenous member of Manitoba's Legislative Assembly, Elijah Harper (1949–2013), delivered the decisive blow when he refused to allow that province's legislature to fast-track debate on the measure before time elapsed (see Chapter 11) (see Cohen 1990; Conway 2004).

The short- and long-term consequences of Meech Lake's failure were immense. Support for Quebec separatism increased (see Bourgault 1991). The Bloc Québécois, formed in the spring of 1990 by a breakaway faction of Mulroney's government when it became apparent the accord would fail, received an immediate boost (Cornellier 1995). Elsewhere, amidst fear and anger, the fortunes of the western-based Reform Party also rose (Harrison 1995). Three years later, the federal Tory party—its political coalition of westerners and Quebecers having evaporated—was dismembered, suffering the greatest electoral defeat by any sitting federal government in Canadian history. In Quebec, the Tory limbs were torn off by the separatist Bloc, which, in a moment of supreme political irony, rose to the position of loyal Opposition to the victorious Liberals. The Reform Party led the slaughter in the West (see Appendix 1).

The failure to ratify the Meech Lake Accord left three principal concerns unresolved—(1) Quebec's role in Canada; (2) western Canada's growing sense of alienation; and (3) Indigenous self-government (Meekison 1993)—and with no clear means of resolution. Canada thus entered a time of constitutional fumbling, culminating in an historical footnote known as the Charlottetown Accord.

The Charlottetown Accord arose out of a meeting of English Canada's nine premiers in July 1992. It was meant to appease the various parties who had opposed the Meech Lake Accord. The Charlottetown Accord gave widespread new powers to the provinces while limiting those of the federal government. It further proposed entrenchment of Indigenous rights and creation of a Triple-E (equal, elected, and effective) Senate. Finally, it also relegated the notion of "distinct society" to a newly proposed Canada clause, whereby its constitutional meaning would be constrained by commitments to "equality of the provinces" and "linguistic duality" (Conway 2004, 140). The new accord did not offer Quebec much. Nonetheless, Quebec Premier Robert Bourassa reluctantly accepted the agreement, with a few minor changes.

Like its predecessor, however, the Charlottetown Accord failed, defeated in a rare Canada-wide referendum, held on October 24, 1992. Why did the Charlottetown Accord fail? In part, after Meech Lake, the chalice of constitutional reform was already poisoned. Charlottetown also failed in part because it was too unwieldy. It attempted to do too much, to address all issues, and to be all things to all people at the same time. In the end, the best thing that could be said about the referendum result was that the accord had been rejected throughout Canada, though the reasons for its rejection varied from person to person and between Quebec and the other provinces.

The Charlottetown Accord's rejection thus ended, for a time, formal constitutional change in Canada. But while many Canadians heaved a sigh of relief, Quebec's relationship with Canada remained unresolved, fuelling a second effort by Quebec nationalists at independence.

A NEAR-DEATH EXPERIENCE: THE 1995 QUEBEC REFERENDUM

On October 30, 1995, Quebecers once more voted in a referendum on sovereignty. Canadians watching on their televisions saw their country come within a few thousand votes of being fundamentally changed, perhaps disintegrating altogether.

The referendum was presaged by three major events. First, the separatist Bloc Québécois (BQ) elected 54 members to Parliament in the 1993 federal election, suggesting widespread support for independence within Quebec (Appendix 1). Second, the BQ's provincial counterpart, the PQ, led by Jacques Parizeau (1930–2015), won the Quebec provincial election in September 1994 with a commitment to pursue sovereignty. Third, the PQ tabled a draft bill on sovereignty, followed by public consultations throughout Quebec during the early part of 1995 (Balthazar 1997; Conway 2004).

It was clear from the beginning that the vote would be close. Polls conducted since the 1994 Quebec election had shown support for sovereignty stable at 45 percent (Conway 2004, 201), a significant base upon which to build. Moreover, the sovereigntist camp believed the referendum question was sufficiently benign as to attract "soft" voters. By contrast, federalists were hamstrung by the fact that they appeared to have nothing concrete to offer Quebecers. The defeat of the Meech Lake Accord had foreclosed the possibility of constitutional renewal. All that Canada's leaders could offer was the status quo, liberally sprinkled with threats, should the *Yes* side prevail (Conway 2004).

Few televisions in Canada were silent on referendum night. In the end, nearly all of Quebec's eligible voters—90 percent, or 4.7 million people—cast ballots, the final result being that 50.6 percent voted *No* while 49.4 percent voted *Yes* (Morton 1997, 340). A swing of less than 30,000 votes would have changed the referendum's outcome (Young 1998).

As in 1980, the 1995 referendum split not only Canada but also Quebec. The *Yes* side won strong support from francophones, about 60 percent of eligible francophone voters (compared with 50 percent in 1980). The *Yes* side also won strong support in Quebec City and rural Quebec, from middle-class and better-educated voters, and from union supporters. In contrast to 1980, the *Yes* side also received some support from business, though business in general remained on the sidelines of the sovereignty debate (Conway 2004). Polls conducted prior to the referendum also suggested that sovereignty appealed especially to those aged 35 to 44 and to men slightly more than to women, though that gap had lessened (Trent 1995). By contrast, the *No* side fashioned its close victory from about 40 percent of francophones and almost all anglophones and allophones, mostly located in

Montreal (Fox et al. 1999), not to mention northern Quebec's small but politically powerful Cree and Inuit peoples (Conway 2004), thus opening up new and important ground for discussing the future of Indigenous peoples within Canadian society (see Part 3).

CONCLUSION

The history of societies, like that of individuals, is one of roads both taken and not taken. Had either the Meech Lake Accord or Charlottetown successor passed, Canada might be very different today. More certainly, had either of the referendums in 1980 or 1995 passed, Canada—and this text—would be very different in discussing the nature of Canadian society.

But roads not taken also leave their mark. Canada was much different at the end of the constitutional years than it was at the beginning, in part because of the Charter of Rights and Freedoms and constitutional promises made to Indigenous peoples. But the two referendums also left scars that would take time to heal—if they healed at all. Moreover, Canadians and Quebecers after 1995 also saw themselves and each other differently from how they had in 1970. Meanwhile, too, new and different pressures for change were coming from sociological forces beyond the political sphere and even beyond Canada's borders. Ultimately, Canadian society was witnessing a shift in power—who has it, what is its basis, how it is expressed—across individuals and social groups, an issue of primary sociological concern. In Quebec and elsewhere, women, Indigenous peoples, and racial and ethnic minorities were demanding a say in the emerging society. The old issues were dying or being recast. In time, the old warriors themselves disappeared.

NOTE

1. It is now known that Trudeau, in his youth, admired the corporatist (and fascist) regimes of Francisco Franco in Spain and Benito Mussolini in Italy (Nemni and Nemni 2006). Trudeau's later conversion to liberalism shows that early socialization is reversible.

CRITICAL THINKING QUESTIONS

1. Why are constitutions important for understanding societies?
2. How might symbolic interaction theorists and post-structural theorists view the importance of language, particularly its ability to arouse strong emotions?
3. To what extent do individuals effect change? To what extent are they products of their time and place?
4. What did Joseph Conrad mean when he said that underlying every great emotion is a great fear?
5. From the perspective of counterfactual history, what might have happened had the Meech Lake Accord been enacted?

RECOMMENDED READINGS

Clarkson, Stephen, and Christina McCall. 1990. *Trudeau and Our Times*, Vol. 1: *The Magnificent Obsession*. Toronto: McClelland & Stewart.
This book is the definitive work on Pierre Trudeau's "obsession" with constitutional reform.

Cohen, Andrew. 1990. *A Deal Undone: The Making and Breaking of the Meech Lake Accord*. Vancouver: Douglas & McIntyre.
Cohen's book details the making and breaking of the Meech Lake Accord.

Gervais, Stéphan, Christopher Kirkey, and Jarrett Rudy. 2011. *Quebec Questions: Quebec Studies for the Twenty-First Century*. Don Mills, ON: Oxford University Press.
A good companion to Behiels and Hayday (2011), with especially useful discussions of memory, identity, citizenship, models of social and economic policy followed in Quebec, and the province's efforts at establishing a presence in the world community.

Harrison, Trevor. 1995. *Of Passionate Intensity: Right-Wing Populism and the Reform Party of Canada*. Toronto: University of Toronto Press.
This book examines the rise of the Reform Party in western Canada in 1987 and its impact on mobilizing opposition to the Meech Lake Accord as well as to the idea of Quebec as a distinct society more generally.

Mills, C. Wright. 1961. *The Sociological Imagination*. New York: Grove Press.
This book is essential reading for any beginning sociologist, outlining Mills's idea of the "sociological imagination."

RELATED WEBSITES

Canadian Constitution Acts, 1867 to 1982
Department of Justice website: www.justice.gc.ca
The Constitution Act of 1982 fundamentally reshaped Canada. In the eyes of some, it also led to Quebec's increased isolation from the rest of Canada.

Official Bilingualism in Canada: History and Debates
www.mapleleafweb.com/features/official-bilingualism-canada-history-and-debates
A useful summary of the history of bilingualism in Canada can be found on Mapleleafweb.

Province of Quebec

www.gouv.qc.ca

> The government of Quebec's website.

CANADIAN SOCIETY ON VIDEO

The Champions Series, Part Three: The Final Battle. 1986. National Film Board of
Canada, 87 minutes, 2 seconds.

Examines the period from 1978 to 1986, including the divisive 1980
referendum on independence and the repatriation of the 1982 Constitution.

CHAPTER 4

The Return of the Nation

Intersection. Photo by Ryoji Iwata on Unsplash.

Canada suffers in many respects from the same ailments as Québec. In fact, Canadian nationalism is also in the process of congealing under the weight of myths and dogmas that are becoming obstacles to the country's evolution.
  —journalist Alain Dubuc, LaFontaine-Baldwin Lecture, 2001

That this House recognize that the Québécois form a nation within a united Canada.
  —motion passed by the House of Commons, November 27, 2006

We coexist by recognizing the volatility and not wanting to disturb it.
  —John Wright, Ipsos Reid polling, 2008

INTRODUCTION

Since the 1970s, Quebec and Canada had held constitutional negotiations designed to address Quebec's grievances and resolve their different visions of the country. The defeat of the Meech Lake and Charlottetown accords removed constitutional change, at least for a time, as a means of doing so; the 1995 referendum, though close, also seemed to end the threat of separation.

Sociologically, however, Quebec and Canada continued to evolve in ways unforeseeable only decades before—one example demonstrating this is the House of Commons's recognition of Quebec as a nation in 2006. This chapter delves deep into sociological questions regarding individual and collective identity, the power exerted by symbols and metaphors in shaping group solidarity and conflict, and the issue of minority rights within a multicultural society. While Quebec provides the focal point of examination, the questions asked are applicable to Canada at large and elsewhere. In anticipation of Part 2 of this book, the issues of nation and state are reconsidered in the context of globalization, traditional notions of sovereignty, and the threat posed by the United States to both the Québécois nation and English Canada.

MULTICULTURALISM, SECULARISM, AND CIVIC NATIONALISM

On referendum night in 1995, the obviously distraught Quebec premier, Parizeau, remarked that the pro-sovereignty side had been defeated by "money and the ethnic vote" (quoted in Conway 2004, 208; see also Balthazar 1997; Morton 1997). Reproached by colleagues and opponents alike for his divisive remarks, a remorseful Parizeau resigned the next day and was succeeded shortly thereafter as premier by Lucien Bouchard.

In broad statistical terms, Parizeau's observations leading to his resignation were correct. Francophones in Quebec *do* disproportionately favour sovereignty; non-francophones *do not* support it. His remarks, however, were divisive in singling out all members of Quebec's allophone community as being opposed to Quebec nationalism—indeed, being unpatriotic (Balthazar 1997). As such, Parizeau's comments unearthed debates within Quebec and the Parti Québécois itself about who a true Québécois is and the nature of Quebec nationalism.

As noted in Chapter 2, traditional Quebec nationalism was cultural and inward looking. It traced its ancestry through bloodlines to the original 10,000 *Canadiens* of the St. Lawrence. It was traditional, tribal, and *Catholic*. Vestiges of the old nationalism still exist today, expressed linguistically through descriptions of people as either *Québécois pur laine* (literally, "pure wool") or *Québécois de souche* ("of the root") (Ignatieff 1993, 172). The old nationalism dominated until after the Second World War and—as we will see—is still prone to resurfacing at times of imagined threat.

But Quebec, like the rest of Canada, changed in the post-war years. The new nationalism that arose in the 1950s was socially progressive, democratic, territorial, pluralistic, and secular, even if (as previously noted) most Quebecers still nominally declared themselves members of the Catholic faith. In theory, the new nationalism welcomed anyone living within Quebec's borders willing to accept the values of Quebec society. This was also the case in practice; many Quebecers today view their nationalism as civic, not ethnic (Ignatieff 1993; Smith 1998). Nonetheless, the debate continues over who is a true Québécois.

An important element of this debate is the role of secularism. As noted, the transformation from old to new nationalism in Quebec was tied to the decline of the Catholic Church's authority. Shortly after this transformation occurred, however, Quebec also began dealing—as did the rest of Canada—with the arrival of new immigrants, many from neither francophone nor anglophone countries, who have still held strong religious beliefs.

The concern expressed by many Quebec francophones is not simply whether new immigrants will support sovereignty (a specifically nationalist concern), but how immigrants can be successfully integrated into modern—and *secular*—Quebec society. These concerns always arise around specific incidents that take on larger symbolic meaning—for example, where a court ruled a Sikh student could carry a kirpan (religious dagger) to school and, in another instance, where a soccer league sought to prevent a youth belonging to the Islamic faith from wearing headgear (a hijab, or head scarf) (see Maclure 2011). Since the terrorist attacks on New York and Washington in 2001, much of the negative response by Quebecers has been directed at people identified as Muslim—a response, it must be noted, also seen in the rest of mainstream Canada and the United States.

In search of an answer to the perceived rise of cultural and religious divisions, in February 2007 the Quebec government established the Consultation Commission on Accommodation Practices Related to Cultural Differences (Government of Quebec 2008). The commission's mandate was to examine accommodation practices in Quebec; to examine similar experiences in other societies; to conduct extensive public consultations on the issue; and "to formulate recommendations to the government to ensure that accommodation practices conform to the values of Québec society as a pluralistic, democratic, egalitarian society" (Government of Quebec 2008, 7).

Co-chaired by a sociologist, Gérard Bouchard, and a liberal philosopher, Charles Taylor, the commission travelled throughout Quebec during the fall of 2007, garnering submissions on the question of **reasonable accommodation**—defined as "a form of arrangement or relaxation aimed at ensuring respect for the right of equality . . . which, following the strict application of an institutional standard, infringes on an individual's right to equality" (Government of Quebec 2008, 7)—of minority cultural and religious rights. In the end, the commission made 37 recommendations based on the notion not of multiculturalism but of "*interculturalisme*," what Saul (2008, 147) describes as "the intercultural dovetailing relationship among four groups: the francophone majority, the anglophone minority, the Indigenous minority, and *the cultural communities*, that is, the newcomers, with French as the central convening language of all four."

Among the commission's specific recommendations were greater cultural awareness, improved intercultural relations, better integration of migrants, and greater effort on the part of government and its institutions to deal with racism and inequality. Its broadest thrust, however, was to recommend Quebec's adoption of "open secularism" based on four principles: (1) the moral equality of persons; (2) freedom of conscience and religion; (3) separation of church and state; and (4) the state's neutrality with respect to religions and deep-seated secular convictions (Government of Quebec 2008, 45). The concept of open secularism was immediately contentious, however, seen by many Quebecers as being at odds with Quebec society as it had developed since the Quiet Revolution (Dickinson and Young 2008). Not only had the province become more secular—**secularization** being a process that occurs when religion "progressively loses its relevance as a social and cultural framework for defining moral values and social conduct"—more fundamentally, Quebec's government since the 1960s had embraced a process of **laicization**, "by which the state deliberately distances itself from religion on an institutional level" (both quotes from Milot 2011, 125).

In November 2013, the Parti Québécois government introduced a bill amending the Quebec Charter of Human Rights and Freedoms. The proposed Quebec Charter of Values, it was argued, would clarify the notion of reasonable accommodation. The bill, which (among other things) would have limited the use of conspicuous religious symbols by public employees and prevented the wearing of face coverings (e.g., hijabs) by anyone providing or receiving a state service, had wide support in Quebec among those who viewed the bill as a necessary defence of secular society. However, many others— including former premiers Jacques Parizeau and Lucien Bouchard—opposed the charter as xenophobic and racist. The bill died in the spring of 2014 with the PQ's electoral defeat at the hands of the provincial Liberals, led by Philippe Couillard (see *Canadian Encyclopedia* 2014).

Quebec's particular concern about the political power of religious institutions has historical roots in the past role of the Roman Catholic Church in that province, but its anxieties, fears, and successes in accommodating cultural difference are also mirrored in the rest of Canada. (During the 2015 federal election, for example, a prominent member of the then-governing Conservative party raised fears of the "barbaric cultural practices" held by immigrants coming to Canada.) In this sense, Quebec's struggles to incorporate minority cultural differences within a framework of civic nationalism are a subset of Canada's struggle to fashion a coherent and cohesive national community that embraces three nations—the English, the French, and the Indigenous—and an assortment of other ethnic groups (Saul 1997, 2008). The struggle to fashion such a framework is not always successful, however, as recent events show.

BILL 21: RELIGIOUS SYMBOLS AND NATIONAL IDENTITY

The earlier controversy of November 2013 over religious symbols was revived in June 2019 when Premier Francois Legault's recently elected Coalition Avenir Québec (CAQ) government passed Bill 21, "An Act respecting the laicity of the State." The bill's exact wording reads as follows (Government of Quebec 2019):

> The purpose of this Act is to affirm the laicity of the State and to set out the requirements that follow from it.
>
> To that end, the Act provides that the laicity of the State is based on four principles: the separation of State and religions, the religious neutrality of the State, the equality of all citizens, and freedom of conscience and freedom of religion. Parliamentary, government and judicial institutions are bound to adhere to all these principles in pursuing their missions, and State laicity requires that all persons have the right to lay institutions and lay public services. . . .
>
> The Act proposes to prohibit certain persons from wearing religious symbols while exercising their functions. . . .
>
> Under the Act, personnel members of a body must exercise their functions with their face uncovered, and persons who present themselves to receive a service from such a personnel member must have their face uncovered when doing so is necessary to allow their identity to be verified or for security reasons. Persons who fail to comply with that obligation may not receive the service.

In short, Bill 21 formally bans public officials from wearing religiously identifiable items (e.g., hijabs or crucifixes) in the course of their duties; further, it requires citizens using public services to uncover their faces. The bill was opposed by the Liberal party and Québec solidaire, as well as many community groups. Uprichard (2019) argues that "while the bill theoretically treats all religious symbols as equal, by far the largest pool of people affected will be non-Christian women who wear scarves or veils, giving it a distinctly xenophobic and sexist edge." Sahi (2019) goes further. Noting that the bill was tabled in April 2019, only a couple of weeks after "an anti-Muslim extremist xenophobe" stormed two mosques in New Zealand, killing 50 Muslims at prayer, and only two years after a right-wing extremist murdered six worshippers and injured nineteen others at a Quebec City mosque in January 2017, Sahi states:

> The tabling of this bill at any time would be controversial and damaging to social cohesion, pitting—within Quebec—a white majority against religious minorities. Outside Quebec, in Canada at large, the bill signals that it's okay to harbour, foster and even legitimize xenophobic thoughts and policies. Essentially, the tabling of Bill 21 empowers populist and far-right nationalist thinking.
>
> It's not about secularism, it's about votes and white Quebec's "neutralization" of its visible and religious minorities.

The issues raised by Bill 21 go beyond the legitimate concerns of critics over individual rights to broader sociological questions of national identity and the role of the state. Morrison (2019) notes that national identity is always unstable and prone to moments of crisis and that, in the case of Quebec, national identity has veered since the Conquest from being religiously Catholic to being culturally secular. Zubrzycki (2016) has similarly examined the transformed symbolism of Quebec's Saint Jean Baptiste holiday (June 24) from an occasion imbued with religious meaning to one celebrating secular nationalism and the state. But Laxer (2017) argues that the changing nature of Quebec's national identity is not a benign or an accidental product of societal changes. It is the result, rather, of political actors vying for power (and legitimacy) using fear to further their political aims—a cultural and secular nationalism whose hidden skeletal frame, despite the Quiet Revolution, remains religiously Catholic (and Christian) and for whom Islam and other non-Western religions are seen as threats to Quebec identity. For Laxer, the Quebec state's recent decisions have taken Quebec identity away from the civic nationalism of the post-Quiet Revolution period toward a less inclusive ethnic nationalism (see the Introduction).

Laxer's argument brings us back to considering the relationship between society and state, and this can be expanded beyond Quebec. It is naive to suggest any state reflects its society. States are mechanisms of power and to a large extent create the societies over which they govern—but they do not do so wholly without some connection to society, or at least connections to some of its social elements. The relationship between the governed and the governing is an elaborate and sometimes tenuous dance, as witnessed in past revolutions in France, the United States, and Russia.

Finally, Laxer's argument also returns us to considering not only Quebec's identity but the often-fragile identity of English-speaking Canada, a product also of successive crises as it has veered between the cultural, political, and economic sway of Britain and the United States—to be explored in the second part of this text.

THE SOVEREIGNTY QUESTION TODAY

How strong is the appeal of Quebec sovereignty today? Data gathered since 1995 are consistent on four points (Trent 1995; Dubuc 2001). First, the vast majority of Quebecers oppose holding another referendum. Second, few Quebecers believe a referendum on sovereignty would pass if held today. Third, support for sovereignty during "normal" periods averages about 42 percent (Léger Marketing 2008). Support for sovereignty rises above this only when Quebecers feel attacked or rejected by English Canada, as during the Meech Lake crisis (earlier mentioned) or when the idea of sovereignty is presented in the abstract or its definition is unclear. And fourth, a large number of Quebecers hold the apparently contradictory belief that Quebec and Canada have reached an impasse *and* that federalism can be renewed.

Looked at another way, about a third of Quebecers are consistent federalists. Another third are hard-core *indépendantistes* who identify with the Quebec state. The remaining third of Quebecers are torn between choosing the Quebec nation or the country of Canada, a predicament captured in the oft-quoted joke of Quebec comedian Yvon Deschamps that "all we want is an independent Quebec within a strong and united Canada" (Colombo 1994, 224). It is on this third of Quebecers that the outcome of any future sovereignty referendum would hinge, should such a vote be held.

At the same time, most analysts agree that compared with the past, sovereignty today invokes little passion in Quebec and even less support. A poll conducted in 2016 is instructive. While Quebecers are less likely than people outside the province to express a deep emotional attachment to the country, a solid plurality of those surveyed in both Quebec and the rest of Canada said that "ultimately, Quebec should stay in Canada" (79 and 84 percent, respectively) and that "the issue of Quebec sovereignty is settled, and Quebec will remain in Canada" (64 percent and 69 percent, respectively) (Angus Reid 2016). What explains these results? In part, the reason seems to be that many of the political, economic, and cultural grievances expressed during the Quiet Revolution have been addressed (Ignatieff 1993).

Since the 1960s, francophones have used their political strength to make gains within Canada's political and labour sectors (Nakhaie 1997). By contrast, while those of British background continue disproportionately to dominate elite positions within Canada, they do not do so unopposed; indeed, it can be argued that British Canada as a sociological construct no longer exists (Gwyn 1996; Igartua 2006). The object of francophone Canada's wrath—white Anglo-Saxon Protestant (WASP) Canada—is today largely an historical artifact—indeed, a myth.

Economically, French-Canadians in general, and francophone Quebecers in particular, no longer experience the second-place status relative to English-Canadians once identified by Porter (1965) and the Royal Commission on Bilingualism and Biculturalism (Government of Canada 1963). Today, much of Quebec's bourgeoisie is francophone and, like the Canadian bourgeoisie at large, wedded to breaking down, rather than defending, national borders. By 1991, in Canada as a whole, workers of French ethnicity were actually earning significantly more than workers of British ethnicity (Lian and Matthews 1998). And, while Quebec is not a "have" province economically, the circumstances of Quebecers overall have gradually improved since the 1960s. As shown in table 4.1, the median income for all census families in Quebec in 2017 (before tax) was $80,550, roughly 95 percent of the Canadian average (calculated from Statistics Canada 2017c), ahead of the Atlantic provinces and equal with Manitoba, though behind (sometimes significantly) many of the western and northern provinces and territories. (The median is the value at the midpoint of a frequency distribution; see Chapter 8.)

Quebec's success in stemming the cultural threat is harder to measure. Though the percentage of French-speaking people in Quebec has stabilized just short of 80 percent (see Chapter 3), many francophone Quebecers remain "linguistically insecure" (Thompson 1995, 78; Dickinson and Young 2008). They particularly fear the impact of allophone immigrants to Quebec who might choose English rather than French as their adopted language,

Table 4.1: Median Total Income (nominal dollars), by Province and Territory (all census families),[1] 2013–2017, and Percentage of Canadian Median Total Income by Province and Territory, 2017[2]

	2013	2014	2015	2016	2017	Percentage of 2017 Canadian Median
Canada	**76,550**	**78,870**	**80,940**	**82,110**	**84,950**	**100**
Newfoundland and Labrador	73,850	77,040	79,260	78,960	79,600	93.7
Prince Edward Island	70,270	72,380	73,910	75,090	77,940	91.7
Nova Scotia	70,020	72,270	73,900	74,590	76,710	90.3
New Brunswick	67,340	69,290	71,040	72,330	74,710	87.9
Quebec	72,240	73,870	75,530	77,670	80,550	94.8
Ontario	76,510	78,790	81,480	83,160	85,900	101.1
Manitoba	72,600	74,790	76,990	78,110	80,530	94.8
Saskatchewan	82,990	85,710	86,970	85,820	87,960	103.5
Alberta	97,390	100,750	100,300	96,470	99,430	117.0
British Columbia	74,150	76,770	79,750	81,370	84,850	99.9
Yukon	95,360	98,540	100,130	103,070	106,440	125.3
Northwest Territories	109,670	112,400	117,100	115,530	118,100	139.0
Nunavut	63,300	65,190	67,860	70,840	74,450	87.6

Notes: 1. Census families include couple families with or without children and lone-parent families. 2. Percentages for 2017 calculated by authors.

Source: Statistics Canada. 2017d. Table 11-10-0017-01: "Census families by family type and family composition including before and after-tax median income of the family."

a fear that ties into concerns about cultural differences generally, as earlier discussed. Still, the level of insecurity concerning language is lower among younger Quebecers, who are used to the protections provided by Quebec's language laws. Moreover, recent census figures suggest that allophone immigrants today are actually strengthening the French language in Quebec by opting to adopt that language (Friesen and Peritz 2012), an outcome strengthened by the provincial government's gaining greater control over immigration, allowing for the recruitment of immigrants from francophone countries.

Beyond Quebec, the world has also changed dramatically since the time of the Quiet Revolution. Liberation politics, drawn from Third World experiences and the writings of Frantz Fanon (1968) and Che Guevara (2003), have little appeal today. Few Quebecers, especially young people, see their province as colonized. In this time of increased global connectedness, as the world seems drawn closer and closer together by economics, technology, cultural exchanges, and trade deals, the very meaning of sovereignty seems unclear. (What would Quebec gain through sovereignty that it does not already possess?) Meanwhile, recent examples of ethnic nationalism gone wrong (e.g., in Yugoslavia and the Middle East) provide stinging counterpoints to the ideal of independence. (What would an independent Quebec lose?) Finally, many young Quebecers—not unlike young people elsewhere—increasingly see themselves as individual consumers and mobile workers. Increasingly, sovereignty is a dream held mainly by the university-educated 55 years and older (Hamilton 2014).

At the same time, it would be a mistake to suggest that Quebec nationalism and the attendant possibility of separation have disappeared. For two centuries, English-speaking Canada has believed that this would be the case. Yet Quebec nationalism and the idea of an independent homeland have continued to stir within the province. Why is this the case? The answer lies in the fact that the issue of French-English, Quebec-Canada relations within the country cannot be addressed by material or even constitutional changes alone. The basis of the issue lies in such intangible, but immanently sociological, issues as self-identity, mutual respect, and the need for recognition.

IDENTITY AND "SELF" IN MODERNITY AND POSTMODERNITY

Who are you? That is, what are the elements that shape who you are and speak to you and others of your "self"? This is a distinctly sociological question, one that emerged in the 19th century with modernity. Riesman and colleagues (1950), for example, observe that notions of individual identity made little sense in pre-modern, feudal societies, where ideas, norms, behaviours, expectations, and outcomes were fairly rigidly controlled by tradition. In the Middle Ages, no one would have sought to "find himself or herself," to use a popular phrase of the 1960s. People of that era were told directly and indirectly who they were from the time they were born. By contrast, in modern societies, individuals not only *seem* to be freer of social restraints, they are also expected to find and express their particular uniqueness.

What are the building blocks used in this construction? For Marx, writing in the mid-19th century, class was the primary factor in a person's identity kit; for Durkheim, occupation was central. More recently, feminist scholars have reminded us how gender is also a primary source of one's identity (Newman 2012). But other factors, such as religion, ethnicity, and sexual orientation, can also inform an individual's self-identity. For people growing up in modern societies, the cache of materials from which to make a "self" is seemingly endless, drawn from television, the Internet, magazines, and so on, even as pressures to express one's identity and to have it accepted as authentic have come to present their own problems (Bauman 1996).

Sociologists view this construction critically, however. First, individual and collective identities are mutually constructed. In a real sense, no one simply chooses an individual identity. Rather, an identity arises out of membership in a group (Tajfel and Turner 1986). Second, both individual and collective identities are highly malleable (Cook 1995, 235). The importance of an identity may lessen over time for a person or group, or events may lead an individual or group to rediscover and reassert their roots. Third, individual identities are neither singular nor exclusive. A person may simultaneously see himself or herself as Italian, a doctor, a soccer player, a conservative, and gay or lesbian.

What does the issue of individual and collective identity have to do with Quebec and Canada? Simply this: Quebec's national culture, broadly conceived, provides many Quebecers with essential materials for their personal identities. Writing in 1951, André Laurendeau (1985) noted that "except for the stateless (and even then!) every being carries the mark of a particular culture. The richer it is, the more it nourishes him [*sic*]."

This notion is at odds (at least on the surface) with dominant Western culture, where private and public spheres are viewed as separate, the individual is sacrosanct, and "the state and civil society are typically understood as facing off against each other" (White 1997, 22). Pierre Trudeau's denunciations of Quebec nationalism as tribal (Chapter 3) were rooted in a supposed separation of individual self and society (Couture 1998), hence his desire to entrench the Charter of Rights and Freedoms in the 1982 Constitution as a means of protecting individuals from collective oppression.

Separating the spheres, however, is difficult, if not impossible. Note, for example, that Canada's Charter of Rights and Freedoms deals with both individual and collective rights (Cook 1995). Likewise, the policies of official bilingualism and multiculturalism enacted by Trudeau similarly protect collective rights over language and culture (Webber 1994; Couture 1998).

It is therefore inaccurate to argue that a necessary opposition exists between the rights of the collective and those of individuals, represented by Quebec and English-speaking Canada, respectively. Repeated surveys show Quebecers have at least as much deep regard for individual rights as other Canadians. Indeed, Quebecers are generally quite liberal in their acceptance of individual differences regarding sexual orientation or marital status (Denis 1993; Dickinson and Young 2008). At the same time, English-speaking Canadians also possess a sense of collective identity, albeit understated, as evidenced quickly if someone tells them they are "just like" Americans.

If the sociological (and political) problem between Quebec and Canada does not lie in an opposition between individual and collective rights, it is even less in an absolute separation of the French and English cultures. French and English identities (and others) in Canada include elements of each other (Dufour 1990; Webber 1994; Saul 1997). Notes Dufour (1990, 81), "Almost by definition, the Quebec identity comprises a more or less significant, more or less conscious, Canadian component." And again, "English is a deeply ambivalent and perturbing element of the Quebec identity" (1990, 97). A majority of Quebecers (though less so among francophones) still see themselves simultaneously as Quebecers *and* as Canadians (see Smith 1998), though the former may take precedence.

What, then, underlies the conflict? For some, the conflict resides in *the right of Quebecers to possess a distinct identity be recognized and respected by the rest of Canada* (Taylor 1993; Coulombe 1998).

There is an apparent paradox in this demand, however, for, as Taylor (1993) and Ignatieff (1993) note, Canada and Quebec have never been closer. Quebec was "more distinct" before the Quiet Revolution than it is today. The paradox of diminishing differences alongside escalating demands for the recognition of difference is partly explained, however, if we consider the impact of neo-liberal globalization upon states, nations (see the Introduction), and, in this instance, group and individual identity.

On the one hand, globalization has accelerated the process of homogenizing cultures. On the other hand, it has left many national groups feeling uneasy and compelled to overemphasize and protect remaining distinctions. This brings us to the problem of identity in postmodernity. While modernity emphasized the fixity of individual identity, postmodernity—alternatively, late modernity, or advanced (or late) capitalism (Morrison 2019)—emphasizes its fluidity. In Bauman's (1996, 18) words, "the postmodern 'problem of identity' is primarily how to avoid fixation and keep the options open." Morrison (2019, 15) notes that in the neo-liberal economy, the postmodern subject does not develop strong or stable attachments with others, as these are disadvantageous, with the result that those identities "that had gained the most prominence and seeming stability in modernity, central among them national identity," have been decentred. Concurrently, however, many people have turned to the apparent solidity offered by national identity, as rooted in modernity, as a means of warding off a host of perceived threats, such as terrorism, migration, automation, and global warming. This result, it will be noted, is not confined to Quebec; it permeates the rest of Canada, the United States, and much of Europe, where inward-looking, often right-wing governments have in recent years been ascendant.

In some instances, the perceived incapacity of multinational states, such as Canada, to protect national cultures has led the latter to seek shelter in smaller units. In line with Daniel Bell's (1993) contention that states today are both too big and too small to deal with important issues, supporters of sovereignty argue that an independent Quebec would be better able to adapt to the demands of the global marketplace (see Bourgault 1991; Parti Québécois 1994).

Such claims are debatable but ultimately beside the point. The question is this: Is it possible for English-speaking Canada to acknowledge Quebec's distinctness in a meaningful way; to grant recognition and respect for Québécois identity; and to give Quebec sufficient powers for its survival within Canada's existing state structures (see Taylor 1993; Denis 1993; Coulombe 1998)? Or—despite the recent lull in the conflict between the two nations—does the flow of history lead inexorably to Quebec sovereignty?

THE RETURN OF THE NATIONAL QUESTION

Suddenly, in the fall of 2006, Canada caught up with its history and, one might argue, with sociology. In an act unimaginable only a few years before, on November 27, 2006, the Canadian House of Commons passed the following motion (by a vote of 266 to 16, the rest abstaining or absent): "That this House recognize that the Québécois form a nation within a united Canada."

How did this turn come about? And to what extent does it represent a "turn" in French-English relations? To unpack the meaning of the Commons's resolution, we need to briefly return to previous discussions.

We have seen that, depending on the time and place, since 1763 Canada's dominant anglophone elite have employed various policies (from coercion and subjugation, to isolation and subtle assimilation, to tentative efforts, beginning in the 1960s, at accommodation and recognition) of dealing with the smaller but nonetheless significant and distinct francophone minority. The prevailing issue underlying these policies is that of the nation.

The Introduction noted the conflation of nation, state, country, and society. Canada is a textbook case of this conflation in practice. The "problem" with which Canada has struggled since its founding is in every sense a modern one: Can it survive as a country administered by a state that accommodates several nations within its territory? As noted in Chapter 1, Lord Durham's Eurocentric background led him to conclude that every nation must have a state, and that no state must have more than one nation, a situation that led to the failed Act of Union of 1841 and then to Confederation in 1867.

The years after 1867 saw the French "fact" in Canada largely isolated (but, thus, also strengthened) within Quebec, while the rest of Canada took on a decidedly English stamp. By the 1960s, arguments about the nature of Canada focused on whether it was a confederation of 10 provinces (of which Quebec was merely one) or a marriage of "two nations," with separatists in Quebec arguing for a third option: that the marriage be dissolved (Chapter 2).

The constitutional discussions of the 1970s and 1980s failed to resolve Quebec's place within Canada. Subsequent efforts to revise the Constitution also failed and even heightened the crisis. English-speaking Canada's rejection in 1990 of the Meech Lake Accord, based primarily on the accord's recognition of Quebec as a "distinct society," increased many Quebecers' sense that they were not accepted by the rest of Canada; the result was a rise in support for sovereignty and the nearly successful vote for separation in 1995 (Chapter 3).

Fast forward to the fall of 2006. Earlier that same year, the governing Liberal Party was defeated in a federal election by the Conservative Party, led by Stephen Harper (1959–), a party resulting from a merger of the Progressive Conservative and Canadian Alliance parties. In the course of the subsequent race to replace Paul Martin (1938–) as Liberal leader, one of the contenders, Michael Ignatieff (1947–) (see Chapter 8), suggested that Quebec be constitutionally recognized as a "nation." Though endorsed by the federal party's Quebec wing, the other Liberal candidates and much of English-Canada's media quickly denounced Ignatieff's proposal, which not only went against the Trudeau legacy of opposing Quebec nationalism in favour of a dual, pan-Canadian ideal, but went further than any previous constitutional effort, including the failed Meech Lake Accord, in recognizing Quebec's distinctiveness (Fidler 2006).

Sensing an opportunity to divide the Liberal Party, however, the Bloc Québécois, which had elected 51 members in the 2006 election, proposed a parliamentary motion along the lines of Ignatieff's position that Quebec constituted a nation within Canada. Likewise, sensing the chance to build support in Quebec while blunting the Bloc Québécois motion, Prime Minister Harper proposed the previously mentioned motion, which the House of Commons subsequently adopted.

At first glance, the proposal appears to be a major step in recognizing Quebec's distinct identity, something that the Reform Party, of which Harper was a prominent member, had vehemently opposed two decades earlier.

Fidler (2006), however, argues that

> the original Bloc motion, which had identified the "Québécois" as a nation, referred to them in English as "Quebeckers." That is, a territorial concept, encompassing everyone who inhabits Quebec irrespective of first language or ethnic origin. This is now the common definition of "Québécois" in Quebec. [Prime Minister] Harper's motion, in contrast, used the term "Québécois" in both French and English versions, an ethnic connotation implying that only those whose first language is French qualified as a "nation."

In short, the House of Commons motion recognized an ethnic definition of the nation, while the Bloc version recognized a civic definition of the nation tied to territory (see the Introduction).

Mere semantics? Perhaps. Linguistic meanings are slippery at the best of times, especially when moving between two languages. Nonetheless, Fidler raises important questions about the exact meaning of the House of Commons resolution. Quoting journalist Pierre Dubuc, Fidler argues that recognition of the Québécois nation is designed to prepare for the partition of Quebec should that province ever vote *Yes* to a referendum on sovereignty. That is, while the Québécois (francophone) nation might vote to separate, the English-speaking areas could likewise vote to remain in Canada. Such a stance would be commensurate with that of previous Canadian governments, both Liberal and Conservative.

In short, the resolution passed by the House of Commons appears to thwart the Bloc's motion by giving symbolic (but not constitutional) recognition to the Québécois nation while simultaneously denying the territorial nationhood of Quebec with all its political implications. Likewise, while the Bloc version would have given particular power to the provincial state as representing and perhaps even constituting the Quebec nation and society, the House of Commons version reserved considerable political power for the Canadian state in this regard. Ultimately, was the House of Commons motion of 2006 too clever by half? Does it offer Quebecers the appearance of recognition but provide something much less? Does it in consequence represent another failed opportunity to recognize Quebec's specific identity and needs?

How do Canadian people view Canada's "nations," not merely that of Quebec, but otherwise? Previous surveys have suggested that anglophones are more likely to recognize ethnic definitions of nationhood, while francophones hold a more territorial or civic definition of nationhood (Léger Marketing 2008). An online survey conducted by Ipsos Reid in the summer of 2008, amid the celebrations of the 400th anniversary of the founding of Quebec City in 1608, found that 70 percent of Quebecers view themselves as "a nation within a united Canada," while only 36 percent of adults in the rest of Canada see them similarly. Likewise, half of Quebecers subscribe to the "two nations" concept of Canada, compared with only one-third in the rest of Canada. Instead, more than 40 percent of those outside of Quebec see Canada as "a nation with one dominant culture and several equal minorities," a view held by only 20 percent of Quebecers (figures from the *Edmonton Journal* 2008). In short, Canada's French and English communities continue to view each other from quite different promontories.

At the same time, fears about the French language's fragility amidst a sea of English continue to plague many francophone speakers in Quebec. A Léger Marketing survey in 2018, conducted for the Quebec Community Groups Network (2018), shows that, within Quebec itself, francophones, anglophones, and allophones hold very different views of intergroup relations, threats to the French language, and the province's historical path for the past fifty years (see box 4.1).

QUEBEC "SOLUTIONS"—AND CANADA'S PROBLEM

In the aftermath of the 1995 referendum, successive federalist forces adopted two strategies to counter the appeal of Quebec sovereignty. These two strategies were referred to as "Plan A" and "Plan B" or, as Conway (2004, 214–215) describes them, the carrot and the stick. Plan A involved attempts to show Quebecers that Confederation works and perhaps, in time, to win Quebecers' hearts and minds. In contrast, Plan B involved a "tough love" approach to Quebec (Conway 2004; Balthazar 1997). Readers of this text will note that variations of these two strategies have been used in the past, going back to 1763.

Even before the sovereignty vote, however, a third strategy, "Plan C," was being proposed in several quarters. Less discussed than either Plan A or Plan B, this strategy aims at a radical **decentralization** of Canada, whereby Quebec's demands would be applied throughout the federation—that is, whatever powers Quebec might obtain are automatically given to every other province. In the words of Gordon Gibson (1994), a former Liberal and Social Credit politician and conservative policy adviser, Plan C would see

Box 4.1: Intergroup Relations and the Importance of History for Quebecers Today

A 2018 Léger Marketing survey discovered the following differences among Quebec residents:

- French-first language speakers in Quebec are much more likely than English-first speakers or Other-first speakers to feel very attached to Quebec (54.8 percent, 24.5 percent, and 24.4 percent, respectively).
- Baby boomers, whether French- or English-first speakers, are more likely to feel very attached to Quebec.
- French-first language speakers in Quebec are much more likely than English-first speakers to be very attached to Quebec and to the Charter of the French Language (Bill 101) and to view protections for the French language as insufficient and the Charter as inadequate.

When asked to name the most important events in Quebec history in the last 50 years, francophones, anglophones, and allophones agreed the Quiet Revolution was the most important (30 percent, 20 percent, and 23 percent). For francophones, the Charter of the French Language was second in importance (26 percent), but for anglophones it was the election of the Parti Québécois in 1976 (17 percent), and for allophones, the 1995 referendum (21 percent). For francophones, the PQ's election was third most important (16 percent), for anglophones it was the FLQ Crisis of 1970 (14 percent), which held very marginal importance for both francophones and allophones, while allophones view the adoption of the Charter (18 percent) as third most important. Other events—such as the repatriation of the Canadian Constitution without Quebec's signature in 1982, the failure of the Meech Lake Accord in 1990, and the Oka Crisis of 1990—were further down the list. Age had an impact on views about the importance of events, though perhaps surprisingly, younger Quebecers viewed the Quiet Revolution as marginally more important than older Quebecers.

Why might individuals hold somewhat different views about intergroup relationships and the importance of historical events? What differences might individuals outside Quebec hold concerning history?

Source: Quebec Community Groups Network. 2018. *Attachment to Quebec and Recent Historic Markers.* Léger Poll conducted for the Association of Canadian Studies and the Quebec Community Groups Network, July 3.

Ottawa reduced to a "service centre," a relatively powerless clearing house with functions residual to those of the provinces.

The idea of decentralization (or devolution) has been around for a long time and appeals to several distinct constituencies, albeit for different reasons. To rigid formalists, decentralization meets Quebec's demands while also maintaining a strict equality of the provinces. To provincial rights advocates, especially in western Canada, decentralization means a return to the division of powers written into the 1867 Constitution, before the Great Depression and two world wars meant the growth of federal powers. To political leaderships in the "have" provinces, it means more money and power that need not be shared with other jurisdictions. To pro-business think tanks (such as the Fraser Institute) and corporations, decentralization means dealing with only one level of government—smaller and often more compliant—regarding, for example, environmental and labour regulations. To some mainstream economists, decentralization embraces the principle of **subsidiarity**—that unless there is a valid reason to the contrary, state functions should be exercised by the lowest level of government (Courchene 1997). Finally, in the years leading up to the financial crisis of 2007 and 2008, some viewed decentralization as an inevitable and perhaps even positive adaptation to globalization (Courchene 1998; Resnick 2000; Ibbitson 2001) that might ultimately strengthen Canadian federalism through greater co-operation.

Decentralization also has critics, however. First, it is argued, Canada is already the world's most decentralized federation (Valaskakis and Fournier 1995), and further decentralization would hinder a unified governmental response to crises, such as the Great Recession of 2008. Second, most Canadians still believe in a strong role for the federal government, particularly in areas of health and social policy. Further decentralization would result in large corporate interests playing regions and provinces against each other, endangering national standards and programs, such as medicare (Laxer and Harrison 1995). Third, the federal government provides one of the few "checks and balances" to provincial power, and vice versa (see Taylor 1993), an equilibrium that decentralization would alter (Romanow 2006). Fourth, as more power flows to the provinces, people's identification with Canada as a whole will lessen, threatening national unity. Fifth, given the nature of Canada's integrated labour market, with goods, services, and people moving from coast to coast (to coast), a similar level of integration seems necessary across such areas as (for example) health, education and retraining, employment, and environmental policy.

Many of these same critics offer a different solution: **asymmetrical federalism** (Laxer 1992; Taylor 1993), or what could be termed "Plan D." Asymmetrical federalism begins from the premise that Quebec is not like the other provinces, that the needs of both Quebec and the other provinces are different, and that federalism cannot be practised in the manner of treating all provinces the same.

How would asymmetrical federalism work? Laxer (1992, 2002) and Webber (1994, 230) suggest that Quebec be given constitutional powers over areas it views as necessary for preserving its national identity, while these same powers for Canadians elsewhere remain "housed" in Ottawa. In effect, Quebec would have more powers than the other provinces, but it would not have powers over the citizens of other provinces, nor would Quebecers have more powers than other Canadians. The change would require two sittings of the House of Commons: an all-Canada sitting in which Quebec members of Parliament (MPs) would participate, and a separate sitting in which Quebec MPs would not participate, dealing with those areas delegated to the Quebec provincial government (Resnick 1991).

In a more complex development of this argument, Resnick (2000) suggests Canada be reconfigured as a country with three tiers that include six provinces (the four Atlantic provinces, Manitoba, and Saskatchewan); three region-provinces with large populations and significant resources (Ontario, Alberta, and British Columbia); and one nation-province (Quebec). These changes could be combined with other political reforms, such as the reform or abolition of the Senate, fixed electoral dates, and the replacement of Canada's first-past-the-post electoral system with proportional representation (Resnick 2000; Conway 2004).

Asymmetrical federalism also has its critics, however (see Cook 1995; Valaskakis and Fournier 1995). First, such a change is politically unacceptable to the other provinces and most Canadians who subscribe to the formal equality of all provinces. Second, Canadian federalism is already asymmetrical in certain respects. Like decentralization, further asymmetry would weaken Canada's federal principle as other provinces quickly seek the same powers as Quebec. Third, by making the government in Quebec City more important to Quebecers, an action not wholly endorsed by many (especially anglophone) Quebecers themselves, the path could be set for further separatist agitation in that province.

Whether asymmetrical federalism could work is debatable. In any case, its program has little support outside of the academic community. By contrast, Plan C—decentralization—is supported by a number of powerful constituencies, including big business and provincial leaders in the larger provinces. Indeed, some observers suggest that since 1995, Canada has embarked on a steady, slow, and largely invisible course of decentralization (see Gregg 2005; Griffiths 2008). Plans A and B got all the press, but Plan C had the greatest impact.

For critics of decentralization, the insistence of dealing with the "Quebec problem" through rigid adherence to symmetrical powers poses the risk that Canada will not end with a bang—the cataclysmic result of Quebec's separation—but with a whimper: with the slow dismantling of Canada into a number of incoherent fiefdoms. In the words of former Saskatchewan premier Roy Romanow, "the soil has been tilled for the sprouting of views at odds with shared destiny, and today there is a palpable momentum toward decentralization, individualism, and privatization, all peddled as a means to forge a stronger nation" (Romanow 2006, 50).

Yet one does not exclude the other. The dissolution of all does not render impossible the separation of one. What if Quebec were to separate? What would it mean for Quebec and for the rest of Canada?

THINKING THE UNTHINKABLE: SEPARATION

Countries, states, nations, and societies change. Though Canada's dissolution would astound and dismay much of the world—as Ignatieff (1993, 147) remarks, "If federalism can't work in my Canada, it probably can't work anywhere"—no country is ordained to last forever. The continued presence of nationalism as a rallying point for many francophone and other Quebecers, combined with the resilience of the Bloc Québécois on the federal scene, as witnessed in the 2019 election, suggests that separatism remains a possible option.

What would Canada and Quebec look like if they separated? In descriptive terms, Canada would cover 8.4 million square kilometres, nearly 85 percent of its previous area, though the Atlantic provinces would be separated from Ontario (Young 1995, 9; Scowen 1999) and the country would have a population of more than 27 million, roughly 50 percent of which would be located in Ontario. Quebec would cover 1.5 million square kilometres and have a population of about 8.2 million people (see table 0.1 for these figures). The economies of both Canada and Quebec would still be large. In constant 2012 dollars, Canada's **gross domestic product (GDP)** in 2018 was $1.6 trillion. Sans Quebec, Canada's GDP in 2018 was $1.3 trillion, while that of Quebec was nearly $332 billion (Statistics Canada 2019c). One cannot assume, however, that GDP would remain the same for either territory after separation. These figures assume no massive transfers of land either way, no large movements of population, and no disruptions to either economy resulting from political unrest. These are big assumptions.

Setting aside the real possibility of violence (see Gibson 1994; Monahan 1995; Martin 1999) with which authorities would have to deal, several key issues would need to be addressed immediately and would likely involve bitter negotiations. These issues would include territorial boundaries (Reid 1992, 37–66); the division of public assets and the national debt, a total of US$925 billion in 2019—for comparison, the United States debt is $19.23 trillion (World Population Review 2019); and determination of citizenship (Bourgault 1991; Scowen 1999). A further key issue would be jurisdiction over and relations with Indigenous peoples (Bourgault 1991; Parti Québécois 1994; Gibson 1994; Conway 2004; Scowen 1999). These issues would only scratch the surface, however. Deeper questions would remain for the citizens of both new countries.

Canada and Quebec would both require new constitutions. Quebec could achieve this task more easily than Canada (Parti Québécois 1994). By contrast, constitutional renewal in Canada would require far more actors and a fundamental rethinking of the country's purpose and structure. Despite arguments sometimes made by sovereigntists that Quebec could retain use of the Canadian dollar, it would in fact need to create its own currency, without which economic independence would be called into question.

Both countries would also have to refashion their international relations. Quebec's task in this case would likely be more difficult than Canada's, though successive Quebec governments have opened international offices and made important contacts.

Quebec would seek a seat at the United Nations, and partnership in all agreements previously signed by Canada (Bourgault 1991; Turp 1993; Parti Québécois 1994). Finally, both Canada and Quebec would need to consider their changed relationship with the United States.

By far, however, the most wrenching adjustment for people in both countries would be psychological. Only a minority of people within Quebec desire outright independence; most hold strong feelings of attachment for Canada. Outside of Quebec, while there is some anti-French, anti-Quebec sentiment, and in recent years a hefty dose of referendum fatigue (Scowen 1999; see also Brimelow 1986; Bercuson and Cooper 1991), most Canadians want Quebec to remain within Canada—though, it must be noted, the level of irritation with Quebec's perceived "demands" increases as one moves westward, with a sizable minority of people on the prairies telling pollsters they would vote to remove Quebec from Canada if they had the chance (Berdahl and Gibbins 2014).

A breakup would be difficult for both parties, though perhaps more so for English-speaking Canada. While Quebecers have had longer to prepare for the event and to define themselves as Québécois, English-speaking Canadians have not prepared themselves for such an eventuality. Their sense of identity includes Quebec, even if many—including western Canadians—refuse to acknowledge this. The fact is that Quebec remains at the heart of most Canadians' psychological map of their country (as noted in Chapter 2).

QUEBEC AND THE "OTHER" ANGLOPHONE STATE

Bourgault (1991, 24) notes that "in Quebec, pro-American feeling is probably stronger than in the rest of Canada." At first, this may seem curious, given the virulent antipathy between New France and the New England states in the years prior to the American Revolution (Chapter 1). After this time, however, Quebec's contacts with the United States gradually became more positive. The American Revolution's ideals appealed to Quebec's intellectual class and fuelled the rebellions of 1837 and 1838 (Conway 2004). From Louis-Joseph Papineau to Louis Riel, French-Canadian "rebels" repeatedly sought safe haven across the border. Nor were they alone. Throughout the 19th and 20th centuries, francophone emigrants, too, chose the eastern United States over the Canadian West.

Meanwhile, American capital also streamed into the province, stimulating Quebec's industrialization (Chodos and Hamovitch 1991). The fact that Prime Minister Brian Mulroney grew up in a Quebec town built by American investment and was president of an American branch plant before entering politics (Sawatsky 1991) is symbolically significant.

The rise of English nationalism in the 1960s (Chapter 7) in counterpoint to Quebec nationalism further (unwittingly) pushed many Quebecers into the American embrace. Anglo-Canadian desires for a strong central government found little support among Quebecers, who viewed the concept of One Canada and the federal state with suspicion. Closer economic links with the United States were furthered by economic development after the Quiet Revolution, especially the expansion of the hydroelectric power industry during the 1970s and by the sovereigntist argument that less dependence upon Canada enhanced the separatist project—at least, such was the basis of Quebec's support of the Free Trade Agreement in the 1988 federal election by some of English-speaking Canada's nationalists (see Resnick and Latouche 1990).

Like people everywhere, Quebecers are large consumers of American culture. Likewise, many Quebecers, including many of its elite, also spend considerable time in the United States, especially Florida (Cook 1995). For them, visits to the rest of Canada hold little attraction, though this sometimes changes once Quebecers have ventured into the other provinces.

Quebec's unconscious relationship with the United States raises interesting questions. As André Laurendeau (1985) argued, "the homogenizing influence of the United States put in question the very existence of both Canadian [French and English] cultures." Unlike English-speaking Canadians, few Quebecers seem concerned about this influence. Some have argued, however, that Quebec's distinct culture has survived against American influence precisely because of its protected place within Canadian Confederation (Dufour 1990; Resnick 1991; Valaskakis and Fournier 1995). In this vein, Brunelle (1999) and Ramonet (2001) suggest that the sovereignty question has distracted Quebecers from examining the impact of neo-liberal globalization and Americanization upon Quebec society, as well as the problems it might face after separation. (One interesting sidelight to the American-led invasion of Iraq in March 2003 was the sudden rise of anti-American sentiment among Quebecers, who, of all Canadians, most opposed the war.)

Interestingly, a similar argument can be made regarding English-speaking Canada: that it has insufficiently valued the role of the French language and culture in differentiating Canada from the United States. Could either Quebec or Canada alone withstand the assimilating influences of the American giant for long? This question and others are addressed in Part 2.

CONCLUSION

Canada and Quebec have travelled a long way since 1960, let alone since 1763. Sometimes in conflict more often than in co-operation, each has shaped the other. Canada's institutions, its decentralized system of governance, its tolerance of cultural differences (not to be overstated), and much of its identity are built upon French foundations. For its part, Quebec—the territory in which the French "fact" was suppressed and contained, and therefore incubated—also contains a hidden English element. Together, Canada's French and English "nations" have withstood absorption into the United States and built, by nearly any standard, one of the best countries and societies on earth.

Canada, it is often said, is an experiment (Bernard 1996; Conway 2004; Saul 1997). Is it possible to break the European model of nation *equals* state *equals* country *equals* society? Is it possible to conceive and create a state structure in which two nations—three, counting Indigenous peoples—exist harmoniously and prosper, housed within a single country? A society in which majority, minority, and individual differences are embraced and respected, and yet political and social coherence are maintained? This has long been Canada's challenge; it is the process of meeting this challenge that has defined Canada's unique identity in the world—a world that continues to watch, wondering whether the grand experiment will succeed.

For sociologists, the relationship between Canada and Quebec, between two distinct cultural communities, provides a wealth of historical events that sociological theories can be used to interpret. The application of conflict theory is self-evident (French-English, Catholic-Protestant, class struggles), but the integrative, functional elements of how both Quebec society and that of the rest of Canada emerged is also relevant. Consider, for example, how Quebec changed from a rural and agricultural-based economy to one that was urban and industrial—and, further, the resultant demographic, political, cultural, class, and gender impacts of this transition. At the same time, much of the conflict between Quebec and the rest of Canada has been rife with symbolism (the Maple Leaf Forever versus the fleur-de-lis; the Richard Riot). Lurking within every material-based conflict lie symbolic meanings of which the combatants are often unaware. Finally, note also the gradual erosion, as post-structuralists suggest, of such authoritative canons as the Catholic Church within Quebec, even as residual elements of religion find their hidden voice within the secular folds of nationalism.

CRITICAL THINKING QUESTIONS

1. Is secularism a kind of modern "religion"?
2. Is it possible to differentiate between individual and collective identities?
3. Why do anglophone and francophone Canadians hold such differing views about the meaning of *nation*?
4. Why do many francophone Quebecers view the United States, another anglophone country, more positively than English-speaking Canada?
5. Does globalization increase or decrease the likelihood of independence movements in Quebec and elsewhere in the world? If so, why?

RECOMMENDED READINGS

Griffiths, Rudyard. 2008. *We're Prying French and English Canada Apart.* Ottawa: The Dominion Institute.
Written by the head of Canada's Dominion Institute, this book argues that recent federal initiatives are tearing apart the country's historic relationship between French and English.

Igartua, José E. 2006. *The Other Quiet Revolution: National Identities in English Canada, 1945–71*. Vancouver: UBC Press.
This book examines the enormous transformation that occurred in English-speaking Canada during Quebec's Quiet Revolution.

Laxer, Emily. 2017. *Unveiling the Nation: The Politics of Secularism in France and Quebec*. Montreal and Kingston: McGill-Queen's University Press.
In the context of Quebec's controversial Bill 21, which limits the wearing of religious clothing and symbols and seems directed at Islam in particular, Laxer's book shows how the struggle of political parties for power and legitimacy shapes the specific articulation of the state's secular boundaries.

Léger, Jean-Marc, Jacques Nantel, and Pierre Duhamel. 2016. *Cracking the Quebec Code: The 7 Keys to Understanding Quebecers*. Montreal: Juniper Publishing.
Using survey data, interviews with provincial leaders, and measured reactions to key words, the authors note seven traits describing the contemporary Quebec character: *joie de vivre*, easygoing, non-committal, victim, villagers, creative, and proud.

Riesman, David, with Reuel Denney and Nathan Glazer. 1950. *The Lonely Crowd: A Study of the Changing American Character*. New Haven, CT: Yale University Press.
Do not let the year of publication put you off. This book remains a classic examination of individualism and the construction of personal identity in modern society.

RELATED WEBSITES

Bouchard-Taylor Commission Report
collections.banq.qc.ca/ark:/52327/bs1565996
In an effort to address perceived cultural and religious divisions, in February 2007 the Quebec government established the Consultation Commission on Accommodation Practices Related to Cultural Differences, otherwise known as the Bouchard-Taylor Commission.

CBC Digital Archives (1995 Sovereignty Referendum)
www.cbc.ca/archives/categories/politics/federal-politics/separation-anxiety-the-1995-quebec-referendum/topic---separation-anxiety-the-1995-quebec-referendum.html
A useful video clip dealing with the 1995 sovereignty referendum is *Separation Anxiety: The 1995 Quebec Referendum*.

Organisation internationale de la Francophonie

www.francophonie.org

The organization representing 88 states and governments where French is the primary or customary language.

CANADIAN SOCIETY ON VIDEO

The Trial 2.0. 2019.

Filmmaker Nadia Zouaoui chronicles the social divisions over secularism, especially within Quebec's feminist movements, arising out of the Parti Québécois government's Charter of Values, launched in 2013. Though never passed into law, the act, which proposed to ban public employees from wearing symbols of their faith, has been carried forward by the current Coalition Avenir Québec government with Bill 21. *The Trial 2.0* is available for paid streaming through Vimeo: vimeo.com/ondemand/thetrial20/339752486.

PART 2

CANADA AND THE UNITED STATES

Part 1 of this book examined conflict and co-operation between Canada's French and English cultures, and how this relationship has shaped—often unwittingly—Canada's political, economic, and cultural landscape. Part 2 examines Canada's—especially English-speaking Canada's—equally complex, often troubled, and even ambivalent relationship with the United States.

The chapters that follow trace the political, economic, and cultural moments defining this relationship. Sometimes, such as during the development of the Canadian economy in the 19th century and during the administration of President Franklin Delano Roosevelt (1882–1945) in the 1930s, the United States has been considered a positive model for Canadian society. At other times, however, such as the turbulent period of the 1960s and the recent war on terrorism, the United States has been seen as a negative model. The result has been a relationship that, if traced, would show two ships occasionally running parallel, and occasionally tacking quite differently into the future.

These chapters do not focus solely on this external relationship, however. They also examine Canada's internal development and deal with such issues as regionalism, the evolution of corporate capitalism, and the development of the Canadian welfare state. Along the way, other changes in Canadian society are detailed, such as Canada's class structure, the role of women in Canadian society, and the country's immigration policy.

Finally, Part 2 examines the recent period of neo-liberal globalization and its impact upon Canada, from issues of free trade and market liberalization to the terrorist attacks on New York and Washington in September 2001 and the subsequent wars in Afghanistan and Iraq.

CHAPTER 5

The Making of English Canada

Fishing Equipment in St. John's. Courtesy Trevor W. Harrison.

The American continents, by the free and independent condition which they have assumed and maintain, are henceforth not to be considered as subjects for future colonization by any European power. . . . [W]e should consider any attempt on their part to extend their system to any portion of this hemisphere as dangerous to our peace and safety.
    —US President James Monroe, Annual Message to Congress, 1823

It is our Manifest Destiny to overspread the continent allotted by Providence for the free development of our multiplying millions.
    —newspaper editor John O'Sullivan, *United States Magazine and Democratic Review,* 1845

*When the experiment of the "dominion" shall have failed—as fail it must—a pro-
cess of peaceful absorption will give Canada her proper place in the great North
American Republic.*
  —publisher Horace Greeley, *New York Tribune*, 1867

INTRODUCTION

The phrase "the world's longest undefended border" is an overused metaphor to describe
Canada's relationship with the United States. No Canadian prime minister, American
president, or accompanying journalist leaves home without some variation on it. While
the phrase is not entirely incorrect, it is historically misleading.

Canadians and Americans often forget that their mutual relationship began less cor-
dially, with a war. The American Revolution spawned the United States, but also led to
the creation of Canada (Lipset 1990). From that time until 1871, the threat of American
invasion was real, and Canadians had frequent cause to anticipate war (Winks 1998).
Even later, until at least 1936, the American Department of Defense regularly updated
invasion plans for Canada (Rudmin 1993).

This chapter traces the development of English-speaking Canada from 1775, when
the American Revolution began, until Confederation in 1867. The chapter concentrates
on the troubled early history of relations between Canada and the United States and how
events in the United States helped spawn the creation of Canada in 1867. Specifically, this
chapter shows that Canadian society has developed socially, economically, and politically,
both for internal reasons and as a defensive response (see Aitken 1959) to the American
threat. Finally, the chapter begins the process of examining English Canada's struggles
to define its identity.

THE BIRTH OF TWO NATIONS

The American War of Independence, popularly known as the American Revolution, began at Lexington, Massachusetts, on April 18, 1775, and ended with the Treaty of Paris
in 1783. Why did the American colonists revolt in 1775?

The American Declaration of Independence of 1776 (*Time* 2020) provides a useful
starting point for answering this question. Like all revolutionary tracts, the declaration
does not shy away from rhetoric: "The history of the present King of Great Britain is a
history of repeated injuries and usurpations, all having in direct object the establishment
of an absolute Tyranny over these States." The declaration lists a series of specific complaints: the general suspension of natural and constitutional rights, unjust trials, press
ganging, the denial of political representation, unlawful taxation, the prevention of trade,
the growth of colonial bureaucracy, general harassment of the people, and the "quartering
of large bodies of armed troops."

Many of these complaints were justified. The American colonists believed strongly that a paternalistic and authoritarian British monarch and his administration had breached constitutional rights guaranteed by the English Bill of Rights of 1689.

Taxation was a particularly vexing issue. From the late 17th century on, the English Crown and Parliament had imposed a series of taxes on the colonies. After 1763, taxation—until then, purely regulatory in nature—became a means of generating revenues (Hofstadter 1958). The colonists were unaccustomed to paying revenue-raising taxes and, in any case, viewed them as potentially ruinous. The colonists also believed that the taxes had been imposed without their consent, given either directly or indirectly, through the will of Parliament (Hofstadter et al. 1957).

The British viewed taxation differently: "The empire was expensive; costly wars had been fought to acquire and defend it; still more money would have to be laid out in the future to garrison it" (Hofstadter 1958, 3). In short, it was time for the colonists to shoulder their fair share of state expenses.

Though frequently the tax measures were withdrawn under protest or otherwise circumvented by the industrious colonists (James 1997), taxes were certainly a major sore point leading up to the revolution. Anti-tax protests were common. In several instances, such as in Boston in 1770, there was violence between British troops and civilians. These confrontations invited further repressive measures. Troops were posted, and dissenters were dealt with harshly.

Nonetheless, as James (1997, 107–109) notes, "Americans in 1774 enjoyed considerable freedom," including a free press, rights of assembly, and the right to travel. Indeed, these freedoms provided much of the basis for the revolution's success. While the issues listed in the declaration were important, they were not intractable before 1775. There was little support for independence, even less for war (Zinn 1995).

The reasons for this lack of support are easy to discern. The American Revolution was less a nationalist fight against foreign oppression than a family squabble. Nine-tenths of the colonies' 2.5 million people were of British descent (James 1997, 101), many of them "excessively proud of their Britishness" (James 1997, 100). At least a third of the American colonists were staunch Loyalists to the Crown, while another third probably were neutral throughout the conflict (Zinn 1995, 76). Many of the colonists were not sure why they were fighting (Hofstadter 1958).

Why, then, did the American colonies revolt? Ironically, part of the reason is that the conclusion of the war with France in 1763 had removed a major threat to the colonies; the British garrisons, for which the colonists were being taxed, served much less of a purpose. But this explanation only provides context, not a substantive cause for the revolution.

More to the point, the consequences of managing the peace created enormous and unexpected conflicts between the British and certain colonists, especially in New England (see Orchard 1998). The colonies that would become Canada were integrally involved in these disputes. Two sections of the Declaration of Independence approved in July 1776 make clear this connection (*Time* 2020, 455). One of the two sections reads as follows:

> For abolishing the free System of English Laws in a neighboring Province, establishing therein an Arbitrary government, and enlarging its Boundaries so as to render it at once an example and fit instrument for introducing the same absolute rule into these Colonies.

The second important section of the declaration reads,

> He [the King] has excited domestic insurrections amongst us, and has endeavored to bring on the inhabitants of our frontiers, the merciless Indian Savages, whose known rule of warfare is an undistinguished destruction of all ages, sexes and conditions.

The reference to exciting "domestic insurrections" refers to a promise made to slaves by Virginia's British governor in November 1775 that they would be freed in exchange for joining the British army—a promise that "deeply disturbed" slave owners, who feared it would "provoke widespread slave revolts" (Ostler 2020). (A slave uprising had occurred in South Carolina in 1739.) More generally, both quoted sections refer to the Quebec Act of 1774. That act, as we have seen (in Chapter 1), restored to the French-Canadians and the Catholic Church certain privileges removed in 1763 by the Royal Proclamation. The resurrection of French Catholicism in North America provoked hysterical alarm among the overwhelmingly Protestant colonists, whose memories of sectarian conflict were fresh. James (1997, 105) notes that, in early 1775, "the New England backwoods buzzed with rumours that Popery was about to be imposed." Among the colonists, papal fears alone might have seemed sufficiently provocative. But the Quebec Act also extended the boundaries of Quebec into the Ohio-Mississippi Indian Territory. While some settler-farmers objected to the limits, "the most potent source of opposition came from colonial elites, especially in Virginia and Pennsylvania, who had invested in companies with claims to lands west of the boundary set by the proclamation" (Ostler 2020), among them George Washington, Thomas Jefferson, and Benjamin Franklin (see Orchard 1998). Only settlement would ensure land title, without which investors would be left with only debt.

Why did the British extend Quebec's boundaries? In part, they did so under pressure from merchants in the Montreal-based fur trade (Innis 1962). But the British also extended the boundaries in hopes of reasserting control over lands designated in the Royal Proclamation of 1763 as specifically "reserved" for the Indians: the lands west of the Appalachian Mountains (see Chapter 11). The expansion-minded colonists and land speculators had consistently ignored the Royal Proclamation Act, resulting in renewed conflict with the Indigenous communities of the Ohio Valley. The British meant, through the Quebec Act, to curtail settlement in the volatile region. In the minds of the colonists, however, the Quebec Act merely incited further conflict with the Indigenous peoples, whom the colonists hated and wanted removed from the territory, hence the declaration's hostile statements quoted previously.

The Quebec Act was passed in the summer of 1774. Shortly after, in September 1774, a continental congress was convened to devise a slate of measures in retaliation to the Quebec Act (James 1997). Events thereafter continued apace. The revolution's first volleys were fired only days before the Quebec Act came into effect, May 1, 1775.

The war dragged on for six years. Untrained colonists fought by unconventional means and the trained British troops used more conventional measures. Long periods of idleness and boredom were punctuated by brief battles of horrific savagery on both sides.

In June 1775, the Americans launched a two-pronged attack on Canada. One American army went along Lake Champlain and captured Montreal, forcing Governor Guy Carleton (1724–1808) to flee to Quebec City. A second American army landed in Maine and proceeded to the shores of the St. Lawrence, where both armies then joined in an assault upon Quebec City. The siege failed the following May, however, when a flotilla of British troops arrived, causing the American forces to withdraw (Conway 2004; James 1997; Orchard 1998).

Thereafter, the war never seriously threatened Canadian territory. Nonetheless, the American colonists believed throughout the conflict that Canada would soon join them in open revolt. The invasion of Canada in 1775, for example, was "advertised as a war of liberation" (James 1997, 113). When the American Articles of Confederation were written in 1777, a special Canada provision (Article 11) was even included:

> Canada, according to this confederation, and joining in the measures of the United States, shall be admitted into, and entitled to all the advantages of this Union: but no other colony shall be admitted into the same unless such admission be agreed to by nine states.

The idea that Canada might join the rebellion was not entirely far-fetched. The people in Nova Scotia, linked by trade and family connections to the New England states, briefly considered joining the cause (Winks 1998). Likewise, many within Montreal's English-speaking business class supported the revolutionary cause (Morton 1997). The larger French-Canadian community—clergy, seigneurs, and merchants alike—remained neutral, however . . . an outcome the British had hoped the Quebec Act would secure.

Which side would emerge victorious was not quite certain until 1778, when France, ever desirous of revenge upon Britain for losses suffered in 1763, joined the conflict. With French assistance in the form of both troops and a naval blockade, the Americans won the last great battle of the war at Yorktown, Virginia, in October 1781 (Hofstadter et al. 1957; Zinn 1995).

The Treaty of Paris saw England recognize American independence. The treaty further set America's borders at the Mississippi River on the west, the 31st parallel (just above Florida) in the south, and the Great Lakes in the north. The treaty also acknowledged American rights to Newfoundland's fisheries. England, however, retained joint privileges with America in navigating the Mississippi. The Americans further agreed to compensate British creditors for private debts owed them and to recommend that individual states restore Loyalist property (Hofstadter et al. 1957).

In 1783, many Americans viewed Canada as a natural extension of their colonies and wanted to remove British influence entirely from the continent. The United States, however, was not strong enough, politically or militarily, to press such demands (Horsman 1993). Moreover, at least some Americans may have viewed a continuing British presence in North America, for all its drawbacks, as a kind of bulwark against possible French and Spanish expansion (James 1997). For these reasons, Canada remained standing, but it was a Canada quickly changing, a Canada that soon faced renewed threats from its youthful American neighbour.

THE WAR OF 1812

The Treaty of Paris did not end disputes between Britain and its former American colonies. A major source of conflict was ended with the signing in 1794 of Jay's Treaty, which saw Britain evacuate the forts it had maintained in the Ohio Valley in defence of Montreal's fur interests (Horsman 1993). Setting a pattern that would repeat itself again in 1814 (the Treaty of Ghent) and in 1846 (the Oregon Treaty), trade—and good relations—with the United States was far more important to Britain than trade with Canada. The interests of Montreal's fur traders, and Canada generally, were expendable.

Still, irritants remained and were heightened after 1793 by the outbreak of yet another war between Britain and France. In their zeal to defeat the French (this time in the person of Napoleon), the British began seizing American ships that traded with France, arresting escaped British seamen, and pressing American seamen into royal service (Berton 1980; Horsman 1993). Understandably, Americans viewed Britain as not only harming American trade but also breaching American neutrality and sovereignty (Bowler 1993). America's still fragile honour was at stake (Horsman 1993).

Once more, Indigenous peoples also featured prominently among American complaints. The British, it was alleged, were encouraging their Indigenous allies, led by the Shawnee Chief Tecumseh (1768–1813) (see Chapter 9), to attack American settlers (Bowler 1993; Hofstadter 1958; Berton 1980; Morton 1997; Granatstein 1996).

As such "provocations" mounted, war fever gripped the United States. During the American congressional debates of 1811 and 1812, legitimate complaints gave way once again to calls that Canada must be liberated. Finally, in June 1812, President James Madison declared the beginning of a second War of Independence (Morton 1997).

As before, many Americans believed Canada would be an easy conquest. Former president Thomas Jefferson stated confidently that "the acquisition of Canada this year . . . will be a mere matter of marching" (Colombo 1994, 29).

As in 1775, such confidence was well placed. In 1812, there were only half a million people in British North America, compared with 7.5 million in the American states (Morton 1997, 33). Moreover, two-thirds of Upper Canada's population were newly arrived Americans (Bowler 1993, 302), largely indifferent to the war. The British themselves were occupied in fighting Napoleon. In short, the 1812 conflict seemed like one that Britain's colonists could not win.

The War of 1812 was fought almost entirely in Upper Canada, though it strayed occasionally into Lower Canada, spawned a few memorable sea battles, and touched off a mini-boom in maritime smuggling (Bowler 1993). Along Upper Canada's main front, the war began in a gentlemanly fashion, continuing indifferently at times—along the invisible border, truck, trade, and personal contacts continued, largely unabated—but became more savage as time progressed (Berton 1980). In April 1813, the Americans sacked and burned York (now Toronto). In revenge, in August 1814, British forces captured and burned the US Capitol building and the presidential mansion at Washington.

In the end, a combination of three things saved Canada from American takeover: American military ineptness, French and Indigenous support at key moments, and the end of the Napoleonic Wars in Europe, which freed regular British troops to come to Canada (Berton 1980; Morton 1997; Horsman 1993).

The Treaty of Ghent in 1814 formally ended the war. The pre-existing borders were restored; the problems that began the war were forgotten or soon disappeared. In the words of historian Desmond Morton (1997, 43), "The war changed no boundaries, brought no reparations, avenged no wrongs." The Battle of Waterloo and Napoleon's subsequent banishment to St. Helena ended Britain's need to seize ships and impress seamen. The severely weakened Indigenous tribes were no longer a threat—if they ever had been—to Americans and the American government's expansionist desires.

The War of 1812 gave English Canada its first heroes: Major-General Sir Isaac Brock (1769–1812) and Chief Tecumseh, who both died in battle, as well Lieutenant Colonel Charles-Michel d'Irumberry de Salaberry (1778–1829) and Laura Secord (1775–1868) (Morton 1997; Bowler 1993; Orchard 1998). The war also strengthened British resolve to protect its North American colonies. It further solidified the alliance of the French, English, and Indigenous peoples, who had fought side by side against the Americans, though the latter received the least reward for their sacrifices (see Chapter 9). Most importantly, however, the War of 1812 took on the status of a founding myth around which English Canada forged the beginnings of its distinct identity.

THE MAKING OF ENGLISH-CANADIAN IDENTITY

We have briefly to reacquaint ourselves with the Loyalists (Chapter 1), especially those 10,000 or so who settled in Canada and caused its division in 1791. Canadians' first impressions were not favourable. Contemporaries used the words "quarrelsome" and "bitter" to describe them. It is time, however, to revisit the Loyalists and ask: Who were they? And, more importantly: What became of them?

To the first question: The Americans portrayed the Loyalists as an "elite of Anglican clergy, bureaucrats, and merchants living off government favours" (Dickinson and Young 2008, 69), an image the Loyalists themselves later encouraged. This image was incorrect, however. The Loyalists were not fundamentally different from the Americans who stayed behind. Most were subsistence farmers, disproportionately young, often poor and illiterate. While most were recent immigrants from Britain, the Loyalists also included various other religious and ethnic minorities (Dickinson and Young 2008; Brown 1993; Granatstein 1996), as well as approximately 3,000 escaped Black slaves, who settled in Nova Scotia, and almost 2,000 Iroquois, who settled north of the Great Lakes, where the city of Brantford today commemorates the name of their leader, Joseph Brant (Wynn 2012, 212–214).

The American Revolution did not merely create two nations; it also created two myths. Not *all* Americans were democrats; not *all* Loyalists were monarchists. Most people on both sides were indifferent, confused, and scared, caught up in events beyond their control (see Granatstein 1996). Yet the Loyalists quickly began to believe their own myths, which brings us to the second question: What became of them? A couple of quotations will point us toward an answer.

The first is taken second-hand from Christian Dufour (1990, 54), who cites a Canadian history text used in English-Canadian high schools in the 1930s as it concludes the episode of the American invasion of 1812: "Once again, the American invaders were repelled, as in 1776, as in 1690." But, asks Dufour, "How can the British Canada that drove back the Americans in 1812 be linked to the New France that stood up to the English in 1690?" Put another way, who were the "Americans" in 1690? They were, of course, the English. (The specific date 1690 refers to a famous incident in which Governor General Louis Frontenac defeated the invading army of Bostonian Sir William Phips.)

The second quotation is from historian P. B. Waite, recalling his days as a schoolboy in Belleville, Ontario, in the early 1930s. In the quotation, Waite (1997, 13) remembers situating his identity within Canada's history:

> We mapped the voyages of Champlain, of La Salle. . . . We rejoiced in the story of Phips' demand . . . and Frontenac's reply. . . . Thus did we English-*Canadiens* fight the Americans and their British allies. And we continued to be *Canadiens*. . . .
>
> Then suddenly, oddly, sharply we became English. It was something of a wrench. Wolfe had laid siege to Quebec in the summer of 1759 and all that summer we stayed with Montcalm fighting off the British. Then, early on the morning of 13 September 1759, we changed sides. We crossed the St. Lawrence with Wolfe and the British in the dark, silent boats, we fought with the British regulars on the Plains of Abraham; and though we mourned both Montcalm and Wolfe, by the time of Montcalm's death the next morning we were already on our way at last to being English-Canadians.

What became of the Loyalists? Upon their arrival, they were defeated and humiliated, indeed, not unlike the French they found in the new land. But they found in the French something of particular value: The French had an identity, one ready-made for appropriation, an identity, moreover, shaped by being the first anti-Americans. Thus, the Loyalists became *Canadiens* and Canadians became (by Loyalist definition and thereafter) anti-Americans.

Of course, we cannot lay the whole weight of appropriation upon the Loyalists. In most provinces, the Loyalists soon found themselves a minority (they never were a majority in Quebec). The sole exception was New Brunswick. Even there, however, after 1812 the Loyalists found themselves engulfed by other immigrants. In 1812, only one-fifth of Upper Canada's population of 100,000 was Loyalist in origin (Brown 1993, 247; see also Wynn 2012). Nonetheless, the Loyalists' myth of rejecting American takeover and their incorporation of French Canada into their identity structure began the process of forging in English Canada a distinctive identity (Brown 1993; Granatstein 1996). After 1812, the people of British North America at last had something in common: British and French, Indigenous and Black alike, they were *not* Americans.

THE MONROE DOCTRINE, MANIFEST DESTINY, AND AMERICAN EXCEPTIONALISM

The Treaty of Ghent did not end tensions between the United States and Britain's North American colonies. Conflict was blunted, it is true, by the signing in 1817 of the Rush-Bagot Convention, which prohibited large warships on the Great Lakes, and by the 1818 Convention, which clarified somewhat international boundary lines. The existing line was extended westward from the Lake of the Woods to the Rocky Mountains along the 49th parallel (Careless 1970).

American expansion continued unabated, however, fuelled by the demands of a growing population (9.6 million people in 1820) (*Time* 2020, 608) and a changing economy. But American expansion also invoked as its justification the notion of "liberating" land and people from the foreign and colonial yoke, even when the people involved did not want to be liberated and viewed the United States as an aggressor, a justification and response sadly not without its recent echoes. Thus, President James Monroe, in his message to Congress in December 1823, introduced what become known as the **Monroe Doctrine** (see this chapter's opening quotation), which declares that the Americas are to be free of foreign influence and that the United States will act to prevent such influence. American expansion also was justified by the notion of **manifest destiny**, a term coined in 1845 by John O'Sullivan, which held that the new country was divinely ordained with a special mission to cover North America (see chapter opening quotation). In turn, such beliefs paved the way for what is often termed **American exceptionalism**, the belief held by many Americans that the United States cannot be judged by the same standards as other countries (see Chapter 8).

The United States expanded steadily across the continent throughout the first half of the 19th century. The process was always similar. American trade with and exploration of new territories was shortly followed by immigration. Soon American land speculators, merchants, and settlers would complain about the actions of local government officials (usually Spanish in origin); then they would lobby Washington to intervene. Covert aid would follow. In time, the existing government would be dethroned (sometimes with the help of American troops), the populace would "ask" to be annexed, and the United States would oblige. Thus, Florida was seized from Spain in 1819; Texas, after years of internal intrigue inspired by the American government, was also seized from Spain in 1845; and New Mexico and California, following an American-provoked war, were annexed from Mexico in 1848 (Hofstadter et al. 1957; Orchard 1998). The annexation from Mexico doubled the size of the United States—not incidentally on the eve of the California gold rush.

Canada was not immune to American intrigues and claims. War nearly erupted in the 1820s after Maine's governor declared New Brunswick's timberlands part of the state and ordered US troops to seize the territory (Orchard 1998). In a prelude to the Mexican wars, in 1844 the United States also claimed, by dint of biblical injunctions, the Oregon territory. The dispute was settled in 1846, again under threat of war, on grounds favourable to the Americans. In 1859, the so-called Pig War erupted over the San Juan Islands in Puget Sound, ending in 1873 with the United States gaining sole ownership of the islands (Lower 1983). Also by the 1850s, Americans settled in the Red River Valley were actively pressing for the United States to annex that territory.

In these ventures, the biggest losers were the Indigenous peoples (see Chapter 9), who were vilified, pacified, assimilated, and often hunted down, sometimes to extinction. Before becoming American president in 1832, Andrew Jackson (1767–1845) earned a well-deserved reputation for savagery directed at Indigenous peoples, terrorizing and killing them by the thousands before taking more than two million acres in northern Alabama (Wright 1993). Another future president, Abraham Lincoln (1809–1865), while sympathetic to the situation of Black people, thought Indigenous people unredeemable and, as a young man, fought briefly in the vicious Illinois Black Hawk War of the 1830s.

By 1853, the United States had nearly achieved its present territorial size. Alaska was added in 1867 and Hawaii in 1898. Canada—a territory once referred to by the French author Voltaire as "a few acres of snow" (quoted in Colombo 1994, 18)—was the only territory in North America unincorporated into the United States.

THE POLITICAL ECONOMY OF BRITISH NORTH AMERICA, 1800–1866

To the unreflecting eye, the British colonies in 1800 must still have seemed not much more than a frozen wasteland. The combined population of the five British North American provinces in 1805 was about 360,000. Of this total, about 230,000 resided in Lower Canada, 46,000 in Upper Canada, 54,000 in Nova Scotia, 25,000 in New Brunswick, and

5,000 or so in Prince Edward Island (Careless 1970, 122; Norrie and Owram 1996, 84, 119; Dickinson and Young 2008). Newfoundland's total population in 1805 was just short of 20,000, but this number included a large number of semi-permanent residents engaged in the seasonal fisheries (see Norrie and Owram 1996, 75).

The end of the Napoleonic Wars, however, saw Britain hit by a depression and rising unemployment. Thus, after 1815 the colonies—except Newfoundland, which itself entered a period of stagnation until the 1850s (see Norrie and Owram 1996)—experienced a massive wave of immigration that lasted four decades. Between 1815 and 1850, nearly 800,000 immigrants, mainly British, arrived in Canada: "discharged soldiers and half-pay officers from Wellington's armies, Irish weavers and paupers, Scottish artisans and dispossessed crofters, English country labourers and factory workers" (Careless 1970, 147).

Few British immigrants remained permanently in Lower Canada. Those who did settled mainly in the Eastern Townships and the growing cities of Montreal and Quebec. Elsewhere, however, British immigration left a permanent mark. Scottish immigration especially filled Nova Scotia, competing with the settled Loyalists and pre-Loyalist New Englanders, and Prince Edward Island, while the Irish, especially after the 1840s, filled New Brunswick (Careless 1970).

Immigration effects were felt most, however, in Upper Canada. There, British immigration rose steadily after 1820, dropped in the mid-1830s due to cholera and the province's political troubles, then rose again sharply during the 1840s. Though all elements of British society—"English, Welsh, Lowland and Highland Scots and Catholic and Ulster Irish" (Careless 1970, 149)—arrived, it was perhaps the Irish who left the greatest impression. Driven from their homeland by poverty, overcrowding, and, finally, the potato famine, the Irish soon found employment building canals and, later, the railways (Morton 1997; see also Pentland 1991; Norrie and Owram 1996).

American immigration to the British colonies generally declined during this period due to westward American expansion. A sole exception to this pattern was the relatively large influx into the Maritimes and Upper Canada of American Black people escaping slavery during the 20 years leading up to that country's Civil War. By 1861, there were about 60,000 Black people in British North America (Winks 1998, 8; Kelly 1997).

As a consequence of immigration and births, British North America's population by 1851 had grown to more than 2.4 million; by 1861, 3.2 million. Upper Canada then had the largest population—nearly 1.4 million—followed by Lower Canada (1.1 million), Nova Scotia (331,000), New Brunswick (252,000), and Prince Edward Island (81,000) (see table 0.1).

Immigration to the colonies, however, began declining in the early 1850s and by the 1860s was actually outpaced by people leaving Canada. Indeed, from 1851 to 1901, while 1.9 million people entered Canada, 2.2 million left, primarily for the United States (McKie 1994, 26).

The British colonies' problem in attracting and retaining people was simple: Their economies were unable to compete with the expanding and rapidly industrializing neighbour to the south. Though economic development occurred, the British colonies generally lacked investment capital; their transportation systems were substandard and internally not integrated; and their separate economies exhibited many of the instabilities characteristic of staple-based, export-driven economies.

Newfoundland, for example, remained an imperial outpost, not even a colony, until 1824. And, though the granting of responsible government in 1855 coincided with a period of growth lasting until the mid-1880s, its economy remained dangerously one-dimensional. In 1858, 89 percent of Newfoundland's labour force worked in the fishery, a statistic that remained relatively constant over the next decade, indicating a single-industry dependence that would sink the Newfoundland economy two decades later (Norrie and Owram 1996, 78–79, 350–351).

The situation elsewhere in the colonies was less bleak but still no cause for optimism. The American Revolution had spurred a short-lived economic boom. Nova Scotia's timber industry developed around producing pine masts for the British navy; shipbuilding, formerly concentrated around local markets, also grew to service trade with the West Indies; and internal markets, especially for agricultural products, arose around the province's increased population, inspired in part by Loyalist immigration. Subsequently, the Napoleonic Wars produced a second Maritime boom, as Britain increased its colonial imports. The fisheries remained important, but now forestry also developed in New Brunswick and spurred forward economic linkages: sawmills and (especially) shipbuilding. By 1860, the Maritimes were one of the world's premier shipbuilding centres. Other important industries that developed included Nova Scotia's trade in coal and agricultural produce (Norrie and Owram 1996).

The years especially after 1815 were not kind to Lower Canada. The fur industry entered a period of decline following the signing of Jay's Treaty in 1794 and left the St. Lawrence Valley altogether following the merger, in 1821, of the North West Company with the Hudson's Bay Company. Wheat became a major export item to Britain and the West Indies during the late 18th century, but early in the next century, it too entered a period of permanent decline occasioned by recurrent crop failures (see Trofimenkoff 1993) and increasing competition from Upper Canada.

These losses were partially offset by other sources of economic growth, notably timber (Norrie and Owram 1996) and power generation. The two major urban centres of Quebec City and Montreal likewise increased in size and importance, the former economy based on shipping, the military, and services; the latter on industry and finance. But much of the province remained rural—indeed, became even more disproportionately so during the century (see Chapter 2)—and underdeveloped, while the benefits of industrialization went almost entirely to the anglophone bourgeoisie.

By contrast, Upper Canada's situation grew decidedly more hopeful as the 19th century progressed. The province was at first economically dependent on British administrative expenditures in the form of direct handouts: subsidies and claims to Loyalists, and military and civil construction. In the words of Norrie and Owram (1996, 123), "the

British government subsidized the initial stages of settlement in Upper Canada." The arrival of the "late Loyalists" (Americans newly arrived in the early 1800s) and of British immigrants after 1820 provided both labourers and consumers. Local domestic markets developed and the timber industry grew. But wheat was Ontario's real story.

Small amounts of wheat were already being shipped down the St. Lawrence as early as 1794 (Norrie and Owram 1996). During the War of 1812, however, wheat became a major export to Britain. Though wheat sales declined after the war, a new market was soon found in Lower Canada, then later again in Britain and the United States. Wheat exports from Upper Canada rose by 500 percent during the 1840s and then doubled again, peaking in 1861 (McCallum 1991, 11).

The importance of wheat to Upper Canada's economy cannot be overestimated. In 1820, more than 95 percent of the province's population was still rural (Norrie and Owram 1996, 126). Locally produced wheat thus fed Upper Canada's population without resort to imports. Capital acquired through exports of surplus wheat, especially after 1840, later fuelled industrial development (McCallum 1991).

Instances of economic development and diversification aside, in the mid-1850s the British colonies were marked by uneven development and export dependency. Nova Scotia's export trade was spread among the other British North American colonies, the United States, and the West Indies. New Brunswick's export trade was heavily tied to Britain. Prince Edward Island's export trade was moderately tied to the other colonies. The Province of Canada's economy was based on agricultural and forestry exports, primarily to the United States. All of the colonies imported a larger percentage of their manufactured goods (Norrie and Owram 1996).

The colonies' resultant economic instability fuelled ongoing political demands, particularly from the Province of Canada's business class, for either annexation by the United States or (at the very least) a reciprocity agreement with the United States that would ensure stable markets. In 1854, they got their wish.

Understanding how the Reciprocity Treaty of 1854 came about requires a brief discussion of changes in economic thinking that had occurred since the 18th century. As the reader will remember (Chapter 1), Canada was founded primarily as a mercantilist adventure. Two centuries later, however, mercantilism was under increasing attack. Adam Smith (1723–1790) launched the first attack in his classic text *The Wealth of Nations*, which, fittingly, came out in 1776, the same year as the American Declaration of Independence. The latter stated a liberal interpretation of political freedom. Smith's text similarly argued for a liberal interpretation of economic freedom.

Smith directed three specific arguments against mercantilism. First, he argued that free trade among countries was mutually beneficial. Second, he argued that trade enhanced specialization in production, leading to increased efficiency. And third, Smith denounced mercantilism on the basis of the "collusive relationship" it encouraged between governments and the merchant classes (La Haye 1993, 535).

Smith's arguments found fertile ground in Britain during the American Revolution. Many British already viewed the colonies as expensive to maintain, administratively and militarily. Now they were a political headache as well.

The outbreak of the Napoleonic Wars in 1793 brought mercantilism a temporary reprieve as Britain became dependent upon its colonies for food and materials—for example, Maritime fish and timber. After 1814, however, Smith's ideas—now augmented by those of a young economist, David Ricardo (1772–1823)—gained momentum. Slowly at first, then with greater alacrity, mercantilism's regulatory walls collapsed. In 1833, Britain abolished colonial slavery, thus creating "free labour." "Free trade" followed in the 1840s with the repeal of timber duties, the Navigation Acts, and the Corn Laws (Norrie and Owram 1996). Britain's policy of preferential trade with the North American colonies ceased after 1846.

Free trade made perfect sense from the British point of view. Britain, after all, was the first industrialized capitalist country. Moreover, it was still a great empire possessing the world's most powerful fleet.

Elsewhere, including in the United States, Smith's and Ricardo's ideas had far less appeal (Laxer 1989; Watkins 1991) (see Chapter 6). The ending of free trade–protected markets was viewed with especial fear in Britain's North American colonies. How did this affect the security of the colonies' exports? The panic climaxed in April 1849.

The Canadian government had been moved the previous year from Kingston to Montreal, the site of Canada's business establishment. In 1849, the Reform government of Baldwin-Lafontaine passed a bill compensating Patriotes and innocent victims of the rebellions of 1837 and 1838 (see Chapter 1) for losses suffered during the conflict. Montreal's English business class, already feeling abandoned by the British government's adoption of free trade and fearing a recession, stormed and burned the new Parliament buildings and threatened the Governor General, Lord Elgin (1811–1863) (Careless 1970; Morton 1997). A manifesto circulated in favour of annexation to the United States. In Chatham, New Brunswick, meanwhile, inhabitants "marched through the streets on July 4, 1849, firing pistols in the air and singing 'Yankee Doodle'" (Wynn 2012, 199–200).

Annexation was not very popular anywhere. Within weeks, talk of joining the United States had subsided. Nonetheless, many in the colonies remained concerned about securing access to the large American market. The Reciprocity Treaty of 1854 was the result. The treaty came into effect in 1855 and lasted until 1866, when the United States terminated it. Specifically, the treaty eliminated the tariff on natural products, including fish.

The signing of the Reciprocity Treaty blunted Montreal merchants' demands for annexation (Winks 1998). The following decade witnessed rapid economic growth throughout the British colonies (Aitken 1959). This period featured the increased economic integration of the St. Lawrence lowlands, the extension of the agricultural area of southern Ontario, the beginning of manufacturing in Ontario and Quebec, and the development of a railway from the Detroit River to the Atlantic seaboard.

How responsible was the Reciprocity Treaty for this period of prosperity? The question is not easily answered. On balance, however, reciprocity seems to have increased the overall volume of trade between the two countries and specifically to have benefited British North American trade in wheat, oats, and flour (Norrie and Owram 1996; see also Careless 1970; Laxer 1989).

By the 1860s, some business and political leaders in the United States had turned against the agreement, believing—with some justification—that Canada had gotten the better deal. Ultimately, however, the Reciprocity Treaty collapsed for reasons other than economic.

CANADA AND THE AMERICAN CIVIL WAR

As the debate over the Meech Lake Accord and "distinct society" heated up in 1989, Reform Party leader Preston Manning repeatedly borrowed American President Abraham Lincoln's phrase warning of the perils of a "house divided" (see Harrison 1995, 173). In the overheated aftermath of the 1995 Quebec referendum, parallels between Canada's situation and events leading up to the American Civil War in 1861 were again advanced (McPherson 1998). The discerning of Canadian parallels, or parables, in the American Civil War was not new. The war was very much on the minds of Canadian politicians in 1864 as they began deliberations on Confederation.

The American Civil War (1861–1865) previewed wars soon to come, introducing trench warfare, advanced weaponry (e.g., the Gatling gun), and calculated terrorism against civilians. Recent estimates suggest the number of Union and Confederate deaths during the American Civil War was 750,000, a total larger than the number of American deaths in any other war (*Time* 2020, 128fn3). As in later wars, a new technological invention—the camera—"brought home" the Civil War to those far removed, including the people of British North America.

British North America was affected by events in the United States even before the war began. In the months leading up to the conflict, some American officials suggested that a war with Britain over Canada might prove a useful diversion and unite the squabbling states. Other Union officials argued that, in the event of losing the South, the conquest of Canada would make for an adequate replacement (Morton 1997; Winks 1998; see also Marquis 2000).

The conflict divided the British colonists. Though slavery had a long history in New France, going back to the early 17th century—nearly 4,200 slaves, mainly Amerindian and Black over two centuries (Trudel 2013, 256)—slavery had been formally abolished in 1833, and most colonists probably supported the North's abolitionist aims on moral grounds (Winks 1998). But while ending slavery was the stated purpose, especially after 1863, the war's first purpose was to save the Union (Hofstadter 1958). The South's argument—that individual states had voluntarily entered into a Confederacy in 1776 and therefore retained the right of self-determination, including the right of exit—struck a responsive chord among some in the colonies, especially those still smarting from the rebellions of 1837–1838.

Inevitably, the British colonies also found themselves caught up in the war's actual dynamics. To the North's displeasure, the British—relying on southern cotton for their clothing industries—continued to trade with the South, while the South used the British colonies as a staging ground for raids against the Union, both by land and sea (Winks 1998; Marquis 2000). In retaliation, and much to British annoyance, northern forces also breached the Canadian border in pursuit of the rebels. Throughout the American Civil War, many in Canada feared, and some in the Confederacy actively hoped, that Britain would be dragged into war with the Union (Winks 1998).

Nor did fears lessen with the conflict's end. British and colonial officials noted the United States had a battle-tested army of 2.3 million men, nearly equal to the entire population of the province of Canada (Martin 1993b, 560), which now could be turned north. Facing the American army was a regular military force of little more than 19,000 (Winks 1998, 282) and perhaps another 10,000 militia. Elaborate plans concerning Canada's defence were made and discussed throughout 1864 and 1865 (see Winks 1998). These plans became more urgent when Irish raiders, known as the Fenians, invaded Canada (with tacit American support) in 1866 (McCue 1999).

Most British officials, including Prime Minister William Gladstone (1809–1898), accepted the obvious: Canada ultimately was not defensible against American attack. So, to avoid provocation, in 1871 Britain removed all its troops from Canadian soil. But the American Civil War, and the threats of invasion that followed, provided the psychological context (Martin 1993b) for getting on with a task long debated: Confederation (see also Winks 1998; Moore 1997).

CONFEDERATION

Confederation in 1867 was intended to address three problems. First, Confederation was meant to provide an "effective defence" against the threat of American invasion. (The fact that such a defence was no more possible after Confederation than before is incidental.) Second, Confederation was meant to create an economic union. Economic union was made necessary by the American government's suspension of the Reciprocity Treaty in 1866 in response to British support for the South during the Civil War. Third, Confederation was meant to deal with French-English political instability in the Province of Canada, where 12 governments had fallen in 15 years (Moore 1997; Romney 1999).

Confederation began as a discussion of Maritime union at Charlottetown, Prince Edward Island, in June 1864. Almost immediately, however, these discussions expanded to include plans for a broader union of all British North America. A follow-up meeting at Quebec City in October that same year drafted the union's essential features. The Quebec

Resolutions were then taken back to the individual colonial legislatures for debate and ratification (Careless 1970; Norrie and Owram 1996; Moore 1997; Silver 1997; Romney 1999).

Confederation's blueprints, and the British North America (BNA) Act of 1867,
which legally constituted the federation, drew heavily from "British precedent and practice" (Norrie and Owram 1996, 210), including an elected federal Parliament and a system of jurisprudence based on the British model. Also, the British monarch remained the
formal head of state, and the highest court for judicial appeals remained in London. But
Confederation also drew upon practices already employed in the Province of Canada and
the American model.

From the Province of Canada was adopted the idea of tariffs, an important element
of the National Policy soon devised (see Chapter 6). Likewise, many of the Dominion's
banking regulations copied legislation developed in the Province of Canada (Norrie and
Owram 1996).

From the American model came the idea of the Senate. Like the American Senate,
which represents individual states (Hofstadter 1958), the Canadian Senate was meant to
represent the provinces (Moore 1997). Unlike American senators, however, Canadian
senators were not to be elected. Why not? The reason, in part, was that the Canadian
Senate was also modelled on the British House of Lords and, in part, that an appointed
Senate left obvious opportunities for patronage, a current criticism. But the Fathers of
Confederation additionally feared that elected senators would possess legitimacy equal to
the elected members of Parliament—the "House of the People"—while threatening the
principle of "one person, one vote" (see Moore 1997, 108; Romney 1999).

The Fathers of Confederation also discerned in the American experience, specifically the recent Civil War, an object lesson (Winks 1998) on the perils of decentralized
government. Here, however, the perceived lesson could only be partially applied (Moore
1997; Silver 1997; Romney 1999). Certainly, Sir John A. Macdonald desired to construct
a strong central government, but this was not possible. Neither the Maritime provinces
nor (especially) Quebec would accept a strongly centralized federation.

The result was a Confederation in which jurisdictional powers were divided between
the federal government and the provinces. The federal government was given powers over
national defence, postal services, the census and statistics, currency and banking, navigation and shipping, fisheries, criminal law, the regulation of trade and commerce, weights
and measures, bankruptcy and insolvency, and taxation. Provincial governments were
given powers over two areas of minimal importance at the time, but hugely important
later on, health and education, as well as generally local matters, such as property and
civil rights, civil law, municipal governments, licences, and the chartering of companies,
as well as direct taxation for government costs. All residual powers lay with the federal
government. Finally, the federal government was further charged with the responsibility of ensuring equitable fiscal assistance to all the provinces to meet their constitutional
functions (Careless 1970; Norrie and Owram 1996).

There was no great outcry of public support in 1867 for Confederation; in some quarters there was significant opposition. Newfoundland and Prince Edward Island rejected Confederation (Careless 1970; Norrie and Owram 1996), while New Brunswick and Nova Scotia were only slowly brought on side (Careless 1970; Moore 1997). In Canada East, opposition remained high despite the implicit and explicit promises of the Conservatives and their leader, George Cartier, that Confederation offered the French a sovereign homeland within a federated state (see Silver 1997; Romney 1999). Only Canada West—festering under the Act of Union, demanding separation from entanglements with Canada East and a system of "Rep by Pop," its gaze fixed on westward expansion—greeted Confederation with something like passion.

Thus, on July 1, 1867, the Dominion of Canada was proclaimed, made up of four provinces: New Brunswick, Nova Scotia, Quebec (formerly Canada East), and Ontario (formerly Canada West). The new country covered 370,045 square miles (958,416.5 square kilometres), a tenth of British North America, and housed roughly four million people— mainly French and English, Catholic and assorted flavours of Protestant. Small clusters of minority populations were growing, however, presaging Canada's multi-ethnic mix of the next century.

Montreal, the site of trade and finance, was the country's largest city, with more than 100,000 people, followed by Quebec City (59,699), Toronto (56,092), Halifax (29,582), and Saint John (28,805) (Morton 1997, 12–19), but the majority of people still lived and worked on rural farms and in small villages.

A significant manufacturing base was developing (Laxer 1989), but most manufactured goods were still imported, and staple exports (fish, wheat, and trees) still ruled Canada's economy (Norrie and Owram 1996). Indeed, the new Dominion remained largely pre-industrial, even pre-capitalist. Probably few people realized immediately that they had become subjects of a new country. Even fewer Indigenous peoples of the West and the North knew that they too would soon be absorbed into something called Canada (see chapters 9 and 10).

CONCLUSION

English Canada was born as a fragment cast off by the American Revolution. The United States became English Canada's "Other," a place of attraction, mystery, awe, and fear. Where few differences marked the Loyalists from other Americans in 1775, war, politics, and economics erected borders that, in time, took on a cultural and psychological reality. Separate histories make separate peoples: Attempts to unite East and West Germans after the Cold War provide a contemporary example.

Confederation made concrete the idea of Canada. Shortly thereafter, American efforts at conquering Canada militarily ceased almost entirely. As Governor General Vincent Massey (1887–1967) later noted, "the disparity of population has made armaments for one country futile and for the other superfluous." Yet Canada's future remained uncertain beside the American behemoth that, on the shores of the 20th century, was flexing its muscles. Much remained to be done if the new country was to thrive.

CRITICAL THINKING QUESTIONS

1. How might North America look different today had the American colonies not revolted in 1775?
2. Why did the notion of manifest destiny arise in the United States, and what is its continued impact today?
3. Why did Canada expand more slowly than the United States?
4. Why did beliefs in free trade arise in England?
5. In light of how the Canadian Senate was originally conceived, how would you deal with more recent controversies about its role?

RECOMMENDED READINGS

Berton, Pierre. 1980. *The Invasion of Canada, 1812–1813*. Toronto: McClelland & Stewart.
Written by one of Canada's great popularizers of history, this book details the events of the somewhat ambiguous War of 1812.

Granatstein, Jack. 1996. *Yankee Go Home? Canadians and Anti-Americanism*. Toronto: HarperCollins.
This book examines the history of anti-Americanism in Canada.

Norrie, Ken, and Douglas Owram. 1996. *The History of the Canadian Economy*. 2nd ed. Toronto: Harcourt Brace and Company, Canada.
This book details the economic history of Canadian development, from resource extraction to industrialization.

Winks, Robin. 1998. *The Civil War Years: Canada and the United States*. 4th ed. Montreal and Kingston: McGill-Queen's University Press.
Winks examines the complex relationship between Canada and the United States during the latter's civil war, 1861–1865.

Zinn, Howard. 1996. *A People's History of the United States: 1492–Present*. New York: Harper Perennial.
One of the United States' best-known radical historians, Zinn provides an historical account of that country's development significantly at odds with conventional narratives.

RELATED WEBSITES

Historica Canada: Black History Canada
www.blackhistorycanada.ca
> A web archive of information on Canada's Black community.

Library and Archives Canada: Confederation
www.collectionscanada.gc.ca/confederation/index-e.html
> Library and Archives Canada holds Canada's national collection of books, historical documents, government records, photos, films, maps, music, and so on. The archives contain valuable documents on Confederation.

Library and Archives Canada: Reciprocity Treaty, 1854
www.collectionscanada.gc.ca/confederation/023001-7101-e.html
> The archives also contain the full text of the Reciprocity Agreement of 1854.

CANADIAN SOCIETY ON VIDEO

Canada: A People's History, "Episode 5: A Question of Loyalties." 2000. Canadian Broadcasting Corporation, 120 minutes.
> Covers the period from 1775 to 1815 and deals with the arrival of the United Empire Loyalists during the American Revolution and the American invasion of Canada in 1812.

Canada: A People's History, "Episode 8: The Great Enterprise." 2000. Canadian Broadcasting Corporation, 120 minutes.
> Covers the period from 1850 to 1867 and the events leading to Confederation.

CHAPTER 6

English Canada in Transition

Horses. Courtesy Bill Jorgensen.

We often say that we fear no invasion from the south, but the armies of the south have already crossed the border. American enterprise, American capital, is taking rapid possession of our mines and our water-power, our oil areas and our timber limits.

    —Sara Jeannette Duncan, *The Imperialist*, 1904

I am for [reciprocity] because I hope to see the day when the American flag will float over every square foot of the British North American possessions clear to the North Pole.

    —Champ Clark, speaker of the US House of Representatives, 1911

The Dominion of Canada is part of the sisterhood of the British Empire. I give you assurance that the people of the United States will not stand idly by if domination of Canadian soil is threatened by any other Empire.

    —US President Franklin Delano Roosevelt, Queen's University, Kingston, 1938

INTRODUCTION

Despite Confederation, immediately after 1867 Canada faced two great challenges: constructing a viable national economy and securing the western region from American advances. Between 1867 and 1905, two internal wars were fought, the economy was transformed, immigrants entered the country in droves, and five new provinces joined the Dominion: Manitoba (1870), British Columbia (1871), Prince Edward Island (1873), and Saskatchewan and Alberta (both 1905). Over the following 40 years, Canada fought in two world wars and suffered through a major economic depression. Canada also changed structurally. Corporate capitalism took hold, mass consumerism flourished, and class conflict intensified. Canada became more urbanized. Women entered the workforce as never before. Slowly, a fledgling sense of Canadian nationalism began emerging from the broad shadows cast by Britain and the United States. This chapter examines these and other events, ending with the Second World War.

THE "AMERICAN SYSTEM" AND THE NATIONAL POLICY

Confederation in 1867 was meant in part to deal with Canada's recurrent economic problems and the threat of American expansion (Chapter 5), but the new nation still faced the question of what specific policy to adopt to meet these goals.

Looking around the world today, models of economic and social development are dominated by "globalization," based on economic liberalism and free trade. In the 19th century, however, several models competed. The British system, with ideas similar to current neo-liberalism—a belief in free markets and limited state involvement in the economy (see Chapter 8)—provided one model, but outside of England it was widely rejected. A European system of economic development existed, based on activist government policies, investment banks, and technical education (Watkins 1991), but it was largely unknown and culturally distant from the Canadian experience. A third model, however, known as the American system, existed next door and was therefore more familiar to Canadian business and political leaders.

The American system employed three elements: (1) high tariffs to protect domestic manufacturers, therefore making it cheaper to buy domestically than to import products, a policy often referred to as **import substitution**; (2) expanded transportation systems (especially railways), built through federal contracts and guaranteed loans to private operators, and designed to bring products to market; and (3) immigration to supply domestic markets (Hofstadter 1958; see also Laxer 1989; Watkins 1991). In 1878, the Conservative government of Sir John A. Macdonald ran on a platform of economic development based on the American system, naming it the National Policy.

The National Policy's specific elements were not new to Canada. Tariffs, for example, were already an established tradition in Upper and Lower Canada by the time of Confederation. Thus, in 1879, tariffs were raised from 17.5 percent to 29 percent on a host of manufactured and agricultural goods, and in 1887 they were raised again, especially on iron, steel, farm machinery, and textiles (Norrie and Owram 1996, 249). Likewise, railway construction was by then another Canadian tradition going back to the boom years of 1850 to 1859 (Norrie and Owram 1996, 191). What was fundamentally different about the National Policy, compared with previous economic policies, was its broader aim of nation building, specifically incorporating the western territories into Canada.

Canadian politicians, and the people of Ontario specifically, had long viewed the lands west to the Pacific as theirs to occupy. By the 1860s, however, competing notions of manifest destiny were evident along the 49th parallel. In British Columbia, 30,000 people were attracted to the Fraser Valley and Cariboo regions by the discovery of gold in 1857 (Norrie and Owram 1996, 213; see also Easterbrook and Aitken 1988). Many of these immigrants were Americans, veterans of the recent California boom, who began pressing for annexation to the United States (see Morton 1997).

Similar pressures were exerted at Red River (later Winnipeg). Between 1850 and 1860, the population of Minnesota, just south of Manitoba, increased by 2,730 percent (Winks 1998, 4). As arable land filled up, Americans pushed further northward into the Red River area, where in 1869 they too pressed for statehood. Caught between the Canadian and American visions for the West were the First Nations and Métis peoples (see Chapter 9). In both cases, John A. Macdonald's vision won out, aided by the use of force in Manitoba and the Territories and the promise of a railway in British Columbia.

Between the two newest provinces lay the vast Northwest Territories. The Territories had long been the Hudson's Bay Company's preserve. Especially after its merger with the rival North West Company in 1821, the entire region, including British Columbia, had fallen under the company's control. By the 1860s, however, the fur trade was dying and the West was coveted by Canadian politicians, for whom the National Policy was already a gleam in the eye, not to mention Americans, who had their own plans for the Territories.

In 1870, the Hudson's Bay Company formally transferred the Territories to Canada, and settlement of the western region slowly began. Immigrants first settled in the "postage stamp" province of Manitoba, so-called because of its shape. When the best land was taken, later settlers pushed further westward into the Territories. In 1883, however, land prices soared, the Canadian Pacific Railway faced bankruptcy, and immigration stopped (see Morton 1997). The word *secession* was voiced in British Columbia (Conway 2014).

The hard times were especially hard on First Nations and Métis peoples of the West. The buffalo were disappearing, the fur trade no longer provided a secure living, and unscrupulous traders were wreaking havoc on the people. In 1885, rebellion in the Territories provided the Canadian government with justification to send in troops (see Chapter 9). The long-promised rail link to British Columbia was completed in time to facilitate their arrival.

Thus, by 1885, Canada had expanded to fill the top shelf of North America from sea to sea. The National Policy's alleged economic benefits, however, had yet to be realized: Public debt was rising, markets were failing, and immigration was stalled. Why was the National Policy slow in delivering expected results?

Several factors limited Canada's economic takeoff. First, beginning roughly in 1873 and lasting for six years, the increasingly integrated world economy entered a prolonged slump that reduced demand for Canadian commodities and hindered the necessary flow of investment capital into Canada (Hobsbawm 1995; Lairson and Skidmore 1997; Saul 1969). Second, the National Policy depended upon the development of western agricultural land, specifically for wheat exports. But development of the Canadian West could not proceed until the more productive lands of the American West were "used up" (Morton 1997) and new strains of wheat were developed to meet the Canadian Prairies' harsh climate and short growing season (Norrie and Owram 1996; see also Laxer 1989). Third, public debt acquired throughout the early 19th century meant that after 1867 the Canadian government employed private interests to build railways by granting them monopoly rights and free land (Laxer 1989). The companies, however, restricted railway construction to areas of profitability and limited land development to keep prices high, with the result that the massive immigration necessary to make the National Policy viable never occurred.

By 1890, the mood in Canada was sour. Many felt the National Policy had failed. Demands were renewed for a reciprocity treaty with the United States; some called for outright annexation.

The federal election of 1891 was held in this context of uncertainty. The Liberal Party under Sir Wilfrid Laurier ran on a platform of unrestricted reciprocity with the United States (Morton 1997; Norrie and Owram 1996). By contrast, the Conservatives under Macdonald appealed to anti-American and pro-British sentiments (Granatstein 1996), arguing that free trade would inevitably lead to Canada's political annexation; they won.

Canada's first free trade election occurred just as the world economy was rebounding. After 1896, investment capital was freed up and circulated throughout the world at an unprecedented rate (Dunning 1983). Internationally, consumer demand increased, while production also expanded in the wake of the second industrial revolution (Norrie and Owram 1996).

At last, the National Policy had its desired result. Fuelled by the Yukon gold rush (see Chapter 10), increased mining in the Canadian Shield, the development of the newsprint industry, and large-scale hydroelectric developments on the Great Lakes and the St. Lawrence, between 1900 and 1913 Canada (especially southern Ontario) experienced its second economic boom (Aitken 1959). While Canada's real gross national product (GNP) grew at a compound rate of only 2.38 percent during the period from 1870 to 1896, between 1896 and 1913 it grew at a rate of 6.48 percent (Norrie and Owram 1996, 218).

Integral to this growth was a change in Canada's labour market. Though still dependent upon primary-sector employment (e.g., resource extraction industries such as agriculture, mining, and forestry), employment in the secondary sector (manufacturing, construction, and the like) also grew under the National Policy, as did employment in the tertiary or service sector, where the commodities exchanged have no tangible form (e.g., teaching, retail trade, hotels, and finance). By 1891, 49 percent of Canada's labour force worked in primary industry, 20 percent in secondary industry, and 31 percent in the service sector.

But the benefits of economic growth were unevenly shared: Indigenous peoples were particularly left out (see Part 3), but others outside the industrialized region of southern Ontario soon also felt the sting of colonization.

REGIONS AND REGIONALISM

Sociological concepts such as class and gender condition the way we see social relations. Within Canada, the concept of region is particularly persuasive as the lens through which Canadian society is often viewed. Such an emphasis is not misplaced, even if the definition of *region*—like so many concepts and the host of terms that stem from it—is unclear (see box 6.1).

Regional (and subregional) divisions already existed at Canada's inception. Quebec and Ontario are obvious examples, with different cultures, histories, and economies, but there were also differences among Canada's three Maritime provinces of Prince Edward

---

Box 6.1: What Is a Region?

A **region** is a territory defined physiologically, geographically, climatically, culturally, politically, or economically. This definition is not as straightforward as it seems, however. Even using the same definition, two people may recognize different regional boundaries. Thus, regions do not exist as physical things. Rather, they are "read into" the landscape, socially constructed (as symbolic interaction theory argues), and then reified (see the Introduction).

The concept of **regional differences** refers to observable variations between two or more regions. For example, the West Coast is wet, while the Prairie provinces are dry. Likewise, Ontario is home to much of Canada's manufacturing, while Alberta is a major producer of oil.

Regionalism refers to an individual's personal identification with a region. In this sense, regionalism provides a sense of who we are, much as nationalism does.

Regional alienation refers to a sense of grievance based on the belief that regional differences are not "natural" but result from the actions of individuals or groups residing outside the region.

Sources: Brodie, Janine. 1990. *The Political Economy of Canadian Regionalism.* Toronto: Harcourt Brace Jovanovich; Westfall, William. 1993. "On the Concept of Region in Canadian History and Literature." In *A Passion for Identity: An Introduction to Canadian Studies,* edited by D. Taras, B. Rasporich, and E. Mandel. Scarborough, ON: Nelson Canada; and Wonders, William. 1993. "Canadian Regions and Regionalism: National Enrichment or National Disintegration?" In *A Passion for Identity: An Introduction to Canadian Studies,* edited by D. Taras, B. Rasporich, and E. Mandel. Scarborough, ON: Nelson Canada.

Island, Nova Scotia, and New Brunswick, and between the people of this region and the two larger provinces, over issues of political control and economic development.

Nova Scotia provides a useful example. Important early on for its geopolitical and military position on the Atlantic coast, by 1867 Nova Scotia was a major economic player with a diversified economy that sported the building of ships and the manufacture of steel, glass, and rope. At the same time, however, the businesses were small, often family affairs. Moreover, they were not well integrated into the British North American economy, instead remaining dependent upon exports to Britain. Consequently, much of the province's business and political elite opposed joining Canada, fearing that Confederation would negatively impact the region's (and their) prosperity, a fear that proved correct in the years after 1885, as the direction of economic flows changed to benefit Ontario's larger manufacturing sector. In effect, Nova Scotia and much of the Maritime region exchanged its status as a colony of Britain for that of being a colony of central Canada.

Canada's fourth Atlantic province, Newfoundland, provides another example. Sparsely populated and less economically diversified than Nova Scotia, economic development in Newfoundland nonetheless increased into the late 19th century, built upon the inshore fisheries and the port city of St. John's. As in Nova Scotia, however, the island experienced a major downturn after 1880 as the importance of the island on shipping routes declined.

Each of these regions faced developmental problems common to the rest of Canada and they responded with similar policies. Economically, they were geographically far from markets, hence subsidies and other inducements were given to private developers to build transportation systems (roads, railways, and canals). As the Atlantic provinces also lacked investment generally, generous inducements were given to companies to settle in these areas. Likewise, land was opened up cheaply to encourage immigration.

Often, however, people in these regions found that development was uneven and centred on a single commodity—the fishery in Newfoundland, for example—resulting in recurrent cycles of boom and bust (Norrie and Owram 1996). (Amid the Great Depression and facing bankruptcy in 1933, the Newfoundland legislature voted to suspend its operations and reverted to a Crown colony of Britain the following year.) In turn, economic instability often resulted in political unrest, with its own distinctive regional characteristics (Clark et al. 1975; Brym and Sacouman 1979). This unrest has had national consequences. As many scholars have pointed out, Canada does not have a national economy, nor even national policies of development, but instead regional policies that too often pit one region against another (see Clement and Williams 1989; Laxer 1991), a situation no more evident than in the history of western Canada.

IMMIGRATION AND THE WEST

Pre-Confederation, in 1861, 3.2 million people lived in British North America. Canada's population stood at only 4.8 million (see table 0.1) 30 years later. By contrast, the population of the United States during this period rose from 31.4 million to nearly 63 million (*Time* 2020, 608). Nature and geography, mercantilist policies, and American competition held Canada's population growth at bay. Indeed, so unattractive was Canada relative to its southern neighbour during the 50-year period from 1851 to 1901 that only 1.9 million people entered Canada while 2.2 million left, most of them for the United States (McKie 1994, 26).

By 1896, however, the American West was virtually filled and the depression over. In Ottawa, administrators fervently pursued immigrants. By 1900, Indigenous peoples of the West had largely been pushed aside (see Chapter 9). Now the prohibitive land regulations (Laxer 1989) were changed, the railways were forced to open up land for settlement, and irrigation construction proceeded, especially in the arid region known as the Palliser Triangle (see Norrie and Owram 1996). Above all, Canadian immigration was promoted as never before. The result was the largest influx of immigrants in Canadian history. Nearly two million immigrants entered Canada between 1901 and 1911 (McKie 1994, 28; Hall 1977); another 375,756 arrived in 1912, and 400,870 more in 1913 (see table 6.1).

The immigrants came primarily from three areas: the United States, Great Britain, and Europe. Of these groups, the first two were viewed as particularly desirable. American immigrants had capital, goods, and Prairie farm experience, and they could "fit in" ethnically in Canada. Thus, the number of American immigrants to Canada increased from 2,400 in 1897 to 12,000 in 1899. Between 1902 and 1905, 40,000 to 50,000 Americans annually entered Canada (Hall 1977, 70). For their part, British immigrants, with the exception of the Irish, were viewed as loyal to the Crown. The immigration boom attracted large numbers of people from the rural areas of England and Scotland. By 1901, however, the great wave of British immigration, fuelled in the early 19th century by a population boom in the old country, was declining. Thus, Canadian immigration officials hesitantly expanded their search for immigrants beyond the traditional Anglo countries, into northern and eastern Europe.

Certain ethnic groups, however, remained restricted from entering Canada. These groups included "Negroes," "Orientals" (including East Indians), "Galicians" (meaning eastern Europeans), Italians, and Jews, who, it was argued, were urban people who could not adjust to the demands of Prairie life and who, in any case, would not fit into Canadian culture. In the case of the Chinese, government policies were explicitly racist. Good enough to be employed as cheap labour in building the railways, and later in British Columbia's mines and forestry industry (Morton 1997), Chinese immigrants were not considered good enough, however, to become citizens. The first of several "head taxes" was enacted on the Chinese in 1885 to prevent workers from being able to afford to bring over family members (Hall 1977).

Immigration moved in waves across the Prairies, leaving distinctive cultural traces that remain today in every province. Between 1871 and 1891, Manitoba's population increased from 25,000 to 153,000, rising to 461,000 by 1911 (see table 0.1). The early days saw Anglo farmers and expatriate elements of Ontario's upper class settle in

Table 6.1: Immigration to Canada, 1852–2019

Year	Immigrants	Year	Immigrants	Year	Immigrants	Year	Immigrants	Year	Immigrants	Year	Immigrants
1852	29,307	1880	38,505	1908	143,326	1936	11,643	1964	112,606	1992	254,790
1853	29,464	1881	47,991	1909	173,694	1937	15,101	1965	146,758	1993	256,641
1854	37,263	1882	112,458	1910	286,839	1938	17,244	1966	194,743	1994	224,385
1855	25,296	1883	133,624	1911	331,288	1939	16,994	1967	222,876	1995	212,865
1856	22,544	1884	103,824	1912	375,756	1940	11,324	1968	183,974	1996	226,071
1857	33,854	1885	79,169	1913	400,870	1941	9,329	1969	161,531	1997	216,035
1858	12,339	1886	69,152	1914	150,484	1942	7,576	1970	147,713	1998	174,195
1859	6,300	1887	84,526	1915	36,665	1943	8,504	1971	121,900	1999	189,951
1860	6,276	1888	88,766	1916	55,914	1944	12,801	1972	122,006	2000	227,456
1861	13,589	1889	44,543	1917	72,910	1945	22,722	1973	184,200	2001	250,637
1862	18,294	1890	75,067	1918	41,845	1946	71,719	1974	218,465	2002	229,048
1863	21,000	1891	82,165	1919	107,698	1947	64,127	1975	187,881	2003	221,349
1864	24,779	1892	30,996	1920	13,824	1948	125,414	1976	149,429	2004	235,823
1865	18,958	1893	29,633	1921	91,728	1949	95,217	1977	114,914	2005	262,242

Year	Number	Year	Number	Year	Number	Year	Number	Year	Number	Year	Number
1866	11,427	1894	20,829	1922	64,224	1950	73,912	1978	86,313	2006	251,640
1867	10,666	1895	18,790	1923	133,729	1951	194,391	1979	112,093	2007	236,753
1868	12,765	1896	16,835	1924	124,164	1952	164,498	1980	143,140	2008	247,247
1869	18,630	1897	21,716	1925	84,907	1953	168,868	1981	128,642	2009	252,172
1870	24,706	1898	31,900	1926	135,982	1954	154,227	1982	121,179	2010	280,689
1871	27,773	1899	44,543	1927	158,886	1955	109,946	1983	89,192	2011	248,748
1872	36,758	1900	41,681	1928	166,783	1956	164,857	1984	88,276	2012	257,887
1873	50,050	1901	55,747	1929	164,993	1957	282,164	1985	84,346	2013	263,160
1874	39,373	1902	89,102	1930	104,806	1958	124,851	1986	99,353	2014	267,920
1875	27,382	1903	138,660	1931	27,530	1959	106,928	1987	152,084	2015	240,760
1876	25,633	1904	131,252	1932	20,591	1960	104,111	1988	161,588	2016	323,190
1877	27,028	1905	141,465	1933	14,382	1961	71,689	1989	191,555	2017	272,710
1878	29,807	1906	211,653	1934	12,476	1962	74,586	1990	216,452	2018	303,257
1879	40,492	1907	272,409	1935	11,277	1963	93,151	1991	232,806	2019	313,580

Sources: Citizenship and Immigration Canada. 1996. "Citizenship and Immigration Statistics 1996." Cat. no. MP22-1/1996. Ottawa: Citizenship and Immigration Canada; and Government of Canada. 2013a. "Facts and Figures 2012—Immigration Overview: Permanent and Temporary Residents." Figures for 2014–2018 from Statista. 2020a. *Number of immigrants in Canada from 2000 to 2019 (in 1,000s)*.

southern Manitoba (Lower 1983), though a sizable Icelandic contingent also moved to Manitoba in 1873, settling north of Winnipeg. Later European immigrants who arrived, finding the best land already taken, settled in the north and west of the province, while Anglo-Americans moved into the southwest (Widdis 1997). But these waves of immigrants to Manitoba were not only ethnically distinct. Over time, they also transformed Manitoba's class structure and political culture. By the start of the First World War, Winnipeg had developed a strong working-class culture, the product of British and eastern European immigrants, paving the way for the strike of 1919 (outlined subsequently) (Wiseman 2007).

The combined population of the entire Territories in 1871 was about 48,000 (not including Indigenous peoples). By 1901, Saskatchewan's population alone had risen to 91,000, while that of Alberta stood at 73,000. Ten years later, these provinces' populations had risen to 492,000 and 374,000, respectively (see table 0.1). Before the turn of the century, there were significant francophone populations in Saskatchewan's north and southwest. Like western Manitoba, however, the early 20th century saw Saskatchewan settled by the second wave of Anglo and European immigrants, not to mention (in the province's southwest) American immigrants (see Wiseman 2007; Widdis 1997).

Alberta, too, at the turn of the century had a large francophone population, located mainly in the northeast. In the late 19th century, however, Anglo-American immigrants moved into southern Alberta, bringing with them populist notions of direct democracy, as well as strong beliefs in possessive individualism (Harrison 2000). American influence in the south was further strengthened after the discovery in 1914 of oil at Turner Valley, a harbinger of events to come. But other ethnic groups also arrived. The mining communities of the southern Crowsnest Pass, for example, filled with southern (especially Italian) and eastern Europeans, while the province's north similarly experienced an influx of central and eastern Europeans.

British Columbia's population growth was slower, but steadier. Approximately 36,000 people (not including those of Indigenous ancestry) lived in BC at Confederation in 1871, rising to 179,000 by 1901 and 393,000 by 1911. Much of this non-Indigenous population was English and Scottish in origin, via Canada's Atlantic region; others were American. In the early stages, settlement was tied to the coastline and Vancouver Island. Later, settlers spread inland, along paths set by the railways. These late arrivals, employed in construction and resource extraction, brought a distinctive working-class consciousness (see Robin 1993). At the same time, sizable numbers of Chinese and Japanese immigrants also came.

There were other distinctive populations throughout the West who were unable or unwilling to be "fitted" easily into the dominant British mould. Black communities developed early on, for example, in Breton, Alberta, and around Maidstone, Saskatchewan. Catholic, Anglican, and other Protestant religious orders dominated Canadian religious and cultural life. Nonetheless, some persecuted religious minorities also found a home in the West. With the moral and financial support of Count Leo Tolstoy, some 7,400

Doukhobors arrived in Canada between December 1898 and April 1899, settling near Yorkton and Prince Albert, Saskatchewan (Mayes 1999). Other religious minorities— Mennonites in southern Manitoba, Hutterites throughout western Manitoba and southern Alberta, and Mormons in southern Alberta—also arrived.

National concern focused on how best to assimilate the "new Canadians," whom James S. Woodsworth (1874–1942), a Methodist minister and later first leader of the Co-operative Commonwealth Federation, in 1909 called the "strangers within our gates" (Woodsworth 1909/1972). Outside Quebec, Canada's immigration and other policies (e.g., education) at the time enforced **Anglo-conformity**—the requirement that subordinate group members express outward compliance with the values and practices of the dominant British group—and reflected broad public sentiment and fears of social discord.

In the early 1900s, "Canadians were more provincial than cosmopolitan, more openly biased than politically correct, and each social grouping more protective of its niche in society" (Lyon 1998, 26). Small differences, even the neighbourhood one lived in, were magnified in importance. There was a recognized pecking order even within the British "tribes": Scots and English on top, Irish Catholics on the bottom.

In extreme cases during the period from 1901 to 1911, **racism** (the belief that one racial category is innately superior or inferior to another) and **xenophobia** (the fear of people who are unfamiliar) resulted in anti-immigrant riots in several cities (see Palmer 1982). Anti-Oriental riots broke out in Vancouver during the recession year of 1907 (Whitaker 1991), for example. In most cases, however, public reaction took the form of occupational or social exclusion, or snickering at the new immigrants' "exotic" and "peculiar" lifestyles. Groups kept to their own turf. Finally, we should keep in mind the well-meaning, if often paternalistic, efforts of many individuals, voluntary agencies, and church groups who assisted the new immigrants' adjustment to Canadian life.

The immigration boom ended in 1913. That year, more than 400,000 immigrants landed on Canada's shores. But the world economy was slowing down, and the war that followed ended immigration almost entirely. In 1914, only 150,484 immigrants entered Canada, and the number declined further during the war years (see table 6.1).

The wartime decline in immigration was presaged in May 1914 by the arrival in Vancouver harbour of a former collier ship, the *Komagata Maru*. Immigration officials met the ship, which carried 376 East Indians, mainly Sikhs, and refused the migrants entry. The ship was held in port for two months, its passengers detained while a Canadian warship kept watch. Finally, 21 of the migrants were allowed to disembark. The rest, however, returned to India on the ship. Arriving there in September, they were greeted by British gunfire. Eighteen died (Jensen 1988).

BETWEEN TWO EMPIRES

Why did many in English Canada view new immigrants as such threats during this period? First, English Canada in 1900 certainly was parochial and ethnocentric. Second, however, English-Canadians remained anxious over the country's future. As we have seen, Canada's hesitant economic development after 1867 raised questions not only about the National Policy but Confederation generally. While some, such as the liberal historian and journalist Goldwin Smith, positively embraced the idea (see Smith 1891/1971), many others feared annexation by the United States.

A group of eminent intellectuals argued for strengthened ties to the British Empire. These "Canadian imperialists"—among them novelist Sara Jeannette Duncan, Presbyterian minister and educator George Monro Grant, humorist and political economist Stephen Leacock, and educator Sir George Robert Parkin—idealized the Loyalist legacy, especially elitism and anti-Americanism. Nostalgic for a simpler life and opposed to the raw materialism, industrialism, and urbanism represented by the United States (Cook 1995), the imperialists saw Canada as having a kind of religious "mission" on Earth (Berger 1976; Romney 1999).

Canadian imperialism and its organizations had some successes in pressuring the Canadian government to increase ties with the Crown. In 1897, Prime Minister Sir Wilfrid Laurier re-established preferential trade with Britain (Norrie and Owram 1996). In 1899, to the chagrin of his French-Canadian supporters, Laurier also sent Canadian soldiers overseas to fight alongside Britain in the Boer War (Miller 1999).

After 1900, however, the United States' economic influence upon Canada steadily increased while that of Britain waned. Trade and investment figures highlight this trend.

Throughout the late 19th century, Canada's trade with the United States and Britain steadfastly shifted toward the former. While British import and export trade with Canada continued to grow during this period, its overall importance to the Canadian economy declined relative to that of the United States. By 1891, Canadian imports from the United States surpassed those from Britain and thereafter never looked back. Export trade took longer to shift, picking up additional steam during the First World War as Canadian industry met British wartime demand. By 1921, however, Canadian exports to the United States, like imports, also surpassed those to Britain (Marchildon 1995; see also Alford 1996).

This shift in trade was, in part, reflected in the amount and form of British and American investment in Canada. Canadian economic development historically has relied upon massive amounts of foreign capital. The boom after 1896 involved especially huge investments, with foreign capital flows into Canada increasing from 2.1 percent of GNP in 1897 to a high of 17.7 percent in 1912 (Norrie and Owram 1996, 241). Until 1922, Britain was Canada's chief source of investment capital. That year, however, American investment totalled $2.6 billion (50 percent of total foreign investment), compared with $2.5 billion (47 percent) from the UK (Norrie and Owram 1996, 324; see also Marchildon 1995; Li 1996). Thereafter, American investment in Canada, both in actual dollars and as a percentage of foreign capital, was never overtaken.

There was also an important difference between American and British foreign investment. Foreign investment takes two forms: portfolio investment (e.g., long-term investments, such as bonds and loans) and direct investment (the actual ownership of productive property). British investment took predominantly the portfolio form. By contrast, American investments abroad were predominantly direct in nature. In Canada, direct investment involved buying up Canadian resources and firms or establishing branch plants. This meant, in practice, that American capital had greater control than British capital over the Canadian economy as a whole, but especially in certain areas of the economy—automobiles, newsprint, metals, and petroleum—that would become important in the 20th century. The increasing number of American firms in Canada also helps explain the rising level of exports to, and imports from, the United States: American firms were trading with themselves.

As always, Canada's need for capital and the prospect of jobs were balanced against the fears of American control leading to annexation (see Sara Jeannette Duncan's quotation at the beginning of this chapter). These fears reached a symbolic climax in 1911.

In 1910, Laurier became the first Canadian prime minister to visit western Canada. There, he heard repeated complaints from farmers regarding the National Policy's tariffs. Remembering his defeat in 1891 but still dedicated to the liberal notion of open markets, Laurier's government worked out a limited reciprocity agreement with the United States (Norrie and Owram 1996). Laurier believed the Conservatives under Sir Robert Borden would not seriously oppose the agreement, as they had for years held out hopes of gaining a similar pact.

The American House of Representatives and Senate gave the agreement swift passage, but the outspoken remarks of several congressmen that the agreement would hasten Canada's annexation (see Champ Clark's quotation at the beginning of this chapter) soon became front-page news in Canada. The election that followed saw Laurier's Liberals defeated by a potent mixture of fear, anti-Americanism, and protectionism (see Granatstein 1996; Orchard 1998; Norrie and Owram 1996). The issue of free trade hence disappeared from public debate, revived only in the late 1980s by the Conservative government of Brian Mulroney (Chapter 7).

Outside of Quebec, Canada in 1914 remained decidedly British, but American economic, cultural, and geopolitical influence over Canada was gradually increasing. The war that followed reinforced this emerging pattern.

A WORLD INTERRUPTED: CANADA AND THE FIRST WORLD WAR

In 1914, years of political posturing, unbridled jingoism, and imperial competition resulted in war. Estimates for the number of people killed in the First World War (1914–1918) range between 8.5 and 16 million; the number of wounded is estimated at more than 21 million (Stearns 1975, 277–278). Russia's casualties were the greatest, made even greater by the revolution and the famines that followed, but Germany, France, and Britain also suffered enormous costs, including in effect the wasting of an entire generation. Many who returned bore wounds that were not always obvious. In strictly monetary terms, the total direct costs of the war were $180 billion and indirect costs $151 billion, substantial amounts for the time (Langer 1948, 951).

Canadian wartime losses amounted to 60,661 Canadian troops dead, among them a host of "war poets," such as John McCrae. Another 1,600 people were killed (6,000 more wounded) at Halifax harbour on December 6, 1917, when an ammunition ship collided with a freighter, exploding with the force of an atomic bomb and destroying much of Halifax. The year following war's end saw nearly as many Canadians die as a result of a worldwide influenza epidemic, caused indirectly by the war.

European places like Ypres, Passchendaele, and Vimy Ridge entered Canada's history, while a small number of individuals—mainly "air aces" like Billy Bishop, William Barker, and A. Roy Brown—became household names for a time. Small towns and villages throughout Canada erected monuments to the dead that still stand, augmented later by more names from other wars. Some towns were named after the battles (such as Vimy, Alberta); however, Berlin, Ontario (founded by people of German ancestry who were now afraid to admit their heritage), was renamed in 1916 after a British war hero, Field Marshal Lord Kitchener, who had died at sea.

Beyond the obvious losses of men, money, and material, the war had several major impacts on Canada, some more immediate than others.

First, the war altered Canada's position relative to other powers within the international state system. The Russian, German, Austro-Hungarian, and Turkish empires were destroyed; the British Empire was hobbled. By contrast, the United States, already the world's leading economy in 1914 (Norrie and Owram 1996), ended the war as the world's leading creditor country (Palmer with Colton 1957), second only to Britain as the world's chief direct investor (Dunning 1983) and in military matters an increasingly formidable power. A series of invasions and military coups after 1898, underpinned by the Monroe Doctrine, had ensured that, in the Americas especially, the United States reigned largely unopposed (Zinn 1995).

Second, the war discredited old institutions and traditional authorities, especially in Europe but also in Canada, paving the way for the rise of new political ideologies and parties during the 1920s and 1930s. Third, at the same time, the role of the state in Canadian society (as elsewhere) expanded. Canadian government spending on goods and services, for example, rose from 10 percent of GDP in 1913 to 14.5 percent of GDP in 1914 and remained at that level throughout the war (Norrie and Owram 1996, 300). The bureaucratic infrastructure of government also expanded, notably through the introduction of the Pension Act of 1919, which provided disability pensions for returning soldiers and which, in turn, gave impetus to later federal intervention in social policy (Rice and Prince 2013). On the revenue side, the Canadian government introduced business and personal income taxes, a temporary wartime measure that soon became a permanent part of Canada's fiscal landscape.

Fourth, the First World War accelerated in all countries a series of social changes. Women, for example, entered the labour force in larger numbers, finding work, especially in the growing public bureaucracies (Lowe 1987). As in most combatant countries, women in Canada also gained the vote (in 1918). (The previous year, Louise McKinney [1868–1931] had been elected to the Alberta legislature, becoming the first woman to hold such an office in the British Empire.) But there were other social changes, notably the continued decline in rural population and the growth of cities, a gradual shift from primary production to secondary manufacturing and services, and the expansion of wage labour.

Fifth, as noted in Chapter 2, the Conscription Crisis became part of the panoply of grievances dividing the French and English in Canada. Sixth, as also noted earlier, the war slowed immigration to Canada—indeed, killing off many who might have come—thus cutting off an important leg of Canada's National Policy.

Finally, the war also sparked in English Canada a fragile sense of independent nationalism. In 1914, Canada was still very much a British colony. Britain's declaration of war on August 4 meant that Canada was itself immediately at war, its troops under British command. By 1918, however, there was a distinct Canadian Corps led by Canadian officers. Canada's separate signing of the Treaty of Versailles in 1919 and garnering of a seat in the newly founded League of Nations further symbolized the country's growing independence from Britain.

CANADA, 1919–1929

The troops returning in 1919 were greeted with high unemployment, rising inflation, declining wages, and mounting anxiety. In Winnipeg in the spring of 1919, a dispute between labourers in the metal and building trades and management over collective bargaining rights, wages, and working conditions escalated into a general strike of 24,000 workers that lasted 40 days. The strike encouraged sympathy strikes (particularly in the West) involving another 88,000 workers. It ended on June 25, amid lingering images of the RCMP on horseback charging into a crowd of strikers at the corner of Portage and Main—causing 30 casualties and at least one death—and of federal troops occupying the streets of Winnipeg (Conway 2014, 86–88).

There was also anxiety in rural Canada, especially in the West. Mass immigration between 1901 and 1911 (see table 6.1) had transformed the Prairie landscape and, in less than two decades, had led to Ontario being supplanted as Canada's wheat-growing region (see Morton 2000; Norrie and Owram 1996). This transformation came at a cost, however.

The West, reliant upon a single commodity, was particularly at the mercy of world markets. When wheat prices collapsed at the end of the war, Canada's agrarians revolted at the ballot box. The United Farmers of Ontario party was elected in 1919. Subsequently, the United Farmers of Alberta gained office in 1921, and the United Farmers of Manitoba in 1922. Meanwhile, at the federal level, in 1921 the newly founded National Progressive Party elected 65 MPs, the most successful showing by a federal "third party" until the Reform Party in the 1990s (see Chapter 8). Among the Progressives was the first woman to be elected to Canada's Parliament, Agnes Macphail (1890–1954).

Why the widespread discontent following the war? The explanation lies in a series of social and economic trends that, beginning in the early 20th century, were rapidly transforming Canadian society.

Think for a moment about life in mid-19th-century Canada. Family and community were the focal point around which people's lives revolved. People, other than arriving immigrants, travelled little in their lifetime. Much of Canada was still rural (80 percent in 1871). The family was still the site of production and consumption, gender roles were largely fixed, markets were mainly local, and few people were full-time wage labourers. Well into the late 19th century, small, paternalistic, family-operated businesses—what Marx termed the "petite bourgeoisie"—dominated the Canadian economy, while family farms were the norm.

After 1900, however, a new form of capitalism emerged: corporate capitalism. Moving beyond the limitations of either petit bourgeois or mercantile or industrial capitalism, corporate capitalism (sometimes also termed "monopoly capitalism") is large-scale, highly capitalized, centralized, and non-competitive (Heron and Storey 1986; Li 1996). Between 1900 and 1920, for example, the number of manufacturing units in Canada fell from 76,000 to 22,000 (Li 1996, 16; Morton 2000, 29). Similarly, the number of Canadian banks went from 36 in 1900 to 22 in 1914 to 10 in 1928 (Li 1996, 20). Canada was quickly transformed from a society of petit bourgeois agrarians and nascent small-time industrialists into one in which large-scale manufacturing (especially in the automobile industry) and services began playing an increasingly large role. At the same time, industrialization and economic development were unevenly distributed, and thus increased regional divisions within Canada.

The rise of corporate capitalism had particular impact in shaping Canada's labour market. Demand for labour grew. Thus, the number and percentage of wage labourers in the overall labour force grew rapidly (see Li 1996, 34). As in the past, labour demand was met in part by new immigrants, but immigration during the 1920s did not recover to prewar levels. Instead, labour demand was met largely through natural population growth, rural migration—hence, in part, the agrarian revolts of 1919 to 1922—and a still largely untapped source: women.

The period leading up to the 1920s saw increasing numbers of women entering the workforce. Between 1911 and 1921, the participation rate for women ages 14 to 65 rose from 16.6 percent to 19.9 percent, compared with a rise from 82 percent to 89.7 percent for men in that age group during the same period. By 1931, the participation rate of women in the labour force was 23 percent, compared with 87.2 percent for men (calculated from Denton 1983). Women's jobs, however, were mostly in the low-paying clerical occupations that arose in the burgeoning bureaucracies of the state and corporations (Lowe 1987; Krahn et al. 2020).

The situation of women was changing at the political level, too. In 1929, five women—Irene Parlby, Louise McKinney, Henrietta Muir Edwards, Emily Murphy, and Nellie McClung—won an especially important legal battle when the Judicial Committee of the Privy Council in Britain (then Canada's highest court) overturned an earlier ruling by the Supreme Court of Canada and declared that women were "persons" under the law and therefore could hold public office (Bellamy and Irving 1981).

Meanwhile, corporate capitalism was also changing Canada's workplaces and workplace relations in important ways. This period saw the introduction of new forms of organization to the workplace. Bureaucratic principles and management techniques based on Frederick Taylor's principles of scientific management were introduced into factories and soon also into white-collar work. These organizational forms increased managerial control over workers and deskilled workers in the name of efficiency and higher profits, but also increased worker alienation and labour conflict (Krahn et al. 2020).

In the long run, concentrated capitalism also meant concentrated labour, resulting in the rise of trade and industrial unions. In the short run, however, these changes led to growing antagonism and intensified class conflict, as evidenced in Winnipeg.

Technology, the war, the increasing role of the state, and the rise of corporate capitalism changed Canada in other ways during this period. Canada gradually became more urbanized. In 1901, 63 percent of Canadians still lived in rural areas. By 1921, however, a nearly equal number of Canadians lived in urban and rural areas (see table 6.2), with the urban population remaining consistently higher than the rural population since 1931. Canada's urbanization had begun.

In 1901, Montreal (population 328,172) and Toronto (population 209,892) were still Canada's largest cities. The next largest city was Quebec City, with 68,840 people. Over the next 10 years, however, Winnipeg grew from 42,340 to 136,035 people, while Vancouver's population increased from 29,432 to 120,847. By 1921, Hamilton and Ottawa also exceeded 100,000 people, joined in 1931 by Quebec City (see Norrie and Owram 1996, 334).

Mass consumption became a reality in the 1920s (Bell 1996; Robbins and Dowty 2019). The automobile was the chief symbol of this new consumer society. Cars had been around for decades; by the 1920s, however, mass production technology, low cost, and easy credit made it possible for more people to own them. The number of cars registered in Canada increased from 275,000 in 1918 to 1.9 million in 1929 (Norrie and Owram 1996, 327), a growth rate far outstripping even the United States (see Hofstadter et al. 1957, 642).

By the 1920s, British influence, though still strong, was waning; the pull of American culture was increasing. Many of Canada's corporations were American-owned. Faintly, however, a more independent Canadian culture was stirring within English-speaking Canada, spearheaded by artists such as Emily Carr and the Group of Seven. Prints of

Table 6.2: Canadian Rural and Urban Population, 1851–2016 (in thousands and percentage)

Year	Total Population	Urban	Rural	Urban (%)	Rural (%)
1851	2,436,297	318,079	2,118,218	13	87
1861	3,229,633	527,220	2,702,413	16	84
1871	3,737,257	722,343	3,014,914	19	81
1881	4,381,256	1,109,507	3,271,749	25	75
1891	4,932,206	1,537,098	3,395,108	31	69
1901	5,418,663	2,023,364	3,395,299	37	63
1911	7,221,662	3,276,812	3,944,850	45	55
1921	8,800,249	4,353,428	4,446,821	49	51
1931	10,376,379	5,572,058	4,804,321	54	46
1941	11,506,655	6,252,416	5,254,239	54	46
1951	14,009,429	8,628,253	5,381,176	62	38
1956	16,080,791	10,714,855	5,365,936	67	33
1961	18,238,247	12,700,390	5,537,857	70	30
1966	20,014,880	14,726,759	5,288,121	74	26
1971	21,568,305	16,410,785	5,157,520	76	24
1976	22,992,595	17,366,970	5,625,625	76	24
1981	24,343,177	18,435,923	5,907,254	76	24
1986	25,309,330	19,352,080	5,957,250	76	24
1991	27,296,856	20,906,872	6,389,984	77	23
1996	28,846,758	22,461,207	6,385,551	78	22
2001	30,007,094	23,908,211	6,098,883	80	20
2006	31,612,897	25,350,743	6,262,154	80	20
2011[1]	33,476,688	27,147,274	6,329,414	81	19
2016	35,151,728	28,576,355	6,575,373	81	19

Note: 1. Starting with the 2011 Census, the term *population centre* replaces the term *urban area*. For more information, please see Statistics Canada's note titled "From Urban Areas to Population Centres," available at www.statcan.gc.ca/subjects-sujets/standard-norme/sgc-cgt/notice-avis/sgc-cgt-06-eng.htm. This note explains the new terminology and classification of population centres. The rural population from 1981 to 2011 refers to persons living outside centres with a population of 1,000 *and* outside areas with 400 persons per square kilometre. Prior to 1981, the definitions differed slightly but consistently referred to populations outside centres with a population of 1,000.

Sources: Statistics Canada. 2011c. "Population, Urban and Rural, by Province and Territory (Canada)." Ottawa: Statistics Canada; Statistics Canada. 2016a. Data Table 98-402-X2016001: "Population and Dwelling Count Highlight Tables." 2016 Census: Population counts, for Canada, provinces and territories, census divisions.

these artists' paintings soon appeared in banks and magazines across the country, promoting images of their land that few Canadians had actually seen.

The first half of the 1920s in Canada, as elsewhere, began with a recession. By contrast, the years between 1925 and 1929 were a time of prosperity, marked by illegal gin, Charleston-dancing flappers, Model T Fords, and jazz. Then, suddenly, the prosperity ended.

THE DEPRESSION YEARS, 1929–1939

In October 1929, the New York stock market crashed. Stock values on the New York Stock Exchange alone fell by 40 percent (Palmer with Colton 1957, 780), and 10 percent of private wealth vanished, virtually overnight (Norrie and Owram 1996, 296). Despite repeated statements by government officials in Canada, the United States, and elsewhere that the economy was sound, the crisis soon spread. As industrial and financial capital collapsed, production fell and unemployment rose, resulting in more uncertainty, a further decline in consumption, and yet more layoffs throughout the industrialized, capitalist world.

During the Depression's worst period (1932–1933), the **unemployment rate**—generally calculated as the number of people out of work and actively looking for work divided by the total number of labour force participants, including the unemployed (Krahn et al. 2020)—reached 23 percent in Britain and Belgium, 24 percent in Sweden, 27 percent in the United States, 29 percent in Austria, 31 percent in Norway, 32 percent in Denmark, and no less than 44 percent in Germany (all rates from Hobsbawm 1995, 90–93). Canadian unemployment rose officially from three percent in 1929 to between 25 and 30 percent in 1933, the peak year (Rice and Prince 2013, 53). How much these official statistics underestimate the problem is open to question, however.

Canada suffered uniquely in the Depression because, first, its economy was export dependent; second, its range of exports was small and lacked diversification; and third, its chief export market was the United States, a country that became highly protectionist during the Depression (Norrie and Owram 1996). Canada's economy was insufficiently developed and not self-contained or integrated enough to withstand the shocks. Consequently, from 1929 to 1933, Canadian industrial production fell by 50 percent, exports by 67 percent, and construction by 90 percent (Rice and Prince 2013, 53).

Within Canada, the Depression hit the West hardest. The region's economy was particularly dependent on wheat for export. Additionally, much of the West experienced a long, harsh drought. The worst-hit area was southwest Saskatchewan, resulting in an estimated quarter of a million people abandoning their farms during the 1930s (Berton 1991, 291). However, for the Maritimes, in semi-permanent recession since the 1880s, and many Indigenous reserves stranded outside the capitalist market system, the Depression hardly seemed a change.

The Depression halted, even reversed for a time, years of social change in Canada. Barter, for example, partially replaced the money economy. Cars morphed into horse-drawn carriages, nicknamed (after Prime Minister R. B. Bennett [1870–1947]) "Bennett buggies." The process of urbanization slowed. Immigration to Canada all but ended; indeed, for the first time since the 19th century, more people left Canada than entered (McKie 1994). Most Canadians did not mind, however. Anti-immigrant sentiment in the 1930s was high. The Canadian government took special steps to halt the entry of people viewed as communist agitators and "troublemakers," or people who were deemed to not fit in. In a replay of the *Komagata Maru* incident, in 1939 the Canadian government refused the disembarkment of 907 Jews aboard the liner *St. Louis*, resulting in their return to Europe and, ultimately, to Nazi Germany's death camps (Abella and Troper 1982; Whitaker 1991).

The Depression damaged Canada's social fabric. Crime rates rose. The year 1931 witnessed an "unprecedented wave of bank holdups" (Berton 1991, 88). Fuelled by Prohibition south of the border, booze became a growth industry throughout Canada, from the Maritime ports to the cities of southern Ontario to the Crowsnest Pass region of Alberta. Suicide rates climbed while birth rates, already dropping in the 1920s, declined further to 3.0 per 1,000 in 1936 and 2.8 per 1,000 in 1941 (see Li 1996, 155), figures not seen again until the 1960s. In the 1930s, few people wanted to have children, not knowing if they could care for them.

Yet Canadians' sense of being part of a larger society also expanded during the Depression. Some young Canadians experienced the country first-hand, hopping freight cars and travelling from community to community in search of work (Berton 1991). Others learned about Canada and the world at large through the cinema, though in the main the silver screen provided not access to but an escape from reality. By contrast, radio played a major role in incorporating Canadians into society. Bennett's government recognized in the early 1930s the importance of radio in nation building and so created the Canadian Radio Broadcasting Commission, which grew in time into the Canadian Broadcasting Corporation (CBC). Radio manufactured an "imaginary collective," creating and sharing common experiences for Canadians from coast to coast, and related to a host of events, from Foster Hewitt's hockey broadcasts, to disasters both real and fake (e.g., *The War of the Worlds* broadcast), to human interest stories (e.g., the Dionne quintuplets).

Bennett's Conservative government expanded the role of the state in other ways, notably through the creation of the Bank of Canada and the Wheat Board. In areas of economic and social concern during the early years of the Depression, however, Bennett followed the policies of his American counterpart, President Herbert Hoover (1874–1964), in steadfastly arguing that governments could not—*should* not—do anything to interfere in the economy. In both countries, problems of the poor, the hungry, and the unemployed were thrown back on local authorities and charities. The role of governments was to balance budgets, protect private property, and maintain social order.

In Canada as in the United States (Zinn 1995), there were strikes and protests by workers throughout the decade. The state did not hesitate to use coercive force to deal with them. At Estevan, Saskatchewan, in 1931, low wages, poor living conditions, and unsympathetic management led to a confrontation between striking mine workers and police in which three strikers were killed, eleven more injured, and five policemen sent to hospital (Berton 1991, 126–127).

As the Depression continued, Canadian governments grew increasingly wary of worker unrest—the mining town of Blairmore, Alberta, twice elected a communist town council in the mid-1930s, which promptly erected Karl Marx Park—and took further steps to curtail political agitation. One such step involved setting up work camps for the unemployed in remote rural areas. Before being shut down in 1936, Canada's relief camps housed 170,248 men and provided 10.2 million worker-days of relief (Howard 1999, 2408), but the food was poor and predictable, the clothing of army issue and distinctly prison-like, and camp control was authoritarian and punitive (Berton 1991). The camps became breeding grounds of hopelessness and anger.

In June 1935, 1,500 young men of various racial and ethnic backgrounds, refugees from the British Columbia camps, set off from the Vancouver waterfront by train, headed for Ottawa, picking up supporters along the way. They were forcibly halted at Regina, however, on Dominion Day. Under orders from Prime Minister Bennett, the RCMP and local police moved into an unsuspecting crowd of 1,500 people on Regina's Market Square to arrest the trek leaders. A panic ensued. By the time it was over, 12 trekkers and five Regina citizens were hospitalized for gunshot wounds, 39 RCMP officers had been hospitalized for injuries (none from gunfire), and one plainclothes detective lay dead. Over 100 people were arrested. Twenty-eight went to trial; eight were eventually convicted and sent to jail (Berton 1991).

In the main, unrest in Canada during the Depression paled in comparison with other countries where strikes, protests, civil violence, and state repression were daily news. Still, it was a time of serious political unrest. Both communism and fascism gained converts in Canada. The authorities treated communists, or those suspected of being communists, far more harshly than fascist sympathizers, who garnered at least tacit support from some members of Canada's political, business, and religious elite (see Robin 1991; Berton 1991).

Two less politically extreme alternatives to communism and fascism arose in western Canada. Like the agrarian parties of the early 1920s, both were **populist parties**—that is, parties built around mass political movements, and mobilized around symbols and traditions congruent with the popular culture, that express a group's sense of threat arising from external elements and directed at the group's perceived "peoplehood."

In Saskatchewan, the Co-operative Commonwealth Federation (CCF), built around a broad coalition of farmers, labourers, religious activists (mainly Protestants), and university-trained intellectuals (mainly economists), melded traditional Prairie populism with democratic socialism. Its leader was James S. Woodsworth (mentioned earlier in the chapter), a former Methodist minister who had been among those arrested in the 1919 Winnipeg Strike and later elected to the House of Commons as a National Progressive in 1921. In 1944, another minister, Tommy Douglas (1904–1986), led the CCF to success in Saskatchewan, bringing to power the first socialist government in North America. In 1961, the CCF became the New Democratic Party (Lipset 1968a; Conway 2014) (see Chapter 7).

In Alberta, Reverend William Aberhart (1878–1943), a radio evangelist, adopted the economic ideas of a British engineer, Colonel Douglas, in founding the Social Credit Party. In 1935, Aberhart's party was elected, defeating the tired and scandal-ridden United Farmers of Alberta. Broadly supported by farmers and workers alike (E. Bell 1993), the party at first mixed populist rhetoric and evangelical zeal, demanding protection against bankruptcy, unemployment insurance, and public health care. Following a series of legislative setbacks, Aberhart's death in 1943, and the discovery of oil in the late 1940s, however, Social Credit became a fairly conventional conservative party opposed to government intervention in the economy (Finkel 1989).

Government policies in Canada in the 1930s were shaped by events in the United States. In 1932, Franklin Delano Roosevelt was elected president. Soon Canadians as well as Americans were hearing Roosevelt over the still-new medium of radio. Canadians liked what they heard. Like Canada, the United States was faced with massive unemployment, civil unrest, and populist agitation. Unlike Bennett, Roosevelt offered solutions to the crisis, embarking on a series of economic and social reforms between 1933 and 1938 that protected farmers, regulated banking, gave relief to the unemployed, extended labour rights, and fuelled the economy through public works projects (Langer 1948; Hofstadter et al. 1957; Zinn 1995).

Facing political pressures, in 1934 Bennett's government launched its own version of Roosevelt's "New Deal": unemployment insurance, minimum wages, legislation dealing with hours of work, marketing legislation, and laws against price-fixing (Langer 1948; Morton 1997). The reforms came too late, however, to save Bennett's government from defeat in 1935 at the hands of William Lyon Mackenzie King's Liberals.

Under King, as under Bennett, the state's role in building Canada grew stronger. The Canadian Radio Broadcasting Commission became the Canadian Broadcasting Corporation, and government-owned Trans-Canada Air Lines was launched (Morton 1997). The economy, however, continued to languish. After a short period of recovery, both Canada and the United States entered a recession again in 1937. Labour and civil unrest persisted. A strike in 1937 by General Motors' workers in Oshawa, Ontario, over poor wages and union recognition led to violence. Meanwhile, ties to the United States grew, symbolized by the signing of a limited reciprocity agreement in 1935, King's almost fawning relationship with Roosevelt, and the latter's comments at Queen's University in 1938, pledging American support in the event of war (Martin 1982).

CANADA AND THE SECOND WORLD WAR

On September 1, 1939, at the end of what English poet W. H. Auden referred to as a "low, dishonest decade," Germany invaded Poland. Within days, much of the world, except the United States and the Soviet Union, was at war with the fascist powers.

It is impossible to overstate the war's human devastation. Hobsbawm (1995, 43) notes that the "losses are literally incalculable" because many of those killed were civilians and "much of the worst killing took place in regions, or at times, when nobody was in a position to count." Gilbert (1991, 746) estimates the total of civilian and military deaths for China, Japan, the Soviet Union, Germany, Poland, and Yugoslavia, and assorted Jewish populations within Europe to be "in excess of forty-six million," suggesting that the total figure for all countries is at least 50 million deaths (Keegan 1990) and perhaps much more.

More than a million Canadian men and women (out of a total population of only 11 million) joined the army, navy, or air force during the Second World War. In total, 42,042 Canadian military personnel were killed and 53,145 wounded. Canada's financial expenditures rose from $118 million in 1939–1940 to $4.5 billion in 1943–1944 (Stacey and Hillmer 1999, 2552). Public debt rose from $5 billion in 1939 to $18 billion by 1945 (Norrie and Owram 1996, 378), resulting in a net federal public debt of nearly 107 percent of GNP in 1946–1947 (Chorney 1989, 43).

Journalist Blair Fraser (1967, 14) later wrote, "The most that could be said was that World War II had done less damage to the fabric of the nation than World War I did." The lasting effects of the Conscription Crisis of the Second World War were less—no "gaping wound," merely "a bruise." There were "no jobless veterans begging or rioting in the streets," no "counterpart of the Winnipeg General strike," though a strike at Windsor in 1945 proved significant for labour relations. Canada's liberal self-image, however, did take a beating for its treatment of ethnic minorities, notably the expulsion and internment of men, women, and children of Japanese extraction.

Yet there were also positive gains. Dragged from their towns and farms, many Canadians saw their own country for the first time; many also gained a sense of their own and Canada's place internationally. Likewise, skills were developed that paid dividends in the post-war years.

The Canadian economy benefited as a whole. The war dragged Canada and the world out of the Depression and set off Canada's third great period of economic growth, a period that continued into the early 1960s (Aitken 1959). Enormous investments in economic infrastructure had turned Canada into a gigantic armament factory, producing thousands of aircraft, tanks, anti-aircraft guns, tracked vehicles, and machine guns (James 1997). These plants were soon refitted to meet peacetime consumer demand. Likewise, Canada ended the war with a huge and disciplined navy and the world's fourth-largest merchant marine, important to export trade. At the same time, however, Canada's military and economy were more integrated than ever into the American orbit.

CONCLUSION

Within a few short decades of Confederation, the world of 1867 had ceased to exist except in memory and old photographs. The basic contours of Canadian society in the second half of the 20th century were forged by events during this early period in Canada, up to the end of the Second World War; the after-effects continue into the 21st century.

First, the United States clearly arose as successor to the British Empire, both internationally and in its influence upon Canada. In the words of Innis (1956), Canada had gone from colony to nation to colony. In this context, new notions of English-Canadian nationalism arose with consequences seen 20 years later (Chapter 7).

Second, English Canada's culture changed during this period, largely as a result of mass immigration in the first decade of the 20th century, to be resumed after 1945. This period set in motion a further decline of English dominance, the distinctive pattern of ethnicity that marks Canadian provinces, and the enactment of Canada's policy of multiculturalism.

Third, corporate capitalism largely replaced petit bourgeois capitalism. No elements of Canadian society, from family size to social values to urban growth, were left unmarked by this event. By the end of the Second World War, the vast majority of Canadians, including large numbers of women, had become part of the paid labour force.

Fourth, the state gradually came to play a larger role in the lives of Canadians. The crumbling of traditional society and its institutions, accelerated by the wars and the Depression, resulted in the deepening and centralizing of state policies, evidenced particularly in the nascent welfare state. More than ever, state and civil society became inseparable.

Canada, in 1945, seemed a land of promise. On its outskirts, however, lay new perils to Canadian identity, harmony, sovereignty, and peace. The next chapter examines Canada's efforts to wend its way through the post-war world's uncertain waters.

CRITICAL THINKING QUESTIONS

1. Why did Canada not adopt the European model of economic development after 1867?
2. In what ways did corporate capitalism benefit from the major wars and other social disasters of the 20th century?
3. Is unemployment a "natural" phenomenon or is it socially produced?
4. In what sense is it possible to think of the First and Second World Wars as one long war?
5. In what ways did the Second World War bring Canada closer into the American economic, social, and political orbit?

RECOMMENDED READINGS

Brodie, Janine. 1990. *The Political Economy of Canadian Regionalism*. Toronto: Harcourt Brace Jovanovich Canada.
   Brodie's book explores the different meanings of regionalism while also tying it to political development.

Finkel, Alvin. 1989. *The Social Credit Phenomenon in Alberta*. Toronto: University of Toronto Press.
This book provides a social and historical account of the rise of the Social Credit Party in Alberta in the 1930s.

Krahn, H., K. D. Hughes, and G. Lowe. 2020. *Work, Industry, and Canadian Society*. 8th ed. Toronto: Nelson.
This is the definitive text on work and industry in Canada.

Laxer, Gordon. 1989. *Open for Business: The Roots of Foreign Ownership in Canada*. Toronto: Oxford University Press.
Winner of the 1991 John Porter Award for best book published in sociology, this book examines empirically the social and political relationships underlying economic development.

Robin, Martin. 1991. *Shades of Right: Nativist and Fascist Politics in Canada, 1920–1940*. Toronto: University of Toronto Press.
Robin's book details the little-known rise of nativist and fascist movements in Canada during the 1930s.

RELATED WEBSITES

Bank of Canada
www.bankofcanada.ca/about/history/
Amid the Great Depression, the Bank of Canada was created in 1934 by an act of Parliament as a means of stabilizing Canada's monetary system. This is a history of the bank.

Canadian War Museum
www.warmuseum.ca
Located in Ottawa, the Canadian War Museum is Canada's national museum of military history.

Museum for Human Rights
humanrights.ca
Though criticized in some quarters for its selectivity, the museum (located in Winnipeg) provides an important venue for highlighting the important issue of human rights.

CANADIAN SOCIETY ON VIDEO

Between Two Wars. 1987. National Film Board of Canada, 87 minutes, 8 seconds.
Three films cover the period from the end of the First World War to the
onset of the Second World War: *The Good, Bright Days* (1919–1927), from the
Armistice of 1918 to the economic boom of the late 1920s (28 minutes,
55 seconds); *Sunshine and Eclipse* (1927–1934), from the end of the boom to the
onset of the Great Depression (28 minutes, 57 seconds); and *Twilight of an Era*
(1934–1939), the years leading up to war in Europe (29 minutes, 3 seconds).

Bloody Sunday: The Winnipeg General Strike of 1919. 2013. CBC, 43 minutes,
39 seconds.
The story of the Winnipeg General Strike in 1919 is told in the context of
broader events occurring at the time, and the film also discusses its legacy.

Reckoning: The Political Economy of Canada, "Part 1: Riding the Tornado." 1986.
National Film Board of Canada, 57 minutes, 22 seconds.
Do not let its date dissuade you: This video explains the phenomenon of boom
and bust cycles related to staples-driven economies better than any video
produced since.

CHAPTER 7

From Colony to Nation—to Colony?

Bucketwheel, Fort McMurray. Courtesy Trevor W. Harrison.

There are two ways to conquer a country—one is by force of arms; the other is by taking control of its economy.
    —American Secretary of State John Foster Dulles in the 1950s

Living with you is in some ways like sleeping with an elephant. No matter how friendly or temperate the beast, one is affected by every twitch and grunt.
    —Prime Minister Pierre Trudeau to the National Press Club in Washington, 1969

We built a country east and west and north. We built it on an infrastructure that deliberately resisted the continental pressure of the United States. For 120 years we've done it. With one signature of a pen, you've reversed that, thrown us into the

north-south influence of the United States and will reduce us, I am sure, to a colony of the United States, because when the economic levers go the political independence is sure to follow.
   —Liberal Opposition Leader John Turner, 1988 free trade debate

Please be serious.
   —Prime Minister Brian Mulroney's response to Turner

INTRODUCTION

The end of the Second World War stimulated in Canada an unprecedented, albeit uneven, period of economic expansion and social and political transformation. Growing demands for skilled labour were ultimately met by immigration and the increased workforce presence of women. Birth rates soared before resuming, in 1956, a longer trend of decline (Li 1996, 70), and family forms changed. The modern welfare state evolved, underpinning a compromise between labour and capital. And, on April 1, 1949, Newfoundland joined Confederation, though some Newfoundlanders joked that their province annexed Canada.

Meanwhile, abroad, the hot menace of fascism was replaced by the Cold War. Anticommunist hysteria gripped the United States and soon found its way across the border. At the Bretton Woods conference held in 1944, Western countries, led by the United States, designed an economic regime meant to rebuild and stabilize the post-war world and—not incidentally—pave the way for orderly capitalist expansion. Key institutions of this plan included the International Monetary Fund (IMF) and the World Bank (also known as the International Bank for Reconstruction and Development). The General Agreement on Tariffs and Trade (GATT), formed to negotiate tariff reductions and the removal of other trade barriers, joined these institutions in the early 1950s (Lairson and Skidmore 1997). Politically, the international post-war era also saw the creation of the United Nations, successor to the failed pre-war League of Nations.

Consumption flourished throughout the next decade, underpinned by continued strong economic growth. Suburban Canada was born, aided by the ubiquitous presence of automobiles. Television invaded family living rooms and bedrooms, creating a more-or-less mass media culture.

In Canada, the prosperous 1950s gave way in the early 1960s to renewed concerns of American control. In the context of growing American defeats abroad and social discord at home, and in contraposition to Quebec's demands for sovereignty, a new nationalism arose in English-speaking Canada. In the 1970s, English-Canadian nationalism paved the way for a further expansion of state involvement in the economy and society, referred to as "Canadianization." By the 1980s, however, debt and internal divisions hobbled the Canadian state, setting the stage for the adoption of free trade and a new developmental paradigm more generally: neo-liberalism.

This chapter traces the key events and changes that occurred in Canadian society between the end of the Second World War and the fateful Canadian election of 1988.

CANADA AND THE UNITED STATES IN THE COLD WAR ERA

In 1945, Canada's 12 million people seemed enviably blessed. The country had a large public debt but also ample resources much in world demand: steel, timber, wheat, and oil, for example. It also had an established industrial and state infrastructure. Abroad, Canada's chief economic competitors lay in ruins. Reconstruction in Europe and the subsequent Korean conflict (1950–1953) fuelled demand for Canadian resources. Meanwhile, at home, a large reservoir of consumer power was ready to be unleashed (Norrie and Owram 1996). The result was generally high economic growth throughout the 1950s, yet the new prosperity also hid real political, economic, and cultural dangers.

To the north, across the Arctic waters, lay the Soviet Union, which only months before had been a staunch ally. Now it was suddenly the enemy. The period was highlighted by the case of Igor Gouzenko, a Soviet embassy clerk who in September 1945 defected with documents revealing Soviet espionage in Canada (Finkel 2012). As in the United States, anti-communist hysteria soon became a staple of Canadian political and cultural life.

To the south lay a more subtle threat, however. The United States ended the Second World War as the globe's lone superpower, possessor of the world's strongest economy and a large battle-hardened military. The United States alone also had the atomic bomb, a fact quickly interpreted by several American politicians and religious figures as symbolizing America's divinely chosen status among countries (Ungar 1991).

More than ever, in 1945 Canada fell under America's sway. Following a secret meeting between Canada's Prime Minister King and US President Roosevelt at Ogdensburg in 1942, the two countries' militaries became strategically linked. These links became more formal in 1949, when Canada became part of the newly formed North Atlantic Treaty Organization (NATO), an anti-communist self-defence bloc headed by the United States. In the 1960s, Canada also became the United States' northern partner in a continental defence pact, the North American Air Defense Command (NORAD).

Economically, wartime production had stimulated Canada's growth but had also increased links with the United States. After the war, American companies began buying up Canada's redundant war factories and retooling them for civilian use. Much the same occurred regarding Canadian resources. In 1952, American President Harry Truman (1884–1972) released the Paley Report (Roberts 1998). The report, issued as the Cold War heated up, suggested Canada's resource wealth made it a potential economic rival to the United States. The report argued further that the American government should do everything in its power to secure Canadian raw materials, especially uranium, in the service of defending the United States.

America's cultural presence in Canada also grew during and after the war through cinema and radio, and it increased again in the 1950s with the rise of television. The fact that a disproportionate number of Canadians found employment in movies and television, both in front of the camera and behind the scenes as writers, technicians, and directors, did not change the impact. The productions were generically American, meant to be sold first into the United States' larger market, then resold abroad to foreigners, including Canadians, who were increasingly entranced by that empire's technology, power, and wealth.

But the American presence in Canada was also increasingly demographic and social. Construction of the Alaska Highway during the Second World War (see Chapter 10) was completed almost entirely with American labour and investment, and the development of large-scale oil production in Alberta after 1947 resulted in a further influx of American money, personnel, and expertise (House 1978; Richards and Pratt 1979). Calgary quickly became the Houston of the North, and an ethos of rugged individualism slowly replaced the settler traditions of co-operation and community. In the long term, the development of Alberta's oil industry set the stage for interprovincial rivalry and federal-provincial hostility, while furthering a continental approach to development at odds with the tenets of the old National Policy.

Internationally, the immediate post-war era saw the start of the divvying up of the world between state communism, represented by the Soviet Union, and corporate capitalism, represented by the United States. During the early period, the final dismantling of colonialism provided opportunities for both superpowers to expand into new territories, notably the Middle East, Africa, and, especially following the French retreat from Vietnam in the late 1950s, Asia. Both the Soviet Union and the United States took measures to secure their strategic borders and expand their influence throughout this period and after. The Soviet Union invaded Hungary in 1956, Czechoslovakia in 1968, and Afghanistan in 1979. Similarly, the United States, acting on the Monroe Doctrine (Chapter 5), continued a long policy after the 1950s of threatening, destabilizing, and sometimes invading sovereign countries throughout the Americas. Occasionally, as during the Cuban missile crisis in 1963, the boundaries of American and Soviet interests intersected, bringing the world close to nuclear war. For Canada, finding its way in this bipolar world was a task not easily accomplished.

There was one notable similarity, however, between communist and capitalist countries: the continued growth of the state. This was no less true in the case of Canada.

FROM STATE TO "WELFARE STATE"

Far from being a nation-state or even a multinational state, Canada may best be described as a state-nation (see the Introduction). That is, the state often came first, and then set about constructing the institutions of nationhood. In the course of this construction, Canadian society was also changed in particular ways.

The Hudson's Bay Company was a kind of prototype for early Canadian development, with other corporations following (e.g., the Canadian Pacific Railway). From building railways and canals, to building defensive fortifications, to the pacification of the West by the North-West Mounted Police to pave the way for immigrants, the Canadian state (including, to a lesser degree, the provinces) acted as chief architect, administrator, and banker. Until the 1930s, much of this involvement was minimalist and remained tied directly or indirectly to furthering private capital accumulation. Slowly, however, the state's involvement in Canadian society entered broader areas of nation building (such as CBC Radio) and social policy.

To a degree, the state's initially minimalist role in Canadian society in 1867 is understandable, given that Canada was a small, still largely pre-capitalist and pre-industrial country. Thereafter, however, the Canadian state and society expanded together. Five periods mark this expansion, transformation, and later retrenchment (see Rice and Prince 2013). The first period occurred between 1867 and 1914, during Canada's initial industrialization and expansion. The second period occurred between the start of the First World War and the end of the post-war boom, from 1914 to 1929, during which corporate capitalism took hold and Canada urbanized (see Li 1996). The third period, from 1929 to 1945, began with the Depression and ended with the close of the Second World War. The fourth period, with which we are primarily concerned here, began in 1945 and continued roughly to 1973 (Rice and Prince 2013), at which time the structural basis of the post-war welfare state came into question, leading to the fifth stage, marked by the retreat of the state under neo-liberal globalization (see Chapter 8).

Each period saw a gradual shift in government functions in areas of social policy. Rice and Prince (2013) note that responsibility for social welfare changed over time in five important ways. First, responsibility shifted from the private to the state sector. Second, responsibility shifted from lower to higher levels (i.e., from municipalities to the provinces or the federal government). Third, the administration and provision of services became more centralized and under the auspices of professional authorities. Fourth, there was a move in policy approaches from remedial to preventive policies.

A fifth related, but gradual, change saw a shift from particularistic to more universal policies, though this was never extensive and has in recent years been curtailed (Chapter 8). The Pension Act of 1919 was Canada's first universal program in the sense that it was provided to all returning soldiers without resort to a means test. A further move toward standardization and universality occurred with the federal government's introduction of the Old Age Pensions Act in 1927.

In Canada, as elsewhere in the industrialized West, the greatest public expansion into social programs, however, occurred after the Second World War (see Turner 1981; Rice and Prince 2013). Influential in this regard were the ideas of British economist John Maynard Keynes (1883–1946), who argued that the state had a role in ensuring economic and, hence, political stability. With full employment as the goal, countercyclical measures to ward off market fluctuations became a standard feature of post-war government planning. In the context of the Cold War, such interventions also proved useful in showing that capitalism could be responsive not only to market demands but also to human needs.

As in other countries, the war enlarged, centralized, and strengthened the Canadian state, increasing its capacity to act. Important models for action were garnered from President Roosevelt's New Deal administration in the United States (Chapter 6) and from the Beveridge Report produced in Britain. Within Canada, the Royal Commission on Dominion-Provincial Relations (the Rowell-Sirois Commission) in 1940 and the federal government's Advisory Committee on Post-War Reconstruction (the Marsh Report) in 1943 provided similar blueprints for reshaping Canada's system of social security.

Pressures for political change came from a variety of sources, particularly unions, social activists, progressive think tanks (such as the League for Social Reconstruction), and the CCF (see Chapter 6). In 1940, these pressures resulted in King's government bringing in Canada's first Unemployment Insurance Act. This was followed in 1944 with the introduction of the Family Allowances Act, a universal program that (at the time) substantially assisted young families in raising their children and, not unintentionally, also encouraged Canada's birth rate.

These tentative steps at reshaping Canada's social security system were nothing compared with what followed, however. Health care provides a specific example of this process of state expansion.

The post-war period saw the Canadian federal government set up a system of national health grants (1948). This was followed in the 1950s by the Old Age Security Act (1951), the expansion of government assistance under the Unemployment Insurance Act (1956), and the passing of the Hospital Insurance and Diagnostic Act (1957), which introduced federal cost-sharing to pay for provincial hospital insurance. In 1965, the government introduced the compulsory Canada Pension Plan and Quebec Pension Plan. The following year, the Guaranteed Income Supplement Plan and Canada Assistance Plan were created, and medicare (a system of public health insurance) was launched with the passage of the Medical Care Act (see Li 1996).

Together, programs such as health care, education, unemployment insurance, social allowance, and others make up what is often referred to as the Canadian "welfare state." What are welfare states, and what do they do?

The term **welfare state**, sometimes called the Keynesian welfare state (KWS) after John Maynard Keynes, refers to a system of state provision of people's social needs outside private markets. Unlike regular commodities that are bought and sold, social needs are de-commodified and provided as a right of citizenship (Esping-Andersen 1990).

In practical terms, the post-war KWS resulted from a compromise between capital and labour. Labour accepted owners' right to a profit and to make decisions regarding company matters. In return, capital (i.e., owners and managers) accepted labour's right to organize and bargain. The state, meanwhile, provided the legal, political, and often financial resources underpinning this compromise. During the Depression and the Second World War, for example, Canada experienced a series of bitter strikes (Roberts 1998).

In 1944, however, the Canadian government passed legislation granting private-sector workers the right to organize, to bargain collectively, and to strike (Panitch and Swartz 1988). This and similar labour legislation and decisions (such as unemployment insurance and the Rand Formula, which requires the deduction of union dues from paycheques even if an employee in a unionized workplace does not want to belong to the union) introduced a period of relative harmony to labour relations. In effect, the state set the rules for Canada's post-war form of capital accumulation, but in doing so, the state also shaped, more broadly, the contours of Canadian society.

The state's greater role in Canadian society after the Second World War was not restricted, however, to areas of health and social security. The late 1960s also saw the state—both federal and provincial—finance a rapid expansion of post-secondary education (Wanner 1999). Between 1971 and 2001, the percentage of Canadians 15 years of age and older with some post-secondary education rose from 17.1 to 35.6, while the percentage of those with university education climbed from 4.8 to 15.4 (City of Toronto 2014). Today, 46 percent of Canadians in the labour force have completed university, college, or another non-university diploma or certificate. Canada's levels of education place it among the very highest in the world.

The state also became more concerned with issues of nation building, social inequality, and social justice. Especially worth noting in regard to these are the Royal Commission on Bilingualism and Biculturalism, also known as the Dunton-Laurendeau Commission (Chapter 2); the Hawthorn Report (Hawthorn 1966/1967) into the Indigenous peoples of Canada (see Chapter 11); and the Royal Commission on the Status of Women in Canada, also known as the Bird Commission. Echoing the call of US President Lyndon Johnson (1908–1973) for a war on poverty, similar efforts were made in Canada, highlighted by a massive government study (Mincome, 1973–1980) into the efficacy of a guaranteed annual income (see Hum 1983), in which many sociologists participated; in fact, one of this text's authors worked on the study.

How does Canada's welfare state compare with those in other countries? Though neo-liberal policies have placed enormous pressures on all welfare states (see Chapter 8), three broad types of welfare states can still be discerned (Esping-Andersen 1990; Wahl 2011): (1) conservative welfare states, such as Austria, France, Germany, and Italy; (2) social democratic welfare states, such as Sweden, Norway, and Denmark; and (3) liberal democratic welfare states, such as the United States and Australia (see also Olsen 2002). In general, social democratic welfare states have high taxes but also extensive and universal social programs, while liberal democratic welfare states have low taxes, few social programs, and programs that are means tested—that is, not available to all. Conservative welfare states fall somewhere in between, with moderate to high taxes and fairly extensive programs, but ones that often are designed to maintain traditional class and gender hierarchies.

Canada's welfare state is a hybrid. Its primary form is liberal, emphasizing means testing, modest levels of social transfers, a belief in individualism, faith in markets, and protection of private profits (Li 1996; Rice and Prince 2013). At the same time, however, Canada's welfare state has embraced some conservative elements (e.g., an emphasis upon maintaining traditional family and gender roles) and social democratic elements (e.g., social equality and, albeit limited, universality) (see Baker 1996; Finkel 2012; Rice and Prince 2013). As many feminist theorists have noted, none of these existing models adequately deals with the problem of poverty for many women, insofar as their situation results from barriers to full participation in the labour force. That is, while de-commodification is not unimportant to issues of equality, it does not address the real inequalities resulting from a stratified labour market (see Olsen 2002).

By European standards, Canada's welfare state programs historically have not been generous or extensive and appear so only when compared with that of the United States (see Finkel 2012; Olsen 2002); moreover, this generosity has declined over time, as we will explore in the next chapter. Closely tied to the rise and fall of Canada's welfare state during the post-war years were also material, cultural, and ideological changes in the role of women.

SEX AND GENDER IN CANADIAN SOCIETY

As the Second World War began, women at last had formal political power, but little actual political, economic, or social power. The war started the process of changing this.

Economically, while many women remained to work the farms left behind by men fighting overseas, many others were pressed into non-traditional occupations, such as welding in wartime factories or taking on higher administrative roles in the growing public service. Fears that the end of war would result in mass unemployment proved unwarranted. Indeed, the demand for skilled labour increased and women now ably filled this demand.

Of course, some women did return to the home and to unpaid labour to raise families; the post-war baby boom was about to start. But a large number of women, single and otherwise, remained in the workplace—though only casually and often shunted to the service end of the labour market—attracted both by the social and economic opportunities. Moreover, the period after 1945 saw an intensification of consumerism that could be met only by families with one-and-a-half (if not two) salaries.

To a degree, women's increased participation in Canada's labour force mirrored that of women in other countries. In the early 1950s, only roughly a quarter of women ages 25 to 54 participated in the labour market, but that rate increased rapidly beginning in the 1960s. Between 1953 and 1990, women's participation rose from 24 percent to 76 percent and continued to climb to 82 percent in 2014. Today, women make up 47.7 percent of Canada's workforce, though their wages remain below that of men (see Chapter 8) (*Catalyst* 2019). In turn, these changes in the female participation rate set off a series of unintended consequences for fertility rates, family structures, gender roles, family and individual finances, and public services, such as the need for child care. After 1975, for example, dual-income families, rather than single-income families, became the Canadian norm.

Other interrelated factors, besides labour economics and increased consumerism, were changing the situation of women, however. The idea of greater individual freedom took hold in Canadian society, as elsewhere. Likewise, the 1950s saw a loosening of cultural prescriptions for male and female gender roles and behaviours, which were sometimes reflected, and sometimes not, in Hollywood films. Technological advances in the 1960s—notably, the contraceptive pill—further changed sexual behaviours and gender relationships. In turn, and over time, these things also began changing family structures. Divorce rates rose while, despite the incidence of the baby boom, average family size declined.

Underlying the changing status of women in Canada (and elsewhere) was also a transformative change in the dominant ideology brought about by feminism. Though far from a unified ideology, the rise of feminism has been broadly viewed as involving three stages or waves. First-wave feminism, beginning in the mid-19th century, sought—largely with success—to gain for women equal property rights and the right to vote. The 1960s brought second-wave feminism, inspired by writers such as Simone de Beauvoir, Kate Millett, and Germaine Greer. Whereas the attention of first-wave feminists had been upon political institutions, second-wave feminists, many of whom had been involved in student protest movements, concentrated on establishing women's organizations from below, in civil society (Corrigall-Brown 2016). Third-wave feminism, begun in the 1990s, critiqued the position of women belonging to ethnic minorities and the dominance of middle-class white women within the feminist movement (Morrow 1994), as well as opening up discussion of sexuality and queer identities. More recently, Kira Cochrane (2013) has argued that a fourth wave of feminism, defined by the use of technology and social media, has emerged whose issues are centred on media sexism, domestic violence, and rape culture (as seen in the MeToo movement).

As in the previous century, those in dominant positions—but also many in Canada at large, including some women—often opposed feminist demands for greater equality. In the mid-1970s, a backlash against the gains made by women began building, finding its political champions in the 1980s and 1990s in a series of New Right political parties and movements. The complaints of these parties and their supporters, which included women, were not just economic but more often cultural. Women's demands (and gains) upset Canada's patriarchy specifically, but discomforted more broadly what Hiller (1987) termed the **symbolic order**—that is, the set of values, beliefs, and behaviours that lend predictability to our everyday surroundings. (One ironic measure of feminism's success, however, was the growing reluctance of many younger women, having not experienced the earlier struggles and wary of some stereotypes, to self-identify themselves as feminists.) More often than not, after the 1970s, these fears were focused not only on the feminist movement but also on Canada's changing ethnic and racial profile.

LABOUR MARKETS, IMMIGRATION, AND MULTICULTURALISM

Canada's KWS, like that of other countries, was predicated on a prosperous national economy and full employment, since employed workers could pay taxes and would not draw upon social security. At the macro level, Canada's finances to pay for these expanded programs remained particularly dependent, however, upon the export of raw resources. Meanwhile, Canada's economy after the Second World War also underwent a substantial transformation.

Most especially, Canada experienced continued change in its labour market, with jobs in the secondary and service industries coming to dominate. As you will recall (Chapter 6), in 1891, 49 percent of Canada's labour force still worked in primary industry, compared with 20 percent in secondary industry, and 31 percent in the service sector. By 1951, however, 31 percent of Canada's labour force worked in the secondary sector, of which the auto industry was key, while 47 percent were employed in services (Krahn et al. 2020).

The following decades saw further growth in Canada's service industries, while the other sectors declined in relative importance to the economy. At the same time, however, the service sector itself became increasingly polarized between jobs in an upper tier (employing well-paid and well-educated people, often "symbolic analysts" able to manipulate data and other information) and a lower tier (frequently employing the young or very old, often marginalized, at low wages in such things as the fast-food, retail, and hostelry industries). In 2012, the service sector employed 78 percent of working Canadians, followed by the secondary sector and the primary sector (Government of Canada 2013b).

Immediately after the Second World War, Canada experienced a heightened demand for labour, especially skilled labour. Some of this demand was met by returning veterans, whom the government retrained under generous financial terms. Women, as noted, also played a large role in filling demand, especially in the growing service industry (Lowe 1987; Li 1996). Canadian industry's demand for labour after the Second World War was inexhaustible, however. Immigration to Canada had virtually ceased during the Depression and subsequent war years (see table 6.1). Now the Canadian government once more opened the immigration door to let in new workers.

At first glance, Canada's post-war immigration policy seems remarkably similar to that during earlier periods of economic expansion (see Chapter 6), especially in favouring immigrants from Britain and western Europe, but there were important differences. While British immigrants at first remained favoured, there were fewer people from that country who wished to come. Also, throughout the 1950s Canada faced increased competition from Australia and the United States for a shrinking pool of labour, especially skilled labour. Thus, Canadian policy gradually stretched to allow more immigrants from non-traditional source countries, first eastern and southern Europeans (especially those escaping communism), and later people from Asia, Africa, and the Caribbean. Changes in the Immigration Act of 1967, which saw the introduction of a point system, furthered this transition. Before this time, race and ethnicity were explicit criteria for entry. After this time, immigration and labour market needs became more closely aligned. The criteria for entry shifted first to educational qualifications, then (by the 1980s) to financial and class (i.e., business) qualifications (Harrison 1996). Table 7.1 compares the birthplaces of immigrants over three periods, beginning with the period before 1971, up to 2016. In the earliest period, slightly more than 78 percent of immigrants came from Europe, especially northern and southern Europe. Between 1971 and 1990, however, this percentage dropped to just under 30, and during the recent period this area constituted the birthplace for less than 12 percent of immigrants. By contrast, the proportion of immigrants from Asia has grown steadily, and made up nearly 62 percent of immigrants in the period from 1991 to 2016, with especially high numbers of arrivals from southeast and southern Asia. But Canada has also experienced a steady, if less spectacular, growth in immigration from Africa and the rest of the Americas in recent decades.

While immigration after 1945 was influenced by the need for skilled workers, after 1960 broader social factors also became influential. Notable among these was the introduction of the birth control pill in the early 1960s, which led to a rapid decline in Canada's birth rate. By the 1970s, some policy-makers feared that Canada's working-age population might one day be insufficient to pay for the expanding services required for an aging population. Immigration thus became tied not only directly to economic needs but also to the growing fiscal requirements of the welfare state (see Li 1996).

The changes to Canada's immigration policy were particularly noticeable in major cities (Toronto, Montreal, Vancouver), where sizable ethnic communities arose as a result of **chain migration**, the tendency of new immigrants to settle in areas already populated by members of their cultural community. This has meant the continued prominence of British ancestry within the East Coast's population, declining generally as one travels westward; the continuance of French ancestry in Quebec (see Part 1); the prominence of people of middle and eastern European heritage on the Prairies; and the larger presence of people of Asian ancestry on the West Coast. Note, in table 7.2, in figures taken from the 2016 census, the relatively large proportion of all immigrants to the Atlantic provinces who come from Europe (more than 30 percent in each case), especially northern Europe (primarily the United Kingdom). Note, similarly, the large proportion of immigrants to British Columbia who arrive from Asia (more than 60 percent).

But ethnic identification in Canada is also increasingly mixed. While a large proportion of Canadians continue to have either British or French ancestry, in many instances these are not exclusive of other heritages, and this blend of heritages also crosses provincial borders, making it inaccurate to summarily categorize any province as, for example, "British."

In 1969, Canada adopted the policy of official bilingualism in response to the rise of Quebec nationalism (Chapter 2). Many people accepted (albeit some grudgingly) the need for two official languages to bind the country together and address the demands of Quebec's sizable francophone population. The notion of two official cultures, however,

Table 7.1: Immigrant Population by Place of Birth and Period of Immigration (total and percentage)[1]

	Number	%	Pre-1971	%	1971–1990	%	1991–2010	%	2011–2016	%
Total	6,775,765	100	1,261,060	100	1,820,660	100	3,694,040	100	1,212,075	100
In Canada	2,220	–	520	–	780	–	915	–	75	–
Outside Canada	6,773,550	100	1,260,540	100	1,819,885	100	3,693,120	100	1,211,995	100
Americas	1,058,010	15.6	132,365	10.5	399,030	21.9	526,625	14.3	152,515	12.6
North America	263,760	3.9	63,640	5.0	80,120	4.4	111,000	2.8	33,070	2.7
Central America	151,630	2.2	3,925	0.3	54,440	3.0	93,260	2.5	27,345	2.3
Caribbean and Bermuda	351,430	5.2	47,530	3.8	152,945	8.4	150,960	4.1	49,510	4.1
South America	291,090	4.3	17,230	1.4	102,520	5.6	171,340	4.6	42,585	3.5
Europe	2,127,785	31.4	987,855	78.3	535,730	29.4	604,200	16.4	140,035	11.6
Western Europe	397,440	5.9	221,945	17.6	72,135	4.0	103,350	2.8	35,670	2.9
Eastern Europe	501,620	7.4	97,390	7.7	116,315	6.4	287,915	7.8	53,005	4.4
Northern Europe	602,120	8.9	318,680	25.3	185,120	10.2	98,310	2.7	31,880	2.6
Southern Europe	626,570	9.2	349,815	27.7	162,150	8.9	114,605	3.1	19,475	1.6

Africa	492,025	7.3	24,530	1.9	107,605	5.9	359,880	9.7	162,795	13.4
Western Africa	76,070	1.1	725	—	10,710	0.6	64,635	1.7	37,515	3.1
Eastern Africa	154,590	2.3	3,605	0.3	55,580	3.1	95,410	2.6	38,770	3.2
Northern Africa	186,745	2.8	15,560	1.2	24,905	1.4	146,280	4.0	59,480	4.9
Central Africa	32,640	0.5	460	—	2,975	0.2	29,205	0.8	20,200	1.7
Southern Africa	41,955	0.6	4,180	0.3	13,430	0.7	24,350	0.7	6,825	0.6
Asia	3,041,100	44.9	106,795	8.5	757,180	41.6	2,177,135	58.9	748,700	61.8
West Central Asia and the Middle East	455,940	6.7	14,805	1.2	99,710	5.5	341,425	9.2	149,630	12.3
Eastern Asia	962,560	14.2	47,395	3.8	225,595	12.4	689,595	18.7	165,685	13.7
Southeast Asia	729,800	10.8	14,965	1.2	257,740	14.2	457,095	12.4	210,345	17.4
Southern Asia	892,760	13.2	29,620	2.3	174,130	9.6	689,010	18.7	223,040	18.4
Oceania	54,530	0.8	8,915	0.7	20,335	1.1	25,285	0.7	7,955	0.7
Other²	700	—	170	—	120	—	350	—	—	—

Notes: 1. Differences within regional totals and between regional totals and Canadian totals due to rounding. 2. Includes all populations not identified elsewhere (i.e., by region).

Sources: Adapted from Statistics Canada. 2011d. Data Table 99-010-X2011026: "Citizenship (5), Place of Birth (236), Immigrant Status and Period of Immigration (11), Age Groups (10) and Sex (3) for the Population in Private Households of Canada, Provinces, Territories, Census Metropolitan Areas and Census Agglomerations." 2011 National Household Survey; and Statistics Canada. 2016b. Data Table 98-400-X2016185: "Immigrant Status and Period of Immigration (11), Place of Birth, Age and Sex for the Population of Private Households of Canada, Provinces, and Territories, Census Divisions and Census Subdivisions, 2016 Census—25% Sample Data."

Table 7.2: Canadian Immigrant Population, by Place of Birth and Province/Territory of Residence, 2016 (in percentages)

Place of Birth	Canada	NL	PE	NS	NB	QC	ON	MB	SK	AB	BC	YT	NT	NU
Americas	15.6	19.7	19.8	20.1	30.1	22.7	16.0	15.1	10.5	13.2	9.7	17.1	13.2	18.4
North America	4.1	13.7	14.7	14.0	24.1	3.1	3.5	3.9	5.1	4.5	5.2	12.9	6.0	8.3
Central America	2.3	1.2	1.2	1.3	1.9	3.5	1.9	4.8	2.1	3.4	1.7	1.6	2.1	1.5
Caribbean and Bermuda	4.9	2.3	2.2	3.2	2.4	9.6	6.0	2.0	1.4	1.9	0.8	1.0	3.5	6.3
South America	4.2	2.6	1.8	1.7	1.7	6.4	4.7	4.4	1.8	3.4	1.9	1.5	1.7	1.9
Europe	27.1	30.3	31.7	35.8	30.6	29.2	28.9	23.9	20.8	22.2	24.0	37.0	21.5	21.4
Western Europe	5.6	6.2	10.0	9.7	11.4	11.8	3.8	6.4	4.2	4.9	5.3	18.0	6.5	4.9
Eastern Europe	6.6	3.4	3.2	3.6	4.2	7.0	7.3	7.4	6.4	6.1	4.6	4.3	2.8	4.4
Northern Europe	7.3	17.4	15.3	19.1	12.8	1.5	7.5	5.5	7.3	7.9	10.6	12.7	9.6	10.2
Southern Europe	7.7	3.3	3.2	3.4	2.2	8.9	10.2	4.7	3.0	3.3	3.5	2.0	2.6	2.4
Africa	8.4	11.6	4.4	6.1	8.2	21.6	5.9	8.2	9.3	10.3	3.3	4.2	12.9	19.4
Western Africa	1.5	3.6	1.6	1.4	2.5	3.1	1.2	2.6	2.6	2.3	0.3	0.5	2.4	6.3
Eastern Africa	2.5	3.1	0.6	1.7	1.7	2.1	2.4	3.4	3.3	4.9	1.4	1.6	6.1	8.7
Northern Africa	3.0	3.2	1.3	1.9	2.3	13.6	1.4	1.0	1.2	1.5	0.4	0.4	2.4	1.0

Central Africa	0.7	0.6	0.3	0.3	1.4	2.7	0.4	0.7	0.6	0.6	0.1	—	—	2.0
Southern Africa	0.6	1.0	0.6	0.8	0.4	0.1	0.5	0.5	1.6	1.0	1.0	1.7	2.0	1.5
Asia	48.0	37.5	43.6	37.1	30.3	26.3	48.8	52.4	58.7	53.0	60.4	39.2	51.1	38.8
West Central Asia and the Middle East	7.7	7.3	7.4	12.2	8.3	9.9	8.7	4.2	5.0	6.0	5.0	1.9	3.2	4.4
Eastern Asia	15.0	10.0	23.6	11.6	11.5	6.1	14.1	7.9	10.0	11.9	29.2	7.6	7.8	4.4
Southeast Asia	11.3	9.3	6.6	5.5	6.6	5.9	9.1	28.3	26.4	19.7	12.6	24.0	30.1	21.4
Southern Asia	14.0	11.0	5.9	7.8	3.8	4.4	17.0	12.0	17.3	15.3	13.6	5.7	10.0	9.7
Oceania	0.9	1.0	0.5	0.9	0.8	0.2	3.7	0.3	0.8	1.3	2.6	2.6	1.2	1.0
Other[1]	—	—	—	—	—	—	—	—	—	—	—	—	—	—

Note: 1. Includes all populations not identified elsewhere (i.e., by region).

Source: Adapted from Statistics Canada. 2016b. Data Table 98-400-X2016185: "Immigrant Status and Period of Immigration (11), Place of Birth (272), Age (7A) and Sex (3) for the Population in Private Households of Canada, Provinces and Territories, Census Divisions and Census Subdivisions, 2016 Census—25% Sample Data."

was received more skeptically by Canadians, particularly visible minorities and Indigenous peoples. The result was Canada's adoption two years later of a policy of **multiculturalism**, whereby no culture is officially privileged over another.

Multiculturalism today is an official mainstay of Canadian identity. Supporters of the policy contend that Canada is leading the way in becoming a postmodern society and that the country's ability to manage cultural differences adds to its strength, economically, culturally, and politically (Adams 2007). The policy also has critics, however. In the eyes of some, multiculturalism merely hides the continuing reality of an ethnic hierarchy in Canada. Others see it as an expensive and destructive policy that encourages people to retain past identities and live in ethnic quarters of Canadian cities rather than forge together a common sense of being Canadian (Bissoondath 1994). It may also undermine universalist social policies as groups call for particularistic programs to meet their unique needs (Rice and Prince 2013).

The impact of the "new ethnics" upon Canadian identity was not particularly evident in the 1960s. Nonetheless, a new sense of identity was already emerging in English-speaking Canada.

THE RISE OF ENGLISH-CANADIAN NATIONALISM

After the Second World War, English-speaking Canada remained very British. It was not until the Canadian Citizenship Act of 1946, for example, that "Canadian citizens" existed. Before that time, Canadians were British subjects, and many—at least those outside Quebec—were quite content to hold British passports.

Into the mid-1960s, Canadian culture outside of Quebec also remained decidedly British. At a time when there were only two television channels (CBC and CTV), a large number of British programs competed with American shows to fill the airwaves. Comedy shows such as *Monty Python's Flying Circus* and English adventure shows such as *Danger Man* and *The Avengers* were standard viewing for many English-speaking Canadians growing up.

Canada's British ties were weakening, however. Economically, bilateral trade between Canada and Britain declined sharply after the Second World War, replaced by trade with the United States (Marchildon 1995; Norrie and Owram 1996). Politically, Canada's ties to the throne were also eroding. In 1951, for example, Canada's Supreme Court replaced Britain's Privy Council as Canada's last court of appeal, setting the stage for Canada's later dropping of other British symbols.

Britain's declining role in Canadian life reflected not only cultural and ethnic changes, brought about by immigration, but also a growing pride and confidence among Canadians themselves. Success in the war caused English-Canadians as a whole to become less parochial and to slough off some of their colonial anxieties. Many wanted Canada to take a greater and more independent role among the victorious states. Thus, after 1945 Canada proudly gained membership in the United Nations, NATO, and other international organizations. Likewise, it participated in the Korean conflict (1950–1953) and took a leading role in settling the 1956 Suez conflict, for which Lester Pearson (prior to becoming prime minister) won the Nobel Peace Prize. But each of these actions also reflected a growing policy convergence with the United States. Thus, as Canada drew away from Britain's embrace, it also found itself increasingly under America's blanket.

In short, by the late 1950s, English-speaking Canada was seeking a new vision of itself, an identity. The result was the rise of English-Canadian nationalism, often referred to as Canadianization. English-Canadian nationalism was not supported by all elements. Business generally disliked or feared nationalism in any form. Francophones viewed English-Canadian nationalism as merely a new variation on assimilation. Regional elements often feared federal intrusions into their areas of jurisdiction (Finkel 2012). Nonetheless, a sizable portion of English Canada's population favoured the heightened nationalism of the time.

The new nationalism was not of one type, however. Some forms expressed nostalgia over the loss of things British (especially the replacement of the Union Jack by the Maple Leaf flag in 1965). Some variations were defensive, a response to the rise of Quebec nationalism or to the increased influence of the United States. Others were frankly imperialist, as when Prime Minister John Diefenbaker invoked his vision of the Canadian North in the 1958 election (see Chapter 10). The new nationalism that gripped English-speaking Canada came in different forms, manifesting itself politically, culturally, and economically.

Politically, English-Canadian nationalism can be divided into formal and popular politics. At the formal level, after 1950, Canadian prime ministers found themselves in a series of delicate skirmishes with their American counterparts. Until Roosevelt, most American presidents had ignored Canada, often viewing it as an extension of the United States, a place of eccentric country cousins. In the context of the Cold War, however, the United States demanded particular obedience from its allies, beginning with Canada. Thus, the Diefenbaker administration's (1957–1963) efforts at an independent defence policy, not to mention encouraging trade with Fidel Castro's Cuba and Communist China, aroused particular antagonism. President John F. Kennedy (1917–1963) had called Prime Minister Diefenbaker an "SOB" and gave encouragement and strategic support to successful Liberal efforts to unseat Diefenbaker in the 1963 Canadian election. Relations between Prime Minister Pearson and President Johnson (following John F. Kennedy's assassination) proved no better, however. Quickly, Canada found itself at odds with the United States over the war in Vietnam and trade policy, especially the 1965 Auto Pact (see Martin 1982; Norrie and Owram 1996). Pearson, like Diefenbaker before and Trudeau after, learned the truth of the axiom that states do not have friends, they have interests. Increasingly, the interests of Canada and the United States were diverging.

English-Canadian nationalism manifested itself politically at the popular level. In keeping with the times internationally, many of these expressions were anti-American and directed at American imperialism in Vietnam and elsewhere, themes often picked up on Canadian campuses (see box 7.1). But there was also widespread revulsion directed at "the

Box 7.1: Canadianization and English Canadian Sociology

Canadianization at large found its mirror in English Canada's universities and colleges beginning in the late 1960s. The immediate catalyst for a nationalist response was the hiring at Canadian institutions of higher learning of a large number of foreign-trained (often American-born) academics to meet the demands of a growing student population. Nationalists sought to bring a Canadian perspective to research and teaching in the academy. Among those involved in the Canadianization movement were a number of sociologists, students, and the Canadian Sociology and Anthropology Association.

Canadianization benefited sociology in at least two ways. First, it led to an increase in Canadian curricula and content being taught. A survey of five disciplines (French, history, political science, economics, and sociology and anthropology) at six universities (Dalhousie, Montreal, Carleton, Alberta, Simon Fraser, and UBC) shows that the number of undergraduate full-time course equivalents with Canadian content increased by 108 percent between 1970–1971 and 1980–1981, with a particularly large increase in sociology and anthropology (Steele and Mathews 2006, 494–495).

Second, Canadianization also impacted the education of sociologists within Canada. In 1970, only 17.5 percent of full-time sociologists in Canada had received their highest degree in Canada, compared with 63.4 percent who received their degree in the United States. By 1980, these percentages had changed to 29.2 percent and 53.2 percent, respectively. In 2005, 52.3 percent of full-time Canadian sociologists had received their highest degree in Canada, while 31 percent had received their highest degree in the United States (Gingras and Warren 2006, 513).

These early successes aside, the turn of the 21st century saw concerns raised by several senior scholars over the state of Canadian sociology. Their concerns centred on declining membership in the Canadian Sociological Association and low status in universities and society in general. But renewed concern also arose regarding fears that Canadian sociology, in the context of globalization, was "becoming diluted into just another participant in the global [read: American and Eurocentric] discipline" (McLaughlin 2019).

At the same time, sociology in Canada continues to change and grow. The "two solitudes" of francophone and anglophone sociology still exist (see Chapter 4) but have lessened. And new practices of a revived feminist scholarship and attention to Indigenous issues, partly through the creation of research clusters within the discipline, suggest that any notion of sociology's demise are greatly exaggerated.

Sources: Steele, James, and Robin Mathews. 2006. "Canadianization Revisited: A Comment on Cormier's 'The Canadianization Movement in Context.'" *Canadian Journal of Sociology* 31(4): 491–508; Gingras, Yves, and Jean-Philippe Warren. 2006. "A British Connection: A Quantitative Analysis of the Changing Relations between American, British, and Canadian Sociologists." *Canadian Journal of Sociology* 31(4): 509–522; McLaughlin, Neil. 2019. "The 'Sociology Wars' in Canada." *Global Dialogue* 9(3).

American way of life" in general, as reflected nightly on American television. Race riots and the killings of civil rights workers and politicians provided an ample "negative model" for Canadians and for between 70,000 and 125,000 American draft dodgers and deserters (Finkel 2012, 154; Rodgers 2014) who wanted to build a better society in North America.

English-Canadian nationalism was also cultural. The Massey Commission outlined the need for Canada to develop its own cultural institutions and distinctly Canadian voice (Stewart and Kallmann 2019). The commission's report in 1951 focused on high culture and drew little initial response, official or otherwise (see Morton 1997). Eventually, however, such institutions as the Canada Council for the Arts, the National Film Board of Canada, and Telefilm Canada were formed to encourage Canadian culture. Whether these institutions were responsible for the spread of cultural nationalism or not is debatable. Nonetheless, except in the area of television and film, which remained largely overwhelmed by American capital and technology, a distinctly Canadian cultural industry slowly emerged in English Canada. In the area of literature, the 1950s and 1960s saw the rise to prominence of a host of writers, including Pierre Berton, Leonard Cohen, Robertson Davies, Timothy Findley, and Margaret Laurence. (A few intellectuals, notably Marshall McLuhan, also became international cultural icons.) Other writers, many of them women (such as Margaret Atwood, Alice Munro, and Carol Shields), followed in the 1970s, joined more recently by Yann Martel, Lisa Moore, Michael Ondaatje, and Rohinton Mistry, pointing also to Canada's increasingly multicultural nature.

There had long been a Canadian popular music scene, stretching from jazz to pop to country. Except at the local and regional level, however, much of it was derivative of American music. Canada's climb aboard the rock 'n' roll bandwagon of the 1950s continued this trend. But the late 1960s saw Canadian music also take a nationalistic turn, assisted by the creation of the Canadian Radio and Television Commission, which legislated Canadian content. Groups such as The Band (headed by Robbie Robertson) became internationally known, as did individual artists such as Neil Young and Joni Mitchell. More importantly, each also remained distinctively Canadian, as often evidenced in their lyrics, setting the stage for bands such as The Tragically Hip in the 1990s and Arcade Fire later on. In keeping with the times, the music of this period sometimes took on an overtly political, often anti-American tenor, as in the words to The Guess Who's "American Woman" and Gordon Lightfoot's "Black Day in July" (about the Detroit riots), continued today in the music, lyrics, and activism of the Portage la Prairie band Propagandhi.

ECONOMIC NATIONALISM, OR THE USES OF GOOD THEORY

Among the sub-genres of nationalism, however, economic nationalism was arguably the most influential. After years of growth, in the late 1950s the Canadian economy entered a recession (Norrie and Owram 1996). In this context, a number of influential Canadians—led by political economist Melville Watkins (1963), conservative philosopher

George Grant (2005), and Liberal finance minister Walter Gordon (1966)—asked (each in his own way) why Canada continued to be "the world's richest underdeveloped country" (Levitt 1970, 25). In particular, many noted that Canada's declining economic performance coincided with increased foreign, mainly American, control of the economy. Were the two events related? For economic nationalists, the answer was a definite *yes*.

Keynes once remarked that there is nothing so practical as a good theory. But good theory arises out of the need to understand real issues. The economic nationalism of the 1960s arose out of genuine concerns over Canada's future; in turn, it provided impetus for a renaissance of investigation into the roots of Canada's economic, political, and social development (see Laxer 1991), a renaissance that ultimately had practical impacts upon Canadian policy.

At least initially, these studies took their inspiration from the work of the Canadian economic historian Harold Innis (1894–1952). Innis's **staples theory** argued that Canada's founding as a hinterland producer of raw exports for world markets curtailed normal economic and political development, resulting in it being prone to being caught in a staples trap. The nature of the trap was that, while staple products (such as cod, furs, trees, and wheat) were often seductively profitable in the short term, their prices were inherently unstable and subject to boom and bust. In Innis's view, an economy built upon raw resources alone did not develop the forward and backward linkages and social structure characteristic of a fully developed economy (see Innis 1995).

Staples theory, based on the historical relationship between the metropolis and the hinterland, bears some relationship to **dependency theory**, which emphasizes the unequal relationship between the core and periphery in the world capitalist system set in motion by early colonialism (see Frank 1975), though the latter also uses a Marxian class analysis. Dependency theory did not fit the Canadian situation well, however. After all, by the 1960s, many parts of Canada were heavily industrialized while residing uneasily with pockets of underdevelopment. Moreover, the benefits of industrialization were—as now—unevenly distributed by gender, race, ethnicity, and region (see Panitch 1977; Laxer 1991; Clement 1997). Hence, the years following the late 1960s saw a "new" tradition of political economy that took analyses of Canadian dependency in different explanatory directions.

Some scholars used **elite theory** to explain Canada's development. Naylor (1975), for example, went back in history to argue that merchants who were concentrated in export industries, especially the fur trade, had conspired against industrial capitalists to hinder economic development (the merchants against industry thesis). Clement (1975), meanwhile, argued that a troika of elites continued to dominate the Canadian economy: a parasite elite (foreign owners and managers), an indigenous elite (Canadian owners and managers), and a comprador elite (Canadians managing companies in Canada for foreign firms).

Others, however, used **class theory** to explain the trajectory of Canadian development. Panitch (1981), for example, argued that, ironically, the relative power of Canada's proletariat during the country's initial stage of industrialization development (1870–1910) hindered capitalism's accumulation of surplus. By contrast, Laxer (1989) argued that Canada had been a successful late industrializing country but had fallen back into dependency due to the political weakness of its agrarian class during this period, which had prevented Canada from adopting the kind of policies (low taxes, easy credit, the targeted construction of railways, and a robust defence policy) that worked successfully in similar countries, notably Sweden.

Many of these studies focused particularly on the impact of the National Policy in Canada's economic development. You will recall that the National Policy's use of tariffs was meant to encourage manufacturing within Canada (Chapter 6). As intended, a number of American branch plants moved to Canada in the early part of the 20th century to feed the Canadian market and also to gain preferential entry at that time into other Commonwealth countries, especially Britain. In the short term, the economy boomed. Employment in new industries soared, out-migration decreased, and banks made profits. The long-term impacts, however, were less rosy.

Economic nationalists pointed out several problems that accompanied these branch plants (Laxer 1991). First, company profits were unavailable for further domestic investment. Finkel (2012) notes that in the 1960s, dividends to American owners exceeded American investment in Canada. American profits, alternatively, were often used to buy up more Canadian companies. Second, branch plants tended to obtain materials and personnel in the home country. Thus, Canada lost the backward and forward linkages, or "multiplier effects," necessary to develop the economy fully. Third, the branch plants were not sources of innovation. Statistics showed Canadian companies invested little in research and development. Instead, Canadian branch plants produced copies of American (or other foreign) products for the local market, a pattern known as the miniature replica effect (Finkel 2012, 163; Levitt 1970).

Ultimately, economic nationalists also saw the issue in broader political terms. As quoted in the beginning of the chapter, American Secretary of State John Foster Dulles (1888–1959) had once opined that there are two ways to conquer a country: by force of arms or by taking over its economy (Laxer 1995). The economic nationalists took Dulles at his word, arguing that no country could remain politically sovereign for long with an economy controlled by a foreign power. But adopting a national strategy faced a seemingly obdurate problem: the fact that national solutions often gave rise to conflicts that pitted provincial interests against national ones, and this even applied to identities (Harrison and Krahn unpublished; see also Chapter 6's discussion of regionalism).

THE NEW WEST

No region of Canada changed more than the West after 1945. The changes were particularly apparent in Alberta and British Columbia, which experienced enormous population growth and industrialization. But all the western provinces changed in important ways, influencing Canada as they did.

In 1941, the populations of the four western provinces were roughly equivalent, ranging from a low of 730,000 in Manitoba to a high of 896,000 in Saskatchewan. By 1971, however, a shift westward was already evident. British Columbia's population had tripled to 2.2 million and Alberta's population had doubled to 1.6 million, both surpassing Manitoba (under one million) and Saskatchewan (932,000). Looking ahead 40 more years, the population changes in the most westerly provinces become even more startling. As of 2016, nearly 4.6 million people reside in British Columbia and nearly 4.1 million in Alberta. By contrast, Manitoba's population has stabilized at around 1.3 million, while Saskatchewan's population, even in the midst of growing prosperity, remains at a little over one million (see table 0.1). Today, about 32 percent of Canadians live in the four western provinces.

These population changes do not tell the whole story. Like the rest of the country, after the war western Canada experienced rapid urbanization (Driedger 1991; see also Chapter 6). This occurred even in Manitoba and Saskatchewan. Winnipeg, for example, grew from 412,000 people in 1956 to 667,000 in 1996. During the same period, Regina's population went from nearly 90,000 to 193,000, while Saskatoon's population increased from 73,000 to 219,000. The greatest urban growth, however, occurred in British Columbia and Alberta. Between 1956 and 1996, Vancouver's population nearly tripled, from 665,000 to more than 1.8 million people. Victoria's population also increased rapidly, from 134,000 to 303,000. In Alberta during this period, Edmonton's population expanded from nearly 255,000 to 862,000, while Calgary's population climbed from 201,000 to nearly 822,000. These figures alone do not indicate the full extent of the growth, however, for many smaller cities and suburbs of larger cities were also spawned during this period. In consequence, the urban centres within areas such as the Vancouver mainland and that between Edmonton and Calgary became largely contiguous.

Today, much of Canada's population (both east and west) is urbanized, with 35 **census metropolitan areas** (CMAs). (A CMA is an area consisting of one or more adjacent municipalities situated around an urban core of at least 100,000 people.) As shown in table 7.3, nine of these 35 CMAs are now located west of Ontario; indeed, the west has three of

Table 7.3: Population of Canada's 33 Census Metropolitan Areas (in Thousands) 2001, 2011, and 2016, and Percentage Change, 2011–2016

	2001	2011	2016	Percentage Increase (2011–2016)[2]
Toronto	4,682.9	5,583.1	5,928.0	6.2
Montreal[1]	3,451.0	3,934.1	4,099.0	4.2
Vancouver	1,987.0	2,313.2	2,463.4	6.5
Calgary[1]	951.5	1,214.8	1,392.6	14.6
Ottawa–Gatineau[1]	1,067.8	1,254.9	1,323.8	5.5
Edmonton	937.8	1,159.9	1,321.4	13.9

	2001	2011	2016	Percentage Increase (2011–2016)[2]
Quebec City[1]	686.6	767.3	800.3	4.3
Winnipeg[1]	676.6	730.0	778.5	6.6
Hamilton	662.4	721.1	747.5	3.7
Kitchener–Cambridge–Waterloo	414.3	496.1	523.972	5.5
London[1]	435.6	474.8	494.1	4.1
Halifax	359.2	390.1	403.1	3.3
St. Catharines–Niagara	377.0	392.2	406.1	3.5
Oshawa	296.3	356.2	379.8	6.6
Victoria	311.9	344.6	367.8	6.7
Windsor	307.9	319.2	329.1	3.1
Saskatoon	225.9	262.2	295.1	12.5
Regina	192.8	211.5	236.5	11.8
Sherbrooke[1]	176.0	202.3	212.1	4.9
St. John's	172.9	197.0	206.0	4.6
Barrie	148.5	187.0	197.1	5.4
Kelowna	147.7	179.8	194.9	8.4
Abbotsford–Mission	147.4	170.2	180.5	6.1
Kingston	146.8	159.6	161.2	1.0
Greater Sudbury/Grand Sudbury	155.6	163.1	164.7	1.0
Saguenay	154.9	158.7	161.0	1.5
Trois-Rivières	137.5	151.8	156.0	2.8
Guelph	117.3	141.1	152.0	7.7
Moncton[1]	118.7	139.3	144.8	4.0
Brantford[1]	118.1	135.5	134.2	–1.0
Saint John	122.7	129.1	126.2	–2.2
Thunder Bay	122.0	121.6	121.6	0.0
Peterborough[1]	110.9	119.0	121.7	2.3
Lethbridge	n/a	106.0	117.4	10.8
Belleville	n/a	101.7	103.5	1.8

Notes: 1. Figures for 2001 adjusted because of boundary change. 2. Percentage change 2001–2016 calculated by authors.

Sources: Adjusted figures for 2001 taken from Statistics Canada. 2007a. *Canada Year Book 2007.* Ottawa: Statistics Canada. Data for 2011 and 2016 taken from Statistics Canada. 2016c. "Focus on Geography Series." 2016 Census.

the six largest areas—Vancouver, Calgary, and Edmonton—with Calgary having the fastest population growth rate between 2011 and 2016 (14.6 percent), followed by Edmonton (13.9 percent), while the lowest rates of population growth for the 35 CMAs occurred in Ontario and Quebec. Altogether, these 35 CMAs represent 71 percent of Canada's population. In short, despite mythology, Canada is a predominantly urban society.

Western Canada's population changed in other ways. Settled by massive immigration in the early 20th century, the West had always been culturally, religiously, and ethnically diverse, but this diversity was often suppressed in the name of Anglo-conformity (Chapter 6). After the 1970s, however, as multiculturalism became Canadian government policy, the West allowed its diversity to emerge more fully (see prior discussion of multiculturalism).

Underlying these population shifts were fundamental economic changes. The Prairie region was originally opened up for agricultural development (Chapter 6). As noted, changes in the farm economy throughout the 20th century resulted in a reduction in Canada's agricultural labour force overall. In 1951, 15.6 percent of Canada's workforce as a whole was employed in agriculture. By 1971, this had fallen to 5.6 percent. By 1991, the proportion of the Canadian workforce employed in agriculture had dropped to 3.6 percent (Li 1996, 45) and is less than 2 percent today. This drop has been less pronounced, though unevenly, on the Prairies, where today 3.7 percent of the labour force in Manitoba, 6.9 percent in Saskatchewan, and 2.1 percent in Alberta hold jobs in agriculture (Statistics Canada 2019d). Yet, while it remains a big part of the Prairie economy and continues to reflect (albeit nostalgically) the cultural history of the West, agriculture—like ranching—is largely a corporate exercise. Economies of scale and the high costs of farm technology have put the farm beyond the reach of families.

The decades after 1945 saw a steady westward shift of population as new industries emerged. Though each province developed somewhat distinctly, economic growth, large or small, in all the western provinces shared certain characteristics. First, it was invariably government-led. Local capital was often scarce, while private, exogenous capital was reluctant to invest in what often seemed tenuous opportunities for profit. Thus, eastern and (more often) foreign capital and expertise were welcomed in under favourable conditions set by the provincial governments. The 1970s, in particular, saw every western government, of every political stripe, engage in what was termed **province building**: an activist approach to economic development on the part of provincial governments.

Second, economic growth in all the western provinces focused on megaprojects, especially in the North (see Chapter 10). Hydroelectricity in Manitoba, potash and uranium in Saskatchewan, the tar sands in Alberta, and hydroelectricity and forestry in British Columbia became the hallmarks of economic development in the West. In classically liberal and typically Canadian fashion, the belief was that these projects would create the capital necessary to diversify the economy and break the cycle of boom and bust so common in the West. Often, however, it meant putting the provinces' eggs in one or two baskets. Too frequently, when the world price of the particular commodity collapsed, individuals and governments, who had backstopped the projects with huge amounts of public capital, were left holding the empty bag. People either sat out the downturn or moved on. No region in Canada better fit Harold Innis's description of a "staples trap" than did the West (Watkins 1963; Drache 1995).

Third, and finally, economic development in the West invariably involved the exploitation of each province's northern region. Flin Flon in Manitoba, Uranium City in Saskatchewan, and Fort McMurray in Alberta are but a few examples. The result sometimes was the building of temporary resource towns that disappeared in time (such as, again, Uranium City). But the impacts of the changes were always permanent, especially for the Indigenous peoples living in those areas. In Canada, as elsewhere around the world, the forces of modernity and capitalism displaced the old ways of living (see Chapter 10).

Population shifts and economic growth brought other political and social changes. In the mid-1960s, Porter (1965) noted that Canada's elite were largely British, represented "old money," were highly interrelated through business, political, school, and even marital ties, and were located primarily in central Canada. His findings were generally validated a few years later by Clement (1975), who traced the corporate interlocks underlying the power of this insular elite.

The emergent power of the new West challenged this elite structure (Richards and Pratt 1979). Throughout the West, but particularly in Alberta, a new regional elite arose, demanding a say in how Confederation should be run. The shift of Sun Life from Montreal to Calgary in the 1970s, followed by the establishment of other financial institutions and corporate head offices in that city, was not merely symbolic. It represented a genuine shift in power—especially corporate power—within Canada, led by Calgary's oil and gas industry (see Chapter 8).

The changes in Canada's West did not come without problems. The increased power of the provinces led to provincial identification replacing regional identification (Gibbins 1979; see also Chapter 8). In some communities, cultural and ethnic diversity created tensions. Expansion into the North disrupted Indigenous communities in particular and created social problems (see Chapter 10). At the same time, economic development did not always lead to security. From the 1970s on, the West's economy continued to experience waves of boom and bust.

Finally, the changes also heightened traditional tensions between western Canada and the other provinces and the federal government over the structure of Confederation. By the 1970s, many in the West, like others in the past, were coming to view the Canadian government as alien and unsympathetic to their views. They resented the "imposition," as they saw it, of policies such as bilingualism and metrification. They believed that Canadian institutions had an eastern bias, and that "national" policies generally meant central Canadian policies—a belief that gained more traction every time the region experienced an economic bust. Thus, the late 1970s and early 1980s saw the rise throughout western Canada, but especially in Alberta, of a number of western separatist movements (Pratt and Stevenson 1981). Later, in 1987, regional alienation combined with right-wing populism to found first the Reform Party (Harrison 1995) and later the Canadian Alliance Party (Harrison 2002), on the way to refashioning the federal Conservative Party in the early 2000s. In short, the re-emergence of regional alienation, as much a staple of western Canada as wheat, became a central feature of Canadian society in the years following the 1970s, and it re-emerged in every decade, including after the 2019 federal election, when voters in Alberta and Saskatchewan overwhelmingly elected Conservative MPs to a minority Liberal parliament (see appendices 1 and 2).

THE ECONOMIC CRISIS OF THE CANADIAN STATE

Taken as a whole, the period from 1945 until the 1990s was a time of spectacular economic growth for Canada. Canada's gross domestic product (GDP) in 1947, for example, was $91.7 billion (constant dollars). By 1992, GDP had grown to $560 billion. Even accounting for the impact of population growth on GDP, the average Canadian in 1992 was three times better off economically than in 1947 (Norrie and Owram 1996, 398).

These figures are misleading, however. For Canada, the period can be broken into two halves, the first signalling the prosperous times of an economic "long wave," the second an economic decline (Watkins 1997). But the recession of the early 1970s was not Canada's alone. Every country in the Western industrial world experienced rising unemployment and increased government debt during this period. In Canada after the early 1970s, personal and corporate bankruptcies skyrocketed while the annual unemployment rate (see Chapter 6) rose steadily, changing also from a temporary or occasional situation to one more long term and chronic. In this context of rising demands but falling revenues, federal and provincial government deficits and debt also spiked. Canada's massive federal debt as a percentage of GDP following the Second World War had declined steadily during the prosperous years. Thereafter, however, it began to rise alarmingly during the 1980s and early 1990s, with interest payments on the debt eating up a growing proportion of revenues (Li 1996, 89). Canada's federal debt peaked in 1997, then steadily declined as a result of severe budget cuts and renewed prosperity throughout the 1990s and early 2000s, before rising again in recent years (see Chapter 8).

What led during this period to the fiscal crisis faced by Western governments and the Canadian government in particular? First, new technologies were displacing workers, hence the rising unemployment that lowered demand for goods and services, while also reducing tax revenues just as state expenditures increased for unemployment insurance and welfare. For Canada, these new technologies cut into jobs in both the primary and secondary sectors. Second, in a preview of globalization (Chapter 8), transnational corporations began shifting finance capital and production to low-wage countries, at the same time avoiding taxation or pressuring governments to lower corporate taxes (Li 1996). In all countries, these factors combined to weaken the full employment policies upon which the welfare state relied.

Also exacerbating the economic recession of the early 1970s, however, were the economic circumstances surrounding a single commodity: oil. Since the beginning of the second industrial revolution, and particularly with the advent of the automobile, oil and natural gas had increased in prominence and power as commodities. Their worldwide importance became quite apparent in 1973 when, following the Yom Kippur War, the Organization of Petroleum Exporting Countries (OPEC) announced it was limiting supply and increasing the price of oil. The OPEC crisis, as it became known, awakened Americans to the fact their country was no longer capable of ensuring a stable and low-priced oil supply. Hence, discussions began on exploration of previously untapped areas under American control, such as Alaska, and means of securing stable supplies from reliable sources, such as Canada.

On the surface, the crisis should have provided a unique opportunity for Canadian development. With large untapped reserves of oil and natural gas, Canada would seem to have been in an ideal position to take advantage of the escalating market price, but Canada was not.

First, 75 percent of Canada's petroleum and natural gas in 1973 were under foreign control, 58 percent under American control (Li 1996, 24–25; see also Fossum 1997). Canada might be the home of large oil and gas reserves, but Canadians had no right of first call on them. Second, while the governments of producing provinces could do quite well from rising prices that translated into increased royalties, non-producing provinces faced only rising costs. The crisis thus pitted the oil-producing provinces, especially Alberta, against the manufacturing provinces of central Canada, with the federal government caught in the middle. But the problem was not merely political. In Canada, as elsewhere, rising oil prices provoked a worldwide phenomenon known as **stagflation**: the simultaneous occurrence of a declining economy and increasing unemployment with rising inflation.

Finally, Canada's fiscal crisis beginning in the 1970s was particularized by its relationship to the United States. In the late 1960s, facing increased competition from the rebuilt economies of Japan and Germany, and in the midst of the widely unpopular Vietnam War, the United States found itself suffering a negative balance of trade with most countries, including Canada. As economic times worsened, the United States government resorted to a time-worn measure: It adopted a series of protectionist measures to buffer American workers, consumers, and companies against the outside world. In 1972, President Richard Nixon (1913–1994) came to Canada bearing news that while the two countries might be good friends, there was no special relationship between them. The United States was going to pursue its own agenda, and Canada should feel free to do the same (Martin 1982).

As an exporting country, with the United States as its major market, Canada was rightly concerned about American protectionism. In 1968, 24 percent of Canada's GDP resulted from exports, a figure six times larger than that of the United States. Moreover,

60 percent of Canada's trade was with its southern neighbour (Finkel 2012, 159–160). Canada was forced—as in 1846, when Britain adopted free trade and took away Canada's assured market for goods, and in 1866, when the United States ended the Reciprocity Agreement—to seek out an alternative policy for economic survival.

THE RISE AND FALL OF CANADIANIZATION, 1972–1982

In the early 1970s, the federal Liberal government of Pierre Trudeau began taking steps to increase the role of central government, politically and symbolically, in an effort to head off the threat of Quebec separatism (Chapter 3). The economic crisis of the same period, in conjunction with the federal election of 1972, which saw the Liberals reduced to a minority government propped up by the left-wing New Democratic Party (Appendix 1), likewise gave the federal government impetus to strengthen its role in the economy. For the Liberal Party, it was a remarkable turnaround. Over many years, the Liberals had developed a solid reputation as pro-business, pro–free trade, and pro-continentalist. Yet during the next decade (1972–1982), the Trudeau government instituted a series of measures designed both to increase the role of government in the economy and to patriate the economy, in much the same way that the Constitution was brought home from Britain in 1982. Later than the Canadianization of some other parts of society, the government began efforts to Canadianize the economy.

These efforts manifested themselves in several ways, including the creation of the Foreign Investment Review Agency (FIRA), designed to oversee foreign takeovers of Canadian companies. At the heart of Canadianization, however, was a series of measures dealing with oil and gas, among them the creation of Petro-Canada. Founded as a Crown corporation, its original mandate was to explore and develop oil reserves, map out the existing reserves in Canada, and generally provide the government with a window on the oil industry.

Canadianization of the economy was a logical extension of the wave of English-Canadian nationalism that swept the country in the 1960s. Certainly, many of the actions taken by the federal Liberals had considerable public support, though this varied from region to region. People in Ontario were the most supportive, while most opposed were people in Quebec and the western provinces, especially Alberta. Many Quebecers, separatist or not, viewed the strengthening of the federal government as threatening their "national" interests. Equally, many in western Canada viewed with suspicion the efforts of the federal Liberals, who had little parliamentary representation in their region. More broadly, many westerners saw Canadian nationalism as disguising central Canadian interests opposed to their own.

The return of the federal Liberals to power in 1980—following the brief rule of Joe Clark's Progressive Conservative government (see Chapter 3)—saw them resurrect efforts to rebuild the central powers of the Canadian state. Thus, a new Constitution was enacted in 1982. Meanwhile, on the economic front, and in the wake of the Iranian Revolution in

1979, which sparked a second major world oil crisis, the Liberals introduced the National Energy Program (NEP) (Fossum 1997).

The NEP had five purposes. First, it was intended, through a series of taxes on the oil industry, to increase federal revenues with which to deal with the growing debt. Second, the NEP was meant to keep Canadian energy prices below world levels, smoothing out the impact of rising prices between producing and consuming provinces. (At the same time, it also placed a floor on prices should they suddenly drop, thereby protecting producing provinces.) Third, the NEP was designed to foster Canadian ownership of oil and gas through a series of monetary incentives. Fourth, the program was meant to encourage exploration of Canadian lands (such as in the North, particularly the Beaufort Sea), therefore increasing energy self-sufficiency. Finally, the NEP also was explicitly meant to promote energy conservation (Finkel 2012; Fossum 1997).

The National Energy Program was the pinnacle of Canadianization. In retrospect, many of its goals (such as its restrictions on foreign ownership and efforts at self-sufficiency) seem modest, the measures common in other countries. However, by 1982, the NEP was dead, though not formally buried by the subsequent Progressive Conservative government of Brian Mulroney until 1986. Why did the NEP fail?

First, the NEP was based on pricing projections that failed to materialize (Fossum 1997). As members of the OPEC cartel began cheating on oil production, the price rapidly declined, throwing economies once more into turmoil and ruining the revenue hopes of both the federal government and the oil-producing provinces.

Second, the NEP, and Canadianization in general, ran afoul of the newly elected administration of Ronald Reagan (1911–2004) in the United States. Reagan's electoral campaign in 1980 was based on a promise to the American people to make that country "strong" again. Economically, he promised to make the United States self-sufficient and, further, to use the power of the state to open doors for American free enterprise and business. Implementation of the NEP resulted in a series of hostile letters to the Canadian government written by high-level individuals in the Reagan administration, warning of retaliation for Canadian actions that harmed American business interests (Clarkson 1985).

Third, competing interests and internal fractures within Canada itself undermined Canadianization. These conflicts were not limited to the federal-provincial or interprovincial level, although these were important. For obvious reasons, American-owned businesses in Canada, including many in western Canada's oil and gas industry, opposed Canadianization. But large private corporations in general opposed Canadianization both on theoretical grounds (they did not like government regulation in general) and because they increasingly favoured open borders for capital.

Today, the NEP remains controversial; in Alberta, it is mythic. In the view of its detractors, the NEP was an unconstitutional intrusion on provincial jurisdiction that stole millions of dollars from the Alberta treasury and led to a subsequent recession (1981–1982). NEP supporters, however, argue that the program was a legitimate effort by the Canadian government to carve out an economic policy independent of the United

States, and they suggest that the policy is unfairly blamed for a downturn that hit all oil-producing regions, including Texas and Oklahoma.

Regardless of the relative merits of these arguments, the fact is that the political and economic failure of Canadianization left the Liberal government, and the Canadian state more broadly, without an economic blueprint for managing the country. Sir John A. Macdonald's National Policy (Chapter 6) of 100 years earlier had led to Canada's industrialization. Its updated equivalent, Canadianization, had attempted to resurrect the role of activist government in shaping the country for the late 20th century. The policy was now in tatters. What path should Canada take?

ADOPTING FREE TRADE

Two items headed the Conservative government's agenda when it took office in 1984: a new constitutional arrangement with Quebec that eventually led to the Meech Lake Accord (Chapter 3) and a new economic policy for Canada. In seeking the latter, Mulroney had to look no further than a study recently commissioned by the defeated Liberals.

The failure of Canadianization led the Liberal Party to set up the Royal Commission on the Economic Union and Development Prospects for Canada in late 1982. The commission's final report, published in 1985, concluded that the Canadian economy needed less government involvement, that businesses and workers in Canada were insufficiently competitive, and that the only solution was greater reliance upon market forces. The report advocated a policy of free trade with the United States to achieve these changes.

To understand fully the significance of this recommendation, one has to go back into Canadian history. The option of free trade with the United States had always been there; indeed, the Reciprocity Treaty of 1854–1866 (see Chapter 6) was a form of managed free trade (Norrie and Owram 1996). After 1867, and particularly after the formulation of the National Policy in 1879, Canadian economic, political, and social development had been nurtured along an east-west grid. But the idea of free trade with the United States persisted, pursued by the Liberal Party and certain supporters, especially western farmers. In the elections of both 1891 and 1911, Sir Wilfrid Laurier's Liberals campaigned on a platform of unrestricted trade with the United States, losing on both occasions to the Tories—the first time to Sir John A. Macdonald, the second time to Sir Robert Borden (Appendix 2). Thereafter, the topic of free trade largely disappeared from sight. Free trade was the ideological plaything of a few academics and "continentalists," those who saw Canada's future within a greater North American whole.

In 1988, the vast majority of Canadians still viewed free trade as a threat to Canadian sovereignty, but two important elements within Canadian society supported the initiative (Doern and Tomlin 1991). First, Canadian business, represented by the Business Council on National Issues (since renamed the Canadian Council of Chief Executives) lobbied hard for free trade, in part because much of Canada's business class was already heavily integrated with its American counterparts and also because it believed such a deal would ensure Canadian access to American markets for export goods and investment capital. Second, several provinces, notably Quebec and Alberta, also supported free trade, the former because its then separatist government believed free trade would loosen that province's dependence upon the rest of Canada and pave the way for sovereignty (see Chapter 3), the latter because it saw free trade as preventing future federal initiatives such as the National Energy Program.

Additionally, Canada faced enormous political and ideological pressures from outside its borders, especially from the United States. The elections of Ronald Reagan as American president in 1980 and of Margaret Thatcher (1925–2013) as British prime minister the year before gave political heft to policies favouring minimal government intervention and the pursuit of free trade.

The 1988 election was highly polarized, comparable only to the conscription election of 1917 (Chapter 2). In the end, though, by a narrow margin (only 43 percent of voters voted for the PCs), Mulroney's Tories won a majority of seats (see Appendix 1). The Free Trade Agreement was ratified. Almost immediately, the newly elected administration of George H. W. Bush (1924–2018) in Washington began pushing for a broader continental agreement that would include Mexico. The United States—militarily, politically, and economically powerful, but resource poor—was poised to access the resources of its two closest neighbours. In the late 20th century, North America quickly emerged as one large trading bloc, with its headquarters in the United States, to compete against other trading blocs that began emerging in Europe and Asia.

Nor was the move to closer ties reversed with the election of a new Canadian government. In 1993, the victorious Liberal Party—which, only five years earlier, had denounced free trade—under new leader Jean Chrétien (1934–), signed the North American Free Trade Agreement (NAFTA), bringing together the economies of Canada, the United States, and Mexico. The economic arrangement was reaffirmed in a new agreement in 2018 and ratified by all three governments in 2020 (see Government of Canada 2018). The years that followed saw Canada pursue further economic ties with the United States, while that country spearheaded efforts to further global free trade. For Canadians, the tepid nationalism of the Trudeau era was quickly swept away.

CONCLUSION

Post-war Canada was built upon an expanding and prosperous economy and a set of welfare state programs to assist the social adjustments necessary to such an economy. These changes in turn resulted in different social arrangements and the emergence of a distinctive English-Canadian identity. Nationalism was the result.

The fiscal crisis beginning in the mid-1970s challenged this vision of Canada. Canadianization was a response to this crisis. In many ways, it was an attempt to create a modern-day National Policy. These efforts crashed, however, against internal regional divisions and pressures exerted by the United States and its business allies. The failure of

Canadianization left Canadian politicians and policy-makers without a clear direction for the country. Much of Canada's political and economic elite sought refuge in closer ties to the United States. The Free Trade Agreement was emblematic of this pursuit.

The future does not unfold as a straight or predictable line, however. Few in 1988 could have guessed that the Cold War was about to end, replaced by a new era marked by neo-liberal globalization, economic uncertainty, and war—an era with particular consequences for Canada, which would raise renewed questions about the country's relationship with the United States and the world.

CRITICAL THINKING QUESTIONS

1. Why do you think Canada's welfare state developed in the way that it did during the 20th century?
2. In what ways do changes in family structure and the economy impact upon each other?
3. To what extent can Canada still be described as having a British culture?
4. Does Canada have a national economy or a regional economy?
5. How important is culture to national identity?

RECOMMENDED READINGS

Clarkson, Stephen. 1985. *Canada and the Reagan Challenge*. Toronto: Lorimer.
    Using official documents, Clarkson details the coercive actions of the American government of President Ronald Reagan in attempting to alter the Canadian government's economic policy in the early 1980s.

Doern, B., and B. W. Tomlin. 1991. *Faith and Fear: The Free Trade Story*. Toronto: Stoddart.
    This book is an essential primer for understanding Canada's adoption of free trade after 1988.

Olsen, Gregg. 2002. *The Politics of the Welfare State: Canada, Sweden, and the United States*. Oxford, UK: Oxford University Press.
    This book compares the different welfare states of Canada, Sweden, and the United States, explaining the variations according to theories in political sociology.

Rice, James, and Michael Prince. 2013. *Changing Politics of Canadian Social Policy*. 2nd ed. Toronto: University of Toronto Press.
    This book examines the relationship between politics and social policy in Canada, beginning in the 20th century and up to 2012, with an emphasis

on the types of programs delivered, who delivered them, and what level of government was involved.

Rodgers, Kathleen. 2014. *Welcome to Resisterville: American Dissidents in British Columbia.* Vancouver: University of British Columbia Press.
Rodgers's book examines a little-known part of Canadian cultural history—the arrival of American draft dodgers during the Vietnam War and the cultural relationship between the resisters and other minority groups in the interior of British Columbia.

RELATED WEBSITES

Canadian Radio-television and Telecommunications Commission
www.crtc.gc.ca
This commission was established by Parliament in 1968, with the role of supervising and regulating Canadian broadcasting and telecommunications.

CBC Digital Archives
www.cbc.ca/archives/categories/economy-business/trade-agreements/canada-us-free-trade-agreement/topic-canada-us-free-trade-agreement.html
This site contains 15 video clips and one radio clip dealing with the Canada-US Free Trade Agreement.

Department of Finance Canada
www.canada.ca/en/department-finance.html
This ministry develops policies and provides advice to the government regarding the economy.

CANADIAN SOCIETY ON VIDEO

America, Love It or Leave It. 1991. Alioli Associates Ltd., 50 minutes.
Examines the exodus of 125,000 American political refugees to Canada during the Vietnam War and their impact upon Canada.

Reckoning: The Political Economy of Canada, "Part 4: In Bed with an Elephant." 1986. National Film Board of Canada, 59 minutes, 48 seconds.
Describes the often-difficult relationship between Canadian prime ministers and American presidents.

CHAPTER 8

Canada in a Neo-Liberal (and Post–Neo-Liberal?) World

Edmonton Bridge. Courtesy Bill Jorgensen.

New World Order
   —term used by US president George H. W. Bush on the occasion of the signing of the North American Free Trade Agreement, 1993

*This, without a doubt, is neoliberalism's single most damaging legacy: the reali-
zation of its bleak vision has isolated us enough from one another that it became
possible to convince us that we are not just incapable of self-preservation but fundamentally not worth saving.*
   —Naomi Klein, 2014

Our plan will put America First. Americanism, not globalism, will be our credo.
    —Donald Trump at the Republican National Convention in July 2016

INTRODUCTION

The global economic order after 1945 can be divided into two major eras. The first period was the Keynesian era, stretching from the end of the Second World War until the OPEC crisis of 1973. The second is the neo-liberal era, a major part of which was Canada's signing of the Free Trade Agreement in 1989 and a number of later regional free trade agreements between developed countries and former Third World states. The beginning of this era coincided with the collapse of the Soviet Union, ending the Cold War as well as the battle between two competing ideologies, capitalism and communism, and heralding the victory of Western liberalism, led by the United States. No sooner had the cheering subsided, however, than neo-liberalism began facing new economic, military, and cultural challenges. These challenges, including the re-emergence of right-wing nationalism, the slow-motion decision by Britain, after the 2016 Brexit referendum, to leave the European Union, and the election of Donald Trump as American president that same year, pose the question of whether a third major era is in the offing.

This chapter examines the rise of neo-liberal globalization and its political, economic, social, and ideological impacts upon Canada. Among the issues specifically examined are questions of employment, social stratification, and Canadian values. More broadly, however, the chapter examines pressures for further political, economic, social, and military integration into the American Empire—even as that empire seems increasingly challenged by other world powers. The chapter begins, however, with a discussion of neo-liberal globalization and its growing discontents.

NEO-LIBERAL GLOBALIZATION

Thesis and Antithesis

The Free Trade Agreement (FTA) of 1989 was enlarged in 1994 under the North American Free Trade Agreement (NAFTA) that brought Mexico into the Canada-US economic partnership. These agreements were followed by several other bilateral or regional trade agreements with Chile and Israel (both in 1997), Costa Rica (2002), and Peru and the European Free Trade Association (both in 2009) (Foreign Affairs, Trade and Development Canada 2013). The election of majority Conservative and Liberal governments in 2011 and 2015, respectively (see Appendix 1), accelerated Canada's efforts to secure new free trade agreements (Stanford 2014). Two extremely large and significant agreements are noteworthy: the Canada–European Union Comprehensive Economic and Trade Agreement (CETA) and the Trans-Pacific Partnership (TPP), both of which—in contrast to the FTA in 1988—few Canadians know anything about because they were crafted in secret and the details have not been released.[1] Finally, in 2018, a new Canada–US–Mexico agreement, building on NAFTA, was also signed and then ratified in 2020 (Government of Canada 2018).

Free trade agreements are only part of broader efforts begun in the late 1970s by Western governments (led by the United States), conservative think tanks, and corporate leaders to remake the world according to a set of liberal political and economic principles based on the ideas of Adam Smith and David Ricardo. This set of ideas is often referred to as **neo-liberalism**—defined as an ideology promoting the efficacy of free markets, limited government, and private property. Proponents of neo-liberal globalization make several assertions.

First, they claim that everyone, consumers and producers alike, benefit in time from free (unregulated) and open trade. Consumers have access to a wider variety of goods and services at lower prices, and resources are used in a more efficient manner than would otherwise occur under protectionist policies. And while those at the top of the economic ladder become wealthier, everyone below also benefits from a larger economic pie and the gradual trickling down of wealth to the bottom. Second, proponents argue that economic freedom is necessary in order to have political freedom and an expansion of human rights. Third, they argue that global economic integration is inevitable, part of the natural history of progress. The words of Britain's then–prime minister Margaret Thatcher, "There is no alternative" (or TINA), quickly became, as post-structural theorists might observe, a discursive means of eliminating debate. At a philosophical level, neo-liberal proponents assert the primacy of the individual over the group or society (see Giroux 2014); as Thatcher also famously remarked, "There is no such thing as society," a statement inherently antagonistic of sociology (see box 8.1). We will return to the cultural implications of neo-liberalism later in this chapter.

Critics of economic globalization dispute these arguments favouring neo-liberalism. They note that the world's wealthiest countries became wealthy historically not through free trade but through protectionist policies (see Chapter 6). They further argue that, as neo-liberalism has proceeded, the economic situation of many countries and individuals has declined while that of the wealthiest has more than prospered (see Piketty 2014). For example, there were 2,057 billionaires in the world in 2019 (*Forbes* 2019). An Oxfam report released in early 2020 argues that the world's 2,153 billionaires possess more wealth than 4.6 billion people (or 60 percent of the world's population)—that, indeed, the world's 22 richest men have more wealth than all the women in Africa (Oxfam International 2020).

Neo-liberalism's advocates have argued since the 1980s that wealth concentrated at the top is reinvested in the economy, resulting in prosperity trickling down to the other classes. Critics argue, however, that "trickle-down theory" is a sham ideology meant to justify economic inequality in the name of alleged benefits to all "down the road" (see Aldred 2019). Indeed, opponents contend that neo-liberal globalization is merely an updated version of global exploitation, going back to mercantilism (Chapter 1) and later colonialism (see Chapter 9). In its current version, neo-liberalism holds countries and their peoples hostage through trade agreements signed by the complicit political elite of

Box 8.1: Neo-Liberalism's Challenge to Sociology

In April 2013, while discussing a recently foiled terrorist plot, Prime Minister Stephen Harper told the House of Commons that it was no time to "commit sociology" (Heath 2013)—a remark that quickly raised eyebrows (and also led to a large number of T-shirts bearing a picture of the prime minister and the phrase being sold at the Victoria meetings of the Canadian Sociology Association that summer). Then, in August 2014, in rejecting calls for a national inquiry into the murder of Tina Fontaine, a 15-year-old Indigenous girl (one of over a thousand murdered and missing Indigenous women), the prime minister stated that Fontaine's murder was a crime that should not be viewed as a "sociological phenomenon." In a narrow sense, as some editorialists quickly noted, the prime minister was correct: Murdering someone is a crime. As Kaye and Béland (2014) noted, however, "crime is a social phenomenon shaped by powerful historical and social forces," and without taking these into account, one cannot adequately frame a public policy response.

The prime minister's comments echo a neo-liberal understanding of human behaviour that rests solely on the individual. This understanding, as Frances Fox Piven (2007, 13–14)—one of the world's best-known and most influential sociologists—has noted, is fundamentally at odds with sociology:

> Although we were slow to recognize it, Thatcher and the neoliberal project she championed declared war on the basic tenets of the sociological enterprise. To be sure, we also study individuals and families, but the sociological enterprise rejects the radical individualism of Thatcher and the personal responsibility [of neo-liberalism]. Our distinctive preoccupation is with the social environments that shape individual and family life.

Piven's response to the challenge is a call for sociologists to take a critical stance regarding political and economic trends, adding that "the early 21st century is reproducing the turmoil of the 19th century, and it is also reviving the moral and political concerns that animated some of the best sociological work in the past" (2007, 15).

What do you think? Is it possible to merge radical individualism with sociology? And what do you think should be the stance of sociologists in the world? Should sociologists merely "interpret the world," or should they, as Marx argued, work to change it?

Sources: Heath, Joseph. 2013. "In Defence of Sociology." *Ottawa Citizen*, April 30; Kaye, Julie, and Daniel Béland. 2014. "Stephen Harper's Dangerous Refusal to 'Commit Sociology.'" *Toronto Star*, August 22; and Piven, Frances Fox. 2007. "The Neoliberal Challenge." *Contexts* 6(3): 13–15.

the subject states (Sassan 2001; Mann 2008). From this perspective, the "freedom" lauded by neo-liberals is that of the wealthy and the powerful to exploit the poor and the weak, unhindered by concerns for democracy, equality, and justice.

Yet even its opponents admit that neo-liberal globalization differs in some significant respects from past periods of capitalist expansion. First, in many instances, neo-liberal globalization has involved a genuine transfer of productive forces from the industrialized North to the underdeveloped South, with consequences for class structures and living conditions both within underdeveloped and developed countries. Second, where capitalist globalization in the past often resulted in intensified conflict between or within the boundaries of the core capitalist countries themselves, or between competing capitalist classes and their patron states (as in the First World War), neo-liberal globalization has reflected a growing convergence of capitalist interests across borders—indeed, a transnational capitalist class (Robinson and Sprague 2018)—even as it has intensified class and other conflicts. Critics of neo-liberal globalization view these gains as only temporary, however, and destined to end—as in the past—in increased social and political conflict.

The Three Periods of Neo-Liberal Globalization

The neo-liberal era can be divided into three relatively distinct periods by decade: (1) ascendancy (the late 1970s and 1980s), (2) triumph (the 1990s), and (3) crisis (the 2000s to present).

The ascendancy period began with the crisis of Keynesianism in the 1970s, followed by the elections of British Prime Minister Thatcher in 1979 and American President Reagan in 1980. Both Thatcher and Reagan avidly promoted neo-liberal policies, such as the privatization of public services, the deregulation of finance capital, attacks on the power of unions, the lowering of personal and corporate taxes, and the shrinking of the post-war Keynesian welfare state. The signing of the Canada–US FTA in 1989 provided a symbolic capstone to the era, launching neo-liberalism's next stage.

Unlike this first period, during which neo-liberal policies were contained largely within Britain, the United States, and the other anglophone countries, including Canada, neo-liberalism's period of triumph saw these policies actively promoted globally. The period was marked symbolically by the collapse of the Soviet Union in 1991, the historic importance of this event captured by then–American President George H. W. Bush in heralding a "New World Order." Lacking an ideological and military adversary, the United States quickly emerged as the "uni-polar" centre of world power. American politicians, economists, and bureaucrats proclaimed neo-liberalism's victory, also known as the "Washington Consensus."

Faced with soaring debts and struggling economies throughout the 1980s and early 1990s, many governments adopted neo-liberal solutions. In the early 1980s, for example, Mexico turned its back on decades of autonomous development and later (in 1993) signed NAFTA with Canada and the United States. Other Latin American countries, such as Argentina, followed suit. Nor was the impact of neo-liberal ideology upon states confined

to the underdeveloped world. The former Soviet Union quickly adopted neo-liberal policies of privatization that saw the emergence overnight of wealthy oligarchs who benefited from scooping up public resources at cut-rate prices. European countries, including
the social democratic welfare states of Scandinavia (see Chapter 7), also felt pressured to
accept the supremacy of market ideology.

Neo-liberalism's good times soon ended, however. A serious recession in the early
1990s was followed in 1997–1998 by an even more serious currency crash that decimated
the emergent middle class in multiple countries. In stark fashion, this crash pointed out
a major peril of globalized capitalism: that economic crises could no longer be isolated to
a single country, region, or even currency. The problem was made worse by the fact that
organizations set up at the end of the Second World War to manage orderly capitalism (i.e.,
the International Monetary Fund, the World Trade Organization, and the World Bank)
had failed miserably; indeed, their active role in deregulating capital flows exacerbated
the crisis and increased inequities across classes, genders, and ethnicities, both within and
between the developed and underdeveloped worlds, resulting in social and political unrest
(see Bello 2002). As the crisis unfolded, governments (especially in Central and South
America) began defaulting on loans and not co-operating with the IMF, setting the stage,
in the years that followed, for several governments in that region to revert to more state-
interventionist policies, breaking away from the laissez-faire American model.

Economic and socio-political instability were not the only problems facing neo-
liberalism as the 1990s came to a close, however. Nature itself began asserting the limits
of economic globalization through a dramatic shift in weather patterns, the concomitant
rise of new diseases and micro-organisms, resource depletion, and global warming (see
Chapter 10). Drawing attention again to the perils of interconnectedness, evolutionary
bio-geographer Jared Diamond (2005, 23) remarked, "Globalization makes it impossible
for modern societies to collapse in isolation. . . . For the first time in history, we face the
risk of a global decline."

Inevitably, the instability was also social and political. Neo-liberalism, in parallel
with structural-functionalist thought, asserted that global markets would create inter-
dependencies that would cement peoples and countries together in mutual benefit. From
a conflict perspective, however, unfettered global capitalism was resurrecting class and
other conflicts that post-war arrangements (e.g., the welfare state) had previously dampened. Karl Polanyi's (1944/2001) *The Great Transformation*, originally published in 1944 as
the Second World War was ending, had earlier articulated the broad, systemic problems
arising from a policy of unregulated markets.

Polanyi argued that the economy is necessarily embedded in society. Efforts to deregu-
late the economy, in the fashion of neo-liberalism, had been tried once before—beginning
in the late 19th century—only to result in what he termed a **double movement**. As the
first movement—that of unregulated markets—proceeded, causing enormous social hardships (e.g., homelessness, unemployment, poverty), a second (double or counter-) movement inevitably arose, comprising individuals, communities, and citizens who protected

themselves by drawing inward. The form of protection they chose varied. Protest parties and unions were one form; fascism, communism, and authoritarianism in general were another. In Polanyi's estimation, the Second World War resulted directly from a social and political breakdown occasioned by deregulated markets over many previous decades.

As Polanyi would have predicted, the late 1990s witnessed an array of double movements arise throughout the world in opposition to neo-liberal globalization, bringing together a cross-section of global society: workers, students, intellectuals, social activists, Indigenous peoples, and others. Drawn from both the Global North and South, the protests represented a host of causes, including peace, the environment, and justice. Ironically, computer technologies (especially the Internet), which had initially fostered capitalist expansion, became a chief means through which mass opposition to it also mobilized.

As the new millennium began, however, nothing could quite prepare the world for the events that followed: a series of brutal wars, a major economic crisis on the scale of the Great Depression, and the political rise of the extreme right.

THE AMERICAN EMPIRE AT WAR

9/11

On September 11, 2001, 19 terrorists aligned with an extreme Islamic fundamentalist group known as Al-Qaeda crashed two passenger planes into New York's World Trade Center, killing roughly 2,800 people. Another plane was flown into the Pentagon in Washington, resulting in the loss of nearly 200 more lives. Though the actual number of people killed was relatively small, the attacks had long-term importance upon world history. As the perpetrators had planned, the attacks pierced the American myth of invincibility, shocking America's collective psyche, and bringing home to some the fact that in the 21st century, terrorism had gone global (Keohane 2002). In Orwellian fashion, the attacks also gave rise to authoritarian impulses both at home and abroad.

Within the United States, fear provided the basis for greater state powers and the disciplining of the population, who surrendered long-held rights in the name of security (Wolf 2007). Likewise, dissent was stifled (see Chomsky 2001). The mainstream media silenced itself and was complicit as an unthinking agent of the state (see Gonzalez 2001). Critics lost their jobs; members of minority groups were sometimes attacked. Some critics warned of creeping authoritarianism, if not fascism, in the land of the free (Wolf 2007; Hedges 2009, 2010).

Abroad, the United States, while still using the discourse of liberal democracy, began exercising its global authority more openly than ever. With the exception of Donald Trump, few American politicians would describe the United States in terms of empire, but several scholars after 9/11 did just that (see Ferguson 2004; Johnson 2006; Mann 2008).

Given geographic proximity, the United States made a series of specific demands of Canada (see Clarkson 2002a, 2002b). Militarily, these demands included the creation of a military zone around North America under American command and control. Politically, the United States demanded that Canada adopt American immigration policies and common security practices, and it also changed the entry requirements for everyone, including Canadians, entering or even flying over the country. Neo-liberal theorists had long envisioned a borderless world (see Ohmae 1990); suddenly, however, borders once again mattered (Laxer 2004).

Canada's Unexpected War: Afghanistan

The United States' demands on Canada and other countries escalated in late 2001, when the United States and a loose coalition of allies invaded Afghanistan, where many members of Al-Qaeda and its leadership resided. That conflict quickly resulted in the defeat of Afghanistan's Taliban government and the Al-Qaeda terrorists dead, imprisoned, or on the run, retreating primarily across the Pakistan border,[2] where Canada was obliged to join the mission under Article 5 of the Treaty of Washington, which states that an attack upon any NATO country is an attack upon all (Stein and Lang 2007, 10–11).

Article 5 aside, why and how did Canada get involved in the Afghanistan mission? Three reasons were paramount. First, the federal Liberal government in 2001 wanted Canada to have a larger symbolic presence on the world stage and saw the Afghan mission as fitting with Canada's imagined identity since the 1960s as an international peacekeeper. Second, the mission had widespread support among much of Canada's military establishment, which wanted Canada to pursue a more "muscular" role in the world and believed that war was necessary in order to turn Canadian troops into real combat soldiers. Third, involvement in the Afghanistan mission was a trade-off for not participating in the then-looming Iraq War, which the United States formally launched in spring 2003. The Afghan mission appeared the "safer" engagement at the time.

Canada's formal involvement began in December 2001; it ended just over 12 years later, on March 12, 2014, when the Maple Leaf flag was lowered at NATO headquarters in Kabul, Afghanistan's capital (CTV 2014). The military mission began with much bellicosity and bravura but gradually morphed into what Stein and Lang (2007) have termed the "unexpected war." The sheer brutality of war (Smith 2013), combined with a growing sense among much of the West's political and military elite that the war was unwinnable by military means (Margolis 2008; Milne 2008) and the inevitable tally of military casualties, gradually eroded public support. The final official count was 158 Canadian soldiers and one diplomat killed during the mission's duration (2001–2014), though there were also several civilian deaths. These numbers, however, do not count the injured—nearly 2,000—or the 160 military suicides that occurred in the period from 2004 to 2014 among soldiers suffering, primarily, the effects of post-traumatic stress disorder (PTSD) (Kilpatrick 2014).

Besides the human toll, the financial costs of war also rose. Mid-way through Canada's involvement, Canada's Parliamentary Budget Officer (2008) estimated the Afghan mission would cost the country between $13.9 billion and $18.1 billion by 2011, or about

$1,500 for every household in the country. Siebert (2014) has since argued that the $18 billion figure is the correct total, though not a final one: Canada remained committed to providing financial support for security and development into 2017.

Canada's role in the Afghan conflict ended not with a bang but a whimper. The war—like so many contemporary conflicts—quickly faded from television screens, replaced by yet another conflict whose complexities and purpose were even more difficult to fathom, even to the most skilled observer.

Iraq: The Illegal War

In September 2002, the administration of President George W. Bush (1946–) released its new National Security Strategy (Government of the United States 2002). The document, popularly called the Bush Doctrine, argues that the terrorist attacks made the principle of launching war purely in retaliation (i.e., for defensive purposes) inoperative. Instead, the document states that the United States will in future attack in pre-emptive fashion any country it believes may possess, or may seek to possess, weapons dangerous to the United States. The Bush Doctrine further argues that, because the threat to American interests is now worldwide, the United States is justified in taking military actions anywhere. (For this reason, some see the Bush Doctrine as an extension of the Monroe Doctrine, discussed in Chapter 5.) Finally, the Bush Doctrine proposes as its aim that no country in the future will be allowed to compete militarily with the United States.

After months of debate at the United Nations, which attempted collectively to implement a peaceful way of disarming Iraq, the United States, Britain, and a handful of smaller countries (most of them financially indentured to the United States) broke with the UN and invaded Iraq in March 2003. The formal war was quickly over, but peace did not come; instead, the next few years witnessed the outbreak of sectarian violence and the deaths of tens of thousands of Iraqi civilians and occupying troops. The war's primary justification—that Iraq had "weapons of mass destruction"—soon proved false. Moreover, no reasonable person believed the other argument: that Iraq had been involved in the 9/11 attacks. It is clear that security and military officials, in consort with the US government, intentionally or otherwise misled the American public and its allied publics. Critics argue that the invasion of Iraq was an illegal act under Chapter 7, Article 39 of the United Nations Charter, though both the United States and United Kingdom, as permanent members of the Security Council, would veto any attempts to rule the invasion as such (United Nations 1945).

Beyond the immediate demands placed on Canada, the 9/11 attacks, and the US response to them, had major impacts on Canada. Canada's decision not to join the subsequent American-led invasion of Iraq proved a good one, but at the time it was contentious. Canada's Liberal government, headed by Jean Chrétien, viewed the mission as foolhardy and unjustified; it was also unpopular at home, being especially opposed by Quebecers. Canada's decision, however, was opposed by powerful forces, including the US administration of President Bush and many political leaders in Canada, among them Alberta's premier, Ralph Klein (1942–2013), and then–federal Conservative Opposition leader, Stephen Harper. Likewise, most of Canada's corporate community disagreed with staying out of the Iraq conflict, fearing that doing so invited American economic reprisals. In the end, no reprisals came, but Canada did experience an onslaught of anti-Canadianism from right-wing talk radio and television commentators (Harrison 2007).

A report by Brown University's Watson Institute for International and Public Affairs found that US spent $6 trillion in fighting wars in Afghanistan and Iraq after 9/11 (O'Connor 2018). The exact body count for these wars is somewhat unclear. The number of US military deaths is about 6,800, with an almost equal number of contract workers killed, but these figures do not include suicides or those wounded (Costs of War 2014a); it likewise does not include the estimated half million Iraqis, mainly civilians, killed since the 2003 invasion (Vergano 2013) or the 21,000 Afghan civilians killed in that country (Costs of War 2014b). More recent accounts suggest that between 480,000 and 507,000 people were killed in the post–9/11 wars in Iraq, Afghanistan, and Pakistan (O'Connor 2018). In the end, the wars to "liberate" Iraq and defeat terrorism in Afghanistan succeeded in neither. Instead, both countries remained consumed by sectarian violence and disorder.

Then, just as it seemed that the world situation could not get worse, the Great Recession—the most serious challenge to global capitalism since the 1930s—began, bringing down long-established financial institutions and leading to massive job layoffs throughout North America and Europe. War made money for some but, in the larger picture, was a further unsustainable drag on the world economy.

In this paired context of war and recession, the United States in 2008 elected its first African-American president, Barack Obama (1961–). His election reflected growing divisions within the American people, along partisan and socio-demographic lines, over the amount of money and American lives spent in fighting the wars—wars that, moreover, seemed increasingly without purpose and led by a governing political class, representing both parties, whose acumen and integrity was now questioned. With its expensive and sophisticated weaponry, the United States could win the war, but it could not win the peace.

President Obama slowly began withdrawing troops from the assorted war zones, the authority of the American Empire carried instead by drones firing from safe distances and guided via satellite. But instability throughout the Middle East increased. Starting in Tunisia in early 2010, protests and popular revolts erupted throughout the region, fuelled by cellphone technology and demands for democracy. But neither democracy nor peace came; instead, the Middle East descended into warfare along nearly the entire length and breadth of its borders, driven by ancient sectarian grievances, geopolitical interests, and an endless supply of lethal weapons provided by Russia and assorted Western governments. In 2014, a new militant group, the Islamic State of Iraq and Syria (ISIS), emerged out of the chaos. Claiming religious authority over all "true" Muslims and declaring its intention to restore a caliphate incorporating much of the land currently part of Syria, Jordan, Israel,

Cyprus, and southern Turkey (*Wall Street Journal* 2014), ISIS began seizing large chunks of Iraq and Syria. The death toll in Syria alone reached 500,000 by 2018 (O'Connor 2018), before ISIS was driven from its territorial base, though perhaps not entirely defeated. In these conflicts, as in Libya in 2011 and in Afghanistan before that, Canada played a small combat role, supplying planes for targeted bombing missions.

War and Society

Wars change societies. Strict obedience to the state is expected; conformity and the dictates of patriarchy are reinforced. Free speech becomes less free; casual social relations less casual or social. Racism and prejudice often flourish. Of course, there are other, less negative—even positive—consequences, too: the advent of many of Canada's social programs being one example. Canada is in many ways a product of past wars: the Conquest of New France, the War of 1812, the First and Second World Wars. In what ways, perhaps subtle, did the Afghan conflict and the war(s) on terrorism change Canada?

Many critics believe the Afghan conflict and the war(s) on terrorism generally have fundamentally changed the country. Author and political activist Murray Dobbin (2008) has argued the endless conflicts since 2001 have not only integrated Canada more tightly into the American Empire, through defence and security policies, but they have also militarized Canada's values and culture. Some contend this change was intentional on the part of the Conservative administration of Prime Minister Harper after 2006: that the government used war to "rebrand" Canada as a military nation with a "glorious" military past (McKay and Swift 2012) and to valorize the role of the warrior in opposition to the "peacekeeper" image established during previous Liberal regimes (Richler 2012). Still others contend that the wars have led, as in the United States, to increased state power in the form of heightened security; restrictions on free speech, even at universities (Turk and Manson 2007); and the use of practices, such as "rendition," that threaten civil liberties.

Are these arguments correct? Is Canada today, at a deep level, a more militarized nation than it was before September 2001? Evidence suggests this may not be the case. For example, while Canada's military budget grew substantially in the years after 9/11 (Staples and Robinson 2008), it later declined to more traditional levels. In 2009, Canadian military expenditures were 1.4 percent of the GDP, and were 1.3 percent in 2018. By contrast, US military expenditures were 4.6 percent of the GDP in 2009, though also slipping to 3.2 percent in 2018 (World Bank 2019). Since the election of Donald Trump as American president, however, Canada has also faced pressure to increase its military spending.

Canada's military industry provides weapons and associated products for both the Canadian military and export. While not small, these industries are not as functionally woven into the fabric of Canadian society in the same way as in the United States. American sociologist C. W. Mills (1956) alluded to the American military's power and influence over that country's political system. His argument was later echoed by President Dwight D. Eisenhower (1890–1969) in warning of the growing power of the

military-industrial complex (Kurth 1993). Still, Canada's military industries, employing thousands and bringing billions of dollars into the Canadian economy, are influential—and controversial, such as when, in September 2019, Global Affairs Canada signed off on the sale of military equipment to Saudi Arabia, a country with a poor human rights record (Project Ploughshares 2019).

For sociologists, the twin wars of Afghanistan and Iraq, like their Asian counterparts of the 1960s and 1970s, point out critical issues of power exercised over civil society by the state through force, ideology, and discourse. But the state also does not stand entirely outside society; it is, rather, a product of interests that might use the mechanisms of the state to forward their ends.

THE GREAT RECESSION AND ITS AFTERMATH

As we have seen, neo-liberalism already faced difficulty as the 9/11 attacks unfolded. Amid the ongoing chaos of war, the world economy in late 2007 entered into its worst crisis since the 1930s. The Great Recession (2008–2010) was set off in the United States by large numbers of homebuyers defaulting on their mortgages. The deeper cause, however, was growing income inequality in the United States and elsewhere (Reich 2010). Deregulation of capital flows, the introduction of new labour-saving technologies, and globalization did as neo-liberalism's exponents expected: shifted political and economic power away from workers to the owners of capital. But capital's "victory" came at a long-term cost.

Capitalism is a system of extracting profits from production by keeping workers' wages low. But the goods produced must also be sold, requiring that sufficient aggregate demand be maintained. Both the unemployed and employed must have sufficient money (through wages or benefits) to purchase the goods produced. In the former case, Keynesian programs, such as employment insurance and social allowance, though eroded since the 1980s, still protected spending to a degree. In the latter case, however, a drop in real wages dampened workers' purchasing power. Increasingly, the spending gap was maintained through central banks' keeping interest rates low and financial institutions' providing easier (and easier) consumer credit. The mortgage crisis was the result.

Quickly, the US crisis reverberated around the world, bringing down banks and other financial institutions. In turn, credit markets seized up, making it harder for businesses to borrow money. They responded by laying off workers. In turn, these unemployed workers/consumers, already in substantial debt, bought fewer goods and services, leading to even more business layoffs as the stock was left unsold. In short, Depression-era economics (Galbraith 1997) returned with a vengeance. To deal with the crisis, Western governments, including Canada's, bailed out many of the world's corporations and financial institutions to the tune of $20 trillion (McNally 2010; Panitch and Gindin 2012). In effect, private debt became public debt, the paying off of which since 2010 has featured low wages, public-sector layoffs, reduced public services, and privatization—in combination, a program of generalized austerity that continues dragging down aggregate demand.

But the Great Recession also signalled a major turning point in neo-liberalism. The promises of endless growth made by proponents had proved hollow. Throughout many Western countries, wages declined and pension funds went insolvent, while the jobs eliminated through globalization were not replaced. Though discontent festered in many countries, it emerged most forcefully in the two countries at the heart of neo-liberal globalization—the United Kingdom and the United States (Harrison 2016). In both countries, the political class, and even political institutions, lost legitimacy. Badly damaged by war and its handling of the economy, the Republican Party in the United States fell victim to an insurgent right-wing populism (Chapter 6), led primarily by older, conservative-minded, working- and middle-class white males, who in 2016 spearheaded Donald Trump's election as president. That same year, a similar demographic of angry voters in England, outside London's financial district, voted to leave the European Union, a desire finally fulfilled in 2020 but in turn putting the United Kingdom at risk as Scotland and Northern Ireland voted to remain.

CANADA AND THE MULTIPOLAR WORLD

The United States remains the world's most powerful empire, militarily, politically, economically, and even culturally. But it is no longer the undisputed world power. China's state-driven economic rise, Russia's resurgence, India's growing nationalism: Each of these states present real challenges to American **hegemony**. In the context of US decline and the unpredictability of the Trump presidency, other regions—notably the European Union—are trying to re-establish independence from American control. The emergent geopolitics of a multipolar world pose real dilemmas for Canada, as shown by the case of Canada's arrest in December 2018 of Meng Qanzhou, chief financial officer of Huawei Technologies Co. Ltd.

Canada arrested Meng at the request of the United States, under an extradition agreement between the two countries. American officials claimed Meng had circumvented US trade sanctions with Iran. It is a classic case of the United States imposing its will on other governments—what is known as **extraterritoriality**—as Ms. Meng faced no charges in Canada.

But there is more to the story. Meng is also the daughter of Huawei's founder, an individual highly connected to Chinese state officials; Huawei is also a large and prominent high-tech company whose growth threatens American-based dominance in that field. While the United States argues, with some legitimacy, that Huawei is a security threat— that its 5G technology may be used for surveillance purposes—the dispute can also be viewed as one between the American and Chinese states.

Canada had attempted to diversify its economy away from dependency on the US. China was an important part of these efforts and a major importer of several Canadian commodities—beef, pork, soybeans, and canola among them (van Praet et al. 2019). These efforts were not opposed by previous US administrations, who pushed for open trade. The

Trump administration is far more protectionist, however, and also insists that its allies pick sides in any dispute.

Canada is caught between a rock and a hard place. In the more distant past, while the country has occasionally stood independent of American policy—on trading with Cuba, harbouring Vietnam draft dodgers, and, later, opposing the Iraq invasion in 2003—Canadian policy moved steadily closer to the United States after the FTA in 1989 and again following the terrorist attacks in 2001. In a unipolar world, such a stance seemed rational for Canada—hence Canada's signing of the extradition agreement.

Meng's arrest, however, starkly reveals Canada's precarious position as a middle power in a world dividing into camps. The political economy and political geography of Canada on the North American continent has already largely determined which camp the country will join. Since Meng's arrest, trade between Canada and China has ground to a halt, along with other cultural exchanges; furthermore, in a tit-for-tat, three Canadians were arrested for alleged violations of Chinese law. The conflict with China came at the time when the Trump administration was also flexing its muscles in demanding revisions to NAFTA.

CANADA'S ECONOMY

The Canada–United States–Mexico Agreement

The FTA and NAFTA were meant to set a long-term path for Canada's future economy. Specifically, supporters argued the agreements would increase cross-border trade between Canada and the United States, increase employment, secure access to American markets, and encourage efficiency, making the Canadian economy better able to compete in world markets. But Canadians today are living in a much more conflicted and unpredictable world than when the new millennium began. Neo-liberalism's crisis combined with the Trump presidency's advocacy of America-first (protectionist) policies have launched Canada's economy once again upon uncertain waters.

As in 1854, 1911, and 1988 (see earlier chapters in Part 2), guaranteed trade with the United States reared its head. Prior to 2016, some trade observers contended that NAFTA needed updating, given changes in the three economies and technological advancements, particularly around the digital economy and e-commerce. The major impetus for the eventual signing of the Canada–United States–Mexico Agreement (CUSMA), however, was the election of Donald Trump as US president in 2016. Trump had campaigned against NAFTA, arguing that it was unfair to the United States and, specifically, had cost American jobs. There was thus a political imperative to do something about the existing agreement. In the lead-up to negotiations, he talked tough, and in May 2018, the United States announced a tariff of 25 percent on certain Canadian steel products and 10 percent on aluminum products. In response, Canada in July 2018 announced that it would impose import surtaxes of C$16.6 billion on steel, aluminum, and other products coming from the United States (Government of Canada 2019a).

After much political posturing, a revised trade agreement between the three countries was achieved. Business interests in Canada were generally pleased with the resulting CUSMA. Access to US markets was maintained, and American efforts to have all trade disputes settled by American courts was rebutted; disputes will be decided by a group not aligned to the interests of any party. The three countries also committed to greater co-ordination of customs procedures, strengthened regulatory practices, and efforts to deal with unfair trade provisions. Action was also taken on addressing digital trade (Moore 2019).

But civil society critics were less sanguine about the CUSMA. The Council of Canadians (2019) acknowledge some gains in the new agreement, notably the "elimination of provisions that allow corporations to sue countries over their public interest laws and policies and the elimination of energy proportionality that set mandatory export quotas for Canadian energy to the US." This latter clause had curtailed Canadian governments' abilities to protect citizens from oil and gas shortages (Laxer and Dillon 2008) and had also worked against efforts at energy conservation and environmental protection (Laxer 2010). Elimination of the clause thus restored a measure of Canadian sovereignty over the country's resources.

But the Council of Canadians (2019) also views with concern the "new corporate-friendly 'regulatory cooperation' provisions that limit government's abilities to regulate in areas such as chemicals, food safety, and the environment"; "concessions on supply management"; and "drug protections that expand Big Pharma's powers to demand exorbitant prices for drugs."

In the end, however, the major question facing both supporters and critics of CUSMA must be these: How robust is the agreement in an age of hyper-protectionism and transactional politics, where even the most solid of agreements melts into air? Are any agreements worth the paper they are written on?

With these considerations in mind, what does Canada's economy look like today?

The United States and International Trade

Even before the adoption of free trade, north-south trade with the United States was increasing in every region of Canada. Free trade only hastened this trend. By the early 2000s, 87 percent of Canada's exports were going to the United States (Grunwald 2002). But while trade in absolute terms has continued to grow between the two countries, the percentage of both exports and imports has declined. In 2018, $432.1 billion in goods and services were exported to the United States (up from $390 billion in 2003), compared with imports of $390.9 billion (up from $240.4 billion in 2003). In 2018, 73.8 percent of Canada's exports went to the United States, while 64.4 percent of Canada's imports came from the United States. In short, both Canadian exports and imports have increased, but trade is more dispersed than in the early 2000s. Other countries, notably the Republic of China, Mexico, South Korea, and Hong Kong, are now major trading partners. In the case of China, that country in 2018 absorbed 29 percent of Canada's exports and made up over 46 percent of Canada's imports (figures from Statistics Canada 2019e)—emphasizing again problems for Canada arising from strained relations with the Asian country.

Still, US trade remains very important to Canada—though the reverse is not so evident. Based on the trade in goods only, US exports to Canada were 18.0 percent of all US exports in 2018, while imports from Canada were only 12.5 percent of all goods coming into that country (Office of the United States Trade Representative 2019). In short, the United States remains more important to the Canadian economy than Canada does to the American economy, with one notable—but perhaps also declining—exception: petroleum (see subsequent discussion). The nature of Canadian trade with the United States returns us to a perennial debate: Is Canada once more caught in a "staples trap" (Stanford 2019; Chapter 7)?

As we have seen, staples can be a source of great wealth when the world economy is booming, as it did during the recent heyday of globalization (the 1990s and early 2000s). Then, the newly emerging economies, in Asia particularly, came calling for Canadian minerals, forestry products, agricultural products, and petroleum. A report by Statistics Canada (2007b) in late 2007 warned, however, that Canada's economy was being driven by commodity prices, though Canadians had become less "hewers of wood and drawers of water" than "conveyers of crude and moilers of metals." As in the past, the boom came at an overall cost to the Canadian economy in terms of stability. The demand for commodities, especially oil, temporarily boosted the economies of western Canada and the Atlantic region, especially Newfoundland and Labrador, but central Canada's manufacturing sector—hit with higher production costs—declined; then the price of oil once more dropped, reversing the polarities of boom and bust. Petroleum is key to understanding many of the economic, political, and environmental issues Canada currently faces.

The Promise and Perils of Petroleum

Petroleum, you will have observed, is not just like any other resource. Next to water, it is today the world's most important resource: one, you will also recall (Chapter 7), that led to the controversial introduction of the National Energy Policy in the early 1980s, arousing passionate anger among many western Canadians, the corporate community, and the American government. Before finally being abandoned by the federal government, it damaged Canadian unity and left scars still easily felt today. After 1988, Canada's petroleum industry boomed, not only in Alberta but also in Saskatchewan and, with the discovery of offshore reserves, Newfoundland and Labrador, Nova Scotia, and the North. In 2018, Canada was the world's fourth largest producer and fourth largest exporter of oil in the world, with 96 percent of its oil exports going to the United States. Nearly 82 percent of all crude oil produced comes out of Alberta, with another 11 percent from Saskatchewan. But conventional oil production has been declining for a while. Today, 64 percent of Canada's production comes from Alberta's oil sands. In fact, 96 percent of Canada's proven oil reserves are in the oil sands (Government of Canada 2020).

These numbers are impressive. In consequence, and not so long ago, Canada's petroleum industry was lauded by business leaders, mainstream economists, and conservative politicians. Canada's oil and gas reserves, and the United States' (and the world's) seemingly insatiable demand for them, appeared to put Canada in the driver's seat, justifying Prime Minister Harper's declaration in 2006 that Canada was a rising "energy superpower." Supporters of carbon-based fuels—centred mainly on oil and gas, but also coal—argued that it produced enormous wealth and provided high-wage jobs to thousands of people both directly and indirectly. They argued further that oil gave Canada a comparative advantage over other non-producing countries and that Canada must exploit the resource now or lose the chance—that the dangers of **climate change**, as raised by critics, were overstated and that, in any case, the world was not getting off oil any time soon. Finally, amid worldwide geopolitical instability, supporters argued that Canada is a reliable and "ethical" producer of oil compared with many other countries, such as Iraq, Iran, or Venezuela (Levant 2011).

Critics dispute the benefits of oil production for Alberta's and Canada's economy. Since the 1990s, much of Canada's oil production has been in the form of heavy oil or unprocessed bitumen, meaning that many of the value-added jobs have been "exported." This oil has been shipped through a growing series of pipelines connecting Canada's North (well beyond the Athabasca oil sands) to refineries in California, Texas, and the American East Coast, with many more planned by 2030 (Laxer and Dillon 2008; see also Laxer 2010). Pipeline construction creates a number of jobs at the front end, but once done, the number of permanent jobs is small (Lee 2012). Even in the extraction phase, overall employment in the oil patch has been declining due to automation. The introduction of self-driving trucks carrying bitumen to Fort McMurray's Syncrude plant provides an example.

The economic arguments in favour of continued—or accelerated—petroleum production faces an even greater challenge, however. Due to distance from markets and difficulty separating the oil from the sand, Alberta's oil is expensive to produce. As a result, Alberta's oil regularly sells at a discount in the range (at least) of $15 per barrel. Alberta's oil is thus uncompetitive with oil produced elsewhere (see box 8.2). Complicating the economics of oil production for Alberta (and Canada) is that, due to the advent of new technologies (such as fracking), the world supply of oil has increased at the same time that demand has lessened as a result of new sources of non-carbon energy and changing consumer preferences. In short, the business case for Alberta's oil industry is questionable.

But critics of petroleum extraction express other concerns. Though dismissed by petroleum supporters, evidence has mounted that CO_2 is the major source of global warming. While per-barrel greenhouse gas (GHG) emissions have dropped by 28 percent since 2000 (Government of Canada 2020), the amount of oil being produced has dramatically increased the overall quantity of GHG being released into the atmosphere, making it virtually impossible for Canada to meet its emissions targets as promised under the 2016 Paris Accord (Government of Canada 2016; see also Chapter 10).

Box 8.2: Not All Oil Costs the Same

The price of oil varies according to its quality (density and sulphur content), marketability (supply and demand for particular oil types), and logistics (distance to markets, available infrastructure and transportation type—e.g., truck, ship, rail, pipe). Western Canadian oil suffers a price differential compared to other types of oil:

Brent: Light, sweet oil, easily transported due to its access to coastal ports; includes European North Sea, Middle East, African, and European oil fields.

West Texas Intermediate (WTI): Light, sweet oil, but produced in land-locked areas of the American south and mid-west.

Western Canada Select (WCS): Heavy (high viscosity) oil, difficult to produce and transport, and far from markets; mixed with blends of bitumen and diluents to help it flow through pipelines.

These differences impact the price of oil and the return to the owners of the product—in Canada, these are the citizens of the respective provinces and levels of government. For example, monthly prices for oil in January 2017 were as follows: Brent, $55.43; WTI, $52.61; and WCS, $38.79. The monthly prices for oil in December 2019 were as follows: Brent, $65.17; WTI, $59.80; and WCS, $38.47. Notably, however, in one period between these dates, November 2018, the price of WCS dropped to $17.71, while the prices of Brent and WTI were $66.11 and $56.69, respectively.

Sources: Alberta Energy. n.d. *Let's Talk Royalties. Not All Oil is Equal: Explaining Price Differences.* Government of Alberta; *Oil Sands Magazine.* 2018. "Oil Sands Pricing Differentials Explained." December 13; *Oil Sands Magazine.* 2020. "Oil and Gas Prices."

Critics also contend that petroleum development contains a number of hidden social and environmental costs. In the Alberta oil sands area, for example, local residents, many of them Indigenous, disproportionately shoulder these costs—a point that questions "ethical oil" arguments (see Marsden 2007; Nikiforuk 2010, 2012; see also Chapter 10). More broadly, critics argue that the market price of oil and gas does not reflect its true cost, that the real costs of production are often passed on to individuals, families, communities, and the ecosystem itself; these costs are treated as **externalities** (see Klein 2014) to those of production. If these costs were included, oil production would not be economically viable. The problem of orphan wells provides an example.

An **orphan well** is defined as "a well for which no owner or operator can be found, or where such owner or operator is unwilling or unable to plug and abandon such well" (Colorado 2013). Alberta has between 90,000 and 155,000 oil and gas wells—no one seems sure how many—with no or declining economic potential, 3,400 of which are orphan wells. Likewise, the total cost to the people of Alberta for reclamation is unclear, but estimates place it between $60 billion and $230 billion (Jones 2020; Green 2019). Some, even within Alberta, have come to question whether the costs of oil and gas development outweigh its benefits.

In boom times, petroleum-producing provinces have done very well. Alberta in particular was even able to use its wealth to flex its political muscle within Confederation. But dependence upon a single resource for provincial revenues poses real risks, as staples theorists warned decades ago (Chapter 7). Prolonged declines in the price of oil inevitably result in severe economic and political crises. The summer of 2015 saw the price of WCS drop to $18 per barrel. While it rose slightly over the next few years, it could not offset the social dislocation that followed. Alberta was particularly hard hit. Unemployment, bankruptcies, and food bank use rose to levels Albertans had not experienced for decades. Blame for the downturn fell upon the provincial NDP and federal Liberal governments, both elected in 2015, and on environmentalists who opposed the building of new pipelines that oil and gas supporters claimed were essential for economic growth. Angry and afraid, some Albertans (and a few residents of Saskatchewan) mused of separating, reenacting protests held 40 years earlier in the midst of another oil price downturn.

A change in government in spring 2019 did not alter the problem of economic dependency, however. The oil patch continued to struggle; then, in early 2020, Canada's oil producers experienced two new threats over which they—and governments—had no control. The first came in the form of a conventional price war between Saudi Arabia and Russia. The second came in the form of a worldwide pandemic (see Chapter 13). The first increased supply, the second—as the world economy contracted—decreased demand. The result was a drop in the price of WCS, for a time, to below $4 per barrel—less, as some people pointed out, than the cost of a high-end Starbucks coffee.

The perils of petroleum development provide a stark example of a larger issue plaguing Canada: the country's growing economic, political, and cultural dependency upon the United States—a dependency that arguably further threatens Canada's future as a sovereign, democratic society.

POLITICAL SOVEREIGNTY AND THE DRIVE FOR "DEEP INTEGRATION"

Free trade supporters in 1988 argued that fears of a loss of political sovereignty were red herrings, that markets are neutral and that Canadian governments would remain able to make decisions in the public interest. By contrast, opponents argued that free trade deliberately removes democratic control of the economy from citizens, placing important decisions instead in the hands of companies, investment dealers, and shareholders who may have little concern for Canada or the public good—that, more broadly, the economic imbalance between Canada and the United States would result in a shift over time of political authority from Ottawa to Washington. Neither argument has been fully realized, though as earlier discussed, Canada has found its leeway compromised on such matters as war or trade disputes with China.

Headed by the Business Council of Canada—made up of Canada's 150 largest companies and pro-business think tanks, like the C. D. Howe Institute, the Fraser Institute, and the Conference Board of Canada—corporate Canada has continued to call for Canada's "deep integration" into the North American economy. A series of papers (termed the *Border Papers*) put out by the C. D. Howe Institute in the early 2000s argued for such things as a common North American tariff and integrated energy, environmental, and regulatory policies (Dymond and Hart 2003; Bradley and Watkins 2003; Hufbauer and Schott 2004). In the words of Dymond and Hart (2003, 1), "The time has come to achieve a seamless border with our neighbour, embraced within a new agreement implementing rules, procedures, and institutions consonant with the reality of ever-deepening, mutually beneficial crossborder integration." Some, such as business commentator Diane Francis (2013, 2017)—like the liberal elites of the 19th century who saw Canada as destined to join the United States (see Chapter 5)—have gone beyond economic integration to calls for a political merger of the two countries. Such calls for Canada to cash in its chips and join the United States are commensurate with neo-liberalism's views of a borderless world where relationships are purely transactional, the result of economic exchanges. But they continue to be heard, as they were in the mid-19th century, when American protectionism drives business interests (in particular) to fear exclusion from US markets.

Has increased economic integration resulted in Canada losing control of its destiny? Nearly two decades after NAFTA, Clarkson (2008) argued that while there is a deepened asymmetry among the three countries, with the United States exercising a growing hegemony over its other partners, both Canada and Mexico also retain "substantial residual autonomy" over their affairs—if they choose to use it. NAFTA, says Clarkson, was meant by its negotiators "to bring down political barriers to trade and investment," but not to fashion the institutions that would further social integration (2008, 459)—that is, to create a *society*.

Canadian nationalists may take some solace from Clarkson's conclusion that formal social and political integration into the American Empire is not yet on the horizon. Nonetheless, might tighter economic integration still pose problems for a united, coherent Canada?

Canada is not an easy place to govern. As economic historian Harold Innis argued years ago, Canada does not have a single, national economy, but rather several regional economies that trade with the United States; Courchene (1998) notes that free trade resulted in a shift from east-west to north-south trade, though interprovincial trade is still the norm. Politically, as well, Canada's system of federal-provincial powers is designed to be fractious and to often follow the regional divides found in the various economies; the last several federal elections have pointed out the regional nature of Canadian politics (see Appendix 2), though these results are also skewed by the country's first-past-the-post electoral system.

What finally tied these regional economies together as a nation—a society—was a network of transport systems, communication systems, and social programs (such as medicare)—many of them arising after 1945—that facilitated positive and ongoing interactions between people within and across the provinces and territories. In short, becoming and remaining a country meant that Canada also had to become a unified *society*. But this did not just happen. Might tighter integration with the United States, even short of a formal merger, lead to Canada's internal fragmentation?

But most view concerns over Canadian independence to be overstated (see Ibbitson 2009). As we will see in the following section, Canadians continue to possess fairly distinct beliefs and values from their American neighbours. This distinctiveness, often reinforced or brought to conscious deliberation by specific political and social events in the United States, causes Canadian nationalists to argue that Canadian identity is strong enough to fend off American influence and continue to bind Canada together as a separate country.

IDEOLOGICAL FOUNDATIONS, VALUES, AND BELIEFS

We previously examined the notion of ideology in relation to the development of modern Quebec (Chapter 2). Here we want to ask: What are Canada's dominant ideological strains? What has shaped Canadian values and beliefs? Have Canadian values and beliefs changed during the time of neo-liberal dominance? To what degree are Canadians values and beliefs similar to those held by Americans?

Arguing that the United States was a product of revolution while Canada was the product of a counter-revolution (the rebellions of 1837–1838), American political sociologist Seymour Martin Lipset (1968b, 1986, 1990, 1996) contended that, in contrast to the United States, Canadians are more elitist (hierarchical), conformist, statist, collectivist, and particularist (group-oriented) (Lipset 1996). Lipset's thesis is contentious on several points. First, recent scholarship suggests there was little to distinguish the revolutionaries from the Loyalists (Grabb et al. 1999; Grabb 2000). Second, Lipset's emphasis upon the revolution as a founding moment ignores other important events in American history, notably the civil war (Chapter 5) and the civil rights movement of the 1960s, while his discussion of Canada ignores the country's French influence. Third, Lipset's thesis lacks a dynamic element, thus freezing both countries in time.

Still, Lipset's depiction of English-speaking Canada's dominant ideological strain may be accurate for a certain period. Research suggests that the War of 1812 and the failed rebellions of 1837 and 1838 did reinforce conservative elements in English-speaking Canada. (Quebec, as we have seen, had its own particular brand of conservatism.) The 19th-century form of English-Canadian conservatism was of a particular type, referred to as Toryism.

In *Lament for a Nation*, Canadian philosopher George Grant (2005) chronicled the importance of Toryism to Canada, arguing that it had been an ideological bulwark against Canada's absorption into the American Empire. Like its British counterpart, English-Canadian Toryism was monarchist, lauded tradition and order, and believed in a natural order of things that extended across class, race, religion, and gender, but it was also balanced by a deep sense of *noblesse oblige* toward those less fortunate—something that, when forged with socialism, gave support to the development of a more extensive welfare state in Canada than is found in the United States (Horowitz 1966).

In Grant's view (2005), Canadian Toryism was also distinguishable from its British forebear. First, Canadian Toryism was staunchly anti-American, thus the Tory party's opposition to free trade in both 1891 and 1911. Second, the Canadian Tory tradition also espoused a particularly strong belief in a positive role for the state, both in the economy and in society at large—hence Prime Minister John A. Macdonald's formulation of the National Policy (Chapter 6) and Prime Minister R. B. Bennett's creation of the Canadian Radio Broadcasting Commission in 1932 (which, as mentioned, led to the founding of the CBC four years later).

By the 1960s, however, Grant viewed the Tory tradition in eclipse due to Britain's fading presence in Canadian life and the growing influence of the United States in promoting liberal ideals and its increased control over the Canadian economy. For Grant, the end of Toryism meant the end of economic nationalism and, hence, Canada's ultimate demise. Both the Liberal and Progressive Conservative parties, he averred, were "liberal" parties that would support continental integration into the larger United States.

Like Lipset, Grant has received criticism, much of it, ironically, from Michael Ignatieff (2009)—George Grant's nephew but also Harvard scholar and briefly leader of the federal Liberal Party—who contends that his uncle misunderstood the importance and endurance of differences between Canadians and Americans regarding such issues as freedom and collective rights. Ignatieff also charges that he ignored the role of Indigenous and Métis peoples and Quebec in shaping Canada, and he further chides Grant for having given up on Canada at the very moment (1965) when Canada was engaged in a major transformation of itself—strengthening the welfare state, adopting a new flag, embracing bilingualism, becoming multicultural, and patriating the Canadian Constitution with a Charter of Rights and Freedoms.

To the short list of arguments about Canada's foundational underpinnings, we may also add those of Resnick (2005) and Saul (2008). Resnick (2005, 89) contends that Canada is essentially a European country, composed of its "European historical connections, a North American geographical setting, multiple national identities, robust social programs, multicultural practices, increasingly secular values, and a multilateral outlook on international affairs," to which he adds one last element setting Canadian political culture off from that of the United States: humility and self-doubt. Saul (2008) refutes Lipset, Grant, and Resnick, instead arguing that Canada is in fact an Indigenous nation (see Chapter 12) that thrives on complexity and nuance. In fact, Saul contends the

United States is the far more European country, with its relatively fixed notions of nation and state.

These deep formative ideological roots are the seedbed for Canadian values and beliefs. Though not permanently fixed, surveys conducted since the 1990s provide evidence that Canadians generally hold value orientations quite distinct from their American counterparts (Nevitte 1996; Adams 1998, 2003; Angus Reid 2016). Compared with Americans, Canadians tend to have the following qualities:

- less deferential to authority
- less conformist
- less formally religious
- less morally conservative
- less characterized by a traditional work ethic
- less accepting of violence
- more desirous of personal autonomy
- more individualistic
- more hedonistic
- more relaxed
- more suspicious of big business

In short, both theory and evidence suggest that Canada is a distinct society on the North American continent. But the distinctness of these value orientations is also mitigated by such sociological factors as class, gender, ethnicity, religion, and region. Work by Grabb and Curtis (2005), for example, describes North America as comprising four value regions: a liberal Quebec, the rest of Canada, a very conservative American South, and the rest of the United States. The authors assert that Quebec draws the rest of Canada in a more liberal direction, while the American South's conservativism filters out to the rest of the United States. This argument is given weight by an Abacus study, conducted in 2016, that found Canadians significantly more "liberal" in their acceptance on a number of issues (abortion, divorce, sex outside of marriage, same-sex relations, pornography, having a baby outside of marriage) than their American counterparts.

Beyond moral differences, perhaps startling is the suggestion made by some researchers that Canadians today are more likely than Americans to believe in and experience the American dream of individual opportunity (Adams 1998, 2003; Corak 2019a; Hood 2008). This conclusion seems also reflected in beliefs held by Canadians and Americans. A comprehensive survey conducted by Angus Reid (2016) found that 64 percent of Canadians said they were satisfied with how things were going but only 36 percent of Americans said the same. The same survey found that 63 percent of Canadians, but only 46 percent of Americans, were optimistic about their country's future. Ideas, values, and beliefs—identity—do not arise out of air. They are the product of material forces, of which Canadian media is central.

CULTURE, THE CORPORATE MEDIA, AND CANADIAN IDENTITY

Just as railroads in the 19th century and airlines and roads in the 20th century came to be understood as the material manifestations that connected Canadian society, cultural institutions as transmitted through the growing array of media became gradually viewed as essential elements in forging a national identity. But the creation of these national bodies—CBC Radio in 1936, the appointment of the Massey Commission in the late 1940s (see Chapter 6), and the development of such organizations as the Canadian Radio and Television Commission later on—as well as financial support for the cultural industries, including media, is controversial. From a neo-liberal perspective, culture is just another commodity—indeed, simply another industry. The United States has repeatedly pressured Canada to drop "protectionist" policies toward its cultural industries. But from a nationalist perspective, America's music, television, film, and publishing industries pose a threat not only to jobs but to the expression of Canada's cultural distinctness (Gardner 2002).

Whether this distinctiveness is national is a point of debate. Pevere and Dymond (1996) have argued persuasively that Canada does not in fact have a national culture; rather, the essence of "Canadian" culture arises from its regions. Canada's proximity to the United States allows many of its artists to mirror American culture and therefore to do very well in that marketplace. (Alessia Cara and Drake provide two examples.) Such artists can "pass" as generically American. In contrast, regional artists (Great Big Sea) and films (*My Winnipeg* or *The Necessities of Life*), or those artists whose content remains too resolutely Canadian (The Tragically Hip), are not as easily sold in the United States. They are "too Canadian." Likewise, one may note the region-specific nature of such acclaimed television shows as *Corner Gas* and *Republic of Doyle*. Nonetheless, in their totality, these regional expressions do appear to capture something of a Canadian identity.

Media plays a key role in cultural production, however. Media in Canada has long played the dual role of both informing Canadians about what is going on in the country and also bringing the rest of world to Canadians. Canada's media has changed markedly in recent decades: much of it is today privately owned; government's role, if any, is regulatory. Mergers, global communications, the Internet (including digital and social media), automation: these factors and others have transformed how information is produced, transmitted, consumed—and understood. In this new landscape, the wall between fiction and non-fiction, entertainment and news (Postman 1985), is increasingly—some would say intentionally—blurred. Modernist notions of a single dominant reality have given way to a postmodern view of multiple realities and no recognized, legitimate authority. What might have seemed only a short while ago indisputable fact may now be dismissed as "fake." The objective reality of any argument is now weighed against its subjective, and individualized, interpretation (Saurette and Gunster 2011). Underpinning much discussion about media are the shifting boundaries of power and the form in which it is exercised.

Who are Canada's media giants? Print media is dominated by TorStar (owner of *The Star*, *Hamilton Spectator*, and *Waterloo Region Record*),[3] Postmedia (owner of the *Edmonton Journal*, *Calgary Herald*, *Montreal Gazette*, *Ottawa Citizen*, *Regina Leader-Post*, *Vancouver Sun*, and *Windsor Star*, as well as tabloid *Sun* papers across Canada), and Woodbridge (the *Globe and Mail*). In Quebec, Quebecor Media operates *Le Journal de Montreal*, *Le Journal de Quebec*, the TVA group, Videotron, and TVA publishing (ClutchPR 2017).

Television and radio are dominated by Rogers Communications (Rogers TV, OMNI, the Shopping Channel, OLN, Sportsnet, and City, along with 53 radio stations and several magazines), Bell Media (CTV, CTV News, Much, Bravo, the Comedy Network, Space, E!, and HBO Canada, as well as several radio stations), Newcap Radio (two radio stations in Newfoundland, 22 in Alberta, and two in Toronto), Shaw (Global, BBC Canada, the Food Network, History, HGTV, Showcase, and Slice), Corus (various children's networks, W, Oprah Winfrey Network Canada, Cosmopolitan TV, and several talk radio stations), Zoomer (several radio stations), CBC (radio and television, French and English), and the APTN (Aboriginal Peoples Television Network) (ClutchPR 2017).

This apparent smorgasbord of media actors obscures the real power of a very few, however. A study conducted by the Canadian Media Concentration Research Project (2015) at Carleton University found that Canada's seventeen largest telecoms, media, and Internet companies accounted for almost 90 percent of all revenues in those industries, and that the "Big 5"—Bell, Rogers, Telus, Shaw, and Quebecor, in that order—accounted for 73.3 percent of all revenues.

Others, however, have noted that such corporate concentration raises concerns that touch on important issues for Canadian society, including, as Gasher (2014) notes, democracy:

> While corporate convergence can be beneficial to companies, there are potential undesirable consequences, including: a reduction in competition; increased barriers to entry for new companies; the further commercialization of the media; and the treatment of audiences as consumers rather than citizens. The substantial costs of corporate mergers have also led converged companies to seek profits through cost-cutting rather than increased investment in communication services.
>
> Corporate convergence also prompts concerns about the quality of corporate journalism, such as: the role of the media in democratic societies to provide objective information and analysis to an informed citizenry; the independence of journalists; the range of voices and diversity of viewpoints on current events; coverage of local issues; and conflicts of interest between properties owned by the same company.

But as large as Canada's media giants are, it is important to recognize that they must also compete against "the US-based globalizing cultural industries" (Mirrlees 2019, 220). Canada's complex array of cultural industries are interconnected and shaped by the capitalist mode of production, the state and civil society, and culture in efforts to forge an ever-shifting definition of Canadian nationalism.

Sociologically, we might ask: Are Canada's cultural industries a source of integration, as structural-functionalists would contend, or a means by which the powerful paper over differences and construct a false consensus? Are Canada's media a vehicle for the expression of legitimate conflicts, or do they manufacture discontent in the service of entertainment? More generally, do Canada's media inform Canadians about what we need to know, or do they function mainly to sell products, to entertain, and even to distract us from the important issues? The answer to all of these competing questions is "Yes."

SOCIAL COHESION: SOCIAL STRATIFICATION AND INEQUALITY

Models of Social Stratification

In recent decades, as several societies have witnessed increased conflict, many sociologists have returned to the age-old question asked by structural functionalists (Introduction): What holds societies together? One such sociologist, Robert Putnam (see Putnam 2000), has coined the term **social capital**, defined as a positive combination of interaction, reciprocity, and trust that bonds people to their communities (see Krahn et al. 2009). In turn, social capital is facilitated by a high degree of **social cohesion**, defined as the bonding effect of society that arises spontaneously out of individuals willingly interacting in order to achieve collective goals. Social cohesion is enhanced when there is a relative equality of income and life chances, while high social and economic equality, in turn, lead to a better economy (Osberg 2003).

We previously examined social stratification in early Canada (Chapter 1). The question of social stratification is important to again examine here, given neo-liberalism's belief in "trickle-down" economics and a minimalist role for the state in reducing social inequalities. What is the nature of Canada's social stratification system today, after nearly 30 years of neo-liberal policies? To what extent are the life chances of Canadian citizens more or less equal?

There are two major paradigms for thinking about social stratification and inequality in society. The first employs the neo-Marxist notion of class, updated to reflect the complexity of today's labour markets and especially the rise of managers and technical experts since Marx's time. The second, termed a measure of **socio-economic status** or SES, combines education, occupation, and income in a composite index (see box 8.3).

There are similarities between Marxian and SES measures of class. Occupation as measured by the SES model, for example, is a reasonable proxy for class in the Marxian sense, but there are also clear theoretical and ideological differences in the manner in

Box 8.3: Neo-Marxist and Socio-Economic Status (SES) Models of Class

Neo-Marxist[1]	SES Model
Capitalist classes	Upper upper
Grand bourgeoisie	Lower upper
Small employers	Upper middle
Petite bourgeoisie	Lower middle
New middle classes	Upper lower
Managers and supervisors	Lower lower
Expert and semi-credentialed workers	
Proletarians	
Underclass	

Note: 1. Capitalists own the means of production in varying degrees but may or may not purchase labour. The managerial and supervisory members of the new middle class may have discretionary control over capital and command labour. All members of this class exercise some degree of job autonomy. The proletarians neither own nor control the means of production, do not command labour, and have no assets in the labour market but their labour.

Sources: Adapted from Wright, Eric Olin. 1985. *Classes.* London, UK: Verso; Knuttila, Murray. 2002. *Introducing Sociology: A Critical Perspective.* Toronto: Oxford University Press.

which each describes systems of social stratification in capitalist societies. First, there is a structural relationship among Marxist classes, especially between (as Marx saw it) the two chief antagonists, the capitalist class (or bourgeoisie) and the workers (or proletariat). There is no such relationship between any of the strata described in the SES model; these are merely continuous statistical categories. Second, and related to the first point, people move through life in the Marxist model as members of a group, with the potential of becoming conscious of this affiliation (i.e., a **social class**), and acting politically upon this knowledge. By contrast, in the SES model people are placed in a category on the basis of their individual credentials, a fact that suggests the model's essentially liberal bias and its congruence with functionalist explanations of social inequality (see the Introduction). Third, whereas the Marxian model implies a relatively closed and static society based on the class position to which one is born, the SES model implies a far more open and fluid social structure where individuals might either rise on the basis of acquired attributes or fall for lack thereof.

On this latter point of **social mobility**—the upward or downward movement of individuals or groups from one position in the social stratification system to another position—both models are somewhat in error with regard to Canadian society. At the top and bottom ends, social mobility in Canada is relatively low, contrary to the implications of the SES model. But the opportunities for members of the working class and new middle class to rise higher in their individual lifetimes (termed **intragenerational mobility**) are greater than envisioned by the Marxist model. Looked at another way, how likely is it that children of one generation will experience greater social mobility than their parents (termed **intergenerational mobility**)? Based on Statistics Canada data, Corak (2019b) argues that "social mobility is twice as great in Canada than in the United States," with particularly low levels of mobility in the northern parts of Canada and southwestern United States. By other comparisons, however, Canada could be doing much better in facilitating social mobility. The World Economic Forum's Global Social Mobility Index 2020 (*National Post* 2020) shows that

> in Denmark, it takes an estimated two generations for those born into a family in the bottom 10 per cent of earners to lift themselves into the mean income range. In Sweden, Norway and Finland it takes three generations; in Canada, it's four; and in the United States and the United Kingdom, it's five.

Fourth, the SES model explicitly ignores wealth (the total amount of money and other financial assets owned by individuals or families) in favour of income (money earned through the sale of labour or through investments). By contrast, the Marxist model concerns all sources of wealth, particularly those that arise out of the ownership of the means of production, for this is also a source of major political power.

Social Stratification in Canada Today

What does Canada's social stratification system look like today? Table 4.1 provides a partial answer to this question, showing that in 2017 the median income of census Canadian families was $84,950 (non-constant dollars); however, note that there is wide variance in incomes across the provinces and territories. Table 8.1 provides additional information to address this question by looking instead at the median net worth of families. The table divides the Canadian population into five groups of 20 percent each (quintiles), from the poorest 20 percent of families to the richest 20 percent of families. Note that the percentage of net worth held by each quintile remained relatively stable over the period 1999–2016 but that total net worth continued to grow at the top while the bottom 20 percent stayed in negative territory.

There are at least two things that, as a sociologist, you should be aware of in examining this table. First, while the median can be a useful statistic, it is only one of three **measures of central tendency**, the others being the mean (or average) and the mode (the most frequently occurring number in a set of numbers). In some instances, each measure will produce similar results. For example, the ratio of women's incomes to men's incomes was roughly the same in 2017 for both the median (.70) and the mean (.69) (Statistics Canada 2020). But this is not always the case. Additionally, note that every

Table 8.1: Net Worth, by Quintile, Canada, 1999, 2005, 2012, 2016 (2016 constant dollars)

	1999		2005		2012		2016		Net Worth Increase, 1999–2016 (Millions $)	Net Worth Increase, 1999–2016 (%)
	Net Worth by Quintile (Millions $)	Net Worth by Quintile (%)	Net Worth by Quintile (Millions $)	Net Worth by Quintile (%)	Net Worth by Quintile (Millions $)	Net Worth by Quintile (%)	Net Worth by Quintile (Millions $)	Net Worth by Quintile (%)		
All Family Units	4,117,887	100.0	5,834,984	100.0	8,518,064	100.0	10,272,540	100.0	6,154,653	149.4
Lowest Quintile	−4,405	−0.1	−7,648	−0.1	−11,479	−0.1	−2,975	0.03	1,430	32.5
Second Quintile	107,652	2.6	131,601	2.3	189,888	2.2	241,480	2.4	133,828	124.3
Third Quintile	362,293	8.8	490,557	8.4	768,598	9.0	935,991	9.1	873,698	241.2
Fourth Quintile	828,725	20.1	1,176,161	20.2	1,825,252	21.4	2,182,630	21.2	1,353,905	163.4
Highest Quintile	2,823,623	68.6	4,044,312	69.3	5,745,805	67.5	6,915,213	67.3	4,091,590	145.0

Source: Statistics Canada. 2019f. Data Table 11-10-0049-01: "Survey of Financial Security (SFS), assets and debts by net worth quintile, Canada, provinces and selected census metropolitan areas (CMAs) (x 1,000,000)." Percentages calculated by authors.

statistic both reveals and simultaneously conceals something about that which it measures. It is important to ask, then, which measure it the most informative and accurate in describing the situation.

Second, consider also that the net wealth reported in table 8.1 is likely not evenly distributed within the quintiles. Take, for example, the fifth quintile. The net worth of those at the very top—the 1 percent, or the 1 percent of the 1 percent—are the primary holders of much of Canada's wealth. In this sense, discussions of the wealth of the top 20 percent miss the point, as much of this wealth is in fact concentrated in the top 1 percent or even the 1 percent of the 1 percent!

In 2017, Canada's richest 33 individuals owned a total of $112 billion. That same year, the two richest Canadian billionaires owned $33 billion, more wealth than the bottom 33 percent of Canadians (Zilio 2018). Since then, the number of Canadian billionaires has continued to grow. Table 8.2 lists the names, as identified by *Forbes* (2019), of Canada's 45 billionaires in 2019—up from 20 in 2009 and 31 in 2014—part of the 2,057 billionaires in the world, as noted earlier.

Table 8.2: Primary Source of Wealth, Estimated Wealth (2009 and 2019), and 2019 World Ranking of Canada's 45 Billionaires

Name	Primary Source of Wealth	Estimated Wealth in Billions $ 2009	Estimated Wealth in Billions $ 2019	World Ranking, 2019
Thompson, David	Inherited, media	13.0	32.5	27
Tsai, Joseph	e-Commerce	n/a	9.5	147
Weston, Galen, Sr.	Retail	5.0	8.4	209
Irving, James	Diversified	n/a	6.2	209
Pattison, Jim	Diversified	2.1	6.0	272
Cheriton, David	Google	1.1	5.8	298
Saputo, Emanuele (Lino)	Cheese	1.3	5.1	343
Camp, Garrett	Uber	n/a	4.6	413
Scheinberg, Mark	Online gambling	n/a	4.5	424
Bouchard, Alain	Retail	n/a	3.7	568
Wilson, Chip	Lululemon	n/a	3.6	597
Irving, Arthur	Oil	n/a	3.3	667
Huang Chulong	Real estate	n/a	3.1	715
Katz, Daryl	Pharmacies	1.5	3.1	715
Gaglardi, Bob	Hotels	n/a	3.0	745
Gilgan, Peter	Homebuilding	n/a	2.9	775

Name	Primary Source of Wealth	Estimated Wealth in Billions $ 2009	Estimated Wealth in Billions $ 2019	World Ranking, 2019
Goldhar, Mitchell	Real estate	n/a	2.7	838
Stroll, Lawrence	Fashion investments	n/a	2.6	877
Coutu, Jean	Drug stores	n/a	2.4	962
Miller, Robert	Electronics	2.1	2.4	962
Bronfman, Charles	Liquor	1.8	2.3	1,008
Fidani, Carlo	Real estate	n/a	2.3	1,008
Godin, Serge	Information technology	n/a	1.9	1,227
D'Amours, Jacques	Retail	n/a	1.8	1,281
Lee-Chin, Michael	Mutual funds	n/a	1.8	1,281
Adams, Marcel	Real estate	n/a	1.7	1,349
Jackman, Hal	Insurance, investments	n/a	1.7	1,349
Pèladeau, Pierre Karl	Media	n/a	1.7	1,349
Jarislowski, Stephen	Money management	n/a	1.6	1,425
Lutke, Tobi	e-Commerce	n/a	1.6	1,425
Schwartz, Gerald	Finance	n/a	1.6	1,425
Edwards, N. Murray	Oil and gas	n/a	1.5	1,511
Louie, Brandt	Drugstores	n/a	1.4	1,605
Smith, Stephen	Finance and investments	n/a	1.4	1,605
Szulczewski, Peter	e-Commerce	n/a	1.4	1,605
Flatt, Bruce	Money management	n/a	1.3	1,717
Reiss, Dani	Canada Goose	n/a	1.3	1,717
Matthews, Terence	Telecom	n/a	1.2	1,818
Sahi, K. Rai	Real estate	n/a	1.2	1,818
Cockwell, Jack	Real estate, private equity	n/a	1.1	1,941
Leonard, Mark	Software	n/a	1.1	1,941
Harary, Ronnen	Toys	n/a	1.0	2,057
Laliberté, Guy	Cirque du Soleil	2.5	1.0	2,057
Rabie, Anton	Toys	n/a	1.0	2,057
Watsa, V. Prem	Insurance, investments	n/a	1.0	2,057

Source: Forbes. 2019. "The World's Billionaires." New York: Forbes Media.

Several things are notable about the *Forbes* list. First, the fact that some individuals may have been on the previous billionaire's list but did not make the current list does not mean they have lost their fortunes. Most simply dropped just below the cut line. Second, note that none of the Canadian billionaires are women; indeed, only 244 women are on the entire world list. Third, while some of those on the list made their money in new kinds of ventures (Cheriton in Google, Camp in Uber), most acquired their wealth in areas of finance capital—investments, e-commerce, and real estate—areas that benefited especially from neo-liberal globalization.

Billionaires often make their money through investments, including owning their companies. Another class of the very wealthy—CEOs—earn their wealth not through direct ownership in a company but through a combination of shares and salary. (In Marxist terms, CEOs hold a contradictory class position.) As researched by Macdonald (2019), Canada's CEOs are generously reimbursed in relation to the workers they oversee. The average pay of the top 100 highest paid CEOs in 2018 was $11.8 million, compared with the average individual income of Canadians, $52,061. From 2008 to 2018, the salaries of Canada's top paid CEOs went up 61 percent, compared to 24 percent over this period for the average paid worker. There again is also a gender component to CEO salaries. Of Canada's top 100 highest-paid CEOs in 2018, only four were women.

In Canada, as elsewhere, the very wealthy obtain most of their wealth through capital investments and lucrative tax breaks on capital gains that reward speculation; this is a phenomenon commensurate with neo-liberalism's veneration of finance capital that, in turn, has seen inequality skyrocket throughout the world in recent decades (see Piketty 2014). Most people otherwise rely heavily on paid income, not investments, a situation made worse by the 2008–2010 recession. While the stock markets rebounded in the years after, this has not been the case for wages, which is a major contributing factor to rising inequality in Canada and increased insecurity felt by the middle class. In fact, the average salary of most workers in Canada has steadily declined in relative terms (and remained largely static in real terms) since the 1980s.

The Labour Market's Periphery

Increased integration of North American production after 1988 meant a significant restructuring of Canada's labour markets as business sought greater efficiencies. Canada's manufacturing sector in particular experienced a significant drop in employment as industry relocated to developing countries with lower wages and poorer environmental standards. Job growth did occur, however, over the following two decades, between the adoption of free trade and the Great Recession, especially in the extractive industries, but this has since levelled off.

Labour force participation and employment in Canada is highly regionalized and tends to increase from Canada's East Coast to the West Coast (Statista 2020b). This trend is primarily the result of job growth in Canada's resource-extraction industries, such as oil production in Alberta, but also reflects demographic differences. Eastern Canada's population tends to be older than that of the western region. By contrast, younger workers—being more mobile—may move to where the jobs are, such as Fort McMurray, or be employed in fly-in work camps; even if they have families back east, they will send their wages "home" to Newfoundland's out-ports (for example). Note, finally, that labour force statistics are also gendered, with participation rates for women being generally lower than for men, while unemployment rates for men are higher than for women.

Critics of labour force statistics are leery of job creation and unemployment numbers, often asking questions about what *kinds* of jobs are being created in Canada. As the second decade of the twenty-first century begins, unemployment rates in both Canada and the United States are low, but far too many jobs are part-time, temporary, insecure, and low paying, part of a trend toward non-standard employment (Krahn et al. 2020). The so-called "gig" economy is not producing jobs that encourage young people to imagine a future—including raising a family or building community. The term **precariat** has been coined to describe a new social class defined by work insecurity, as experienced especially by many young people (Standing 2011, 2014; see following discussion of social stratification).

For those wholly outside of, or only tangentially tied to, the labour market, the decline in living standards has been even greater. Compare, for example, the net wealth of the bottom quintile in 1999 and 2016 as shown earlier in table 8.1. As noted in Chapter 7, the Keynesian welfare state, created after 1945 to deal with the inevitable fluctuations of a capitalist (market) economy, worked well until the mid-1970s. But globalization, beginning in the 1980s, has shifted economic power to capital. Unable—or unwilling—to challenge capital's power, many countries have reduced the role and capacity of welfare states to address the needs of the most vulnerable (Wahl 2011).

This reduction has also occurred in Canada (see McBride and Whiteside 2011; Rice and Prince 2013). Shortly after the adoption of free trade in 1989, Canada began making changes and cuts to its social safety net. These changes have given greater power to "the market" and have had the effect of disciplining workers to accept a reduction in wages, other benefits, and protections. Individuals and families who rely upon non-market sources of income have been especially impacted by these changes. There has been a steady increase, for example, in the use of food banks throughout Canada. Canadians visited food banks 1.1 million times in March 2018 alone. Of these visitors, 35 percent were children, while 45 percent of users were from single-family households (Food Banks Canada 2019).

Similarly, homelessness has also become a common feature of Canadian urban life, even in very small towns. A 2016 report estimates that "at least 235,000 Canadians experience homelessness in a given year" but notes "the actual number is potentially much higher, given that many people who are unhoused live with friends or relatives, and do not come into contact with emergency shelters" (Canadian Observatory on Homelessness 2019).

It is important to note, moreover, that many who use food banks or who are homeless are employed. Many users, often young people, for example, do in fact have part-time or temporary—but also poorly paying—jobs: again, members of the precariat. Food Banks Canada (2019) estimates that one in six food bank users are employed.

As a sociologist, you will have observed that, when it comes to great poverty, great wealth, and positions in between, not all people are treated equally (Grabb et al. 1999). In 2019, the median salary for women in Canada was 79 percent of that earned by men, up roughly 5 percent since 2015. If calculated, however, on the basis of same job and qualifications, women's median income for the same year was 98 percent of that earned by men. This shows that labour laws have had a positive impact in ensuring gender equity (PayScale 2020). What has not been adequately addressed is structural or systemic bias. Women remain often concentrated in lower-level, lower-paying jobs, or in occupational and educational areas not valued as those of men, who tend to hold jobs in higher-paying occupations (Krahn et al. 2020). The median salaries of women belonging to visible ethnic and racial groups also tend to be lower than white women.

At the other end of the scale, women also disproportionately number among Canada's poor, especially those on some form of public assistance. Income and poverty rates are particularly high for single-parent female-headed families and single, widowed, or divorced female seniors (Curtis et al. 1999; Morissette and Zhang 2001). The fact that women are disproportionately represented among the poor has led some policy-makers to speak of the **feminization of poverty**. As with wealth, poverty is cross-cut by other variables, such as age, education, disability, occupation, region of residence, and immigration status.

While the impact of ethnicity and race is not as stark—except in the case of Indigenous persons (see Part 3)—as when John Porter published his seminal tome, *The Vertical Mosaic*, in 1965 (see Nakhaie 1997; Lian and Matthews 1998), they still play a major role in inequality. A recent study by Block et al. (2019) is instructive. Using Statistics Canada census data, the authors found that, despite being more active in the labour force than non-racialized workers, racialized workers were more likely to be unemployed and to have significantly lower incomes from work or from capital gains and investments. Intersecting with gender, racialized women having lower incomes than racialized men or non-racialized men and women. The same intersecting effect was noted for immigrants (compared with non-immigrants).

CONCLUSION AND SUMMARY OF PART 2

Part 2 has shown the importance of using an historical sociological approach to understanding the present. English-speaking Canada is the product of a history of contestation and accommodation, first with the people of New France (Part 1) and later the emerging country of the United States. The marks of this latter engagement can be seen in Canada's trade and immigration policies, welfare programs, cultural products, political debates, and values and beliefs, and on a host of battlefields strewn across the globe.

From a sociological perspective, Canada's relationship with the United States reflects both conflict and compromise, but also the various forms of power—economic, political, and cultural—that a more dominant actor can exert upon a smaller entity. However, it also demonstrates the ways in which the latter might still attempt to maintain its sphere of independence—for example, in building alliances with other actors. But Part 2 also reflects the internal conflicts and compromises that make up Canada internally, between the federal and provincial governments, as well as various groups of citizens. Finally, Part 2 also shows again the importance of symbols, both as sources of conflict and co-operation, but also in the construction of meaning and identity. The Canadian flag is a prime example here, even as—from a post-structuralist perspective—the power and coherence of symbols seems to be eroding.

Canadians have long faced the task of carving out an existence and an identity as a northern people on the margins of the world economy and under the aegis of empire. But Canada's fate lies not in the stars or in the inexorable workings of some imaginary manifest destiny imposed by others; rather, it lies in the will of its people to find or create new reasons to continue as a society, a country, and a different kind of nation. In this quest, they might look no further for answers than among the Indigenous peoples of Canada, who, earlier than most, faced the onslaught of global imperial forces.

NOTES

1. For a list of free trade agreements signed by Canada and the value of all merchandise imported or exported, see Statistics Canada (2019g).
2. In May 2011, Osama bin Laden—Al-Qaeda's leader and mastermind of the 9/11 attacks—was killed by a special operations unit of the US Central Intelligence Agency.
3. As of writing, TorStar is in process to be sold to Fairfax Financial Holdings Ltd., a financial services holding company.

CRITICAL THINKING QUESTIONS

1. Why did neo-liberalism become the dominant ideology of the late 20th and early 21st centuries?
2. In what ways is the American Empire similar to or different from past empires?
3. Are values and beliefs the creators or products of a society's material conditions?
4. Which model of stratification described in Chapter 8 fits Canada best?
5. Are the cultural industries synonymous with the concept of culture?

RECOMMENDED READINGS

Alberta, Tim. 2019. *American Carnage: On the Front Lines of the Republican Civil War and the Rise of President Trump.* New York: Harper.
This book argues that the rise of Donald Trump to the presidency was the culmination of a decade-long civil war inside the GOP and of a parallel sense of cultural, socio-economic, and technological disruption occurring in American society during the same period.

Diamond, Jared. 2005. *Collapse: How Societies Choose to Fail or Succeed.* New York: Viking.
This very readable book presents a wealth of case studies on how human behaviour can result in ecological disasters that impact the survival of societies.

Grant, George. 2005. *Lament for a Nation: The Defeat of Canadian Nationalism.* 40th anniversary Edition. Originally published in 1965. Montreal and Kingston: McGill-Queen's University Press.
Though often disputed, Grant's lament for Canada remains, nearly a half-century on, a keystone of philosophical discourse on Canada's relationship to the United States.

Klein, Naomi. 2014. *This Changes Everything: Capitalism vs. the Climate.* Toronto: Knopf Canada.
One of Canada's and the world's foremost critics, Klein argues that the Earth is imperilled by the logic and practice of neo-liberal capitalism.

Smith, Graeme. 2013. *The Dogs Are Eating Them Now: Our War in Afghanistan.* Toronto: Knopf.
Written by an acclaimed journalist, this book brings home to readers the horror and senselessness of war.

RELATED WEBSITES

LittleSis
littlesis.org
Founded in 2009 and located in Buffalo, New York, LittleSis (i.e., not "Big Brother") is a non-profit, grassroots watchdog network that collects information on government and corporate connections, including lobbyists, think tanks, and board directorships.

World Economic Forum
www.facebook.com/worldeconomicforum
The WEF works with global society's political, business, and other leaders with the aim of improving the state of the world through public-private co-operation.

World Social Forum
wsf2018.org/en/english-world-social-forum-2018/
A counterpart to the World Economic Forum, this loose global organization of non-governmental, non-partisan social movements meets every year in Brazil to discuss alternatives to neo-liberalism.

CANADIAN SOCIETY ON VIDEO

The Afghan Mission. 2017. Government of Canada.
    A collection of 132 short video clips that document the experiences of
    Canadian soldiers during their tour in Afghanistan.

Capitalism: A Love Story. 2009. Dog Eat Dog Films and the Weinstein Company.
    127 minutes.
    Directed by Michael Moore, the film centres on the financial crisis of 2008–
    2010 and the recovery stimulus, while also indicting the current economic order
    of the United States and unfettered capitalism in general.

Oil Bonanza. 2014. SBS Australia, 15 minutes, 38 seconds.
    Produced a few years before the downturn in the price of oil and missing some
    recent elements of the controversy regarding oil sands development, this video
    nonetheless deals well with environmental, employment, and wider economic
    issues, including the situation of Indigenous peoples in the Fort McKay and
    Fort Chipewyan communities.

PART 3

CANADA AND THE INDIGENOUS NATIONS

It may seem a bit unorthodox to discuss the First Nations of Canada at the end of this volume rather than at the beginning. Our argument, however, is that Indigenous peoples not only should not be historicized, but should be seen as constituting, if Canadians play fairly, the sector with the most promising future. Indeed, Indigenous peoples are a youthful and thriving cultural, political, and economic force that holds a key to Canada's future as a whole.

In Part 1, we examined Canada's French and English "solitudes." But Indigenous and non-Indigenous peoples in Canada constitute another pair of solitudes, separated by history, culture, class, and experience. This separation continues even though Indigenous people, especially in western Canada, are increasingly part of the urban landscape. Instead, state institutions such as the federal Department of Crown-Indigenous Relations and Northern Affairs Canada (CIRNAC) (formerly the Department of Indian Affairs),[1] children's service agencies, welfare agencies, and the courts often mediate this relationship, with the result that the knowledge possessed by non-Indigenous people of their Indigenous neighbours is largely abstract or anecdotal—indeed, stereotypical.

Part 3 of this book explores relations between Indigenous and non-Indigenous peoples in Canada. As in the previous two sections, the first chapter of Part 3, Chapter 9, provides an historical overview. Chapter 10 then examines a part of Canada not yet discussed here in detail: the North, a place where Indigenous peoples still predominate and yet a region that is a prime source of Canadian identity. Chapter 11 examines the genesis of recent Indigenous demands and growing militancy. Finally, Chapter 12 concludes with a portrait of Indigenous peoples today in Canada, an examination of the major issues still to be resolved in this area, and a discussion of the profound impact that Indigenous people may have in shaping Canadian society in the future.

NOTE

1. In 2019, the Department of Indian Affairs and Northern Development was broken into two departments: Crown-Indigenous Relations and Northern Development Canada (CIRNAC), whose mandate is to meet the Canadian government's obligations and commitments to First Nations, Inuit, and Métis and for fulfilling the federal government's and constitutional responsibilities in the North; and Indigenous Services Canada (ISC), whose mandate is to provide high-quality services to First Nations, Inuit, and Métis.

CHAPTER 9

When Cultural Worlds Collide

Fort Qu'Appelle Industrial School, Lebret, Saskatchewan, Unknown Date. Credit: Canada. Dept. of Mines and Technical Surveys / Library and Archives Canada / PA-023092.

We had a cross made thirty feet high, which was put together in the presence of a number of the Indians on the point at the entrance to this harbour, under the cross-bar of which we fixed a shield with three fleurs-de-lys in relief, and above it a wooden board, engraved in large Gothic characters, where was written, LONG LIVE THE KING OF FRANCE. We erected this cross on the point in their presence and they watched it being put together and set up.
—Jacques Cartier; Diary, 1534

But the face of the red man is now no longer seen. All traces of his footsteps are fast being obliterated from his once favourite haunts, and those who would see the aborigines of this country in their original state, or seek to study their native manners and customs, must travel far through the pathless forest to find them.
—artist Paul Kane, 1859

All men were made by the same Great Spirit Chief. They are all brothers. The earth is the mother of all people, and all people should have equal rights upon it.
    —Chief Joseph, Nez Perce Nation, 1877

INTRODUCTION

On June 11, 2008, Prime Minister Stephen Harper issued a formal apology to the First Nations, Inuit, and Métis in Canada for the government's treatment of Indigenous children in residential schools. Among other things, Harper said, "The treatment of children in Indian residential schools is a sad chapter of our history. Some sought, as was infamously said, to 'kill the Indian in the child.' This policy was wrong, caused great harm, and has no place in our country."

Reactions to the prime minister's announcement varied greatly. Some Indigenous leaders and interested observers demanded immediate concrete action—fearing more empty promises—to ameliorate social problems emanating from residential school experiences. Others were more positive, believing the apology was a good start toward creating better relations between Indigenous peoples and other citizens.

Finding ways to improve relations between Indigenous and non-Indigenous peoples is a huge task, however. The vast majority of non-Indigenous people have little knowledge of Indigenous history or Indigenous ways. As the late Cree leader Harold Cardinal (1945–2005) put it, "We have been fighting for so long now that the original misunderstandings and differences [that] have created this conflict have been forgotten" (Cardinal 1977, 7). Moreover, unlike other minority groups of whom Canada's dominant cultures also have little understanding, Indigenous peoples face a range of challenges, including economic underdevelopment, substandard education, often deplorable social conditions, and public misunderstanding, prejudice, and racism.

How did we—Indigenous and non-Indigenous peoples alike—get to where we are? And how will we get to the future? In order to understand, we have to retrace our steps. This chapter examines the cultural world of Indigenous peoples before and after the arrival of Europeans, including the political economy of the two peoples' early relations. The discussion examines how the dominant-subordinate relationship between the non-Indigenous and Indigenous peoples became institutionalized, with consequences for both parties and for Canadian society as a whole.

PRE-CONTACT INDIGENOUS SOCIETIES

Archaeologists inform us that the Indigenous peoples of North America have been on this continent for 10,000 to 12,000 years, but the truth is that no one really knows when the first Indigenous peoples arrived. Some evidence points to an arrival as long as 30,000 to 50,000 years ago (Dickason 2002, 6).

For decades, the prevailing theory was that Indigenous peoples arrived in North America thousands of years ago via an ice bridge that temporarily linked Asia to this continent. The Bering Strait theory may explain some migrations, but this theory is now seriously questioned. Today, evidence suggests the first immigrants may have arrived by various routes, by boat or raft, across both major oceans.

Initial encounters between the Europeans and Indigenous North Americans were limited to the south and central regions of the continent. Northern contact occurred much later. The first Europeans who arrived often failed to make distinctions among resident tribes, but in fact the people they encountered represented a variety of different civilizations and cultures.

In what is today Canada, six distinct cultural areas may be identified among the Indigenous peoples. These include the Northwest Coast, the North, the Plateau, the Plains, the Mackenzie District, and the Eastern Woodlands. Authorities differ regarding linguistic variation, but today three language groups comprise most Indigenous language families (Wilson and Urion 1995, 32). The first of the three major linguistic groups is the Algonquian, which includes most of Canada's Indigenous people and the vast majority in southern Canada east of the Rockies. Two Algonquian groups, Cree and Ojibway, are closely related, implying recent separation. The Blackfoot also appear to be distantly related.

The second major language family in Canada is Athapaskan, with the majority of speakers occupying much of northwestern Canada and Alaska. Because of the limited diversity among this language group, linguists believe this area was fairly recently occupied.

The third language family is Eskimo-Aleut, represented in Canada by Inupik (Inuktitut), is identified only in the region from northern Alaska across to eastern Greenland. Apart from any archaeological evidence, this seems to imply that the region has only recently been occupied (see Chapter 10).

Addicted as we are to the magic of the technological age, it is sometimes hard to realize the dramatic cultural changes that have occurred over the last several centuries in Canada. The impact on Indigenous cultures has been considerable, and while many First Nations have successfully harnessed elements of the technological revolution to serve their communities and campaigns, others are still determining how to maintain their unique identities and practices amid this transition.

Cultures may differ materially and non-materially (through their particular languages, values, beliefs, norms, and behaviours) in ways passed on from one generation to the next. From a structural functionalist perspective, however, all cultures, Indigenous or other, possess certain elements (Durkheim 1912/1978; Wissler 1923). These elements include (1) language; (2) artifacts (i.e., physical objects) that serve functional purposes; (3) social organization; (4) authority and decision-making arrangements; (5) underlying spiritual or religious beliefs and structures; (6) forms of welfare arrangements whereby the aged, the sick, and the young are taken care of; (7) arts and music; (8) forms of property ownership or usage; and (9) a means of educating the young to assure perpetuation of the system.

Pre-contact Indigenous lifestyles represented a very present-oriented way of life. They enjoyed day-to-day living and took time for leisure activities. Unlike their 21st-century counterparts, First Nations were never in a hurry to get somewhere else; they were already where they needed to be. They did not have the luxury of placing things in a freezer to save for another day, though they had ways of preserving many foods. Nor did they make use of such future-oriented facilities as savings accounts, pension plans, or registered retirement savings plans; they relied instead on each other and the environment around them. Primary to all considerations was their relationship to nature, the elements—sun, earth, water, wind, fire—and the cycle of natural growth and change.

Indigenous peoples' awe of nature did not hinder them from developing elaborate metaphysical belief systems or developing complex forms of food gathering, food preparation, art, and weaponry. Often these cultural elements were related. Food gathering and religion, for example, were highly related activities in nearly all pre-technological societies, but people were still able to live a satisfying way of life. The late Chief Walking Buffalo (Tatanga Mani) of the Stoney (Nakoda Sioux) Nation put it as follows (Friesen 1998, 30):

> We were on pretty good terms with the Great Spirit and Ruler of all. . . . We saw the Great Spirit's work in almost everything: sun, moon, trees, wind and mountains. Sometimes we approached Him through these things. Was that so bad? Indians living close to nature and nature's Ruler are not living in darkness.

While many communities had their own unique forms of organization, European settlers reported the primary unit of traditional social structure among Indigenous peoples as the **band**, often considered a subunit of a tribe (now called a "First Nation"). The chiefs who headed the bands often possessed valuable talents, with varying gifts for leadership in hunting or war, or in other contexts. Chiefs were mentors or servants of the people rather than managers or rulers (Snow 1977). Real authority within the bands or tribe, however, might reside with the elders, individuals perceived as having wisdom or medicinal knowledge gathered through years of living (Meili 2012). Likewise, the Europeans did not recognize the importance of women in Indigenous societies—a lack of appreciation that continued into future treaty negotiations (Hall 2019). This diffuse power structure confused the Europeans, who were used to rigid, patriarchal, and hierarchical authority structures.

Bands were often formed on the basis of numbers; if a band got too large to set up or shut down camp easily, the people might divide into two subunits. Hunting and gathering bands tended to be small. By contrast, bands engaging in horticulture could accommodate larger populations. Other factors—disagreements or the emergence of a charismatic leader with a following—could also lead to the division of a band. The nomadic bands of the Prairies would sometimes meet during the summer months to renew acquaintances, socialize, or celebrate the sun dance.

The Indigenous peoples of the West Coast and Eastern Woodlands developed elaborate clan systems of social organization. The clans were exogamous and bore animal names such as "Bear" or "Turtle." They were subdivided on a matrilineal basis, and clan mothers were guardians of clan traditions and sacred practices. Clan mothers alone had the right to select and depose chiefs and councils, and they had primary authority in such matters as land allotment, supervision of field labour, care of the treasury, the ordering of feasts, and dispute settlement (Johnston 1964). Chieftainships were not primarily hereditary along patrilineal lines, so a man might pass on his office to his sister's son, the latter not being a member of the chief's clan (Trigger 1969).

FIRST CONTACT

Beginning in the 15th century, a series of European visitors reached North America. They represented a host of states and nationalities, including Spain, Portugal, England, and France. They arrived unprepared to meet a people whose way of life featured an entirely different view of social organization and government, grounded in a spirituality and lifeway intimately connected to the Earth and natural systems. The Europeans ignored these differences. Armed with a strong sense of **ethnocentrism**, the tendency of people to see the world only from their own cultural perspective, they boldly proceeded across the continent.

Jacques Cartier and Samuel de Champlain were the most important of these Europeans in early Canadian history because of their role in fostering further explorations of the New World. In the mid-16th century, when Cartier returned to France with descriptions of the new land and its inhabitants, the whole of France attended him with extraordinary interest. As proof of his feats, Cartier even kidnapped two young Indigenous men, the sons of Iroquois Chief Donnacona, and brought them back to France with him. Later he returned and endured a most severe winter, but thanks in large part to assistance from the Iroquois, he and his crew managed to survive an onslaught of scurvy. This experience could have dampened the enthusiasm Cartier displayed in his first evaluation of the potential of the new country, but explorations continued. Following Cartier's lead, when Champlain arrived at the beginning of the 17th century, he made friends with the Iroquois and established colonies in Acadia and New France (Chapter 1).

In 1610, the English built their first colony in the New World, in Newfoundland. Further settlements followed along the eastern coast and along the St. Lawrence, heightening contact, competition, and conflict between the French, the English, and their Indigenous allies.

In Newfoundland, the Europeans (mainly English, Portuguese, and French) encountered the Beothuk. The Beothuk's practice of colouring everything in red ochre—clothing, belongings, weapons, burial goods, and so on—resulted in the phrase "Red Indian" (Friesen 1997, 49). There was intense conflict between the two cultures, and in the early 19th century, the last Beothuks disappeared, though there is disagreement about whether or not this resulted from intentional **genocide**, an organized attempt by one society to eradicate another society or subgroup, often, but not always, violently (see Dickason 1984; Cook 1995).

Yet not all contacts were negative. By contrast, for example, early European contact with the Mi'kmaq, a neighbouring tribe of the Beothuk, was by all accounts mutually beneficial. The invaders were quite impressed with the Mi'kmaq way of life, particularly their well-built wigwams, their methods of procuring food from both the land and the sea, and their socio-political structures.

Moreover, it was not immediately obvious that contacts between Indigenous peoples and the Europeans, beginning in the late 15th century, would prove disastrous to the former (Cook 1995). Indigenous peoples were central to the fur trade (see the following section) and also instrumental politically and militarily during both the European wars for dominance of the trade in North America and post-revolutionary America's attempt to take over Canada. However, as Cook (1995, 22) remarks, "the long-term advantages . . . lay with the Europeans: a growing economy, an increasingly complex technology, an expanding population, and a centralized political system supported by military power." Indigenous power, in relation to the Europeans, rose and fell with the fur trade.

THE FUR TRADE

Early 20th-century writings portrayed Indigenous peoples as victims of the fur trade, but more recent writings provide a more complex view. Cook (1995) stresses three points concerning the fur trade. First, trade among the Indigenous tribes in North America preceded the coming of the Europeans and was occasionally accompanied by conflict. The arrival of the Europeans only intensified the level of both. Second, insofar as eastern and coastal tribes had more immediate contact with Europeans than did the more western and inland tribes, the latter were able to preserve their cultures and base of power for a longer period. Third, Indigenous peoples were not passive participants in the fur trade, but willing and motivated, and in the early period they frequently did very well in bargaining. Not only did they quickly learn to demand better quality in the goods they were purchasing, but they became quite discriminating about the quantity of goods offered to them. Experience was a good teacher.

The beaver was central to the fur trade. Beaver pelts could be "felted" and used for making what became the treasured beaver pelt hat. The popularity of this unique item persisted in the 17th and 18th centuries, becoming a badge of social status (Innis 1962). Everyone in Europe with pretensions to "respectability" wanted a beaver hat, and when the hats began to age, they were refurbished and shipped to South America to grace less particular heads. As Lower (1977, 99) puts it,

So close was the relationship between the fur trade and the beaver hat that when early in the eighteenth century fashion in Europe decreed that brims should be a little narrower, a crisis ensued in the backwoods of Canada.

When the first Europeans settled along the eastern coast of North America, the First Nations brought them furs in exchange for European goods. Almost immediately, some Indigenous peoples became intermediary traders between their counterparts further inland and the newcomers. Very soon, this established pattern had to be altered as the heavy European demand for furs resulted in a scarcity of pelts, which drove the fur traders further inland. As Innis (1962) later observed, the search for staples—in this case, furs—led to Canada's economic development.

The Europeans quickly learned the value of Indigenous peoples and their culture in procuring the desired furs. Indigenous peoples not only trapped and transported the pelts, but, more importantly, they knew how to survive in the New World. They knew the habits of the sought-after animals, which plants were suitable as food and medicine, and the best routes to take (Cook 1995). Indigenous women, in particular, also proved adept as translators and trade negotiators, not to mention valued companions to the European traders (van Kirk 1999; Saul 2008). For these reasons, it was to the advantage of Europeans in Canada, unlike the Spanish invaders to the far south, to develop harmonious relations with the Indigenous peoples (Conrad et al. 1993).

The fur trade gradually carried dangerous consequences for the Indigenous peoples. Little did the First Nations realize that the enterprise was soon to heap devastating consequences on their traditional way of life through institutional restructuring, deadly diseases, revisionist philosophies, and severe changes to their economic circumstance.

Intensified conflict, with both Europeans and each other, was one obvious consequence. The introduction of guns raised conflict to new levels and changed the balance of power between Indigenous Nations. No less lethal were the recurrent epidemics unleashed by the Europeans. In 1634, smallpox and measles killed large numbers of Montagnais and Algonquians. Similarly, between 1636 and 1639, a series of epidemics reduced the Huron population from 25,000 to around 10,000 (Dickinson and Young 2008, 20). In the main, the devastation experienced by Indigenous peoples from epidemics was unintentional, with a single, notable exception: During the Seven Years War (1756–1763), General Jeffery Amherst (1717–1797) appears to have been the first person to utilize germ warfare when he ordered blankets contaminated by smallpox to be distributed among France's Indigenous allies.

Liquor was another danger. Motivated by economic desires, the fur traders did whatever it took to obtain furs. Various items were traded or even given as gifts, but liquor was easily the most damaging. The English traded rum, while the French relied on brandy. Not familiar with either commodity, Indigenous people did not differentiate between the liquids, which made the traders quite happy, particularly since the two were equally effective as trade items. The long-term effects of the dispersal of liquor led to the alcoholism that eventually destroyed the structure of tribal life.

As the fur trade flourished, European traders used the arrangement to enhance the status of tribal leaders in the eyes of their people and to reward them for their efforts on behalf of the trading companies (Ray 1974). If a band later failed to obtain a sufficient quantity of furs or provisions to pay off its debts, the leader was denied the symbols of office. If, on the other hand, the crop was ample or abundant, Indigenous leaders were paid in more generous terms.

In the latter years of the 16th century, France attempted to form a monopoly on trade. The attempt failed. Over the next two centuries, France and England repeatedly went to war, ending with the former's final defeat in 1763 (Chapter 1).

THE ROYAL PROCLAMATION

The end of war saw the British government pass the Royal Proclamation of 1763. Fully one-third of the Royal Proclamation was devoted to matters pertaining to First Nations (Johnston 1989) and remains the founding legal document for all written negotiations between First Nations and the federal government of Canada. Some critics argue that the Royal Proclamation was intended to dispossess First Nations of both their sovereignty as well as their lands. According to Boldt (1993, 3), the document was based on the "self-serving, villainous doctrine which held that, by right of 'first discovery' a Christian nation was Divinely mandated to exercise dominion over conquered 'non-Christian primitives.'"

The Royal Proclamation decreed that Indigenous people would be allowed to live unmolested on their traditional lands at the Crown's pleasure, the British government thus being established as protector of those lands that "have not been ceded or purchased by us." Boldt (1993, 4) states that the Royal Proclamation set forth five important principles. First, the Crown legally held title to all Indigenous lands. Second, the Crown allowed Indigenous peoples **usufructuary rights** (i.e., rights of possession) to their traditional lands. Third, possession of these lands could be surrendered only to the Crown; thus, incoming settlers could take over Indigenous lands and use them for their own purposes only after these legal rights had been surrendered by formal agreements such as treaties with the Crown (and, by later extension, the federal government of Canada). Fourth, the Crown could extinguish Indigenous rights of possession at its discretion, subject to reasonable compensation. And fifth, selected lands described as reserves would be set aside for Indigenous domicile (on these points, see also Angus 1991, 67). None of these conditions included the entrenchment of Indigenous rights as a principle of justice for First Nations, as we will later note.

Yet, before leaving the Royal Proclamation, it should be noted that Indigenous peoples do not view the document as entirely negative. Some view it as also protecting their legal rights. A document prepared by the Union of Ontario Indians (UOI) in 1970 argues that while the British colonial legal system denied Aboriginal sovereignty, it did not deny the existence of Aboriginal rights as grounded in the possession of tribal lands; in fact, the Royal Proclamation of 1763 arose out of efforts to protect these territory rights that had led to conflict during the preceding seven years (Plain 1988; see earlier discussions of the Seven Years War in Chapters 1 and 5).

In short, the UOI views the Royal Proclamation, the first constitutional document for British North America, as recognizing the existence of Aboriginal peoples' rights and establishing legal procedures for the surrender of land (Plain 1988, 31). Likewise, the Penner Commission, formed in 1983 to study Aboriginal self-government (see Chapter 11), argued that the subsequent writing of treaties was based on the principles of the Royal Proclamation of 1763 (Russell 2000, 7), but that the treaties in practice did everything the Royal Proclamation said not to do (Krotz 1990, 166).

The Royal Proclamation is legal; whether its interpretation and application have always been just is another question. As the UOI document notes further, many lands in Canada were never ceded or purchased by the colonial power. Today, as new treaties are being signed, will the procedures established by the Royal Proclamation be applied for the ceding of Indigenous lands? In Chapter 12, we will examine the making of new treaties.

DECLINE, RESPONSE, AND THE BIRTH OF THE MÉTIS

The end of war and France's defeat did not immediately change the contours of the fur trade and so did not immediately impact the economic basis of Indigenous peoples' existence. The French merchants were soon replaced in Montreal by a new organization of American and British merchants and French-Canadian voyageurs. The North West Company, as it was called, challenged the Hudson's Bay Company for supremacy in the fur trade, especially in the West.

Nonetheless, the fur trade was in trouble. By the early 19th century, overharvesting, changes in European fashion, and the impact of settlement upon habitat were taking their toll (Innis 1962). After a long and sometimes bloody struggle (including the battle at Seven Oaks in 1816) to gain control of the fur trade, the Hudson's Bay Company and the North West Company merged in 1821. The merger ended the bitter rivalry between the two companies, but it did not end the fur trade's decline. Thus, the company's new governor, George (later Sir George) Simpson (1792–1860), made several policy changes. To increase profits, he ordered that cheaper goods be traded for furs, reduced the use of alcohol as a trade item, and forbade the use of steel traps. He also tried to dissuade Indigenous people from trapping endangered species and taking furs out of season. This augured poorly with the Indigenous trappers, whose way of life now revolved around the fur economy and who reasonably insisted they had no choice but to keep on trapping in areas where food was in short supply.

The Cree and Ojibway peoples were not unaware of the need for long-term planning or conservation, but the changes to their way of life from colonial expansion had them caught between a rock and a hard place. Ignoring this very real predicament, Simpson requested that the British government place the First Nations on permanent, well-defined territories as a means of better implementing his policies and—not incidentally—paving the way for a process of dispossession through the reserve system. In time, Simpson took even more extreme measures by closing redundant trading posts. By the middle of the 19th century, the fur trade labour force was cut back by as much as two-thirds (Ray 1974, 205).

The Simpson incident is reminiscent of previous Indigenous expressions of opposition to European actions. Indigenous bitterness over land-grabbing had been growing since 1760, when Pontiac (1720–1769), an Ottawa chief, organized a pan-Indigenous confederacy to oppose British policy ("Pontiac's Rebellion," as White historians named it) (Francis et al. 1988, 166). In 1811, Shawnee Chief Tecumseh led an Indigenous confederacy of some 30 nations on a series of raids to challenge the cessions of territory, particularly those in Indiana. The raids helped pave the outbreak of the War of 1812 (Chapter 5).

In western Canada, Indigenous resistance arose on another front. One of the unexpected results of the cultural clash between European fur traders and First Nations was the birth of the Métis people. Among the Europeans, the French proved the most inclined to merge culturally and biologically with the local Indigenous population. Traditionally, intermarriage between French settlers and Indigenous wives has been attributed to a shortage of women in New France and the value of securing interests in the fur trade. More recently, however, Saul (2008, 3) has argued that "by marrying into the indigenous world, most of the newcomers were marrying up. They were improving their situations socially, politically, and economically." And though Dickason (1984, 147) suggests that "Amerindians and French were still distinct entities at the end of the French Regime in 1760," Saul (2008, 2) contends that "anyone whose family arrived before the 1760s is probably part Aboriginal."

Children of these unions were commonly called "half-breeds" or Métis, meaning "mixed." Eventually, there were enough Métis people to be identified as a separate cultural group. Morton (1970) has described the Métis as hunters, trappers, fishermen, voyageurs, horsemen, and farmers, but above all, soldiers. Between 1820 and 1869, the Métis settlement at Red River, in what became Manitoba, was one of the most populated settlements in the West (Sprague 1988). The Métis represented the chief labour force of the western fur trade and were hit particularly hard by that trade's demise.

The Métis resented previous British indifference to their fate and worried that Canada's politicians would do no better. In consequence, the charismatic Métis leader Louis Riel and his colleagues set up a provisional government and took control of the Red River region. This first act of Indigenous resistance in western Canada ended more or less peacefully, with Manitoba's entry into Confederation (1870), though Riel was forced to flee to the United States. The second act played out 15 years later at Batoche (near Prince Albert), with Riel and his followers—Métis and First Nations peoples together—defeated, and Riel tried and hanged.

Riel today remains a controversial figure. Was he a traitor or a hero? Was he insane or not (Flanagan 1977; Braz 2003)? Was he tried fairly, or was he railroaded (Thomas 1977)? We continue to reassess the meaning and place of historical figures within our collective imaginations (see box 11.2, regarding Sir John A. Macdonald).

Métis resistance has often been portrayed in the victor's derogatory terms, such as *rebellion*, *insurrection*, or *defiance*, but a strong counter-argument is that the Métis—like the Indigenous peoples who rose up again in 1885, Oka militants who took up arms in Quebec in 1990, or pipeline protesters today in British Columbia's Wet'suwet'en territory (see Chapter 11)—were simply defending their native lands. The Manitoba Métis hold a unique place in Canadian history, being the only charter group in the country with a history of national political independence before joining Confederation. Under Riel's leadership, the Métis formulated the charter of the province of Manitoba (Friesen and Friesen 2004).

Despite these accomplishments, it was only in 1972 that the Canadian federal government acknowledged the Métis as a separate national entity. Since then, the Métis have worked hard to attain additional historical and cultural recognition through political action. This was partially achieved in 2003, when the Supreme Court of Canada declared that the Métis were to be regarded as an Indigenous people. In April 2016, the Court ruled further that "the federal government has jurisdiction over Métis people, and that both members of the Métis Nation and Non-Status Indians are 'Indians' as defined by the *Constitution Act*" (Gaudry 2019). In June 2019, the federal government formally signed agreements recognizing the Métis right to self-government in Alberta, Ontario, and Saskatchewan (Fida 2019).

CONFEDERATION AND THE NUMBERED TREATIES

The conflict in Red River and Manitoba's entry into Confederation were only the beginning of Canadian expansion, growth that necessarily involved the signing of treaties in the western provinces (see Chapters 2 and 5). By 1870, treaty making in Canada was well established, with Indigenous Nations having often engaged in friendship treaties and treaties concerning territorial and hunting rights with each other prior to European contact, and even having engaged in treaties with Europeans on a nation-to-nation basis going back more than two centuries (Warry 1998).

Still, the form and intent of these treaties had changed over time. The early treaties between the Indigenous peoples and Europeans were conducted on the stated basis of "friendship and peace." After that, the treaties focused primarily on land (Dickason and Newbigging 2010). The later pre-Confederation treaties carried out in the Maritimes generally dealt with military and political arrangements involving land transfers, annuities, or compensation for rights that were given up (Frideres and Gadacz 2001). In contrast, the post-Confederation treaties, conducted in the West, dealt explicitly with the transfer of land from Indigenous peoples to the Canadian government. (The BNA Act of 1867 refers to Aboriginal [Indigenous] rights as follows: "Section 91[24] gives the federal government exclusive jurisdiction to make laws in relation to Aboriginal tenure and rights in lands reserved for Aboriginals. No constitutional authority exists for provincial jurisdictions to make laws concerning lands reserved for Aboriginals.")

The opening up of the West for agricultural settlement involved the "work and labour of settler colonialism [that] in its early or initial deployments, incorporates the socio-spacial practices of clearing, claiming, and keeping" (Smith 2019, 181) and meant the displacement of the Indigenous peoples of the region. In counterpoise to the American experience, where a century of warfare and forced internment cleared the way for settlement, the displacement of the Indigenous peoples in Canada (with the notable exception of 1885) resorted to signing what are known as the "numbered treaties"—a deployment, as it were, of socio-legal weaponry (see Smith 2019; Hall 2019).

Treaty No. 1, signed in 1871, involved the Ojibway (Saulteaux) people on the Peguis Reserve, a tribe of Swampy Cree, and others in southern Manitoba (see box 9.1). Treaty No. 1 is called the Stone Fort Treaty because negotiations took place at Lower Fort Garry, which was built of stone. This began the process by which the government hoped to justify the formation of the province of Manitoba as a place for incoming non-Indigenous settlers to reside (Dickason and Newbigging 2010).

Box 9.1: Key Provisions of Treaties No. 1 and No. 2, Signed with the Peguis (Ojibway) First Nation in 1871

Treaties 1 and 2 were the first of 11 numbered treaties negotiated between 1871 and 1921. Treaty 1 was signed August 3, 1871, between Canada and the Anishinabek and Swampy Cree of southern Manitoba. Treaty 2 was signed August 21, 1871, between Canada and the Anishinaabe of southern Manitoba. Although some were later restricted, key provisions included the following points:

1. Cession, release, surrender, and yield of specified land to Her Majesty the Queen; in return,
2. Continuance of using the land in the surrendered tract for traditional pursuits, such as hunting, trapping, and fishing (later restricted);
3. Each band to receive a reserve large enough to provide 160 acres for each family of five (or in like proportion for smaller or larger families);
4. Each man, woman, and child to be given a gratuity (or one-time payment) of three dollars, and a yearly annuity totalling $15 per family of five (later increased to five dollars each);
5. The government also agreed to maintain a school on each reserve and to prohibit the introduction or sale of liquor on reserves;
6. The provision of animals such as bulls, cows, boars, and sows, and equipment such as plows and harrows, and buggies (unfulfilled).

Source: Albers, Gretchen. 2015. "Treaties 1 and 2." *Canadian Encyclopedia*, September 25.

By 1877, six more treaties had been signed; by 1899, three more were signed; an 11th treaty was signed in the Northwest Territories in 1921. These numbered treaties were not like earlier ones, however. Whereas previous treaties implied an agreement between equals, the numbered treaties imposed the will of the new colonial government. Thus, Indigenous peoples were enjoined to divide themselves into bands and elect chiefs and councillors to govern themselves. Likewise, Status Indians who wanted to have a vote in Canada or even leave a reserve and go to a bar would have to disavow their "Indian-ness." It is not an exaggeration to suggest that these treaties determined virtually every aspect of Indigenous peoples' everyday lives.

Racism underpinned the Canadian government's approach to treaty making, informing two particular considerations. First, the government wanted to set aside specific areas for European settlement; by contrast, as Chief John Snow (2005) points out, the land set aside for Indian reserves was very poor and unsuitable for farming. Second, establishing reserves constituted a convenient way for governments to manage Indian affairs, since the nomadic First Nations would be settled on relatively small pieces of land (Melling 1967).

The terms offered in these numbered treaties were generally similar. Terms included surrender of Indigenous rights and title to traditional lands in addition to the creation of reserves not to exceed one square mile (1.6 square kilometres) per family of five. The government also agreed to provide a measure of military protection, a small per-capita annuity, instruction in the basics of farming, and some form of education (Buckley 1993). The location of each reserve was determined, after consultation with First Nations, by someone sent by the chief superintendent of the Indian Affairs Branch (IAB) of the Department of Indian Affairs and Northern Development. Other terms included a ban on intoxicating beverages, a guarantee of hunting and fishing rights, the provision of a school, and the annual award of a few dollars per individual. In Treaty No. 6, for example, the amount was $12 per year. In addition, the government would make provisions of implements, twine, and farm animals so that the reserve residents could take up agriculture.

There is evidence that, far from being weak or passive victims of the process, the Indigenous leaders made the best of an admittedly difficult situation. Friesen (1986) points out that some Indigenous leaders discussed the terms of the agreements handed to them and, when necessary, manoeuvred, stalled, appeased, and compared offers to get the best deal. Some chiefs objected to the amounts of land prescribed for them and voiced their objections. The chiefs rejected the terms of Treaty No. 6 three times before signing it, for example, and the negotiations ended with a fourfold increase in assigned lands, as well as a "medicine chest."

However, the treaties remain contentious. Until recently, the standard interpretation has been that government officials believed they were negotiating the surrender of Indigenous lands, while Indigenous peoples believed they were simply arranging the sharing of the land in return for benefits. Krasowski (2019, 1) terms this the **cultural misunderstanding thesis** and argues that it is wrong—there was no ambiguity about what had taken place: successive governments simply did not live up to their part of the agreement. Focusing on numbered treaties 1 to 7 and relying on previously ignored first-hand accounts, recently published secondary sources, and oral histories, Krasowski argues Indigenous peoples "agreed to share the land so that settlers could make a living by farming," in exchange for which "First Nations received a number of benefits" (2019, 277). Others have similarly argued that, in many cases, the government never recognized or honoured the hard-won oral promises that Indigenous leadership had gained during the treaty signing (Frideres and Gadacz 2001). Indigenous activist and Métis leader Howard Adams (1921–2001) argues that, because they were aimed primarily at furthering the process of colonization, the treaties are worthless (Adams 1989).

As flawed in content and application as they might be, in the eyes of some Indigenous leaders, the treaties nonetheless represent a binding—albeit broken—contract. In the words of former president of the Indian Association of Alberta, Harold Cardinal (1969), the treaties are an Indigenous "Magna Carta" because they were entered into with faith and hope for a better life. In a speech two months before the first ministers' meetings held in Ottawa on March 15 and 16, 1983, Chief John Snow (1988, 42) stated,

> The Indian treaties with the Crown are real, and we must see to it that the terms of those treaties and related documents are fully included with the new constitution. Without our treaties we would be in the same unfortunate situation as the non-Status and non-treaty Indians. I remind all treaty and registered Indians that the treaties are sacred covenants; they are binding documents and they must not be altered unilaterally by the Government of Canada.

FROM HUNTING AND GATHERING TO AGRICULTURE

As the conditions brought about by the treaties gradually became reality, the Indigenous peoples were informed that they would soon become sedentary farmers instead of nomadic hunters. Father Albert Lacombe, missionary to the Blackfoot, urged Chief Crowfoot (1830–1890) to lead his people to a way of life that would eventually provide them with a new kind of prosperity. Chief Starblanket (1816–1896) of Saskatchewan optimistically stated, "We Indians can learn the ways of living that made the white man strong" (Buckley 1993, 34).

A decade after the first treaty signing, Indigenous peoples on the Prairies were increasingly motivated to adopt an agricultural mode of economy with the demise of the "supermarket of the plains," as the buffalo has been called. Many Indigenous leaders could not fathom what was happening to their way of life. Competition among First Nations for the remaining bison grew. Many former warriors resisted the idea of digging in the ground with a stick. Others grasped at spiritual straws, some believing their religious leaders when they spoke of the Great Spirit's anger with humankind for replacing hunting with ploughing, while some prophets also predicted the eventual return of the animal, perhaps in some other form. (A few years ago, a spokesman for the Smallboy band of Cree in Alberta declared that the buffalo were now coming back out of the ground in the form of oil and gas.)

These incidents aside, how enthusiastic were Indigenous farmers in the West toward the idea of taking up an agrarian lifestyle? Early historian G. F. G. Stanley (1936/1975) fostered the view, later promoted by Hanks and Hanks (1950) in their study of the Blackfoot reserve in Alberta, that Indigenous warriors and hunters looked upon farming with disdain and shunned the concepts of steady work and acquisitiveness promoted by the dominant Euro-Canadian society, though some chiefs changed their minds about farming when they saw the rewards that could be theirs: axes, blankets, and beads. This view, replicating early 20th-century Euro-centric approaches,[1] has since been successfully challenged.

Carter (1993) argues that this Euro-centric view is based on a dualism theory that recognizes two distinct and largely independent thinking patterns, modern and traditional. In this view, the modern perspective is characterized by high productivity, a market orientation, is quite receptive to change, and pursues rational and maximizing aims. In contrast, the more traditional (Indigenous) perspective is regarded as pre-capitalist, subsistence-oriented, primitive, and small-scale. It is depicted as present-oriented, resistant to change, and affected by incentives quite different from the modern model—a view that ignored the ways in which Indigenous peoples had long integrated adaptive practices into their lifeways.

Against the views of Stanley and others, Carter (1993) presents evidence that East Coast Indigenous peoples were long involved in horticulture and agriculture; for example, Woodland First Nations were already solidly entrenched in agriculture (growing corn, beans, and squash) when the first Europeans arrived. Similarly, the Iroquois received acceptable land grants on the Grand River in Upper Canada and met with success in farming comparable to that of their Euro-Canadian neighbours.

Citing studies by Tobias (1977) and Carlson (1981), Carter contends that many Plains First Nations in the West were actually quite anxious to take up farming. The Cree people, for example, adopted farming, and much of the political activity of their leaders involved concerns about the lack of promised assistance rendered to them in that regard. Likewise, the Dakota of Manitoba initially showed great enthusiasm about farming until environmental setbacks and government restrictions brought about a period of stagnation (Laviolette 1991). Lobbied by settler colonists fearing competition, the Department of Indian Affairs intentionally prevented Indigenous farmers in the West from acquiring the proper seeds and supplies and the latest in agricultural machinery (Carter 1993) that might allow them to prosper. Indigenous farming became marginal to the new economy, the government leaving the people increasingly impoverished and starving.

As a final note, however, we might also question the privileging of farming over hunting and gathering. The stages of economic development, from one to the other and ending in industrialism, is very much a European model. Prior to colonization, however, hunting on the Prairies in the form practised by Indigenous peoples was aligned with long-term sustainability and a steady work ethic commensurate with the seasons. Only when the settlers arrived and often deliberately killed off bison herds did that way of life become unsustainable.

COLONIALISM

With the collapse of the fur trade, its replacement by an agricultural and industrial economy, and the easing of tensions with the Americans, the British government in 1830 transferred management of Aboriginal affairs in Canada from military to civil authority. Indigenous peoples, lacking an economic base for continued political control of their lives, experienced an abrupt change as civil authorities now sought to "take care of" (i.e., dominate) them.

Until Confederation, the protection of First Nations and their lands was the paramount goal. The notion that Indigenous peoples needed to become civilized gained in importance, but assimilation was regarded as a gradual and long-term process. In 1869, the goals of civilization and assimilation were officially added to government objectives with the passing of the Act for the Gradual Enfranchisement of Indians (Tobias 1983). Thereafter, Indigenous peoples were denied any of the original or residual political power recognized in the Royal Proclamation's treaty process. Colonial interests simply dictated that plenary power would be centralized in the Constitution (Schouls 2003). What is colonialism?

Colonialism is a complex national system of racial, cultural, and political domination that produces privileges beyond the surplus value generated by capitalism (Adams 1999, 7). As a process, colonialism shapes the culture and life of both the colonizer and the colonized, with the important difference, of course, that the former assumes a superior position and assigns the latter an inferior status. Frideres and Gadacz (2001, 4–7) delineate the process of colonization in terms of seven characteristics.

The first characteristic is a colonizing group's invasion of a geographic territory occupied by an indigenous group (see Chapter 6). The second characteristic is a campaign of deliberate destruction of the indigenous group's social, economic, and cultural structures. Formal programs to carry out destructive policies were enacted between 1830 and 1875, particularly involving religious denominations and the provision of education, designed to assimilate the Indigenous peoples into European values and norms (Surtees 1969). In the years after 1870, the Canadian government engaged in a "state-sponsored attack on Indigenous communities" (Daschuk 2013, 186) that saw tens of thousands of Indigenous people die from famine and disease.

The third and fourth characteristics of colonialism are the interrelated processes of exerting external control while encouraging economic dependency among the conquered people. Typically, the invading nation sends out governors to run things in the newly acquired territory, rather than assigning such responsibilities to leaders of the colonized peoples. In Canada the federally appointed "Indian agent" filled this role, but frequently became a most despised foreign despot among the reserve residents, whose lives he made miserable (Halliday 1935). Nearly every activity on a reserve had to be approved by the Indian agent, including requesting seed, farm implements, or livestock, or even leaving the reserve on a temporary basis.

The fifth characteristic of colonialism is the provision of low-quality social services, including health, education, and welfare. This characteristic continues to be manifested in First Nations communities in a host of statistics showing reduced life expectancy, high mortality rates, poverty, inadequate education, a high incidence of infectious diseases such as tuberculosis, poor housing, and heavy reliance on social assistance, not to mention alcohol and substance abuse, suicide, physical assaults, child abuse, and family breakup.

The last two characteristics of colonialism are the practice of racism (see Chapter 6) and the establishment of a "colour line." Analytically, racism may be defined as the perspective that tends to stress the real or alleged features of race and supports the use of them as grounds for group and intergroup action (Fairchild 1967, 246). In practice, this means that some people simply believe one racial category is innately superior or inferior to another. If the practice of **endogamy** (marriage within one's own group) is any indication, the enforcement of a colour line has certainly worked in Canada; Indigenous peoples have the highest rate of marriage within their own ranks—almost 94 percent (Frideres and Gadacz 2001, 7).

Colonialism continues today, though it is more subtle—what some observers suggest is a form of **settler colonialism**,[2] the process of continuing settler control and domination of Indigenous peoples (Smith 2019). Ponting (1986, 86) points to several indicators of this form of colonialism: (1) manipulation of information as a form of social control; (2) excessive secrecy or overburdening band members with information; (3) obstructionism versus facilitation insofar as getting information is concerned; (4) manipulation of discretionary funds; (5) withholding of funds; and (6) other means of socio-fiscal control.

Adams (1999) similarly insists that colonialism is alive and well but argues it is often fostered by Indigenous organizations themselves. He alleges that leaders in these organizations often manipulate government grants to benefit themselves and not band members. In turn, this arrangement works well for government: By using reactionary Indigenous regimes, governments can hide their own colonial policies while crushing Indigenous efforts toward self-sufficiency by dispersing and disorganizing the population.

Echoing Adams's concerns, Boldt cautions Indigenous peoples to carefully monitor their own leaders if they are to attain justice, arguing that their leaders "often manifest the same degree of paternalism, authoritarianism, self-interest and self-aggrandizement in their leadership as their non-Native counterparts" (Boldt 1993, 141). A corollary to this concern is the matter of accountability. Flanagan (2000) argues that Indigenous leaders will never be held accountable by their people as long as the money they spend comes from the public treasury; thus, a new definition of Indigenous self-government is needed. This advice seems questionable, however, given the many negative legacies of colonialism (impoverishment, substandard housing, inadequate sanitation, addiction, etc.). Some degree of economic self-sufficiency is required for self-government to succeed, and this is unfortunately largely lacking on most Indigenous reserves.

THE RESERVE SYSTEM

Indigenous reserves in Canada were first established following negotiation of the treaties in the late 19th century between representatives of Queen Victoria and the various Indigenous chiefs. Wuttunee (1971) argues that reserves were designed to take Indigenous peoples away from their traditional territories and segregate them on small parcels of land so that the surrounding areas would be safe for incoming settlers. Melling (1967) supports this argument, noting, for example, that no reserves were created in areas where settlers did not migrate, such as the Yukon, Labrador, or the Northwest Territories. It also could be argued that reserves were at least partially designed for the administrative convenience of government. It was a lot easier to deal with Indigenous "problems" if they were all located on a specific plot of land rather than trying to minister to the needs of a group of nomadic wanderers.

Whatever the underlying reasons, it is clear that much of the land reserved for the Indigenous population was chosen—quite intentionally—for its unsuitability for farming. Thus, the period after the treaty signings saw Canada prosper under the National Policy (see Chapter 6), while Indigenous peoples languished. The reserve inhabitants suffered from malnutrition and disease in primeval silence (Krasowski 2019), often far from the hurly-burly of mainstream Canadian life and thus unseen, in semi-permanent havens from the modern world.

Until the 1960s, there was practically no economic development on Indigenous reserves. Were it not for government transfer payments such as relief family allowance, youth allowances, blind and disabled people's allowances, and old age assistance, few Indigenous peoples would have survived, though it can be cogently argued that the money provided was insufficient to launch them out of dependency. In 1959, the average yearly income of Indigenous people in Saskatchewan was $200, one-sixth that of the average yearly income of $1,245 earned by all the province's citizens.

There were exceptions. In contrast to their western counterparts, the Algonquian and Iroquois nations did quite well, when given the opportunity. The same was the case in other areas of economic life. For example, Indigenous males who had previously been successful voyageurs became river pilots, guiding boats and barges loaded with supplies through the rapids to the port of Montreal. When the Grand Trunk Railway began building the Victoria Bridge, some of the same river men learned the skills of the high-beam steel workers, a prestigious occupation that many Iroquois continued to practise today. In short, Indigenous people in eastern Canada had built up over time a repertoire of skills employable in the changing economy.

By contrast, as we have seen, Indigenous people in the West were actively opposed by the Department of Indian Affairs in their efforts to become farmers (Carter 1993). Similarly, when the railway cut through the western plains, the surplus of Indigenous workers at hand was ignored for employment. The reserve system, so heavily concentrated in the West, promoted the public's view that Indigenous people constituted an alien and dying society (Buckley 1993).

INDIGENOUS EDUCATION

Colonialism is not merely an economic or political phenomenon; it is also cultural. Where colonial systems have been most successful, they have entered into the psychology of the colonized. The truly colonized individual "apes" the language, beliefs, and behaviours of the colonizer while denigrating his or her own cultural heritage (Fanon 1968). Educational institutions have always played a key role in this process.

The campaign to colonize Indigenous culture via schooling has a long history in Canada. Mission schools were tried in early New France but soon proved unsuccessful due to low attendance. An alternative plan saw young Indigenous boys and girls sent directly to France, where they could be "properly educated" and later returned as teachers for their own people, but again, the results were not favourable; more often than not, the young Indigenous individuals became marginalized, unable to function in either society. A few died. By 1639, scarcely a dozen had returned to the colony to assist the missionaries. As a result, the practice was ended (Cornish 1881; Hawthorn 1966/1967; Jaenen 1986).

The Hudson's Bay Company operated Canada's first schools designed to educate Indigenous children. The company built and operated them primarily for the children of their employees, but a few Indigenous children were enrolled. Later, religious orders became the main administrators of schools for Indigenous students. In 1658, Sister Marguerite Bourgeoys (1620–1700), who later founded the Ursulines, opened a school for French girls in a converted stable, where eventually Indigenous children were also enrolled (Chalmers 1974). Around this same period, the Jesuits developed day schools in permanent settlements in New France and tried to lure Indigenous students, with a view to teaching them the Catholic faith and French culture.

The Catholic oblates, founded in the 1840s, dominated the early stages of missionary schools in Canada. The Grey Nuns (Sisters of Charity), responsible for the education of Indigenous girls, established their first school, St. Joseph's Academy, in St. Boniface in 1845. Further west, a host of well-known individuals, Catholic and non-Catholic alike, laboured for the same cause. These included James Evans, Robert Rundle, Father Albert Lacombe, Henry Steinhauer (an Indigenous missionary), and others. Typical of the educational philosophy of the time, Methodist missionaries George McDougall and his son John strove to "Christianize, educate and civilize" Indigenous peoples—in their case, the Woodland Crees and the Stoneys (McDougall 1903).

A dramatic shift in policy occurred in 1830 with a scheme to assimilate Indigenous peoples. Alongside the plan to establish First Nations in permanent settlements and commence instruction so that an agricultural form of lifestyle would be possible, missionaries and schoolmasters were brought in to instruct the children and to teach them to pray, read the Scriptures, and pursue "moral lives" (Friesen 1991, 14). In 1857, legislation to design education for Indigenous peoples was passed, entitled An Act for the Gradual Civilization of the Indian. The Civilization and Enfranchisement Act followed in 1858.

This same period saw the start of Canada's experiment in residential schooling for Indigenous children. Between 1833—when missionary Peter Jones petitioned the Methodist Church to build a residential school among the Ojibway people of Ontario—and 1996—when the last residential school in Canada closed (the Gordon Residential School in Punnichy, Saskatchewan)—80 such schools operated.

Among the first of these were industrial schools, begun shortly after 1830, when the civil branch of government took over Indigenous matters from the military (Titley 1992). The industrial school experiment in Indigenous education was short-lived, however.

Late enrolment for many students, short periods of attendance, and lack of funds to support the students in jobs after graduation were some of the problems. With justification, Indigenous parents disliked their children's removal to places often very far away; the industrial schools' deliberate attempts to convert and "civilize" them at the cost of their heritage; restrictions on the use of Indigenous languages; the teaching of "women's chores" to young men (rather than teaching them to read and write); and the industrial schools' work component, arguing that their children had been sent to school to learn literary skills, not to become unpaid apprentices with full-time jobs (Miller 1987)—complaints that echoed through the other types of residential schools that followed.

Confederation in 1867 saw the federal government become responsible for educating Indigenous youth. The treaties signed shortly thereafter specified that Her Majesty (Queen Victoria) agreed to maintain schools for instruction in such reserves (Brookes 1991), but the quality and mode were not specified. Given governmental objectives to eradicate Indigenous culture, why bother providing them with a first-class education? Besides, since the missionaries were already involved in the enterprise; why not continue to finance the residential schools for a few more years until they were no longer required?

Despite significant Indigenous protest, the push to have residential schools continued, and by the end of the 19th century every region of the nation had boarding schools for Indigenous children. Promoted by Egerton Ryerson (1803–1882), who in 1844 became the first superintendent of schools in English-speaking Canada, the federal government financed these schools while churches provided spiritual guidance and management. Ryerson suggested that Indigenous children could not attain civilization without a "religious feeling," and thus "the animating and controlling spirit of each residential school should be a religious one" (Brookes 1990, 20). The Province of Canada endorsed Ryerson's plan, acknowledging "the superiority of the European culture and the need to raise them [Indigenous peoples] to the level of the whites" (Haig-Brown 1993, 29).

A shift in policy was signalled in 1947 in a paper entitled (with admirable honesty), *A Plan to Liquidate Canada's Indian Problem in Twenty-Five Years* (Pauls 1984, 33). The scheme outlined a plan to transfer the authority for the operation of Indigenous schools from federal to provincial governments, a stance later reiterated in the White Paper of 1969 (see Chapter 11). Integration, rather than assimilation, was to be the basis of the new policy, though given that "integration" was still to be one way, it seemed a distinction without difference. Indigenous students would interact with their non-Indigenous peers, thereby slowly absorbing the values of dominant European culture (Allison 1983).

In 1949, the federal government placed the administration of residential schools directly in the hands of government bureaucrats instead of religious leaders. That same year, the Special Joint Committee of the Senate and the House of Commons recommended that, wherever possible, Indigenous children should be educated in association with other children (Friesen 1983). Despite considerable input from Indigenous leaders, however, education according to the traditional European format was still perceived as a vehicle for assimilating First Nations (Hawthorn 1966/1967). Likewise, despite mounting criticism, residential schools continued to operate; the last one closed in 1996.

LIFE IN A RESIDENTIAL SCHOOL

Indian residential schools conformed to what the Canadian sociologist Erving Goffman (1961, xiii) terms a **total institution**: a place of residence and work where a large number of like-situated individuals, cut off from the wider society for an appreciable period of time, together lead an enclosed, formally administered round of life.

Although only 30 to 35 percent of Indigenous children attended residential schools (Steckley and Cummins 2008, 191), many of them remember with deep pain the experiences they suffered in those institutions (Friesen 1999). Life in residential schools meant participating in an entirely different cultural milieu, replete with such alien features as corporal punishment, severe discipline, punishing work schedules, loneliness, and confinement. But worse—as a slew of testimony later revealed—many of the schools were places of severe emotional, psychological, physical, and sexual abuse. The cemeteries abetting the many schools provide evidence of the many children who died as a result of rampant illness, malnutrition, and medical experimentation.

A common feature of total institutions is **identity stripping** (Goffman 1961), essentially the removing of articles, personal identification, and other elements that tell individuals who they are. Children arriving at residential schools were often given Christian names to replace their own (though students in some schools were referred to only by assigned numbers), stiff uniforms in place of their Indigenous clothing, and a haircut, the latter a sufficient form of insult to a culture that revered long hair. The children also quickly learned that use of their native language was forbidden, and that using it would result in severe punishment, including beatings. The intent of stripping was to make Indigenous children ashamed of their culture and heritage.

Students quickly found themselves confronted with a highly structured hierarchical institution. Church-employed staff constituted the power structure and the ideological ethos of the school. Many of them were from lower socio-economic backgrounds, were minimally educated, and were often only recent immigrants to Canada, with little understanding of Canada's history or value system, and knew even less about Indigenous lifeways (King 1967). They were armed with a strong sense of mission that, when frustrated, found vent in aggression and outright violence toward the children. Since their identity was derived theologically, they held more authority than parents or students, surpassed in status only by school administrators.

Daily activities in a residential school were quite crude and very public. Initially the huge brick buildings, heavily occupied and built on the factory model, had sealed windows; this no doubt contributed to the spread of diseases, notably tuberculosis, that took a fearful toll on Indigenous youth, and the buildings often had a rank odour. At other times, the residences were cold and drafty (Grant 1996). Bathing was a group activity, with the younger students bathing first. The water was often scalding hot when they started the ritual, but by the time the older students got their turn, the water was cold and dirty.

The quality of residential food was poor, the quantity scanty, and former residents frequently recall long periods of hunger. Given food shortages and rationing, students sometimes wolfed down their food as fast as possible. Sometimes, they stole bread from the kitchen, though the punishment for theft was severe if caught; thus, stealing food became a complex operation involving a number of participants in a particular institutional subcultural practice (Haig-Brown 1993). Due to the poor quality of much of the food, children's digestion was often poor, and so daily laxatives began to be administered whether children needed them or not. Likewise, many residential schools were sites of government-sanctioned medical testing/medication and nutritional experimentation.

Even more than in non-Indigenous schools of the period, the curriculum of the residential schools was primarily based on the three R's—readin', 'ritin', and 'rithmetic—plus a fourth staple, large doses of religion, the latter indubitably the most important of the four components (Perley 1993). As in the old industrial schools, there was also gender-specific work in some areas: farming and trades for boys, and housekeeping, mending, and knitting for girls. As noted, however, the use of Indigenous languages was forbidden; likewise, the history or cultures of First Nations was completely ignored. Music and songs reflected only the themes of the dominant settler society.

Learning was by rote and academic achievement low, mirroring the similarly very low expectations the largely inexperienced teachers had of their Indigenous students. But as Barman and colleagues (1986) and Grant (1996) argue, residential school education was never intended in any case to truly educate Indigenous youngsters. Had they been properly educated, Indigenous children may have become so well prepared that they might successfully enter the socio-economic order and become a threat to dominant society. The real purpose of residential schooling was to "kill the Indian in the child"; the real lessons to be learned every day were discipline and obedience to settler society. When students later transferred to provincial schools for high school training, they were often ashamed of their poor records; small wonder that less than 3 percent of those children attending residential schools ever graduated from high school.

Residential schools did provide some training in communication arts imported from Europe, and today many Indigenous leaders can trace their literary beginnings to the years they spent in residential schools. This in no way justifies the existence of that form of teaching and learning, but it offers some measure of consolation. In addition to mastering the basic forms of communication required to negotiate effectively with governments, many students formed lasting friendships with their peers that have endured to this day. (It is interesting, though not necessarily reassuring, to note that the majority of Indigenous leaders today are products of residential schools.) In some ways these bonds may have partially alleviated painful memories of the cruelties and hardships endured in residential schools.

Perhaps surprisingly, a few residential school survivors have quite positive memories of the experience and today even speak highly of the education they received. For example, interviews conducted with 80 elders from the Kainai (Blood) reserve in southern Alberta, authorized by the Kainai administration in 1995 and 2003, convey several instances of pride and gratitude felt by some former residents (Sikotan and Mikai'sto 1995; Sikotan, Mikai'sto, and Omahksipootaa 2003).

These few positive memories are far eclipsed, however, by the devastating and long-term impacts of residential schools upon the vast majority of those who attended. According to Grant (1996), these impacts include an inability to express feelings, apathy, values confusion and culture shock, anti-religious attitudes, and significant long-term trauma that has affected succeeding generations. Many former residential school students have had to work very hard to overcome the psychological, spiritual, and sexual abuses they suffered, and sadly, those abused in residential schools often became abusers themselves (O'Hara 2000). The cycle continued with many former students transmitting the abuses they witnessed and experienced at the hands of the staff and teachers on to their own children.

Why did Indigenous parents enrol their children in such harmful environments? The fact is, parents had no real choice. Often, the children were taken away by members of the Royal Canadian Mounted Police. Some parents, having a difficult time supporting their families largely due to the effects of colonization and having to live on reserves, grudgingly released their children in hopes they might have a better chance in life if they attended the school and developed their skills (Furniss 1995). Still others followed the local Indian agent's advice, perhaps in the belief that doing so might gain the agent's approval.

The residential system ended due to increased government intervention motivated by citizen concern (King 1967). As a first step toward liquidation, schools run by missionaries were taken over by government bureaucrats in the 1950s, but this stage was brief. Indigenous parents, some of them educated in residential schools themselves, grew increasingly involved in the education of their children. In 1970, the residential school in St. Paul, Alberta, was turned over to local control after nearly 300 Indigenous people conducted a sit-in at the school (Persson 1986). Fifteen years later, two-thirds of reserve schools in Canada were either partly or completely managed by Indigenous school boards.

Over the years, many of the closed residential schools were simply torn down, though some were converted to other purposes. First Nations bands managed a few; in 1995, for example, Indigenous management operated six residential schools in Saskatchewan. Several former residential schools became cultural centres, adult learning centres, or private schools. When administration of these schools was transferred to Indigenous control, the influence of Indigenous input was quickly evident. It is more than symbolic that, at the final closing exercises of several residential schools in the 1980s—for instance, at Qu'Appelle Indian Residential School in Saskatchewan—Indigenous dancing and social events often took precedence over denominational activities (Gresko 1986).

CONCLUSION

Contact between Indigenous and non-Indigenous peoples in North America occurred in several stages. During the first stage, Indigenous peoples had a degree of control over the relationship. The outsiders wanted a valuable commodity: furs. They also relied on local know-how in learning how to live in inclement climates. The Indigenous tribes were pleased to supply furs and expertise in return for various imported products, but the fur trade also soon exposed them to dangers such as disease and war, including conflict between the tribes. Over the long term, the fur trade also eroded Indigenous culture.

By the time the fur trade collapsed in the early 19th century, the relationship between Indigenous and non-Indigenous peoples was no longer that of equals. Excluded from the new modes of economy, subject by government decree to policies and practices designed to cause their languages and cultures to disappear, Indigenous peoples in Canada were rolled over as the country expanded after 1867, first westward, to the Prairies, then to the coast, and, finally, to the North. Viewed by successive governments as a dying people, Indigenous Nations gradually vanished from the Canadian landscape into places of physical and psychological retreat and subjugation. They were shut out of modernity, though the consequences of colonialism remained: scars often visible in the forms of poverty, unemployment, interpersonal violence and abuse. Thankfully, however, the story does not end there, as we will see in the chapters that follow.

NOTES

1. The alleged contrast between traditional and modern societies was a standard element of early sociology, including the work of Emile Durkheim and Max Weber (see Chapter 1). It continued in the later work of Talcott Parsons (1902–1979) and other post-1945 proponents of modernization theory whose implicit aim was to make Third World countries into economic and institutional mirrors of the industrialized western countries (see Parsons 1966).

2.   The term "settler colonialism" is used in preference to the older and less precise term "internal colonialism."

CRITICAL THINKING QUESTIONS

1.   How does the existence of Indigenous peoples complicate our conventional notions of the nation-state?
2.   How does the dominant mode of economic production shape the organizational structure of a society?
3.   What lessons does the fur trade hold for Canadian economic development as a whole?
4.   What are the similarities and differences between residential schools and other types of total institutions?
5.   In what ways are Indigenous peoples in Canada still subjects of colonial rule?

RECOMMENDED READINGS

Cardinal, Harold. 1977. *The Rebirth of Canada's Indians*. Edmonton: Hurtig Publishers.
  Considered somewhat of a classic over time, this book, by a young Indigenous leader, reached back into history to reveal the many shortcomings of both Canadians and their government in negotiating with Indigenous peoples.

Daschuk, James. 2013. *Clearing the Plains: Disease, Politics of Starvation, and the Loss of Aboriginal Life*. Regina: University of Regina Press.
  In arresting but harrowing prose, this book examines the roles that Old World diseases, climate, and Canadian politics—the politics of ethnocide—played in the deaths and subjugation of thousands of Indigenous people in the realization of Sir John A. Macdonald's "National Dream."

Friesen, John W., and Virginia Lyons Friesen. 2005. *First Nations in the Twenty-first Century: Contemporary Educational Frontiers*. Calgary: Detselig.
  The authors explore six educational challenges facing First Nations in Canada today: (1) spirituality, (2) leadership, (3) language maintenance, (4) Indigenous self-identity, (5) school curriculum, and (6) preparation of teachers.

Helin, Calvin. 2006. *Dances with Dependency: Indigenous Success through Self-Reliance*. Vancouver: Orca Spirit Publications and Communications.
  This book is touted as somewhat of a bible for Indigenous economic success, and Chief Helin, the author, is a strong proponent of Indigenous-originated and operated business and economic development.

Steckley, John I., and Bryan Cummins. 2008. *Full Circle: Canada's First Nations.* 2nd ed. Toronto: Pearson Education Canada.

Written in everyday language, this text is a good primer for those not acquainted with Indigenous affairs in Canada. Topics include prehistory and traditions, culture areas, legal definitions, effects of colonialism, and contemporary issues.

RELATED WEBSITES

Historical Society of St. Boniface
www.shsb.mb.ca/en

This is the oldest francophone historical society in western Canada. Among its online offerings is information on Louis Riel.

McGill University's Digital Library
digital.library.mcgill.ca/nwc

This library contains a large number of documents and maps dealing with the fur trade in Canada.

Métis National Council
www.metisnation.ca

Recognition of the Métis people as one of Canada's three distinct Indigenous peoples in the Constitution Act, 1982, paved the way for the creation in 1983 of the Métis National Council. Today, the MNC represents the Métis Nation nationally and internationally.

CANADIAN SOCIETY ON VIDEO

The Learning Path. 1993. National Film Board of Canada, 56 minutes, 50 seconds.

A moving film that describes the devastating effects of residential/boarding schools on Indigenous communities in Canada and the widespread sexual and physical abuse to which they were subjected. One of five videos in the *As Long as the Rivers Flow* series produced by the NFB.

Maïna. 2012. Telefilm Canada, 100 minutes.

A movie set in pre-European times, it follows the story of the daughter of an Innu chief as she tries to rescue a boy stolen by Inuit from her community. The film is in English, Inuktitut, and Inupiaq with English subtitles.

Olive Dickason's First Nations. 2006. Villagers Media Productions, 48 minutes.

This video captures the acclaimed work of Métis scholar Dr. Olive Dickason as she unearthed the buried history of First Nations culture in North America.

CHAPTER 10

Keepers of the North

Sled Dogs. Courtesy Bill Jorgensen.

What happens in the North will . . . tell us what kind of a country Canada is; it will tell us what kind of people we are.
    —Justice Thomas Berger, 1977

Canadians have never strayed far either physically or spiritually from the Canada-US boundary. We are [a] northern nation in fantasy and imagery only.
    —Ken Coates, P. Whitney Lackenbauer, William R. Morrison, and Greg Poelzer, 2008

What would a north where we actually respected Indigenous and treaty rights look like? It will take an enormous popular struggle to answer a question that no one in the highest reaches of power today wants to hear.
    —Peter Kulchyski, activist and author, 2013

INTRODUCTION

The vast majority of Canadians live within about 240 kilometres of the American border. Few have ever travelled to any of the territories, yet the North holds a special place in most Canadian hearts. It is a source of national identity.

Unlike elsewhere in Canada, Indigenous peoples predominate throughout much of the North, and they represent a majority in the Northwest Territories and Nunavut. While making up only 3.8 percent of the Canadian population as a whole, Indigenous peoples constitute roughly 24 percent of the resident population of the Arctic and subarctic regions (Harrison 2012). In fact, were a horizontal line drawn across Manitoba's 53rd parallel—roughly the latitude of Edmonton—73 percent of that province's population living north of the line identify as Indigenous (Indigenous Economy Report n.d.). Many Canadians at large see the North as part of Canada but also as overwhelmingly Indigenous land, with Canadians as its guardians.

The North is also a major source of Canada's present and future, a treasure trove of minerals and oil and gas reserves. But it is threatened—first by global warming and second by international challenges to Canada's jurisdiction from other polar countries. For all of these reasons, the North is very much in the news today.

This chapter briefly explores the peoples and history of the North, as well as the changing relationship of the region with the rest of Canada. We focus on the state's role in the North's gradual integration into Canada and the North's social, economic, political, and environmental challenges.

A PORTRAIT OF THE NORTH

Outsiders to the far north are amazed that anyone could enjoy life in an environment almost entirely void of trees and surrounded by great amounts of snow and ice. For about eight months of the year, most of the Arctic is covered with snow and extensive portions of its seas are frozen. The subarctic seems only slightly more hospitable, a place of pesky blackflies in summer and cold winter twilight. To those raised in the North, however, life in the crowded, fast-paced urban centres of the South seems equally strange and even tantamount to suicide. Besides, the long periods of daylight in Inuit country balance the long, bleak winter.

Canada's North consists of Arctic and subarctic regions and stretches north from 60 degrees latitude to the North Pole. The Arctic comprises three million square kilometres of ice, water, and tundra, while the subarctic includes more than 4.5 million square kilometres of land. Combined, these regions amount to nearly 80 percent of the land and water mass of Canada, an area populated by nearly 1.5 million people. While these areas together make up the largest geographic region in Canada, they have by far the smallest economy and population.

The Arctic's unique physical environment is primarily a result of the sun's relative absence. The tilt of the earth on its axis keeps the northern area facing away from the sun throughout the winter months and facing toward the sun throughout the summer months. For as long as four consecutive months, from mid-October to mid-February, the Arctic is plunged into darkness.

During the summer, snow melts, plants grow, and it becomes the land of the midnight sun, experiencing constant daylight for a few short months. Spring and fall are virtually non-existent in the area. Most Arctic regions experience January temperatures as cold as −40°C or −45°C with a mean temperature of only 12°C during the warmest months, though this is rapidly changing (see further in this section). The 200 varieties of vegetation in the Arctic (shrubs, scrub trees, herbs, and lichen) are low to the ground, grow away from the wind, and thrive in brief and intense growing periods.

The Arctic Ocean and surrounding lakes and rivers begin to freeze over in October and remain frozen until May in most areas. The frozen ocean extends the Arctic coastline by hundreds of kilometres, but the ice is not always safe to travel on and in recent years has been growing thinner. Strong winds often drive vast floating fields of ice across the waterways, and they may crash into one another, creating upheavals. A sudden spring breakup can create ice floes that may carry off unsuspecting hunting parties or migrating families (Osborn 1990).

Traditionally, the peoples of the Arctic relied on a variety of game and birds for food. This included the Arctic hare, the Arctic fox, the muskox, and birds such as rock ptarmigans, sandpipers, plovers, elder ducks, red-throated loons, and ruddy turnstones. Little-appreciated life forms included a variety of obnoxious insects such as small flies, mosquitoes, and bees. Today, many Arctic species, such as the polar bear, are threatened by climate change.

An obvious treeline separates the subarctic from the Arctic and consists of four distinct zones: (1) the wooded tundra, (2) the lichen woodland, (3) the closed boreal forest, and (4) the forest parkland. The wooded tundra forms the transition zone. This wooded area contains sporadic patches of spruce and larch trees, and the lichen woodland has a few stands of spruce and pine. The closed boreal forest offers a denser stand of fir, spruce, and pine, while the forest parkland combines elements of forest and grass milieu (Bone 1992). Subarctic wildlife is more plentiful and includes some 50 species of birds and 600 species of plants.

Bone (1992) points out that the North's fragile physical environment poses unique challenges. Its cold climate and slow rate of natural growth means it takes longer to recover from industrial accidents such as oil spills. Unfortunately, industrial development in the North often does not fully consider the environment and people there.

THE NORTH'S INDIGENOUS PEOPLES

Indigenous peoples in the North are made up of three primary groups: (1) the Inuit of the Arctic, (2) the Algonquian-speaking people of the eastern subarctic (the Cree, the Naskapi, and the Montagnais, with those located in Labrador referred to as Innu), and

(3) the Athapaskan-speaking people (the Dene), located in the western subarctic (Brody 1987). The latter two groups also span the northern portions of several provinces, including Quebec and Labrador, as well as the western provinces.

The Inuit

Most historians and archaeologists today believe the Inuit are descendants of the Thule Inuit, who spread from the northern coast of Alaska to the Mackenzie Delta in the 11th century, replacing the Dorset people (Crowe 1974; Wilson 1976; Purich 1992). Linguistically, the Inuit language is unique, with no discernible relationship with any other Indigenous people on the continent. The language probably diverged from Aleut about 6,000 years ago and thereafter evolved into two distinct subfamily units, Yupik and Inupik. This includes all dialects between western Alaska and Greenland (Jennings 1978).

The land of the Inuit is divided into a western portion, which includes the Aleut on the Aleutian Islands as well as the Inuit of Alaska, and a central and eastern region, which embraces all of the Inuit from the Mackenzie River Delta east to Greenland. At the time of first contact with Europeans, some 22,000 Inuit lived in the North. The groups broadly identified as Inuit include Mackenzie, Copper, Netsilik, Sadliq, Caribou, Iglulik, South Baffin Island, Ungava, and Labrador (Crowe 1974; Brody 1987). There is evidence of a fairly widespread exchange of various minerals, including soapstone, iron, and copper, and products made from raw materials like ivory, among the tribes before the arrival of Europeans (Crowe 1974).

Essentially an ocean-oriented culture, the Inuit obtained most of their food supply from the sea. Seals and other sea mammals were a chief source of food, though in the summer months fishing and caribou hunting supplemented the Inuit diet. Taylor (1974) describes a typical annual cycle used by the Netsilik around the turn of the 20th century. The sea began to freeze around October, the caribou herds departed southward, and the building of snow houses commenced. The Netsilik continued fishing char from the sea until the middle of November, and the women were busy making winter clothes. During December and January, people generally remained at home, relying on provisions made the previous summer and fall. The breathing-hole seal hunting began in February when the snow on the ice was deep; other hunting techniques were employed when April and May arrived. These included sneaking up on the seal or catching new pups at the breathing holes. A few stray caribou showed up, and in June when the snow houses caved in from the hot sun, the people moved into tents. Kayaks were prepared for caribou hunting, which continued until the herd disappeared south again.

The Inuit had a sophisticated culture that suited the materials and circumstances of their climate and geography. The Alaskan Inuit and Aleuts, for example, developed the two-holed kayak and, in place of the toggling harpoons that other Inuit used for large sea mammals, also devised a multi-barbed harpoon dart head (Dumond 1977). Housing construction—from portable summer tents made of seal or caribou skin, to winter homes of the classic igloo type (Baldwin 1967), to (in the south) rectangular, semi-subterranean, turf-covered houses of logs—reflected a firm grasp of such things as ventilation and insulation.

The Inuit have traditionally been unique among Indigenous people in functioning with a simple social system, unencumbered by elaborate hierarchical forms of governing individuals or bodies. They have historically had no chiefs among them. Contrary to the Western dichotomy of individualism versus collectivism, the traditional Inuit way of life involved a form of **individual egalitarianism**: when food was scarce, supplies were stretched as far as possible and a spirit of goodwill prevailed. Friendliness was expected; anger was viewed as a form of madness (Coates et al. 2008). Age and gender determined one's status, though the sexes were more equal than in European countries of the day. In hunting, for example, women assisted their husbands in driving animals into an ambush. Still, women had the chief role in raising children and preparing food (Giffen 1930). Inuit clothing was unisex, consisting of loose-fitting fur trousers and shirts, usually made of caribou hide, but sometimes of polar bear or other animal fur (Josephy 1968).

Polygyny, the marriage of one man to more than one woman, was not uncommon. Since the Inuit sometimes practised female infanticide, however, there was often a scarcity of women. This being the case, on occasion, and subject to strict clan-related rules, a man might lend the use of his wife to a friend on a short-term basis, a practice that elicited both sensationalist intrigue and condemnation among European outsiders (Mowat 1952; Balikci 1970; McMillan 1995).

Storytelling, along with everyday modelling, were means of transmitting valued Inuit cultural beliefs and values to the young. In some tribes storytellers were designated, while in others both men and women of respect could relate stories. Among the Labrador Inuit, each village had a designated storyteller, while in Alaska certain old men monopolized this art (Giffen 1930).

The Dene

The Dene (sometimes spelled Dinneh) today number 65,000 people, nearly 70 percent concentrated in Saskatchewan. They speak a dialect of the Athapaskan language (Chapter 9), part of a language family comprising the Apache and the Navajo of the American Southwest. Abel (1993) suggests the northern peoples traditionally used the word *Dinneh* to identify the larger population and distinguished a wide range of separate groups by adding the name of a river or lake associated with their particular hunting ground. Irwin's (1994) comprehensive list of Dene tribes includes the Chipewyan of the Canadian interior (not to be confused with the Chippewa-Ojibway of Lake Superior); the Dogrib, between Great Slave Lake and Great Bear Lake; the Beaver, who lived along the lower Peace River in northern Alberta; the Slavey, along the southern shore of Great Slave Lake; the Hare, northwest of Great Bear Lake; the Klaska or Nahani, west of the headwaters of the Mackenzie River; the Sekani, in central British Columbia; the Carrier (named for their widows' custom of carrying the charred bones of their dead husbands on their backs) of north-central British Columbia; the Chilcotin, who were south of Carrier lands; the

Tahlan, on the upper Stikine River in northwestern British Columbia; and the Tuchone in southern Yukon Territory (see also Crowe 1974; Ryan 1995; Massey and Shields 1995).

Like the Inuit, the Dene have traditionally been hunters and trappers. Huge herds of caribou and moose were vital components of Dene diet and culture, supplemented by the fish of lakes and rivers. Predictability of supply was important. The Chipewyan people, for example, followed the migration patterns of the caribou, and if there was even a slight shift in their migration paths, the band's food supply was affected. In fall, these animals were slaughtered by waiting hunters as they passed a certain point, and the meat was cut into strips, dried in the sun, and pounded into pemmican for the winter food supply (McMillan 1995).

The Dene traditionally have specific kinship patterns. For example, the Hare, so named for their use of rabbit skins for clothing and shelter, lived in small extended families that divided relatives into two groups: Cross-relatives were in-laws, while parallel relatives were akin to parents, siblings, or one's own children (Ives 1990). A similar situation prevailed in Slavey country, where the people identified two kinds of relatives—kinsmen and in-laws.

The Dene also had quite explicit social rules (Ryan 1995), covering three specific areas: (1) natural resources, (2) families, and (3) governance or decision-making. In turn, these rules were intertwined with the Dene's holistic view of the universe. Rule-breakers were punished in various ways. For minor offences, an elder might deal verbally with the guilty party. Individuals committing more serious offences were often made the subject of a gathering in which they were required to admit guilt and make restitution, followed by a process of reconciliation. If this failed, shunning—and even death, though rarely used—was possible.

A 19th-century visitor to Dene country, Father Petitot, noted that Dene beliefs were reflected in daily practices but not formalized (Savoie 1970). A series of celestial beings were worshipped as deities: the midnight sun, for example, was a real national and tutelary god, supremely recognized and worshipped. Father Petitot described the Dene as having a primordial knowledge of a Good Being who was placed above all other beings and possessed a multitude of names, the most common one being Bettsen-nu-unli ("He by whom the earth exists"). Frequently, spirit beings would personify themselves in the form of birds, such as the eagle; the male spirit brought the day and the female spirit brought the night (Savoie 1970). As in the South, the trickster was recognized in the form of a raven, as a creator, culture hero, and miracle worker (Merkur 1991).

Roman Catholic priests who later arrived in Dene territory introduced concepts that blended well with traditional Dene beliefs: love your spouse, be kind to your neighbours, take good care of your children and raise them well, and stay together forever (Ryan 1995). In many instances, priests were perceived as emissaries from God possessing spiritual power and authority, and served as wisdom elders, providing advice and direction, resolving disputes, and meting out disapproval for acts of violation.

There is little doubt that conflict with European society caused some First Nations cultural and spiritual traditions to be altered or even lost (Brody 1987). Many sacred practices that the priests frowned upon continued in secret; sometimes, as well, Christianity merged with Indigenous beliefs—in a process known as **syncretism**—in ways the missionaries did not recognize. In short, Christianity had important effects on Indigenous cultures, but Indigenous peoples also took what they wanted from the new religion while retaining many of their old beliefs and values, the shoots of which are seen today in a strong cultural and spiritual renaissance in most Indigenous communities (Lincoln 1985; McGaa 1990).

THE COMING OF THE EUROPEANS

Initial contact between the northern people and Europeans in the 10th century were not friendly. Erik the Red, a Norwegian who explored Greenland, and whose son, Leif, later returned to establish a colony in Newfoundland, viewed the locals as quite primitive "little people" who had no iron and used missiles made of walrus tusks and sharp stones for knives (Osborn 1990, 77). It was a pattern of contact repeated several centuries later with the arrival of a new band of explorers.

Among these early explorers were John Cabot (in 1497 and 1498), Martin Frobisher (in 1576, 1577, and 1598), John Knight (in 1606), and Henry Hudson (in 1609 and 1610). Why did they come? In part, they were searching for precious metals, especially copper and gold, but they also had a larger quest: finding a northwest passage to the Orient.

European exploration, beginning in the 15th century with Cabot, was inextricably linked to mercantilism (Chapter 1). In today's context, we can see this period as an early expression of globalization, with its search for new products and markets, and the expansion of trade. While considerable trade occurred overland between Europe and Asia, it also occurred by sea. But a ship sailing to the Orient from Europe, either eastward around Africa or westward around South America, might journey more than a year. By contrast, a passage more directly westward would save time and money, hence the search for what Pierre Berton (1988) termed "the Arctic Grail."

Ultimately, the North-West Passage was found. It was not mastered, however, until Norwegian Roald Amundsen sailed his sloop, the *Gjoa*, through the ice in 1905 (Berton 1988). By then, the North had claimed a host of explorers and their ships. Among these was Hudson, who steered a course into a strait that later bore his name and became icebound, whereupon his crew mutinied and set him and a few loyal crewmen adrift in a small boat, never to be seen again. Hudson's lurid fate and that of other disastrous expeditions that followed—from Jens Munk in 1619 to Sir John Franklin in 1845 to 1849 (Beattie and Geiger 1987)—did not dissuade outsiders, however. Far from it, in fact—the North became transformed into a place both mystical and mythical. (Note that Mary Shelley's monster in *Frankenstein*, published in 1819, dies on an Arctic ice floe.) Where mysterious allure failed to attract, profit proved a siren call to Europeans.

And profit there was. In 1665, two disgruntled fur traders from New France, Pierre-Esprit Radisson and Médard Chouart des Groseilliers, having been turned down by the French government, went to London to meet King Charles II and local merchants to seek their support. The English were more responsive to Radisson and des Groseilliers, and shortly thereafter, in 1670, Charles II issued the Hudson's Bay Company charter, granting the company rights to all lands whose waters drained into Hudson Bay. The Hudson's Bay Company (HBC) thus became "the vastest empire any private company ever controlled" (Morton 1997, 75; Newman 1998).

The HBC did not immediately thrive. Over the next decades, the French captured company forts and burned them to the ground several times, only to see them rebuilt. Gradually, however, the company grew. Defeat of the French in 1763 and amalgamation with the rival North West Company in 1821 left the entity unassailable in the North. For roughly the next 50 years, the HBC represented a kind of quasi-government, making rules and regulations, enforcing order, and even providing social services such as education.

With the advent of the fur trade, the lifestyle and political economy of the northern Indigenous peoples changed dramatically. Some initially did quite well with the arrangement. For a hunting people, rifles and ammunition were a real advantage. Likewise, certain tribes also initially did well, notably the Cree, who quickly became middlemen and spread westward across Canada. But, as noted in Chapter 9, the fur trade also brought negative consequences. In the words of Brody (1987, 199), the "fur trade was built upon the economics of dependency." Trade with the forts became habitual. Hunters became trappers and changed their lifestyles accordingly. The role of women also changed, as they now had to clean and tan additional furs for market.

Not all northern peoples were brought into the world economy all at once. Beginning in the 17th and 18th centuries, some tribes in the subarctic had initial contact with fur traders pushing north from the St. Lawrence and whalers arriving from the North Atlantic. Others, however, experienced their first contact only in the 19th century. At that time, European ships began regular trips to the Arctic to garner whale oil, baleen (whalebone, used in making corsets), and walrus ivory. In the 1850s, the ships began to winter over, and contact between Europeans and Inuit intensified. The establishment of whaling stations upset the seasonal economic cycle of the settlements, which became handout stations, soon known as places where "weekly biscuits were handed out" (Wilson 1976, 85).

This increased contact brought other material and cultural changes. By the time commercial whaling came to an end (around 1912), "hunters were using rifles, telescopes, sheath knives, jack-knives, hatchets, saws, drills, awls, steels and files. Women cooked in metal pots and kettles, and used steel needles, cotton thread and metal scissors in sewing" (Brody 1987, 193). Clothing materials and styles also changed, as did music and dancing.

Some changes were decidedly negative, although the Indigenous people further west were less affected (Finnie 1948). Overhunting depleted the whale pods and led to starvation in some instances. Alcoholism, suicide, and disease also devastated communities. As early as 1887, Father Emile Petitot quoted a chief of the Chiglit Eskimos on the terrible living conditions among the Inuit: "We are all dying. . . . [W]e are getting snuffed out day by day and nobody cares about us. No one looks after our sick or pities our misfortunes" (Petitot 1999, 15). In 1912, Captain Henry Toke Munn described the Inuit of Baffin Island as a "passing race" destined for extinction because of the coming blight of complex European civilization, without whose influence he felt they would be better off. Brody (1987, 193) notes that around this same period, the Inuvialuit of the Mackenzie Delta were reduced from a community of 2,000 to about 30.

Northern peoples were about to experience even further changes, however. As so often in the history of the Americas (Wright 1993), the catalyst for change was gold.

THE YUKON GOLD RUSH

The California gold rush of 1849 begat the British Columbia gold rush of 1858, followed in 1896 by the discovery of gold on a tributary of the Klondike River by George Washington Carmack and his two Indigenous brothers-in-law, Skookum Jim and Tagish Charley. Even earlier, Robert Campbell, a trader with the Hudson's Bay Company, found gold in the gravel near his trading post at the junction of the Yukon and Pelly rivers in the early 1850s. An Anglican missionary, Robert McDonald, reported traces of gold in Birth Creek near the Yukon-Alaska border in the 1870s (Cruikshank 1998). This time, however, gold fever became a pandemic.

By the summer of 1897, however, hordes of men (women were scarce) were swarming over the Yukon region, some arriving by water, many taking the arduous journey over the White Pass and Chilcoot Pass, then down the Yukon River by a colourful assortment of handmade boats and rafts. By 1898, a total of 30,000 people lived in the Klondike region, about 16,000 of whom resided in Dawson City, which became the Yukon's capital. Most of the newcomers knew only three things about the Yukon: it was cold, it was remote, and gold nuggets were available for the picking.

While many of the fortune seekers sought female companionship among the locals, few of these relationships lasted very long. Most of the men soon drifted back south, often leaving children behind them. Those who stayed and struck it rich were few. Like other booms, it was the traders, hoteliers, or other providers of goods and services, not to mention the con artists, who made money (Cruikshank 1998; Berton 1958). Most of those who remained ended up working for wages, their stay occasioned by either a love of the North or dreams still nursed of becoming wealthy (Fried 1969).

The 1896 gold rush ended quickly. The boom-and-bust pattern of Canadian development, so familiar to the South, was replicated in the North. Dawson City's fortunes and population experienced a steep decline. Between 1902 and 1903 alone, $12 million left the northern territories, but—for all the wealth generated—little remained to be invested locally. Residents blamed both an uninterested government and lack of local control for this loss of revenue.

First, the gold rush augured the North's full integration into the world capitalist economy. It was a slow process. The fur economy remained strong throughout the 1920s, bringing considerable wealth to the Yukon and Northwest Territories. Fur towns like Aklavik sprang up, and a few local families got rich, but prosperity was again short-lived. For many people tied only tangentially to the labour market, however, the downturn was not critical. Meanwhile, companies were increasingly entering the region, searching for exploitable resources. Gold remained in high demand, leading to the foundation of towns at Noranda, Quebec; Kirkland Lake, Ontario; and Flin Flon, Manitoba. Other minerals such as radium and uranium were mined in places like Great Bear Lake, high in the Northwest Territories (Careless 1970).

It had long been known that the North possessed rich pockets of oil. Writing in his diary in the 18th century, explorer Peter Pond wrote about the thick pitch oozing from the Athabasca River's banks in what is today northern Alberta. In 1907, Alfred von Hammerstein, known as "the Count," acquired surface and mineral rights to about 48,600 hectares of freehold land downstream of where Fort McMurray now stands, and he set about drilling wells. He was unsuccessful. In 1920, however, the Imperial Oil Company announced the discovery of large amounts of oil at Norman Wells. The announcement temporarily spurred the Canadian government to seek a treaty with the local Dene to pave the way for development. The small amount of oil produced soon discouraged the government from further development in the area.

Second, while the North's economy as a whole was being transformed, local Indigenous peoples were frequently left on the margins of these changes. The pattern began with the gold rush and was repeated in the 1920s and 1930s, which saw an influx of white southerners seeking their fortunes at a time when jobs "back home" were growing scarce (Brody 1987). Locals now found themselves hard pressed to find employment, while incoming outsiders claimed jobs in the new economy: mining, oil, and government bureaucracies.

Third, the gold rush signalled the growing involvement of the Canadian government in the lives of northerners. Canada had gained jurisdiction over the West, Rupert's Land, and the Northwest Territories in 1870. In 1880, the British government ceded responsibility over the Arctic Islands to Canada, in large part to thwart American and other efforts to claim Baffin Island (Purich 1992). Canada's failure to enforce jurisdiction, however, subsequently resulted in claims pressed by other countries. Thus, the late 19th century saw a host of countries—particularly Britain, the United States, and Norway—sending polar expeditions, ostensibly in the name of exploration, but also to "plant their flags" (see Coates et al. 2008).

The Canadian government responded to these threats in various ways—for example, in 1897, by sending a reconnaissance mission to Hudson Bay and Baffin Island, where Captain William Wakeham declared Canada's sovereignty over that and surrounding islands. Similar missions followed, leading up the First World War. Between 1913 and 1918, the Canadian government also funded the research of Vilhjalmur Stefansson, whose work quickly popularized for Canadians "their" northern heritage. The government also expanded the number of North-West Mounted Police (NWMP) posts in the Arctic, the first having been established two years before the Yukon gold rush (Coates et al. 2008), increasing to three by 1903, and several more by the 1920s.

In 1922, the Canadian government instituted a yearly patrol of the eastern Arctic to enforce its claims to sovereignty over the North (Purich 1992; see also Brody 1987). The NWMP, now expanded and renamed the Royal Canadian Mounted Police in 1920, played an important role in this enforcement while performing a multitude of other functions and roles, including the North's administrators, social workers, and, perhaps most importantly, explorers. From 1940 to 1942, the RCMP vessel *St. Roch*, a kind of floating detachment, travelled the Northwest Passage from west to east, then from east to west in 1944, becoming the first ship to navigate the passage in both directions while also engaging in unofficial wartime reconnaissance.

In less than 50 years, Canada's North had been transformed from a peripheral and even exotic appendage to a politically, economically, culturally, and administratively integrated colony of the South. In 1939, the North also began its military integration into the Western world's geopolitics.

THE SECOND WORLD WAR AND THE POST-WAR SOUTH

The Second World War and subsequent Cold War brought renewed but brief interest in the North, this time not only for its resources but more immediately for strategic reasons. A major supply route for oil and other military supplies for Alaska moved down the Mackenzie River and along a new highway. Local centres like Fort Smith and Whitehorse suddenly burgeoned population-wise, and Frobisher Bay became a vast military complex. A former ghost town, Churchill, Manitoba, became a military base with a satellite town of skilled and unskilled non-Indigenous workers and a large number of unemployed Indigenous people whom the former viewed, ironically, as "squatters."

The Second World War saw a number of large-scale construction projects launched in the North. These included the construction of a series of landing fields, a military base at Goose Bay, the expansion of oil production at Norman Wells, the building of a pipeline from Norman Wells to Whitehorse, and the construction of the Alaska Highway. Both Goose Bay and Gander became strategic links in the North American chain of defence and, between them, supplied more than 900 warplanes to the United Kingdom (Bone 1988, 1992).

The Alaska Highway was a particularly monumental task for its time. Originally proposed in the 1930s, construction began finally in the 1940s, partially motivated by the Japanese bombing of Pearl Harbor in December 1941. The road was built both to supply Russians with needed materials to fight the Nazi invasion of their country and as a safeguard against a Japanese invasion of North America. The road was over 2,500 kilometres in length, built over muskeg and unstable fields of tundra, and required 11,000 men, including US army engineers and civilians, to complete the job. Although 80 percent of the highway was built on Canadian soil, the United States government paid the entire cost of $133 million while Canada absorbed the costs of upkeep. The road had two long-term impacts outlasting the war: It stimulated oil and gas exploration in the North, and the construction itself reinforced American influence in western Canada, especially Alberta (see Chapter 7).

As important as the military intrusion into the North was, the role of the Canadian government was more crucial in bringing about change (Vallee 1971). This presence increased markedly after 1945, with the federal government taking over direct responsibility for economic and social affairs as the Hudson's Bay Company no longer felt obligated to buffer Indigenous people from the economic swings in the marketplace.

Soon government facilities existed for services that touched on every aspect of Indigenous life. To some extent, this intervention improved the local way of life, as housing standards rose and famine became virtually a thing of the past. As colonization increased the precarity of hunting and trapping, new sources of Indigenous income were necessary, including wage labour programs, the sale of handicrafts, family allowances, various pensions, and social assistance.

Education was a key area of increased government involvement. As in the South, missionary schools had long existed in the North. Mission schools were opened as early as 1867 at Fort Providence on Great Slave Lake, and in 1874 at Fort Chipewyan on Lake Athabasca (Fisher 1981). Others followed, with a spate of residential schools set up by missionaries for Arctic and subarctic children in the 1940s and 1950s (Brody 1987). The purpose of the "new education" was acculturation and assimilation (see also Chapter 9). Local language training was prohibited, and religious practices related to Indigenous culture and spirituality discouraged. Boys no longer hunted or trapped with their fathers, and girls were removed from situations where they could take up traditional domestic responsibilities (Cline 1975). Health and educational facilities were virtually non-existent in northern regions (Rea 1968), although a federally sponsored program to train young women as nurses in mission hospitals was initiated in the Northwest Territories in 1939 (Drees 2013). After the 1950s, however, government intervention increased in the form of social and educational assistance as a means of assimilating Indigenous peoples into the body of national life. During the 1930s and 1940s, for example, the fur economy was still a mainstay of northern families. After 1947, however, the price of furs collapsed and remained low until the 1960s. Many Canadian officials viewed trapping as a dying way of life and were determined to drag the North and its residents into the "modern world." Education and economic development were seen as key elements of this process.

Increasingly, the Dene and Inuit found themselves backed into a corner by the realities of a shrinking resource base, their own geography, and the forces of international markets (Abel 1993). In the 1950s, settlements based on the fur industry declined. Farther north, some were able to live off the land, living in fishing camps in the summer and organizing hunting parties in the winter (Massey and Shields 1995), part of what Stabler (1989) has identified as a **dual economy**, a livelihood earned by both traditional and modern means. (In 1989, two-thirds of family breadwinners in the Northwest Territories still hunted and trapped.) In the southern subarctic, however, planned resource towns like Thompson, Manitoba, became major producers of minerals, attracted sizable populations, and sometimes employed local Indigenous peoples (Bone 1992).

NORTHERN VISIONS

In the late 1950s, English-speaking Canada was beginning to discover or, rather, create itself. Having broken with Britain over the period of the two world wars, Canada was also in the early stages of trying to separate itself from the United States. In part, these efforts were economic. Thus, in the elections of 1957 and 1958, Conservative leader John Diefenbaker spoke out regarding Canada's need to diversify trade, seek out new markets in Asia, and revive those in Britain. But Diefenbaker also lit a fire in many Canadians' imaginations with visions of opening up the North in much the same way that Sir John A. Macdonald had opened up the West in the 19th century. Like past federal colonizing efforts, the Diefenbaker government saw the North as a treasure trove of export commodities: forest products, minerals, and energy. The plan was to transform the fur-trading economy of the North into a resource-based, urban-like economy.

Under Diefenbaker's leadership, Indigenous Canadians garnered unconditional federal voting rights. Before 1960, they had to surrender their Indian Status, a process known as **enfranchisement**, if they wanted to vote as Canadian citizens. During the Diefenbaker years, assimilation as an official government policy toward First Nations was also downplayed. For these and other liberating manoeuvres, some observers have jokingly referred to Diefenbaker as "the Lincoln of the North" (McMillan 1995, 314).

By the late 1950s, Diefenbaker's "northern vision" had growing cultural support. Years before, Vilhjalmur Stefansson's 1921 book *The Friendly Arctic* and his subsequent speeches, as well as Robert Flaherty's 1922 silent film *Nanook of the North*, the world's first full-length documentary, had popularized the North among Canadians and non-Canadians alike (Brody 1987; Srebrnik 1998). (*Nanook* began touring Canada again in 2014, with a new soundtrack featuring the sounds of Tanya Tagaq, an Inuk throat singer.) The harrowing tales of bush pilots in the years after, followed by the popular writings of people like Farley Mowat and Pierre Berton in the 1950s, added further lustre to the North's reputation and its role in Canadian identity.

From the beginning, however, development of the North has faced economic challenges unlike those of any other area of the country. First, the terrain (largely muskeg or rock) is unwieldy. Second, the North's summer season, when outside work is most feasible, is very short. Third, a lack of skilled labour has meant bringing in people from outside the region. Fourth, the North is far from markets and supplies, resulting in high transportation costs in both directions. Fifth, economic development in the North requires a lot of capital investment, supplied in the past by the state, either directly or through loans, or by private, often foreign, investors who frequently demand generous terms or conditions that ignore the environment and local job creation and training.

Beyond these purely economic factors, there are also significant political, social, and environmental considerations that came to the fore after the 1970s. On the one hand, Indigenous peoples increasingly developed the political organization and skills to press their demands for a greater role in economic development and the use of their lands (see Chapter 11). On the other hand, the period from 1965 to 1975 also witnessed a renewed interest in the North on the part of many provincial governments, driven by a belief in activist government and a spirit of province building (Chapter 7). Megaprojects, featuring employment in large-scale industries, became a feature of the northern part of nearly every province: forestry in British Columbia, the oil sands in Alberta, potash and uranium in Saskatchewan, hydroelectricity and mining in Manitoba and Quebec, and mining in Ontario.

In the early 1960s, the Quebec government began searching for a northern supply of power (see Chapter 2). These ideas were finally realized in 1971 with Premier Robert Bourassa's announcement of a land agreement between the Cree First Nation at James Bay and the Quebec government that would allow construction of a dam (see Chapter 11). A key part of the agreement was Indigenous employment in the project. Later, however, there were criticisms that the project involved massive unforeseen social and environmental costs, borne largely by the Cree people (Clerici 1999; see also Frideres and Gadacz 2001).

Similar stories arise from other projects, such as the Nelson River Hydroelectric Project at Pike Lake, Manitoba, the Dryden Chemicals plant at Dryden, Ontario, and the oil sands developments in Fort McMurray. When the Pike Lake project began, local Indigenous peoples were told that tremendous benefits would accrue from the project. The end result, however, was that little job training took place and instead outside labour was brought in. At Dryden, the plant flushed its waste of chlorine and other chemicals directly into the Wabigoon River, creating a relatively high level of mercury. Eventually, the mercury worked its way up the local food chain, severely damaging the mental and physical health of people in the local Indigenous communities who ate the contaminated fish (Bone 1992). The Indigenous peoples of Fort Chipewyan in northern Alberta, meanwhile, have been experiencing high rates of unusual cancers attributed by many to contaminated water runoff from the Fort McMurray oil sands seeping into the Athabasca River (see Marsden 2007; Nikiforuk 2010).

In the 1970s, however, the people of the North reacted to the devastating results of modernization. The oil crises of that decade suddenly made financially feasible the possibility of shipping northern oil and gas to southern markets via an overland pipeline crossing Yukon and the Northwest Territories. Large companies were eager to exploit the moment. Federal government approval was required, however, and though technically able to make decisions for the northern territories, which lack the status of provinces, the federal government suddenly became sensitive to northern residents' concerns. The government struck a commission of inquiry.

The Mackenzie Valley Pipeline Inquiry (better known as the Berger Inquiry, after its chair, Justice Thomas Berger) went on for three years (1974–1977) and may properly be described as the first significant public study of the environmental and social effects of economic development ever conducted in Canada. Altogether, 1,000 people, including 300 experts in 35 communities, testified at the hearings, which resulted in 204 volumes of relevant data. Berger's final recommendation was blunt. He outright rejected the pipeline proposal, based on the threat of damage to the local ecosystem, and recommended an alternative route through the Mackenzie Valley. There were also a number of charges, which have since been resolved, about development not being ceded by treaty, involving residents in Inuvialuit, Nunavut, Nunatsiavut, and Nunavik in Yukon as well as certain areas in the Northwest Territories (Frideres 2011).

Today, the North—if not its populace—is nearly fully integrated into the rest of Canada and the world economy. Many traditional jobs have been replaced by work in the new economy: the hydrocarbon industries (including diamonds), government bureaucracies, tourism, and the manufacture of cultural products (such as narwhal carvings and beadwork). Unemployment remains stubbornly high, however: The official unemployment rate for the three northern territories in 2011 was over 9 percent and over 15 percent in Nunavut (Canadian Northern Economic Development Agency 2013), but hope for improvement lingers on the horizon (Cooke and Long 2011).

To an extent, cultural integration is also happening. Most northern peoples today live in permanent settlements. The pickup truck and the snowmobile have long replaced the dog team, and the same assortment of large stores, schools, churches, hospitals, sports arenas, and other institutions found in many small Canadian towns in the South can be seen in the North (Condon 1987).

Moreover, Indigenous languages (see Chapter 12) and cultures are no longer being explicitly attacked; they are instead encouraged (Brody 1987). The training of Indigenous teachers, including work with community elders, has been undertaken, and curricula have been amended to reflect local themes.

But old problems resulting from colonization remain, to which new ones—especially acute in Nunavut—have been added: poor housing, food insecurity, poor health—as evidenced by diseases such as diabetes and the return of an old nemesis, tuberculosis—school absenteeism, and unemployment. These social problems in turn interact with alarmingly high rates of sexual violations against children, homicide, violence against women, and suicide (Hicks 2013; *Nunatsiaq News* 2019). Regarding the latter, the suicide rate per 100,000 in Nunavut in 2018 was 54.7, 27.2 in the Yukon, and 24.7 in the Northwest Territories, compared to 10.3 for Canada as a whole (Centre for Suicide Prevention 2020).

Amid these changes and challenges, and in the context of renewed fears about world energy shortages, the idea of a northern pipeline was revisited early in the new century (Gregoire 2007, 58). The project garnered support from northern people, including Indigenous peoples; former Justice Berger even came out in support of a pipeline, saying the North was now ready to handle the associated difficulties while taking advantage of the opportunity. The opening for development soon closed, however: reflecting once more the precariousness of staples dependency (see chapters 7 and 8), the low price of natural gas on world markets has rendered the Mackenzie Valley pipeline no longer finan-cially viable. The project has been permanently shelved.

Nonetheless, the original Berger Inquiry stands as a landmark in Canada's relations with the North and its peoples. The inquiry was the first time the wishes of local north-erners themselves became central to decision-making. The North gained a voice, but the inquiry also had the effect of informing many Canadians elsewhere about the North and about environmental issues generally. In this sense, the North has played a role in shaping Canadians' growing concern over environmental matters; a concern, one might add, that has slowly worked its way into sociology (see box 10.1).

Box 10.1: The Ecological Challenge to Sociology

Catton and Dunlap (1980) argue that traditional sociology is premised on a set of assumptions that human society is exempt from ecological considerations, a broader rubric they term the human exemptionalist paradigm, which comprises four central beliefs:

1. Humans have a cultural heritage in addition to (and distinct from) their genetic inher-itance, and thus are quite unlike all other animal species.
2. Social and cultural factors, including technology, are the major determinants of hu-man affairs.
3. Social and cultural environments are the crucial contexts for human affairs, and the biophysical environment is largely irrelevant.
4. Culture is cumulative; thus, technological and social progress can continue indefin-itely, making all social problems ultimately soluble.

By contrast, they argue for a new ecological paradigm, based on four very different assumptions:

1. While humans have exceptional characteristics (e.g., culture, technology), they remain one among species that are interdependently involved in the global ecosystem.
2. Human affairs are influenced not only by social and cultural factors, but also by intri-cate connections of cause, effect, and feedback in a web of nature; thus, purposive human actions have many unintended consequences.
3. Humans live in and are dependent upon a finite biophysical environment that imposes physical and biological restraints on human affairs.
4. Although the inventiveness of humans, and the powers derived from this inventiveness, may seem for a while to extend carrying capacity limits, ecological laws cannot be repealed.

Source: Catton, William R., and Riley E. Dunlap. 1980. "A New Ecological Paradigm for Post-Exuberant Sociology." *American Behavioral Scientist* 24(1): 34.

GLOBAL WARMING AND THE NORTH

There is near consensus in the scientific community that **global warming** is occurring and that human activity, specifically the burning of fossil fuels, is a major contributor to a rise in average temperatures worldwide.[1] Since 1988, when it was founded, the United Nations Intergovernmental Panel on Climate Change (IPCC) has compiled the scientific evidence dealing with global warming, and it continues to put out new reports warning of the planetary dangers of continued carbon dioxide emissions. The National Aeronautics and Space Administration (NASA) in 2020 summarized data from the IPCC and other scientific organizations regarding global warming and climate change:

Global Temperature Rise: The planet's average surface temperature has risen about 1.62 degrees Fahrenheit (0.9 degrees Celsius) since the late 19th century, a change driven largely by increased carbon dioxide and other human-made emissions into the atmosphere. The five warmest years on record have taken place since 2010.

Warming Oceans: The oceans have absorbed much of this increased heat, with the top 700 metres (about 2,300 feet) of ocean showing warming of more than 0.4 degrees Fahrenheit since 1969.

Shrinking Ice Sheets: The Greenland and Antarctic ice sheets have decreased in mass. Greenland lost an average of 286 billion tons of ice per year between 1993 and 2016, while Antarctica lost about 127 billion tons of ice per year during the same time period.

Glacial Retreat: Glaciers are retreating almost everywhere around the world— including in the Alps, Himalayas, Andes, Rockies, Alaska, and Africa.

Decreased Snow Cover: The amount of spring snow cover in the northern hemisphere has decreased over the past five decades and snow is melting earlier.

Sea Level Rise: The global sea level rose about eight inches in the last century; the rate, however, has nearly doubled in the last two decades and is accelerating slightly each year.

Declining Sea Ice: Both the extent and thickness of Arctic sea ice has declined rapidly over the last several decades.

Ocean Acidification: Since the beginning of the Industrial Revolution, the acidity of surface ocean waters has increased by about 30 percent. The amount of carbon dioxide absorbed by the upper layer of the oceans is increasing by about two billion tons per year.

What are the causes of climate change? The IPCC's 2014 report is clear: (1) "The largest contribution to total radiative forcing is caused by the increase in the atmospheric concentration of CO_2 since 1750," and (2) "It is extremely likely that human influence has been the dominant cause of the observed warming since the mid-20th century" (United Nations 2014, 2020).

According to some authorities, global warming will result in a massive loss of human and animal life as rising sea levels inundate much of the planet, while many other areas would be rendered uninhabitable due to heat and drought. In turn, these temperature changes will have enormous economic, social, and political impacts, including dramatic population shifts and intensified competition for scarce resources, leading, some predict, to war (Dyer 2008). A briefing note prepared by researchers for the Center for Climate & Security (a branch of the US Central Intelligence Agency) noted that climate change is both directly and indirectly a "national security threat." Two of the centre's researchers, Femia and Werrell (2014, 4) conclude the following:

> There is a high enough degree of certainty that climate change is, and has the capacity to be, a multiplier of direct and indirect threats to the United States. That's why US national security planners put time, personnel and resources into mitigating and adapting to its effects. Climate change as a security threat is not just a narrative, or a political talking point. It's a reality. The US military and the US intelligence community get it. Our policy-makers should too.

It is not just the military that is concerned about global warming. Alerted by increasing payouts, insurance companies have begun factoring climate changes into their financial calculations.

While global warming, accompanied by changes in precipitation, will impact all of Canada, Lemmen and Warren (2004) argue the impacts will hit the northern regions and the south-central Prairies the most. In addition to environmental concerns, many of these impacts have geopolitical implications for Canadian jurisdiction and sovereignty. Chief among these are (1) the opening up of the Northwest Passage for year-round shipping, which poses both environmental risks from oil leaks and other forms of contamination as well as risks to Canadian jurisdiction; and (2) disputes over subsurface rights in the Arctic, which geological surveys suggest may hold as much as 25 percent of the world's undiscovered oil and gas, as well as valuable minerals such as diamonds. But it is the United States, not other northern states (e.g., Russia, Norway, and Denmark), that is Canada's main opposition, with Alaska giving the United States its foothold (legal and otherwise) to make claims (Burke 2018).

In response to threats to Canada's jurisdiction, then–prime minister Stephen Harper announced in 2007 plans to "build military ice-breakers, upgrade underwater and aerial surveillance capabilities, build a deep-water port, and expand Canada's military presence in the area" (Coates et al. 2008, 172; see also see Griffiths, Huebert, and Lackenbauer 2011). This was followed in 2009 with a document outlining Canada's "Northern Strategy," which continues to be revised (Government of Canada 2014). To date, however, few of the promises embedded in these policy statements have been implemented; the North remains a prime backdrop for political photo-ops and symbolic speeches, but with little real or meaningful action (Byers 2014).

Indeed, in terms of mitigating the environmental impacts facing Canada's North, some view Canada's political leadership and the actions it has taken as not only woefully indifferent but even at times in direct opposition to this goal. A report by the Commissioner of the Environment and Sustainable Development (CESD) (2014) stated the federal government did not have a defined national plan, in conjunction with the provinces and territories, on how to achieve Canada's international greenhouse gas emission reduction target.

The failure to implement meaningful environmental policies and initiatives to deal with global warming is not specific to any single governing party. The previous Liberal governments of Jean Chrétien and Paul Martin, as well as the later Conservative government of Stephen Harper, failed to seriously tackle the issue, and the latter is viewed as being especially hostile to the scientific evidence (Turner 2013; Linnitt 2013).

The causes of government failure to protect the ecological commons are complex and often involve political and economic considerations concerning the value of the petroleum industry to Canadian governments, corporations, and individuals. Former Prime Minister Harper stated in June 2014, for example, that his government viewed the environment and economic growth as largely incompatible issues: "No country is going to undertake actions on climate change, no matter what they say . . . that is going to deliberately destroy jobs and growth" (*Maclean's* 2014). Others question, however, whether one can speak of an economy separate from a healthy and sustainable climate and environment.

The current Liberal government of Justin Trudeau has voiced stronger recognition of the problem. It has brought in a (controversial) carbon tax designed to use market mechanisms to move consumers away from carbon-based forms of energy to green alternatives. It has also established a clearer system of regulatory oversight. These actions have been denounced as insufficient by environmentalists and too restrictive by the business community, especially pro-oil supporters.

Canada continues to lag behind earlier commitments to reduce greenhouse gas (GHG) emissions, the chief cause of global warming. Canada's current level of GHG emissions is marginally below that of 2005, largely due to declines in Ontario's electricity generation. It is far off, however, the targets set when Canada signed the 2009 Copenhagen Accord through the United Nations Framework Convention on Climate Change—targets that will be further from Canada's reach if the plethora of pipelines from the oil sands get approved (see the previously mentioned CESD report).

What does global warming mean for the people of the far north? Put simply, it could prove particularly disastrous. As Grossman and Parker (2013, 13–14) suggest, "Climate change is already here . . . climate change is a potential culture killer"—a harsh verdict, if correct, for northern peoples.

According to Ford and Wandel (2013, 114), communities in Nunavut are particularly vulnerable to changes brought about by global warming, including "the erosion of traditional Inuit knowledge, weakening of social networks, and reduced harvesting flexibility" that have lessened people's adaptive capacity. In response to the looming crisis, the government of Nunavut began consultations in the summer of 2014, working with "communities, Inuit organizations and university researchers" to start mapping areas vulnerable to climate change (Government of Nunavut 2014). More broadly, Indigenous communities in the North have increasingly begun mounting legal challenges against the actions—and inaction—of Canadian governments that have failed to deal with climate change (Sniderman and Shedletzky 2014).

At the same time, the issues surrounding climate change have rekindled debate regarding **Indigenous ecology** and whether First Peoples have ever lived up to Western-imposed ecological stereotypes (Porter 2012, xiii).

INDIGENOUS ECOLOGY

After anthropologist Shepard Krech III published *The Ecological Indian* in 1999, the book garnered considerable criticism for questioning whether Indigenous peoples in North America were naturally ecologically minded prior to colonization and whether Indigenous cultural practices automatically account for the complexities of natural systems, waste, or future sustainability. Krech was criticized initially for being anti-environmental and anti-Indian. Harvey Feit (2007, 95–96), for example, contends that Krech ignores the historical context of colonization, the fur trade, and the policy choices and politics of Indigenous rights today, even misleading readers "about present circumstances and possibilities for North Americans and Native Americans." Others have suggested more recently, however, that Krech's argument be viewed as a critique of European colonialist imagery harkening back to tropes about the "noble savage" (Conway 2017). Outside of criticisms of Krech, his book can be claimed to have stimulated much debate regarding Indigenous culture and Indigenous ways of seeing and experiencing the world.

Hull University historian Joy Porter (2012, xv) stated that "it is not argued here that native thinking about American land is always necessarily better that Euro-American thinking, rather it is suggested that a close examination of each is fruitful and important if we are to think anew of the most pressing issues of the future." Porter's approach may be seen as less than even-handed, given her defence of a whale hunt undertaken by the West Coast Makah First Nation, opposed by 350 groups from 27 countries (Porter 2012, 33). But Porter justified the whale hunt as environmentally sound, saying that it invigorated the Makah community, providing it with symbolic and intercultural power, and can be viewed as highlighting a people's right to determine its way of life.

Against such efforts to bridge the gap, Christine Elsey (2013) of the University of the Fraser Valley emphasizes the polarity that exists between traditional Indigenous and Western thought. Elsey argues that the former perspective views the natural world not simply as resources to exploit but as connected spiritual gifts from the Creator. This expression of difference is echoed in the work of retired anthropologist Julie Cruikshank, who has worked extensively with the Athapaskan and Tlingit elders who have cautioned newcomers to the region to respect the glaciers that tradition suggests are living, sentient beings. The glaciers, Cruikshank observes, "were seen as animate as any animals. . . . They responded to people. They took offence easily. You had to be very circumspect in the way you behaved around them, or you would be served catastrophic consequences" (quoted in Montgomery 2007, 76). Kathleen Absolon (2011) concurs, pointing out that the contemporary age is not particularly attuned to appreciate a holistic and relational viewpoint; in the view of many Indigenous people in the North, issues of the environment are not merely scientific and certainly not purely economic; they are inherently spiritual.

Others also note, however, the connection of this spirituality to the land and to local control. Citing a report by the United Nations' Intergovernmental Science-Policy Platform on Biodiversity and Ecosystems, Sneed (2019) notes that while millions of species face immanent extinction around the world, the "decline is happening at a slower rate on indigenous peoples' lands." Sneed notes further the report's recommendation that Indigenous and other local communities' partner with scientists and policy-makers to "stem the tide of biodiversity loss."

These issues are highlighted again in Chapter 11, which looks at the Wet'suwet'en dispute that has pitted traditional cultural practices against pipeline development on their unceded territory, and in Chapter 12, where traditional and modern value orientations are explored.

CONCLUSION

For most Canadians, Canada's North remains solely a place of fantasy and imagery only, a land rich in symbolism and myth but largely unknown, yet it is important to all of Canada in ways that Canadians have not yet recognized.

Since the 1980s, Canada has started to forge a new relationship with the North and its peoples, but progress has been slow and uneven, and there are still many problems as well as possibilities. The creation of Nunavut in 1999 was an important step; some land claim issues there have been settled, though many remain. Among the most important issues remaining are calls for self-government. This call is likewise voiced elsewhere in Canada by Indigenous peoples—a call that, unheeded, has often led to conflict in recent decades—the subject of the chapter to follow.

NOTE

1. Nineteen of the 20 warmest years have occurred since 2001, with the exception of 1998. The year 2016 ranks as the warmest on record (National Aeronautics and Space Administration 2020a, 2020b).

CRITICAL THINKING QUESTIONS

1. Why do places such as the North gain such a hold on the human imagination?
2. What examples of syncretism can you identify from other cultures?

3. In what ways are the kinds of megaprojects in the Canadian North similar to those under way in many countries of the Global South?
4. How might Catton and Dunlap's "new ecological paradigm," if adopted, alter the way sociologists look at issues?
5. Is climate change only an issue for northern Indigenous communities, or should it be an important issue to Canadians as a whole?

RECOMMENDED READINGS

Bone, Robert. 1992. *The Geography of the Canadian North: Issues and Challenges.* Toronto: Oxford University Press.
> Considered a watershed work on Canada's North, this book expertly details the topography of the region and outlines the challenges faced by people living there.

Coates, Ken S., P. Whitney Lackenbauer, William R. Morrison, and Greg Poelzer. 2008. *Arctic Front: Defending Canada in the Far North.* Toronto: Thomas Allen.
> This book provides an environmental, historical, political, and economic overview of the issues facing the Canadian North today.

Grossman, Zoltán, and Alan Parker, eds. 2013. *Asserting Native Resilience: Pacific Rim Indigenous Nations Face the Climate Crisis.* Corvallis, OR: Oregon State University Press.
> This book offers a series of perspectives on Indigenous responses to climate change.

Harkin, Michael E., and David Rich Lewis, eds. 2007. *Native Americans and the Environment: Perspectives on the Ecological Indian.* Lincoln, NE: University of Nebraska Press.
> The focus of this book is to elaborate the environmental perspectives of a group of interdisciplinary scholars.

Porter, Joy. 2012. *Native American Environmentalism: Land, Spirit, and the Idea of Wilderness.* Lincoln, NE: University of Nebraska Press.
> This book explores the conflict between traditional Indigenous attitudes toward nature and that of Christian environmentalists.

RELATED WEBSITES

Environment Canada

weather.gc.ca

> The official Canadian body collecting and reporting on weather conditions across Canada.

Government of Nunavut

www.gov.nu.ca

> The official website for the government of Nunavut.

Intergovernmental Panel on Climate Change

www.ipcc.ch

> The United Nations Environment Programme and the World Meteorological Organization established the Intergovernmental Panel on Climate Change (IPCC) in 1988 to provide scientific information on the current state of climate change and its potential environmental and socio-economic consequences.

CANADIAN SOCIETY ON VIDEO

The Necessities of Life. 2008. 102 minutes.

> The film traces the removal by boat of an Inuit hunter (played by Natar Ungalaaq) from Baffin Island to a Quebec City sanatorium in 1952.

People of the Ice. 2003. National Film Board of Canada, 52 minutes.

> Examines the Inuit way of life and how it is threatened by global warming today.

Vanishing Point. 2012. 82 minutes, 23 seconds.

> The film examines the unprecedented changes facing all Arctic peoples. A stunning scene features a dog team pulling an Inughuit family across the vast sea ice of Greenland. As the team forges ahead, the terrain melts beneath them, and the dogs break through the surface, plunging into frigid polar waters.

CHAPTER 11

The Fight for Justice

Idle No More Protest, Comox Valley. Courtesy Bill Jorgensen.

The day will come when Indians will not be concerned with struggling for their basic rights only, but for the basic rights of all.
    —Cree lawyer William Wuttunee, 1971

However noble and necessary justice is to our struggles, its gaze will always be backward. By itself, the concept of justice is not capable of encompassing the broader transformations needed to ensure coexistence. Justice is one element of a good relationship; it is concerned with fairness and right and calculating moral balances, but it cannot be the end goal of a struggle.
    —author and professor Taiaiake Alfred, 2005

It is those who are being healed within their deepest wounds who will be the strongest healers. They will be the most generous for it is they who, blessed as they are, respond so completely in it. They will be the new Persons, the New Indians, so long awaited.
    —Joseph E. Couture, 2013

INTRODUCTION

Well into the 20th century, Indigenous peoples remained hidden from mainstream Canadian society. Occasionally, some—like Tom Longboat—became quite famous athletes, or found employment in towns and cities, and thus left the reserves. The two world wars of the 20th century provided yet another opportunity to leave. During the Second World War, some 4,000 Status Indians and an unknown number of Métis and other Indigenous peoples enlisted, with several of them becoming quite decorated for their valour (see Winegard 2012). In general, however, the colonial reserve system fulfilled its function of segregating Indigenous peoples from Canadian society. Gradually, though, Indigenous peoples have begun reclaiming their voices. This chapter examines current treaty-making processes, land claims settlements, and demands for self-government. More broadly, the chapter looks at the processes of self-reclamation and the search for justice, processes that continue today, sometimes with conflict, sometimes in co-operation. The chapter begins with a discussion of the emergence of Indigenous organizations capable of fighting for positive change.

INDIGENOUS CAPACITY AND THE HAWTHORN REPORT

Under the Indian Act, enacted in 1876, members of Indian organizations were prevented from meeting together by a pass system that forbade individuals from leaving their reserves without permission of the Indian agent (see Chapter 10). Under Section 141 of the same act, introduced in 1927, it was an offence to raise money for the purpose of advancing Indigenous claims (Purich 1986).

Despite these impediments, a few Indigenous organizations *did* emerge in Canada during the 1930s and 1940s. These included the Native Brotherhood of British Columbia, the Indian Association of Alberta, and, with the encouragement of Saskatchewan's CCF government, the Union of Saskatchewan Indians. In the 1960s, the federal government's decision to fund Indigenous organizations meant the growth of additional organizations. The National Indian Brotherhood (NIB) was formed in 1968 when the National Indian Council split into two factions, the NIB and the Canadian Métis Society. These and other, newer, Indigenous organizations experienced some success through lobbying, organizing, and protesting. Together, these organizations drew attention to a wider range of concerns that went beyond individual First Nations (Frideres and Gadacz 2001) and finally convinced governments to take a hard look at a community within Canada that had been too long ignored. The result was the Hawthorn Report.

In 1963, the federal government asked University of British Columbia anthropologist Harry Hawthorn to study the living conditions of Indigenous peoples. This was at a time when Canada was rapidly becoming urbanized, but Indigenous peoples, rural and confined to reserves, still made little impression upon most Canadians. Hawthorn's subsequent report (1966–1967) stunned everyone, including government leaders. Few knew or had taken the time to find out about the devastating conditions under which most Indigenous peoples were living. The Hawthorn Report catalogued the plight of Indigenous peoples, from high rates of unemployment and poverty to health problems, including malnutrition, and a resultant life expectancy that was dismally below that of other Canadians. It made clear that Indigenous housing was substandard and education was inadequate. Importantly, the report called for Indigenous peoples to be extended the same rights as other Canadian citizens *but also* be assured that their legal rights as Status Indians be honoured, a plea captured in the term **citizens plus**.

The Hawthorn Report was delivered in a time of political unrest and growing demands for the recognition of human rights and fundamental freedoms. Civil rights protests and demonstrations against the Vietnam War in the United States spilled over into Canada, where renewed focus was given to social issues and neglected minorities. This focus often reflected a liberal bias: a sincere, if paternalistic, belief in the state providing opportunities for neglected communities to "join" the rest of society. Too often, these efforts implied that all responsibility for accommodation lay within the minority camp and further assumed that education and good teaching alone might achieve the twin aims of equalizing opportunity and minimizing differences (Friesen 1993). In 1969, while clutching the Hawthorn Report, Pierre Trudeau's Liberal government made public its new Indigenous policy in a White Paper.

WHITE PAPER, RED PAPER

The Liberal administration of Pierre Trudeau was modernist to a fault; that is, it believed firmly in the role of the state in society and, at the same time, the values of liberal individualism and economic progress. In this vein, the Liberal government decided to adopt a new Indigenous policy, the intent of which was to resolve Indigenous land claims and to eliminate distinctions between Indigenous peoples and other Canadians. Indigenous peoples were to be made individually self-reliant. Indian Status was to disappear as a meaningful term in law (Boldt 1993).

The White Paper (Government of Canada 1969) proposed the following measures: abolishing the Department of Indian Affairs and Northern Development; repealing the Indian Act; transferring all responsibility for Indian programs to provincial administration; providing economic assistance to those reserves that are furthest behind; formulating a policy to end treaties; appointing an Indian claims commissioner; and recognizing the contributions that Indian people have made to Canadian society.

Many Indigenous leaders immediately and vigorously denounced the government's White Paper and were joined in their repudiation by a number of non-Indigenous social and political organizations. In his book *The Unjust Society*, a prominent young Indigenous leader, Harold Cardinal, contrasted the White Paper with Pierre Trudeau's vision of a "just society," calling the White Paper "a programme which offers nothing better than cultural genocide" (Cardinal 1969, 1).

The first official reaction to the White Paper came from the Indian Chiefs of Alberta (1970), who claimed that it was a document of despair, not hope, and its proposals (if implemented) would see Indigenous peoples within a generation or two left with no land and threatened by complete assimilation. The Indian Chiefs' "Red Paper," as it was called, itself drew strong criticism, however, notably from Cree lawyer William Wuttunee (1928–) in his book *Ruffled Feathers* (1971), which accused the Alberta Chiefs of being too dependent on government money and fostering nostalgia for traditional culture.

A second major paper (the "Brown Paper") critical of the White Paper emanated from the Union of British Columbia Indian Chiefs. The Brown Paper argued that the special relationship between Indigenous peoples and the federal government, developed through the years, should not be negated; indeed, this relationship carried immense moral and legal force and should constitute the foundation for future co-operative policy-making. The Brown Paper also made reference to the principle of self-determination and suggested that bands should take over aspects of reserve administration at local levels. The authors of the Brown Paper joined with other Indigenous organizations in asking Indian Affairs to provide the necessary financial resources to develop their plans, programs, and budgets toward that end.

Government officials were surprised and dismayed by the response of the Indigenous community to the White Paper; their reaction was not only forceful but incredibly articulate and organized in its expression. Faced with such opposition, in 1970 the federal government decided not to proceed with implementing the White Paper (Purich 1986).

In retrospect, the White Paper and Indigenous organizations' response to it set the stage for several important changes in Canadian society. First, the White Paper resulted in a profound growth of Indigenous organizations on the Canadian scene. Second, under pressure from these organizations, the federal government began the process of instituting a comprehensive land claims policy recognizing two broad categories of claims: **comprehensive claims** based on Indigenous rights, and **specific claims** based on specific legal commitments—claims backed up by funding made possible through a newly established Office of Native Claims. In consequence, the Dene of the Northwest Territories in 1975 became one of the first Indigenous groups to claim First Nation Status. The following year, the Inuit Tapirisat proposed a land claim settlement that would eventually give birth to the territory of Nunavut on April 1, 1999 (Geddes 2001) (see Chapter 12). The response of Indigenous organizations to the White Paper had an important third, if gradual, impact: It educated many in the non-Indigenous community for the first time about pressing issues facing Indigenous peoples. This public awareness was reinforced and expanded on many occasions over the next 45 years, most immediately in the rewriting of Canada's constitution.

INDIGENOUS PEOPLES AND THE 1982 CONSTITUTION

In February 1980, Prime Minister Trudeau declared his intention to bring home Canada's Constitution (Chapter 3). Immediately, a number of Indigenous organizations began lobbying both the federal government and the British Parliament to include Indigenous rights in the process of patriation. The lobbying worked—in January 1981, the Canadian government introduced an amendment to the proposed Constitution that would "recognize and affirm" the Aboriginal and Treaty Rights of Canada's Indigenous peoples. The amendment included in its recognition the existence of First Nations, Inuit, and the Métis. The amendment also pledged that a conference to define Aboriginal rights be held within two years of the completion date of the patriation process.

These amendments soon ran into problems, however. Agreement by all provinces except Quebec (see Chapter 3) to repatriation was achieved only when it was agreed that the word *existing* be added to recognition of Aboriginal rights. In effect, Aboriginal peoples could expect no new rights; the Constitution endorsed only those rights they already possessed. Many feared that this condition would hinder the development of **Aboriginal self-government**—fears that have since proved well justified.

On April 17, 1982, Canadians could finally say that they had their own Constitution. For Indigenous peoples, while the new Constitution remained incomplete, it nonetheless represented an important step. It affirmed existing Indigenous rights in broad terms and thus opened the door for making land claims. For the first time, the Métis, along with the Inuit, garnered specific mention in Canada's Constitution. The document also set out a process of ongoing constitutional conferences aimed at defining Indigenous rights and giving Indigenous peoples the opportunity to present their views. Finally, the Canadian Charter of Rights and Freedoms not only recognized and affirmed Indigenous and Treaty Rights, it also highlighted what some observers saw as the Indian Act's prejudicial provisions against Indigenous peoples, including gender-based discrimination.

The Constitutional Conferences

Part IV of the newly minted Constitution committed the federal government to hold two future constitutional conferences on Indigenous peoples and the representatives of Yukon and the Northwest Territories. These conferences were duly held on March 15 and 16, 1983, and were followed by three additional conferences. From the beginning, at least one practical problem beset these conferences: that of representation. Through tradition and the Indian Act, Status Indians had a recognized seat at the gatherings. This was not the case, however, for Métis people and non-Status Indians. In the past, the Native Council of Canada (NCC) had spoken for Métis people, but the Métis disagreed with the NCC's definition of Métis (anyone of mixed blood) and wanted a more explicit definition, including the origins and domicile of the Métis in the Red River area. Similarly, non-Status Indians demanded equal rights with Status Indians. By contrast, the Métis were not requesting Status rights; they simply wanted to be recognized as a distinct Indigenous group.

In the end, Prime Minister Trudeau asked the NCC to represent Métis interests, a move that further split the Indigenous community. A new organization, the Métis National Council, was then formed by a group of dissidents who launched a court case to demand that their interests also be represented at constitutional conferences. When the first conference was over, it was agreed that no constitutional changes affecting Indigenous rights would be made without a constitutional conference for that explicit purpose, to which Indigenous representatives would be invited (Schwartz 1986). It was further agreed that future land claims would include a definition of "existing rights" and that sexual equality would be guaranteed, hence the later passing of Bill C-31.

Indigenous Women and Bill C-31

The Indian Act, established in 1876, governs who is defined as an Aboriginal. On "the day that the government counted the Indians," all who "stood in line" became Status Indians by law. This afforded them the privilege of having matters pertaining to health, education, and welfare delivered directly through federal auspices. This practice discriminated, however, against Indigenous peoples who were not counted on that day, and was even more discriminatory toward Status Indian women who married non-Status men (either Indigenous or non-Indigenous) and their subsequent offspring. While children born to Status Indians were added to the Indian Register, a Status woman who "married out" lost her Status rights, and children born to her were also deprived of Status. This was not true for males, however. In fact, if a Status Indian man married a non-Status woman (either Indigenous or non-Indigenous), that woman became a Status Indian. The 1973 case of *A. G. (Can) v. Lavell* upheld this discriminatory provision of the Indian Act. In 1975, however, Sandra Lovelace took her complaint about the act's gender discrimination to the Human Rights Committee of the United Nations, and in 1981, the committee decided that her case was one of "an unjustifiable denial of her rights under the United Nations' Covenant on Civil and Political Rights" (Miller 2000, 357–358). The terms of this case may have influenced the subsequent shaping of Canada's Charter of Rights and Freedoms.

The issue of how Indigenous peoples traditionally viewed women's rights is complex. Of eight national First Nations organizations, only four endorsed Bill C-31, the equal rights amendment that would end Status women's loss of their rights through marriage to non-Status males. Indigenous women were themselves not unanimous in endorsing the bill. One group of Indigenous women launched a demonstration in Ottawa protesting against it, and some argued that women who married "outside" knew very well what they were doing. Insofar as Indigenous peoples believe tribal spirituality is mainly transferred through women, who alone have the power to give life, some viewed those who married out, whether male or female, as disregarding the spiritual welfare of the band. Hence, some believed that women doing so deserved to lose their Status and should not be permitted to opt back in. Some bands refused to return band membership to women despite their regaining Status through the auspices of Bill C-31. The result has been a new division in First Nations communities. This is illustrated by a remark made by an Indigenous individual to one of the authors when a neighbour regained Status: "Oh, so now she is a Bill C-31 Indian!"

But the arguments put forward by those who objected to Bill C-31 were decidedly out of step with Canadian society and with most in the Indigenous community. In 1985, Bill C-31 was passed, eliminating sexual discrimination, abolishing the concept of enfranchisement, and providing for those who had lost their Indian Status to gain partial reinstatement. The bill had the almost immediate effect of greatly enlarging the Indigenous population of Canada: By 2001, more than 105,000 people had regained Indian Status under Bill C-31 (Frideres and Gadacz 2001, 35) (see Chapter 12).

FROM MEECH LAKE TO OKA AND BEYOND

The failure of the Meech Lake Accord in 1990 had important consequences for Quebec-Canada relations (Chapter 3). But the Meech Lake Accord likewise had important consequences for Indigenous peoples and Canada.

From the beginning, groups of First Nations opposed the Meech Lake Accord. They feared that the accord's provisions recognizing Quebec's specificity would lead to a similar delegation of powers to the other provinces, including jurisdiction over Indigenous affairs. Symbolically, the phrase respecting Quebec as a "distinct society" also rankled many Indigenous peoples, who believed that the accord completely overlooked their historical traditions; indeed, it identified Quebec as the "foremost distinct society" in Canada, implicitly building on the notion of "two founding races" (French and English) while ignoring the pre-existence of Indigenous peoples on the continent. Members of the Indigenous community were further upset that Canada's first ministers had long rejected the entrenchment of Indigenous rights on the grounds that the concept was too vague and undefined, yet suddenly they were quite willing to grant similar rights to the province of Quebec (York 1989).

Technically, the Meech Lake Accord died on the East Coast when the Newfoundland legislature failed to vote on it. In fact, as earlier recounted (Chapter 3), the accord's final defeat came at the hands of Elijah Harper, an Indigenous NDP member of the Opposition in the Manitoba legislature. By the spring of 1990, the House of Commons and most provinces had given the accord approval. Newfoundland and Manitoba had not, however, and time was running out. The agreed-upon procedure required that for the Manitoba legislature to vote on the accord, and to thus make the deadline, there had to be unanimous approval by the members. When the proposal to cut debate short was put forward, however, Harper stood alone in refusing approval, without which the accord could not be passed in time. Newfoundland's government already knew of this outcome on the day that it also refused to vote on the accord.

The accord's failure had profound consequences for Indigenous-non-Indigenous relations, not only in Quebec but elsewhere in Canada. The first consequence of this failure was a series of actual confrontations between Indigenous peoples and Canadian governments that escalated, in several instances, to armed conflict.

The most immediate and famously publicized of these conflicts occurred in Oka, Quebec. Cross and Sévigny (1994, 80) describe the events:

> Everything began on a nice day in March 1990, when the Municipal Council of the Village of Oka [outside Montreal] adopted the proposal to expand the area's golf course. In one stroke, Oka's Pines and Mohawk cemetery at Kanehsatàke were threatened. To protect their land and the graves of their ancestors, the Mohawks erected a barricade to make the Whites understand that they intended to protect their land against all invaders.

As with any conflict, however, the roots of the Oka Crisis (as it quickly became known) were much older. In fact, the conflict dated back to 1717, when King Louis XV of France granted the land in question to the Seminary of St. Sulpice to set up a mission for the Indigenous residents, mainly Huron, Algonquin, and Iroquois. By French law (which never recognized **Aboriginal title**), later confirmed by British and Canadian governments, the lands of Kanehsatàke (Oka) did not legally belong to the Indigenous inhabitants; to Indigenous peoples, however, this was their land (Dickason 2002). Indeed, for many Mohawks and their supporters, such legal decisions merely reinforced the notion that law and justice are often strangers and that the Canadian legal system is simply another tool for state oppression—an idea with which many conflict theorists would sympathize.

The crisis escalated into violence when the Quebec police decided to attack and take down the barricades, resulting in the death of a police officer, although the exact circumstances of the incident are uncertain to this day. The Canadian government quickly sent in 2,500 soldiers to surround the reserve, which was now guarded by khaki-clad Mohawk members bearing automatic rifles. Sympathy barricades arose on other Mohawk reserves nearby. The crisis lasted 11 weeks, during which many people, Indigenous and non-Indigenous alike, feared a bloodbath (Alfred 1995); fortunately, this did not occur. On September 26, 1990, the crisis ended with the Mohawk warriors putting down their weapons and walking out from behind the barricade. Only a few dozen Mohawk warriors were tried in court; a few were convicted on minor offences and sentenced to short periods in jail.

Today, there remains a great deal of mistrust between Mohawks and the Quebec and federal governments, as well as between Mohawks and the surrounding non-Indigenous community. But there are also fractures within the Mohawk community between moderate and hard-line Mohawk nationalists, worsened since 1990 by the emergence of criminal gangs thriving on gambling and smuggling (primarily of cigarettes, but also guns). As for the disputed land, in June 2000 the Kanehsatàke Mohawk band signed a deal with Ottawa, gaining control (but not legal title) of their affairs, while the Mohawk band council gained the right to establish bylaws, zoning regulations, and a process for resolving disputes on those lands, a situation akin to self-government, as we will see.

The Oka Crisis must be viewed in a larger context of Indigenous resistance dating back centuries (Chapter 9). Indigenous peoples have never given up—nor can they give up—the fight (whether militantly or politically expressed) for self-governance. Long before Oka, there were similar confrontations. In 1969, for example, Mohawk Indians from the St. Regis Reserve blocked the international bridge between Canada and the United States near Cornwall, Ontario. And months prior to Oka, in September 1989, the Barriere Lake Algonquin of Quebec blockaded six logging roads in an effort to save their traditional hunting grounds and way of life. After Oka, however, the number and prevalence of confrontations grew (see box 11.1).

Box 11.1: Indigenous–Non-Indigenous Conflict in Recent Decades

---

Lubicon Lake Cree, Northern Alberta. The land claims dispute dated back to 1899 but escalated as a result of resource development and exploitation on the unceded lands. Amid high-profile protests and barricades, a settlement was finally reached in 2018 with the province's then-NDP government. The Lubicon peoples received 2,346 square kilometres of land and $113 million combined from the federal and provincial governments.

Ipperwash Provincial Park, Ontario. Several members of the Stoney Point Ojibway band occupied the park in 1995 to assert their claim to nearby land expropriated during the Second World War. The ensuing confrontation with Ontario Provincial Police resulted in the killing of an unarmed Indigenous protester, Dudley George. Following a provincial inquiry, the Ontario government in 2009 formally signed over the 56-hectare park to the Chippewas of Kettle and Stony Point First Nation. In 2016, the bands also received a settlement of $95 million.

Gustafsen Lake, British Columbia. This 1995 conflict involved the RCMP (representing the government of Canada), a non-Indigenous land owner, and Indigenous peoples of the Shuswap nation over sacred and unceded lands. It ended after violence, the shooting of one individual, and a cost of $5.5 million. Fifteen Indigenous and non-Indigenous individuals were charged, convicted, and sentenced from six months to eight years in jail.

Burnt Church, Nova Scotia. Violence flared in 1999 after the Mi'kmaq First Nation won a Supreme Court ruling that members could fish out of season. Heavily armed non-Indigenous fishers responded with blockades against Indigenous fishers to keep them from going out to sea, and a ceremonial boat was sunk. Standoffs occurred between the RCMP and Indigenous fishers. The dispute ended when members of the non-Native community were allowed to fish, but only for subsistence purposes.

Jenpeg Dam, Manitoba. In 2014, Indigenous members of the Pimicikamak Cree Nation reserve occupied a generating station in protest of the Manitoba government's failure to live up to a 1977 agreement to eradicate mass poverty and unemployment on the reserve, but the dispute revolved more broadly around unfulfilled promises arising from Treaty 5 in 1875. The dispute ended with a new agreement.

Enbridge Northern Gateway Pipeline. Beginning in the early 2000s, the proposed 1,177-kilometre pipeline carrying natural gas and diluted bitumen would have stretched from Bruderheim, Alberta, to Kimimat, British Columbia. It was opposed by numerous First Nations, including the Haisla, Gitga'at, Haida, Gitxaala, Wet'suwet'en, Nadleh Whut'en, Nak'azdli, and Takla Lake, as well as environmental groups, municipalities, and anti–oil sands groups. The dispute finally ended in 2016 with the pipeline proposal being shelved, in part because declining oil prices made the project economically not viable.

Caledonia, Ontario. The dispute revolved around a 385,000-hectare tract of land granted in 1784 by the British Crown to the Six Nations band. Henco Industries, a real estate developer, later claimed Six Nations surrendered rights in 1841 and bought the land from the government. Six Nations argued they had never relinquished title. Protests intensified in 2006 when Henco began development. Eventually, the Ontario government purchased the land from Henco, but conflict continued, including assaults, between Six Nations protesters and local residents. The conflict wound down in 2014 with the removal of a Native blockade.

Two things are observable from this pattern of conflicts. First, many of them have deep historical roots. Second, most of them revolve around resource development projects, often connected to energy—oil, gas, or hydro—from which Indigenous peoples rarely benefit but too often bear the costs.

These patterns are not new, however. So why have Indigenous protests increased in recent decades? Clearly, the protests reflect a great deal of frustration on the part of Indigenous peoples. Anger and discontent do not alone lead to political action, though. Examining the increase in Indigenous protests in recent years, sociologist Howard Ramos (2006) has concluded that the increase in Indigenous-launched protests is positively related to the number of Indigenous organizations; that is, while a pan-Indigenous ideology (or consciousness) of relevant issues may be necessary, this is an insufficient factor in explaining Indigenous political action—the necessary factor is organization, including the financial resources that go with it.

Oka and other conflicts alarmed many Canadians, whether Indigenous and non-Indigenous. (Regrettably, in some quarters, racism and prejudice also reared their heads.) The sight of Canadian soldiers and police squaring off against Indigenous protesters has revealed starkly the divide between Canada's other "two solitudes" and the possible dangers if that gulf is not addressed. Within government circles, a heightened sense of urgency has emerged—if in ebbs and flows—over treaties, land claims, and the Indigenous right to self-government (Mercredi and Turpel 1993). The creation of the Royal Commission on Aboriginal Peoples (RCAP) in 1991 was a tangible result of this changed mood.

THE ROYAL COMMISSION ON ABORIGINAL PEOPLES

Chaired by former Assembly of First Nations (AFN) Chief George Erasmus and Quebec Judge René Dussault, the RCAP included seven members, four of them Indigenous and three of them non-Indigenous. The commission held a number of public meetings, analyzed transcripts, and undertook a great deal of research, though it is clear both from the structure of the report and from the public hearings that the commissioners regarded their task as an exercise in public education as well as a government investigation (Miller 2000). Altogether, the commission cost $50 million, and its final report in 1996 consisted of five volumes, more than 3,500 pages, and 400 recommendations (Royal Commission on Aboriginal Peoples 1996).

The report recommended a major reconstruction of Canadian society so that justice and equality would be better assured for Indigenous peoples in Canada. It noted two specific and urgent concerns: the high suicide rates in Indigenous communities and the high incidence of incarceration for Indigenous peoples, especially in the western provinces, which raised issues regarding the fairness of Canada's criminal justice system. The report recommended swift action in these areas, starting with a meeting of the various law societies and lawyers' associations. It also urged increased government spending on preventive programs.

More broadly, the RCAP also recommended rewriting the principles of the Royal Proclamation to reflect the new nation-to-nation concept of negotiation, as well as a new constitutional foundation by which to perceive past treaty-making processes. In the words of University of Calgary sociologist Rick Ponting (1997a, 470), the report recommended at its core "the re-balancing of political and economic power between Aboriginal nations and Canadian governments." Among its many recommendations was the formation of an Aboriginal parliament with advisory but no law-making authority. This was seen as a first step toward creating a House of First Peoples as the third chamber of the Parliament of Canada. The commission also recommended the abolition of the Department of Indian Affairs and Northern Development and its replacement by two departments: the Department of Aboriginal Relations and the Department of Indian and Inuit Services (this has since been accomplished).

The RCAP also recommended creating a number of new organizational structures, including an Aboriginal peoples' international university along with Indigenous student unions and Indigenous residential colleges, as well as an Indigenous languages foundation, which would parallel the work of the international university and supplement its efforts to maintain Indigenous languages and culture.

The Liberal government's response to the report was to set up, in 1998, a special healing fund in the amount of $350 million to be used over a four-year period as a token of the government's apology for the treatment of Indigenous peoples in residential schools; it also approved an increase of $250 million in the next year's budget as a means of supporting Indigenous causes. However, the response of others was often critical.

While Phil Fontaine (1944–), then grand chief of the AFN, generally approved of the recommendations, suggesting that they were the best that one could hope for at the time, most Métis, Inuit, and non-Status Indians were critical of it and subsequent government actions, such as favouring Status Indians. Others noted the report's lack of emphasis on the situation of Indigenous peoples in urban settings, privileging reserve life and cultural persistence over solving socio-economic problems across the board (Allan Cairns cited in Miller 2000)—a particularly important consideration, since more than one-half of First Nations in Canada now live in urban centres (see Chapter 12).

Likewise, the report also met with strong criticism in the non-Indigenous community. University of Calgary political scientist Thomas Flanagan (2000) is one of the report's harshest critics. Flanagan disagrees with the assumption that first habitation gives Aboriginals any particular rights over later arrivals; he argues that because Aboriginal peoples never continuously settled the land but were nearly always in motion, they have no legitimate territorial claims. Flanagan contends that Aboriginal peoples are not nations, but rather subordinate communities within the nation of Canada, and hence lack a legitimate basis for claims to self-government.

While Flanagan acknowledges the current plight of Aboriginal peoples and their communities, he argues the solution does not lie in collective, racially based claims for political status and Aboriginal community property rights. Instead, he argues for a "realistic" interpretation of the ongoing relationship between Aboriginals and non-Aboriginals, including a full integration of Indian peoples into the modern economy, implying a willingness to leave the reserves, if necessary, and relocate to where there are jobs and investment opportunities (Flanagan 2000, 7).

What can we make of Flanagan's criticisms? Setting aside counters to his particular arguments, the interesting foundations of his position are the "modernist" values upon which they are based. Seen this way, Flanagan's arguments point to the wide cultural gap remaining between Indigenous and non-Indigenous understandings of such things as social relationships, individualism, private property, capitalism, and notions of state and nation.

While many of the Royal Commission's recommendations remain unimplemented, the report nonetheless set Canadian society on a new path in handling several Indigenous issues, including dealing with residential school claims, the establishment of a Truth and Reconciliation Commission to deal with the schools' impact, revising or eliminating the Indian Act, settling existing land claims, signing recent treaties, and defining and implementing self-government.

Residential School Claims

We have seen the negative role that residential schools played in the colonization of Indigenous peoples (Chapter 9). While not all Indigenous peoples are products of Canada's residential schools, the vast majority of those who attended them experienced years of physical, sexual, and psychological abuse, the effects of which were often visited upon later generations, with enormous community ramifications.

Seeking legal redress for the abuses they suffered, former residents of the schools were encouraged to bring forward their demands for justice. In response, the Canadian government established a fund of $1.9 million in 2005 to address these claims. In 2007, the Indian Residential Schools Settlement Agreement, the largest class action settlement in Canadian history, was negotiated and approved, covering nine jurisdictions and 139 schools, including 64 Roman Catholic–, 35 Anglican–, and 14 United Church–run schools. The settlement agreement was meant to reach reconciliation with an estimated 80,000 former students still living (Edmond 2014). It contains the following elements:

- a common experience payment, to be paid to all eligible former students who resided at a recognized Indian residential school
- an independent assessment process for claims of sexual or serious physical abuse
- the introduction of the Truth and Reconciliation Commission
- commemoration activities
- measures to support healing, such as the Indian Residential Schools Resolution Health Support Program and an endowment to the Aboriginal Healing Foundation

By the 2012 deadline, Canada had received "over 105,000 applications for Common Experience Payments, of which over 79,000 were found eligible and paid, the average amount being $19,412" (Edmond 2014). Sadly, in too many cases, the plaintiffs received little of the money won through litigation; lawyers were often the big winners.

The Truth and Reconciliation Commission (TRC)

The TRC was established in June 2008 as a separate part of the residential school agreement. Based on the court-like restorative justice body assembled in South Africa after the abolition of Apartheid in that country, the TRC was given a budget of $60 million over five years to travel across Canada and receive submissions from former residential school students regarding claims of mistreatment and abuse at government-run residential schools dating back to the 1870s. The TRC's focus was also on "promoting healing, educating, listening, and the preparation of a report for all parties that includes recommendations for the Government of Canada regarding the Indian Residential School system, experience and legacy." Its final report (Truth and Reconciliation Commission of Canada 2015) was released in December 2015. Its preface begins with these words:

> These residential schools were created for the purpose of separating Aboriginal children from their families, in order to minimize and weaken family ties and cultural linkages, and to indoctrinate children into a new culture—the culture

of the legally dominant Euro-Christian Canadian society, led by Canada's first prime minister, Sir John A. Macdonald. The schools were in existence for well over 100 years, and many successive generations of children from the same communities and families endured the experience of them. That experience was hidden for most of Canada's history, until Survivors of the system were finally able to find the strength, courage, and support to bring their experiences to light in several thousand court cases that ultimately led to the largest class-action lawsuit in Canada's history. (v)

The Report's preface concludes with the following message:

Getting to the truth was hard, but getting to reconciliation will be harder. It requires that the paternalistic and racist foundations of the residential school system be rejected as the basis for an ongoing relationship. Reconciliation requires that a new vision, based on a commitment to mutual respect, be developed. It also requires an understanding that the most harmful impacts of residential schools have been the loss of pride and self-respect of Aboriginal people, and the lack of respect that non-Aboriginal people have been raised to have for their Aboriginal neighbours. Reconciliation is not an Aboriginal problem; it is a Canadian one. Virtually all aspects of Canadian society may need to be reconsidered. (vi)

The TRC report calls the Canadian government to act on several legacy issues, including the number of Aboriginal children currently in the child welfare system, educational and employment gaps between Aboriginal and non-Aboriginal Canadians, protection of Aboriginal language rights, Aboriginal health, and the justice system. The report also calls for several measures dealing with reconciliation, including that "federal, provincial, territorial, and municipal governments . . . fully adopt and implement the Declaration on the Rights of Indigenous Peoples as the framework for reconciliation" and further "develop a national action plan, strategies, and other concrete measures to achieve the goals of the United Nations Declaration on the Rights of Indigenous Peoples." A particularly interesting recommendation is that

the Government of Canada, on behalf of all Canadians . . . jointly develop with Aboriginal peoples a Royal Proclamation of Reconciliation to be issued by the Crown. The proclamation would build on the Royal Proclamation of 1763 and the Treaty of Niagara of 1764, and reaffirm the nation-to-nation relationship between Aboriginal peoples and the Crown. (199)

The TRC report makes clear that the process of reconciliation must be national, bringing together governments, public servants, private business, sports organizations, the media, churches, educational institutions, community-based youth organizations, and cultural institutions (such as museums and archives). It further recommends the creation of a national centre for truth and reconciliation, where the history and legacy of residential schools and information about missing and buried Indigenous children can be collected, and the establishment of a statutory holiday, the National Day for Truth and Reconciliation. Finally, the report calls upon the Government of Canada to amend the Oath of Citizenship to read:

> I swear (or affirm) that I will be faithful and bear true allegiance to Her Majesty Queen Elizabeth II, Queen of Canada, Her Heirs and Successors, and that I will faithfully observe the laws of Canada, including Treaties with Indigenous Peoples, and fulfill my duties as a Canadian citizen. (217)

Healing of the kind described in the TRC report can only come about in any society through a frank and honest understanding of its history and current context; in Canada, this includes the history and continued embeddedness of racism and oppression in many of the country's political, legal, and cultural institutions, including its symbolic representations.

This latter recommendation can be seen in the context of wider discussions in recent years regarding public statues to historical figures. Violent protests and counter-protests broke out in several southern US states in 2017 about efforts to remove statues raised to Confederate heroes. Similar arguments have occurred in Canada over statues raised to such historical figures as General Amherst and General Cornwallis. No individual epitomized this issue more starkly, however, than Canada's first prime minister, Sir John A. Macdonald (see box 11.2).

Box 11.2: What to Do with a Problem Like John A. Macdonald—and Other Statues?

Sir John A. Macdonald was a self-admitted alcoholic, a taker of political bribes, a racist who opposed Chinese immigration and voting rights, and the man who ordered Louis Riel be hung, and who continued the practice of building residential schools while in office. Macdonald was also the major architect—though certainly not alone—of Canada, who rescued the country from American clutches after 1865, crafted the National Policy (Chapter 6) in the years after, and even bridged the seemingly obdurate divide between French and English. What to do with the many statues and other symbols—including the ten-dollar bill—designed in his honour? *Canada's History* addressed the controversy in a special article in early 2019. Four qualified individuals—a professor of political science (Frederic Boily), a non-fiction author (Charlotte Gray), a poet and professor in Indigenous studies (Lee Maracle), and a Canadian historian (Christopher Moore)—debated Macdonald's controversial legacy and how it should be recognized. Without ignoring Macdonald's personal flaws, Boily notes the difficult political context surrounding his decisions at the time, a note Gray echoes: "We need to be more tolerant of the moral failings of our predecessors—not as an act of charity to them but as an act of charity to ourselves." Rather than expunging Macdonald's presence, Maracle argues that statues and buildings provide the opportunity for starting a genuine conversation about Macdonald's legacy, and she suggests a plaque be added, "bearing his name, explaining his role in forming the residential school system"—and, while one is at it, also "thinking about how to honour overlooked Indigenous heroes." Finally, placing Macdonald's real legacy in present context, Moore states:

> It is not shameful to respect John A. Macdonald's contribution to the building of Canadian Confederation or his years as prime minister. What would be shameful would be to remove Macdonald statues around the country—without addressing Canada's responsibility for the poverty, dispossession, and alienation of Indigenous peoples that he helped to create and that we maintain.

What do you think? What should we do with statues to flawed historical figures? Are plaques enough? Or is the problem that we do not have enough statues to Indigenous and other forgotten or ignored peoples?

Source: Boily et al. (2019). "The trials of John A." *Canada's History,* February-March, 20–31.

LAW, VOICE, AND POWER: LESSONS FROM THE WET'SUWET'EN 2020 STANDOFF

Throughout early 2020, Canadians watched as protesters across Canada set up solidarity blockades in support of the Wet'suwet'en in British Columbia, who have been opposing the building of a liquid natural gas (LNG) pipeline through their unceded territory. The pipeline, to be built by Coastal GasLink, is to carry natural gas from northern British Columbia to the LNG Canada export facility in Kitimat, but it crosses Wet'suwet'en traditional territory, an area of 22,000 square kilometres. The issues immediately underlying the dispute went back to 2010, when the territory's Hereditary Chiefs had set up a cabin on the pipeline's planned route. In the intervening years, Coastal GasLink had obtained legal approvals from federal and provincial authorities, and in late 2018 obtained a temporary injunction against the blockade. In early 2019, heavily armed RCMP moved into Wet'suwet'en territory to enforce the injunction; 14 protesters are arrested, setting off several solidarity protests in Canadian and American cities. In December 2019, Canada's

Supreme Court issued a further injunction, but protests and continued and expanded, notably in Quebec, where the Mohawk communities of Kahnawake and Kanehsatàke, abutting Montreal, set up solidarity blockades, bringing back memories of the Oka Crisis of 1990 (timeline in *Star Calgary* 2020). Similar actions ensued across Canada, shutting down rail traffic as well as ferry terminals, major roads, and government offices. Ironically, what had long been a political liability for Indigenous mobilization—the non-contiguous nature of Indigenous communities—became a strength as protests were no longer confined to single territories.

As the days passed, tempers and angry confrontations flared between Indigenous peoples (with their non-Indigenous supporters) and those opposed to the blockades. Several talk shows and some mainstream newspapers demanded that force be used to end the conflict. A few conservative politicians cited the need to restore "law and order." Others, however, remembering previous confrontations between the Canadian state and Indigenous peoples, called for calm and continued dialogue to settle the dispute peacefully, even if it took several weeks. The dispute appeared to wind down in late February 2020, with the Canadian government signing a draft agreement with the Hereditary Chiefs that recognized the legitimacy of the Wet'suwet'en governance structure and its authority over the unceded lands (Cecco 2020). However, the federal and provincial governments have also continued to proceed with pipeline construction and so tensions remain high. In June 2020, a Hereditary Chief complained of RCMP intimidation after armed officers were seen outside his smokehouse.

As the initial dispute unfolded, several larger issues concerning Indigenous and non-Indigenous relations were highlighted; indeed, the conflict provided a veritable university course in history, sociology, and constitutional law. As in so many similar cases, the Wet'suwet'en dispute traces directly to the Royal Proclamation of 1763, which recognizes the existence of Aboriginal title over land unless purchased by the Crown. This recognition continued after 1867 on those western lands transferred to Canada by the Hudson's Bay Company; hence, the need, as the government perceived it, to sign the numbered treaties in preparation for non-Indigenous settlement (see Chapter 6). British Columbia and some other parts of Canada remained unceded territories, however. The Supreme Court decision in the case of *Delgamuukw v. British Columbia* in 1997 reaffirmed the ancestral right of Aboriginal title protected by Section 35(1) of the Constitution Act, 1982, and the decision has been the basis of several subsequent agreements, notably the Nisga'a Comprehensive Agreement.

In short, the *Delgamuukw* decision is part of Canadian law—indeed, Canada's highest law, the Constitution, meaning that the actions of Wet'suwet'en Hereditary Chiefs in blocking the pipeline construction were entirely legal—an ironic twist to demands by some that the dispute be ended by force in order to respect the rule of law; such a demand speaks less to the rule of law and more to the convenience of (colonial) rulers.

But the actions of the Hereditary Chiefs are also tied up in another bequest of colonialism, the Indian Act. The act establishes in Canadian law a system of leadership selection based on individual voting, a political practice valorized in Western democracies as the central measure of democracy. By this rubric, the idea of hereditary leadership appears archaic, undemocratic, and—in a Weberian sense—even irrational. From the perspective of traditional societies, however, a hereditary system—common to many Indigenous tribes in Canada, not only British Columbia—is viewed as ensuring respect for tradition and continuity, and even a kind of deeper wisdom. As noted by Gunn and McIvor (2020), the Wet'suwet'en are governed by both a traditional governance system, represented by Hereditary Chiefs, and a system of governance established under the Indian Act, represented by elected chiefs and council. The former have authority over lands not ceded—that is, lands over which Aboriginal title exists—while the latter have authority over decisions within reserve lands.

The dual systems of governance need not be opposed. A useful comparison might be the House of Commons and the Senate. But in the case of the GasLink pipeline, there is a real difference of interests and jurisdiction. According to Jang and Hager (2020), all 20 elected First Nations councils along the pipeline route support the project, but eight of the nine Hereditary Chiefs—there are 13 in total, with four positions unfilled—oppose it. For project supporters, the assent of the elected officials outweighs that of the Hereditary Chiefs. For project opponents, the decision of the Hereditary Chiefs holds sway over the territory outside the reserves and must be respected not only on the basis of tradition but on the basis of law.

Project supporters argue that the Hereditary Chiefs are not being true to the governance model (Macdonald 2020). But project opponents point out that, until 2015, there were no disagreements between the elected chiefs and Hereditary Chiefs, as both rejected the pipelines—a point to which project supporters respond that further consultations and contractual agreements have since dealt with environmental concerns. In a final argument, opponents counter that these "agreements" were not legal, as they were made under duress—many of the reserves overseen by the elected chiefs are impoverished, lacking sanitary water or adequate housing.

The Wet'suwet'en dispute holds a mirror up to more general disputes between Indigenous peoples and non-Indigenous peoples and their governments across Canada, as well as to the issues that all Canadians must face in going forward, one of which remains the Indian Act.

THE INDIAN ACT

The Indian Act has not been substantially changed since its enactment in 1876. The federal government has on several occasions suggested either revising or even abandoning the act, most notably in the White Paper of 1969 and again in 1999. Indigenous responses to the idea of changing the Indian Act have been mixed, with most First Nations and their organizations rebuffing these suggestions, a response that will likely surprise non-Indigenous readers. Why is this the case? Why are many Indigenous peoples reluctant to eliminate an act at the heart of colonial oppression?

While some Indigenous leaders clearly view the Indian Act as hindering efforts to get ahead, others view it as actually protecting certain of their rights, while still others support changing the Indian Act but dislike the federal government's process for making changes, especially efforts at speaking over the heads of the AFN leadership to the Indigenous grassroots directly. They want the government to work through the AFN, which represents about half of all Indigenous peoples in Canada.

Disagreements aside, most Indigenous peoples nonetheless view three key issues in the Indian Act as needing redress. First, the Indian Act does not make clear the powers of chief and council or the legal standing and capacity for Aboriginal bands and band councils to sue, contract, borrow, and so on. Second, as we have seen, the act does not outline a clear and consistent system of determining band leadership selection and voting rights. Some bands follow procedures outlined in the Indian Act for the election of chiefs and councils, while others continue to follow a hereditary system of appointment, through which the government has no power under the Indian Act to interfere. Additionally, while the Indian Act allows off-reserve Indigenous peoples to vote in band elections, they cannot run for the office of counsellor but can apply for the office of chief; in fact, one does not have to live on a reserve or even be a band member to run for that office. Third, the Indian Act has few rules ensuring that First Nations communities will be run in a fair and equitable manner. While many First Nations bands have in place their own systems of accountability, these vary in structure and function, with many Indigenous band members feeling that they have no control or say in bylaws, annual reports, accounting, and band budgeting. Many Indigenous people likely agree that changes to the Indian Act are required in these three areas.

The push for changes to the Indian Act has gained momentum from recent court rulings in such areas as reserve elections and matrimonial and property rights for Indigenous women. Today, legislation to replace the Indian Act continues winding its way through Parliament. A few years ago the government set aside a budget of $13 million for the project, though the recent economic downturn has hindered attempts at making progress.

Existing Land Claims and Modern Treaties

We have previously examined the historical development of treaties in Canada (Chapter 9). Two types of claims under the treaty process need differentiation. Indigenous peoples' claims under negotiation with the federal government involving promises not fulfilled or interpretations of what was promised by either the treaties or scrip are referred to as specific claims (see the case of Burnt Church). Indigenous peoples' claims involving lands that they have never legally surrendered are referred to as comprehensive claims (see the case of the Lubicon Cree).

The need to deal with both specific and comprehensive claims has intensified in recent decades for two reasons. First, as Canadian economic development has shifted northward (Chapter 10), governments and companies have wanted to ensure jurisdiction. This has been the case in nearly every instance of a stalled pipeline project in recent years.

Second, Indigenous peoples themselves are today more politically aware, unified, and adept at pressing their claims. An example of this is a pact signed in 2000 between the Blood, Peigan, and Siksika of Alberta and the Blackfeet of Montana nations, all members of the once mighty Blackfoot Confederacy that, before Treaty No. 7 was signed in 1877, controlled the southern third of Alberta, stretching into Saskatchewan and Montana. The pact was meant to draw the government's attention to their concerns, including honouring Indigenous rights, renewing tribal customs, and restoring lands they insisted were wrongfully appropriated from the Confederacy (*Edmonton Journal* 2000).

It is the settlement of comprehensive claims that has raised the most issues, however. As noted in Chapter 10, the first comprehensive agreements were signed in the late 1970s by the Quebec government with the James Bay Cree of northern Quebec. The Inuvialuit agreement, dealing with lands in Canada's far north, followed in 1984, extinguishing Aboriginal title to the western Arctic in return for ownership of 96,000 square kilometres of territory and $55 million (combined) in benefits and money for economic development (Dickason 2002, 405). After 14 years of negotiation, a similar agreement regarding the Dene/Métis Western Arctic land claim was cancelled by the federal government, which refused to renegotiate the extinguishment of Aboriginal title (Dickason 2002; see also Geddes 2001). This was quickly followed, however, by a series of other, smaller, agreements signed with bands in the Yukon and Northwest Territories.

Finally, the territory of Nunavut was created in 1999 (see Chapter 10). Nunavut (meaning "our land") began as a proposal submitted in 1976 by the Inuit Tapirisat of Canada organization. After years of exhaustive negotiations, boundary disputes, and meetings with Dene and Métis representatives who had their own agendas, the residents of the Northwest Territories passed their own plebiscite on the issue in 1992 (Momatiuk and Eastcott 1995). The federal government eventually accepted the proposal, and in 1999 Nunavut became the permanent home of the Inuit. The Inuit population in Canada is over 65,000; of this total, 73 percent reside in Nunavut, meaning that 85 percent the territory's population is of Inuit heritage. The area comprises more than 2.2 million square kilometres, more than one-fifth of Canada's land surface, and is the largest land claim in Canada's history (Dickason and Newbigging 2010).

As many of these comprehensive agreements have dealt with sparsely populated northern lands inhabited mostly by Indigenous peoples, far away from non-Indigenous Canadians, the agreements have raised few questions. As in Quebec before the Second World War, the two solitudes scarcely came into meaningful contact. Not so, however, in the case of treaty claims and land settlements further south, especially in British Columbia.

The situation of treaty negotiations in British Columbia is unique. Aside from 14 minor treaties signed with Governor James Douglas in the middle of the 19th century, and the overlapping of Treaty No. 8 into their territory, British Columbia had never, until recently, negotiated treaties with First Nations. For years, the province of British Columbia denied having any legal obligations to Indigenous peoples. In 1992, however, a newly elected New Democratic government opened discussions pertaining to 47 land claims, promising to resolve them (Dickason and Newbigging 2010).

The total area of British Columbia is 932,000 square kilometres. By October 1999, negotiations were in process for claims amounting to 703,832 square kilometres of the province (Frideres and Gadacz 2001, 223). The Nisga'a of northern British Columbia, whose claim was settled in 1999, provide a useful case study of contemporary land claims.

The Nisga'a were never militarily defeated, nor did they ever sign a treaty with the Government of Canada ceding their lands. They first pressed their claims in 1887, when a group of Nisga'a chiefs travelled to Victoria. The government ignored them and took no action until 1976. Even then, it was a token acknowledgement. Twenty years later, in March 1996, the government and the Nisga'a leadership signed an agreement in principle. The agreement gave the Nisga'a a cash payment of $190 million (later increased to $500 million) and established a Nisga'a central government with administrative, municipal-like responsibilities for 2,000 square kilometres of land in the Nass River Valley. Additionally, Nisga'a ownership of surface and subsurface resources was safeguarded, as well as rights to salmon stocks and wildlife harvests. In 1999, the 5,000 members of the Nisga'a First Nation ratified the treaty, and in April of the same year, the British Columbia government and federal Parliament passed the agreement into law. The Senate passed the bill on April 13, 2000, completing the treaty process (Steckley and Cummins 2008).

In a bold subsequent move, the Nisga'a in November 2013 became the first Indigenous Nation in British Columbia to privatize land (Lynch 2013). Some observers believe that when individuals are able to take loans against home equity in order to establish a business, more opportunities will be provided for the Nisga'a to move out of poverty. Critics worry, however, that private ownership means that citizens can transfer, sell, or will their property to anyone, including non-Nisga'a—an issue of obvious importance to Indigenous culture, community, and identity.

Beyond these concerns, the Nisga'a treaty has also encountered criticism, not least from some Indigenous peoples who dislike the fact that, under the agreement, federal and provincial income tax laws, the Charter of Rights and Freedoms, and the Criminal Code now apply to Nisga'a government. By far the strongest criticisms of the Nisga'a and similar treaties have come, however, from the non-Indigenous community (Frideres and Gadacz 2001).

Many non-Indigenous concerns over comprehensive claims are unfounded. There is no chance, for example, that Indigenous peoples will confiscate the lands on which Vancouver sits and have non-Indigenous people evicted, as some have argued. Likewise, the Supreme Court has rejected Smith's (1995) argument that there is no legal basis for comprehensive land claims.

Smith's other four concerns, however, bear consideration: (1) that such land claims agreements are actually constitutional agreements that are binding upon subsequent generations and therefore do not provide for sufficient flexibility; (2) that such agreements open the way for endless negotiations, ever-escalating demands, the creation of more bureaucracy, and mounting costs; (3) that land claims raise jurisdictional concerns, including whether Indigenous people under the agreements will be subject to Canadian law, including the Constitution's Charter of Rights and Freedoms; and (4) that the land claims agreements (and concomitant rights and benefits provided to Indigenous peoples) are race-based and will actually hinder the chances of ordinary Indigenous people from entering fully into Canadian society.

The latter concern—that comprehensive land claims are race-based, of which the Nunavut agreement establishing an Inuit "home" provides an example—remains a point of debate for some (see Flanagan 2000), though the alleged practical implications appear unclear. As to the other concerns, with the passage of time, their cogency has diminished. Yes, the agreements are indeed constitutional documents, but this in no way places a stop on further changes, any more than other constitutional changes over the years have rendered; yes, there have been ongoing negotiations, but these have resulted, if slowly, in real settlements and not ongoing stalemates; and, finally, a set of Supreme Court decisions has clarified the meaning of self-government. For example, while recognizing the Nisga'a agreement's validity, the Supreme Court also established that nation's self-government as nonetheless fitting "into the wider constitutional fabric of Canada" (Nisga'a Lisims Government 2013). Another Supreme Court decision, this time dealing with Tsilhqot'in First Nation of British Columbia, provides a similar conclusion. While that decision grants the Tsilhqot'in Nation title to historic lands (Stueck 2014), albeit possibly shared with other First Nations (Pemberton 2014), it also appears to have determined the meaning and extent of Aboriginal self-government in a manner that ends talk of Aboriginal sovereignty (Mulgrew 2014). These rulings suggest the idea of government-to-government or nation-to-nation discussions has been replaced by one in which Indigenous jurisdiction is confined within Canada (on the limits of Indigenous self-government, see Frideres and Gadacz 2001; Frideres 2011). Despite this clarification, real questions and barriers remain if Indigenous peoples are going to gain a meaningful say over their futures.

THE ROAD TO SELF-GOVERNMENT

Indigenous peoples in Canada had successful governance structures long before the arrival of Europeans. Historical examples of self-government in Indigenous communities include the Iroquois Confederacy, circa 1570 (from which some elements of the American Constitution were drawn) and the eastern Maritime Mi'kmaq First Nation, which existed prior to European contact and operated a seven-state democratic system presided over by seven chiefs and a grand chief who lived on Cape Breton Island. Subsequent colonialism destroyed many of these organizational structures, but First Nations peoples have never ceased their fight to regain control over their lives.

Indigenous claims for self-government rest on three planks (Schouls 2003). First, as originally sovereign nations, Indigenous Nations have an inherent right to create and maintain their own identities, cultures, languages, values, and practices, and therefore they should have the right to choose their own form of governance. Second, even though Indigenous peoples live under the Crown's protection, this in no way reduces or diminishes their historical right to self-government. The original agreements between government and First Nations (treaties) were signed as equal partners—nation to nation. Therefore, any model of self-government must constitute more than mere self-administration. Third, because the original treaty-making process was initiated on principles of reciprocity and consent, there is no valid reason to ignore or even seek to improve this arrangement; the original agreements should simply be adhered to. Ultimately, the desire for self-government may also be justified as a means of redressing the harm done by a "foreign" government—that of Canada—and ensuring it does not happen again (Buckley 1993).

Indigenous peoples have been demanding the right of self-government within Canada for quite some time, but these demands either have been ignored or have faltered amid efforts to arrive at a workable application of the meaning of self-government. In language reminiscent of Jean Lesage's Liberals in Quebec in the early 1960s (see Chapter 2), the Union of British Columbia Indian Chiefs, for example, defined its position on self-government as follows (cited in Wall 2000, 144):

> We must be masters in our own house, in order to survive as Indian people. There is no basis in the laws of Canada to restrict the recovery of Aboriginal rights because we have never given up our rights to control our own lives and means to live.

Paternalism, an offshoot of colonialism, has continued to infuse government-Indigenous relations. During the constitutional discussions in the early 1980s, however, real efforts were begun in earnest to define self-government.

In 1983, the federal government released a report the Special Committee on Indian Self-Government in Canada (also known as the Penner Report) (Government of Canada 1983). The Penner Report dismissed the terms and intent of the Indian Act as being out of date and ineffective for contemporary negotiations and made several recommendations, calling for the government to establish a new kind of relationship with Indigenous peoples based on the notion of Aboriginal self-government. Among specific recommendations, the report recommended that Indigenous governments be made accountable to their own people; that bilateral federal-Indigenous agreements govern respective jurisdictions, with the federal government ceding all areas of competence required for First Nations, Inuit, and Métis to govern themselves effectively and ensuring that provincial laws would not apply to Indigenous land except with Indigenous consent; and that complete control be given to

First Nations over their lands and resources, with financial backing through federal grants and the settlement of land claims. Finally, the report also originated the concept of a third order of governance with respect to Indigenous self-government (Tennant 1988).

The federal government's response to the Penner Report was to try to entrench Aboriginal self-government for Status Indians at a first ministers' meeting in 1984. At that meeting, Prime Minister Pierre Trudeau pursued the report's initiatives but found little agreement among the premiers. Brian Mulroney's government made similar proposals in 1985 and 1987, but again consensus was lacking. The governments of Alberta, British Columbia, Newfoundland, and Saskatchewan in particular were reluctant to support federal proposals for Indigenous self-government without a full definition of costs and terms (Miller 1988).

Additionally, some Indigenous organizations have found self-government proposals inadequate while, for its part, the federal government appears to only tacitly recognize the "inherent right" of Aboriginal peoples to negotiate for self-government (Asch 2000, 67), a recognition that carries no fundamental meaning. (Ottawa has left the door open for the negotiation of self-government in the Dene-Métis and Yukon claims, but only on condition that this right not receive the same constitutional protection accorded to other settlements, meaning that any constitutional recognition of the Indigenous right to self-government gained by the Dene-Métis constituency cannot be used as a precedent in any other sector of the Aboriginal community.)

Several contentious and interrelated issues lie at the heart of the problems of defining and implementing self-government.

Timing

There is little doubt that First Nations communities in Canada—weary of being regarded as wards of the government—desire self-government (Kulchyski 2005). Thus far, however, government departments overseeing First Nations and Indigenous affairs generally have shown a reluctance to shed paternalistic control, often arguing that bands are not ready for self-government.

Territoriality

The intent of recent land claims settlements has been to define the idea of Indigenous self-government. Implementing self-government is difficult enough when confined to a single, uncontested geographical space, but it is less clear how one might implement self-government in, say, urban areas, where a significant and growing number of Indigenous peoples live, including some on urban reserves (Barron and Garcea 1999) (see Chapter 12). It is even more problematic when different institutions and rules govern different groups of people within the same space.

Level and Form of Government

The Canadian government has tended to view "self-government" as approximating the level of Canadian municipalities, often transferring certain responsibilities to local

Indigenous bands and councils, which, in turn, act as financial administrators (Asch 2000). By contrast, Indigenous organizations want assurances that the Constitution will protect their actual institutions—unlike municipal government bodies, which are not protected—and that such self-governing institutions are more or less on the level of provincial counterparts. The Supreme Court decisions outlined previously suggest for Indigenous governance a status between that of municipal and provincial government. As Kulchyski (2005) argues, many Indigenous leaders view self-government as not simply a matter of transferring powers from government to local bands, but of clarifying and determining the kind of governance that will be initiated.

Governance Structure

Whatever form it takes, if Indigenous self-government is ever realized, there will have to be a recognized authority structure (Angus 1991). As the discussed case of the Wet'suwet'en shows, existing governmental structures based on Euro-Canadian practices are not necessarily appropriate or functional for Indigenous communities (Kulchyski 2005).

Jurisdiction

Angus (1991) states that in order for Indigenous self-government to succeed, the Canadian government must recognize Indigenous authority in specific areas of jurisdiction. Similarly, Kulchyski (2005) argues that to be effective, Indigenous self-government must be tailored to meet local needs. These arguments suggest again that the form of self-government will need to fall somewhere between that of a municipality and a province, with commensurate jurisdiction. In this vein, Fleras (2007) suggests that Indigenous jurisdiction will likely include control over (1) the delivery of social services such as policing, education, and health and welfare; (2) resources and use of land for economic development; (3) the means to protect and promote distinct cultural values and language systems; (4) band membership and entitlements; and (5) local expenditures according to Indigenous priorities rather than those of government or bureaucracy, with some variation at play regarding different Indigenous communities.

Economic Self-Sufficiency

Recent years have seen some First Nations establish agreements ensuring benefits from economic development on their land. For example, the Fort McKay First Nation's oil field and service companies, in partnership with non-Indigenous companies, today employ 1,300 individuals (Fort McKay Group of Companies n.d.). Such instances remain a rarity, however. Except where local resources are today in wide demand (e.g., oil), many of Canada's reserves are situated on land intentionally determined under earlier treaties to be of little value, and thus they lack a strong economic base. While large numbers of Indigenous peoples have moved or are moving to Canadian cities in search of jobs and other opportunities (see Chapter 12), many of those remaining are supported by government social assistance and welfare. Such a situation defies any meaningful sense of self-government;

indeed, as Boldt (1993, 261) argues, such a situation is a mockery that encourages a "culture of dependence" designed for continued subordination and paternalism.

From Self-Government to Self-Determination

It has often been said that Canada does not work in theory, but it does in practice. Despite seemingly interminable debates about how it will work and a number of issues to be addressed, at the concrete level things are progressing. In 1986, for example, the Sechelt band of British Columbia gained a form of self-government that has since served as a model for other bands. Sechelt assumed powers to legislate matters that range from zoning and land use to on-reserve education. Today, both federal and provincial governments respect the application of these rights so long as they are consistent with federal and provincial laws. Moreover, the Sechelt agreement has paved the way for similar recognition of rights for all bands in Canada that previously had to negotiate with the federal government over even peripheral matters (Russell 2000; Asch 2000; Bird et al. 2000). While tedious, real progress toward Indigenous self-government has been made (Hylton 1999).

But the debate over self-government may also obscure the more important notion of self-determination. In the words of McDonnell and Depew (1999, 353), "The processes associated with self-government are so powerfully unilateral in their focus that they have all but displaced considerations relating to self-determination." As Boldt (1993) noted some years ago, beyond self-government, the survival of Indigenous cultures requires Indigenous peoples to develop a clear vision and consensus about their own future. This means assessing the damage inflicted by colonialism in the past and as it continues today; creating ways to stop the ongoing processes of assimilation and acculturation; critically evaluating what must be done; and, finally, mobilizing efforts toward making a revitalized identity a reality. Self-government alone will not do these things.

CONCLUSION

Canadian society is at a crossroads in its relationship with Indigenous peoples. A series of conflicts over the past 30 years, including the recent Wet'suwet'en dispute in British Columbia, have highlighted the economic, political, and social stakes for everyone. There is no going back, but what is the way forward? The Royal Commission on Aboriginal Peoples and the Truth and Reconciliation Commission provide some guidance, but the journey will not be easy for anyone, Indigenous or non-Indigenous. There has been conflict and this will likely occur again. But as conflict theorists would argue, conflict has also paved the way for dealing with a host of problems previously ignored. In this still-early part of the 21st century, a path for renewal has been set, a path that will define Canada for decades to come—but will both communities accept it? The following chapter examines a set of transformations occurring within Indigenous society today and how these transformations may also change the rest of Canada.

CRITICAL THINKING QUESTIONS

1. Why did so many studies like the Hawthorn Report arise in Canadian society during the 1960s?
2. Are there common lessons to be learned from the series of conflicts involving Indigenous peoples and governments since the 1990s?
3. Why have so few of the Royal Commission's recommendations been enacted?
4. What problems do notions of Indigenous self-government pose for mainstream ideas of state and nation?
5. What problems and opportunities might arise from the introduction of individual property ownership on Nisga'a territory?

RECOMMENDED READINGS

Bird, John, Lorraine Land, and Murray MacAdam, eds. 2000. *Self-Government in the New Millennium: Nation to Nation: Aboriginal Sovereignty and the Future of Canada*. Toronto: Irwin Publishing.
This is one of the first books to address the question of Aboriginal self-government and does so from the perspective of informed authorities.

Davis, Wade, K. David Harrison, and Catherine Herbert Howell, eds. 2008. *Book of Peoples of the World: A Guide to Cultures*. Washington, DC: National Geographic.
The book examines the rapid disappearance of ethnic identities, including the many Indigenous cultures around the world, in the midst of encroaching modernity.

Dickason, Olive Patricia, and William Newbigging. 2010. *A Concise History of Canada's First Nations*. 2nd ed. Don Mills, ON: Oxford University Press.
Written from an Indigenous perspective, this book delivers what its title professes.

Snow, Chief John. 2005. *These Mountains Are Our Sacred Places: The Story of the Stoney People*. Calgary: Fifth House.
Although primarily an in-depth case study of the Stoney First Nation in Alberta, the narrative outlines much broader implications for other First Nations as well.

Warry, Wayne. 2007. *Ending Denial: Understanding Aboriginal Issues*. Peterborough, ON: Broadview Press.
This is an in-depth, objective appraisal of a variety of legal and socio-economic frontiers faced by First Nations communities in Canada.

RELATED WEBSITES

Canadiana
www.canadiana.ca
> This is a national body made up of distinguished scholars and representatives of major research libraries from across Canada. The organization hosts a digital archive, Canada in the Making, containing a collection of narrative text, primary documents, maps, and photos.

Royal Commission on Aboriginal Peoples
www.bac-lac.gc.ca/eng/discover/aboriginal-heritage/royal-commission-aboriginal-peoples/Pages/introduction.aspx
> In the wake of the Oka Crisis, the Canadian government established the Royal Commission on Aboriginal Peoples. The commission's final report can be found on this site.

The Truth and Reconciliation Commission of Canada
www.rcaanc-cirnac.gc.ca/eng/1450124405592/1529106060525
> This is the website of the commission's final report.

CANADIAN SOCIETY ON VIDEO

The Invisible Nation. 2012. National Film Board of Canada, 93 minutes, 20 seconds. The lifestyle of Canada's Algonquin was changed forever when Europeans arrived. Today, barely 9,000 Algonquin are left. They live in about 10 communities and are suffering threats to their very existence in silence. Richard Desjardins and Robert Monderie have decided to sound the alarm before it's too late.

Is the Crown at War With US? 2002. National Film Board of Canada, 96 minutes. This film by Alanis Obomsawin looks at the conflict in Burnt Church, New Brunswick, in 2000 between the Mi'kmaq and non-Indigenous fishermen. Obomsawin delineates the complex roots of the conflict with passion and clarity, building a persuasive defence of the Mi'kmaq position while criticizing the role of the federal fisheries department.

The Journey of Nishiyuu. 2013. Grand Council of the Crees, 14 minutes, 18 seconds. *Nishiyuu* means "human beings" or "modern people" in the Cree language. Between January and March of 2013, a group of Cree youth walked from northern Quebec to Ottawa, a distance of more than 1,600 kilometres, in support of the Idle No More movement.

CHAPTER 12

New Learning Paths

Eagle. Courtesy Bill Jorgensen, photographer, and Wes Seeley, sculptor.

Our people have come into their own—there's no doubt about it—but now we have to build an audience. We have to do what we can to ensure that the beautiful power of our voices is heard. . . . Our stories are full of both sorrow and joy and it is important that we share them.
    —actor Gary Farmer, 2005

It is only a matter of time for this growing cultural self-confidence to express itself, and be listened to, in other arenas as well. A key area is education, and the First Nations have demonstrated their effectiveness in taking control of the schooling of their children.
    —Olive Patricia Dickason and William Newbigging, 2010

The fact of Native existence is that we live modern lives informed by traditional val-
ues and contemporary realities and that we wish to live those lives in our terms.
   —Thomas King, 2012

INTRODUCTION

There is much unfinished business surrounding Indigenous and non-Indigenous relations: land claims, new treaties, the eventual abolition of the Indian Act, and the implementation of genuine self-government, not to mention real economic and social equality. Above all, there is the need for healing. But this is all to be expected. Every society has unfinished business, although matters pertaining to Indigenous peoples have specific urgency. In this regard, Drees (2013, 121) emphasizes that Indigenous peoples should be encouraged to heal in accordance with traditional Indigenous "medicines" that—although not always visible—are very much available. As noted in the Introduction, societies are not static; they are a process, and in this instance, the process of healing will require that non-Indigenous peoples listen more closely to Indigenous voices.

This concluding chapter of Part 3 examines Indigenous society in all its complexity today, including some of the current experiments going on in Indigenous communities and among emerging Indigenous leaders. Along the way, the chapter also explores how Indigenous values embedded within traditional lifeways view might fit into today's Canada, and it alludes to how Canadian society could benefit—if it chooses—from rediscovering its Indigenous roots. To begin, however, the chapter provides a necessary demographic profile of Indigenous peoples in Canada.

POPULATION DYNAMICS

When Columbus first arrived from Europe, the total population of North and South America was about 57 million people, 4.5 million of whom lived north of Mexico (Cook 1995, 33). Of these, about 500,000 lived in what is today Canada. Shortly after Confederation, however, the Indigenous population of Canada sank to 102,000 (Ponting 1997b, 68) and did not rise again until the 1940s. Since then, however, the population of Status Indians in Canada has steadily risen. As shown in table 12.1, the number of First Nations people in Canada today totals 977,235, while nearly 1.7 million people report Aboriginal ancestry.[1] While the First Nations population remains the largest segment, the largest increase in recent years has occurred among the Métis, who now comprise just over 35 percent of Indigenous peoples in Canada.

The growth of the Indigenous population can be measured against the country's population as a whole. In 2016, Indigenous peoples made up roughly 4.9 percent of the Canadian population, up from 3.8 percent in 2006 (see table 12.2). As a proportion of total population, the greatest increase in Indigenous peoples has occurred in Newfoundland and the Prairie provinces, but increases have occurred in nearly all parts of the country.

Table 12.1: Aboriginal Identity Population, Canada, 2016

Aboriginal Identity Population	Number	Percentage
Total Aboriginal identity population	1,673,780	100
Single Aboriginal responses	1,629,800	97.4
First Nations (North American Indian)	977,235	58.4
Métis	587,545	35.1
Inuk	65,025	4.0
Multiple Aboriginal responses	21,305	1.3
Aboriginal identities not included elsewhere	22,670	1.4

Source: Statistics Canada. 2016d. "Aboriginal Peoples Highlight Tables, 2016 Census Aboriginal identity population by both sexes, total—age, 2016 counts, Canada, provinces and territories, 2016 Census—25% Sample data." Percentages calculated by authors.

Why has the Indigenous population in Canada increased so rapidly in recent years? The increase is particularly impressive given both the high infant mortality rate that stalks many First Nations communities and the much lower life expectancy generally for Indigenous peoples. (The **infant mortality rate** is calculated as the number of infants who die during their first year after birth for every thousand live births within a certain population.) In their 2010 report, Smylie and colleagues (2010, 147) noted, for example, that the infant mortality rate for "Status Indians living off-reserve and Inuit IMRs ranged from 1.7 to over 4 times the over-all Canadian and/or non-Aboriginal rates." For example, the infant mortality rate for Inuit in 2017 was 12.3 per 1,000 in 2004–2006, compared to 4.4 per 1,000 for non-Indigenous Canadians (Inuit Tapiriit Kanatami 2018, 11–12).

Infant mortality rates impact the calculation of life expectancy rates if done long-term. For example, life expectancy among Inuit of both sexes in 2017 was 72.4 years compared to 82.9 years for non-Indigenous Canadians (Inuit Tapiriit Kanatami 2018, 11–12). Thus, at age one, the life expectancy of males and females among First Nations and Inuit peoples in 2011 was roughly 9 to 11 years less than non-Indigenous Canadians, and between 4.5 to 5 years less for male and female Métis compared to their non-Indigenous counterparts. In contrast, when calculated after age 20, the life expectancy gap narrowed to 4.6 and 6.2 years for First Nations and Inuit, and between 2.7 and 3.8 years for Métis (Tjepkema et al. 2019). Nonetheless, these differences remain significant.

Given these dire statistics, what are the causes of the Indigenous population increase? First, the passage of Bill C-31 in 1985 (see Chapter 11) allowed many Indigenous women to regain their status. A little more than a decade after Bill C-31 was passed, some 105,000 individuals had regained their status (Frideres and Gadacz 2001, 35). Second, a growing sense of pride in Aboriginal ancestry has led to an increase in voluntary identification

Table 12.2: Indigenous and Non-Indigenous Populations by Provinces and Territories, Canada, 2006 and 2016

	2006						2016					
	Total Population	Indigenous Population		Non-Indigenous Population			Total Population	Indigenous Population		Non-Indigenous Population		
	Persons	Persons	%	Persons	%		Persons	Persons	%	Persons	%	
Canada	**31,241,030**	**1,172,790**	**3.8**	**30,068,240**	**96.2**		**34,460,060**	**1,673,785**	**4.9**	**32,786,280**	**95.1**	
Newfoundland and Labrador	500,610	23,450	4.7	477,155	95.3		512,255	45,725	8.9	466,525	91.1	
Prince Edward Island	134,205	1,730	1.3	132,475	98.7		139,690	2,740	2.0	136,945	98.0	
Nova Scotia	903,090	24,175	2.7	878,915	97.3		908,340	51,490	5.7	856,850	94.3	
New Brunswick	719,650	17,655	2.5	701,995	97.5		730,710	29,385	4.0	701,325	96.0	
Quebec	7,435,905	108,430	1.5	7,327,475	98.5		7,965,450	182,885	2.3	7,782,565	97.7	
Ontario	12,028,900	242,495	2.0	11,786,405	98.0		13,242,160	374,395	2.8	12,867,765	97.2	
Manitoba	1,133,515	175,395	15.5	958,120	84.5		1,240,695	223,310	18.0	1,017,390	82.0	
Saskatchewan	953,850	141,890	14.9	811,960	85.1		1,070,560	175,020	16.3	895,540	83.7	
Alberta	3,256,355	188,365	5.8	3,067,990	94.2		3,978,145	258,640	6.5	3,719,505	93.5	
British Columbia	4,074,385	196,075	4.8	3,878,310	96.2		4,560,240	270,585	5.9	4,289,650	94.1	
Yukon	30,190	7,580	25.1	22,610	74.9		35,110	8,195	23.3	26,920	76.7	
Northwest Territories	41,055	20,635	50.3	20,420	49.7		41,135	20,860	50.7	20,275	49.3	
Nunavut	29,325	24,920	85.0	4,410	15.0		35,580	30,550	85.9	5,025	14.1	

Source: Northwest Territories Bureau of Statistics. 2017. "Indigenous Peoples" (released November 2); data generated from Statistics Canada Census 2006 and 2016.

among Indigenous peoples. Most researchers, however, attribute the primary cause of the population increase to birth rates that remain higher than the Canadian average within the Indigenous community. A further consequence of high birth rates is that Canada's Indigenous population, again compared with the general population, is also very young. As shown in table 12.3, the percentage of Indigenous peoples in the age groups between newborn and age 34 is higher than that of non-Indigenous people in these same groups, the shift in percentages occurring as the respective populations grow older. While some of this difference may be attributable to a lower age of mortality among Indigenous people, thus increasing the proportion of people in the lower age groups, the finding is also congruent with higher birth rates. But note also the differences within the three Indigenous identity groups—First Nations, Métis, and Inuit—which speak to the differential life chances within the overall Indigenous community.

Looking ahead, demographers with Statistics Canada (Morency et al. 2015) have mapped out four possible future scenarios for Canada's Indigenous population. Employing such variables as fertility and mortality rates and intergenerational migration and ethnic mobility (factors that might impact self-identification), demographers project Canada's Indigenous population to be between 1,965,000 and 2,633,000 in 2036. In the latter scenario, Indigenous people would constitute 6.1 percent of the total Canadian population.

The importance of Indigenous peoples in shaping Canadian society in the future is not solely related to numbers per se, but also to geographic location. Just as a population shift is occurring throughout Canada (Chapter 7), as people migrate to the West, a similar shift is occurring within the Indigenous population of Canada, though it is birth rates, rather than interprovincial migration, that is the primary factor. As shown in table 12.2, while Ontario has the largest Indigenous population (374,395), nearly half of Indigenous peoples in Canada today live in the four western provinces, where birth rates are also among the highest in Canada. Birth rates among the North's Inuit peoples are similarly high, roughly three times that of the total Canadian population.

Administratively, governments describe First Nations communities as tribes with subdivisions known as bands. As of March 2019, there were 619 recognized First Nations. Traditionally, the term band referred to small cultural and linguistic groups living together, or coming together at various seasons and times, as part of a larger Indigenous society, such as the Cree, Blackfoot, or Inuit. Today, however, the term describes a local unit of administration operating under the Indian Act (see Chapter 11). Most bands consist of about 500 members, but some—such as Six Nations in Ontario, with over 27,000 members, and the Kainai Nation in southern Alberta, with over 12,000 members—are quite large.

While many Indigenous peoples in the northern parts of Canada's provinces and in the territories continue to live in rural areas, there is also a second population shift of both Status and non-Status Indigenous peoples increasingly relocating to Canada's cities and towns. Today, slightly more than half of Status Indians (52 percent) (Indigenous and Northern Affairs Canada 2017) live off reserve, mainly in urban centres. The urbanization

Table 12.3: Age Distribution for Selected Aboriginal Identity and Non-Aboriginal Populations, Canada, 2016

Age Groups	Non-Aboriginal Identity Population		Aboriginal Identity Population		First Nations (North American Indian)		Métis		Inuk (Inuit)	
	Number	%	Number[1]	%	Number	%	Number	%	Number	%
Total age groups	32,786,280	100	1,673,780	100	977,235	100	587,545	100	65,025	100
0–14 years	5,368,180	16.4	448,865	26.8	285,825	29.2	130,990	22.1	21,490	33.0
15–24	3,948,340	12.0	283,385	16.9	170,700	17.5	94,105	16.0	11,995	18.4
25–34	4,340,675	13.2	235,900	14.1	136,925	14.0	83,585	14.2	9,910	15.2
35–44	4,304,915	13.1	202,860	12.1	116,625	11.9	74,185	12.6	7,475	11.5
45–54	4,779,785	14.6	212,190	12.7	117,945	12.1	82,065	14.0	6,805	10.5
55–64	4,686,150	14.3	168,905	10.1	87,140	8.9	71,505	12.2	4,285	6.6
65 years and over	5,358,245	16.3	121,665	7.2	62,070	6.4	51,115	8.7	3,060	4.7

Note: 1. The estimates for the three Aboriginal groups do not add to the total Aboriginal identity population because only selected Aboriginal identity categories are shown.

Source: Statistics Canada. 2016d. "Aboriginal Peoples Highlight Tables, 2016 Census Aboriginal identity population by both sexes, total—age, 2016 counts, Canada, provinces and territories, 2016 Census—25% Sample data." Percentages calculated by authors.

of Indigenous peoples in Canada has received increased attention from sociologists over the last three decades—much of it unfortunately negative, however, and focused on the great difficulties that Indigenous peoples may have in adjusting to urban life. Despite these difficulties, which are exacerbated by discrimination, prejudice, and racism, Indigenous peoples continue to migrate to Canada's cities, drawn by educational and employment opportunities as well as cultural and community factors (Cooke and Bélanger 2006; Frideres 2011). A significant consequence of this migration has been the emergence of **urban reserves**.

URBAN RESERVES

Saskatchewan is the birthplace of urban reserves. In 1976, the Saskatchewan and federal governments and Indigenous leaders signed an agreement, the Saskatchewan Formula, through which land equity would be worked out. A change of provincial government (from NDP to Conservative) saw the deal temporarily abandoned, but the NDP's later re-turn to power assured the signing of the Saskatchewan Treaty Land Entitlement Frame-work Agreement in 1992. The agreement set aside $446 million to purchase land on which to develop urban reserves (Barron and Garcea 1999, 26). That same year, 28 of Saskatchewan's 70 Indian bands signed on, and 28 urban reserves were created, nine of them in larger centres (Steckley and Cummins 2008, 141). Today there are more than 120 Indigenous urban reserves operating throughout Canada (Indigenous and Northern Affairs Canada 2017).

Barron and Garcea (1999) state three reasons for the creation of urban reserves. The first reason is that they are directly related to treaties and treaty land entitlement. When treaties 4, 6, and 7 were drawn up (see Chapter 9), the conditions were that every family of five would be awarded a full section of land, but the federal government often failed to live up to this arrangement and simply shortchanged Indigenous peoples. A century after the first 10 numbered treaties were signed, Indigenous peoples made up a full 3 percent of Canada's population but possessed only 0.02 percent of available land. (In Saskatchewan alone, almost 30 bands were shortchanged when land entitlements for reserves were nego-tiated.) In effect, the 1992 agreement settled an outstanding claim by offering bands com-pensatory funds with which to buy private real estate holdings.

A second reason is that urban reserves are closely associated with First Nations' desires to develop and diversify economic opportunities. Federal land was found for eco-nomic development in Saskatoon, for example, and transferred, after negotiations, to Indigenous ownership.

Third, for many Indigenous peoples, urban reserves are a territorial expression of the inherent right of self-government. They want to be full players in the dominant society, not as assimilated members of that society, but as people with their own distinct cultural identity. Urban reserves function as an extension of a band's national land patrimony and authority to make decisions over their lives.

On this latter point, urban reserves clearly tie into demands for self-government (see Chapter 11). The concept of a bonded community offers not only strong encouragement for economic development but also the opportunity necessary for participants to formulate some kind of self-government to determine rules for living and to set community goals.

Indigenous peoples on urban reserves continue to face stiff opposition, however, particularly from local non-Indigenous politicians, though politicians at other levels have also expressed resistance. This opposition often stems from concerns that any form of reserve government could establish rules and laws that might contradict those passed by city council, that the establishment of a different kind of neighbourhood might affect federal and provincial grants to cities and towns, and that urban reserves might turn into ethnic ghettos. Without doubt, some of these objections are grounded in prejudice and discrimination. But urban reserves do raise some legitimate jurisdictional questions, reflecting the complexity and newness of such ventures (Frideres 2011). A recent report by Poholka (2016) highlights some of the benefits and challenges of urban reserves:

- Benefits for First Nations include increased job opportunities, revenue generation, jurisdiction over new reserve land, increased economic self-sufficiency, and increased quality of life.
- Benefits for municipalities include revenue from urban reserve service provisions, job opportunities, and positive relationships with Indigenous peoples.
- Challenges for First Nations include high financial risk, limited financial resources, fragmentation of band members as some move closer to urban centres and away from the parent reserve, and discrimination in urban centres.

In addition, Poholka notes several general challenges, including a lack of clarity regarding the federal government's Additions to Reserve (ATR) policy, the often drawn-out process of land purchases, and friction between municipalities and First Nations in setting up service agreements.

Despite challenges, and perhaps above all, urban reserves hold the promise of bringing together the two solitudes of Indigenous and non-Indigenous peoples in the pursuit of providing equal opportunities for education, employment, adequate housing, and other social benefits.

HEALTH AND SOCIAL CONDITIONS

A report by the National Collaborating Centre for Aboriginal Health (2013, 4) notes that Indigenous peoples experience several major health problems at higher rates than their non-Indigenous counterparts, among them,

> high infant and young child mortality; high maternal morbidity and mortality; heavy infectious disease burdens; malnutrition and stunted growth; shortened

life expectancy; diseases and death associated with cigarette smoking; social problems, illnesses and deaths linked to misuse of alcohol and other drugs; accidents, poisonings, interpersonal violence, homicide and suicide; obesity, diabetes, hypertension, cardiovascular, and chronic renal disease (lifestyle diseases); and diseases caused by environmental contamination (for example, heavy metals, industrial gases and effluent wastes).

These results are largely attributable to conditions of poverty on many First Nations reserves or in the North that mirror those found in underdeveloped countries far beyond Canada's borders. On-reserve housing, for example, is generally substandard and often poorly ventilated. (For example, in November 2007, 31 people on the Peigan reserve in southern Alberta were evacuated from five homes that were condemned in part due to serious mould problems.) The homes are too hot in summer and too cold in winter. Running water is frequently a luxury. Many First Nations' reserves have limited capacity when natural disasters strike, as occurred in the spring of 2013 in southern Alberta, when a massive rain-fed flood forced 1,000 people from the Siksika (Blackfoot) reserve to evacuate their homes, and 510 homes on the Stoney Nakoda Reserve, west of Calgary, were similarly flooded, contributing to hazardous health conditions for some families that remained.

We must also keep in mind that, while on-reserve conditions are generally poor, the situation of Indigenous people migrating to urban areas is often not much better. Though cities may provide some families with increased opportunities and more accessible services (see previous section on urban reserves), many Indigenous people also find they have to contend with myriad other challenges, such as cultural alienation and racism (Buckley 1993; Fox and Long 2000).

Sociologists and health care providers in recent years have come to understand and identify important linkages between health outcomes and other social and economic factors—what collectively are now termed the **social determinants of health**. The Canadian Public Health Association (2020) lists 14 such determinants, one of which in Canada is Aboriginal Status. The other 13 are income and income distribution; education; unemployment and job security; employment and working conditions; early childhood development; food insecurity; housing; social exclusion; social safety network; health services; gender; race; and disability.

Recognizing that health is not an individual or even a purely physical and biological issue but is tied to a complex web of social factors is, almost by definition, sociological. But the web of connections can be extended even further. As noted in the Truth and Reconciliation Report, a disproportionate number of Indigenous children are taken into care by provincial welfare agencies, many simply because their parents are considered too poor to provide care. This is particularly the case in western Canada (Sinha and Kozlowski 2013). Submitted in support of Bill C-92, a government report to deal with the issue states that "Indigenous children make up 7.7% of all children under 15 but account for 52.2% of children in foster care in private homes" (Government of Canada 2019b). Most explanations for this overrepresentation emphasize the negative historic impact of residential schools upon Indigenous parents and the social conditions under which too many Indigenous children are raised. But let's spool out the thread a little further.

Not surprisingly, perhaps, there is also a near perfect correlation between the disproportionate number of Indigenous adults in custody in Canada and the same disproportion of Indigenous children who wind up in welfare institutions. In 2010 and 2011, Indigenous adults made up 27 percent of the population in provincial and territorial custody, and 20 percent in federal custody (Dauvergne 2012)—meaning that the proportion of Indigenous people in custody is about seven to eight times that of adult Indigenous people in Canada as a whole. Those who had been wards of the state as children also make up a disproportionate number of inmates within adult correctional institutions.

Amid this darkness, however, genuine beams of light are shining. Indigenous peoples across Canada are gaining more control over the social, economic, and political factors shaping their lives (see box 12.1). The report of the National Collaborating Centre for Aboriginal Health (2013, 5) notes that "Aboriginal approaches to health are often rooted in a holistic conception of well-being involving a healthy balance of four elements or aspects of wellness: physical, emotional, mental and spiritual." The report contends that

Box 12.1: Profiles in Aboriginal Leadership

The Osoyoos Indian band of south-central British Columbia is a storied economic success. Led by Chief Clarence Louie (1961–), one of the emerging generation of Indigenous leaders, the Osoyoos band boasts nearly a dozen successful local businesses, including a golf course/hotel/residential complex, a vineyard, a campground, a recreational vehicle park, a construction company, a ready-mix concrete company, a gas bar, and a convenience store. Together, these business ventures bring in revenues of more than $15 million annually—seven times the revenue it receives from the federal government.

Similar success stories can be found throughout Canada:

- The Dokis First Nation in north-central Ontario negotiated a river hydro project that was completed through the creation of its own land code under the First Nations Land Management Act.
- The Membertou First Nation of Sydney, Nova Scotia, successfully diversified its economy. The reserve today features a convention centre, gaming centre, gas bar, business centre, hotel, and other investments within the community, as well as the Membertou Sports and Wellness Centre.
- In July 2008, the Stoney Nation of Morley, Alberta, opened a $65 million resort and casino complex.

these four elements are key to restoring the health and well-being of Indigenous peoples "at both the individual and the community levels."

LABOUR FORCE PARTICIPATION AND INCOME

As seen in Chapter 8, an individual's life chances are much influenced by his or her place in the labour market. This is particularly true for Indigenous peoples, whose percentage of the labour force has increased in recent years. At the same time, the economic circumstances of various Indigenous communities in Canada are not uniform, affected—as in the non-Indigenous community—by such factors as place of residence, gender, and class. Indigenous peoples in the Atlantic region and Quebec tend to have lower employment and participation rates compared with their counterparts in the West, notably in the oil sands region of Alberta; Indigenous women tend to earn less than Indigenous men; and, within First Nations bands, there are sometimes also class and status differences.

One obvious factor influencing successful employment is whether First Nations people remain on reserve or not. On-reserve individuals are less likely than their off-reserve counterparts to enter the labour force, and for a very good reason: There are fewer jobs to be had. Unfortunately, however, the employment situation for off-reserve Indigenous people is often not much better.

Frideres (2011, 214) notes that the overall unemployment rate for First Nations people in Canada is three times that of the general population, a point given further emphasis by data looking at the impact of the recent economic downturn (discussed in Chapter 8) on the Indigenous labour force. Between 2010 and 2016, Indigenous workers experienced a decrease in labour force participation and employment, and an increase in unemployment exceeding that of their non-Aboriginal counterparts. This decline in employment was most acute for individuals during their prime working years, 25 to 54 (Usalcas 2011; Statistics Canada 2016e)

Nonetheless, Indigenous peoples are participating in the labour market more today than in the past, a fact raising an important point for Canada's future. One of Canada's fast-emerging challenges is its aging population, with consequences, among other things, for the country's labour force needs. Might Indigenous workers be the solution? More broadly, might the Indigenous birth rate rescue Canada from demographic decline? Politicians and corporate leaders (e.g., the Canadian Chamber of Commerce 2013) have noted this possibility and, in some instances, made well-publicized efforts to open up opportunities for Indigenous people in the workforce. But is this increased participation in the labour market reflected in Indigenous peoples' economic circumstances?

The most recent comparative data, drawn from the 2016 census, indicates that the median income for people of Aboriginal identity was $25,526 compared with $34,604 for non-Aboriginal identifiers, a difference of 26.2 percent; while the average income for Aboriginal identifiers was $36,043 compared with $47,981 for non-Aboriginals, a difference of 24.9 percent (Statistics Canada 2016e). The same data shows, however, that

Indigenous incomes are also stratified, with Métis individuals generally having higher medium and average incomes, Inuk (Inuit) individuals next, and First Nations people at the bottom. In the case of Inuk identifiers, the relatively higher incomes likely result from higher wages in the North, to compensate for a higher cost of living—meaning that such individuals may not be further ahead in terms of personal finances. In the case of First Nations individuals, there may be some variance between the incomes of on- and off-reserve residents, though as noted, employment opportunities are sometimes not improved by moving to urban environments.

Credit for much of the progress that has been made can be attributed to several First Nations bands, led by a new generation of young, entrepreneurial leaders who are changing the culture of First Nations reserves, as well as to several Indigenous-led civil society organizations, such as the Indigenous Leadership Development Institute and Indspire, a national charity funded by the Toronto-Dominion Bank in support of education for Indigenous youth.

EDUCATION

Level of education correlates positively with occupational attainment and income. The educational levels of Indigenous peoples have historically lagged behind those of other Canadians, thus explaining much about the former's reduced economic circumstances. Today, however, educational achievement among Indigenous youth is at an all-time high.

The 1996 Report of the Royal Commission on Aboriginal People indicated that 4.2 percent of Aboriginal individuals held university degrees and that 21 percent of Aboriginal peoples had completed college certificates. Recent data suggest the level of educational attainment among Indigenous peoples continues to increase, especially for Indigenous women. In 2016, nearly 9 percent of Aboriginal identifiers 25 years and older held university degrees in 2016, while more than 20 percent held college diplomas or university certificates below a bachelor's level. Another 11 percent were educated in the trades, perhaps not surprising given the number of jobs involved in the northern resource extraction industries (Statistics Canada 2016f).

Nonetheless, Indigenous educational attainment continues to trail that of non-Aboriginal Canadians, whose post-secondary levels have also risen since 1991. Moreover, a large proportion of Aboriginal people, nearly 34 percent, had less than high school equivalency, compared with a (still high) nearly 18 percent of non-Aboriginal identifiers (Statistics Canada 2016f). However, we should also note the role of gender across these differences. Like their non-Indigenous counterparts, Indigenous women are attaining generally higher education than are men. Within the Aboriginal-identifying community, women today make up nearly two-thirds of all university degree-holders, a proportion consistent across the other higher education levels.

The increasing educational success of Indigenous peoples reflects in part the growing responsiveness of universities to Indigenous needs. According to a Universities Canada survey, "Since 2013 there has been a 55% increase in the number of academic programs that include an Indigenous focus or are designed for Indigenous students" (Universities Canada 2017). Every major university across Canada today has courses dealing with Indigenous peoples, and many grant Indigenous Studies degrees. In fall 2008, for example, York University began sanctioning graduate research in Indigenous languages, with graduate students now able to defend their research in any of 50 Indigenous languages. Elsewhere, special pre-medicine courses for Indigenous students are available, and medical faculties are beginning to accept mature students with community-based experiences in place of university degrees (Warry 2007). These victories have begun showing positive results. Finally, Regina is home to the First Nations University of Canada, established in 1976, and whose main campus was designed by world-famous Indigenous architect Douglas Cardinal.

The seeds of later educational success are sewn early. Even greater efforts at innovation and experimentation have been undertaken at the K–12 level. Some schools in British Columbia, for example, are inviting local elders to share their knowledge and celebrate ceremonies with students and teachers. The Qualicum School District even has an elder-in-residence program, in which an elder will spend one day a week in local schools, demonstrating traditional cultural activities and teaching life lessons.

From the point of view of Indigenous communities, the meaning of education touches on its broader relation to culture and identity. Education in the non-Indigenous world is often viewed as merely a means to occupational attainment. This view is not entirely incorrect, as previously noted, since education is positively correlated with high occupational and economic attainment. Within Indigenous communities, however, there is a focus on the right to educate youth in the ways of their traditional knowledge and heritage (Battiste and Henderson 2000).

In Part 1, we noted the importance of language in debates regarding the preservation of French cultural heritage and identity in Canada. Similarly, many today view the revival of Indigenous languages as key to the transmission and survival of Indigenous knowledge and culture (Kirkness 1998a). While there has been some success in restoring and preserving Indigenous languages in Canada, which today are spoken by 260,550 people, the fact is that only three particular languages dominate: Cree, with 96,575 speakers (37.1 percent); Inuktitut, with 39,770 speakers (15.3 percent); and Ojibway, which has 28,130 speakers (10.8 percent) (Statistics Canada 2017e). (Both Cree and Ojibway are part of Canada's largest language group, Algonquin.) These three languages will likely persist into the 22nd century. Research shows that for these languages to prevail, however, they must first become a priority within Indigenous communities themselves (Friesen and Friesen 2005). In 2019, the Canadian government also passed the Indigenous Languages Act. Among other things, the act is designed to "support the reclamation, revitalization, strengthening and maintenance of Indigenous languages in Canada" and establishes the Office of the Commissioner of Indigenous Languages (Government of Canada 2019c).

Indigenous concerns related to linguistic matters involve a broader understanding that includes self-esteem, cultural pride, and indeed the very survival of the community

(Antone 2000). Effective cultural renewal goes beyond simply adding Indigenous components, even language, to the content of non-Indigenous curricula in schools; Indigenous teachings must have a broad cultural foundation (Witt 1998; see also Marker 2000). As Verna Kirkness (1998b), Cree Professor Emeritus at the University of British Columbia, argues, the survival of Indigenous culture must move beyond mere rhetoric to the actual practice of culture in everyday life beyond the school.

Things are gradually improving. Indigenous youth are increasingly aware of their history, assisted by elders who pass on cultural lessons, often in traditional ways—through storytelling, modelling, and hands-on training—and by Indigenous teachers who have been trained to work in their own communities. Likewise, there have been improvements in educational facilities, local control of schooling, counselling services, and support groups, and school curricula have been revised to include culturally relevant content. From kindergarten to Grade 12 and beyond, Indigenous peoples are slowly gaining control of their own schools, their own education, and their own lives. In doing so, Indigenous peoples are also preserving a way of being in the world that challenges Western non-Indigenous values.

CONTRASTING WORLD VIEWS

Classical sociologists, such as Émile Durkheim (see the Introduction), often contrasted the fundamental values and beliefs of Indigenous societies with those of the emergent industrial society; that is, they contrasted the overarching **world view** by which each society defined reality.

It is simplistic—and sometimes dangerous—to dichotomize world views, yet if we employ them as Weberian "ideal types" and do not reify them, such descriptions can serve a heuristic purpose.

At the macro-level of cultural analysis, several differences can be identified between the world views held by traditional and modern societies, differences that often continue to manifest in day-to-day misunderstandings between Indigenous peoples and their non-Indigenous counterparts in Canada.

The Sacred and the Profane

Durkheim (1912/1978) described two exclusive philosophical worlds existing side by side. The first is the **profane world**: the world of the everyday, the expected, the mundane, and the explainable. The second is the **sacred world**: the world of mystery, uncertainty, and even danger. The latter existed before time and will continue to live after; it is perpetual. According to Durkheim, the sacred cannot and should not be approached with the idea of exploitation or domination, nor should one tamper with the elements or workings of the universe. The sacred is to be treated with awe, even reverence. This contrast between the sacred and the profane well describes a fundamental difference between traditional and modern societies, between traditional Indigenous and dominant Canadian societies. However, it yields nothing to the notion of flexibility or transition, a fact readily visible in contemporary Indigenous communities.

The early European invaders underestimated the extent to which spirituality was valued by Indigenous peoples in their daily lives (Friesen 1995; Witt 1998; Hanohano 1999). This emphasis on spirituality likewise remains minimized—even trivialized—and misunderstood by Canada's non-Indigenous citizens, who long ago abandoned the spiritual roots of their society. For many Indigenous leaders, their spirituality serves as a foundation for education, land claims, and language revitalization programs, though some Indigenous leaders have altered this stance in the interests of coping with and even expanding economic development in their communities.

Many other differences between the two solitudes follow from Indigenous culture's greater acceptance of this spiritual or sacred realm.

Spiritual Holism versus Scientific Empiricism

In contrast to current Western science, which often seeks to study and test elements in isolation, traditional cultures experience no uneasiness at the thought of multiple realities, spiritual or phenomenological, operating at once. Yet, these multiple realities nonetheless also form a single, if complex, world. In this world, dreams, visions, and other spiritual experiences are also considered valid sources of knowledge and derived truths, though many successful Indigenous entrepreneurs today often augment their traditional repertoire of knowledge with such things as university research, innovation, and strategic economic planning.

Cyclical versus Linear Notions of Time

The Industrial Revolution and the advent of capitalism resulted in a changed conception of time ("wasting time," "lost time," "time is money") that sees time as linear, a direct offshoot of the notion of "progress," that "every day, in every way, things must get better and better." Prior to this transformation, traditional peoples everywhere—including Europe—viewed time as cyclical, tied to hunting and growing seasons. In many such societies, including those of Indigenous peoples of Canada, time was symbolically represented in the form of a wheel. The notion of progress, or permanent change, was peculiar, as everything returned to whence it came. "Progress" to traditional societies is an illusion—perhaps even a dangerous delusion, a thought Canadians may wish to ponder.

Acceptance versus Dominance of Nature

Much of the current Western world tends to view nature as alien, a source of either danger or of profit—perhaps both. But given the right tools and approaches, nature can be controlled—even improved upon and tailored to advantage. By contrast, people in traditional societies view themselves as part of a great chain of existence in which all elements of creation are interrelated and interdependent (Ross 1992). If any single element is subjected to pressures or is otherwise tampered with, there are sure to be repercussions in the grand scheme of things. This notion—which, one may note, is not incongruent with structural functionalist approaches—leads also to what sociologists refer to as **unintended**

consequences (Merton 1968). In this manner, traditional cultures provide an inherent warning against attempts to dominate or exploit nature, but advise rather to respect and work in harmony with it (Suzuki 1992)—a warning again perhaps worth heeding, given escalating concerns over the environment or the recent COVID-19 pandemic.

The Collective versus the Individual

As previously noted (Chapter 4), modernity's greatest invention, and perhaps also its greatest illusion, is that of the "individual," often contrasted with the "collective." Traditional cultures are viewed as restrictive and conformist; modernity, it is alleged, has liberated people to act on their own free will. This notion ignores, however, the enormous barriers—economic, racial, gender, and others—facing most people. Moreover, a casual look around us quickly reveals the profoundly conformist nature of current society, from styles of dress to musical tastes to faddish diets—even to our political views.

This dominant view of people in traditional society is simplistic, to say the least. Family loyalty *does* have a high priority, and the collective good *is* extolled. Among Indigenous peoples, the individual *is* expected to submit to group and community demands (Dion 1979; Surtees 1969). And yes, these expectations *do* put limits on one's individual achievements as tallied by contemporary capitalist society. (Corporate managers are rarely sympathetic to individuals who take time off to tend to personal family matters—though perhaps they should be, if we are to embrace a healthier work-life balance.)

There is a paradox, however. Beyond these restraints, the community also guarantees the individual emotional security, support, and a particular assigned identity, though this is sometimes amended or, if need be, taken away from the individual. While individuals are "put in line" if they "show off" (too much), and in extreme cases may even be shunned as punishment, this is not absent in Western society; consider, for a moment, the practice of cyber-bullying. In the main, however, traditional societies, such as those in Indigenous communities, practise a subtle kind of non-interference.

Egalitarianism versus Hierarchy

If democracy means anything in practice, it means equality of voice. Whether within political institutions, corporations, universities, or even many families, decision-making within Western societies tends to be hierarchical rather than egalitarian. By contrast, traditional societies, including those of Indigenous peoples in Canada, have been exceedingly democratic. Age and sex were the only certain markers of unequal status; otherwise, authority rules tended to be complex and shifting. This practice confused the Europeans, whose own feudal traditions were born of a caste system, and they still confuse many Euro-Canadians today.

Few non-Indigenous people, accustomed to *Robert's Rules of Order* (a widely used guide to Parliamentary procedure), for example, could appreciate a traditional Indigenous meeting. The rules guiding such meetings are profoundly different from those governing non-Indigenous meetings. Elders, chiefs, and respected spokespeople prescribe the procedures for a meeting simply by their behaviour, and no one takes issue with this. In the most traditional format, every challenge faced by a tribe must be resolved communally. Western business and government negotiators frequently become quite impatient with such processes—witness the consternation surrounding the time required to settle the recent Wet'suwet'en dispute (Chapter 11). Where hierarchy—and authoritarianism—provide for *an* answer, a quick answer, democracy is inherently slow in its attempt to provide *the* answer. (It may sometimes even require a lengthy sweet-grass or tobacco ceremony before deliberations can proceed.) Given these differences, one can easily agree with Augie Fleras (2007, 347), who writes that future discussions between the two cultures may require a "rewriting of rules and attitudes."

SEEKING A THIRD WAY

We have previously noted (Chapter 9) that the intent of the original non-Indigenous educational establishment—both residential as well as day schools—was to silence expressions of Indigenous culture. Over time, the process of educational imperialism had a crushing effect on Indigenous communities. Several generations lost their languages and transformed their cultures, sometimes resulting in psychological and social upheaval for community members. In recent years, a crescendo of Indigenous voices has emphasized the importance of reviving traditional knowledge and spirituality (Cajete 1994; Couture 1991; McGaa 1995; Johnston 1995; Bear Heart 1998; Weaver 1998; Battiste 2000; Battiste and Henderson 2000; Meili 2012). But there have also been repeated calls from some, within both Indigenous (Helin 2006) and non-Indigenous communities (Flanagan 2000), for Indigenous people to adopt Western ways, or to "get with the program." Is it possible to combine traditional Indigenous world views and values with those of modernity, to adapt them to the dominant socio-economic environment? Is there a third way between the constructed polarities of traditional and modern values? This is a major challenge facing not only Indigenous peoples but Canadians as a whole. Yazzie (2000) argues that if First Nations want to retain elements of their traditional belief systems, they must first throw off the yoke of epistemological colonialism and commence the truth-finding process within themselves. According to this notion, political self-determination begins with internal sovereignty, which means taking control of one's personal, family, clan, and community life. Essentially, this requires valuing tradition while integrating aspects of contemporary Euro-Canadian value systems. This task will not be easy. As Findley (2000) notes, despite increasing criticisms from Euro-Canadian and Indigenous scholars alike, modernity's orthodoxies remain dominant and are even expanding their domain. Maintaining or retrieving traditional Indigenous culture is made problematic by the fact that many First Nations today are significantly "modernized," while others are marginalized between their traditional and Western cultures.

How have Indigenous peoples adapted to the challenges of Western, capitalist society? Friesen and Friesen (2005) and Schultz and Kroeger (1996) describe five types of responses by groups within Indigenous communities.

Traditionalists make up the first group, and they respond to the challenge by clinging tenaciously to "the old ways" and ignoring or denying any form of change. Traditionalists have strong ties to the past, culturally as well as spiritually, and are therefore able to ignore societal changes while continuing to live with both eyes on the past.

The second group is made up of lost-identity individuals who feel powerless in the current of socio-economic change and often fall prey to social and cultural breakdown. They often develop confused identities; exhibit characteristics of deprivation, grief, and dependency; and often drift into poverty.

The third group are new traditionalists or "born-again" Indigenous persons with little knowledge of the old ways, but who like to dress traditionally by wearing braids, sporting ribbon shirts, and displaying items of beadwork. Unaware of the impracticality and difficulty of such an existence today, they nonetheless often extol the virtues of hunting, gathering, and fishing societies. Often youthful, articulate, and college-educated, members of this group seek a cultural renaissance of sorts.

The fourth group are those assimilated completely into the Western world, albeit often unconsciously. This requires adopting new norms and forming new social alliances. For this group and its proponents, maintaining an Indigenous cultural identity is secondary to economic development (Helin 2006).

The fifth group comprises those who might be called internationally minded persons of Indigenous background. (There are increasing contacts among Indigenous peoples in Australia, New Zealand, South America, Scandinavia, the United States, and Canada.) These individuals seek to balance and appreciate the contributions of both Indigenous and non-Indigenous cultures, placing a great deal of value on their own heritage without belittling those of others. They are often quite open to alternative ways of thinking, such as finding ways to protect the environment while also supporting technological and industrial advancement.

Mainstream Canadian society need not romanticize traditional Indigenous culture or its values; nor, however, can these aspects be ignored. As we have detailed, there is a large gap between the values and beliefs embedded in Indigenous culture and those of the dominant society. The latter has little understanding and even less appreciation for a lifestyle focused on living in harmony with nature, respecting the Earth, believing in the interconnectedness of all living phenomena, and honouring the Creator in one's daily life (Friesen 1995; Brascoupé 2000). In the words of well-known Métis architect Douglas Cardinal, Indigenous culture amounts to a "different way of being human" (Buckley 1993, 174). The question for non-Indigenous Canadians at the start of the 21st century is whether they are open enough to accommodate, learn from, and perhaps even embrace such a differing world view.

WE ARE YOU: CANADA AS AN INDIGENOUS SOCIETY

In Chapter 8, we looked at how various political philosophers have described the nature of Canadian society. For Lipset (1990), you will recall, Canada is a British Tory country; for Grant (2005), Canada was a Tory country but is now a modern Liberal (and, hence, American) country; while for Resnick (2005), Canada is a European country; and on and on.

More recently, John Ralston Saul (2008) proffered a very different, even radical, thesis: that Canada is a Métis civilization, an Indigenous country. Saul initially points out the many practical contributions that Indigenous peoples have made to Canada, from various kinds of foods to canoes. But Saul's argument goes beyond an historical homage to a lost culture; rather, he argues that Indigenous ways of thinking and behaving, of solving problems, continue in the kind of society that Canada has become. He argues that several strategic elements linked to this unrecognized heritage have shaped how Canadians see themselves (Saul 2008, 54–55):

> Our obsession with egalitarianism. Our desire to maintain a balance between individuals and groups. The delight we take in playing with our non-monolithic idea of society—a delight in complexity. Our tendency to try to run society as an ongoing negotiation, which must be related to our distaste for resolving complexities. Our preference, behind a relatively violent language of public debate, for consensus—again an expression of society as a balance of complexity, a sort of equilibrium. Our intuition that behind the formal written and technical face of our society lies something more important, which we try to get at through the oral and through complex relationships. Our sense that the clear resolution of differences will lead to injustice and even violence. And related to that, our preference for something that the law now calls minimal impairment, which means the obligation of those with authority to do as little damage as possible to people and to rights when exercising that authority.

Ultimately, Saul's call is for Canadians to escape colonially imposed ways of thinking, to thereby see—to imagine—ourselves based on the truth of how Canada has been built; if we are unable to do this, Canadian society may continue to stumble and fail.

In issuing his call, however, Saul also reverses a centuries-old practice of Euro-Canadian ethnocentrism. There are many observers, sympathetic or otherwise, who claim that Indigenous traditions and practices have no relevance in a competitive, market-oriented society (Flanagan 2000). Indeed, they argue that Indigenous peoples have "much to learn" from Euro-Canadian society, that the way forward lies in becoming more like the dominant culture. Saul's critique (2008), and that of Davis (2009), takes us in a more interesting and challenging direction, enjoining us to ask such questions as "What by way of modernity have we lost?" and "What, if anything, can traditional cultures teach us?"

What lessons might non-Indigenous Canadians learn from the values and heritage of Indigenous peoples? We provide one example, dealing with crime and justice.

Despite a general decrease in actual incidence of crime, many Canadians remain fearful of being victims of it; due to this fear, Canadians are often persuaded that the solution lies in more police officers, stiffer sentences, and bigger jails. Most criminologists view such policies as ineffective except in dealing with a few select types of crime; the United States is a shining testament to the failure of "tough on crime" policies, leading even many conservative voices in that country to rethink such a strategy, as well as for greater public calls to "de-fund" police and move the money to other services. Beyond focusing on the criminal, however, such policies often leave victims of crime feeling unsatisfied—sometimes even revictimized—by a legal system that seems remote and uncaring.

Consider, then, the practice of traditional Indigenous justice. In pre-contact days, Indigenous peoples employed storytelling, ridicule, and shaming as methods to keep people in line. In more serious cases, they would put an offender in a circle of elders, who would offer advice and mete out punishment to the offender (Warry 2007). This gathering of elders would demand change in the offender's behaviour and determine an appropriate punishment for the misdeed.

Sometimes called a **sentencing circle** or healing circle, this approach—though altered slightly—has been revived in many Indigenous communities. Such circles are part of a broader concept of restorative justice. They involve a formal court process that includes offenders, victims, community members, and justice professionals who meet and discuss the offences face to face, aiming to ensure that all involved feel that justice is being administered (Chiste 2005). Re-established in the Yukon in the 1990s, where some 300 sentencing circles soon emerged, the practice has since been revived in Saskatchewan, British Columbia, Manitoba, and Quebec (Steckley and Cummins 2008). The central purpose of sentencing circles is to encourage the offender to deal directly with the victim and the community at large. Wrongdoing involves a tearing of the social fabric; the intent of the sentencing circle is therefore to repair the harm done. Might such an approach also work better than conventional, non-Indigenous approaches to crime, which often separate and alienate the offender from the community?

CONCLUSION

Our world continues to change at an accelerating speed. Ironically, however, many of the biggest changes in Canada today and in the foreseeable future involve Indigenous peoples—those who were there at the forefront of changes 400 years ago, then forgotten, are now once more prominent.

But this is not a situation peculiar to Canada. Throughout many parts of the world long ago colonized, Indigenous peoples have begun reasserting their political rights and cultural identities. This has particularly been the case in the former British colonies—Canada, the

United States, Australia, and New Zealand (see Fleras and Elliott 1992)—but is also seen in the growing resurgence of Indigenous peoples in many parts of Latin America since the 1990s (e.g., Mexico's Zapatista movement) and in Asia (e.g., the Ainu of Japan).

We began our search for Canadian society with a discussion of the concepts of country, nation, and state. We noted the problematic nature of these terms, and the uniqueness of Canada in trying to fit them into the Canadian experiment. The case of Indigenous peoples in Canada provides perhaps the most striking example. Canada remains a country, and it also constitutes, we would argue, a unique society. Part of Canada's uniqueness, however, resides in the complex manner in which Canada has accommodated more than one nation into its grand design.

One thing is particularly clear: Canada's Indigenous Nations will play a major role in shaping the kind of society Canada will become in the remaining years of the 21st century. As Phil Fontaine, former grand chief of the Assembly of First Nations, has observed, "The future of First Nations and Canada's future are intricately linked."

NOTE

1. The nomenclature of *Aboriginal* used here, rather than *Indigenous*, reflects the term used by Statistics Canada in this and other tables.

CRITICAL THINKING QUESTIONS

1. As Indigenous communities in Canada change and adapt, what kinds of conflicts might we expect to arise within those communities?
2. What factors might explain the differences in educational attainment between men and women in both Indigenous and non-Indigenous communities?
3. Are the inequalities between Indigenous and non-Indigenous peoples in Canada more similar to a class system or a caste system?
4. Is a "third way" between traditional and modern (Western) world views possible? What might it look like?
5. What lessons from Indigenous societies might assist non-Indigenous societies in meeting the challenges of the 21st century?

RECOMMENDED READINGS

Davis, Wade. 2009. *The Wayfinders: Why Ancient Wisdom Matters in the Modern World*. Toronto: House of Anansi.

Destined to be a classic, Davis's book, the 2009 Massey Lecture, examines traditional cultures around the world and "why ancient wisdom matters."

Drees, Laurie Meijer. 2013. *Healing Histories: Stories from Canada's Indian Hospitals.* Edmonton: University of Alberta Press.
This book traces the formation, development, and operation of Canada's Indian hospitals while carefully mingling traditional Indigenous healing philosophies and techniques.

Frideres, James S. 2011. *First Nations in the Twenty-First Century.* Don Mills, ON: Oxford University Press.
This book offers a comprehensive view of First Nations' legal and historical identity as well as an analytic treatment of contemporary issues affecting Indigenous communities.

Friesen, John W., and Virginia Lyons Friesen. 2008. *Western Canadian Native Destiny: Complex Questions on the Cultural Maze.* Calgary: Detselig.
The authors document a series of contemporary Indigenous issues, including urban adjustment, health, justice, education, cultural identity, land claims, economic development, and self-government.

Warry, Wayne. 2007. *Ending Denial: Understanding Aboriginal Issues.* Peterborough, ON: Broadview Press.
Warry examines the problems and obstacles that confront First Nations in Canada in their quest to wrest control of their institutions from the federal government.

RELATED WEBSITES

Assembly of First Nations
www.afn.ca
The Assembly of First Nations is the national representative organization of First Nations in Canada.

Indigenous Leadership Development Institute (ILDI)
www.ildii.ca
The ILDI is a non-profit organization that has been promoting and supporting good self-governance and capacity building within the Indigenous community since its incorporation in 2000.

Turtle Island Native Network
www.turtleisland.org/news/news-justice.htm
One of Canada's Indigenous news and information networks.

CANADIAN SOCIETY ON VIDEO

Circles. 1997. National Film Board of Canada, 57 minutes, 45 seconds.
Circles examines justice and community healing, hope, and transformation, bringing together a traditional Indigenous justice circle and the Canadian justice system.

Mohawk Girls. 2005. National Film Board of Canada, 62 minutes, 45 seconds.
This film examines the lives of three teenage Mohawk girls on the Kahnawake reserve and the hope, despair, heartache, and promise of growing up Indigenous at the beginning of the 21st century.

Nîpawistamâsowin: We Will Stand Up. 2019. National Film Board of Canada, 98 minutes.
The film examines the gunshot death of a young Cree man, Colten Boushie, in August 2016, after he entered Gerald Stanley's rural Saskatchewan property with his friends, and Stanley's subsequent jury acquittal. Boushie's death is woven into a broader narrative of the filmmaker's own adoption, the stark history of colonialism on the Prairies, and an analysis of the racism embedded within Canada's legal system.

CONCLUSION

Canada in the World and in the Future

Pandemic—Physical Distancing. Courtesy Trevor W. Harrison.

The function of sociology, as of every science, is to reveal that which is hidden.
    —French sociologist Pierre Bourdieu, 1998

We have been living in a bubble, a bubble of false comfort and denial. . . . The temptation, when this pandemic has passed, will be to find another bubble. We cannot afford to succumb to it. From now on, we should expose our minds to the painful realities we have denied for too long.
    —British journalist George Monbiot, 2020

Information is shock resistance. Arm yourself.
    —Canadian author and activist Naomi Klein, 2007

INTRODUCTION

In the introductory chapter, we defined *society* as

> the product of relatively continuous and enduring interactions, within a political
> territory, between people more or less identifying themselves as members of
> the society, these interactions being maintained by an ensemble of political,
> economic, cultural, and other institutions, the sum of such interactions being in
> excess of interactions occurring with similarly defined societies external to the
> given territory.

We have taken as a given throughout this text the notion that something termed "Canadian society" exists as a sociological construct amenable to study. As guiding principles
for this study, the text has emphasized three themes: First, the study of society cannot be
adequately conducted without consideration of its historical context. Second, the study of
society cannot be hived off from its relation to the state and to the market. Third, if subtly
expressed throughout the text, sociological theory must not be employed in a decorative
or didactic fashion (i.e., "Look here: an example of conflict theory!"), but used reflectively
as a genuine lens for examining and understanding events and issues. This chapter briefly
revisits these three themes and then moves on to highlight the value of sociology in examining a current issue facing Canada and the global community: the coronavirus—or
COVID-19—pandemic.

THE ROLE OF HISTORY RE-EXAMINED

This text has used an historical sociological approach to examining Canadian society.
As defined in the text's Introduction, historical sociology is based on the notion that *our
material institutions, actions, and beliefs are shaped, though not determined, by past events and
our understanding (or misunderstanding) of those events*. Karl Marx (1977c, 300) famously
wrote that people "make their own history . . . under circumstances directly encountered,
given, and transmitted from the past." The text provides several examples of historical circumstances structuring our lives and the importance of employing history in sociological
analyses. To give one broad example, played out across the text's three parts, the Royal
Proclamation of 1763 led to a series of other acts, treaties, and institutional practices that
later shaped Canadian society. But history is also a living thing, living not only in its
material forms but also in the memories and meanings that people attach to historical
events and actors. Max Weber, in his famous *Protestant Ethic and the Spirit of Capitalism*,
emphasized how the meanings we attach to events lead to action. We can see this linkage
between meaning and action in the continuing presence of the Conquest in Quebec nationalism (Part 1), of regional alienation in western Canada (Part 2), and in the traumatic
memories of residential schooling held by many Indigenous peoples (Part 3).

THE TRIAD OF STATE–SOCIETY–MARKET

In the introductory chapter, we reviewed theories about the relationship of the modern state to the market and society: whether it is responsive to a plurality of social interests, an instrument of capital, a relatively autonomous actor vis-à-vis the economy, or a wholly independent entity with its own powers, goals, and interests. The internal workings of this triadic relationship are never static and often uneasy. Instances of the state facilitating business interests are not difficult to find. Mercantilism represented a cozy relationship between merchants and the monarchial state. The National Policy's establishment in 1878 was a contrivance of the fledgling Canadian government and the country's fledgling capitalists. The pursuit of free trade in the 1980s was the result of Canadian capitalists and neo-liberal politicians, conservative and liberal alike.

But the state was forced to take a more independent stance during the 1930s and again during the Great Recession of 2008–2010. Moreover, the response of actors within civil society sometimes shaped and even overturned some outcomes. Thus, the apparent victory of mercantilism was later offset by intellectuals, professionals, and the working class demanding a greater say in how Canada was governed. Likewise, the inequities of the National Policy in time gave rise to political parties and movements opposing the relationship between the federal state and industrialists: Elements within civil society— charitable groups, intellectuals, unions, artists—continued their fight against the neo-liberal agenda that free trade signalled in the years after 1988. This fight continues today in the context of the grinding austerity that neo-liberal governments imposed after the recent Great Recession.

SOCIOLOGICAL THEORY IN PRACTICE

This text provides numerous examples of sociological theory in practice.

Consider, for example, structural-functionalism. According to structural-functionalist theory, all elements of society should operate in relative harmony with each other. A change in one element will inevitably result in changes to the other elements in order to restore the balance. Part 1 examined the interrelated changes to Quebec society as its economy shifted from agricultural to industrial production and how this change was also mirrored in demographic (rural to urban, large families to small), political, and ideological shifts culminating two centuries later in the Quiet Revolution. Part 2 described the creation of the welfare state in the 20th century as a means of integrating and socializing elements in society as it was disrupted by changes in the labour market and economy more generally. Part 3 examined the ripples upon Indigenous society caused by the loss of hunting, gathering, and particularly the fur trade, as well as the subsequent destruction of their family structures through colonial practices.

Consider also conflict theory. The essence of conflict theory is that conflict, in a variety of forms, is inevitable but also in the long run positive as it addresses problems in the system. All three parts provided examples of violence and physical conflict, from the Conquest, the American Revolution, the War of 1812, the rebellions of 1837–1838, the Red River Rebellion of 1869, the North-West Rebellion of 1885, the two world wars of the 20th century, the 1919 Winnipeg Strike, the FLQ Crisis of 1970, and the Oka Crisis of 1990. But conflict is most often psychological and ideological, unconscious and subtle, as exhibited through class, gender, racialization, and other means of dominance and subordination. The text provides ample examples of these conflicts as well.

Or consider symbolic interaction theory, which argues that the meaning of human behaviour is collectively constructed and defined in the course of interactions through sets of more-or-less agreed upon symbols. Language itself is a symbol, a set of sounds pointing toward a meaning. But language is also a larger symbol of personal and group identity, as seen through efforts by Quebec's francophone community since the Conquest to preserve French (Part 1) and renewed efforts by the Indigenous community in recent years to reclaim their traditional languages (Part 3). We can also point to the Canadian flag or medicare (Part 2) as things that, for many Canadians, are an expression of a deep, symbolic attachment to what it means to be Canadian. Finally, however, symbols can also be sources of division, as noted regarding such historic figures as Louis Riel and Sir John A. Macdonald.

Post-structural theory may seem at first more difficult to recognize. In essence, post-structuralism rejects symbolic interaction theory's notion of any symbol having a constant or even solid referent. Meanings are fluid and always contested. In late modernity, moreover, there appear to exist no institutions having the recognized authority to provide the answer to existential questions, let alone the path to take. Part 1 provides one example in the form of Quebec's gradual rejection of the Catholic Church's dictates. Indigenous peoples' increased questioning of the settler-colonial construction of Canada provides another example (Part 3).

Theories are tools for looking at phenomena in different ways. They need not be at odds with each other. Consider the issue of climate change as discussed at length in Chapter 10. For many, the impact of climate change necessitates a series of economic, social, and political adaptations (structural-functionalism). For many, too, climate change pits the world's wealthiest populations, mainly in the industrialized North, against the poorest in the southern hemisphere (a conflict perspective). For some, climate change is not merely about preserving the human race but it is part of a spiritual quest to protect Mother Earth (a symbolic interaction perspective). Finally, climate change deniers may view the entire premise as a hoax perpetrated by egghead scientists and other pseudo-experts (a distinctly post-structural perspective).

THE GLOBAL PANDEMIC—AND AFTER

As 2020 began, the world heard stories emanating out of China of a virus. Ignored at first by politicians and much of the public, the virus gradually and then quickly spread. On March 11, the World Health Organization officially declared it a **pandemic**: a disease occurring over a wide geographic area and affecting a large proportion of the population. The coronavirus, quickly known as COVID-19, moved rapidly across the globe. By mid-April, the official number of people infected worldwide was over two million, the number of dead over 100,000, a death rate well above usual predictions of 1 to 2 percent. The countries of Brazil, China (especially Wuhan province), Italy, Spain, the United Kingdom, and the United States were particularly impacted, but this was a truly global pandemic. By late January 2021, over 99 million people worldwide had been infected, resulting in 2.1 million deaths (Statista 2021). Given epidemiological predictions that the pandemic has not reached its peak—a peak that will vary from country to country, season to season, and might last beyond 2021—the total number of infections and deaths is uncertain. Canadian political scientist Thomas Homer-Dixon (2020) contends, however, based on competing lethality rates of 0.5 to 3.0 percent, that the number of deaths worldwide could be between 12 million and 150 million. By late January 2021, US cases alone had neared 2.6 million. Early estimates by top US health officials that American deaths would reach 200,000 (Brest 2020) proved seriously low, as the number of coronavirus deaths eclipsed 429,000. By late January 2021, Canada's official count stood at 747,000 cases of infection and just over 19,000 deaths (Government of Canada 2021), but predictions hold that these numbers will be well eclipsed before the pandemic runs its expected course in the coming year.

The world has experienced numerous pandemics in the past, among them the Black Death in the 14th century, which claimed 200 million lives, and smallpox in the 16th century, which claimed another 56 million (all figures from LePan 2020). The most famous pandemic in recent memory was the Spanish Flu epidemic of 1918–1920. It took the lives of between 50 and 100 million people worldwide—more than the First World War (see Chapter 6). Canada's death toll was 55,000, mostly young adults, nearly as many deaths as from the war (Government of Canada n.d.).

While the coronavirus is a medical event, it is also much more than that. Armstrong et al. (2020) argue that the world's most recent pandemics have all involved diseases ("zoonotic diseases")—HIV, Ebola, Zika, Hendra, SARS, MERS, and the bird flu among them—that jumped from animals to humans as the result of human decisions and actions.

Consider, first, the causal factors behind the outbreak, its transmission, and spread. Today, the world's population stands at roughly 7.8 billion and is growing. The regions of greatest population increase are some of the world's poorest, a fact commensurate with demographic studies showing that birth rates tend to level off and decline only as living standards—and personal expectations—increase. Increased population means the need for more food, but food in poor countries is often limited by climate, technology, and other factors, among which are economies based on cash crops (tea, coffee, etc.) producing goods for Global North markets. The hunt for country foods, such as monkeys, rats, or various reptile species, is a product not of exotic tastes but of growing populations of hungry people in crowded circumstances.

Moreover, unless climate change is addressed (see also Chapter 10), Monbiot (2020) warns that this food crisis will only become worse. Global heating, he warns, "in combination with a rising human population, and the loss of irrigation water, soil and pollinators . . . could push the world into structural famine."

Monbiot adds that the starvation and malnourishment faced by millions of people is a result of "the unequal distribution of wealth and power." Oxfam's annual report (Oxfam International 2020), cited in Chapter 8, catalogues the enormous and growing gap between the world's wealthiest and the world's poorest. The report argues further that a "care crisis" is emerging—a crisis falling particularly upon women and girls—in the world's poorest regions. Released just as the pandemic was hitting, the report presages the difficulties faced by many countries, to which Homer-Dixon (2020) adds a lack competent governments, resources, adequate public health, and necessary urban water and sanitation systems. Forebodingly, Homer-Dixon remarks that "these regions also risk becoming 'epidemiological pumps'—vast reservoirs of the disease that reintroduce it regularly, in mutated form, into parts of the world that might have otherwise brought it under some control." These remarks emphasize what sociologists and health experts have long known: Disease thrives in conditions of economic and social inequality, and it is not confined to the individual (Pickett and Wilkinson 2011).

These factors—global inequality and climate change, combined with a series of senseless wars (see Chapter 8)—have in turn led to the growing phenomenon of stateless refugees (Dyer 2018). If these underlying factors are not addressed, there will be a deluge of refugees and people otherwise seeking escape. In recent years, right-wing politicians throughout Europe, the United Kingdom, and the United States have used fear of "the Other" as a stepping stone to power (Ehmsen and Scharenberg 2018); the appeal of xenophobia may become even worse in years to come.

These fears and anxieties are occurring in a particular economic context. As noted, the past 30 or more years of neo-liberalism have witnessed a vast accumulation of wealth at the top, profound immiseration at the bottom, and a hollowing at the centre (Piketty 2014, 2020). This wealth transfer is due in part to financial regulations that privilege investors and shareholders at the expense of workers, as well as through criminal activities, such as money laundering and bribery, that have contributed to governments lacking the means to level social inequalities, while also mixing with drug and sex trafficking. For Canada alone, an estimated $50 to $130 billion is laundered every year (Cohen 2019).

But the declining economic circumstances of workers are also attributable to two other factors: automation (Cameron 2017) and the reorganization of the labour market under neo-liberalism, which has created a new class of workers, the precariat (Standing 2011), as described in Chapter 8. Already marginally employed, workers in this so-called **gig economy** (Woodcock and Graham 2019)—those working a series of non-permanent "gigs"—have often been a casualty of the pandemic's forced shutdown of the economy. At the same time, might the pandemic prove the catalyst for broader changes in public policy? Along with a more equal distribution of incomes, might the work week be lessened (Booth 2019)? Might some form of guaranteed income be introduced, or an even more broad expansion of human rights (Standing 2014)? Might there be existential changes in the way people view work and leisure, even their identities, and relationship to others?

Communication systems like television, radio, and the Internet have altered the way people understand and relate to each other. Such interactive platforms as Skype, Zoom, and Facebook have allowed for the creation of virtual communities, especially during the pandemic, as millions of people have been confined to their homes. These same technologies have also allowed governments to inform people about the pandemic and how to prevent its spread (e.g., through "physical distancing"). The Internet has not been an unbridled good, however. Even before the pandemic, such technologies allowed for both greater state surveillance of individuals and the spreading of false information, conspiracy theories (Stiegler 2019; Doctorow 2019), and a more general revolt against the Enlightenment project of reason (Babones 2018), out of which sociology arose, the dark side of which is an erosion of trust—a central pillar of society.

These examples—touching on demography, health, globalization, the economy, work, gender, immigration, inequality, poverty, crime, politics, media, knowledge, trust, and technology—are all areas of sociological interest and inquiry and suggest the breadth of the discipline. This text's authors encourage sociologists, both established and budding, to commit to using insights from the field to study the wide array of real-world issues and problems.

But the foregoing discussion also points to tensions and possibilities in the concept of society. As noted in the Introduction, it arose in the mid-19th century as an explanatory category for an abstract social phenomenon residing outside of the state and market. As these latter two have grown, so has society, tied together by such factors as trade, communications, and travel. In this context, advocates of neo-liberalism, in particular, until recently have waxed eloquent about globalization bringing about a borderless and harmonious world, a "global village." To manage and assist these connections, world governments, corporations, and civil society groups have formed a number of organizations, such as the United Nations, World Bank, International Labour Organization, Amnesty International, and Aga Khan Development Network. But globalization, as it has happened historically, is not necessarily a one-way street; deglobalization, through war, political design, or disease is also possible. Might people in future begin seeing their society in a more limited way, both spacially and psychologically? Alternatively, might the (presumed) continuance of computer technologies foster new forms of sociability across distances, bridging the geographic divide?

Noted sociologist Daniel Bell (quoted in Swedberg 1990, 222) once remarked that "people can only identify with society if the society feels a responsibility to them." Recent years suggest that too many people believe the form of globalization fashioned by neo-liberalism does not care about them—that it is about power and profit alone. In consequence, at least some people have retreated in fear into their tribal communities, protected by strong, authoritarian figures of a Hobbesian bent (Hobbes 1651/2014). The society of hope, implicitly promised by neo-liberalism, has given way to what Bude (2017) describes as a "society of fear." But it need not be so. Human beings are not determined by their history or their material circumstances. We can decide the kind of society—and the future—we want.

CONCLUSION

For several hundred years, the people inhabiting the political territory of Canada have interacted, sometimes in hostility, sometimes in amity, often in tolerance, and perhaps even more often in unconsciousness. The creation of Canadian society has meant the intensification of these interactions and knowledge (or at least imagined knowledge) of a large assortment of others, from Cape Spear to Vancouver Island to the Arctic Circle. No society remains static, however, and even less so in the 21st century.

Even before the current pandemic, Canada faced many challenges. These challenges—such as ensuring that all citizens are included culturally, socially, politically, and economically—will be accentuated in the years to come. Likewise, efforts will be necessary to ensure the enactment of deep democracy as the lived experience of all Canadians in their daily lives, no matter their class, race, gender, or religion and whether in their workplaces, their homes, or their communities.

Canada is one of the world's wonders. Against many odds, Canadians through the centuries have constructed a society that, though not perfect, is prosperous and tolerant, progressive and civil. The torch is thus passed to future generations to continue the Canadian experiment into the coming decades.

CRITICAL THINKING QUESTIONS

1. Which sociological theory or theories do you believe provide(s) the best understanding of society? Why?
2. How might an historical sociological approach help us understand the pandemic that began in early 2020?
3. Is a global society possible?
4. What types of things can be globalized, and what things should not?
5. What do you think Canada will be like in 2050?

RECOMMENDED READINGS

Bell, Daniel. 1996. *The Cultural Contradictions of Capitalism*. 20th anniversary ed. New York: Basic Books.
Bell's book remains a classic in sociology, arguing that capitalism brings about cultural changes that, in turn, destroy capitalism's underpinnings.

Brown, Wendy. 2019. *In the Ruins of Neoliberalism: The Rise of Antidemocratic Politics in the West*. New York: Columbia University Press.
    Quoting numerous scholars and political theorists, Brown traces how neo-liberal ideas designed to free the market have had the unintentional consequence of unleashing white male rage and attacking the foundations of liberal democracy.

Dyer, Gwynne. 2018. *Growing Pains: The Future of Democracy (and Work)*. London: Scribe.
    Dyer examines how inequality, poverty, joblessness, and automation have contributed to the rise of populism, as well as some solutions to these problems.

Pickett, Kate, and Richard Wilkinson. 2011. *The Spirit Level: Why Greater Equality Makes Societies Stronger*. London, UK: Bloomsbury Press.
    Pickett and Wilkinson present a strong case that individuals, both rich and poor, are healthier and happier with a greater degree of equality in the society around them.

Piketty, Thomas. 2020. *Capital and Ideology*, trans. A. Goldhammer. Boston: Harvard University Press.
    A sequel to his much lauded 2014 book *Capital in the Twenty-First Century*, Piketty argues that inequality is produced not by technological or material factors, but it is the result of ideology.

RELATED WEBSITES

Central Intelligence Agency (CIA)
www.cia.gov/index.html
    This agency was established in 1947 as a civilian intelligence agency of the United States government. As such, it gathers a huge amount of information, much of which can be found on its site.

International Labour Organization (ILO)
www.ilo.org/global/lang--en/index.htm
    This is a United Nations organization that deals with labour issues.

World Health Organization
www.who.int
    The World Health Organization was created in April 1948. It employs today more than 7,000 people from more than 150 countries working in 150 countries, in six regional offices, and at its headquarters in Geneva. The WHO's mandate includes the promotion worldwide health, to keep the world safe, and to serve the vulnerable.

WORLD SOCIETY ON VIDEO

The Coming Pandemic. 2018. BBC. 50 minutes.
    This documentary, released two years before the coronavirus outbreak, provides
    a prescient look at pandemics.

The Panama Papers. 2018. Great Point Media. 94 minutes.
    The Panama Papers refers to the leak by a German newspaper in 2016 of
    11.5 million encrypted confidential documents, property of Panama-based
    law firm Mossack Fonseca. This documentary examines the biggest global
    corruption scandal in history and the hundreds of investigative journalists who
    risked their lives to break the story.

The Street. 2019. Zed Nelson. 94 minutes.
    Following its inhabitants over a four-year period, this documentary charts the
    toxic collision of gentrification, austerity, and the nation's slide into Brexit.

APPENDIX 1

Canadian Federal Election Results since Confederation

Year	Conservatives	Liberals				Other	Total
1867	101	80					181
1872	103	97					200
1874	73	133					206
1878	137	69					206
1882	139	71					210
1887	123	92					215
1891	123	92					215
1896	89	117				7	213
1900	78	128				8	214
1904	75	139					214
1908	85	133				3	221
1911	133	86				2	221
		Liberals	**Unionists**				
1917		82	153				235
	Conservatives	**Liberals**	**Liberal Conservatives**	**Progressives**		**Other**	
1921		116	50	65		4	235
1925	116	101		24		4	245
	Conservatives	**Liberals**	**Liberal Progressives**	**Progressives**	**United Farmers**	**Other**	
1926	91	116	9	13	11	5	245
1930	137	88	3	2	10	5	245

	Conservatives	Liberals	CCF	Social Credit		Other	
1935	39	171	7	17		11	245
1940	39	178	8	10		10	245

	Progressive Conservatives	Liberals	CCF	Social Credit		Other	
1945	67	125	28	13		12	245
1949	41	190	13	10		8	262
1953	51	170	23	15		6	265
1957	112	105	25	19		4	265
1958	208	48	8			1	265

	Progressive Conservatives	Liberals	NDP	Social Credit		Other	
1962	116	99	19	30		1	265
1963	95	129	17	24			265

	Progressive Conservatives	Liberals	NDP	Social Credit	Créditistes	Other	
1965	97	131	21	5	9	2	265
1968	72	155	22		14	1	264
1972	107	109	31		15	2	264
1974	97	136	17		9	5	264
1979	136	114	26		6		282
1980	103	147	32				282
1984	211	40	30			1	282
1988	169	83	43				295

	Progressive Conservatives	Liberals	NDP	Reform	Bloc Québécois	Other	
1993	2	177	9	52	54	1	295
1997	20	155	21	60	44	1	301

	Progressive Conservatives	Liberals	NDP	Alliance	Bloc Québécois	
2000	12	172	13	66	38	301

	Conservatives	Liberals	NDP		Bloc Québécois	Other	
2004	99	135	19		54	1	308
2006	124	103	29		51	1	308
2008	143	77	37		49	2	308
2011	166	34	103		4	1	308
	Conservatives	**Liberals**	**NDP**	*Green*	**Bloc Québécois**	**Other**	
2015	99	184	44	1	10		338
2019	121	157	24	3	32	1	338

Source: Elections Canada On-Line, "Past Elections," https://www.elections.ca/home.aspx

APPENDIX 2

Canadian Prime Ministers, Governments, and Major Policies since Confederation

Prime Minister	Party	Dates of Administration	Major Policies/Events
Sir John A. Macdonald	C	July 1867–Nov. 1873	Confederation; Red River Rebellion; Manitoba, British Columbia, and Prince Edward Island join Canada
Alexander Mackenzie	L	Nov. 1873–Oct. 1878	Supreme Court of Canada established; Intercontinental Railway completed; first Indian Act passed
Sir John A. Macdonald	C	Oct. 1878–June 1891	National Policy; North-West Rebellion; Louis Riel hanged
Sir John J. C. Abbott	C	June 1891–Nov. 1892	
Sir John S. Thompson	C	Dec. 1892–Dec. 1894	
Sir Mackenzie Bowell	C	Dec. 1894–Apr. 1896	
Sir Charles Tupper	C	Apr. 1896–July 1896	
Sir Wilfrid Laurier	L	July 1896–Oct. 1911	Manitoba Schools Act; Klondike Gold Rush; Boer War; free trade election (lost)
Sir Robert Borden	C	Oct. 1911–Oct. 1917	First World War; Conscription Crisis; income tax introduced
Sir Robert Borden	U	Oct. 1917–July 1920	War ends; white women gain federal vote; Winnipeg general strike
Arthur Meighen	U	July 1920–Dec. 1921	
W. L. Mackenzie King	L	Dec. 1921–June 1926	King-Byng Constitutional Affair
Arthur Meighen	C	June 1926–Sept. 1926	

Prime Minister	Party	Dates of Administration	Major Policies/Events
W. L. Mackenzie King	L	Sept. 1926– Aug. 1930	Great Depression begins; Cairine Wilson appointed Canada's first female senator
R. B. Bennett	C	Aug. 1930– Oct. 1935	Statute of Westminster; Co-operative Commonwealth Federation (CCF) founded; Regina riot; Social Credit elected in Alberta
W. L. Mackenzie King	L	Oct. 1935– Nov. 1948	Second World War; beginning of welfare state; second Conscription Crisis; CCF elected in Saskatchewan
Louis St. Laurent	L	Nov. 1948– June 1957	Korean War
John Diefenbaker	PC	June 1957– Apr. 1963	Avro Arrow cancelled; Canadian Bill of Rights; Status Indians gain vote
Lester Pearson	L	Apr. 1963– Apr. 1968	Maple Leaf flag; medicare
Pierre Trudeau	L	Apr. 1968– June 1979	Bilingualism; multiculturalism; the FLQ Crisis; capital punishment abolished; PQ elected
Joe Clarke	PC	June 1979– March 1980	
Pierre Trudeau	L	March 1980– June 1984	Quebec Referendum; National Energy Program; Constitution Act, 1982
John Turner	L	June 1984– Sept. 1984	
Brian Mulroney	PC	Sept. 1984– June 1993	Free Trade Agreement; Meech Lake Accord, Charlottetown Accord and Referendum; Goods and Services Tax (GST); Oka Crisis
Kim Campbell	PC	June 1993– Oct. 1993	First female prime minister
Jean Chrétien	L	Oct. 1993– Nov. 2003	North American Free Trade Agreement; Quebec referendum; Clarity Act; 9/11 attacks; Canadian military involvement in Afghanistan War
Paul Martin	L	Nov. 2003– Feb. 2006	Gomery Inquiry; same-sex marriage becomes law

Prime Minister	Party	Dates of Administration	Major Policies/Events
Stephen Harper	C	Feb. 2006–Oct. 2015	GST cuts; end of Afghan War; recognition of Quebec as "nation"; political scandals (robocalls, expenditures, the Senate-Duffy affair); residential schools apology; increased use of omnibus bills and prorogation; petroleum policies
Justin Trudeau	L	Oct. 2015–	United States–Mexico–Canada (USMCA) free trade agreement; federal carbon tax; political scandal (SNC-Lavalin affair); Trans Mountain pipeline; conflict with Conservative-headed provincial governments; minority government, 2019–

Legend: C = Conservative; L = Liberal; U = Unionist; PC = Progressive Conservative

Source: "Elections and Prime Ministers." *Canadian Encyclopedia.* https://www.thecanadianencyclopedia.ca/en/timeline/elections-and-prime-ministers

Glossary

Aboriginal self-government: formal structure through which Indigenous communities may control the administration of their people, land, resources, and related programs and policies, through agreements with federal and provincial governments

Aboriginal title: inherent Aboriginal right to land or a territory

American exceptionalism: belief that the United States is unique or exceptional when compared with the historical development of other countries and thus cannot be judged by the same standards as other countries

Anglo-conformity: requirement that subordinate group members express outward compliance with the values and practices of the dominant British group

asymmetrical federalism: federal system in which the division of powers (and specific arrangements pertaining to them) are not the same from province to province

band: governing unit of Indigenous people in Canada instituted by the Indian Act of 1876. The act defined a "band" as the basic unit of government for First Nations peoples subject to the act

census metropolitan area (CMA): area consisting of one or more adjacent municipalities situated around an urban core of at least 100,000 people

chain migration: tendency of new immigrants to settle in areas already populated by members of their cultural identity

charisma: extraordinary quality viewed as existing within a person

citizens plus: term used in the Hawthorn Report, arguing that Indigenous peoples be extended the same rights as other Canadian citizens but also be assured the honouring of their legal rights as Status Indians

class theory: political theory arguing that power in society is based on the particular mode of production and ownership of the means of production

clerico-nationalism: a traditionalist, religious form of French-Canadian nationalism focused in Quebec on the Roman Catholic Church. In France, a similar ideology was referred to as National Catholicism

climate change: long-term change in the Earth's climate, especially shifts due to an increase in the average atmospheric temperature (see also **global warming**)

colonialism: complex national system of racial, cultural, and political domination that produces privileges beyond the surplus value generated by capitalism

compact theory: see **two nations theory**

comprehensive claims: claims made by Indigenous peoples involving lands never legally surrendered (see also **specific claims**)

conflict theory: political theory arguing that tensions and conflicts arise when resources, status, and power are unevenly distributed between groups in society, but that these conflicts are also the cause of social change

constitution: the institutions, practices, and principles that define and structure a system of government and the written document that establishes or articulates such a system

counterfactual history: a simulation based on calculations about the relative probability of plausible outcomes

country: a territorial area, politically recognized as a country both by people within the territory and by governments outside it, on the basis of historical, material, and geographic factors

cultural misunderstanding thesis: idea that government officials and Indigenous peoples had different interpretations of what was being negotiated in land treaties

decapitation thesis: holds that the Conquest destroyed New France's "embryonic bourgeoisie," leading to underdevelopment

decentralization: idea that many powers held by the federal government should be turned over to the provinces

dependency theory: political theory that emphasizes the unequal relationship in the world capitalist system between the core and periphery, set in motion by early colonialism

distinct society: political notion used during constitutional debates over the Meech Lake and Charlottetown accords, referring to the uniqueness of Quebec, particularly its language, laws and culture

double movement: the term coined by Karl Polanyi in his book *The Great Transformation* to describe the twin processes of a push for an unregulated market economy, resulting in a turn in counter-movements within civil society seeking social protection against market instability

dual economy: simultaneous operation of traditional and modern ways of making a living—for example, living off the land versus fulfilling the role of factory worker

elite theory: political theory arguing that all societies are inescapably divided between a dominant minority and a dominated majority

endogamy: custom of marrying only within the limits of a local community, clan, or tribe

enfranchisement: legal process for terminating a person's Indian Status and conferring full Canadian citizenship. The practice ended in 1961

ethnocentrism: judging another culture based on preconceptions that are found in the values and standards of one's own culture

externalities: cost or benefit to a third party (including the natural environment) that has no control over how that cost or benefit was created

extraterritoriality: (1) exemption of an individual or group from the jurisdiction of local law, usually as the result of diplomatic negotiations; or (2) ability of a state to pass laws having authority beyond its borders

feminization of poverty: tendency for women to experience poverty at rates disproportionately higher than men and the factors that contribute to this phenomenon

francophone proletariat: referred to francophone workers in Quebec who, prior to the Quiet Revolution, were often employed by the dominant Anglophone business class

genocide: the deliberate and systematic destruction of a racial, political, or cultural group

gig economy: an economic sector consisting of part-time, temporary, and freelance jobs

globalization: a series of integrative economic, political, and cultural changes, sometimes contradictory and even opposed, occurring throughout the world

global warming: increase in Earth's average surface temperature due to rising levels of greenhouse gases; distinguished from climate change (see also **climate change**)

gross domestic product (GDP): total value of all goods and services produced by a country in a year

hegemony: the political dominance or authority of one nation or group over another, often supported by legitimating norms and ideas

historical sociology: branch of sociology that studies changes in societies over time, the historical events and contingencies underpinning these changes, and the trajectories for subsequent societal development arising from these changes

identity stripping: intentional removal of articles, personal identification, and other elements that tell individuals who they are; generally associated with total institutions such as prisons, mental asylums, and religious cults

ideology: a more or less integrated set of ideas, attitudes, and beliefs held by individuals and groups that guide their actions

import substitution: development strategy emphasizing the replacement of imports with domestically produced goods, rather than the production of goods for export, to encourage the development of domestic industry; generally implemented through tariff protections and subsidies

Indigenous ecology: notion that Indigenous approaches to the environment were more harmonious with nature than European approaches

individual egalitarianism: manner of living that balances individual aims with collective goals; typical of traditional Inuit culture

infant mortality rate: ratio of deaths in the first year of life to the number of live births occurring in the same population during the same period of time

institutional bilingualism: requirement under the Official Languages Act declaring the "equality of status" of both English and French in Parliament and the Canadian public service, including all federal departments, judicial and quasi-judicial bodies, and administrative agencies and Crown corporations established by federal statute

***interculturalisme*:** concept within Quebec that the relationship among the francophone majority, the anglophone minority, the Indigenous minority, and allophones is dovetailing, with French being the central convening language

intergenerational mobility: degree of social mobility experienced from one generation to the next

intragenerational mobility: degree of social mobility experienced by an individual in their lifetime

laicization: process of the state deliberately distancing itself from religion on an institutional level

manifest destiny: term coined in 1845 by John O'Sullivan that held that the United States was divinely ordained with a special mission to cover North America

mapism: tendency of English-speaking Canadians to identify with the shape of Canada as learned in school by looking at the map

measures of central tendency: measures that describe the central tendency of a data set, including the mean (or average, the sum of all values in a data set divided by the number of values), median (the middle value in a data set arranged in ascending order), and mode (most frequently occurring value in a data set)

mercantilism: economic system in which the state was deeply involved in the operation of the economy, providing subsidies, bounties, and monopolistic privileges to individual companies (such as the Hudson's Bay Company) through the assignment of exclusive privileges and trading rights

military-industrial complex: informal alliance of the military and related government departments with defence industries that is held to influence government policy

Monroe Doctrine: declaration made by President James Monroe, in his message to Congress in December 1823, that the Americas are to be free of foreign influence and that the United States will act as the guarantor to prevent such influence; used repeatedly since the 19th century to justify American political and military operations in Latin and South America

multiculturalism: policy recognizing the equal rights and opportunities of all cultural or racial groups within society

nation: a mass of individuals who define themselves collectively as a people

neo-liberalism: ideology promoting the efficacy of free markets, limited government, and private property

orphan well: an oil well for which no owner or operator can be found, or where such owner or operator is unwilling or unable to plug and abandon the well

pandemic: disease occurring over a wide geographic area and affecting a large proportion of the population

patriarchy: system of male domination in society

polygyny: marriage of one man to more than one woman

populist parties: parties built around mass political movements—and mobilized around symbols and traditions congruent with the popular culture—that express a group's sense of threat arising from external elements and directed at the group's perceived "peoplehood"

post-structural theory: philosophical theory holding that language does not connect individuals directly with a "truth" or "reality" outside, but it is instead a structure or code, whose parts derive their meaning from their contrast with one another and thus lack a solid referent

power: ability to impose one's will upon others, even against their resistance

praxis: purposeful action in contrast to abstract theorizing

precariat: new social class defined by work insecurity (e.g., those working in the gig economy; see also **gig economy**)

profane world: world of the everyday, the expected, the mundane, and the explainable; contrasts with the **sacred world**

province building: activist approach to economic development on the part of provincial governments; commonly employed in the 1960s and 1970s

racism: belief that one racial category is innately superior or inferior to another

reasonable accommodation: form of arrangement or relaxation aimed at ensuring respect for the right of equality, which, following the strict application of an institutional standard, infringes on another individual's right to equality

region: territory defined physiologically, geographically, climatically, culturally, politically, or economically

regional alienation: a sense of grievance based on the belief that regional differences are not "natural" but result from the actions of individuals or groups residing outside the region

regional differences: observable variations between two or more regions, such as geographic or economic

regionalism: an individual's personal identification with a region

reification: process of coming to believe that our mental constructs actually exist materially

sacred world: the world of mystery, uncertainty, and even danger; contrasts with the **profane world**

secularization: process that occurs when religion progressively loses its relevance as a social and cultural framework for defining moral values and social conduct

sentencing circle (alternatively, a healing circle): formal court process that includes offenders, victims, community members, and justice professionals who meet and discuss face to face the offences committed and determine ways to ensure that justice is administered

settler colonialism: distinct type of colonialism that functions through the replacement of Indigenous populations with an invasive settler society that, over time, develops a distinct identity and sovereignty

sexism: belief that one sex is inherently superior to another

social capital: positive combination of interaction, reciprocity, and trust that bonds people to their communities

social class: group of people with similar levels of wealth, influence, and status (see also **class theory**)

social cohesion: bonding effect of society that arises spontaneously out of individuals willingly interacting in order to achieve collective goals

social determinants of health: economic and social conditions—and their distribution among the population—that influence individual and group differences in health status

social mobility: upward or downward movement of individuals or groups from one position in the social stratification system to another position

social norms: more or less agreed-upon societal rules and expectations that guide ways of behaving in society

social stratification: system by which a society ranks categories of people (e.g., occupation, race, ethnicity, or gender) in a hierarchy involving inequalities of various sorts

society: the product of relatively continuous and enduring interactions within a political territory, between people more or less identifying themselves as members of the society, these interactions being maintained by an ensemble of political, economic, cultural, and other institutions, and the sum of such interactions being in excess of interactions occurring with similarly defined societies external to the given territory

socio-economic status (SES): combination of education, occupation, and income

sociological imagination: ability to grasp history and biography as well as the relations of the two within society

sociology: the study of human social behavior, especially the study of the origins, organization, institutions, and development of human society

specific claims: claims by Indigenous peoples involving promises not fulfilled or interpretations of what was promised by either treaties or scrip (see also **comprehensive claims**)

stagflation: simultaneous occurrence of a declining economy and increasing unemployment with rising inflation

staples theory: asserts that the export of natural resources, or staples, from Canada to more advanced economies has a pervasive impact on the economy as well as on social and political systems

state: set of institutions successfully claiming a monopoly over political rule-making and the legitimate use of violence and coercion within a given territory (i.e., a country)

structural functional theory: sees society as a complex system whose parts work together to promote solidarity and stability

subaltern: lower classes and social groups at the margins of a society whose perspectives are often ignored

subsidiarity: principle that unless there is a valid reason to the contrary, state functions should be exercised by the lowest level of government

symbolic interaction theory: deals with the role of symbols in facilitating interactions between individuals and small groups

symbolic order: set of values, beliefs, and behaviours that lend predictability to our everyday surroundings

syncretism: merging or assimilation of several originally discrete traditions, especially in the theology and mythology of religion, thus asserting an underlying unity and allowing for an inclusive approach to other faiths

territorial bilingualism: idea that while Canada is bilingual within federal institutions, the predominance of language in everyday usage differs across the provinces, regions, and territories

terrorism: deliberate use of acts of violence or the threat of violence by individuals, groups, or the state for the purpose of furthering political ends

total institution: place of residence and work where a large number of like-situated individuals, cut off from the wider society for an appreciable period of time, together lead an enclosed, formally administered round of life

two nations theory (compact theory): the view that Canada's founding was based on an equal partnership of two peoples, the French and the English

unemployment rate: number of people out of work and actively looking for work divided by the total number of labour force participants, including the unemployed

unintended consequences: set of results that was not intended as an outcome

urban reserves: Indigenous reserves within or adjacent to an urban centre

usufructuary rights: legal right to use and derive profit from property belonging to someone else, provided that the property itself is not injured in any way

verstehen: process of interpreting meanings

welfare state: social system whereby the state assumes primary responsibility for the welfare of its citizens, as in matters of health care, education, employment, and social security

world view: overall perspective from which one sees and interprets the world

xenophobia: strong and unreasonable dislike or fear of unfamiliar people coming from other cultures and countries

References

Abel, Kerry. 1993. *Drum Songs: Glimpses of Dene History*. Montreal and Kingston: McGill-Queen's University Press.

Abella, Irving, and Harold Troper. 1982. *None Is Too Many: Canada and the Jews in Europe, 1933–1948*. Toronto: Lester and Orpen Dennys.

Abrams, Philip. 1988. "Notes on the Difficulty of Studying the State." *Journal of Historical Sociology* 1(1): 58–89.

Absolon, Kathleen E. (Minogiizhigokwe). 2011. *Kaandossiwin: How We Come to Know*. Halifax, NS: Fernwood.

Adams, Howard. 1989. *Prison of Grass: Canada from a Native Point of View*. 2nd ed. Saskatoon: Fifth House Publishers.

Adams, Howard. 1999. *Tortured People: The Politics of Colonization*. Revised ed. Penticton, BC: Theytus Books.

Adams, Michael. 1998. *Sex in the Snow: Canadian Social Values at the End of the Millennium*. Toronto: Penguin.

Adams, Michael. 2003. *Fire and Ice: The United States, Canada, and the Myth of Converging Values*. Toronto: Penguin.

Adams, Michael. 2007. *Unlikely Utopia: The Surprising Triumph of Canadian Pluralism*. Toronto: Viking.

Aitken, Hugh G. J. 1959. "The Changing Structure of the Canadian Economy." In *The American Economic Impact on Canada*, 3–35. Durham, NC: Duke University Press.

Albers, Gretchen. 2015. "Treaties 1 and 2." *Canadian Encyclopedia*, September 25.

Alberta, Tim. 2019. *American Carnage: On the Front Lines of the Republican Civil War and the Rise of President Trump*. New York: Harper.

Alberta Energy. n.d. *Let's Talk Royalties. Not All Oil Is Equal: Explaining Price Differences*. Government of Alberta. open.alberta.ca/dataset/5e6f425a-e1c7-441a-9aa0-64890e4ecade/resource/b7080f88-f748-45f0-8294-81d32a7a834c/download/13-Explaining-oil-price-differentials-formatted.pdf

Albrow, Martin. 1997. *The Global Age: State and Society beyond Modernity*. Stanford, CA: Stanford University Press.

Aldred, Jonathan. 2019. "The Evils of Bad Economics." *Guardian Weekly*, June 14, 42–43.

Alford, B. W. E. 1996. *Britain in the World Economy since 1880*. London, UK: Longman.

Alfred, Gerald R. 1995. *Heeding the Voices of Our Ancestors: Kahnawake Mohawk Politics and the Rise of Native Nationalism*. Toronto: Oxford University Press.

Alfred, Taiaiake. 2005. *Wasáse: Indigenous Pathways to Action and Freedom*. Peterborough, ON: Broadview Press.

Allain, Kristi A. 2012. "'Real Fast and Tough': The Construction of Canadian Hockey Masculinity." In *Rethinking Sociology in the 21st Century*, 3rd ed., eds. M. Webber and K. Bezanson, 359–372. Toronto: Canadian Scholars' Press.

Allison, Derek. 1983. "Fourth World Education in Canada and the Faltering Promise of Native Teacher Education." *Journal of Canadian Studies* 18(3): 102–119.

Anderson, Benedict. 1983. *Imagined Communities*. London, UK: Verso.

Angus, Murray. 1991. *And the Last Shall Be First: Native Policy in an Era of Cutbacks*. Toronto: NC Press.

Angus Reid. 2016. "What makes us Canadian? A study of values, beliefs, and identity." *Canadian Public Opinion Poll*, October 3. angusreid.org/canada-values/

Antone, Eileen M. 2000. "Empowering Aboriginal Views in Aboriginal Education." *Canadian Journal of Native Education* 24(2): 92–101.

Armstrong, Fiona, Anthony Capon, and Ro McFarlane. 2020. "Coronavirus Is a Wake-Up Call: Our War with the Environment Is Leading to Pandemics." *The Conversation*, March 30. theconversation.com/coronavirus-is-a-wake-up-call-our-war-with-the-environment-is-leading-to-pandemics-135023?fbclid=IwAR3EiNy_-Pw9j7HILWwyKMEwLoC_EHVcdLRderuP2w7s23A-VWIwI6hG0lY

Asch, Michael. 2000. "Self-Government in the New Millennium." In *Nation to Nation: Aboriginal Sovereignty and the Future of Canada*, eds. J. Bird, L. Land, and M. MacAdam, 65–73. Toronto: Irwin.

Babones, Salvatore. 2018. *The New Authoritarianism: Trump, Populism, and the Tyranny of Experts*. Cambridge, UK: Polity.

Baker, Maureen. 1996. "Social Assistance and the Employability of Mothers: Two Models from Cross-National Research." *The Canadian Journal of Sociology* 21(4): 483–504.

Baldwin, Gordon C. 1967. *How Indians Really Lived*. New York: G. P. Putnam's Sons.

Balikci, Asen. 1970. *The Netsilik Eskimo*. Garden City, NY: The American Museum of Natural History.

Balthazar, Louis. 1993. "The Faces of Quebec Nationalism." In *A Passion for Identity: An Introduction to Canadian Studies*, eds. D. Taras, B. Rasporich, and E. Mandel, 92–107. Scarborough, ON: Nelson Canada.

Balthazar, Louis. 1997. "Quebec and the Ideal of Federalism." In *Quebec Society: Critical Issues*, eds. M. Fournier, M. Rosenberg, and D. White, 45–60. Scarborough, ON: Prentice-Hall Canada.

Barman, Jean, Yvonne Hébert, and Don McCaskill. 1986. "The Legacy of the Past: An Overview." In *Indian Education in Canada*, Vol. I: *The Legacy*, eds. J. Barman, Y. Hébert, and D. McCaskill, 1–22. Vancouver: UBC Press.

Barron, F. Laurie, and Joseph Garcea. 1999. "The Genesis of Urban Reserves and the Role of Governmental Self-Interest." In *Urban Indian Reserves: Forging New Relationships in Saskatchewan*, 22–52. Saskatoon: Purich.

Battiste, Marie. 2000. *Reclaiming Indigenous Voice and Vision*. Vancouver: UBC Press.

Battiste, Marie, and James (Sa'ke'j) Youngblood Henderson. 2000. *Protecting Indigenous Knowledge and Heritage*. Saskatoon: Purich.

Bauman, Zygmunt. 1996. "From Pilgrim to Tourist—Or a Short History of Identity." In *Questions of Cultural Identity*, eds. S. Hall and P. du Gay, 18–36. London: Sage.

Bear Heart. 1998. *The Wind Is My Mother: The Life and Teachings of a Native American Shaman*. New York: Berkley Books.

Beattie, Owen, and John Geiger. 1987. *Frozen in Time: Unlocking the Secrets of the Franklin Expedition*. Saskatoon: Western Producer Prairie Books.

Behiels, Michael D., and Matthew Hayday. 2011. *Contemporary Quebec: Selected Readings and Commentaries*. Montreal and Kingston: McGill-Queen's University Press.

Bell, Daniel. 1993. "The Third Technological Revolution and Its Possible Socioeconomic Consequences." In *Sources: Notable Selections in Sociology*, eds. K. Finsterbusch and J. Schwartz, 351–365. Guilford, CT: Dushkin.

Bell, Daniel. 1996. *The Cultural Contradictions of Capitalism*, 20th anniversary ed. New York: Basic Books.

Bell, Edward, 1993. *Social Classes and Social Credit*. Montreal and Kingston: McGill-Queen's University Press.

Bellamy, Donald, and Allan Irving. 1981. "Pioneers." In *Canadian Social Welfare*, eds. J. Turner and F. Turner, 27–46. Don Mills, ON: Collier Macmillan Canada.

Bello, Walden. 2002. *Deglobalization: Ideas for a New Economy*. London, UK: Zed Books.

Bercuson, David, and Barry Cooper. 1991. *Deconfederation: Canada without Quebec*. Toronto: Key Porter Books.

Berdahl, Loleen, and Roger Gibbins. 2014. *Looking West: Regional Transformation and the Future of Canada*. Toronto: University of Toronto Press.

Berger, Carl. 1976. *The Sense of Power: Studies in the Ideas of Canadian Imperialism, 1867–1914*. Toronto: University of Toronto Press.

Bernard, Paul. 1996. "Canada as a Social Experiment." *Canadian Journal of Sociology* 21(2): 245–258.

Berton, Pierre. 1958. *The Klondike Fever: The Life and Death of the Last Great Gold Rush*. New York: Knopf.

Berton, Pierre. 1980. *The Invasion of Canada, 1812–1813*. Toronto: McClelland & Stewart.

Berton, Pierre. 1988. *The Arctic Grail*. Markham, ON: Penguin.

Berton, Pierre. 1991. *The Great Depression, 1929–1939*. Toronto: Penguin.

Bird, John, Lorraine Land, and Murray MacAdam, eds. 2000. *Self-Government in the New Millennium: Nation to Nation: Aboriginal Sovereignty and the Future of Canada*. Toronto: Irwin Publishing.

Bissoondath, Neil. 1994. *Selling Illusions: The Cult of Multiculturalism in Canada*. Toronto: Penguin.

Black, Conrad. 1977. *Duplessis*. Toronto: McClelland & Stewart.

Block, Sheila, Grace-Edward Galabuzi, and Ricardo Tranjan. 2019. *Canada's Colour-Coded Inequality*. Ottawa: Canadian Centre for Policy Alternatives. December. www.policyalternatives.ca/sites/default/files/uploads/publications/National%20Office/2019/12/Canada%27s%20Colour%20Coded%20Income%20Inequality.pdf

Boily, Frederic, Charlotte Gray, Lee Maracle, and Christopher Moore. 2019. "The Trials of John A." *Canada's History*, February-March, 20–31.

Boldt, Menno. 1993. *Surviving as Indians: The Challenge of Self-Government*. Toronto: University of Toronto Press.

Bone, Robert M. 1988. "Cultural Persistence and Country Food: The Case of the Norman Wells Project." *Western Canadian Anthropologist* 5: 61–79.

Bone, Robert M. 1992. *The Geography of the Canadian North: Issues and Challenges*. Toronto: Oxford University Press.

Booth, Rob. 2019. "Are We Prepared for the Four-Day Week?" *Guardian Weekly*, March 22, 28–29.

Bourdieu, Pierre. 1998. *On Television*. Trans. P. P. Ferguson. New York: The New Press.

Bourgault, Pierre. 1991. *Now or Never: Manifesto for an Independent Quebec*. Toronto: Key Porter Books.

Bowler, Arthur. 1993. "Introduction." In *Reappraisals in Canadian History: Pre-Confederation*, eds. A. D. Gilbert, G. M. Wallace, and R. M. Bray, 291–309. Scarborough: Prentice-Hall Canada Inc.

Boyer, Robert, and Daniel Drache, eds. 1996. *States against Markets*. London, UK: Routledge.

Bradley, Paul G., and G. Campbell Watkins. 2003. "Canada and the US: A Seamless Energy Border?" *The Border Papers*, no. 178, April. Toronto: C. D. Howe Institute.

Brascoupé, Simon. 2000. "Aboriginal Peoples' Vision of the Future: Interweaving Traditional Knowledges and New Technologies of the Heart." In *Canadian Aboriginal Issues*, eds. D. Long and O. P. Dickason, 411–432. Toronto: Harcourt Canada.

Braz, Albert. 2003. *The False Traitor: Louis Riel in Canadian Culture*. Toronto: University of Toronto Press.

Brest, Mike. 2020. "Deborah Birx predicts coronavirus death toll up to 200,000 'if we do things together well, almost perfectly.'" *Washington Examiner*, March 30. www.washingtonexaminer.com/news/deborah-birx-predicts-coronavirus-death-toll-up-to-200-000-if-we-do-things-together-well-almost-perfectly

Brimelow, Peter. 1986. *The Patriot Game*. Toronto: Key Porter Books.

Brodie, Janine. 1990. *The Political Economy of Canadian Regionalism*. Toronto: Harcourt Brace Jovanovich Canada.

Brody, Hugh. 1987. *Living Arctic: Hunters of the Canadian North*. Vancouver: Douglas & McIntyre.

Brookes, Sonia. 1990. An Analysis of Indian Education Policy, 1960–1989. Master's Thesis. Calgary: University of Calgary.

Brookes, Sonia. 1991. "The Persistence of Native Educational Policy in Canada." In *The Cultural Maze: Complex Questions on Native Destiny in Western* Canada, ed. J. W. Friesen, 163–180. Calgary: Detselig.

Brown, Wallace. 1993. "Victorious in Defeat: The American Loyalists in Canada." In *Reappraisals in Canadian History: Pre-Confederation*, eds. A. D. Gilbert, G. M. Wallace, and R. M. Bray, 241–250. Scarborough, ON: Prentice-Hall Canada.

Brunelle, Dorval. 1999. "Free Trade Illusions in Quebec." *Le Monde Diplomatique* (April), 15.

Brunet, M. 1993. "The British Conquest and the Decline of the French-Canadian Bourgeoisie." In *Reappraisals in Canadian History: Pre-Confederation*, eds. A. D. Gilbert, G. M. Wallace, and R. M. Bray, 198–215. Scarborough, ON: Prentice-Hall Canada.

Brym, Robert. 2020. *SOC+*. 4th ed. Toronto: Nelson.

Brym, Robert J., and R. James Sacouman, eds. 1979. *Underdevelopment and Social Movements in Atlantic Canada*. Toronto: New Hogtown Press.

Buckley, Helen. 1993. *From Wooden Ploughs to Welfare: Why Indian Policy Failed in the Prairie Provinces*. Montreal and Kingston: McGill-Queen's University Press.

Bude, Heinz. 2017. *Society of Fear*. Cambridge, UK: Polity Press.

Burbach, Roger, Orlando Nunez, and Boris Kagarlitsky. 1997. *Globalization and Its Discontents.* London, UK: Pluto Press.

Burke, Danita Catherine. 2018. *International Disputes and Cultural Ideas in the Canadian Arctic: Arctic Sovereignty in the National Consciousness.* New York: Palgrave.

Byers, Michael. 2014. "The North Pole Is a Distraction." *Globe and Mail*, August 20, A11.

Cajete, Gregory. 1994. *Look to the Mountain: An Ecology of Indigenous Education.* Durango, CO: Kivaki Press.

Cameron, Nigel. 2017. *Will Robots Take Your Job?* Cambridge, UK: Polity Press.

Canadian Chamber of Commerce. 2013. *Opportunity Found: Improving the Participation of Aboriginal Peoples in Canada's Workforce.* Ottawa: Canadian Chamber of Commerce.

Canadian Encyclopedia. 2014. "Quebec Values Charter." www.thecanadianencyclopedia.ca/en/article/the-charter-of-quebec-values

Canadian Media Concentration Research Project. 2015. "Canada's Top Media, Internet, and Telecom Companies by Market Share (2014)." Ottawa: Carleton University, October. www.cmcrp.org/canadas-top-media-internet-telecom-companies-by-market-share-2014/

Canadian Northern Economic Development Agency. 2013. "Northern Economic Index, 2011–12." Ottawa: Canadian Northern Economic Development Agency. www.cannor.gc.ca/eng/1387900596709/1387900617810

Canadian Observatory on Homelessness. 2019. "Homelessness Hub: How many people are homeless in Canada?" Toronto, ON: York University. www.homelesshub.ca/about-homelessness/homelessness-101/how-many-people-are-homeless-canada

Canadian Public Health Association. 2020. "What are the social determinants of health?" www.cpha.ca/what-are-social-determinants-health

Cardinal, Harold. 1969. *The Unjust Society: The Tragedy of Canada's Indians.* Edmonton: Hurtig.

Cardinal, Harold. 1977. *The Rebirth of Canada's Indians.* Edmonton: Hurtig.

Careless, J. M. S. 1970. *Canada: A Story of Challenge.* Toronto: Macmillan and Company.

Carlson, Leonard. 1981. *Indians, Bureaucrats, and Land: The Dawes Act and the Decline of Indian Farming.* Westport: Greenwood Press.

Carr, Edward H. 1990. *What Is History?* Markham, ON: Penguin Books.

Carter, Sarah. 1993. *Lost Harvests: Prairie Indian Reserve Farmers and Government Policy.* Montreal and Kingston: McGill-Queen's University Press.

Catalyst. 2019. "Women in the workforce—Canada: Quick take." May 28. www.catalyst.org/research/women-in-the-workforce-canada/

Catton, William R., and Riley E. Dunlap. 1980. "A New Ecological Paradigm for Post-Exuberant Sociology." *American Behavioral Scientist* 24(1): 15–47.

Cecco, Leyland. 2020. "Canada: Wet'suwet'en and ministers agree tentative deal in land dispute." *Guardian*, March 2. www.theguardian.com/world/2020/mar/02/canada-wetsuweten-indigenous-land-dispute-deal-agreement

Central Statistics Office (Ireland). n.d. "European statistical system." www.cso.ie/en/aboutus/pagesforfoi/europeanstatisticalsystem/

Centre for Suicide Prevention. 2020. *Suicide Stats for Canada, Provinces, and Territories.* February 3. www.suicideinfo.ca/resource/suicide-stats-canada-provinces/

Chalmers, J. W. 1974. "Marguerite Bourgeoys, Preceptress of New France." In *Profiles of Canadian Educators*, eds. R. S. Patterson, J. W. Chalmers, and J. W. Friesen, 4–20. Toronto: DC Heath.

Chiste, Katherine Beaty. 2005. "Getting Tough on Crime the Aboriginal Way: Alternative Justice Initiatives in Canada." In *Hidden in Plain Sight: Contributions of Aboriginal Peoples to Canadian Identity and Culture*, eds. D. Newhouse, C. Voyageur, and D. Beavon, 218–232. Toronto: University of Toronto Press.

Chodos, Robert, and Eric Hamovitch. 1991. *Quebec and the American Dream*. Toronto: Between the Lines.

Chomsky, Noam. 2001. *9–11*. New York: Seven Stories Press.

Chorney, Harold. 1989. *The Deficit and Debt Management: An Alternative to Monetarism*. Ottawa: Canadian Centre for Policy Alternatives.

Citizenship and Immigration Canada. 1996. "Citizenship and Immigration Statistics 1996." Cat. no. MP22-/1996. Ottawa: Citizenship and Immigration Canada.

City of Toronto. 2014. "Labour Force Survey Data—Educational Attainment." Toronto: Data Centre.

Clark, Samuel D., J. Paul Grayson, and Linda M. Grayson. 1975. *Prophecy and Protest: Social Movements in Twentieth-Century Canada*. Toronto: Gage.

Clarkson, Stephen. 1985. *Canada and the Reagan Challenge*. Toronto: Lorimer.

Clarkson, Stephen. 2002a. *Uncle Sam and Us: Globalization, Neoconservatism, and the Canadian State*. Toronto: University of Toronto Press.

Clarkson, Stephen. 2002b. "What Uncle Sam Wants. . . ." *Globe and Mail*, December 2, A13.

Clarkson, Stephen. 2008. *Does North America Exist?* Toronto: University of Toronto Press.

Clarkson, Stephen, and Christina McCall. 1990. *Trudeau and Our Times*, Vol. 1: *The Magnificent Obsession*. Toronto: McClelland & Stewart.

Clement, Wallace. 1975. *The Canadian Corporate Elite*. Toronto: McClelland & Stewart.

Clement, Wallace, ed. 1997. *Understanding Canada: Building on the New Canadian Political Economy*. Montreal and Kingston: McGill-Queen's University Press.

Clement, Wallace, and Glen Williams. 1989. *The New Canadian Political Economy*. Montreal and Kingston: McGill-Queen's University Press.

Clerici, Naila. 1999. "The Cree of James Bay and the Construction of Their Identity for the Media." In *Futures and Identities*, ed. M. Behiels, 143–165. Montreal: Association for Canadian Studies.

Cline, Michael S. 1975. *Tannik School: The Impact of Education on the Eskimos of Anaktuvuk Pass*. Anchorage: Alaska Methodist University Press.

ClutchPR. 2017. *Who Owns What in the Canadian Media Landscape?* clutchpr.com/canadian-media-landscape/

Coates, Ken S., P. Whitney Lackenbauer, William R. Morrison, and Greg Poelzer. 2008. *Arctic Front: Defending Canada in the Far North*. Toronto: Thomas Allen.

Cochrane, Kira. 2013. *All the Rebel Women: The Rise of the Fourth Wave of Feminism*. London: Guardian Books.

Cohen, Andrew. 1990. *A Deal Undone: The Making and Breaking of the Meech Lake Accord*. Vancouver: Douglas & McIntyre.

Cohen, James. 2019. "How Canada Helps Advance Global Corruption." *Globe and Mail*, May 13.

Collins, Randall. 1982. *Sociological Insight: An Introduction to Non-Obvious Sociology*. Oxford, UK: Oxford University Press.

Colombo, John Robert. 1994. *Colombo's All-Time Great Canadian Quotations*. Toronto: Stoddart.

Colorado. 2013. Oil and Gas Conservation Commission, Practice and Procedure, Code of Colorado Regulations, 2 CCR 404-1, February.

Commissioner of the Environment and Sustainable Development. 2014, October 7. *Commissioner of the Environment and Sustainable Development Releases Fall 2014 Report.* Ottawa: Office of the Auditor General of Canada.

Condon, Richard G. 1987. *Inuit Youth: Growth and Change in the Canadian Arctic.* Newark, NJ: Rutgers University Press.

Conrad, Margaret, Alvin Finkel, and Cornelius Jaenen. 1993. *History of Canadian Peoples: Beginnings to 1867.* Toronto: Copp Clark Pitman.

Conway, John. 2004. *Debts to Pay: The Future of Federalism in Quebec.* 3rd ed. Toronto: James Lorimer and Company.

Conway, John. 2014. *The Rise of the New West: The History of a Region in Confederation.* 4th ed. Toronto: James Lorimer and Company.

Conway, Philip. 2017. "'The Ecological Indian' and the History of Environmental Ideas." The Disorder of Things, November 14. thedisorderofthings.com/2017/11/14/the-ecological-indian/

Cook, Ramsay. 1995. *Canada, Quebec, and the Uses of Nationalism.* 2nd ed. Toronto: McClelland & Stewart.

Cooke, Martin, and Daniéle Bélanger. 2006. "Migration Theories and First Nations Mobility: Towards a Systems Perspective." *Canadian Review of Sociology and Anthropology* 43(2): 141–165.

Cooke, Martin, and David Long. 2011. "Moving Beyond the Politics of Aboriginal Well-Being, Health, and Healing." In *Visions of the Heart: Canadian Aboriginal Issues*, 3rd ed., eds. David Long and Olive Patricia Dickason, 292–327. Don Mills, ON: Oxford University Press.

Corak, Miles. 2019a. "If There Is Such a Thing as the 'Canadian Dream,' It Would Look Very Much Like What Americans Say Is the 'American Dream.'" *Economics for Public Policy*, April 15. milescorak.com/2019/04/15/if-there-is-such-a-thing-as-the-canadian-dream-it-would-look-very-much-like-what-americans-say-is-the-american-dream/

Corak, Miles. 2019b. "Intergenerational Mobility between and within Canada and the United States." *Economics for Public Policy*, April 15. milescorak.com/2019/04/15/intergenerational-mobility-between-and-within-canada-and-the-united-states/

Cormier, Ryan. 2014. "Alberta Court of Appeal Rules Provincial Laws Don't Have to Be Bilingual," *Edmonton Journal*, February 21.

Cornellier, Manon. 1995. *The Bloc.* Toronto: James Lorimer and Company.

Cornish, George H. 1881. *Encyclopedia of Methodism in Canada.* Toronto: Methodist Book and Publishing Company.

Corrigall-Brown, Catherine. 2016. *Imagining Sociology: An Introduction with Readings.* Don Mills, ON: Oxford University Press.

Costs of War. 2014a. "US and Allies Killed." Watson Institute.

Costs of War. 2014b. "Afghanistan: At Least 21,000 Civilians Killed." Watson Institute.

Coulombe, Pierre A. 1998. "Quebec in the Federation." In *Challenges to Canadian Federalism*, eds. M. Westmacott and H. Mellon, 187–197. Scarborough, ON: Prentice-Hall Canada.

Council of Canadians. 2019. *CUSMA: The New NAFTA.* canadians.org/nafta

Courchene, Thomas. 1997. *The Nation State in a Global/Information Era: Policy Challenges.* Kingston: John Deutsch Institute for the Study of Economic Policy, Queen's University.

Courchene, Thomas. 1998. *From Heartland to North American Region State: The Social, Fiscal, and Federal Evolution of Ontario.* Toronto: University of Toronto Press.

Couture, Claude. 1998. *Paddling with the Current: Pierre Elliott Trudeau, Etienne Parent, Liberalism, and Nationalism in Canada*. Edmonton: University of Alberta Press.

Couture, Joseph E. 1991. "The Role of Native Elders: Emergent Issues." In *The Cultural Maze: Complex Questions on Native Destiny in Western Canada*, ed. J. W. Friesen, 201–218. Calgary: Detselig Enterprises.

Creighton, Donald. 1970. *Canada's First Century, 1867–1967*. Toronto: Macmillan of Canada.

Cross, Ronald, and Héléne Sévigny. 1994. *Lasagna: The Man behind the Mask*. Vancouver: Talonbooks.

Crouch, Colin. 2018. *The Globalization Backlash*. Hoboken, NJ: Wiley.

Crowe, Keith J. 1974. *A History of the Original Peoples of Northern Canada*. Montreal: Queen's University Press.

Cruikshank, Julie. 1998. "Discovery of Gold on the Klondike: Perspectives from Oral Tradition." In *Reading beyond Words: Contexts for Native History*, eds. J. S. H. Brown and E. Vibert, 435–458. Toronto: Broadview Press.

CTV. 2014. "Timeline: Canada's Involvement in Afghanistan." *CTV News*. www.ctvnews.ca/canada/timeline-canada-s-involvement-in-afghanistan-1.1814698

Curtis, James, Edward Grabb, and Neil Guppy. 1999. *Social Inequality in Canada: Patterns, Problems, and Policies*. Scarborough, ON: Prentice-Hall Allyn and Bacon Canada.

Daschuk, James. 2013. *Clearing the Plains: Dosearse, Politics of Starvation, and the Loss of Aboriginal Life*. Regina: University of Regina Press.

Dauvergne, Mia. 2012. "Adult Correctional Statistics in Canada, 2010/2011." *Juristat*. Ottawa: Statistics Canada. www.statcan.gc.ca/pub/85-002-x/2012001/article/11715-eng.htm#r11

Davis, Wade. 2009. *The Wayfinders: Why Ancient Wisdom Matters in the Modern World*. Toronto: House of Anansi Press.

Denis, Claude. 1989. "The Genesis of American Capitalism: An Historical Inquiry into State Theory." *Journal of Historical Sociology* 2(4): 328–356.

Denis, Claude. 1993. "Quebec-as-Distinct-Society as Conventional Wisdom: The Constitutional Silence of Anglo-Canadian Sociologists." *Canadian Journal of Sociology* 18(3): 251–270.

Denton, Frank. 1983. "The Labour Force." *Historical Statistics of Canada*. 2nd ed. Ottawa: Statistics Canada.

Deutsch, Karl W., ed. 1980. *Politics and Government: How People Decide Their Fate*. Boston: Houghton Mifflin.

Diamond, Jared. 2005. *Collapse: How Societies Choose to Fail or Succeed*. New York: Viking.

Dickason, Olive Patricia. 1984. *The Myth of the Savage and the Beginnings of French Colonialism in the Americas*. Edmonton: University of Alberta Press.

Dickason, Olive Patricia. 2002. *Canada's First Nations: A History of Founding Peoples from Earliest Times*. Toronto: McClelland & Stewart.

Dickason, Olive Patricia, and William Newbigging. 2010. *A Concise History of Canada's First Nations*. Don Mills, ON: Oxford University Press.

Dickinson, John, and Brian Young. 2008. *A Short History of Quebec*. 4th ed. Montreal and Kingston: McGill-Queen's University Press.

Dilthey, Wilhelm. 1961. *Pattern and Meaning in History*. London, UK: Harper and Row.

Dion, Joseph F. 1979. *My Tribe: The Crees*. Calgary: Glenbow Museum.

Dobbin, Murray. 2008. "Afghanistan Transforms Canada: To Play Junior Partner to Empire, We've Militarized Our Identity." *The Tyee*, August 11. thetyee.ca/Views/2008/08/11/ AfghanCan

Doctorow, Cory. 2019. "Why Do People Believe the Earth Is Flat?" *Globe and Mail*, September 21, O4.

Doern, B., and B. W. Tomlin. 1991. *Faith and Fear: The Free Trade Story*. Toronto: Stoddart.

Drache, Daniel. 1995. "Introduction: Celebrating Innis: The Man, the Legacy." In *Staples, Markets, and Cultural Change: Selected Essays*, ed. D. Drache, xiii–lix. Montreal and Kingston: McGill-Queen's University Press.

Drees, Laurie Meijer. 2013. *Teaching Histories: Stories from Canada's Indian Hospitals*. Edmonton: University of Alberta Press.

Driedger, Leo. 1991. *The Urban Factor: Sociology of Canadian Cities*. Oxford, UK: Oxford University Press.

Dubuc, Alain. 2001. "The Lafontaine-Baldwin Lecture: Canadian Nationalism." In *Dialogue on Democracy: The LaFontaine-Baldwin Lectures 2000–2005*, ed. R. Griffiths. Toronto: Penguin Canada.

Dufour, Christian. 1990. *A Canadian Challenge: Le defi quebecois*. Halifax: Oolichan Books and the Institute for Research on Public Policy.

Dumond, Don E. 1977. *The Eskimos and Aleuts*. London, UK: Thames and Hudson.

Duncan, Sarah J. 1971. *The Imperialist*. Originally published in 1904. Toronto: McClelland & Stewart.

Dunn, Christopher. 1995. *Canadian Political Debates*. Toronto: McClelland & Stewart.

Dunning, John. 1983. "Changes in the Level and Structure of International Production: The Last One Hundred Years." In *The Growth of International Business*, ed. M. Casson, 84–139. London, UK: George Allen and Unwin.

Durkheim, Émile. 1964. *The Division of Labor in Society*. Originally published in 1893. New York: The Free Press.

Durkheim, Émile. 1978. *Elementary Forms of Religious Life*. Originally published in 1912. London: George Allen and Unwin.

Dyer, Gwynne. 2008. *Climate Wars*. Toronto: Random House Canada.

Dyer, Gwynne. 2018. *Growing Pains: The Future of Democracy (and Work)*. London: Scribe.

Dymond, Bill, and Michael Hart. 2003. "Canada and the Global Challenge: Finding a Place to Stand." *The Border Papers* 180 (March). Toronto: C. D. Howe Institute.

Easterbrook, W. T., and Hugh G. J. Aitken. 1988. *Canadian Economic History*. Toronto: University of Toronto Press.

Eccles, W. J. 1993a. "The French Forces in North America during the Seven Years War." In *Reappraisals in Canadian History: Pre-Confederation*, eds. A. D. Gilbert, G. M. Wallace, and R. M. Bray, 162–174. Scarborough, ON: Prentice-Hall Canada.

Eccles, W. J. 1993b. "The Society of New France, 1680s–1760." In *Reappraisals in Canadian History: Pre-Confederation*, eds. A. D. Gilbert, G. M. Wallace, and R. M. Bray, 40–48. Scarborough, ON: Prentice-Hall Canada.

Edmond, John. 2014. "Indian Residential Schools: A Chronology." *Law Now*, July 7. www. lawnow.org/indian-residential-schools-chronology

Edmonton Journal. 2000. "New Confederacy Aims to Restore Blackfoot Nation," August 13, A8.

Edmonton Journal. 2008. "Separatism Dormant but Not Forgotten: Survey," June 2, A5.

Ehmsen, Stefanie, and Albert Scharenberg, eds. 2018. *The Far Right in Government: Six Cases from across Europe.* New York: Rosa Luxemburg Stiftung.

Elsey, Christine J. 2013. *The Poetics of Land and Identity among British Columbia Indigenous Peoples.* Black Point, NS: Fernwood.

Esping-Andersen, Gøsta. 1990. *The Three Worlds of Welfare Capitalism.* Princeton: Princeton University Press.

Fairchild, Henry Pratt, ed. 1967. *Dictionary of Sociology and Related Sciences.* Totowa, NJ: Littlefield, Adams, and Company.

Fairclough, Norman. 1989. *Language and Power: Language in Social Life.* London, UK: Longman.

Fanon, Frantz. 1968. *The Wretched of the Earth.* New York: Grove Press.

Feit, Harvey A. 2007. "Myths of the Ecological Whitemen: Histories, Science, and Rights in North American—Native American Relations." In *Native Americans and the Environment: Perspectives on the Ecological Indian*, eds. M. E. Harkin, M. E. and D. R. Lewis, 95–122. Lincoln, NE: University of Nebraska Press.

Femia, Francesco, and Caitlin E. Werrell. 2014. "UPDATE: Climate and Security 101: Why the US National Security Establishment Takes Climate Change Seriously." *Briefer* 23: 1–4. Washington, DC: Center for Security and Climate.

Ferguson, Niall, ed. 2003. *Virtual History: Alternatives and Counterfactuals.* London, UK: Pan Books.

Ferguson, Niall. 2004. *Colossus: The Price of America's Empire.* New York: Penguin.

Fida, Kashmala. 2019. "Métis Nations in Alberta, Ontario, and Saskatchewan Sign Historic Self-Government Agreements with Ottawa." *Star Edmonton*, June 27.

Fidler, Richard. 2006. "A 'Québécois Nation'? Harper Fuels an Important Debate." *Global Research*, December 22. www.globalresearch.ca/index.php?context=va&aid=4244

Findley, L. M. 2000. "Foreword." In *Reclaiming Indigenous Voice and Vision*, ed. M. Battiste, ix–xiii. Vancouver: UBC Press.

Finkel, Alvin. 1989. *The Social Credit Phenomenon in Alberta.* Toronto: University of Toronto Press.

Finkel, Alvin. 2012. *Our Lives: Canada after 1945.* 2nd ed. Toronto: Lorimer.

Finnie, Richard. 1948. *Canada Moves North.* Toronto: Macmillan Company of Canada.

Fisher, A. D. 1981. "A Colonial Education System: Historical Changes and Schooling in Fort Chipewyan." *Canadian Journal of Anthropology* 2(1): 37–44.

Flanagan, Thomas. 1977. "Louis Riel: Insanity and Prophecy." In *The Settlement of the West*, ed. H. Palmer, 15–36. Calgary: Comprint.

Flanagan, Thomas. 2000. *First Nations? Second Thoughts.* Montreal and Kingston: McGill-Queen's University Press.

Fleras, Augie. 2007. *Unequal Relations: An Introduction to Race, Ethnic, and Aboriginal Dynamics in Canada.* 5th ed. Toronto: Pearson Canada.

Fleras, Augie, and Jean Leonard Elliott. 1992. *The Nations Within: Aboriginal-State Relations in Canada, the United States, and New Zealand.* Toronto: Oxford University Press.

Food Banks Canada. 2019. "Hunger Facts." Mississauga, ON: Food Banks Canada. www.foodbankscanada.ca

Forbes. 2019. "The World's Billionaires." New York: Forbes Media. www.forbes.com/billionaires/list/

Ford, James, and Johanna Wandel. 2013. "Responding to Climate Change in Nunavut: Policy Recommendations." In *Moving Forward, Making a Difference*, Vol. 3, eds. Jerry P. White, Susan Wingert, Dan Beavon, and Paul Maxim, 103–115. Aboriginal Policy Research Series. Toronto: Thompson Educational.

Foreign Affairs, Trade and Development Canada. 2013. "The Economic Impact of the Canada-Chile Free Trade Agreement." Ottawa: Foreign Affairs, Trade and Development Canada. www.international.gc.ca/economist-economiste/analysis-analyse/studies-etudes/canada_chile-canada_chili/econo_impact_toc-tdm.aspx?lang=eng

Fort McKay Group of Companies. n.d. fortmckaygroup.com

Fossum, John Erik. 1997. *Oil, the State, and Federalism: The Rise and Demise of Petro-Canada as a Statist Impulse*. Toronto: University of Toronto Press.

Foucault, Michel. 1973. *Madness and Civilization: A History of Insanity in the Age of Reason*. New York: Vintage Books.

Foucault, Michel. 1977. *Power/Knowledge: Selected Interviews and Other Writings, 1972–1977*, ed. C. Gordon. New York: Pantheon.

Foucault, Michel. 1980. *The History of Sexuality*, Vol. 1: *An Introduction*. New York: Vintage Books.

Fournier, Marcel. 2001. "Quebec Sociology and Quebec Society: The Construction of a Collective Identity." *Canadian Journal of Sociology* 26(3): 333–347.

Fournier, Marcel, Michael Rosenberg, and Deena White, eds. 1997. *Quebec Society: Critical Issues*. Scarborough, ON: Prentice-Hall Canada.

Fox, John, Robert Andersen, and Joseph Dubonnet. 1999. "The Polls and the 1995 Quebec Referendum." *Canadian Journal of Sociology* 24(3): 411–424.

Fox, Terry, and David Long. 2000. "Struggles within the Circle: Violence, Healing, and Health on a First Nations Reserve." In *Visions of the Heart: Canadian Aboriginal Issues*, eds. D. Long and O. P. Dickason, 271–301. 2nd ed. Toronto: Harcourt Canada.

Francis, Daniel. 1997. *National Dreams: Myth, Memory, and Canadian History*. Vancouver: Arsenal Pulp Press.

Francis, Diane. 2013. *Merger of the Century*. Scarborough, ON: HarperCollins.

Francis, Diane. 2017. "The Big Idea: Why Canada and the US Should Merge." *Daily Beast*, July 11. www.thedailybeast.com/the-big-idea-why-canada-and-us-should-merge

Francis, R. Douglas, Richard Jones, and Donald B. Smith. 1988. *Origins: Canadian History to Confederation*. Toronto: Holt, Rinehart, and Winston of Canada.

Frank, Andre Gunder. 1975. *On Capitalist Underdevelopment*. Bombay, India: Oxford University Press.

Fraser, Blair. 1967. *The Search for Identity: Canada: Postwar to Present*. Toronto: Doubleday Canada.

Frideres, James S. 2011. *First Nations in the Twenty-First Century*. Don Mills, ON: Oxford University Press.

Frideres, James S., and Rene R. Gadacz. 2001. *Aboriginal Peoples in Canada: Contemporary Conflicts*. 6th ed. Scarborough, ON: Prentice-Hall Canada.

Fried, Jacob. 1969. "Boom Towns . . . Must They Bust?" In *People of the Light and Dark*, ed. M. van Steensel, 38–42. Ottawa: Department of Indian Affairs and Northern Development.

Friesen, Jean. 1986. *Magnificent Gifts: The Treaties of Canada with the Indians of the Northwest, 1869–70.* Transactions of the Royal Society of Canada, Series 5, Vol. 1, 41–51. Toronto: University of Toronto Press.

Friesen, Joe, and Ingrid Peritz. 2012. "New Bilingualism Taking Hold in Canada." *Globe and Mail*, October 24. www.theglobeandmail.com/news/national/new-bilingualism-taking-hold-in-canada/article4650408

Friesen, John W. 1983. *Schools with a Purpose.* Calgary: Detselig.

Friesen, John W. 1991. "Introduction: Highlights of Western Canadian Native History." In *The Cultural Maze: Complex Questions on Native Destiny in Western Canada*, ed. J. W. Friesen, 1–22. Calgary: Detselig.

Friesen, John W. 1993. *When Cultures Clash: Case Studies in Multiculturalism.* 2nd ed. Calgary: Detselig.

Friesen, John W. 1995. *You Can't Get There from Here: The Mystique of Plains Indians' Culture & Philosophy.* Dubuque: Kendall/Hunt.

Friesen, John W. 1997. *Rediscovering the First Nations of Canada.* Calgary: Detselig.

Friesen, John W. 1998. *Sayings of the Elders.* Calgary: Detselig.

Friesen, John W. 1999. *First Nations of the Plains: Creative, Adaptable, and Enduring.* Calgary: Detselig.

Friesen, John W., and Virginia Lyons Friesen. 2004. *We Are Included: The Métis People of Canada Realize Riel's Vision.* Calgary: Detselig.

Friesen, John W., and Virginia Lyons Friesen. 2005. *First Nations in the Twenty-First Century: Contemporary Educational Frontiers.* Calgary: Detselig.

Frisby, David, and Derek Sayer. 1986. *Society.* London, UK: Ellis Horwood/Tavistock.

Fukuyama, Francis. 1992. *The End of History and the Last Man.* New York: The Free Press.

Furniss, Elizabeth. 1995. *Victims of Benevolence: The Dark Legacy of the Williams Lake Residential School.* Vancouver: Arsenal Pulp Press.

Gagnon, Lysiane. 2000. "The October Crisis: Singular Anomaly." *The Beaver* 80(5): 6–7.

Galbraith, John Kenneth. 1997. *The Great Crash 1929.* Boston: Mariner.

Gardner, Dan. 2002. "The First Casualty of Hollywood . . . Is Truth." *Edmonton Journal*, February 9, A16.

Gasher, Mike. 2014. "Media Convergence." Revised by A. McIntosh. *Canadian Encyclopedia.* Historica Canada. www.thecanadianencyclopedia.ca/en/article/media-convergence

Gaudry, Adam. 2019. "Métis." Revised by M. A. Welch and D. Gallant. *Canadian Encyclopedia.* Historica Canada. www.thecanadianencyclopedia.ca/en/article/metis

Geddes, John. 2001. "Northern Son." *Maclean's*, April 23, 16–21.

Gervais, Stéphan, Christopher Kirkey, and Jarrett Rudy. 2011. *Quebec Questions: Quebec Studies for the Twenty-First Century.* Don Mills, ON: Oxford University Press.

Gibbins, Roger. 1979. *Prairie Politics and Society: Regionalism in Decline.* Toronto: Butterworths.

Gibson, Gordon. 1994. *Plan B: The Future of the Rest of Canada.* Vancouver: Fraser Institute.

Giddens, Anthony. 1984. *The Constitution of Society: Outline of the Theory of Structuration.* Cambridge, UK: Polity Press.

Giddens, Anthony. 1987. "Structuralism, Post-Structuralism, and the Production of Culture." In *Social Theory Today*, eds. A. Giddens and J. Turner, 195–223. Stanford, CA: Stanford University Press.

Giffen, Naomi Musmaker. 1930. *The Roles of Men and Women in Eskimo Culture*. Chicago: University of Chicago Press.

Gilbert, Martin. 1991. *The Second World War*. New York: Holt.

Gingras, Yves, and Jean-Philippe Warren. 2006. "A British Connection? A Quantitative Analysis of the Changing Relations between American, British, and Canadian Sociologists." *Canadian Journal of Sociology* 31(4): 509–522.

Giroux, Henry A. 2014. "Neoliberalism and the Machinery of Disposability." Truth-Out.Org, October 7. www.truth-out.org/opinion/item/22958-neoliberalism-and-the-machinery-of-disposability

Goffman, Erving. 1961. *Asylums*. Garden City, NY: Anchor Books.

Gonzalez, Roberto J. 2001. "Lynne Cheney-Joe Lieberman Group Puts Out a Blacklist." *San Jose Mercury News*, December 13.

Gordon, Walter. 1966. *A Choice for Canada: Independence or Colonial Status?* Toronto: McClelland & Stewart.

Government of Canada (Parks Canada). n.d. "The Spanish Flu in Canada (1918–1920)." www.pc.gc.ca/en/culture/clmhc-hsmbc/res/doc/information-backgrounder/espagnole-spanish

Government of Canada. 1963. *A Preliminary Report of the Royal Commission on Bilingualism and Biculturalism*. Ottawa: Queen's Printer.

Government of Canada. 1969. *The White Paper*. Statement of the Government of Canada on Indian Policy. Published under the Authority of the Honourable Jean Chrétien, Minister of Indian Affairs and Northern Development. Ottawa: Indian Affairs Branch.

Government of Canada. 1982. *The Canadian Constitution*. Ottawa: Public Works.

Government of Canada. 1983. *Indian Self-Government in Canada: Report of a Special Committee*. Ottawa: House of Commons.

Government of Canada. 2013a. "Facts and Figures 2012—Immigration Overview: Permanent and Temporary Residents."

Government of Canada (Global Affairs Canada). 2013b. "Canada and Trade in Services." www.international.gc.ca/trade-agreements-accords-commerciaux/topics-domaines/services/canada.aspx?lang=eng

Government of Canada. 2014. "Canada's Northern Strategy." Ottawa: Government of Canada. www.canada.ca/en/news/archive/2013/08/canada-northern-strategy.html

Government of Canada. 2016. "The Paris Agreement." www.canada.ca/en/environment-climate-change/services/climate-change/paris-agreement.html

Government of Canada. 2018. "CUSMA: Canada–United States–Mexico Agreement." www.international.gc.ca/trade-commerce/trade-agreements-accords-commerciaux/agr-acc/cusma-aceum/index.aspx?lang=eng

Government of Canada (Department of Finance) 2019a. "Updated—Countermeasures in Response to Unjustified Tariffs on Canadian Steel and Aluminum Products." www.canada.ca/en/department-finance/programs/international-trade-finance-policy/measures-steel-aluminum-businesses/countermeasures-response-unjustified-tariffs-canadian-steel-aluminum-products.html

Government of Canada. 2019b. "An Act respecting First Nations, Inuit and Métis children, youth and families." www.canada.ca/en/indigenous-services-canada/news/2019/02/an-act-respecting-first-nations-inuit-and-metis-children-youth-and-families.html

Government of Canada. 2019c. "Indigenous Languages Legislation." www.canada.ca/en/canadian-heritage/campaigns/celebrate-indigenous-languages/legislation.html

Government of Canada (Natural Resources Canada). 2020. "Crude Oil Facts." March 30. www.nrcan.gc.ca/science-data/data-analysis/energy-data-analysis/energy-facts/crude-oil-facts/20064

Government of Canada. 2021. *Coronavirus Disease (COVID-19)*. www.canada.ca/en/public-health/services/diseases/coronavirus-disease-covid-19.html

Government of Nunavut. 2014. "Climate Change Community Consultations." Government of Nunavut News Release, August 26. www.gov.nu.ca/eia/news/climate-change-community-consultations

Government of Quebec. 2008. "Building the Future: Abridged Report of the Bouchard-Taylor Commission." Quebec: Government of Quebec.

Government of Quebec. 2019. *Bill 21: An Act respecting the laicity of the State*. Quebec: Government of Quebec. www2.publicationsduquebec.gouv.qc.ca/dynamicSearch/telecharge.php?type=5&file=2019C12A.PDF

Government of the United States. 2002. *The National Security Strategy of the United States of America*. Washington: Government of the United States.

Grabb, Edward. 2000. "Defining Moments and Recurring Myths: Comparing Canadians and Americans after the American Revolution." *Canadian Review of Sociology and Anthropology* 37(4): 373–420.

Grabb, Edward, Douglas Baer, and James Curtis. 1999. "The Origins of American Individualism: Reconsidering the Historical Evidence." *Canadian Journal of Sociology* 24(4): 511–534.

Grabb, Edward, and James Curtis. 2005. *Regions Apart: The Four Societies of Canada and the United States*. Toronto: Oxford University Press.

Granatstein, Jack. 1996. *Yankee Go Home? Canadians and Anti-Americanism*. Toronto: HarperCollins Publishers.

Grant, Agnes. 1996. *No End of Grief: Indian Residential Schools in Canada*. Winnipeg: Pemmican Publications.

Grant, George. 2005. *Lament for a Nation: The Defeat of Canadian Nationalism*. 40th anniversary ed. Montreal and Kingston: McGill-Queen's University Press.

Gray, John. 1994. *Lost in North America: The Imaginary Canadian in the American Dream*. Vancouver: Talonbooks.

Green, Kenneth P. 2019. "Alberta's abandoned well needs tending." Fraser Institute, February. www.fraserinstitute.org/article/albertas-abandoned-wells-need-tending

Gregg, Allan. 2005. "Quebec's Final Victory." *The Walrus*, February, 50–61.

Gregoire, Lisa. 2007. "People of the Delta." *Canadian National Geographic* 127(3): 42–58.

GRES. 1997. "Immigration and Ethnic Relations in Quebec: Pluralism in the Making." In *Quebec Society: Critical Issues*, eds. M. Fournier, M. Rosenberg, and D. White, 95–122. Scarborough, ON: Prentice-Hall Canada.

Gresko, Jacqueline. 1986. "Creating Little Dominions within the Dominion: Early Catholic Indian Schools in Saskatchewan and British Columbia." In *Indian Education in Canada*, Vol. 1: *The Legacy*, eds. J. Barman, Y. Hébert, and D. McCaskill, 88–109. Vancouver: UBC Press.

Griffiths, Franklyn, Rob Huebert, and P. Whitney Lackenbauer. 2011. *Canada and the Changing Arctic: Sovereignty, Security, and Stewardship*. Waterloo, ON: Wilfrid Laurier University Press.

Griffiths, Rudyard. 2008. *We're Prying French and English Canada Apart*. Ottawa: The Dominion Institute.

Grossman, Zoltán, and Alan Parker, eds. 2013. *Asserting Native Resilience: Pacific Rim Indigenous Nations Face the Climate Crisis*. Corvallis, OR: Oregon State University Press.

Grunwald, Michael. 2002. "Security Fears Have US and Canada Rethinking Life on the Border." *Guardian Weekly*, January 10–16, 29.

Guevara, Che. 2003. *Che Guevara Reader: Writings on Politics & Revolution*. Ed. D. Deutschmann. Melbourne, Australia: Ocean Press.

Gunn, Kate, and Bruce McIvor. 2020. "The Wet'suwet'en, Aboriginal Title, and the Rule of Law: An Explainer." February 13.

Gwyn, Richard. 1996. *Nationalism without Walls: The Unbearable Lightness of Being Canadian*. Toronto: McClelland & Stewart.

Haig-Brown, Celia. 1993. *Resistance and Renewal: Surviving the Indian Residential School*. Vancouver: Tillacum Library.

Hall, D. J. 1977. "Clifford Sifton: Immigration and Settlement Policy, 1896–1905." In *Settlement of the West*, ed. H. Palmer, 60–85. Calgary: Comprint Publishing Company.

Hall, Rebecca Jane. 2019. "A Feminist Political Economy of Indigenous-State Relations in Northern Canada." In *Change and Continuity: Canadian Political Economy in the New Millennium*, eds. M. P. Thomas, L. F. Vosko, C. Fanelli, and O. Lyubchenko, 185-202. Montreal and Kingston: McGill-Queen's University Press.

Halliday, W. M. 1935. *Potlatch and Totem and the Recollections of an Indian Agent*. London, UK: J. M. Dent and Sons.

Hamelin, J. 1993. "What Middle Class?" In *Reappraisals in Canadian History: Pre-Confederation*, eds. A. D. Gilbert, G. M. Wallace, and R. M. Bray, 215–223. Scarborough, ON: Prentice-Hall Canada.

Hamilton, Graeme. 2014. "A Dying Dream: Most Quebec Voters Want Nothing to Do with Sovereignty." *National Post*, April 5. nationalpost.com/opinion/graeme-hamilton-a-dying-dream-most-quebec-voters-want-nothing-to-do-with-sovereignty

Hanks, Lucien M., Jr., and Jane Richardson Hanks. 1950. *A Study of the Blackfoot Reserve of Alberta*. Toronto: University of Toronto Press.

Hanohano, Peter. 1999. "The Spiritual Imperative of Native Epistemology: Restoring Harmony and Balance to Education." *Canadian Journal of Native Education* 23(2): 206–219.

Harkin, Michael E., and David Rich Lewis, eds. 2007. *Native Americans and the Environment: Perspectives on the Ecological Indian*. Lincoln, NE: University of Nebraska Press.

Harrison, Trevor. 1995. *Of Passionate Intensity: Right-Wing Populism and the Reform Party of Canada*. Toronto: University of Toronto Press.

Harrison, Trevor. 1996. "Class, Citizenship, and Global Migration: The Case of the Canadian Business Immigration Program." *Canadian Public Policy* 22(1): 7–23.

Harrison, Trevor. 1999. "Globalization and the Trade in Human Body Parts." *Canadian Review of Sociology and Anthropology* 36(1): 21–36.

Harrison, Trevor. 2000. "The Changing Face of Prairie Politics: Populism in Alberta." *Prairie Forum* 25(1): 107–122.

Harrison, Trevor. 2002. *Requiem for a Lightweight: Stockwell Day and Image Politics*. Montreal: Black Rose.

Harrison, Trevor. 2007. "Anti-Canadianism: Explaining the Deep Roots of a Shallow Phenomenon." *International Journal of Canadian Studies* 35: 217–240.

Harrison, Trevor. 2012. "Resources and the Northern Colonies." Presentation to the 16th Annual Parkland Institute Conference, Edmonton, Alberta, November 24.

Harrison, Trevor W. 2016. "A Tale of Two (Global) Cities: London, New York, and the Rise of Finance Capital." In *International Political Economy*, eds. G. Anderson and C. Kukucha, 311–328. Oxford: Oxford University Press.

Harrison, Trevor, and Harvey Krahn. Unpublished. *Provincial Versus National Identity in Alberta*.

Hawthorn, Harry B. 1966/1967. *A Survey of the Contemporary Indians of Canada*, Parts I and II. Ottawa: Indian Affairs.

Heath, Joseph. 2013. "In Defence of Sociology." *Ottawa Citizen*, April 30. spon.ca/in-defence-of-sociology/2013/05/01/

Hedges, Christopher. 2009. *Empire of Illusion: The End of Literacy and the Triumph of Spectacle*. Toronto: Vintage.

Hedges, Christopher. 2010. *Death of the Liberal Class*. Toronto: Vintage.

Heilbroner, Eric. 1992. *Twenty-First Century Capitalism*. Concord, ON: Anansi.

Helin, Calvin. 2006. *Dances with Dependency: Indigenous Success through Self-Reliance*. Vancouver: Orca Spirit Publications and Communications.

Hemberger, Suzette. 1993. "Constitution." In *The Oxford Companion to Politics of the World*, ed. J. Krieger, 189–190. Oxford, UK: Oxford University Press.

Henderson, Robert, ed. n.d. *A Soldier's Account of the Campaign on Quebec, 1759*. Taken from *A Journal of the Expedition up the River St. Lawrence*. Originally published in 1759. Manotick, ON: Discriminating General.

Heron, Craig, and Robert Storey. 1986. "On the Job in Canada." In *On the Job*, eds. C. Heron and R. Storey, 3–46. Montreal and Kingston: McGill-Queen's University Press.

Hicks, Jack. 2013. "The Dissociative State of Nunavut." *Canadian Dimension* 47(31): 14–15.

Hiller, Harry. 1987. "The Foundation and Politics of Separation: Canada in Comparative Perspective." *Research in Political Sociology* 3: 39–60.

Hobbes, Thomas. 2014. *Leviathan*. Ed. N. Malcolm. Originally published in 1651. Toronto: Oxford University Press.

Hobsbawm, Eric. 1992. *Nations and Nationalism since 1780*. 2nd ed. Cambridge, UK: Cambridge University Press.

Hobsbawm, Eric. 1995. *Age of Extremes: The Short Twentieth Century, 1914–1991*. London, UK: Abacus.

Hofstadter, Richard, ed. 1958. *Great Issues in American History*, Vol. I: *1765–1865*. New York: Vintage Books.

Hofstadter, Richard, William Miller, and Daniel Aaron. 1957. *The United States: The History of a Republic*. Englewood Cliffs, NJ: Prentice-Hall.

Holloway, John. 1994. "Global Capital and the National State." *Capital and Class* 18(1): 23-49.

Homer-Dixon, Thomas. 2020. "Coronavirus Will Change the World. It Might Also Lead to a Better Future." *Globe and Mail*, March 5.

Honan, William. 1998. "Historians Warming to Games of 'What If?'" *New York Times*, January 7, B7.

Hood, Duncan. 2008. "How Canada Stole the American Dream." *Maclean's*, July 7, 51–54.

Horowitz, Gad. 1966. "Conservatism, Liberalism, and Socialism in Canada: An Interpretation." *Canadian Journal of Economic and Political Science* 32: 143–171.

Horsman, Reginald. 1993. "On to Canada: Manifest Destiny and United States Strategy in the War of 1812." In *Reappraisals in Canadian History: Pre-Confederation*, eds. A. D. Gilbert, G. M. Wallace, and R. M. Bray, 272–291. Scarborough, ON: Prentice-Hall Canada.

House, John D. 1978. *The Last of the Free Enterprisers*. Toronto: MacMillan of Canada.

Howard, V. 1999. "Unemployment Relief Camps." *Canadian Encyclopedia*. Year 2000 ed. Toronto: McClelland & Stewart.

Hufbauer, Gary C., and Jeffrey J. Schott. 2004. "The Prospects for Deeper North American Integration." *The Border Papers* 195 (January). Toronto: C. D. Howe Institute.

Hum, Derek. 1983. *Federalism and the Poor: A Review of the Canada Assistance Plan*. Toronto: Ontario Economic Council.

Hylton, John H. 1999. "Future Prospects for Aboriginal Self-Government in Canada." In *Aboriginal Self-Government in Canada*, 432–455. Saskatoon: Purich.

Ibbitson, John. 2001. *Loyal No More: Ontario's Struggle for a Separate Destiny*. Toronto: HarperCollins.

Ibbitson, John. 2009. *Open and Shut: Why America Has Barack Obama, and Canada Has Stephen Harper*. Toronto: McClelland & Stewart.

Igartua, José E. 2006. *The Other Quiet Revolution: National Identities in English Canada, 1945–71*. Vancouver: UBC Press.

Ignatieff, Michael. 1993. *Blood and Belonging: Journeys into the New Nationalism*. Toronto: Penguin.

Ignatieff, Michael. 2009. *True Patriot Love: Four Generations in Search of Canada*. Toronto: Viking.

Indian Chiefs of Alberta. 1970. *Citizens Plus: A Presentation by the Indian Chiefs of Alberta to the Right Honourable P.E. Trudeau, Prime Minister and the Government of Canada*, a.k.a. "The Red Paper." Edmonton: Indian Association of Alberta.

Indigenous Economy Report. n.d. *Look North*. A joint report of Manitoba's Rural Development Institute, Brandon University, and the Manitoba Keewatinowi Okimakanak Inc. www.brandonu.ca/rdi/files/2019/04/Look-North-Ind-Econ-FINAL-compress.pdf

Indigenous and Northern Affairs Canada. 2017. "Urban reserves." April 11. www.aadnc-aandc.gc.ca/eng/1100100016331/1100100016332

Innis, Harold. 1956. "Great Britain, the United States, and Canada." In *Essays in Canadian Economic History*, ed. M. Q. Innis, 394–412. Toronto: University of Toronto Press.

Innis, Harold. 1962. *The Fur Trade in Canada*. Toronto: University of Toronto Press.

Innis, Harold. 1995. "Recent Trends in Canadian-American Relations." In *Staples, Markets, and Cultural Change: Selected Essays*, ed. D. Drache, 262–270. Montreal and Kingston: McGill-Queen's University Press.

Inuit Tapiriit Kanatami. 2018. *Inuit Statistical Profile 2018*. www.itk.ca/wp-content/uploads/2018/08/Inuit-Statistical-Profile.pdf

Irwin, R. Stephen. 1994. *The Indian Hunters*. Blaine, WA: Hancock House.

Ives, John W. 1990. *A Theory of Northern Athapaskan Prehistory*. Boulder, CO: Westview Press.

Ivison, John. 2020. "Canadians Had Better Brace Themselves for an Alarming New Post-COVID Economic World." *National Post*, April 3.

Jaenen, Cornelius. 1986. "Education for Francization: The Case of New France in the Seventeenth Century." In *Indian Education in Canada*, Vol. I: *The Legacy*, eds. J. Barman, Y. Hébert, and D. McCaskill, 45–63. Vancouver: UBC Press.

James, Lawrence. 1997. *The Rise and Fall of the British Empire*. London, UK: Abacus.

Jang, Brent, and Mike Hager. 2020. "Indigenous Supporters of Coastal GasLink Speak Out on Division and Backlash." *Globe and Mail*, February 22, A13.

Jaszi, Oszkar. 1961. *The Dissolution of the Habsburg Monarchy*. Originally published in 1929. Chicago: University of Chicago Press.

Jennings, Jesse D. 1978. *Ancient Native Americans*. San Francisco: W. H. Freeman and Company.

Jensen, Joan. M. 1988. *Passage from Indian: Asian Indian Immigrants in North America*. New Haven, CT: Yale University Press.

Jessop, Bob. 1993. "Towards a Schumpeterian Workface State? Preliminary Remarks on Post-Fordist Political Economy." *Studies in Political Economy* 40: 7–39.

Johnson, Chalmers. 2006. *Nemesis: The Last Days of the American Republic*. New York: Holt.

Johnston, Basil. 1995. *The Manitous: The Spiritual World of the Ojibway*. Toronto: Key Porter Books.

Johnston, Charles M., ed. 1964. *The Valley of the Six Nations: A Collection of Documents on the Indian Lands of the Grand River*. Toronto: University of Toronto Press.

Johnston, Darlene. 1989. *The Taking of Indian Lands in Canada: Consent or Coercion?* Saskatoon: University of Saskatchewan Native Law Centre.

Jones, Jeffrey. 2020. "Idle Wells, Tailings Ponds Are Alberta's Mess." *Globe and Mail*, February 1, B4.

Josephy, Alvin M., Jr. 1968. *The Indian Heritage of America*. New York: Alfred A. Knopf.

Kaye, Julie, and Daniel Béland. 2014. "Stephen Harper's Dangerous Refusal to 'Commit Sociology.'" *Toronto Star*, August 22. www.thestar.com/opinion/commentary/2014/08/22/stephen_harpers_dangerous_refusal_to_commit_sociology.html

Keegan, John. 1990. *The Second World War*. New York: Penguin.

Kelly, W. E. 1997. "Canada's Black Defenders." *The Beaver* 77(2): 31–34.

Keohane, Robert O. 2002. "The Globalization of Informal Violence: Theories of World Politics, and the 'Liberalism of Fear'." *Dialogue IO* (Spring): 29–43.

Kilpatrick, Sean. 2014. "Suicide Claims More Soldiers than Those Killed by Afghan Combat." *Toronto Star*, September 17. www.thestar.com/news/canada/2014/09/16/suicide_claims_more_soldiers_than_those_killed_by_afghan_combat.html

King, A. Richard. 1967. *The School at Mopass: A Problem of Identity*. New York: Holt, Rinehart, and Winston.

King, Thomas. 2012. *The Inconvenient Indian: A Curious Account of Native People in North America*. Toronto: Doubleday Canada.

Kirkness, Verna J. 1998a. "Our Peoples' Education: Cut the Shackles; Cut the Crap; Cut the Mustard." *Canadian Journal of Native Education* 22(1): 10–15.

Kirkness, Verna J. 1998b. "The Critical State of Aboriginal Languages in Canada." *Canadian Journal of Native Education* 22(1): 93–107.

Klein, Naomi. 2014. *This Changes Everything*. Toronto: A. A. Knopf Canada.

Knuttila, Murray. 2002. *Introducing Sociology: A Critical Perspective*. Toronto: Oxford University Press.

Knuttila, Murray, and Wendee Kubik. 2000. *State Theories: Classical, Global, and Feminist Perspectives*. Halifax: Fernwood.

Korten, David. 2001. *When Corporations Rule the World*. 2nd ed. San Francisco: Berrett-Koehler.

Krahn, Harvey, Trevor Harrison, Michael Haan, and William Johnston. 2009. "Social Capital and Democratic Political Engagement." *International Journal of Contemporary Sociology* 46(1): 51–76.

Krahn, Harvey, K. D. Hughes, and G. Lowe. 2020. *Work, Industry, and Canadian Society*. 8th ed. Toronto: Nelson.

Krasowski, Sheldon. 2019. *No Surrender: The Land Remains Indigenous*. Regina: University of Regina Press.

Krech, Shepard, III. 1999. *The Ecological Indian: Myth and History*. New York: Norton.

Krotz, Larry. 1990. *Indian Country: Inside Another Canada*. Toronto: McClelland & Stewart.

Kulchyski, Peter. 2005. *Like the Sound of a Drum: Aboriginal Cultural Politics in Denendeh and Nunavut*. Winnipeg: University of Manitoba Press.

Kulchyski, Peter. 2013. "Focus: The North." *Canadian Dimension* 47(31): 13.

Kurth, James. 1993. "Military-Industrial Complex." In *The Oxford Companion to Politics of the World*, ed. J. Krieger, 587–588. Oxford, UK: Oxford University Press.

La Haye, Laura. 1993. "Mercantilism." In *The Fortune Encyclopedia of Economics*, ed. D. R. Henderson, 534–538. New York: Warner Books.

Lairson, T. D., and D. Skidmore. 1997. *International Political Economy: The Struggle for Power and Wealth*. Toronto: Harcourt Brace.

Lane, Jan-Erik, and Svante O. Ersson. 1994. *Politics and Society in Western Europe*. London, UK: Sage.

Langer, W. L. 1948. *An Encyclopedia of World History*. Boston: Houghton Mifflin Company.

Laurendeau, André. 1985. "The Conditions for the Existence of a National Culture." In *Canadian Political Thought*, ed. H. D. Forbes, 255–269. Toronto: Oxford University Press.

Laviolette, Gontran. 1991. *The Dakota Sioux in Canada*. Winnipeg: DLM Publications.

Laxer, Emily. 2017. *Unveiling the Nation: The Politics of Secularism in France and Quebec*. Montreal and Kingston: McGill-Queen's University Press.

Laxer, Gordon. 1989. *Open for Business: The Roots of Foreign Ownership in Canada*. Toronto: Oxford University Press.

Laxer, Gordon, ed. 1991. *Perspectives on Canadian Economic Development*. Toronto: Oxford University Press.

Laxer, Gordon. 1992. "Distinct Status for Quebec: A Benefit to English Canada." *Constitutional Forum* 3(3): 57–61.

Laxer, Gordon. 1995. "Social Solidarity, Democracy, and Global Capitalism." *Canadian Review of Sociology and Anthropology* 32(3): 287–314.

Laxer, Gordon. 2000. "Surviving the Americanizing Right." *Canadian Review of Sociology and Anthropology* 37(1): 55–76.

Laxer, Gordon. 2002. "Alternatives to Secession." *Review of Constitutional Studies* 7(1/2): 272–293.

Laxer, Gordon. 2010. "Superpower, Middle Power, or Satellite? Canadian Energy and Environmental Policy." In *Canada's Foreign and Security Policy: Soft and Hard Strategies of a Middle Power*, eds. N. Hynek and D. Bosold, 138–161. Toronto: Oxford University Press Canada.

Laxer, Gordon, and John Dillon. 2008. *Over a Barrel: Exiting from NAFTA's Proportionality Clause*. Edmonton: Parkland Institute.

Laxer, Gordon, and Trevor Harrison, eds. 1995. *The Trojan Horse: Alberta and the Future of Canada*. Montreal: Black Rose.

Laxer, James. 2004. *The Border*. Toronto: Anchor.

Lee, Marc. 2012. "Northern Gateway Pipeline Jobs Far from the Number Promised." *CCPA Monitor* 19(1): 12–13.

Léger Marketing. 2008. "Referendum Voting Intentions in Quebec." Montreal: Léger Marketing.

Lemmen, Don, and Fiona Warren. 2004. *Climate Change Impacts and Adaptation: A Canadian Perspective*. Ottawa: Government of Canada.

LePan, Nicholas. 2020. "Visualizing the History of Pandemics." *Healthcare*, March 14. www.visualcapitalist.com/history-of-pandemics-deadliest/

Levant, Ezra. 2011. *Ethical Oil: The Case for Canada's Oil Sands*. Toronto: McClelland & Stewart.

Levitt, Kari. 1970. *Silent Surrender: The Multinational Corporation in Canada*. Toronto: Macmillan of Canada.

Li, Peter. 1996. *The Making of Post-War Canada*. Toronto: Oxford University Press.

Lian, Jason Z., and David Ralph Matthews. 1998. "Does the Vertical Mosaic Still Exist? Ethnicity and Income in Canada, 1991." *Canadian Review of Sociology and Anthropology* 35(4): 461–482.

Lincoln, Kenneth. 1985. *Native American Renaissance*. Berkeley, CA: University of California Press.

Linnitt, Carol. 2013. "Harper's Attack on Science: No Science, No Evidence, No Truth, No Democracy." *Academic Matters: OCUFA's Journal of Higher Education* (May). www.academicmatters.ca/2013/05/harpers-attack-on-science-no-science-no-evidence-no-truth-no-democracy

Lipset, Seymour M. 1968a. *Agrarian Socialism: The Co-operative Commonwealth Federation in Saskatchewan*. Garden City, NY: Doubleday.

Lipset, Seymour M. 1968b. *Revolution and Counter-Revolution*. New York: Basic Books.

Lipset, Seymour M. 1986. "Historical Conditions and National Characteristics." *Canadian Journal of Sociology* 11(2): 113–155.

Lipset, Seymour M. 1990. *Continental Divide*. New York: Routledge.

Lipset, Seymour M. 1996. *American Exceptionalism: A Double-Edged Sword*. New York: W. W. Norton.

Lowe, Graham S. 1987. *Women in the Administrative Revolution*. Toronto: University of Toronto Press.

Lower, Arthur R. M. 1977. *Colony to Nation: A History of Canada*. Toronto: McClelland & Stewart.

Lower, J. Arthur. 1983. *Western Canada: An Outline History*. Vancouver: Douglas & McIntyre.

Lynch, Laura. 2013. "BC's Nisga'a Becomes Only First Nation to Privatize Land." *CBC News*, November 4. www.cbc.ca/news/canada/british-columbia/b-c-s-nisga-a-becomes-only-first-nation-to-privatize-land-1.2355794

Lyon, John Tylor. 1998. "'A Picturesque Lot': The Gypsies of Peterborough." *The Beaver* 78(5): 25–30.

Macdonald, David. 2019. *Fail Safe: CEO Compensation in Canada*. Ottawa: Canadian Centre for Policy Alternatives.

Macdonald, Nancy. 2020. "Second Wet'suwet'en Hereditary Subchief Speaks Out against Protest Leaders." *Globe and Mail*, February 23.

Maclean's. 2000. "Trudeau: His Life and Legacy." Special commemorative ed. Toronto: Maclean's.

Maclean's. 2014. "Economy Trumps Climate Change Actions, PM Says," June 9. www.macleans.ca/news/canada/economy-trumps-climate-change-actions-pm-says

Maclean's. 2016. "Statistics Canada Eyes the End of the Short-Form Census," September 25, 36.

MacLennan, Hugh. 1959. *The Watch That Ends the Night*. Toronto: Macmillan.

MacLennan, Hugh. 1974. *The Rivers of Canada*. Toronto: Macmillan of Canada.

MacLennan, Hugh. 1998. *Two Solitudes*. Toronto: Stoddart.

Maclure, Jocelyn. 2011. "Quebec's Culture War: Two Conceptions of Quebec Identity." In *Quebec Questions: Quebec Studies for the Twenty-First Century*, eds. S. Gervais, C. Kirkey, and J. Rudy, 137–148. Don Mills, ON: Oxford University Press.

MacMillan, Margaret. 2008. *The Uses and Abuses of History*. Toronto: Viking.

Manchester, William. 1992. *A World Lit Only by Fire: The Medieval Mind and the Renaissance*. Boston: Little, Brown.

Mann, Michael. 2008. "American Empires: Past and Present." *Canadian Review of Sociology* 45(1): 7–50.

Marchak, M. Patricia. 1988. *Ideological Perspectives on Canada*. Toronto: McGraw-Hill Ryerson.

Marchildon, Gregory. 1995. "From Pax Britannica to Pax Americana and Beyond." In *Being and Becoming Canada: The Annals of the American Academy of Political and Social Science* 538, eds. C. Doran and E. Babby, 151–169.

Margolis, Eric. 2008. "Time to Face Facts in Afghanistan." *Toronto Star*, October 6.

Marker, Michael. 2000. "Economics and Local Self-Determination: Describing the Clash Zone in First Nations Education." *Canadian Journal of Native Education* 24(1): 30–44.

Marquis, Greg. 2000. *In Armageddon's Shadow: The Civil War and Canada's Maritime Provinces*. Kingston and Montreal: McGill-Queen's University Press.

Marsden, William. 2007. *Stupid to the Last Drop: How Alberta Is Bringing Environmental Armageddon to Canada (and Doesn't Seem to Care)*. Toronto: Alfred A. Knopf.

Martin, Ged. 1993a. "The Influence of the Durham Report." In *Reappraisals in Canadian History: Pre-Confederation*, eds. A. D. Gilbert, G. M. Wallace, and R. M. Bray, 437–448. Scarborough, CA: Prentice-Hall Canada.

Martin, Ged. 1993b. "History as Science or Literature: Explaining Canadian Confederation." In *Reappraisals in Canadian History: Pre-Confederation*, eds. A. D. Gilbert, G. M. Wallace, and R. M. Bray, 543–570. Scarborough, ON: Prentice-Hall Canada.

Martin, Lawrence. 1982. *The Presidents and Prime Ministers*. Markham, ON: Paper Jacks.

Martin, Lawrence. 1993. *Pledge of Allegiance: The Americanization of Canada during the Mulroney Years*. Toronto: McClelland & Stewart.

Martin, Lawrence. 1999. "Canada Was on the Brink of Civil Strife Four Years Ago." *Edmonton Journal*, A19.

Marx, Karl. 1977a. "The Communist Manifesto." In *Karl Marx: Selected Writings*, ed. D. McLellan, 221–268. Oxford, UK: Oxford University Press.

Marx, Karl. 1977b. "Theses on Feuerbach." In *Karl Marx: Selected Writings*, ed. D. McLellan, 156–158. Oxford, UK: Oxford University Press.

Marx, Karl. 1977c. "The Eighteenth Brumaire of Louis Napoleon." In *Karl Marx: Selected Writings*, ed. D. McLellan, 300–325. Oxford, UK: Oxford University Press.

Massey, Don, and Patricia N. Shields. 1995. *Canada: Its Land and People*. 2nd ed. Edmonton: Reidmore Books.

Mayes, Hubert G. 1999. "Resurrection: Tolstoy and Canada's Doukhobors." *The Beaver* 79(5): 39–44.

McBride, Stephen, and Heather Whiteside. 2011. *Private Affluence, Public Austerity: Economic Crisis and Democratic Malaise in Canada*. Halifax: Fernwood.

McCall-Newman, Christina. 1982. *Grits: An Intimate Portrait of the Liberal Party*. Toronto: Macmillan of Canada.

McCallum, John. 1991. "Agriculture and Economic Development in Quebec and Ontario until 1870." In *Perspectives on Canadian Economic Development*, ed. G. Laxer, 10–20. Toronto: Oxford University Press.

McCue, William Westaway. 1999. "Crossing the Line." *The Beaver* 79(1): 16–21.

McDaniel, Susan, and Heidi MacDonald. 2012. "To Know Ourselves—Not." *Canadian Journal of Sociology* 37(3): 253–272.

McDonald, Kevin. 1994. "Globalisation, Multiculturalism and Rethinking the Social." *Australian–New Zealand Journal of Sociology* 30(3): 239–247.

McDonnell, R. F., and R. C. Depew. 1999. "Self-Government and Self-Determination in Canada: A Critical Commentary." In *Aboriginal Self-Government in Canada*, ed. J. H. Hylton, 352–376. Saskatoon: Purich.

McDougall, John. 1903. *In the Days of the Red River Rebellion*. Toronto: William Briggs.

McGaa, Eagle Man, ed. 1990. *Mother Earth Spirituality: Native American Paths to Healing Ourselves and Our World*. New York: HarperCollins.

McGaa, Eagle Man, ed. 1995. *Native Wisdom: Perceptions of the Natural Way*. Minneapolis: Four Directions Publishing.

McKay, Ian, and Jamie Swift. 2012. *Warrior Nation: Rebranding Canada in an Age of Anxiety*. Halifax: Between the Lines.

McKie, Craig. 1994. "A History of Emigration from Canada." *Canadian Social Trends* 35: 26–29.

McLaughlin, Neil. 2019. "The 'Sociology Wars' in Canada." *Global Dialogue* 9(3). globaldialogue. isa-sociology.org/the-sociology-wars-in-canada/

McMillan, Alan, D. 1995. *Native Peoples and Cultures of Canada*. 2nd ed. Vancouver: Douglas & McIntyre.

McNally, David. 2010. *Global Slump: The Economics and Politics of Crisis and Resistance*. Oakland, CA: PM Press.

McPherson, James. 1998. "Quebec Whistles Dixie." *Saturday Night* (March): 13–14, 18, 20, 22–23, 72.

Meekison, J. Peter. 1993. "Canada's Quest for Constitutional Perfection." *Constitutional Forum* 4(2): 55–59.

Meili, Dianne. 2012. *Those Who Know: Profiles of Alberta's Aboriginal Elders.* Edmonton, AB: NeWest Press.

Melling, John. 1967. *Right to a Future: The Native Peoples of Canada.* Toronto: T. H. Best Printing Co.

Mercredi, Ovide, and Mary Ellen Turpel. 1993. *In the Rapids: Navigating the Future of First Nations.* Toronto: Viking Press.

Merkur, Daniel. 1991. *Powers Which We Do Not Know: The Gods and Spirits of the Inuit.* Moscow, ID: University of Idaho Press.

Merriam-Webster, Incorporated. 2003. *Merriam-Webster's Collegiate Dictionary.* 10th ed. Springfield, MA: Merriam-Webster.

Merton, Robert. 1968. *Social Theory and Social Structure.* New York: The Free Press.

Miliband, Ralph. 1969. *The State in Capitalist Society.* New York: Basic Books.

Miller, Alan D. 1988. *Native Peoples and Cultures of Canada.* Vancouver: Douglas & McIntyre.

Miller, Carman. 1999. "Canada's First War." *The Beaver* 79(5): 6–7.

Miller, J. R. 1987. "The Irony of Residential Schooling." *Canadian Journal of Native Education* 14(2): 3–14.

Miller, J. R. 2000. *Skyscrapers Hide the Heavens: A History of Indian-White Relations in Canada.* 3rd ed. Toronto: University of Toronto Press.

Mills, C. Wright. 1956. *The Power Elite.* Oxford, UK: Oxford University Press.

Mills, C. Wright. 1961. *The Sociological Imagination.* New York: Grove Press.

Mills, Sean. 2005. "Modern, Postmodern, and Post-Postmodern." *The Beaver* (April/May): 11–12.

Milne, Seumas. 2008. "Civilian Dead Are a Trade-Off in Nato's War of Barbarity." *Guardian Weekly*, October 16.

Milot, Micheline. 2011. "That Priest-Ridden Province? Politics and Religion in Quebec." In *Quebec Questions: Quebec Studies for the Twenty-First Century*, eds. S. Gervais, C. Kirkey, and J. Rudy, 123–136. Don Mills, ON: Oxford University Press.

Mirrlees, Tanner. 2019. "A Political Economy of the Cultural Industries in Canada." In *Change and Continuity: Canadian Political Economy in the New Millennium*, eds. M. P. Thomas, L. F. Vosko, C. Fanelli, and O. Lyubchenko, 203–228. Montreal and Kingston: McGill-Queen's University Press.

Mittelman, J. H. 1996. "The Dynamics of Globalization." In *Globalization: Critical Reflections*, 1–19. International Political Economy Yearbook, Vol. 9. Boulder, CO: Lynne Rienner Publishers.

Moffett, Samuel E. 1972. *The Americanization of Canada.* Originally published in 1908. Toronto: University of Toronto Press.

Momatiuk, Yva, and John Eastcott. 1995. "'Nunavut' Means 'Our Land.'" *Native Peoples* 9(1): 42–48.

Monahan, Patrick. 1995. *Cooler Heads Shall Prevail: Assessing the Costs and Consequences of Quebec Separation.* Toronto: C. D. Howe Institute.

Monbiot, George. 2020. "Covid-19 Is Nature's Wake-Up Call to Complacent Civilization." *Guardian Weekly*, March 20.

Montgomery, Charles. 2007. "When Mountains Crumble." *Canadian National Geographic* 127(3): 68–78.

Moore, Christopher. 1997. *1867: How the Fathers Made a Deal*. Toronto: McClelland & Stewart.

Moore, Christopher. 2012. "Colonization and Conflict: New France and Its Rivals (1600–1760)." In *The Illustrated History of Canada*, ed. Craig Brown, 95–180. Toronto: Key Porter Books.

Moore, Dene. 2019. "Post NAFTA Post-Mortem: Is Canada Better Off under the New, Less Catchy CUSMA." *Globe and Mail*, October 28. www.theglobeandmail.com/featured-reports/article-post-nafta-post-mortem-is-canada-better-off-under-the-new-less/

Morency, Jean-Dominique, Éric Caron-Malenfant, Simon Coulombe, and Stéphanie Langlois. 2015. "Projections of the Aboriginal population and households in Canada." Tables: 91-552-X, September 17. Ottawa: Statistics Canada. www150.statcan.gc.ca/n1/en/catalogue/91-552-X

Morissette, Rene, and Xuelin Zhang. 2001. "Experiencing Low Income for Several Years." *Perspectives* (Summer): 25–35. Cat. no. 75-001-XPE. Ottawa: Statistics Canada.

Morrison, Ian A. 2019. *Moments of Crisis: Religion and National Identity in Quebec*. Vancouver: UBC Press.

Morrow, Ray. 1994. "History of Sociological Theory." In *An Introduction to Sociology*, eds. W. Meloff and D. Pierce, 1–22. Scarborough, ON: Nelson.

Morton, Desmond. 1997. *A Short History of Canada*. Edmonton: Hurtig Publishers.

Morton, Desmond. 2000. "1900: A New Century Begins." *The Beaver* 79(6): 23–29.

Morton, William Lewis. 1970. "The Battle at Grand Coteau, July 13 and 14, 1851." In *Historical Essays on the Prairie Provinces*, ed. D. Swainson, 45–59. Toronto: McClelland & Stewart.

Mowat, Farley. 1952. *People of the Deer*. Toronto: McClelland & Stewart.

Mulgrew, Ian. 2014. "First Nations Mistaken in Their Celebration of Supreme Court Ruling." *Vancouver Sun*, June 29. www.vancouversun.com/life/Mulgrew+First+Nations+mistaken+their+celebration+Supreme+Court/9986954/story.html

Murray, Jane Lothian, Rick Linden, and Diana Kendall. 2017. *Sociology in Our Times*. 7th Canadian ed. Toronto: Nelson.

Nakhaie, M. Reza. 1997. "Vertical Mosaic among the Elites: The New Imagery Revisited." *Canadian Review of Sociology and Anthropology* 34(1): 1–24.

National Aeronautics and Space Administration (NASA). 2020a. *Climate Change: How Do We Know?* climate.nasa.gov/evidence/

National Aeronautics and Space Administration (NASA). 2020b. *Global Temperature*. Updated April 7. www.climate.nasa.gov/vital-signs/global-temperature/

National Collaborating Centre for Aboriginal Health. 2013. "An overview of Aboriginal health in Canada." www.ccnsa-nccah.ca/docs/context/FS-OverviewAbororiginalHealth-EN.pdf

National Post. 2015. "Supreme Court Says Alberta Doesn't Have to Make Its Laws in Both English and French." November 20. nationalpost.com/news/canada/supreme-court-says-alberta-doesnt-have-to-make-its-laws-in-both-english-and-french

National Post. 2020. "World Economic Forum Research: It's Easier to Get Ahead in Canada than in the US." January 21.

Naylor, R. T. 1975. *The History of Canadian Business, 1867–1914*, 2 vols. Toronto: Lorimer.

Nemni, Max, and Monique Nemni. 2006. *Young Trudeau: 1919–1944: Son of Quebec, Father of Canada*. Toronto: Douglas Gibson.

Nevitte, Neil. 1996. *The Decline of Deference*. Peterborough, ON: Broadview Press.

Newman, Peter C. 1998. *Empire of the Bay: The Company of Adventurers That Seized a Continent.* Toronto: Penguin Books.

Newman, Zoë. 2012. "Bodies, Genders, Sexualities: Counting Past Two." In *Power and Everyday Practices*, eds. D. Brock, R. Raby, and M. P. Thomas, 61–85. Toronto: Nelson.

Nikiforuk, Andrew. 2010. *Tar Sands: Dirty Oil and the Future of a Continent.* Vancouver: Greystone.

Nikiforuk, Andrew. 2012. *The Energy of Slaves: Oil and the New Servitude.* Vancouver: Greystone.

Nisga'a Lisims Government. 2013. "Supreme Court of Canada refuses to hear challenge to the constitutionality of the Nisga's Treaty." August 22. www.nisgaanation.ca/news/ supreme-court-canada-refuses-hear-challenge-constitutionality-nisgaa-treaty

Norrie, Ken, and Douglas Owram. 1996. *The History of the Canadian Economy.* 2nd ed. Toronto: Harcourt Brace and Company, Canada.

Northwest Territories Bureau of Statistics. 2017. "Indigenous Peoples." Data generated from Statistics Canada Census 2006 and 2016. www.statsnwt.ca/census/2016/Indigenous_ Peoples_2016_Census.pdf

Nunatsiaq News. 2019. "Homicide in Northern Canada: It's Who You Know, StatsCan Says." December 3. www.nunatsiaq.com/stories/article/homicide-in-northern-canada-its-who-you-know-statcan-says/

O'Connor, Tom. 2018. "US Has Spent Six Trillion Dollars on Wars That Killed Half a Million People since 9/11, Report Says." *Newsweek*, November 14.

Office of the United States Trade Representative. 2019. "Canada: US-Canada Trade Facts." ustr. gov/countries-regions/americas/canada

O'Hara, Jane. 2000. "Abuse of Trust." *Maclean's*, June 26, 16–21.

Ohmae, Kenichi. 1990. *The Borderless World: Power and Strategy in the Interlinked Economy.* New York: Harper Business.

Ohmae, Kenichi. 1995. *The End of the Nation State: The Rise of Regional Economies.* New York: The Free Press.

Oil Sands Magazine. 2018. "Oil Sands Pricing Differentials Explained." December 13. www. oilsandsmagazine.com/market-insights/crude-oil-pricing-differentials-why-alberta-crude-sells-at-deep-discount-to-wti

Oil Sands Magazine. 2020. "Oil and Gas Prices." www.oilsandsmagazine.com/energy-statistics/ oil-and-gas-prices

Olsen, Gregg. 2002. *The Politics of the Welfare State: Canada, Sweden, and the United States.* Oxford, UK: Oxford University Press.

Orchard, David. 1998. *The Fight for Canada.* 2nd ed. Westmount, QC: Robert Davies Multimedia Publishing.

Orum, Anthony M., and John G. Dale. 2009. *Political Sociology: Power and Participation in the Modern World.* 5th ed. Oxford, UK: Oxford University Press.

Orwell, George. 2008. *1984.* Toronto: Penguin.

Osberg, Lars, ed. 2003. *The Economic Implications of Social Cohesion.* Toronto: University of Toronto Press.

Osborn, Kevin. 1990. *The Peoples of the Arctic.* New York: Chelsea House.

Ostler, Jeffrey. 2020. "The Shameful Final Grievance of the Declaration of Independence." *The Atlantic*, February 8. www.theatlantic.com/ideas/archive/2020/02/americas-twofold-original-sin/606163

Ouellet, Fernand. 1993. "The 1837/38 Rebellions in Lower Canada as a Social Phenomenon." In *Reappraisals in Canadian History: Pre-Confederation*, eds. A. D. Gilbert, G. M. Wallace, and R. M. Bray, 356–379. Scarborough, ON: Prentice-Hall Canada.

Oxfam International. 2020. World's Billionaires Have More Wealth Than 4.6 Billion People. January 20. www.oxfam.org/en/press-releases/worlds-billionaires-have-more-wealth-46-billion-people

Palmer, Howard. 1982. *Patterns of Prejudice: A History of Nativism in Alberta*. Toronto: McClelland & Stewart.

Palmer, R. R., with Joel Colton. 1957. *A History of the Modern World*. New York: Alfred A. Knopf.

Panitch, Leo. 1977. *The Canadian State: Political Economy and Political Power*. Toronto: University of Toronto Press.

Panitch, Leo. 1981. "Dependency and Class in Canadian Political Economy." *Studies in Political Economy* 6: 7–33.

Panitch, Leo, and Sam Gindin. 2012. *The Making of Global Capitalism: The Political Economy of American Empire*. London, UK: Verso.

Panitch, Leo, and Donald Swartz. 1988. *The Assault on Trade Union Freedoms: From Consent to Coercion Revisited*. Toronto: Garamond.

Paquet, Gilles. 1997. "States, Communities, and Markets: The Distributed Governance Scenario." In *The Nation State in a Global/Information Era: Policy Challenges*, ed. T. J. Courchene, 25–46. Kingston: Queen's University Press.

Parliamentary Budget Officer. 2008. "The Fiscal Impact of the Canadian Mission in Afghanistan." October 9. Ottawa: Office of the Parliamentary Budget Officer.

Parsons, Talcott. 1951. *The Social System*. Glencoe, IL: The Free Press.

Parsons, Talcott. 1966. *Societies: Evolutionary and Comparative Perspectives*. Englewood Cliffs, NJ: Prentice-Hall.

Parti Québécois. 1994. *Quebec in a New World: The PQ's Plan for Sovereignty*. Trans. R. Chodos. Toronto: James Lorimer and Company.

Pauls, Syd. 1984. "The Case for Band-Controlled Schools." *Canadian Journal of Native Education* 12(1): 31–37.

PayScale. 2020. *The State of the Gender Pay Gap 2019*. www.payscale.com/data/gender-pay-gap

Pemberton, Kim. 2014. "University of Victoria Puts First Nations Land Claim Mapping in the Spotlight." *Vancouver Sun*, August 11. www.vancouversun.com/news/University+Victoria+puts+First+Nations+land+claim+mapping+spotlight/10109738/story.html#ixzz3CmKhuXAr

Pentland, Clare. 1991. "The Transformation of Canada's Economic Structure." In *Perspectives on Canadian Economic Development*, ed. G. Laxer, 296–310. Toronto: Oxford University Press.

Perley, David G. 1993. "Aboriginal Education in Canada as Internal Colonialism." *Canada Journal of Native Education* 20(1): 118–128.

Persson, Diane. 1986. "The Changing Experience of Indian Residential Schooling: Blue Quills, 1931–1970." In *Indian Education in Canada*, Vol. I: *The Legacy*, eds. J. Barman, Y. Hébert, and D. McCaskill, 150–167. Vancouver: UBC Press.

Petitot, Father Emile. 1999. *Among the Chiglit Eskimos*, trans. E. Otto Höhn. Edmonton: Boreal Institute for Northern Studies.

Pevere, Geoff, and Greig Dymond. 1996. *Mondo Canuck: A Canadian Pop Cultural Odyssey.* Scarborough, ON: Prentice-Hall.

Pickett, Kate, and Richard Wilkinson. 2011. *The Spirit Level: Why Greater Equality Makes Societies Stronger.* London, UK: Bloomsbury Press.

Piketty, Thomas. 2014. *Capital in the Twenty-First Century*, trans. A. Goldhammer. Cambridge, MA: Belknap.

Piketty, Thomas. 2020. *Capital and Ideology*, trans. A. Goldhammer. Boston: Harvard University Press.

Piven, Frances Fox. 2007. "The Neoliberal Challenge." *Contexts* 6(3): 13–15.

Plain, Fred. 1988. "A Treatise on the Rights of the Aboriginal Peoples of the Continent of North America." In *The Quest for Justice: Aboriginal Peoples and Aboriginal Rights*, eds. M. Boldt and J. A. Long, 31–40. Toronto: University of Toronto Press.

Poholka, Holli. 2016. First Nation Successes: Developing Urban Reserves in Canada. Master's Thesis. Kingston: Queen's University, School of Urban and Regional Planning Department of Geography and Planning.

Polanyi, Karl. 2001. *The Great Transformation: The Political and Economic Origins of Our Time.* Originally published in 1944. Boston: Beacon Press.

Ponting, J. Rick. 1986. "Relations between Bands and the Department of Indian Affairs: A Case of Internal Colonialism." In *Arduous Journey: Canadian Indians and Decolonization*, 84–111. Toronto: McClelland & Stewart.

Ponting, J. Rick. 1997a. "Getting a Handle on Recommendations of the Royal Commission on Aboriginal Peoples." In *First Nations in Canada: Perspectives on Opportunity, Empowerment, and Self-Determination*, 445–472. Toronto: McGraw-Hill Ryerson.

Ponting, J. Rick. 1997b. "The Socio-Demographic Picture." In *First Nations in Canada: Perspectives on Opportunity, Empowerment, and Self-Determination*, 68–114. Toronto: McGraw-Hill Ryerson.

Porter, John. 1965. *The Vertical Mosaic.* Toronto: University of Toronto Press.

Porter, Joy. 2012. *Native American Environmentalism: Land, Spirit, and the Idea of Wilderness.* Lincoln, NE: University of Nebraska Press.

Postman, Neil. 1985. *Amusing Ourselves to Death.* Toronto: Penguin.

Potts, Karen, and Leslie Brown. 2016. "Becoming an Anti-Oppressive Researcher." In *Rethinking Sociology in the 21st Century: Critical Readings in Sociology*, 4th ed., eds. M. Webber and K. Bezanson, 90–106. Toronto: Canadian Scholars' Press.

Poulain, Michel, and Anne Herm. 2013. "Central Population Registers as a Source of Demographic Statistics in Europe." *Population* 68(2): 183–212.

Poulantzas, Nicholas. 1973. *Political Power and Social Classes*, trans. T. O'Hagan. London, UK: New Left Books.

Pratt, Larry, and Garth Stevenson, eds. 1981. *Western Separatism: The Myths, Realities, and Dangers.* Edmonton: Hurtig.

Project Ploughshares. 2019. *Global Affairs Canada Report on Saudi Exports Puts Economic Benefits before Human Rights.* November 28. ploughshares.ca/2019/11/global-affairs-canada-report-on-saudi-exports-puts-economic-benefits-before-human-rights/

Purich, Donald. 1986. *Our Land.* Toronto: James Lorimer.

Purich, Donald. 1992. *The Inuit and Their Land.* Toronto: Lorimer and Company.

Putnam, Robert. 2000. *Bowling Alone: The Collapse and Revival of American Community*. New York: Simon and Schuster.

Quebec Community Groups Network (QCGN). 2018. *Attachment to Quebec and Recent Historic Markers*. Léger Poll conducted for the Association of Canadian Studies and the Quebec Community Groups Network, July 3. www.qcgn.ca/association-for-canadian-studies-and-the-quebec-community-groups-network-powerpoint-presentation-attachment-to-quebec-and-recent-historic-markers/

Ramonet, Ignacio. 2001. "The Changing Face of Separatism." *Le Monde diplomatique* (February): 1.

Ramos, Howard. 2006. "What Causes Canadian Aboriginal Protest? Examining Resources, Opportunities, and Identity, 1951–2000." *Canadian Journal of Sociology* 31(2): 211–234.

Ramp, William, and Trevor W. Harrison. 2012. "Libertarian Populism, Neoliberal Rationality, and the Mandatory Long-Form Census: Implications for Sociology." *Canadian Journal of Sociology* 37(3): 273–294.

Ray, Arthur J. 1974. *Indians in the Fur Trade: Their Role as Trappers, Hunters, and Middlemen in the Lands Southwest of Hudson Bay, 1660–1870*. Toronto: University of Toronto Press.

Rea, K. J. 1968. *The Political Economy of the Canadian North*. Toronto: University of Toronto Press.

Reich, Robert. 2010. *After-Shock: The Next Economy and America's Future*. New York: Alfred A. Knopf.

Reid, Scott. 1992. *Canada Remapped*. Vancouver: Arsenal Pulp Press.

Resnick, Philip. 1991. *Toward a Canada–Quebec Union*. Montreal and Kingston: McGill-Queen's University Press.

Resnick, Philip. 2000. *The Politics of Resentment: BC Regionalism and Canadian Unity*. Vancouver: UBC Press.

Resnick, Philip. 2005. *The European Roots of Canadian Identity*. Peterborough, ON: Broadview Press.

Resnick, Philip, and Daniel Latouche. 1990. *Letters to a Quebecois Friend*. Montreal and Kingston: McGill-Queen's University Press.

Rice, James, and Michael Prince. 2013. *Changing Politics of Canadian Social Policy*. 2nd ed. Toronto: University of Toronto Press.

Richards, John, and Larry Pratt. 1979. *Prairie Capitalism: Power and Influence in the New West*. Toronto: McClelland & Stewart.

Richler, Noah. 2012. *What We Talk about When We Talk about War*. Fredericton, NB: Goose Lane Editions.

Rickman, H. P. 1961. "General Introduction." In *Pattern and Meaning in History*, ed. W. Dilthey, 11–63. London, UK: Harper Row Publishers.

Riesman, David, with Reuel Denney and Nathan Glazer. 1950. *The Lonely Crowd: A Study of the Changing American Character*. New Haven, CT: Yale University Press.

Rioux, Marcel. 1978. *Quebec in Question*. Toronto: James Lorimer and Company.

Rioux, Marcel. 1993. "The Development of Ideologies in Quebec." In *A Passion for Identity: An Introduction to Canadian Studies*, eds. D. Taras, B. Rasporich, and E. Mandel, 72–91. Scarborough, ON: Nelson Canada.

Robbins, Richard H., and Rachel A. Dowty. 2019. *Global Problems and the Culture of Capitalism*. 7th ed. Toronto: Pearson.

Roberts, Joseph K. 1998. *In the Shadow of Empire: Canada for Americans*. New York: Monthly Review Press.

Robin, Martin. 1991. *Shades of Right: Nativist and Fascist Politics in Canada, 1920–1940*. Toronto: University of Toronto Press.

Robin, Martin. 1993. "British Columbia: The Company Province." In *A Passion for Identity: An Introduction to Canadian Studies*, eds. D. Taras, B. Rasporich, and E. Mandel, 480–488. Scarborough, ON: Nelson Canada.

Robinson, William I., and Jeb Sprague. 2018. "The Transnational Capitalist Class." In *The Oxford Handbook of Global Studies*, eds. M. Juergensmeyer, M. Steger, S. Sassen, and V. Faesse, 309–327. Oxford, UK: Oxford University Press.

Rodgers, Kathleen. 2014. *Welcome to Resisterville: American Dissidents in British Columbia*. Vancouver: UBC Press.

Romanow, Roy. 2006. "A House Half Built." *The Walrus*, June, 48–54.

Romney, Paul. 1999. *Getting It Wrong: How Canadians Forgot Their Past and Imperilled Confederation*. Toronto: University of Toronto Press.

Ross, Rupert. 1992. *Dancing with a Ghost: Exploring Indian Reality*. Markham, ON: Reed Books.

Rotstein, Abraham. 1978. "Is There an English-Canadian Nationalism?" *Journal of Canadian Studies* 13: 109–118.

Royal Commission on Aboriginal Peoples. 1996. *Final Report*. Ottawa: Government of Canada.

Rudmin, Floyd. 1993. *Bordering on Aggression*. Hull, QC: Voyageur Publications.

Rummel, R. J. 1994. *Death by Government*. New Brunswick, NJ: Transaction.

Russell, Dan. 2000. *A People's Dream: Aboriginal Self-Government in Canada*. Vancouver: UBC Press.

Russell, Peter H. 2017. *Canada's Odyssey: A Country Based on Incomplete Conquests*. Toronto: University of Toronto Press.

Ryan, Joan. 1995. *Doing Things the Right Way: Dene Traditional Justice in Lac La Martre, NWT*. Calgary: Arctic Institute of North America.

Sahi, Ahmad. 2019. "Quebec's Unthinkable Bill 21." *Maclean's*, April 9.

Said, Edward. 1993. *Culture and Imperialism*. New York: Vintage Books.

Sassan, Saskia. 2001. "Governance Hotspots: Challenges We Must Confront in the Post-September 11 World." Social Science Research Council. essays.ssrc.org/sept11/essays/sassen.htm

Saul, John Ralston. 1997. *Reflections of a Siamese Twin: Canada at the End of the Twentieth Century*. Toronto: Penguin Books.

Saul, John Ralston. 2008. *A Fair Country: Telling Truths about Canada*. Toronto: Viking.

Saul, S. B. 1969. *The Myth of the Great Depression, 1873–1896*. London, UK: Macmillan.

Saurette, Paul, and Shane Gunster. 2011. "Ears Wide Shut: Epistemological Populism, Argutainment and Canadian Conservative Talk Radio." *Canadian Journal of Political Science* 44: 195–218.

Savoie, Donat, ed. 1970. *The Amerindians of the Canadian North-West in the 19th Century, as seen by Émile Petitot: The Loucheux Indian*, Vol. II. Ottawa: Northern Science Group, Department of Indian Affairs and Northern Development.

Sawatsky, John. 1991. *Mulroney: The Politics of Ambition*. Toronto: Macfarlane Walter & Ross.

Sayer, Derek. 1987. *The Violence of Abstraction: The Analytic Foundations of Historical Materialism*. Oxford, UK: Basil Blackwell.

Schouls, Tim. 2003. *Shifting Boundaries: Aboriginal Identity, Pluralist Theory, and the Politics of Self-Government*. Vancouver: UBC Press.

Schultz, Marylou, and Miriam Kroeger, eds. 1996. *Teaching and Learning with Native Indians: A Handbook for Non-Native American Adult Educators*. Phoenix, AZ: Adult Literacy and Technology Resource Center.

Schwartz, Bryan. 1986. *First Principles, Second Thoughts: Aboriginal Peoples, Constitutional Reform, and Canadian Statecraft*. Montreal: Institute for Research on Public Policy.

Scott, John, and Gordon Marshall. 2005. "Post-Structuralism." In *Oxford Dictionary of Sociology*, eds. J. Scott and G. Marshall, 510–512. Oxford, UK: Oxford University Press.

Scowen, Reed. 1999. *Time to Say Goodbye: The Case for Getting Quebec Out of Canada*. Toronto: McClelland & Stewart.

Showalter, Dennis E., and Harold C. Deutsch, eds. 2010. *If the Allies Had Fallen: Sixty Alternate Scenarios of World War II*. New York: Skyhorse Publishing.

Siebert, John. 2014. "Canada and the Failure to End the 'Thousand Little Wars' in Afghanistan." *The Ploughshares Monitor* 35(2): 4–9.

Sikotan (Flora Zaharia) and Mikai'sto (Leo Fox). 1995. *Kitomahkitapiiminnooniksi: Stories from Our Elders*, Vol. 1. Kainaiwa Board of Education. Edmonton: Donahue House Publishing.

Sikotan (Flora Zaharia), Mikai'sto (Leo Fox), and Omahksipootaa (Marvin Fox). 2003. *Kitomahkitapiiminnooniksi: Stories from Our Elders*, Vol. 4. Kainaiwa Board of Education. Edmonton: Donahue House Publishing.

Silver, A. I. 1997. *The French-Canadian Idea of Confederation, 1864–1900*. 2nd ed. Toronto: University of Toronto Press.

Silver, Jim. 1996. *Thin Ice: Money, Politics, and the Demise of an NHL Franchise*. Halifax: Fernwood.

Sinha, Vandna, and Anna Kozlowski. 2013. "The Structure of Aboriginal Child Welfare in Canada." *The International Indigenous Policy Journal* 4(2): 1–21.

Sklair, Leslie. 2002. *Globalization: Capitalism and Its Alternatives*. Toronto: Oxford University Press.

Skocpol, Theda. 1979. *States and Social Revolutions*. Cambridge, UK: Cambridge University Press.

Smith, Adrian. 2019. "Toward a Critique of Political Economy of 'Sociolegality' in Settler Capitalist Canada." In *Change and Continuity: Canadian Political Economy in the New Millennium*, eds. M. P. Thomas, L. F. Vosko, C. Fanelli, and O. Lyubchenko, 167–184. Montreal and Kingston: McGill-Queen's University Press.

Smith, Donald. 1998. *Beyond Two Solitudes*. Halifax: Fernwood.

Smith, Goldwin. 1971. *Canada and the Canadian Question*. Originally published in 1891. Toronto: University of Toronto Press.

Smith, Graeme. 2013. *The Dogs Are Eating Them Now: Our War in Afghanistan*. Toronto: Knopf.

Smith, Melvin H. 1995. *Our Home OR Native Land? What Government Aboriginal Policy Is Doing to Canada*. Toronto: Stoddart.

Smylie, Janet, Deshayne Fell, Arne Ohlsson, and the Joint Working Group on First Nations, Indian, Inuit, and Métis Infant Mortality of the Canadian Perinatal Surveillance System Surveillance System. 2010. "A Review of Aboriginal Infant Mortality Rates in Canada: Striking and Persistent Aboriginal/Non-Aboriginal Inequities." *Canadian Journal of Public Health* 101(2): 143–148.

Sneed, Annie. 2019. "What Conservation Efforts can Learn from Indigenous Communities." *Scientific American*, May 29. www.scientificamerican.com/article/what-conservation-efforts-can-learn-from-indigenous-communities/

Sniderman, Andrew Stobo, and Adam Shedletzky. 2014. "Aboriginal Peoples and Legal Challenges to Canadian Climate Change Policy." *University of Western Ontario Journal of Legal Studies* 4(2). ir.lib.uwo.ca/uwojls/vol4/iss2/1

Snow, Chief John. 1977. *These Mountains Are Our Sacred Places: The Story of the Stoney Indians*. Toronto: Samuel Stevens.

Snow, Chief John. 1988. "Identification and Definition of Our Treaty and Aboriginal Rights." In *The Quest for Justice: Aboriginal Peoples and Aboriginal Rights*, eds. M. Boldt and A. Long, 41–46. Toronto: University of Toronto Press.

Snow, Chief John. 2005. *These Mountains Are Our Sacred Places: The Story of the Stoney People*. Calgary: Fifth House.

Sprague, D. N. 1988. *Canada and the Métis, 1869–1885*. Waterloo, ON: Wilfrid Laurier University Press.

Srebrnik, Henry F. 1998. "The Radical 'Second Life' of Vilhjalmur Stefansson." *Arctic* 51(1): 58–60.

Stabler, Jack. 1989. "Dualism and Development in the Northwest Territories." *Economic Development and Cultural Change* 37(4): 805–840.

Stacey, C. P., and Norman Hillmer. 1999. "World War II." In *The Canadian Encyclopedia*, ed. James A. Marsh, 2551–2553. Toronto: McClelland & Stewart.

Standing, Guy. 2011. *The Precariat: The New Dangerous Class*. London, UK: Bloomsbury Academic.

Standing, Guy. 2014. *A Precariat Charter: From Denizens to Citizens*. London, UK: Bloomsbury Academic.

Stanford, Jim. 2014. "European Trade Deal Would Make a Bad Situation Worse for Auto Sector, with Spillover Effects throughout the Economy." *Canadian Centre for Policy Alternatives Monitor* 21(2): 1, 10–12.

Stanford, Jim. 2019. "Staples Dependence Renewed and Betrayed: Canada's Twenty-First Century Boom and Bust." In *Change and Continuity: Canadian Political Economy in the New Millennium*, eds. M. P. Thomas, L. F. Vosko, C. Fanelli, and O. Lyubchenko, 79-105. Montreal and Kingston: McGill-Queen's University Press.

Stanley, George F. G. 1975. *The Birth of Western Canada: A History of the Riel Rebellion*. Originally published in 1936. Toronto: University of Toronto Press.

Staples, Steven, and William Robinson. 2008. *More Than the Cold War*. Ottawa: The Rideau Institute.

Star Calgary. 2020. "Key Moments in the Coastal GasLink and Wet'suwet'en Conflict: A Timeline." February 11. www.thestar.com/news/canada/2020/02/11/key-moments-in-the-coastal-gaslink-and-wetsuweten-conflict-a-timeline.html

Statista. 2020a. *Number of Immigrants in Canada from 2000 to 2019 (in 1,000s)*. https://www.statista.com/statistics/443063/number-of-immigrants-in-canada/

Statista. 2020b. "Unemployment rate in Canada in 2019, by province." January 22. www.statista.com/statistics/442316/canada-unemployment-rate-by-provinces/

Statista. 2021. "Number of novel coronavirus (COVID-19) cases worldwide as of January 27, 2021, by country." www.statista.com/statistics/1043366/novel-coronavirus-2019ncov-cases-worldwide-by-country/

Statistics Canada. 1983. Data Table 11-516: *Historical Statistics of Canada*. Ottawa: Statistics Canada.

Statistics Canada. 2001. Canada Year Book. Cat. no. 11-402. Ottawa: Statistics Canada.

Statistics Canada. 2006. "Population by Mother Tongue, by Province and Territory." 2006 Census. Ottawa: Statistics Canada.

Statistics Canada. 2007a. *Canada Year Book 2007*. Ottawa: Statistics Canada.

Statistics Canada. 2007b. "Study: The New Underground Economy of Resources." *The Daily*, October 11.

Statistics Canada. 2011a. "Focus on Geography Series." 2011 Census. Ottawa: Statistics Canada. www12.statcan.gc.ca/census-recensement/2011/as-sa/fogs-spg/Index-eng.cfm

Statistics Canada. 2011b. Data Table 99-010-X2011032: "Religion (108), Immigrant Status and Period of Immigration (11), Age Groups (10) and Sex (3) for the Population in Private Households of Canada, Provinces, Territories, Census Metropolitan Areas and Census Agglomerations." 2011 National Household Survey.

Statistics Canada. 2011c. "Population, Urban and Rural, by Province and Territory (Canada)." Ottawa: Statistics Canada.

Statistics Canada. 2011d. Data Table 99-010-X2011026: "Citizenship (5), Place of Birth (236), Immigrant Status and Period of Immigration (11), Age Groups (10) and Sex (3) for the Population in Private Households of Canada, Provinces, Territories, Census Metropolitan Areas and Census Agglomerations." 2011 National Household Survey.

Statistics Canada. 2013. "History of the Census of Canada." Ottawa: Statistics Canada. www12.statcan.gc.ca/census-recensement/2011/ref/about-apropos/history-histoire-eng.cfm

Statistics Canada. 2016a. Data Table 98-402-X2016001: "Population and Dwelling Count Highlight Tables." 2016 Census: Population counts, for Canada, provinces and territories, census divisions. www12.statcan.gc.ca/census-recensement/2016/dp-pd/hlt-fst/pd-pl/Table.cfm?Lang=Eng&T=703&S=87&O=A

Statistics Canada. 2016b. Data Table 98-400-X2016185: "Immigrant Status and Period of Immigration (11), Place of Birth (272), Age (7A) and Sex (3) for the Population of Private Households of Canada, Provinces, and Territories, Census Divisions and Census Subdivisions, 2016 Census—25% Sample Data." www12.statcan.gc.ca/census-recensement/2016/dp-pd/dt-td/Rp-eng.cfm?LANG=E&APATH=3&DETAIL=0&DIM=0&FL=A&FREE=0&GC=0&GID=0&GK=0&GRP=1&PID=110526&PRID=10&PTYPE=109445&S=0&SHOWALL=0&SUB=0&Temporal=2017&THEME=120&VID=0&VNAMEE=&VNAMEF=

Statistics Canada. 2016c. "Focus on Geography Series." 2016 Census.

Statistics Canada. 2016d. "Aboriginal Peoples Highlight Tables, 2016 Census: Aboriginal identity population by both sexes, total—age, 2016 counts, Canada, provinces and territories, 2016 Census—25% Sample data." www12.statcan.gc.ca/census-recensement/2016/dp-pd/hlt-fst/abo-aut/Table.cfm?Lang=Eng&T=101&S=99&O=A

Statistics Canada. 2016e. Data Table 98-400-X2016268: "Aboriginal Identity (9), Employment Income Statistics (7), Highest Certificate, Diploma or Degree (11), Major Field of Study—Classification of Instructional Programs (CIP) 2016 (14), Work Activity during the Reference Year (3), Age (10) and Sex (3) for the Population Aged 15 Years and Over in Private Households of Canada, Provinces and Territories, 2016 Census—25% Sample Data." www12.statcan.gc.ca/census-recensement/2016/dp-pd/dt-td/Rp-eng. cfm?APATH=3&DETAIL=0&DIM=0&FL=A&FREE=0&GC= 0&GID=0&GK=0&GRP=1&LANG=E&PID=110682&PRID=10&PTYPE= 109445&S=0&SHOWALL=0&SUB=0&THEME=123&Temporal=2016&VID= 0&VNAMEE=&VNAMEF=

Statistics Canada. 2016f. Data Table 98-400-X2016178: "Aboriginal Identity (9), Highest Certificate, Diploma or Degree (11), Income Statistics (17), Registered or Treaty Indian Status (3), Age (9) and Sex (3) for the Population Aged 15 Years and Over in Private Households of Canada, Provinces and Territories, Census Metropolitan Areas and Census Agglomerations, 2016 Census—25% Sample Data." www150.statcan.gc.ca/n1/en/ catalogue/98-400-X2016178

Statistics Canada. 2017a. Data Table 98-316-X2016001: "Canada [Country] and Canada [Country] (table). Census Profile." 2016 Census. www12.statcan.gc.ca/census-recensement/2016/dp-pd/prof/details/page.cfm?Lang=E&Geo1=PR&Code1=01&Geo2= PR&Code2=01&SearchType=Begins&SearchPR=01&B1=Population&type=0

Statistics Canada. 2017b. "2016 Census of Population Long-Form Guide." www.statcan.gc.ca/ eng/statistical-programs/document/3901_D18_T1_V1

Statistics Canada. 2017c. "English–French bilingualism reaches new heights." August 2. www12. statcan.gc.ca/census-recensement/2016/as-sa/98-200-x/2016009/98-200-x2016009-eng.cfm

Statistics Canada. 2017d. Data Table 11-10-0017-01: "Census families by family type and family composition including before and after-tax median income of the family."

Statistics Canada. 2017e. "The Aboriginal languages of First Nations people, Métis and Inuit." www12.statcan.gc.ca/census-recensement/2016/as-sa/98-200-x/2016022/98-200-x2016022-eng.cfm

Statistics Canada. 2019a. Table 18-10-0057-01: "Projected population, by projection scenario, age and sex, as of Jul 1 (x 1,000)." doi.org/10.25318/1710005701-eng

Statistics Canada. 2019b. "Language Highlight Tables, 2016 Census: Mother tongue by age (Total), 2016 counts for the population excluding institutional residents of Canada, provinces and territories, 2016 Census—100% Data." www12.statcan.gc.ca/census-recensement/2016/ dp-pd/hlt-fst/lang/Table.cfm?Lang=E&T=11&Geo=00

Statistics Canada. 2019c. Table 36-10-0222-01: Gross domestic product, expenditure-based, provincial and territorial, annual (x 1,000,000). doi.org/10.25318/3610022201-eng

Statistics Canada. 2019d. Table 14-10-0287-03: "Labour force characteristics by province, monthly, seasonally adjusted." Month of September 2019. doi.org/10.25318/1410028701-eng

Statistics Canada. 2019e. "Canada at a Glance 2019: International Trade, Table 25: Major goods trading partners, 2018." www150.statcan.gc.ca/n1/pub/12-581-x/2019001/it-ci-eng.htm

Statistics Canada. 2019f. Data Table 11-10-0049-01: "Survey of Financial Security (SFS), assets and debts by net worth quintile, Canada, provinces, and selected census metropolitan areas (CMAs) (x 1,000,000)." doi.org/10.25318/1110004901-eng

Statistics Canada. 2019g. Data Table 12-10-0140-01: "Canada's international merchandise trade by free trade agreement." www150.statcan.gc.ca/n1/daily-quotidien/190904/dq190904d-eng.htm

Statistics Canada. 2020. Table: 14-10-0324-01: "Average and median gender pay ratio in annual wages, salaries and commissions." *Geography*: Canada, Geographical region of Canada, province or territory. www150.statcan.gc.ca/t1/tbl1/en/tv.action?pid=1410032401

Stearns, P. N. 1975. *European Society in Upheaval.* 2nd ed. New York: Macmillan Publishing.

Steckley, John I., and Bryan D. Cummins. 2008. *Full Circle: Canada's First Nations.* 2nd ed. Toronto: Pearson Education Canada.

Steele, James, and Robin Mathews. 2006. "Canadianization Revisited: A Comment on Cormier's 'The Canadianization Movement in Context.'" *The Canadian Journal of Sociology* 31(4): 491–508.

Stefansson, Vilhjalmur. 1921. *The Friendly Arctic.* New York: Macmillan.

Stein, Janice Gross, and Eugene Lang. 2007. *The Unexpected War: Canada in Kandahar.* Toronto: Viking.

Stewart, J. D. M., and Hellmut Kallmann. 2019. "Massey Commission." *Canadian Encyclopedia*, November 12. www.thecanadianencyclopedia.ca/en/article/massey-commission-emc

Stiegler, Bernard. 2019. *The Age of Disruption: Technology and Madness in Computational Capitalism.* New York: Polity.

Strange, Susan. 1996. *The Retreat of the State.* Cambridge, UK: Cambridge University Press.

Stubbs, R., and G. R. D. Underhill, eds. 1994. *Political Economy and the Changing Global Order.* Toronto: McClelland & Stewart.

Stueck, Wendy. 2014. "Ruling over Land in BC Has Ripple Effects across Canada." *Globe and Mail*, June 27. www.theglobeandmail.com/news/british-columbia/ruling-over-land-in-bc-has-ripple-effects-across-canada/article19357334

Surtees, R. J. 1969. "The Development of a Reserve Policy in Canada." *Ontario Historical Society* 61: 87–99.

Suzuki, David. 1992. "A Personal Foreword: The Value of Native Ecologies." In *Wisdom of the Elders*, eds. P. Knudtson and D. Suzuki, xxi–xvi. Toronto: Stoddart.

Swedberg, Richard. 1990. *Economics and Society.* Princeton, NJ: Princeton University Press.

Tajfel, Henri, and John C. Turner. 1986. "The Social Identity Theory of Intergroup Behavior." In *Psychology of Intergroup Relations*, eds. S. Worchel and W. A. Austin, 7–24. Chicago: Nelson-Hall.

Taylor, Charles. 1993. *Reconciling the Solitudes.* Montreal and Kingston: McGill-Queen's University Press.

Taylor, J. Garth. 1974. *Netsilik Eskimo Material Culture: The Roald Amundsen Collection from King William Island.* Oslo: Universitetsforlaget.

Teeple, Gary. 2000. *Globalization and the Decline of Social Reform: Into the Twenty-First Century.* 2nd ed. Toronto: Garamond.

Tennant, Paul. 1988. "Aboriginal Rights and the Penner Report on Indian Self-Government." In *The Quest for Justice: Aboriginal Peoples and Aboriginal Rights*, eds. M. Boldt and A. Long, 321–332. Toronto: University of Toronto Press.

Thomas, Lewis H. 1977. "A Judicial Murder: The Trial of Louis Riel." In *The Settlement of the West*, ed. H. Palmer, 37–59. Calgary: Comprint.

Thompson, Dale. 1995. "Language, Identity, and the Nationalist Impulse: Quebec." In *Being and Becoming Canada: The Annals of the American Academy of Political and Social Science* 538, eds. C. Doran and E. Babby, 69–82. SAGE Publications.

Time. 2020. *The World Almanac and Book of Facts 2020*. New York: Infobase.

Titley, E. Brian. 1992. "Red Deer Industrial School: A Case Study in the History of Native Education." In *Exploring Our Educational Past*, eds. N. Kach and K. Mazurek, 55–72. Calgary: Detselig.

Tjepkema, Michael, Tracey Bushnik, and Evelyne Bougie. 2019. "Life expectancy of First Nations, Métis, and Inuit household populations in Canada." Statistics Canada, December 18. www.doi.org/10.25318/82-003-x201901200001-eng

Tobias, John L. 1977. "Indian Reserves in Western Canada: Indian Homelands or Devices for Assimilation?" In *Approaches to Native History in Canada*, ed. D. A. Muise, 89–103. Ottawa: National Museum of Man Mercury Series.

Tobias, John L. 1983. "Protection, Civilization, Assimilation: An Outline History of Canada's Indian Policy." In *As Long as the Sun Shines and Water Flows: A Reader in Canadian Native Studies*, eds. Ian A. L. Getty and Antoine Lussier, 39–55. Vancouver: UBC Press.

Tönnies, Ferdinand. 1957. *Community and Society*, ed. and trans. C. P. Loomis. Originally published in 1887. New York: Harper and Row.

Trent, John E. 1995. *The 1995 Quebec Referendum: A Practical Guide*. Ottawa: Dialogue Canada.

Trigger, Bruce G. 1969. *The Huron: Farmers of the North*. New York: Holt, Rinehart, and Winston.

Trofimenkoff, Susan. 1993. "For Whom the Bell Tolls." In *Reappraisals in Canadian History: Pre-Confederation*, eds. A. D. Gilbert, G. M. Wallace, and R. M. Bray, 380–392. Scarborough, ON: Prentice-Hall Canada.

Trudeau, Pierre. 1996. *Against the Current: Selected Writings 1939–1996*, ed. G. Pelletier. Toronto: McClelland & Stewart.

Trudel, Marcel. 2013. *Canada's Forgotten Slaves: Two Hundred Years of Bondage*, trans. G. Tombs. Montreal: Véhicule Press.

Truth and Reconciliation Commission of Canada. 2015. *Honouring the Truth, Reconciling for the Future: Summary of the Final Report of the Truth and Reconciliation Commission of Canada*. nctr.ca/reports.php

Turk, James L., and Allan Manson, eds. 2007. *Free Speech in Fearful Times: After 9/11 in Canada, the US, Australia, and Europe*. Ottawa: Canadian Association of University Teachers.

Turner, Chris. 2013. *The War on Science: Muzzled Scientists and Wilful Blindness in Stephen Harper's Canada*. Vancouver: Greystone.

Turner, Joanne. 1981. "The Historical Base." In *Canadian Social Welfare*, eds. J. Turner and F. Turner, 49–57. Don Mills, ON: Collier Macmillan Canada.

Turp, Daniel. 1993. "Solutions to the Future of Canada and Quebec after the October 26th Referendum: Genuine Sovereignties within a Novel Union." *Constitutional Forum* 4(2): 47–49.

Ungar, Sheldon. 1991. "Civil Religion and the Arms Race." *Canadian Review of Sociology and Anthropology* 28(4): 503–525.

United Nations. 1945. *Charter*. www.un.org/en/sections/un-charter/un-charter-full-text/

United Nations. 2014. *United Nations Intergovernmental Panel on Climate Change*. Fifth Assessment Report. New York: United Nations. www.ipcc.ch/index.htm

United Nations. 2020. *United Nations Intergovernmental Panel on Climate Change*. Sixth Assessment Report. New York: United Nations. www.ipcc.ch/index.htm

Universities Canada. 2017. "Indigenous student education." www.univcan.ca/priorities/ indigenous-education/

Uprichard, Lucy. 2019. "What Is Quebec's Secularism Law—And How Does It Affect Women?" *Chatelaine*, June 17.

Usalcas, Jeannine. 2011. "Aboriginal People and the Labour Market: Estimates from the Labour Force Survey, 2008–2010." Labour Statistics Division, Statistics Canada. Cat. no. 71-588-X, no. 3. www.statcan.gc.ca/pub/71-588-x/71-588-x2011003-eng.pdf

Valaskakis, Kimon, and Angeline Fournier. 1995. *The Delusion of Sovereignty: Would Independence Weaken Quebec?* Montreal: Robert Davies Publishing.

Vallee, Frank. 1971. "Eskimos of Canada: A Minority Group." In *Native Peoples*, ed. Jean Elliott Leonard, 75–88. Don Mills, ON: Prentice-Hall of Canada.

Vallières, Pierre. 1971. *White Niggers of America*. Toronto: McClelland & Stewart.

van den Berghe, Pierre. 1992. "The Modern State: Nation-Builder or Nation-Killer?" *International Journal of Group Tensions* 22: 191–208.

Van der Pijl, Kees. 1998. *Transnational Classes and International Relations*. London: Routledge.

van Kirk, Sylvia. 1999. *Many Tender Ties: Women in the Fur Trade Society, 1670–1870*. Winnipeg: Watson and Dwyer.

van Praet, Nicolas, David Parkinson, and Nathan Vanderklippe. 2019. "It Wasn't Supposed to Be Like This: Inside Canada's Unravelling Ties with China, and What Happens Next." *Globe and Mail*, September 21, B6.

Vergano, Dan. 2013. "Half-Million Iraqis Died in the War, New Study Says." *National Geographic*, October 15. news.nationalgeographic.com/news/2013/10/131015-iraq-war-deaths-survey-2013

Wahl, Asbjørn. 2011. *The Rise and Fall of the Welfare State*. London, UK: Pluto.

Waite, P. B. 1997. "In Loyalist Ontario: A Schoolboy's Recollections, 1930–1933." *The Beaver* (February–March): 12–13.

Wall, Denis. 2000. "Aboriginal Self-Government in Canada: The Cases of Nunavut and the Alberta Métis Settlements." In *Visions of the Heart: Canadian Aboriginal Issues*, eds. D. Long and O. P. Dickason, 143–166. 2nd ed. Toronto: Harcourt Canada.

Wallerstein, Immanuel. 1997. "World-Systems Analysis." In *Social Theory Today*, eds. A. Giddens and J. Turner, 309–324. Stanford, CA: Stanford University Press.

Wall Street Journal. 2014. "The Short Answer: What Is Islamic State?" June 12. blogs.wsj.com/ briefly/2014/06/12/islamic-state-of-iraq-and-al-sham-the-short-answer

Wanner, Richard A. 1999. "Expansion and Conscription: Trends in Educational Opportunity in Canada, 1920–1994." *Canadian Review of Sociology and Anthropology* 36(3): 409–442.

Warry, Wayne. 1998. *Unfinished Dreams: Community Healing and the Reality of Aboriginal Self-Government*. Toronto: University of Toronto Press.

Warry, Wayne. 2007. *Ending Denial: Understanding Aboriginal Issues*. Peterborough, ON: Broadview Press.

Waters, Malcolm. 1994. "Introduction: A World of Difference." *Australian–New Zealand Journal of Sociology* 30(3): 229–234.

Watkins, Melville. 1963. "A Staple Theory of Economic Growth." *Canadian Journal of Economics and Political Science* 29(2): 80–100.

Watkins, Melville. 1991. "The 'American System' and Canada's National Policy." In *Perspectives on Canadian Economic Development*, ed. G. Laxer, 148–157. Toronto: Oxford University Press.

Watkins, Melville. 1997. "Canadian Capitalism in Transition." In *Understanding Canada: Building on the New Canadian Political Economy*, ed. W. Clement, 19–42. Montreal and Kingston: McGill-Queen's University Press.

Weaver, Jace, ed. 1998. *Native American Religious Identity: Unforgotten Gods*. Maryknoll, NY: Orbis Books.

Webber, Jeremy. 1994. *Reimagining Canada*. Montreal and Kingston: McGill-Queen's University Press.

Weber, Max. 1958. *From Max Weber: Essays in Sociology*, eds. H. Gerth and C. W. Mills. New York: Oxford University Press.

Westfall, William. 1993. "On the Concept of Region in Canadian History and Literature." In *A Passion for Identity: An Introduction to Canadian Studies*, eds. D. Taras, B. Rasporich, and E. Mandel, 335–344. Scarborough, ON: Nelson Canada.

Whitaker, Reg. 1987. "Neo-Conservatism and the State." In *Socialist Register*, eds. R. Miliband, L. Panitch, and J. Saville, 1–31. London, UK: The Merlin Press.

Whitaker, Reg. 1991. *Canadian Immigration Policy since Confederation*. Ottawa: Canadian Historical Association.

White, Deena. 1997. "Quebec State and Society." In *Quebec Society: Critical Issues*, eds. M. Fournier, M. Rosenberg, and D. White, 17–44. Scarborough, ON: Prentice-Hall Canada.

Whyte, Donald. 1992. "Sociology and the Constitution of Society: Canadian Experiences." In *Fragile Truths: 25 Years of Sociology and Anthropology in Canada*, eds. W. Carroll, L. Christiansen-Ruffman, R. Currie, and D. Harrison, 313–319. Ottawa: Carleton University Press.

Widdis, Randy. 1997. "American-Resident Migration to Western Canada at the Turn of the Twentieth Century." *Prairie Forum* 22(2): 237–261.

Wilson, C. Roderick, and Carl Urion. 1995. "First Nations Prehistory and Canadian History." In *Native Peoples: The Canadian Experience*, eds. R. B. Wilson and C. R. Morrison, 22–66. 2nd ed. Toronto: McClelland & Stewart.

Wilson, Roger, ed. 1976. *The Land That Never Melts: Auyuittuq National Park*. Ottawa: Minister of Supply and Services.

Winegard, Timothy C. 2012. *For King and Kanata: Canadian Indians and the First World War*. Winnipeg: University of Manitoba Press.

Winks, Robin. 1998. *The Civil War Years: Canada and the United States*. 4th ed. Montreal and Kingston: McGill-Queen's University Press.

Wiseman, Nelson. 2007. *In Search of Canadian Political Culture*. Vancouver: UBC Press.

Wissler, Clark. 1923. *Man and Culture*. New York: Thomas Crowell.

Witt, Norbert. 1998. "Promoting Self-Esteem, Defining Culture." *Canadian Journal of Native Education* 22(2): 260–273.

Wolf, Naomi. 2007. *The End of America: Letter of Warning to a Young Patriot*. White River Junction, VT: Chelsea Green.

Wonders, William. 1993. "Canadian Regions and Regionalisms: National Enrichment or National Disintegration?" In *A Passion for Identity: An Introduction to Canadian Studies*, eds. D. Taras, B. Rasporich, and E. Mandel, 345–366. Scarborough, ON: Nelson Canada.

Woodcock, Jamie, and Mark Graham. 2019. *The Gig Economy: An Introduction*. Cambridge, UK: Polity Press.

Woodsworth, J. S. 1972. *Strangers within Our Gates*. Originally published in 1909. Toronto: University of Toronto Press.

World Bank. 2019. "Military Expenditures (% of GDP)." data.worldbank.org/indicator/MS.MIL.XPND.GD.ZS

World Population Review. 2019. "Debt to GDP Ratio by Country 2019." www.worldpopulationreview.com/countries/countries-by-national-debt

Wright, Eric Olin. 1985. *Classes*. London, UK: Verso.

Wright, Ronald. 1993. *Stolen Continents: The New World through Indian Eyes*. Toronto: Penguin.

Wuttunee, William I. C. 1971. *Ruffled Feathers: Indians in Canadian Society*. Calgary: Bell Books.

Wynn, Graeme. 2012. "On the Margins of Empire 1760–1840." In *The Illustrated History of Canada*, ed. Craig Brown, 181–276. Toronto: Key Porter Books.

Yazzie, Robert. 2000. "Indigenous Peoples and Post-Colonial Colonialism." In *Reclaiming Indigenous Voice and Vision*, ed. M. Battiste, 39–49. Vancouver: UBC Press.

York, Geoffrey. 1989. *The Dispossessed: Life and Death in Native Canada*. Toronto: Lester and Orpen Dennys.

Young, Robert A. 1995. *The Secession of Quebec and the Future of Canada*. Montreal and Kingston: McGill-Queen's University Press.

Young, Robert A. 1998. "Quebec Succession and the 1995 Referendum." In *Challenges to Canadian Federalism*, eds. M. Westmacott and H. Mellon, 112–126. Scarborough, ON: Prentice-Hall Canada.

Zilio, Michelle. 2018. "Two Richest Canadians Own More than Bottom 30% of Population, Report Finds." *Globe and Mail*, March 21. www.theglobeandmail.com/news/politics/report-makes-recommendations-to-achieve-economy-that-works-for-all-canadians/article33629405/

Zinn, Howard. 1995. *A People's History of the United States: 1492–Present*. New York: Harper Perennial.

Zubrzycki, Geneviève. 2016. *Beheading the Saint: Nationalism, Religion, and Secularism in Quebec*. Chicago: University of Chicago Press.

Index